AMERICAN

BIOGRAPHICAL NOTES,

BEING

Short Notices of Deceased Persons,

CHIEFLY THOSE NOT INCLUDED IN ALLEN'S OR IN DRAKE'S BIOGRAPHICAL DICTIONARIES,

GATHERED FROM MANY SOURCES,

AND ARRANGED BY

FRANKLIN B. HOUGH.

ALBANY:
JOEL MUNSELL.
1875.

EDITION 130 COPIES.

PREFACE.

This volume owes its origin to an accidental circumstance. Nearly twenty years ago, the undersigned had occasion to ascertain the date of death of a person who many years before had been a distinguished citizen of Albany, holding an important public office, and filling a prominent place in social circles in the day in which he lived. All existing biographical collections failed to give the information desired, and an extended course of personal inquiry among aged citizens of Albany elicited nothing but this, that while all remembered the fact that he had lived, none could give the slightest information as to when or where he died. At length a man was found who thought, that by looking in the files of a newspaper, published some forty years before, the date desired might be found, and accordingly, after a lengthy search, it was discovered, but several years earlier than the year which the informant had indicated.

Now this incident must have had its parallel in the experience of every one who has had occasion to find obituary dates. It impressed upon the writer the importance of saving, in form for convenient reference, these dates scattered all along the course of passing time, and daily coming under our notice to be read, laid aside and forgotten. Accordingly at leisure moments, these passing facts, with a brief note, and often a reference, were written down upon slips of paper of uniform size, and kept in alphabetical order until the practice became a habit; and the collection extended to several thousand in number, without the slightest thought of its ever being used by any one but the writer. These abstracts were carried through several series of magazines and scientific periodicals, and through many volumes that came within our range of reading, without professing to be exhaustive in any case as to number or extent; they being in fact nothing but brief notes, with such further references as might happen to be convenient.

In this form it lay until, upon its being incidentally mentioned to the publisher, its printing was undertaken, in the hope that it might form a convenient index to dates most widely scattered, and often most difficult to find. In the course of its collection, the names already given in Rev. William Allen's *American Biographical Dictionary* had been avoided, and during the years in which, at scattered moments, the series had been forming, the *Dictionary of American Biography* of Mr. Francis A. Drake had been published. When its printing was decided upon, it was thought proper to throw out all the names that had been included in the latter, unless we were able to present some additional facts, and in this event, to refer to it for fuller information. In some instances also, a name contained in Allen's Dictionary has been more fully given in this book. With this qualification, therefore, the present work may be regarded as a supplement to these two series of American biographies, but without pretensions to fullness, or to that editorial care which has been bestowed upon them.

It is in fact, as its title claims, nothing but a series of notices, always brief, and in no case in any way approaching to that standard of completeness that would be required in a full biographical sketch.

From the prevalent custom of copying notices from one newspaper into another, without sufficiently indicating the day first intended, it sometimes becomes impossible to fix with accuracy the true date. If our newspaper editors, instead of noticing an event as occurring " on Thursday last," or " on the 7th inst.," would give the *year*, *month* and *day* (which could generally be done within less space than the indirect method above alluded to), a much more satisfactory result would be obtained.

There are doubtless many errors arising from this source, but generally we have preferred to leave the date indefinite as to the day, or even the month, rather than assume to decide in a case of doubt. Of course a series of notes made like this at wide intervals, cannot pretend to any uniformity of style, in the arrangement of the facts that they contain.

A further difficulty has occurred in the printing of the volume, from the fact that the greater part has been done without revision of proofs by the editor, and although reasonable care has been given to this by the publisher and his proof-readers, it cannot be claimed as entirely free from those defects which the writer of a manuscript could alone detect.

We wish to return our thanks to several friends who have sent us notices of deceased persons, more especially to Dr. Moses M. Bagg, of Utica, Col. Charles Whittlesey of Cleveland, O., and Hon. Winslow C. Watson of Port Kent, N. Y. To the former, especially, we are indebted for many notices of early citizens of Oneida county, and central New York, which, without his kind coöperation, would not have been included.

FRANKLIN B. HOUGH.

LOWVILLE, N. Y., *October* 21, 1875.

AMERICAN

BIOGRAPHICAL NOTES.

ABBEY, Mrs. Dillia, d. Oct. 28, 1840, in her 103d year, retaining her mental faculties till the close of life.

ABBOT, Caleb Fletcher, d. at Toledo, O., April 24, 1855, a. 43; b. in Chelmsford, Mass., Sept. 8, 1811; graduated at Harvard University in 1827; in 1836, settled as a lawyer in Toledo, O., where he gained a high rank in his profession. He was mayor of the city and prosecuting attorney for third judicial district.

ABBOT, Rev. Jacob, minister of Hampton Falls; drowned at Windham, N. H., Nov. 2, 1834; grad. at H. U. in 1792 and was settled as a clergyman in 1795.

ABBOT, John Lovejoy, clergyman, grad. at H. U. in 1805; some years college librarian; in 1814 ordained at Boston, and d. in 2 years.

ABBOT, Stephen, officer of the revolution, resided in N. H., and lived to an advanced age.

ABBOTT, Dr. Henry, collector of a valuable series of Egyptian antiquities, now in the rooms of the New York Historical Society; d. near Cairo, March 30, 1859, a. 47; b. in London, had been a surgeon in the British navy, and was long engaged in practicing his profession at Cairo.

ABBOTT, Joel, commodore, U. S. N., d. Dec. 14, 1855, at Hong Kong, China; was commanding the U. S. squadron in the East Indies, and had entered the service in 1812; was an officer of ability, brave and energetic.

ABEEL, Capt. David, an officer on board the Alliance frigate in the revolutionary war, d. Oct., 1840, at New Brunswick, N. J.

ACKER, Jacob, formerly sheriff of New York city, d. Nov. 6, 1849, a. 56.

ACKLEY, Dr. Horace, prof. of surgery for many years in the Cleveland Med. Coll.; d. suddenly April 23, 1859, in his 48th year.

ADAMS, Daniel, d. in Charlestown, Mass., March 27, 1846, a. 95 years 6 months, being at the time, the oldest man in that town.

ADAMS, David, b. at Waxhaws, S. C., Jan. 28, 1766; served at the close of the revolution in S. C.; settled in Ga.; served against the Creeks as maj., brig. gen. and maj. gen.; served the state in several commissions; was in the legislature more than 25 years, and was often speaker. (*White's Hist. Ga.*, p. 501.)

ADAMS, Dr. Ira, d. at Lowville, N. Y., March 8, 1857, a. 65.

ADAMS, George B., of Pa., consul for the U. S. at Alicant, Spain; d. Sept. 10, 1834.

ADAMS, JAMES, a native of Mass., and a soldier of the revolution, d. at Hartford, Susquehannah co., Pa., March 27, 1849, a. 104 years.

ADAMS, JOHN, financier, for many years at the head of the mercantile firm of Clendenning & Adams of N. Y., and later was pres. of the Fulton Bank, filling this office from 1827 to his death; was for a time treas. of the Am. Bible Soc., and 37 years treas. of the N. Y. Hospital; d. in 1855, a. 83.

ADAMS, J. C., noted bear tamer, familiarly known as Old Adams, of California, d. Oct. 26, 1860, at Neponset, Mass., having long suffered from injuries received from a grizzly bear in California.

ADAMS, REV. JOHN W., d. at Syracuse, N. Y., April 1, 1850, a. 54.

ADAMS, ROBERT H., senator in congress from Mississippi, d. at Natchez, July 2, 1830.

ADAMS, SAMUEL, patriot and surgeon in revolution; native of Killingly, Ct.; studied medicine and settled at Truro, Mass.; served as surgeon through the war, and settled at Bath, Me., where he died in 1819, a. 74. (*Bradford's N. E. Biog.*)

ADAMS, SAMUEL, in 1844 was presiding officer of the Arkansas senate, and for a short time acting governor; was afterwards state treas., and held that office till a short time before his death which occurred Feb. 27, 1850.

ADAMS, STEPHEN, native of Pennsylvania, was a senator in that state; removed to Mississippi, and was elected to the legislature; a judge of the circuit court, and from 1852 to 1857, a senator in congress; d. at Memphis, Tenn., May 11, 1857.

ADAMS, THOMAS BOYLSTON, son of Pres. John A., grad. at H. U., in 1790; engaged in law practice; was a judge of com. pleas, and in 1811 one of the executive council; d. in 1832.

ADAMS, DR. ZABDIEL BOYLSTON, d. in Boston, Mass., Jan. 25, 1855; b. in Roxbury, Feb. 1793; grad. at H. U. in 1813, and was a skilful and successful physician.

ADAN, JOHN R., grad. at H. U., in 1813; read law with Judge Wm. Prescott; several years pres. of the city council; represented Suffolk co. in the senate; was several times a counselor of the government; d. at Boston, July 4, 1849. (*Stryker's Am. Regr.*, iii, 233.)

ADDISON, DANIEL DULANY, loyalist capt. in Md., in 1782; at the peace was a maj., and went to England, where he d. in London in 1808.

AGNEW, REV. JOHN, rector of the parish of Suffolk, Va.; was called to account Mar. 24, 1775, for his tory principles; soon left and became chaplain of the Queen's Rangers; settled in New Brunswick; d. near Fredericton in 1812, a. 85. (*Sabine's Loyalists.*)

AGNEW, STAIR, loyalist captain in Queen's Rangers, and it is thought a son of Rev. John A. of Va.; settled at Fredericton, New Brunswick, where he d. 1821, a. 63; was a half pay officer, and was a prisoner for some time. (*Sabine's Loyalists.*)

ALBEERS, SOLOMON G., a merchant of Baltimore, Md., d. Oct. 19, 1839, in his 63d year.

ALBURTIS, WILLIAM, capt. 2d U. S. Infantry; kd. at the siege of Vera Cruz, March 11, 1847; served with reputation in the Florida war.

ALBRIGHT, John, d. at East Homer, N. Y., March 2, 1845, a. 85; served in the revolution; was twice a prisoner with the enemy, once at Fort Montgomery and once by the Indians at Fort Stanwix.

ALDERSON, Col. James C., d. at Holly Springs, Mississippi, 1850, having filled many offices of trust and honor in the state; at the time of his death, he was pres. of the Northern Bank of Mississippi.

ALDIS, Asa, grad. Brown U.; eminent lawyer; in 1815 chief justice of the sup. court of Vermont; d. at St. Albans, Oct. 18, 1847, a. 77.

ALEXANDER, Andrew, d. near Lexington, Va., Feb. 6, 1847; a. 75; he had been a member of the state legislature and took much interest in internal improvements.

ALEXANDER, Elijah, a native of Mecklenburg, N. C.; when 16 or 17 years old joined the army as a vol., and served several months; d. in Tennesse, Nov. 10, 1850, at the age of 90.

ALEXANDER, Mrs., d. at Winchester, N. H., July, 1835, aged 100.

ALFRED, Asahel, rev. soldier, settled in Columbia, Herkimer co., N. Y., in 1791, from Ct.; d. June, 1853, a. 93; was in the battle of Monmouth, and taken prisoner at the Cedars in Canada and encountered many perils. (*Benton's Herkimer Co.*, p. 390.)

ALICE, a female slave, b. in Philadelphia, of parents that came from Barbadoes, d. at Bristol, Pa., in 1803, a. 116. She was quite blind at 100, but gradually regained her sight at 102. (*Kirby's Museum*, ii, 271.)

ALLAIRE, Anthony, tory; in 1782, a lieut. in the Loyal Am. Regt., and at the peace a captain; he settled in New Brunswick, received half pay, was a grantee of St. John, but removed to the country, and d. in Ct., in the parish of Douglas, in 1838, a. 84.

ALLEN, Adam, tory officer in the Queen's Rangers; went to St. Johns, N. B., rec'd half pay, and in 1798 was in command at Grand Falls on the St. Johns; d. in York co., N. B., in 1823, a. 66. (*Sabine's Loyalists.*)

ALLEN, Andrew, son of Chief Justice Wm. A., of Pa.; was early in the revolution a whig, and served in congress in 1775–6, and on the com. of safety; in 1776 he became tory, and during the war went to England where he d. in London in 1825, a. 85. (*Sabine's Loyalists.*)

ALLEN, Capt. A., an early settler at Jefferson, O., was capt. of a vol. co., in war of 1812; served under Gen Harrison; d. May 26, 1850.

ALLEN, Benjamin, LL.D., an eminent classical teacher, and formerly prof. of mathematics in Union College, Schenectady; d. at Hyde Park, N. Y., July 22, 1836.

ALLEN, Rev. Beverly, removed from Va., merchant in Elbert co., Ga.; became a self taught and effective preacher; upon going in 1794 to Augusta to purchase goods, with his brother Billy, he resisted and killed the marshal (Robert Forsyth, father of the celebrated John F.), fled to Elbert co., was arrested, lodged in jail, rescued by a mob, and fled to the extreme western frontier; d. at an advanced age, apprehensive to the last of being arrested for killing Forsyth. (*White's Hist. Ga.*, p. 448.)

ALLEN, Chilton, born in Albemarle co., Va., settled when a lad in Kentucky; in 1807, removed to Winchester, where he studied law and settled; was elected to the state legislature in 1811, and subsequently served in both houses many years; was in congress from 1831 to 1837;

in 1837–8 was pres. of the board of internal improvement in Ky.; d. at Winchester, Ky., Sept. 3, 1858, a. 73.

ALLEN, GEN. ETHAN, rev. patriot, brig. gen., b. in Litchfield, Ct., Jan. 10, 1737; removed young to Vermont; took a bold and active part as a leader of the Green Mountain Boys in opposition to the government of New York, and captured Ticonderoga by surprise May 10, 1775, aided by 83 Vermonters; in the fall of 1775 he visited Canada twice, was taken prisoner to Halifax, and thence to N. Y., where he was exchanged for Col. Campbell May 6, 1778; was active in procuring the recognition of Vermont as a separate state; d. at his home in Burlington, Vt., Feb. 12, 1789. The state of Vermont, in 1858, erected a monument to his memory at Burlington. (*Rogers's Am. Biog.; Hist. Mag.*, ii, 256.) *Allen's Biog. Dict.*, 2d ed. says Ethan was born at Roxbury. *Pease and Niles's Gazetteer of Conn. and R. I.*, Cornwall. *Blake's Biog. Dict.*, Salisbury. *Sparks's Life of Allen and Barber's, Conn.*, Litchfield. *Cothren's Hist. of Woodbury*, says Woodbury. The records of the town of Litchfield contain the register of his birth, Jan. 10, 1737–8. (*Hist. Mag.*, ii, p. 49.)

ALLEN, ETHAN A., last surviving son of Col. Ethan A., of the rev., grad. at West Point in 1806; was lieut. Oct. 1809, and capt. of 1st Artillery in 1814; was disbanded in 1821; d. at his home in Norfolk co.; Va., Dec. 6, 1854, in his 70th year. (*N. Y. Eve. Post.*)

ALLEN, GEORGE F., pres. of trustees of N. Y. Inst. for the Blind; d. Aug. 1, 1863.

ALLEN, HEMAN, b. in 1776; was a resident of Milton, Vt.; studied law, and was elected to congress from 1827 to 1829, and again from 1833 to 1839; afterwards removed to Burlington; d. there Dec. 11, 1844; at one time minister to Chili.

ALLEN, DR. JAMES, health officer of Halifax; d. at Halifax, Sept. 1, 1857, a. 35.

ALLEN, JAMES, a general officer in the Texan war of independence, and pioneer settler in California; d. at Washoe, Nevada ter., Oct. 30, 1863.

ALLEN, JAMES BOWDOIN, member of the Suffolk bar; d. at East Boston, Mass., Dec. 23, 1853, a. 29; post master at East Boston at the time of his death.

ALLEN, JENNINGS, a soldier of the rev.; d. in Fairfield dist., S. C., Jan. 1835, a. 114.

ALLEN, JOHN, socialist, native of N. E., and formerly a Universalist preacher; he early adopted the former doctrine, became a popular orator and was connected with the experiment at Brook farm, and upon its failure removed to Patriot, Ind.; engaged in vine raising; d. Oct. 15, 1858. (*Hist. Mag.*, ii, 350.)

ALLEN, RICHARD C., judge of the U. S. dist. court of Apalachicola; d. at St. Joseph's, Florida, July 30, 1841.

ALLEN, SAMUEL, M.D., of Mass., settled at Lowville, N. Y., April, 1809, and in 1811 in Copenhagen, N. Y., as a merchant and manufacturer; d. June 12, 1849, a. 66; he possessed fine social wit and pleasing manners. (*Hough's Hist. Lewis Co., N. Y.*, p. 82, with portrait.)

ALLEY, DR. JOHN BURROUGHS, d. in Boston, Mass., April 29, 1862, a. 41; grad. at Yale, and at the Har. Med. Sch.; several years supt. of the Boston Dispensary; at one time sec. of the Mass. Med. Soc.

ALLEY, SAUL, a leading merchant and capitalist of N. Y. city; d. Oct. 21, 1852, a. 74.

ALLSTON, WILLIS, mem. of congress from N. C., from 1799 to 1815, and from 1825 to 1831; d. at Gretna Green, N. C., April 10, 1837; b. in Halifax co.; served several years in the state legislature.

ALLSTON, WILLIAM MOORE, brother of the distinguished artist; d. at Newport, R. I., May 29, 1844, a. 62.

ALLYN, CAPT. FRANCIS, a leading citizen of New London, Conn.; d. in that city, Aug. 23, 1862. He brought Lafayette to America in 1824.

ALMADA, DON DOMINGO, a wealthy Cuban, d. at New York, April 13, 1870, a 83.

ALSOP, JOHN, a venerable member of the society of Friends; d. at Ledyard, N. Y., April 28, 1835, a. 84.

ALSTON, JOHN ASHE, son of Wm. Algernon A., of Georgetown, La., and nephew of Washington A. he was educated at the Va. Univ.; resided at Georgetown as a planter, and was several years in the legislature of La.; in 1854 he removed to New Orleans, his native city; d. at Sullivan's island, Oct. 8, 1848, in his 42d year.

ALSTON, COL. WILLIAM, d. in Charleston, S. C., June 26, 1839, a. 83; was a captain under Marion; in the state senate and a presidential elector, and father of the late Gov. Joseph Alston. (*Am. Almanac*, 1840, p. 305.)

ALTHOUSE, JOHN., of N. Y., tory, and in 1782 capt. of N. Y. Vols.; he went to New Brunswick where he d.; his son John A. jr., was, in 1782, an ensign in the N. Y. Vols.

ALVEAR, DON CARLOS DE, envoy ex., and minister plenipoten. of the Argentine republic to the U. S.; d. in N. Y. city, Nov. 4, 1852.

ALVORD, ELIJAH, d. at Greenfield, Mass., Sept. 9, 1840; had formerly been clerk of the county court of Franklin co.

ALVORD, JAMES C., elected mem. of the 26th congress for the Franklin dist.; d. at Greenfield, Mass., Sept. 27, 1839; grad. at Dartmouth in 1827; a lawyer of good standing; served in both branches of the state legislature.

AMES, NATHANIEL, a soldier of the rev.; b. in Killingly, Conn., April 25, 1761; d. at Rome Corners, Wis., Oct. 27, 1863.

AMES, MRS. SARAH, d. at Waterford, Ct., Dec. 14, 1840, a. 105.

AMHERST, WILLIAM, bro. of Sir Jeffrey A., b. in 1732; lieut. Sept. 21, 1757, and capt. of the 1st Regt. Foot Guards; aid to the commander at Louisburgh in 1758; in 1759 lt. col; in 1760 at Oswego; appointed to the command of the Light Infantry battalion; in 1762 was sent to expel the French from Newfoundland, and in 1766 became col. in the army and aid-de-camp to the king; in 1774 became lieut. gov. of St. Johns, N. F., and in 1755, col. of the 32d Foot; in 1777 was major gen.; in 1779 lieut. gen.; d. May 13, 1781; his son succeeded to the title of Earl of Amherst. (*Com. Wilson's Orderly Book*, *Munsell's Hist. Series*, i, 34.)

AMORY, JOHN, d. N. Y., Aug. 11, 1780; native of N. Y. city; left his property near Albany as a loyalist refugee in 1777, and joined Burgoyne's army; went to Canada after the surrender, whither after great hardships his family followed him. (See *Rivington's Gazette*, Aug. 16.)

AMORY, THOMAS C., merch. in Boston, d. in 1812, a. 45.

ANDERSON, DR. ALEXANDER, pioneer wood engraver, and distinguished for the abundance and excellence of his work which he continued to produce till near the end of life: d. at N. Y., Jan. 17, 1870, a. 95. (See *Lossing's Memoir.*)

ANDERSON, ANDREW, M. D., pres. of the Southern Life Ins. and Trust Co.; formerly of N. Y.; d. Nov. 7, 1839, at St. Augustine, Fla.

ANDERSON, CORNELIUS V., formerly chief eng. of the fire dept. of N. Y. city; at the time of his death, one of the board of ten governors; d. in N. Y. city, Nov. 29, 1868.

ANDERSON, JACOB, a militia officer in the rev.; d. in Hunterdon co., N. J., May 11, 1837, a. 84.

ANDERSON, JAMES B., ed. of the *New Orleans Sun;* d. at New Orleans, May, 1840.

ANDERSON, JOHN, a tory, of Thickety Creek, S. C.; accepted an office in 1780; a lieut. in 1782, and at the peace capt. in the King's Rangers; his estate was confiscated.

ANDERSON, GEN. ROBERT E., of the U. S. A., and the hero of Fort Sumter; d. at Nice, Italy, Oct. 26, 1871.

ANDERSON, SAMUEL, formerly an associate judge of the king's bench; at the rev., he joined the royal cause; was capt. in the King's Royal Regt. of N. Y., and after the peace settled at Cornwall, Canada; d. in Canada, Oct. 6, 1836, a. 101.

ANDERSON, DR. SAMUEL, mem. of the 20th congress from Chester, Pa.; often served in the state legislature, and in 1849 was a speaker in the house of representatives; d. at Chester, Pa., Jan. 17, 1850, in the 77th year of his age.

ANDERSON, SIMEON H., mem. of congress from Kentucky from 1839 to 1841; d. near Lancaster, Ky., Aug. 11, 1840.

ANDERSON, THOMAS O., formerly a lieut. in the U. S. navy; d. in Newton, Sussex co., N. J., April 14, 1844, a. 60; was one of the company under Decatur who captured and burned the frigate Philadelphia in the harbor of Tripoli.

ANDERSON, WALKER, a native of Va.; res. many years in Florida; for a time chief justice of the supreme court of that state; d. at Pensacola, Fl., Jan. 13, 1857.

ANDERSON, DR. WILLIAM, b. in Princeton; where he grad. in 1789; rem. to Schenectady, N. Y., practiced medicine with Dr. Joseph W. Hegeman; went to New Orleans; d. of yellow fever in returning in 1811. (*Tr. N. Y. St. Med. Soc.*, 1857, p. 29; *Munsell's Ann. Alb.*, ix, 93.)

ANDERSON, WILLIAM E., formerly a judge in Tennessee; d. at Vicksburgh, Miss., a. 50; a distinguished lawyer, and much esteemed.

ANDREWS, ASA, d. in Ipswich, Mass., Jan. 13, 1856; b. in Shrewsbury, Mass., in 1762; grad. at Cambridge in 1783; settled at Ipswich, where he spent his life; collector there from 1794 till 1829.

ANDREWS, CHARLES, d. in Paris, Me., April 30, 1852, a. 38; a rep. in congress from the 4th dist. of Maine; b. in Paris, in 1814; admitted to the bar in 1837, and settled in Turner; in the state legislature from 1839 to 1843, and in 1842 was speaker.

ANDREWS, ISAAC, served in the last war with Great Britain; d. at Newark, N. J., March 4, 1850, a. 76.

ANDREWS, JAMES, consul of several foreign states ; d. in Boston, Mass., Feb. 24, 1842.

ANDREW, REV. JAMES OSGOOD, bp. of the M. E. Ch. S. ; b. near Washington, Wilkes co., Ga., May 3, 1794 ; his father, a soldier of the rev., was the first native Georgian who entered the itinerant ministry of the M. E. Ch. ; the son was admitted as a preacher in 1812, and labored with success on various circuits until in 1832 he was ordained bp. at Phila. ; in 1844 the Gen. Conf. at N. Y., passed resolutions for deposing him unless he would cease owning slaves, which he had received by legacy and marriage, this led to the division of the M. Ch. into N. and S., the division resting chiefly upon the slavery question ; d. at Mobile, Ala., March 2, 1871. (*White's Hist. Ga.*, p. 515, with portrait.)

ANDREWS, JOANNA, d. in Gloucester, Mass., Jan. 20, 1847, a. 102.

ANDREWS, REV. SAMUEL, P. E. minister in Ct. ; became tory ; went to N. B. ; was first rector at St. Andrews, and after a ministry of 58 ys. d. there, Sept. 26, 1818, a. 82. (*Sabine's Loyalists.*)

ANDREWS, ISAAC, d. in Newark, N. J., Feb., 1850, a. 76 ; he commanded a regt. of N. J. militia in the war of 1812, and was stationed for a time at Sandy Hook, for the defense of the coast, and harbor of N. Y. ; was afterwards brig. gen., and for nearly thirty years a magistrate in his county, and a mem. of the Pres. ch.

ANSLEY, OZIAS, a tory ; in 1782 an ensign in the 1st battalion of N. J. vols. ; he settled in N. Brunswick ; rec'd half pay ; was a magistrate and a judge of com. pleas several years ; d. at Staten Island, N. Y., in 1828, a. 85 ; his son Rev. Tho. A., a P. E. minister of Nova Scotia ; d. at St. Andrews, N. B., in 1831, a. about 65. (*Sabine's Loyalists.*)

ANTHON, DR. CHARLES CHRISTIAN, native of Germany ; grad. at Amsterdam ; was in the service of the Dutch W. I. Co. ; Lord Amherst appointed him hosp. surg., at N. Y., and from thence was transferred to Detroit, where he remained through the French and Indian wars ; he settled in N. Y., in 1784, and died in 1815, a. 81 ; was the father of Prof. Chas. A., of Columbia Coll. (*Hist. Mag.*, iv, 97.)

ANTHONY, JOSEPH B., pres. judge of the 8th dist. court of Pa., and mem. of the 23d and 24th congresses ; d. at Williamsport, Pa., Jan. 17, 1851.

APPLEGATE, A. J., ex-lieut. gov., d. at Mobile, Ala., Aug. 22, 1870.

APPLETON, GEN. JAMES, d. in Ipswich, Mass., Aug. 25, 1862 ; b. at that place Feb. 14, 1785 ; served in the legislature ; removed to Portland, where he was also elected to the legislature ; in the war of 1812, he was a col. of militia, and became a brig. gen.

APTHORP, CHARLES WARD, mem. of the council of N. Y., and held property in Mass., which was confiscated, by law, on account of his tory principles.

ARCHER, SAMUEL, a mer. of Phila., and for many years a successful importer of East India and China goods ; d. 1839, a. 68.

ARCULARIUS, PHILIP I., mem. of assembly in 1798, 9, 1801, 2, 5, and a citizen of great worth ; d. in N. Y., August, 1849.

ARDEN, JOHN B., of N. Y., late attaché of the U. S. emb., at Berlin ; killed by a rail road accident near Minden, Germany, Jan. 21, 1851. (*Stryker's Am. Reg.*, vi, 208.)

ARMISTEAD, ANTHONY, a soldier of the rev.; d. Feb. 10, 1841, in Wilkinson co., Miss., a. 83.

ARMISTEAD, CAPT. WILLIAM, d. in Clark co., Ala., March 1, 1842, a. 83; was present at the battles of Monmouth and Stony Point.

ARMSTRONG, AMZI, d. in Petersburgh, Va., April 12, 1845, a. 38; b. in Mendham, N. J.; grad. at Princeton; studied law with T. Frelinghuysen; a mem. of the council of the state of N. J., and of the court of errors and appeals.

ARMSTRONG, JOHN, a rev. soldier, and many years a judge of com. pleas; d. in Warren co., N. J., May 7, 1836, a. 87.

ARMSTRONG, ROBERT L., mem. of the bar of N. J.; d. at Trenton, Sept. 21, 1838.

ARMSTRONG, SAMUEL T., held many offices of trust; was lieut. gov. and for a time acting gov. of Massachusetts; a mem. of the state senate and mayor of Boston; was a well known bookseller and publisher, and a useful mem. of A. B. C. F. mission; d. at Boston, March 26, 1850, a. 66. (*Stryker's Am. Reg.*, iv, 453; *Am. Almanac*, 1851, p. 310.)

ARMSTRONG, WILLIAM, was a loyalist capt. in the rev.; settled in N. Y. at the peace; in 1806 he joined Miranda's expedition as col. of riflemen, and a q. m. gen.; he got involved in quarrels with every one about him, and finally quit without leave and went to London. (*Sabine's Loyalists.*)

ARNOLD, EDWARD, rev. soldier; d. at Little Falls, N. Y., Oct. 29, 1842, in his 83d year.

ARNOLD, BENEDICT, the Descendants of. Very little is known in this country respecting the descendants of Benedict Arnold. Arnold's treason was not looked upon in England in the same light as Americans viewed it; there he was regarded as a man who had repented of his error and had returned to the allegiance of his king. Occasionally he met with persons who did not fail to express their contempt for him, but the majority of people were inclined to put the best construction on his actions. The popular idea that he died unknown in a foreign land, and that his descendants have dropped out of the recollection of men, is not in accordance with the actual state of the case. Arnold m. first in early life, —— Mansfield, who died at New Haven about 1775. By this marriage he had three sons:

1. BENEDICT, who is described as a violent and headstrong youth, held a commission in the British army, and d. in the West Indies.
2. RICHARD, was a merchant; a lieut. of cav., in the Am. Legion in 1782, commanded by his father, and his history down to 1829, is identical with that of his brother Henry. It is believed that the store at St. Johns was burned to obtain a fraudulent insurance; is supposed to have died in Canada. (*Sabine's Loyalists.*)
3. HENRY, was a merchant; joined the king's service after his father's treason; was lieut. col. of cavalry in the Am. Legion and accompanied his father to St. Johns, where he was in business; his store was burnt on a night when he slept in it, yet was thought to have been fired by his own hand; afterwards resided in Troy, N. Y.; went to Canada, where in 1829, he was reputed rich; rec'd half pay, and a grant of lands from the British government, and is supposed to have died in Canada. (*Sabine's Loyalists.*)

Arnold m. 2d, April 8, 1779, Margaret, dau. of Judge Edward Shippen of Penna., and d. in 1801, having had issue as follows:

4. EDWARD SHIPPEN, lieut. 6th Bengal Cavalry; paymaster at Muttra; d. at Singapore, India, Dec. 13, 1813.
5. JAMES ROBERTSON, b. in the U. S.; an infant when his father fled from West Point; m. Virginia, dau. of Bartlett Goodrich, of Saling Grove, Essex, which lady d. July 14, 1852; he entered the British army, was col. of eng. and was stationed at Bermuda in 1816–18, and at Halifax in 1818–23; was lieut. gen. K. H. and K. C., and aid-de-camp to Queen Victoria; d. 1834.
6. GEORGE ARNOLD, lieut. col., 2d Bengal Cav.; m. Anne Brown; d. in India, Nov. 1, 1828.
7. WILLIAM FITCH, the only one of his sons who left issue, was born June, 25, 1794. He was a captain in the 19th Lancers, and m. May 19, 1819, Elizabeth Cecilia, only dau. of Alexander Ruddach, of the island of Tobago, capt. in the royal navy, and had issue:
    1. Edwin Gladwin Arnold, the present head of the family, is a clergyman of the established church of England, and rector of Barrow in Cheshire; was b. April 25, 1823; m. April 27, 1852, Charlotte Georgiana, eldest dau. of Lord Henry Cholmondeley (a younger son of the Marquis Cholmondeley), and has issue as follows: 1. Edward Cholmondeley Arnold, b. Dec. 15, 1854. 2. William Henry Arnold, b. March 23, 1856; midshipman royal navy. 3. Charles Lowther Arnold, b. Dec. 28, 1859. 4. Henry Abel Arnold, b. Aril 5, 1861. Arthur Seymour Arnold, b. April 24, 1865. 6 Herbert Tollemachel Arnold, b. April 5, 1867. 7. Maria Elizabeth Arnold. 8. Emma Charlotte Georgiana Arnold. 9. Mabel Caroline Frances Arnold.
    2. William Trail Arnold, b. Oct. 23, 1826, capt. 4th regt.; killed at Sebastopol, May 5, 1855.
    3. Margaret Stewart Arnold, m. to the Rev. Robert H. Rogers.
    4. Elizabeth Sophia Arnold, m. to the Rev. Bryant Burgess.
    5. Georgiana Phipps Arnold, m. to the Rev. John Stephenson.
    6. Louisa Russell Arnold, m. to the Rev. J. Cecil Rogers.

8. SOPHIA MATILDA, m. to Col. Pownall Phipps, of the East Indian army (related to the Earl of Mulgrave's family,; d. 1828.

The estate and seat of the family is Little Missenden Abbey, Buckinghamshire, a property which had previous to the reformation belonged to the church. Arnold received from the British government several grants of land in Canada, one of them being situated near what is now the city of Toronto; this, after being held by the family for a long series of years, has recently become of great value. The present Edward Gladwin Arnold inherited it from his father, who came into possession of, it on the death of his elder brother Gen. James Robertson Arnold. Whatever may have been the failings of Arnold, there is no denying the fact that his sons and grandsons were high-minded and honorable men. (*Albany Argus.*) This notice has been extended because no where else so fully and correctly stated.

ARNOLD, REV. OLIVER, b. in Ct.; grad. at Yale in 1776; went to St. John, N. B., after the rev.; labored as a missionary and became rector of Sussex, N. B., where he d. in 1834, a 79; he was ardently attached to the Epis. ch. (*Sabine's Loyalists.*)

ARNOT, Hugh, came to America as lieut. in 42d Highlanders in 1756; became capt., Dec. 27, 1757; served at Ft. Wm. Henry, under Amherst in 1759; continued in the army till 1769. (*Wilson's Orderly Book*, 143.)

ARRINDELL, Sir William, chief justice of Demarara; d. Jan. 27, 1863.

ARUSMONT, D' Madame, better known as Fanny Wright; d. in Cincinnati, O., Dec. 4, 1852; a native of Dundee, Scotland; b. in 1795, and was well known on account of her teachings in socialism and her peculiar theological views.

ASHBARNER, Luke, d. in Stockbridge, Mass., June 17, 1844; b. in India, on the Malabar coast, of an affluent English family, and educated in England; returned to India, but in 1817, came to the U. S.; settled with his family at Stockbridge, where he res. till his death.

ASHE, Richard, of Beaufort, S. C.; after the surrender of Charleston, in 1780, accepted a British commission and his estate was confiscated.

ASHLEY, Gen. Turner, of the confed. army; killed near Harisonburg, Va., June 6, 1862; b. at Rose Hill, Fauquier co., Va., about 1824; res. at Markham, Va., when the war begun; he was a dashing and brave brave cav. officer, and was made brig. gen. in May, 1862.

ASHLEY, Chester, U. S. senator from Arkansas; d. at Washington, D. C., April 29, 1848, a. 58; b. in Westfield, Mass., June 1, 1790; removed in infancy to Hudson, N. Y., where he lived till 27; then emigrated, and after practicing successfully as a lawyer about two years he went to the ter. of Arkansas, and established himself at Little Rock; in 1844 was chosen senator, and was chairman of the judiciary committee.

ASHMAN, George, d. at Springfield, Mass., July 16, 1870, a. 66; b. in Brandford, Mass., Dec. 25, 1804; grad. at Yale in 1823, and studied law at Greenfield; was in the state legislature in 1833, 5, 6, 8, 41, and in the latter year was speaker; in cong. from 1845 to 1851.

ASHTON, Col. Henry, marshal of the Dist. of Columbia; d. at Washington, Feb. 24, 1834.

ATIATONHARONKWEN, or Atayataghronghta. (See *Cook, Louis.*)

ATKINS, Charles, in 1774, was one of the com. of corres., in Charleston, S. C.; became a tory, and in 1780 applied with others for arms; in 1782, he was an officer of vols.; was banished and his property confiscated; he went to England. (*Sabine's Loyalists.*)

ATKINS, Rev. Elisha, pastor of Cong. ch. in Killingly, Conn; d. June 11, 1839; was a chaplain in the rev. war.

ATKINS, Quintus F., removed from Connecticut to Ohio: was a pioneer on the Western Reserve, and a lieut under Gen. Harrison; d. in Brooklyn, Ohio, Jan. 23, 1859, a. 77.

ATKINSON, Daniel C., d. at Sandbornton Bridge, N. H., April 4, 1842; he was many years judge of probate in Strafford county.

ATKINSON, Thomas C., b. in Baltimore, and for 9 years a resident of Alexandria; chief engineer of the Orange and Alexandria R. R., from the beginning of the work; d. at Alexandria, Dec. 6, 1858.

ATTWATER, Russell, pioneer agent and settler of Russell, N. Y.; b. June 20, 1762, at Chester, Ct.; settled at Russell, St. Lawrence co., N. Y., as agent in 1804; became county judge in 1808, and was com'r for building several roads; he was state senator in 1813–6, and pres. elector in 1816; d. at Norfolk, N. Y., June 16, 1851. (*Hough's Hist. St. Law. and Fr. Cos. N. Y.*, p. 584.)

AUDUBON, JOHN W., only surviving son of J. J. Audubon, the great naturalist; d. at N. Y., Aug., 1862; he was preparing a new edition of the *Birds of America.*

AUGUSTUS, GEORGE H., b. near St. Stephens, Ala., Nov. 12, 1802; bred to the law, and elected to the legislature of Mississippi in 1831; a judge of probate in Noxubee co., in 1833; afterwards elected to the house, and to the state senate, of which latter body he was pres.; d. in Kemper co., Miss., Oct. 28, 1850, a. 48.

AUSTIN, JOHN, M. D., a native of Barbadoes and formerly a surgeon in the British navy and practitioner at Barbadoes and Demarara; d. at Philadelphia, Pa., Dec. 25, 1837, a. 67.

AUSTIN, SAMUEL, b. in Boston and spent his life in that city; in 1815 entered mercantile business and continued so employed through life; was largely engaged in the Calcutta trade, and amassed a large fortune; elected to the state legislature in 1827, and was reëlected the next six years; a mem. of the com. council in 1829–30, and a director of the State bank, from 1824 till his death, Sept. 15, 1858, a. 65.

AVEL, REV. STEPHEN M., R.C., b. at Cabazat, Fr., 1822; ordained priest in 1847; appointed pastor at Santa Fe., and in July, 1858, was sent to a large mission in N. Mex.; d. Aug. 3, 1858, a. 36, of poisoned wine used in the service. (*Metropolitan Cath. Almanac*, 1859, p. 248.)

AVERILL, COL. PERRY, d. in Washington, Conn., July 10, 1842, a. 88; was an officer in the Connecticut line in the rev. war.

AVERY, REV EPHRAIM, Episcopal, of Pomfret, Ct.; grad. at Yale in 1767; succeeded Mr. Punderson as minister at Rye, N. Y., in 1765; he became obnoxious to the whigs in the rev., and his property was plundered; he d. Nov. 5, 1776; was a step son of Gen. Putnam. (*Doc. Hist. N. Y.*, iv, 409.)

AVERY, JULIUS, d. in Illinois, Nov. 27, 1870.

AXTELL, REV. HENRY, D.D., b. at Morristown, N. J., in 1784; grad. at Princeton in 1796; settled in Geneva, N. Y.; taught school; studied theology with Rev. J. Chapman, and was licensed by the Presbytery of Geneva, Nov. 1, 1810; in 1812 became pastor of a ch. at Geneva, and held till Feb. 11, 1829, when he died. (*Hotchkin's Western N. Y.*, p. 271.)

AYCINENA, DON ANTONIO DE, late consul gen. of Guatemala to the U. S.; d. in Washington, D.C., June 20, 1852.

AYLETT, ELIZABETH, wid. of Philip Aylett of Montville, and dau. of the orator Patrick Henry; d. Sept. 24, 1842, in King William co., Va., in her 74th year.

AYLETT, PATRICK HENRY, a lawyer; d. at Richmond, Va., April 27, 1870.

AYMAR, FRANCIS, b. in N. Y. city in 1759, was one of the grantees of St. John, N. B., where he settled in 1783, and lived there; lived also at Eastport, Me., New York, and St. Andrews; d. at the latter place in N. B, Oct., 1843, a. 84. (*Sabine's Loyalists.*)

AYRES, DR. DANIEL, b. at New Braintree, Mass., May 17, 1787; settled in Salisbury, N. Y., in 1792; studied medicine and settled at St. Johnsville, in N Y.; rem. to E. Canada Creek; in 1837 to Amsterdam, N. Y.; d. May 25, 1853. (*Tr. N. Y. St. Med. Soc.*, 1855, p. 170.)

AYRES, STEPHEN, b. at Braintree, Mass., Feb. 16, 1770; came with his father Jabez, to Salisbury, N. Y., in 1792; settled that year in Fairfield, N. Y.; in 1836 he was in the assembly; d. Sept. 17, 1850, a. 81. (*Benton's Herkimer Co.*, p. 294.)

BABCOCK, CHARLES, M.D., b. in Stonington, Ct., June, 1787; studied medicine in Phila., in 1808–9, and settled at New Hartford, N. Y.; d. July 4, 1850. (*Tr. N. Y. St. Med. Soc.*, 1851, p. 193.)

BABCOCK, REV. LUKE, youngest s. of Joshua B., Ch. Jus. of Sup. Court of R. I.; b. at Westerly, R. I., July 6, 1738; grad. at Yale in 1755; studied divinity; went to England for holy orders in 1769; licensed as a missionary Feb. 2, 1770, and the next year went to Philipsburg, N. Y.; becoming a tory, his person and papers were seized in 1776, he was detained several months, and Feb., 1777, was ordered to remove within the enemy's lines; d. Feb. 18, 1777. (*Bolton's Church in West Chester Co.*, p. 504; *Doc. Hist. N. Y.*, iv, 491.)

BACHE, THEOPHYLACT, of N. Y., a determined loyalist; his bro. Richard m. Sarah, dau. of Dr. Franklin and was a whig; resided at Flatbush, N. Y., was abducted in 1778; in 1782 vice pres. of the N. Y. Chamber of Commerce; d. in N. Y., in 1807, a. 78. (*Sabine's Loyalists*).

BACKER, BENJAMIN, sen., of Charleston, S. C., a tory, was banished and lost his estate under the act of 1782; d. soon after.

BACKER, JOHN, jr., of Marshfield, Mass., a tory; went to Halifax in 1776, and was proscribed and banished in 1778, but was afterwards in the U. S.

BACKUS, FREDERICK FANNING M.D., b. in Bethlehem, Ct.; June 15, 1794, s. of Rev. Azel Backus, D.D., Pres. of Ham. Coll., grad. at Yale in 1813; studied with Dr. Eli Ives, received a medical degree in 1816, and settled in Rochester, then a small village, and engaged in a laborious practice; in 1844–7, was in the state senate, where his influence procured the establishment of the Western House of Refuge at Rochester, and a state asylum for idiots; since removed to Syracuse; d. Nov. 4, 1859, a. 64. (*Tr. N. Y. St. Med. Soc.*, 1860, p. 176; *Hist. Mag.*, ii, 367).

BACKUS, a negro slave, d. in King George co., Va., March 26, 1840, a. 110.

BACON, EPAPHRODITUS CHAMPION, d. at Seville, Spain, Jan. 11, 1845, while traveling for his health, a. 33; grad. at Yale in 1833; studied law, and evinced a taste for historical researches.

BACON, JOHN, b. in Canterbury, Conn.; grad. at the Coll. of N. J., in 1765; preached in Md., and in Boston; left the pulpit and became representative in the legislature; presiding judge of com. pleas; senator and pres. of state senate, and from 1801 to 1803 mem. of cong.; d. in Berkshire co., Mass., Oct. 25, 1820.

BACON, JOHN F., b. in Mass., settled in law, at Albany; in 1814 clerk of the senate and held by annual appointment till 1840; appointed by Pres. Polk, U. S. consul at Nassau, N. P., and resigned about 1856; he afterwards spent his summers at Castleton, Rens. co., and winters at Nassau, where he d. Feb. 25, 1860, a. 71. (*Hist. Mag.*, iv, 157.)

BACON, RICHARD jr., poet, b. at Northington now Avon, Ct., and soon rem. with his parents to Simsbury; d. insane at the Hartford Asylum, Dec. 29, 1838, a. 24. (*Griswold's Biog. Annual*, 1841, 121.)

BADGER, REV. MOSES, grad. at Harv., in 1761, m. a dau. of Judge Saltonstall; was an Episcopal minister and a loyalist; went to Halifax in 1776, and was at one time chaplain to De Lancey's 2d battalion; became rector of King's chapel, Prov., R. I., after the war; d. there in 1792. (*Sabine's Loyalists.*)

BAGBY, ARTHUR P., b. in Va., in 1794, and studied law; settled in Alabama in 1818; was in the state legislature in 1820, and 1822, and governor of the state from 1837 to 1841; senator in congress, from 1843 to 1849, and minister to Russia in 1849, where he remained four years; d. at Mobile, Ala., Sept. 21, 1858, a. 64.

BAILEY, ADAMS, rev. officer, of Scituate, Mass., was a capt., and d. at an advanced age. (*Bradford's N. E. Biog.*)

BAILEY, ADAMS, b. in Scituate, Mass., and except 2 years, held office in the Boston Custom House, 42 years, and for nearly half this time dep. coll; was for many years secretary of the Mass. Soc. of Cincinnati, and d. in Boston, Nov. 20, 1858, a. 69.

BAILEY, CAPT. DANIEL, a soldier of the rev., d. at Goshen, N. Y., May 16, 1841, a. 84.

BAILEY, GEN. MOUNTJOY, an officer of the rev.; d. at Washington, D.C., March 22, 1836, in his 82d year.

BAILEY, GOLDSMITH F., member of cong.; d. at Fitchburgh, Mass., May 8, 1862.

BAILEY, HENRY, a lawyer of distinction, and formerly attorney general of S. Carolina; d. at Charleston, April 28, 1849.

BAILEY, JOHN, mem. in congress from Mass., from 1823 to 31; d. at Dorchester, Mass., June 26, 1835.

BAILEY, LIEUT. MOSES, d. March 14, 1842, at Andover, Mass.; his descendants then living amounted to 135 persons.

BAILEY, REV. WINTHROP, Unit. clergyman; d. at Deerfield, Mass., March 16, 1835, a. 51.

BAILEY, WILLIAM, tory, was capt. lt. of Loyal Am. regt., in 1782; settled in New Bruns. after the war, and received half pay; d. on the St. John, near Fredericton, in 1832, a. 97.

BAKER, CAPT. RICHARD BOHUN, d. at Ft. Moultrie, S. C., Nov. 6, 1837, a. 80; last survivor of those who defended that fort in the rev. war.

BAKER, DR SAMUEL, pres. of the Medico-chirurgical soc., and formerly prof. of Materia Medica in the Univ. of Md.; d. Oct. 16, 1835, a. 50.

BAKER, MAJ. JAMES N., b. in Phila., and was an officer in the war of 1812, where he rose to the rank of major; in 1820, was mayor of Phila.; in 1829, collector of that port, which office he held till 1838, when he was appointed first comp. of the treas.; he held this place some years, and remained in the treas. dep. till his death March 9, 1858; he was a dramatic and literary writer.

BAKER, THEOPHILUS, native of Yarmouth, Mass., and a patriot of the rev.; d. at Eden, N. Y., April, 1838, a. 90.

BAKER, VERY REV. R. S., D.D., d. at Charleston, S. C., March 6, 1873, a. 63.

BALCH, REV. STEPHEN BLOOMER, d. at Georgetown, D. C., Sept. 22, 1833, a. 87.

BALCH, THOMAS, d. at Waterloo, N. Y., Jan. 17, 1840, a. 75; served under Paul Jones in the rev.

BALDWEEN, JOHN, served the king through the rev., sought refuge in Charlotte co., N. Bruns.; d. at St. George, N. B., Aug., 1840, a. 91. (*Sabine's Loyalists.*)

BALDWIN, ABRAHAM, b. in Conn.; grad. at Yale in 1772; tutor from 1775 to 1779; studied law and settled in Savannah; was in state legislature; was founder of the Univ. of Georgia; in continental congress from 1785 to 1788, and a member of the convention for preparing the constitution of the U. S.; was in cong. from 1789 to 1799, and in the U. S. senate from 1799 to 1807; d. March 4, 1807, a. 53.

BALDWIN, ABRAHAM DUDLEY, d. May 20, 1862, in Boston; b. in Woburn, Mass., April 29, 1782; became a civil eng. in which his father and bro. both named Loamini were engaged; was engaged in various public works. (*National Almanac*, 1863, p. 326.)

BALDWIN, BRISCOE G., d. in Staunton, Va., May 18, 1852; one of the judges of Court of Appeals of Va.; b. in Winchester, Va., Jan. 4, 1789; elected by the legislature to the trust in which he d. in 1842.

BALDWIN, CHRISTOPHER C., lib. of the Am. Antiquarian Soc. of Worcester Mass.; killed at Norwich O., Aug. 20, 1835, by the upsetting of a stage coach.

BALDWIN, DR. JONAS C., b. in Windsor, Mass., June 3, 1768; studied medicine and was for a time professionally employed at Little Falls; in 1797, he removed to Ovid; in 1801 or 2 to Onondaga, East Hill, and in 1807 to Lysander and founded the village of Baldwinsville; d. March 3, 1827. (*Clark's Onondaga*, ii, 159 with portrait.)

BALDWIN, EDMUND, late a mem. of N. Y. assembly; d. in West Indies, May 3, 1861, a. 57.

BALDWIN, GRANT B., d. at Elmira N. Y., Feb. 1840, in his 48th year; formerly first judge of Tioga co., N. Y.

BALDWIN, HARVEY, pioneer settler of Onondaga co., N. Y., b. Feb. 4, 1797; d. in Syracuse, Sept., 1863; a son of Dr. Jonas C. Baldwin, and largely interested in business at Baldwinsville.

BALDWIN, REV. METHUSELAH, d. in Scotchtown, Orange co., N. Y., March 27, 1847, a. 84; was licensed to preach by the presbytery of Newark in 1791; ordained in Dutchess co., in 1793 and settled.

BALDWIN, REV. THERON, D.D., d. at Orange, N. J., April 10, 1870.

BALDWIN, WILLIAM, M.D., naval surgeon and botanist, son of Tho. B., b. in Newlin, Chester co., Pa., Mar. 29, 1779; in 1805 became surg. in a merchant ship to Canton; in 1807, grad. at Phila.; m. and settled at Wilmington, Del.; became a zealous botanist and continued so through life; June, 1812, was appointed surg. in the navy; was stationed at St. Mary's, Flor. 2 ys.; in 1817 his reputation as a botanist led to his being sent with a frigate to South America; in 1819 he went with Maj. Long's ex. up the Missouri, but his constitution was unequal to the labor; d. at Franklin on the Missouri, Sept. 1, 1819, a. 41. (*Reliquae Baldwinianae, by Wm. Darlington*, Phila., 1843, 12 mo., p. 346, with portrait.)

BALENTINE, ALEXANDER, tory, from the U. S.; went to St. John N. B.; and was one of the grantees of that city.

BALFOUR, HENRY, became lieut. in 2d Battalion Royal Foot, Mar. 15, 1755; capt. Oct. 8, 1761; major in July 15, 1768, and left the regiment in July, 1769; served in America in the French war.

BALLARD, GEN. KRADAH, an officer of the rev.; d. in Gates co., N. C., in Jan. 16, 1834, in his 86th year.

BALLARD, JOHN PARKER, formerly of Pepperell, Me.; grad. of Harv. in 1829; d. in Clinton, La., Jan., 1845.

BALLARD, JOSEPH A., for many years connected with the shipping department of the *Boston Daily Advertiser;* d. at Boston, Oct. 1, 1858, a. 53.

BALL, DR. MOTTROM, d. Aug. 23, 1842, at Woodbury, Va.; educated at Edinburgh and Glasgow, and practiced med. for a long time in his native county with great success.

BALL, ELIAS, of S. C.; two tories of S. C. of this name, one of Wambaw, and the other of Curmantee, held commissions under the crown after the surrender of Charleston, and both lost their property by confiscation.

BALL, JOHN, an ens. in the rev. war; d. near Parsippany, N. J., Dec. 15, 1838, a. 93.

BALL, RICHARD, d. Sept. 25, 1780, at N. Y.; surgeon's mate in gen. hospital (British); in America in the last war; several years surgeon to the British consul at Algiers, where he took an exact map of the city, mole and fortifications, which was published. (*Rivington's Gazette*, Sept. 30.)

BALL, WILLIAM LEE, b. in Lancaster co., Va., and in cong. from Virginia 1817 to 1824; d. Feb. 29, 1824, a. 43.

BALLINGALL, ROBERT, of S. C., a tory, and held a commission under the crown after the fall of Charleston in 1780; his estate was confiscated.

BANGS, EDWARD P., d. at Worcester, Mass., April 2, 1838; was many years sec. of commonwealth of Mass.

BANKS, HENRY, d. at Kentucky, Dec. 22, 1833, at an advanced age.

BANKS, LINN, accidentally drowned, Feb. 24, 1842, in Madison co., Va.; for 20 successive years speaker of the house of del. of Va.; he retired in 1838 and was elected to cong., in that year, to complete the unexpired term of Mr. Patton who was chosen councilor. (*Am. Almanac*, 1843, p. 307.)

BARBARIE, JOHN, in 1782, was capt. in 2d bat., of N. Y. Vol. (Loyalists), went to St. John, N. B. on the peace, was a grantee, and drew half pay; was col. of militia and a magistrate of the co. of York; d. at Sussex Vale in 1818, a. 67; his son Andrew, was a member of the house of assembly of N. B.

BARBARIE, OLIVER, in 1782 a lieut. in the Loyal Am. regt.; he settled at St. John, N. B., in 1783, and was a grantee; d. at Sussex Vale, N. B.

BARBER, JOHN H., editor of the *Newport Mercury*, with which he was connected 60 years; d. at Newport, R. I., Feb. 25, 1850. His paper was begun in 1758, by James Franklin jr., and was the second oldest existing paper in the country.

BARBER, NOYES, d. in Groton, Conn., Jan. 5, 1844, a. 43; was mem. of cong., from Conn., from 1821 to 1835.

BARBOUR, JAMES, eldest s. of James B., gov., of Va., from 1813 to 1815; d. in Barbourville, Va., Nov. 7, 1857, a. 58; b. Dec. 22, 1798; grad. at Harv. Coll., in 1818; went with his father to Europe in 1828, the former having been appointed minister to England, and enjoyed unusual opportunities for literary studies; after his return home, continued to pursue literature in the intervals of his leisure through life.

BARBOUR, PHILIP N., brev. maj. 3d U. S. Inf.; b. in Ky., and grad. at West Point, in 1834; served in the Florida war; killed at Monterey, Mex., Sept. 21, 1846. (*Am. Almanac*, 1848, p. 343.)

BARCLAY, MORDECAI, ex-gov. of Ohio; d. at Mansfield, O., Oct. 9, 1870, a. 84.

BARCLAY, THOMAS H., son of Rev. Henry B., of Trin. Ch., N. Y., was b. Oct. 12, 1753; grad. at King's Coll., studied law with John Jay; entered the British army under Sir Wm. Howe, as capt. in Loyal Am. regt., was promoted by Sir Henry Clinton, in 1777, and in active service till the peace; his estate was confiscated in 1779, and he fled to Nova Scotia; he was there adj. gen. of militia and speaker in the house of assembly; from 1796 to 1828 he held civil offices of trust and honor, was com'r, under Jay's treaty, consul gen., for the northern and eastern states, commissary for the exchange of prisoners, and again boundary comr., under the treaty of Ghent; d. in N. Y., April, 1830, a. 77. His son Col. Delancy B., an aid-de-camp of Geo. IV, d. in 1826. (*Sabine's Loyalists.*)

BARCULO, SEWARD, judge of the supreme court for the first judicial dist., of the state of New York; d. in N. Y. city, June 17, 1854, a. about 50; succeeded Judge Ruggles as circuit judge, and was chosen justice of the supreme court at the first judicial election under constitution of 1846.

BARCULO, SEWARD, a just. of the sup. court of N. Y., for the 2d jud. dist.; d. at Poughkeepsie, N. Y., June 17, 1854.

BARDSLEY, ABEL, a tory, from Fairfield co., Ct., arrived in St. John, New Brunswick, in 1783.

BARKER, DAVID, jr., mem. of cong. from N. H., in 1827–9; d. at Rochester, N. H., April 1, 1834, a. 37.

BARKER, GEN. JOHN, of Phila.; formerly mayor of that city, and high sheriff; d. April 3, 1818, a. 72.

BARKER, GEORGE P., a prominent lawyer and politician; was in the N. Y. assembly from Erie co., in 1836, and afterwards att. gen.; d. at Buffalo, Jan. 27, 1848, a. 39.

BARKER, JOSEPH, grad. at Yale in 1771; in cong. from Mass., from 1805 to 1809; d. 1815.

BARNARD, HEZEKIAH, of Nantucket, held many responsible offices, among which were those of rep. to the gen. court, senator and state treas.; d. March 25, 1849, a. 86. (*Stryker's Am. Reg.*, ii, 498.)

BARNARD, JOHN, rev. patriot in Ga., and major; d. in Chatham co., Ga., a. 65.

BARNARD, REV. JEREMIAH, d. at Amherst, N. H., Jan. 15, 1835, a. 84.

BARNARD, TIMPOOCHEE, maj. in the Creek nation; son of Timothy B., and an Uchee woman; took an active part with the Americans against the hostile Creeks in 1814, and commanded as major; he was in several engagements and was twice wounded. (*White's Hist. Ga.*, p. 166, with portrait.)

BARNES, BAXTER, ex-mem. of cong.; d. at West Brookfield, Mass., Dec. 28, 1863.

BARNES, DAVID LEONARD, judge in U. S. dist. court, R. I.; s. of Rev. Dr. B.; grad. at Harv. in 1780; settled as a lawyer in Providence, and was appointed U. S. dist. judge in 1802 and held until his death in 1812. (*Bradford's N. E. Biog.*)

BARNES, HENRY, a tory merchant of Marlborough, Mass.; was proscribed and banished in 1778; he is supposed to have d. in London, in 1808, a. 84. (*Sabine's Loyalists.*)

BARNES, JOHN, a comedian, well known throughout the U. S., as Old Jack Barnes; d. at Halifax, N. S., Aug. 28, 1841, a. 61.

BARNES, LEVI, a mem. of the house of rep., and of the sen. of Conn., on repeated occasions, and a judge of probate, until disqualified by age; d. at Southington, Ct., March 8, 1860, a. 88.

BARNES, SAMUEL, many years editor of a paper in Frederick, Md., and more recently of the *Baltimore Clipper*; d. in Baltimore, Dec. 15, 1858, a. 72.

BARNEY, JOHN, son of Commodore Joshua B.; a mem. of cong. from Baltimore from 1825 to 1827; d. in Washington, D. C., Jan. 26, 1857, a. 72.

BARNITZ, CHARLES A., was elected a senator to the Pa. legislature, in 1815, and in 1832 to cong. from the York dist.; in 1837, was selected as a sen. delegate to the state convention; many years pres. of the York bank and sustained the reputation of an accomplished scholar and an able lawyer; d. at York, Pa., Jan. 8, 1850, a. 62. (*Stryker's Am. Reg.*, iv, 442.)

BARNITZ, CHARLES A., d. at York, Pa., March, 1850; in cong. from Pa., from 1833 to 1835.

BARNUM, DAVID, the well known proprietor of Barnum's hotel in Baltimore, Md.; d. at that city, May 10, 1844, a. 74.

BARR, REV. JOSEPH WELSH, missionary, b. July 22, 1802, in Liberty, Trumbull co., O.; grad. at the W. R. coll., Hudson, O., in 1830; studied at Andover and Princeton, was ordained for the missionary service of the western for. mis. soc., on the coast of Africa; d. at Richmond, Va., Oct. 28, 1832, when about to embark. (*Memoir of Rev. J. W. B., by E. P. Swift*, Pittsburg, 1833, 18mo, pp. 292.)

BARRADALL, EDWARD, an eminent lawyer of Va., att. gen., judge of admiralty, and incumbent in other offices of trust; d. in 1743, and buried at Williamsburg, Va.

BARREMORE, MANSFIELD, maj. of the Loyal Westchester Refugees, d. N. Y., Dec. 27, 1780, from wounds received in an encounter in the month of November. (*Rivington's Gazette*, Dec. 30, 1780.)

BARRINGER, GEN. PAUL, d. June 20, 1844, in Lincolnton, N. C., a. 65; he was of Cabarras co., and long a mem. of the legislature of N. C., in which he served in both houses.

BARRON, REV. EDWARD, D.D., Cath. miss. bish. of the west coast of Africa; d. at Savannah, Ga., of yellow fever, Sept. 12, 1854.

BARRON, REV. SAMUEL, cong. minister at Sharon, Vt.; d. March 17, 1837, a. 61.

BARROW, ALEXANDER, U. S. senator from La., d. at Baltimore, Md., Dec. 29, 1846, a. about 45; b. at Nashville, studied law and settled in Louisania where he was repeatedly elected to the state legislature, and served with reputation; he entered the U. S. senate in 1841. (*Am. Almanac.* 1848, p. 344.)

BARROWS, DR. CHARLES, b. in Mansfield, Conn., Sept. 11, 1793; d. at Clinton, Oneida co., Sept. 2, 1870; practiced medicine at the latter place 36 years. (*Trans. N. Y. State Med. Soc.*, 1872, p. 346.)

BARROWS, WILLIAM, d. at Hebron, Me., Nov. 22, 1837, in his 82d year; a soldier of the revolution.

BARRINGER, DANIEL L., b. in Mechlenburg co., N. C., Oct. 1, 1788; studied law, served in the legislature of N. C., in 1813, and from 1819 to 1822; was in congress from 1826 to 1835, and from 1843 to 1849; removed to Tennessee, and was elected speaker of the house of rep. in that state; d. Oct. 16, 1852.

BARRY, REV. EDMUND D., D.D., rect. of St. Mathew's ch. in Jersey City, N. J.; d. at that place April 20, 1852, a. 76.

BARRY, JOHN A., ex-gov. of Mich.; d. Jan. 19, 1870, a. 68.

BARRY, ROBERT, a tory, went from N. Y., to Shelburne, Nova Scotia after the rev.; became eminent as a merchant, and established branch houses in various parts of the province; d. at Liverpool, N. S., Sept., 1843, a. 84. (*Sabine's Loyalists.*)

BARSTOW, GIDEON, d. at St. Augustine, Fla., Mar. 26, 1852, a. 69; was a native of Mass.,and had gone south for his health; had served in both houses of the state legislature, and was a member of cong. from Mass., from 1821 to 1823.

BARTLE, COL. ——, an early settler and formerly a leading merchant of Cincinnati, O.; d. at that place in hospital Dec., 1859.

BARTLETT, DR. JOSIAH, d. at Stratham, N. H., April 14, 1838, a. 70. Was in congress from New Hampshire in 1811–13, and was son of Josiah B., of Kingston, first governor of N. H., under the constitution.

BARTLETT, DR. ZACCHEUS, vice pres. of the Pilgrims' Society, d. at Plymouth, Mass., Dec., 25, 1855, a. 70.

BARTLETT, ISRAEL, d. at Haverhill, N. H., April 21, 1838; was a rev. soldier and several years in the state senate.

BARTLETT, JAMES, formerly a mem. of the sen. of New Hampshire, and register of probate; d. at Dover, N H., July 17, 1837.

BARTLETT, REV. WILLARD, F. W. Bap. preacher. Moved from Vt. to Canada when young, was ordained in Wheelock, Vt., a. 33; soon removed to Melbourne, C. E., and preached statedly till old age; he d. Aug. 31, 1855, a. 73. (*F. W. Bap. Reg.*, 1857, p. 87.)

BARTLETT, Richard, formerly sec. of state of New Hampshire; d. at New York city, Oct. 23, 1837, a. 45.

BARTON, Cyrus, d. near Concord, N. H., Feb. 7, 1855; was editor of the *Concord Reporter;* died suddenly after concluding a speech at a political meeting.

BARTON, David, senator in congress from 1821 to 1831; d. near Boonville, Mo., Sept. 28, 1837.

BARTON, Rev. Thomas, b. in Ireland in 1730; grad. at Dublin, in 1754, was appointed mis. in York and Cumberland counties, Pa.; was chaplain in the expedition to Ft. Duquesne in 1758; became a loyalist, and after two years' confinement fled to N. Y.; d. May 25, 1780, a. 50; Prof. Barton of Phila., was his s.; m. a sister of Mr. Rittenhouse, the mathematician, whose memoirs were written by his s. William B.; Benj. Smith Barton, was another s. (*Doc. Hist. N. Y.*, iv, 361; *Sabine's Loyalists.*)

BARTON, Rev. Thomas, Am. loyalist from Lancaster, Pa.; d. N. Y. city, May 25, 1780; a soc. mis.; had been compelled to leave his family and take refuge in N. Y.; was buried in the chancel of St. George chapel.

BARTON, Roger, d. near Holly Springs, Miss., March 4, 1855, a. about 55; was a native of East Tennessee, but for twenty years had lived in Miss., where he was a distinguished lawyer; served in both houses of the legislature.

BARTON, Seth, formerly solicitor of the treas., and chargé d'affairs to Chili under Pres. Polk; d. at New Orleans, La., Dec. 29, 1854.

BASS, Henry, d. April 4, 1842, at Boston, Mass., a. 70; Mr. Bass had for several years been one of the permanent assessors of that city.

BASS, Samuel, d. Feb. 1, 1842, at Randolph, Mass., a. 88; grad. of H. U., and much esteemed.

BASSE, Jeremiah, clerk of the council, sec. of the province and prothonotary of the supreme court of N. J.; had been gov. under the proprietaries; in 1716, was elected a rep. of Cape May; in 1719, att. gen. of the prov. (*Coll. N. Y. Hist. Soc.*, i, 156; *ib.*, iii, 83.)

BASSET, Rev. John, b. at Bushwick, L. I., Oct. 1, 1764; grad. at Columbia coll.; settled as colleague of Rev. E. Westerlo at Albany, in 1787, and installed Nov. 25; in Dec., 1804, became pastor at the Boght (Watervliet, N. Y.), and afterwards at Bushwick, where he d. Sept. 4, 1824 (*Rogers's Hist. Discourse*, p. 32.)

BATCHELDER, Dr. John P., of N. Y. city; d. April 7, 1868, a. 82.

BATEMAN, Simon, a soldier of the rev.; served through the war; d. Aug. 7, 1841, at Houston co., Ga.; was a col. of militia. (*White's Hist. Ga.*, p. 497.)

BATES, Barnabas, was a native of England, and came to this country in childhood; became a Bapt. preacher in R. I., but afterwards Unitarian; was for a short time collector of the port of Bristol, under Pres. Adams, but in 1825 removed to N. Y., and started the *Christian Inquirer*, which was discontinued in a few years; being appointed by Pres. Jackson to a position in the N. Y. P. O., his attention was called to the subject of cheap postage for which he labored earnestly and successfully; d. in Bost., Oct. 11, 1853, a. 66.

BATES, JOHN, theatre manager; d. at Cincinnati, O., July 27, 1870, a. 75.

BATES, PHINEAS P., rem. to Canandaigua, N. Y., in 1790, with his father, and afterwards continued to reside at that place; in 1812, he was appointed lieut. col., and served with reputation under Gens. Porter and Brown; in 1818 was in assembly and in 1819 was appointed sheriff of Ontario co., to which office he was twice elected after 1821; in 1828 was the dem. nominee for cong.; d. Dec. 11, 1857.

BATES, WALTER, a tory from Stamford, Ct., went to St. John, N. B.; in 1783; settled in Kings co., N. B.; was several years its sheriff; d. at Kingston, N. B., in 1842, a. 82.

BAXTER, GEORGE, a distinguished lawyer; d. at Lexington, Va., Nov. 1835.

BAXTER, REV. GEORGE, D.D., prof. of theo. in the Union Theo. Sem., in Prince Edward co., Va.; formerly president of Wash. Coll. at Lexington; d. in Va., April 24, 1841.

BAXTER, SIMON, tory, of N. H., was proscribed, banished, and his estate confiscated; arrested by the whigs, condemned and led out to execution, but fled with the rope about his neck and reached Burgoyne's army; went to New Brunswick; d. at Norton, Kings co., N. B., in 1804, a. 74. (*Sabine's Loyalists.*)

BAXTER, STEPHEN, a tory of Jamaica, N. Y., went to Nova Scotia in 1783.

BAYARD, C. C., of the U. S. navy, son of ex-senator Bayard of Del.; d. at Naples, Feb. 21, 1850, from lock jaw occasioned by a wound from a stone thrown from the crater of Vesuvius, which he was visiting during an eruption.

BAYARD, ROBERT, of N. Y., a tory, was judge of the admiralty court, and was attainted and banished by act of Oct. 22, 1779.

BAYARD, SAMUEL, d. at Princeton, N. J., May 12, 1840, a. 76; formerly a judge of the court of com. pleas, and author of two law books.

BAYARD, SAMUEL, of N. Y., in 1776 was taken pris., in N. Y., as a tory; entered the service of the crown, and in 1782 was major of the king's Orange Rangers; his son Samuel jr., was dep. sec. of the col. of N. Y., previous to the rev., and was considered in office in 1782.

BAYARD, SAMUEL VETCH, was a tory, and held a military office under the crown during the rev.; d. at Wilmot, Nova Scotia, in 1832, a. 75.

BAYARD, WILLIAM, sympathised with the early patriot movements in N. Y., in the rev. sided with the tories, and was attainted and banished, Oct. 22, 1779.

BAY, DR. WILLIAM, d. Sept. 7, 1865, a. 91. (*Munsell's Hist. Coll. Albany*, iii, 263; *Trans N. Y. S. Med. Soc.*, i, p. 317.)

BAYEUX, THOMAS, in 1782, was an officer in the superintendent depart. at N. Y.

BAYLEY, DR. JOSEPH, d. in N. Y. city, Dec. 7, 1836, a. 61.

BAYLIES, HODIJAH, rev. officer, grad. at Harv. in 1777; entered the army and acted as aid to Gen. Lincoln, whose daughter he m.; became an aid to Washington, and in 1804 was made judge of probate in Bristol co.; resigned in 1835 at the age of 78; then retired to private life; he was brother of Dr. Wm. B. of Dighton; d. at Dighton, Mass., April 26, 1843, a. 86. (*Bradford's N. E. Biog.*)

BAY, Rev. Andrew, Second Pres. minister at Albany; rem. from Ireland to Md.; belonged to the Newcastle Presb., and succeeded Rev. Mr. Hanna at Albany, holding 5 years; rem. to Newtown, L. I.; was dismissed from the N. Y. Presb., in 1774; supposed to have gone to Charleston, S. C., where his son Elisha Hall Bay was afterwards judge. (*Doc. Hist. N. Y.*, iv, 384.)

BAY, Samuel Mansfield, d. in Mo., July 1, 1849; late att. gen. of that state, and an accomplished lawyer.

BAYNTON, Benjamin, in 1782 a lieut. in the Pa. Loyalists.

BEACH, Capt. Jedediah, a soldier of the rev.; d. at Springfield, N. Y., May 23, 1841, a. 86.

BEACH, Gen. Ebenezer S., d. in Rochester, N. Y., March 14, 1850, a. 65; was largely engaged in milling and speculations in grain and flour in which he was widely known.

BEACH, Rev. Horace, d. at Woodville, Miss., Sept. 1, 1844; pastor of the Pres. Ch.

BEACH, Rev. John, of Newtown, Ct., Cong., b. in 1700; grad. at Yale in 1721; was ordained in Eng., and appointed to the miss., of Newtown, Ct., where he arrived Sept. 1732; continued there till his death, March 19, 1782; a steadfast loyalist till the end, and wrote upon polemic and doctrinal theology. (*Doc. Hist. N. Y.*, iii, 1053; *Sabine's Loyalists.*)

BEACH, William, of Auburn, mem. of the N. Y. senate in 1850–3; d. at the Delavan House, Albany, March 14, 1860.

BEALLS, William, of the *Boston Post*; d. Dec. 8, 1870, a. 86.

BEAN, Ebenezer, rev. pensioner; d. at Conway, N. H., March, 1846, a. 90 years 6 months; was in the battle of Bunker hill, and served in Capt. Aaron Kinsman's co., Col. John Stark's regiment.

BEAN, Thomas, a tory, went from N. Y. to St. John, N. B., in 1783; and was a grantee in that city; d. at Portland, N. B., in 1823, a. 79. (*Sabine's Loyalists.*)

BEARD, Albin, printer, and editor of *New Hampshire Telegraph;* post master at Nashua, and twice mayor of that city; d. in Nashua, Aug. 16, 1862.

BEARD, Robert, a tory of Charleston, S. C.; was banished, and in 1782, his property was confiscated.

BEARDSLEE, John, b. in Sharon, Ct., Nov., 1759; left in 1781; tarried for a time in Sheffield, Mass., and in Vt.; built a bridge at Schaticoke, N. Y., a church at Schoharie, then settled in Whitestown; finally settled at Manheim, N. Y., and became extensively engaged in Central N. Y., as a bridge builder, millwright and architect; d. Oct. 3, 1825. (*Benton's Herkimer Co.*, p. 435.)

BEARDSLEY, Cyrus H., d. at Fairfield, Conn., Aug. 13, 1852, a. 53; b. in Huntington, Conn., and grad. at Yale in 1818; studied law, but entering political life, was a mem. of both branches of the legislature, and speaker of the house, and judge of the county court of Fairfield co.

BEARDSLEY, REV. JOHN, a tory; in 1872, chap. of the loyal Am. regt.; went to N. Brunswick; was settled as Epis. clergyman at Mangerville, and d. there.

BEASLEY, REUBEN G., U. S. consul at Havre, France; d. in that city June 1, 1847.

BEATTY, WILLIAM, rev. officer, b. in Frederick co., Md., June 19, 1758, the eldest of 12 brothers; in 1776 he was appointed ens. in the Md. flying camp and served in N. Y.; his merits earned him a commission of lieut. and of capt. and his bravery was often proved in battle; he was killed at the battle of Hobkirk's hill near Camden, S. C., April 25, 1781. (*Rogers's Am. Biog.*)

BEAUMONT, ANDREW, b. in Penn.; was in cong. from that state from 1833 to 1836, and d. at Wilkesbarre, Pa., Oct. — 1853.

BECK, ABRAHAM, a lawyer, brother of Dr. T. Romeyn Beck; d. at St. Louis, Mo., 1821.

BECK, NICHOLAS FAIRLY, bro. of Dr. T. Romeyn Beck, d. June 30, 1830, a. 34, while holding the office of adj. gen. of the state of New York.

BECK, WASHINGTON, d. at New Orleans, La., Sept. 11, 1837, a. 32; was formerly of Georgetown, D. C.

BECKETT, CAPT. JOHN, was many years a mem. of the legislature of Md., and an officer in the war of 1812; at the battle of York he bore from the field the wounded Pike, and at the capture of Ft. George affair, at Stony Creek and the battle of Crysler's field he acted an honorable part; d. at Locustgrove, Calvert co., Md., May 26, 1850, in the 59th y. of his age. (*Stryker's Am. Reg.*, iv, 464.)

BECKMAN, CAPT. SOLOMON, a rev. officer d. near Zebulon, Pike co., Ga., March 25, 1839, a. 76.

BECKWITH, COL. JOHN, a revolutionary soldier d. at Poughkeepsie, N. Y., Sept. 12, 1834, a. 83.

BECKWITH, DR. JOSIAH G., of Litchfield, Conn.; d. Mar. 21, 1871, a. 68.

BECKWITH, SIR JENNINGS, known as the *Leather Stocking* of the Northern Neck; d. at Mount Airy, Richmond co., Va., Nov. 13, 1835, a. 72.

BEECHER, GEN. PHILEMON, b. in Litchfield, Conn.; d. at Lancaster, O., Nov. 30, 1839, in his 64th year; a lawyer, and an early settler of Ohio, where he filled several public offices with ability, from 1817 to 1821, and from 1823 to 1829, he was in cong.; was of the Federal school of politics.

BEEKMAN, FLETCHER M., d. at Hudson, N. Y., April 9, 1835.

BEELEN, CONSTANTINE ANTOINE, son of the Baron de Beelen de Bertholf; came to this country with his father who was sent soon after the peace of 1783 in a public capacity by the emp. of Austria; resided at Phila., several years; political difficulties preventing their return, the parents remained and d. in Penn.; the subject of this notice settled at Pittsburg at an early age, where he resided through life and d. Dec. 16, 1850, in his 84th year.

BEERS, NATHAN, d. at New Haven, Conn., Feb. 10, 1849, a. 96; b. in Stratford, Conn., in 1753; rem. in early life to New Haven, and served in the rev.; he was for a time in mercantile business, and for many years steward of Yale Coll. (*Am. Almanac*, 1840, p. 323.)

BEERS, TIMOTHY PHELPS, M. D., prof. in Yale med. sch.; b. Dec. 25, 1789, grad. at Yale in 1808; was surg. in the army in 1812; prof. of obstetrics at Yale from 1830 to 1856, and d. at New Haven, Ct., Sept. 22, 1858; was son of Dea. Nathan Beers. (*Hist. Mag.*, ii, 348.)

BEHN, JAMES B., Belgian consul at N. O.; d. in that city, Sept. 9, 1852.

BELKNAP, ANDREW ELIOT, son of the late Rev. Dr. B., and for many years a respectable merchant in Boston; d. in that city Jan. 25, 1858, a. 78; took great interest in hist. matters, especially such as related to Boston and wrote frequently for the newspapers, over the sig. of *A Boston Boy.*

BELKNAP, EZEKIEL, son of Moses B. and an officer of the rev.; d. at Atkinson, N. H., Jan. 5, 1836, a. 100 years and 10 days; his father d. in 1803, a. 99 ys. 5 mos.; his grandmother, Hannah Belknap Atkinson, d. a. 107.

BELKNAP, GEN. CHAUNCEY, d. at Newburgh, N. Y., June 8, 1840, a. 73.

BELLAMY, JOSEPH H., d. in Bethlehem, Conn., Nov. 1, 1848, a. 60; grad. at Yale in 1808; was repeatedly in the state legislature, and a senator from the 16th dist.

BELL, ANDREW, d. at Perth Amboy, N. J., June 4, 1843, a. 86; was many years surveyor gen. to the proprietors of East Jersey.

BELL, GEORGE HENRY, m. a sister of Gen. Herkimer, and was a prominent man in the Mohawk valley before the rev.; he was a capt. in the battle of Oriskany and a wound there received disabled him for life; his two sons Joseph and Nicholas were in the battle; the former was killed and the latter fled; he was many years a justice of the peace, and lived on Fall hill, Herkimer county. (*Benton's Herkimer Co. N. Y.*, p. 131.)

BELLINGER, CHRISTOPHER, b. at German Flats, was a wealthy farmer, held several town offices many years; in May, 1812, as col. of militia he was sent to Sackets Harbor, and commanded that post several months; in 1814 was again upon the frontiers as col.; in 1810, 11, 14, 22, 24, was in assembly; in politics he was a Jeff. rep. and later a bucktail; d. about 1839 at Little Falls, at an advanced age. (*Benton's Herkimer Co. N. Y.*, p. 134.)

BELLINGER, FREDERICK, merchant in Herkimer co., N. Y., and in assembly in 1836; d at Mohawk, German Flats; he was a major of militia. (*Benton's Herkimer Co. N. Y.*, p. 139.)

BELL, JAMES, many years in the legislature of Vt.; a lawyer, and much noted as a political speaker; d. at Walden, Vt., April 23, 1852, a. 76.

BELL, JOSEPH, d. at Saratoga, N. Y., July 25, 1851, a. 64; b. in Bedford, N. H.; grad. at Dartmouth, in 1807, and practiced law with eminent success at Haverhill, N. H.; removed to Boston, in 1841.

BELL, JOSHUA F., d. at Danville, Ky., Aug. 20, 1870, b. in Kentucky, and a rep. to congress, 1845–7.

BELL, RICHARD H., entered the army in 1808, was made capt. in 1813, and was wounded at Lyons creek, N. C., Oct. 19, 1814, retained in 1815, and resigned in May, 1817; d. at Norfolk, Va., May 9, 1835.

BELL, ROBERT, an early auctioneer and bookseller of Phila.; d. in Richmond, Va., in 1784.

BELL, SAMUEL, was educated at D. Coll.; studied law under Judge Samuel Dana, and after presiding in both branches of the legislature of N. H., was appointed judge of sup. court in 1816; in 1819, he was elected gov. and in 1823, senator in cong., where he remained till 1834; d. at Chester, N. H., Dec. 23, 1850, a. 81.

BELLOWS, BENJAMIN, founder of Walpole, N. H.; b. May 26, 1712, at Lunenburg, N. H.; having with others bought a tract on the Conn. river at the Great falls, he rem. in 1752, built a fort and organized a town. The place suffered from Indian wars, but improved rapidly after 1761; Col. B., d. July 10, 1777; his descendants consecrated a monument to his memory, Oct. 11, 1854. (*Hist. Sketch of Col. B...... with an account of the gathering of* 1854.)

BELSER, JAMES E., mem. of cong., from Alabama, in 1844–7; d. at Montgomery, Ala., Jan. 16, 1859.

BELTON, JONATHAN, of S. C., a tory, and after the surrender of S.C. held a commission under the crown; his estate was confiscated.

BELTON, THOMAS, d. at Newark, N. J., July, 1840, a. 108 years; he was a soldier of the revolution.

BELTRAMI, GIACOMO COSTANTINO, b. at Bergamo, Italy in 1779. Having gained a judicial office under the gov., he became involved in political affairs and was obliged to live in exile in 1821; he came to the U. S., traversed Mexico, and ascended the Miss., of one of the principal sources of which he was the first discoverer; he went to Lond., in 1826, or 7, and after res. some years on the continent, returned to Italy, and d. in Feb., 1855; he published in N. O., in 1824 an account of his discoveries on the upper Miss., and several other works in Phila. and Lond.; the legislature of Minn., have named a county in his memory, and the municipality of Bergamo in 1865, published a memoir of Beltrami, which is dedicated to the Minn. Hist. Soc. (*Coll. of Minn. Hist. Soc.*, 1867, p. 13.)

BENDER, JOHN, a native of Germany, and soldier of the rev.; d. at Woolwich, near Swedesborough, N. J., Dec. 25, 1840, a. 108.

BENEDICT, AMOS, 2d dist. atty. of Jeff., Lewis and St. Law. counties, N. Y., native of Middlebury, Ct.; grad. at Yale in 1800, settled at Watertown, N. Y., in 1807; was dist. att'y in 1810, 13, 15, and d. in 1816. (*Hough's Hist. Jeff. Co., N. Y.*, p. 420.)

BENEDICT, DR. ABIJAH G., of Redhook, N. Y.; d. Oct. 4, 1862, a. 72. (*Transac. N. Y., State Med. Soc.*, 1864, p. 447.)

BENEDICT, DR. N. D., St. Augustine, Florida; d. April, 1871.

BENEDICT, LEWIS, a prominent citizen of Albany, d. July, 1862, a. 77. (*Munsell's Hist. Coll. Albany*, ii, 114.)

BENEDICT, COL. LEWIS, son of preceding, killed at battle of Pleasant hill, 9 April 1864, a. 46. (*Ib.*, iii, 465.)

BENEDICT, THOMAS B., militia col., in the war of 1812–15, b. at Woodbury, Ct., Oct. 23, 1783; settled at De Kalb, N. Y., as a merchant, and commanded the militia at Ogdensburgh in the summer of 1812; d. in De Kalb, March 11, 1829. (*Hough's Hist. St. Law. and Fr. Cos.*, 584.)

BENHAM, JOSEPH S., d. in Cincinnati, O., July, 1840, a. 43; was a distinguished mem. of the bar in that place.

BENJAMIN, JONATHAN, d. Aug. 26, 1842 in Union, Licking, co., O.; at the age of sixteen he enlisted in the army where he served for several years. The Indians broke in upon his family and killed and took prisoner three entire families, his only son escaping to the fort; he came to Ohio in 1804 where he resided until his death.

BENJAMIN, SARAH, d. a. 114 ys. 5 mo. 3 d. at Mt. Pleasant, Pa., April 20, 1858; maiden name Sarah Matthews; b. in Goshen, N Y., Nov. 17, 1743; her first husb., Wm. Reed, d. of a wound in the rev.; 2d husb.. Aaron Osborn of Goshen, a soldier in the rev. (*Hist. Mag.*, ii, 216; *Phren. Jour.*, Nov., 1854.)

BENNEHAN, THOMAS G., d. near Raleigh, N. C., June 24, 1847, a. 65; grad. at the U. of N. C., and was for many years before his death one of its trustees; one of the most extensive planters of the state.

BENNETT, REV. BENJAMIN, d. at Middletown N. J., Oct. 8, 1840, a. 78; was a Bap. minister, and from 1815 to 1819, mem. of cong. from N. J.

BENNETT, JAMES, d. Sept. 4, 1842, in Billerica, Mass. a. 84; he served as ensign in the army during five years of rev. war.

BENNETT, JAMES GORDON, founder and editor of the *New York. Herald*, b. about 1800; d. June 1, 1872. (*Drake's Dict. Am. Biog.*)

BENNETT, REV. ALFRED, b. in Mansfield, Ct., Sept. 26, 1780, and settled as a Bap. preacher at Homer, N. Y., where he remained in that office and as senior agent of the Am. Bap. Miss. Union, until his death May 10, 1851. (*Missionary Magazine; Memoir by H. Harvey*, 12mo, pp. 232, N. Y., 1852.)

BENNETT, REV BARTLETT, d. in Cincinnati, O., Oct. 12, 1842, a. 99; b. in Albemarle, Va.; a Bap. minister from the a. of 25; was one of the early pioneers in the state of Kentucky.

BENOIST, CATHARINE, an original settler of St. Louis, dau. of Chas. Sanguinet, and gr. dau. of Dr. Conde, a French surg., who came to St. Louis in 1755; d at St. Louis, Dec. 9, 1859. (*Hist. Mag.*, iv, 60.)

BENSON, BARRY W., d. at Columbus, Miss., June 11, 1839, a. 27; sec. of state of Mississippi.

BENTLEY, REV. WILLIAM, D D., native of Boston; grad. at H. Coll., in 1778; 3 years teacher of Greek in the coll., and in 1783, was ordained over the 2d ch. of Salem, where he served till his death in 1819, a. 63. (*Bradford's N. E. Biog.*)

BENTON, JOHN RANDOLPH, d. at St. Louis, Mo., March 17, 1852, a. 22; only son of Senator Thomas H. Benton.

BENTON, SAMUEL, bro. of Thomas H. B., of Mo.; d. in San Augustine, Tex., Sept. 29, 1846, a. about 60; was b. in N. C., and rem. to Texas from St. Louis about 1822; a distinguished supporter of the rights of Texas, and a mem. of cong., in the republic, before admission.

BENZEL, ADOLPHUS, son of Archbishop Ulric B. of Upsal; came to America in 1749 and settled at Wilmington, Del., in 1750; served as an officer in the British army from 1755 to 1770, when he was appointed inspector of H. M. woods, forests and unappropriated lands, on Lake Champlain and in Canada. (*Doc. Hist. N. Y*, iv, 854.)

BERGMAN, REV. JOHN E., b. in Germany, served the cong. of Salzburgers at Ebenezer, Ga., 36 y. and d. at an advanced age.

BERIOT, MADAME MALIBRAN DE,— Maria Felicitas, eldest dau. of Señor Manuel Garcia,— known in Europe and America as an opera singer; b. in Paris, in 1808; came with her family to New York in 1826, and was married to M. Malibran; she d. at Manchester, Eng., Sept. 23, 1836. (*American Almanac*, 1838, p. 298.)

BERKELEY, DR. CARTER, d. in Hanover co., Va., Nov. 3, 1839, a. 72, a descendant of Sir William B.; grad. at the Edinburgh Med. Sch.

BERNARD, SIR JOHN, son of Sir Francis B., gov. of Mass.; was a whig, and remained in America, and reduced to abject poverty; his father had given him the agency of a landed estate in Maine, but this was confiscated in 1778; he lived at Bath and Machias Me., and after the peace at Pleasant Point near Eastport in a hut with no companion but his dog; he became insane and afterwards the legislature of Mass. released to him one half of the island of Mt. Desert, which had belonged to his father; he res. several years about Boston, visited Maine occasionally and late in life held British offices at Barbadoes and St. Vincent, and was known as Sir John Bernard, baronet; d. in the West Indies in 1809. (*Sabine's Loyalists.*)

BERNARD, SIR THOMAS, Bt., third son of Sir Francis B., gov. of Mass.; grad. at H. U. in 1767, went to England, m. a lady of fortune, and on the death of his brother John succeeded to his title; he was a man of great benevolence, d. in Eng. in 1818; the Univ. of Edin. conferred on him the degree of LL.D. (*Sabine's Loyalists.*)

BERRY, CHARLES C., d. in Brooklyn, N. Y., June 22, 1852, a. 39; com. of the steamship United States, and for many years connected with the merchant marine service of N. Y.

BERRY, DR. J. L., of Memphis, Tenn., a vol. in the yellow fever epidemic at Portsmouth, Va., in the autumn of 1855, and fell a victim to the disease.

BERRY, LAURENCE W., a lawyer of reputation and atty. for the commonwealth in several of the state courts of Va.; d. at Fredericksburg, Va., Feb. 3, 1846, a. 52; a native of King George co., Va.

BERRY, MAJ. JACK, d. at Jack-Berrytown, Buffalo Creek Reservation, N. Y., July 3, 1839; a distinguished chief of the Seneca tribe of Indians.

BERRY, NATHANIEL, d. in Gardiner, Me., Aug. 22, 1850, a. 94; a soldier of the rev.

BESANCON, GEN. LORENZO A., d. on board a steamboat on his way from N. O., to Baton Rouge, La., July 23, 1853, was a prominent newspaper editor of the Southern Rights party; in the Mex. war, he was a capt. of dragoons.

BESANZON, PETER, rev. pat.; b. near Besanzon France; came to America, a. 16, with La Fayette, and served through the war; res. many years at Butternuts, N. Y., and rem. to Perry and Pike, N. Y., where he d. July 1855, a. 93.

BETHUNE, DR. NORTON, d. March 29, 1842, in Philadelphia, Pa., a. 39; grad. at H. U., in the class of 1821.

BETHUNE, GEORGE, one of the oldest citizens of Bos.; d. Oct., 1859, a. 90; his father m. a niece of Peter Faneuil, and he inherited the family plate, pictures, etc., of the Faneuil family. (*Hist. Mag.*, iii, 354.)

BETHUNE, MRS. JOANNA, wid. of Divie B., and mother of the Rev. Dr. B., of Brooklyn, b. at Ft. Niagara, in 1768, a dau. and an assistant of

Mrs. Isabella Graham, a well known teacher of N. Y.; in 1796 she m. Divie Bethune a merchant and man of great liberality; their early efforts in behalf of Bible and tract distribution, Sunday schools, and the relief of orphans and poor women, were assiduous and successful, leading to the formation of societies for these objects; about 1827, she became interested in infant schools, and wrote several books for them, and in a school at the Five Points became herself a teacher; she edited her mother's letters, and correspondence; d. at N. Y., July 28, 1860, in her 92d year. (*Hist. Mag.*, iv, 285.)

BETTON, Silas, grad. at Dart., in 1787, was rep. in cong., from New Hampshire, from 1803 to 1807; d. in 1822, a. 58.

BETTYS, Joseph, a noted tory of the rev.; at the beginning of the war lived at Ballston, N. Y., and was a whig, and in Arnold's naval battle on Lake Champlain was captured and taken to Canada; he entered the royal service, became a spy, was arrested, tried and condemned to the gallows, but pardoned by Washington; he returned to the enemy and began a course of burning and murder of the most successful and atrocious character, and was at last captured in 1782, taken to Albany and hung as a spy. (*Sabine's Loyalists.*)

BEVERIDGE, Col. Noble, d. in Middlebury, London co., Va., Dec. 8, 1844, in his 67th year; was formerly a merchant, and acquired a large fortune.

BEVERLEY, Carter, d. at Fredericksburg, Va., Feb. 10, 1844, a. 72.

BEYRICK, Dr., —— naturalist and traveler from Germany; d. at Ft. Gibson, Mo. Ter., Oct. — 1834; was going westward with the design of crossing the Rocky mountains.

BIBBINS, Dr. William Burr, d. in N. Y., Jan. 1, 1871; b. in Fairfield, Conn., Aug. 8, 1823; grad. at Yale in 1845, and at the coll. of phys. and surg. N. Y., and became an eminent phys. in the city of N. Y. (*Transactions N. Y. State Med. Soc.*, 1872, p. 327.)

BIBIGHANS, Thomas M., d. in Lebanon, Pa., June 18, 1853, a. 37; mem. of cong. from Penn., in 1851–3.

BIDDLE, CHARLES, late commissioner from the U. S. gov., for exploring a route between the Atlantic and Pacific oceans; d. at Phila., Pa., Dec. 21, 1836, a. 49.

BIDDLE, JOHN, of Bucks co., Pa., was coll. of excise and a dep. har. mast. under the whigs; became tory in 1777, and his estate was confiscated.

BIDDLE, Jonathan William, a mem. of the Phila. bar; d. in Phila., Jan. 21, 1856.

BIDLACK, Benjamin A., a native of Penn.; in cong. from 1841 to 1845; was chargé d'affaires to New Grenada, and d. at Bogotá, Feb. 29, 1849; had formerly been in the state legislature, and his home residence was Wilkesbarre, Luzerne co.

BIDWELL, Marshall S., lawyer; removed from N. Eng., to Kingston, Canada, and was several years in the prov. parliament; being a leader in the liberal party before the rebellion of 1837, he was ordered to leave Canada, and accordingly rem. to N. Y. city, where he afterwards lived; was an able lawyer, and prominent mem. of various literary and benevolent societies; d. Oct., 1872.

BIGELOW, ABIJAH, was b. in Westminster, Mass.; grad. at D. C., in 1795; studied law and practiced in Leominster; a mem. of cong. from 1811 to 1815, and clerk of the courts for Worcester co., from 1817 to 1834; d. at Worcester, April 4, 1860, a. near 85.

BIGELOW, ABRAHAM, of Cambridge, Mass., d. in N. Y. July 7, 1832.

BIGELOW, ALPHEUS, a distinguished citizen of Mass.; b. in Weston, Mass., about 1784, and d. in that place Sept. 23, 1863.

BIGELOW, HARDIN, d. in San Francisco, Cal., Nov. 27, 1850; mayor of Sacramento, displayed great vigor and bravery in quelling squatter riots and in enforcing the laws, in which he lost an arm; being reduced from this cause, he fell a victim to the cholera.

BIGELOW, TIMOTHY, an eminent lawyer, son of Col. Timothy B.; grad. at H. U., in 1786, and settled as a lawyer at Groton, Mass., was long in the legislature and several years speaker of the house; a state senator for some time, and member of the council; d. in 1821, a. 54. (*Bradford's N. E. Biog.*)

BILES, SAMUEL, sheriff of Bucks co., Pa., and a tory in the rev.; estate confiscated in 1779.

BILLINGS, ASAHEL, d. at Hardwick, Mass., July 16, 1839, a. 100; a lieut. in the rev., present at the capture of Burgoyne.

BILLINGS, DR. BENJAMIN, a surg. in the rev., and med. practitioner in Mansfield, Mass., for more than fifty years, d. in that town Oct. 9, 1842, a. 82.

BILLOP, CHRISTOPHER, a man of wealth and influence on Staten Island, N. Y.; from 1769 to 1775 in the gen. assembly; commanded a corps of loyalists or of loyal militia and was actively engaged on the loyal side; was attainted and banished Oct. 22, 1779, fell into the hands of the whigs and was heavily ironed and closely confined on bread and water for his cruel treatment of prisoners; in 1782 he was sup't. of police on Staten Island; went to New Brunswick and became prominent there; was a member of the assembly and of the council, and on the death of Gov. Smythe in 1823 claimed the presidency of the government, but did not hold it; d. at St. John in 1827 a. 90; his two sons settled in N. Y., as merchants. (*Sabine's Loyalists.*)

BILLOP, THOMAS, son of Christopher B., res. on Staten Island, with his brother, was a merchant in N. Y.; upon the occurrence of the yellow fever, his br. being single remained in the city to look after the property and died; in 1806 he joined Miranda's expedition as captain, and was taken prisoner by the Spaniards and executed. (*Sabine's Loyalists.*)

BINGHAM, JEREMIAH, d. Feb. 1842 in Cornwall, Vt., a. 94; he was born in Norwich, Conn.; in early life he was a schoolmaster and taught in many towns in Mass., and N. H.; rem. to Cornwall at the close of the rev. war, when there was not another inhabitant in the town, and in 1785, by his encouragement and assistance a church was organized there of eight members.

BINKLEY, COL. ADAM, d. in Davidson co., Tenn., Feb. 28, 1837, a. 136; at the time of the rev. he was m. and had eleven children. (*S. W. Christian Advocate.*)

BINNEY, COL. AMOS, was b. at Hull, Mass., in 1768, was left an orphan at an early age and entered upon the duties of life without education; he supplied this want by his own enterprise; became a distinguished mem. of the Meth. Ep. ch. and a liberal promoter of public and private charities; was navy agent for the port of Boston, and d. at Bost., Jan. 10, 1833, a. 65. (*Am. An. Reg.* 1832, 3, Ap., 427).

BINNEY, DR. BARNABAS, a surg. of the rev., b. in Bost. in 1751; grad. at R. I. Coll, in 1774, and studied medicine in Europe; his health became so impaired in the rev. that he lived but a few years after, and d. June 21, 1787.

BINNEY, HIBBERT NEWTON, d. July 21, 1842, in Halifax, a. 76; for fifty years collector of impost and excise at that port.

BINNEY, HORACE, JR., pres. of the loyal league of Philadelphia, d. Feb. 8, 1870.

BIRCH, REV. ROBERT, d. in New Brunswick, N. J., Sept. 12, 1842, a. 34: pastor of the Presb. ch. at that place.

BIRCH, WILLIAM YOUNG, b. in Manchester, Eng., a bookseller and publisher in Phila.; began trade in 1793, and in 1800, became a partner with Abraham Small; their business was large for that day; left a large estate, of which about $180,000 went to the Penn. In. for Ins. of the Blind.

BIRCHARD, DR. SOLOMON, an eminent physician of Baltimore, d. in that city, Nov. 30, 1836, a. 77.

BIRD, JOHN, son of Dr. Seth Bird, b. in Litchfield, Ct.; grad. at Yale in 1786; was admitted to the bar in Ct., and settled in Troy, N. Y., in 1794; in the assembly in 1796–7, 8, and in cong. from 1799 to 1803; d. in 1806, a. 38; was brilliant but eccentric, often impatient and passionate without cause, and at times blasphemous; (*Woodworth's Troy*, 94).

BIRDSALL, JOHN, judge and atty. gen., of Texas, settled in Greene, N. Y., in 1816 having grad. at Williams the year before, studied law with Robt. Monell; became eminent at the bar; settled at Mayville, N. Y., where he was appointed, Apr. 18, 1826, circuit judge of the 8th circuit, and resided in Rochester; resigned in 1829, returned to Mayville, was in the state senate in 1832, res. June 5, 1834, and in 1837 emigrated to Texas; became law partner of Sam Houston, and was atty. gen. of the Lone Star rep. till his death in 1839. (*Chenango American*, Jan., 1858.)

BIRDSEYE, VICTORY, of Pompey, Onondaga co., N. Y.; in assembly in 1823, 1838 and 1840; in the senate in 1827–8, and in congress from 1815 to 1817, and from 1841 to 1843; d. in Wayne co., N. Y., Sept. 16, 1853, a. 71.

BIRDSILL, BENJAMIN, a tory of N. Y.; went to New Brunswick, in 1783, and settled in Queens co.; d. at Gagetown, in 1834, a. 91. His widow d. in 1843, a. 97. (*Sabine's Loyalists.*)

BISHOP, CLEMENT, d. at Avon, N. Y., Feb. 5, 1840, a. 92; formerly of Montville, Conn., and a soldier of the rev.; was captain of a company of Minute Men when New London was burned.

BLACK, EDWARD, a mem. of the soc. of Friends, and the oldest inhabitant in town, d. Oct. 29, 1841, a. 96, at New Egypt, Mon. co., N. J.

BLACK, EDWARD J., b. in Beaufort, S. C. in 1806; studied law and settled in Ga., where he served in the state legislature; was in cong. from 1839 to 1845; d. in Barnwell dist., S. C., whither he had gone for a change of scene in 1849.

BLACK, JAMES A., of S. C., a mem. of the 30th cong.; d. at Washington, D. C., April 1848.

BLACK, JAMES, d. in Winchester, Va., Aug. 29, 1854; was late of La., and from 1834 to 1838 a sen. in cong. from Miss.

BLACK, JAMES R., judge of the superior court of Del.; d. at Newcastle, Del., Sept. 3, 1839.

BLACK, JOHN, was at one time a res. of Louisiana, but rem. to Miss. where he was chosen senator to cong. from 1834 to 1838; d. in Winchester, Va., Aug. 29, 1854.

BLACK, JOSEPH, of S. C., was a tory, and held a crown office after the surrender of Charleston; estate was confiscated.

BLACK, REV. A. W. a prominent divine of the Ref. Presbyterian church, and a prof. of biblical literature in the Theo. Sem. of that sect in Phil.; d. at Pittsburg, Pa., Sept. 10, 1858.

BLACK REV. JOHN, the oldest minister of the Ref. Protestant Dutch ch., and one of the oldest inhabitants of Pittsburg; d. at that place Nov. 1849, a. 82.

BLACK-COAT, a Cherokee chief, d. in Scott co., Kentucky, on a journey, March 29, 1855.

BLACKBURN, GEN. SAMUEL, an eminent lawyer of Va.; d. Mar. 2, 1835, in Bath co., a. 77. He was for many years a conspicuous member of the state legislature, and at his death liberated 46 slaves, and charged his estate with their removal to Liberia.

BLACKBURN, GEN. WILLIAM, b. in Md., rem. to Penna., and afterwards became an early settler in Ohio. He commanded a co. of vols. in 1812; was in the Ohio legislature in 1817, and reëlected annually till 1835, when he was appointed receiver of public moneys in Lima, O., where he held till 1843; was again in the legislature in 1851; d. May 7, 1858, a. 70.

BLACKBURN, SAMUEL, of Irish descent, taught an academy at Washington, Wilkes co., Ga., and studied law; m. Gov. Matthews's dau. and settled on Broad river in Ellert co.; afterwards rem. to Va., and d. in 1835.

BLACKLEDGE, WILLIAM S., d. in Newbern, N. C., March 21, 1857, a 64; in gen. assembly from Craven co., 1820, and the same year was elected to cong. and was reëlected the following year; held various offices of trust in Craven co. such as commissioner, warden of the poor, clerk of the superior court, and chairman of the county court.

BLACKMAN ELEAZER, one of the survivors of the massacre of Wyoming, d. at Hanover, Pa., Nov. 4, 1845, a. 85.

BLACKSHEAR, DAVID, b. in Jones co., N. C., Jan. 31, 1764; was active against the tories; settled in Ga., in 1790, and had several conflicts with the Indians; prior to 1813 he was brig. gen. and commanded a line of forts in Twiggs, Pulaski and Telfair co's.; served in the Creek war with an army of 2,500 men, and received a vote of thanks from the Ga. legislature; was in the legislature, and a presidential elector, and d. in Laurens co., Ga., July 4, 1837, a. 74. (*White's Hist. Ga.*, p. 510; *Am. Almanac*, 1838, p. 314.)

BLAIR, DR. ARBA, of Rome, N. Y.; d. June 20, 1863, a. 82. (*Transac. N. Y. State Medical Soc.*, 1869, p. 443.)

BLAIR, Gen. James, mem. of cong. from S. C. in 1821–2, and from 1829 to 1834; d. at Washington by his own hand March 27, 1834.

BLAIR, John, a British spy, executed in 1778, at Hartford, Ct.; had a large amount of counterfeit continental money in his possession.

BLAIR, Robert, a tory merchant of Bost. was pros. and banished.

BLAIR, Robert, a tory of S. C.; held a commission under the crown after the surrender of Charleston, and lost his estate.

BLAKE, Col. Thomas H., d. in Cincinnati, O., Nov. 28, 1849, native of Calvert co., Md.; rem. when young to Washington; and on formation of state gov. in Ind., settled at Terre Haute; was many years in the legislature, a judge, dist. atty., and from 1827 to 1829, mem. of cong.; under Pres. Tyler, was com'r of gen. land office, and at the time of his death had recently returned from England as financial agent of the state, and a trustee of the Wabash and Erie canal.

BLAKE, Dominie T., a native of Ireland, and for thirty-six years a mem. of the N. Y. bar; d. in the city of N. Y., Nov. 6, 1839.

BLAKE, George, for many years U. S. attorney for the dist. of Mass.; d. at Boston, Oct. 6, 1841, a. 73.

BLAKE, Gen. John, d. Jan. 21, 1842 at Bangor, Me., a. 89; was an officer in the rev. known as Black Jack; also commander-in-chief in the eastern section during the war of 1812.

BLAKE, Jacob Edmund, lieut. top. engineers U. S. A., of Pa., grad. at West Point in 1833; was made 2d lt. 6th Infantry, July 1, 1833, assist. com. of subsist. May, 1835, Q. M. A. 1835 to 1836; 1st lt. Sept. 1837; 1st lt. top. engineers July 1838; before the battle of Palo Alto he rode boldly along the enemy's lines to observe their force; killed by the accidental discharge of his own pistol, May 9, 1846. (*Thorpe's Army of the Rio Grande*, p. 193.)

BLAKE, Rev. Caleb, d. in Westford, Mass., May 11, 1847, a. 85; grad. at H. U. in 1784, and was a settled minister at Westford, 45 years.

BLANCHARD, Andrew, d. Feb. 14, 1839, a. 100, in Mon. co., N. J.

BLANCHARD, John, b. in Caledonia co., Vt., Sept. 30, 1787; grad. at D. C., in 1812; rem. to Penn., taught school, studied law, and was in congress from 1845 to 1849; d. at Columbia, Lancaster co., Pa., March 8, 1849.

BLANCHAND, Nathaniel, a native of Peacham, Vt., and a lawyer at Fayetteville, Ga.; d. at Hardwick, Vt., Aug. 11, 1836, a. 37.

BLANCHARD, William A., an eminent book publisher of Phila.; d. Oct. 6, 1874, a. 70. He was principally noted as a financier, possessing none of the literary taste and ability of his partners, Lea and Baird, the grandson of Matthew Carey. (*Publishers' Weekly*.)

BLANDING, Col. Abraham, d. at Sullivan's Island, S. C., Sept. 20, 1839, a. 60; He was of Columbia, S. C., pres. of the south-western railroad bank; was b. at Rehoboth, and grad. at Brown U. in 1796. (*Am. Almanac*, 1841, p. 275.)

BLAND, Theodoric, ancestor of Blands of Va.; was a merch. at Luars in Spain; came to Va. in 1654; settled at Westover on the James river, and d. April 23, 1671, a. 41; He was buried in the chancel of a church which he built and gave to the Co. with 10 acres of land, a court house and a prison; was one of the king's council in Va., and a man of talent and fortune; his wife was a dau. of Gov. Bennett; he left a son, Richard. (*Campbell's Va.*)

BLATCHFORD, DR. THOMAS W., a prominent phys. of Troy, N. Y.; d. Jan. 7, 1866, a. 71. (*Transac N. Y. State Med. Soc.*, 1866, p. 322.)

BLATTERMAN, GEORGE, d. in Charlottesville, Va., Jan. 1, 1850; prof. of mod. languages in the Uni. of Va., from 1825 to 1833.

BLEAKLEY, JOHN, a wealthy and liberal Philadelphian, distinguished for his benevolence and zeal for the promotion of literary objects, for which he made liberal bequests.

BLEAN, URIAH, was an ensign in the 3d batt. of N. J. vols. (Loyalists) in 1782.

BLEAN WALDRON, was a capt. in the 3d N. J. vols. (Loy.) in 1782.

BLEECKER, ANTHONY, b. in N. Y. city, Oct. 1770; grad. at Columbia Coll.; bred a lawyer, possessed a literary taste and wrote much for the press; He wrote out Capt. Riley's narrative of the brig Commerce, and was constantly engaged in literary researches and studies; d. in 1827, a. 56. (*Hist. Mag.*, ii, 46.)

BLEECKER, BARENT, d. at Albany, June 1, 1840; pres. of the Bank of Albany.

BLEECKER, HARMANUS, minister to the Netherlands; b. Oct. 19, 1779; was admitted to the bar in Albany in 1801, a. 22; became eminent in his prof.; was in cong. in 1811, 13, and in assembly in 1814, 15; was many years a regent, and acted as com'r for settling the line of N. Y. and N. J.; was appointed minister at the Hague by Van Buren; his library and portrait are preserved in the N. Y. State Library; he d. at Albany, July 19, 1849. (*Munsell's An. Alb.*, i, 276; *Rogers's Hist. Discourse*, p. 105.)

BLISS, DANIEL, tory of Concord, Mass., son of Rev. Samuel B.; b. 1740; grad. at H. U. in 1760; was a barrister, and pros. and appointed commissary in the British army; settled in New Brunswick; became a mem. of the council and chief justice of the inferior court of com. pleas; d. near Fredericton, N. B., in 1805, a. 66; his widow d. in 1807, a. 60; Samuel B., his br., d. at St. George, N. B., in 1803. (*Sabine's Loyalists.*)

BLISS, DR. JOHN, drowned at Cooperstown, N. Y., June 26, 1858, a. 55.

BLISS, GEORGE, grad. at Yale Coll. in 1784, and settled as a lawyer at Springfield, Mass., his native place; several years a representative, senator and counselor. (*Bradford's N. E. Biog.*)

BLISS, JONATHAN, of Springfield, Mass., grad. at H. U., in 1763, and d. at Fredericton, N. B., in 1822, a. 80; his wife and Mrs. Fisher Ames were sisters; in 1768, he was a mem. of the gen. court of Mass., and one of the 17 rescinders, and in 1778 was pros. and banished; in N. B. he became chief just. and pres. of the council. (*Sabine's Loyalists.*)

BLISS, JOHN MURRAY, son of Daniel B., native of Mass., from whence, being a tory, he rem. at the beginning of the rev.; settled in N. B. in 1786; practiced law several years; represented the co. of York in assembly, and, in 1816 was elevated to a seat in his majesty's council; in 1824, he became pres. and commander-in-chief of the colony, and held nearly a year; d. at St. John, Aug. 1834, a. 63, being then senior justice of the supreme court. (*Sabine's Loyalists.*)

BLODGET, JESSE, pioneer settler in Denmark, N. Y.; d. Jan. 9, 1848, nearly 84 years of age; his wife d. Aug, 5, 1844.

BLOOD, ISAIAH, state senator of N. Y.; d. at Ballston, N. Y., Nov. 30, 1870, a. 60.

BLOODGOOD, FRANCIS, d. at Albany, March 5, 1840, a. 72; pres. of the state bank, and formerly clerk of the sup. court, and may. of Albany.

BLOODGOOD, FRANCIS A., d. at Ithaca, N. Y., Dec. 1842, a. 67; studied law at Albany, with John V. Henry, and settled in Oneida co.; was appointed co. clerk and clerk in chan.; state sen. from 1809 to 1816, and an active friend of the Erie canal project. (*Am. Alm.* 1844, p. 308.)

BLOODGOOD, SIMEON DE WITT, sometime editor of *The True Sun* in N. Y., and other newspapers, and an author; d. July 14, 1866, a. 66. (*Munsell's Hist. Coll. Albany*, iii, 319.)

BLOOMER, REV. JOSHUA, grad. at Kings Coll. N. Y. in 1761; was a maj. in the prov. service and a merchant; went to Eng. in 1765 for orders; succeeded Dr. Seabury at Jamaica, N. Y., to which were attached Newtown and Flushing; d. at Jamaica, June 23, 1790, a. 55. (*Thompson's Hist. L. I.*, ii, 125; *Sabine's Loyalists.*)

BLUE-SKY, JOHN, sachem of the Hawk band of the Senecas; rendered important services to the Americans at the battle of Queenston Heights; he d. at Tonawanda, N. Y., April 30, 1850.

BLUNT, NATHANIEL BOWDITCH, d. at Lebanon Springs, N. Y., July 16, 1854; an eminent lawyer of the N. Y. bar, and dist. atty. for the city of N. Y. at the time of his death.

BLUNT, SIMON FRAZER, lieut. U. S. N.; d. at Baltimore, Md., April 27, 1854, a 34; appointed midshipman in 1831.

BLYTHE, CALVIN, a native of Adams co., Pa.; in 1813, entered into the service as a private and served through the war; having studied law he settled at Mifflintown, from whence he was elected to the legislature and served in both houses; was appointed sec'y of the commonwealth, and was twice appointed pres. judge of the judicial dist. embracing Dauphin, Lebanon and Schuylkill co's; was twice appointed collector of the port of Phila., where he afterward settled as a lawyer; d. June 27, 1849. (*Stryker's Am. Reg.*, iii, 231.)

BOARDMAN, DR. DANIEL H., d. at New Orleans, Oct. 13, 1835; was a native of New Milford, Conn.

BOARDMAN, ELIJAH, b. in New Milford, Conn., March 7, 1760; was a successful merchant and repeatedly in the leg. and council of Conn.; sen. in cong. from 1821 to 1823; d. in Boardman, O., Oct. 8, 1823.

BODISCO, ALEXANDER DE, Russian minister to the U. S.; d. at Georgetown, D. C., Jan. 23, 1854; he had filled important offices in Russia, and had served seventeen years in the office in which he died.

BODLE, CHARLES, mem. of cong. from New York from 1833 to 1835; d. in New York city, 1836.

BOEL, HENRY, d N. Y. Oct. 10, 1780; many years a clerk in general post office.

BOGARD, ABRAHAM, a native of Delaware; d. in the poor house Maury co., Tenn., June 14, 1833, a. 118 years, 4 days.

BOGGS, JAMES, of Pa., a tory, went to St. John, N. B. after the rev.; was a grantee of that city, and in 1792 a magistrate of Queens co.

BOGUE, REV. PUBLIUS V., a Presb. clergyman; d. in Oneida co., N. Y., Aug. 28, 1846, a. 73.

BOHLEN, JOHN, an eminent shipping merch. and importer at Phila. and a native of Germany; d. at Phila., March 11, 1850, a. 80.

BOIES, JEREMIAH SMITH, d. in Boston, March 29, 1851, a. 89; grad. at H. U., in 1783, of which class he was the last survivor; was connected with cotton mills and part owner of the first large one in the state; under difficulties that can now be hardly appreciated, it became eminently successful. (*Stryker's Am. Reg.* vi, 222.)

BOILEAU, ALEXANDER, sec. of state of Arkansas; was appointed to fill a vacancy from death of Maj. D. B. Greer, and d. Jan. 18, 1860.

BOILEAU, NATHANIEL B., at an early age was an active mem. of the Pa. leg., and took a leading part in the well known impeachment of the judges in 1805, 6; was sec'y of state under Gov. Snyder nine years, and was an unsuccessful candidate for gov. in 1847; d. at Abington, Pa., March 16, 1850, a. 88. (*Stryker's Am. Reg.*, iv, 453.)

BOISSEAU, JAMES, of S. C., held an office under the crown after the surrender of Charleston, in 1780, and his estate was confiscated.

BOKEE, DAVID A., mem. of cong. from N. Y. from 1849 to 1851; d. in Washington, D. C., March 15, 1860.

BOKER, CHARLES S., an eminent merchant and financier of Phila.; d. Feb. 10, 1858 (*Sargent's Eminent Philadelphians*, with portrait.)

BOKER, JOHN G., importing wine merch. of N. Y.; the collector of the fine paintings of the Dusseldorf school, long exhibited in N. Y., and came prominently before the public a few years before his death by the eccentric marriage of his dau. to his coachman Dean; d. March 3, 1860.

BOLLES, MRS. MARY C., d. at Montville, Conn., Jan. 4, 1862, a. 104.

BOLLES, REV. LUCIUS, D. D., d. in Boston, Jan. 5, 1844, a. 64; formerly pastor of the First Baptist church in Salem, and many years senior sec'y of the American Bap. board of foreign missions.

BOLLING, ROBERT, m. Jane Rolfe, the only grandchild of Pocahontas; was b. Dec. 1646, came to Va. Oct. 1660, and d. July 1709, a. 62; Col. B. left an only son, Maj. John B., father of Col. John B., and several daughters, who m. Col. Richard Randolph, Col. John Fleming, Dr. Wm. Gay, Tho. Eldridge and James Murray.

BOLTON, NATHANIEL P., late U. S. consul at Geneva, and long connected with the press in Ind.; d. at Indianapolis, Ind., Nov. 26, 1858.

BOLZIUS, REV. JOHN MARTIN, a teacher and leader of the Salzburgers who settled in Effingham co. Ga; reached Charleston, S. C., March 1734, and soon settled near the Savannah, 25 miles by water, above the city, at Ebenezer. (*White's Hist. Ga.*, p. 928, with portrait.)

BONAPARTE, LOUIS NAPOLEON, emperor of the French; d. Jan. 9, 1872, a. 64; was some time resident of the United States.

BOND, DR. THOMAS, a physician and philosopher of considerable eminence in Phila.; d. in that city, in 1784, a. 72.

BOND, GEORGE, d. in Phila., May 23, 1842, a. 53; was a merchant of Boston, and noted for his benefactions.

BOND, PHINEAS, several years British consul in Phila.; d. in London, Dec. 29, 1815.

BONFILS, SAUVIER F., d. in Lexington, Ky., July 6, 1849, a. 54; was prof. mod. languages and literature in Transylvania University, and many years in the same depart. in the Univ. of Ala., at Tuscaloosa; was a native of France, but for the last 30 years a teacher of French in Am.

BONGARS, GEN. THEODORE VARIEN THOMAS, COUNT DE, d. in New York, Feb. 1, 1862, a. 70; formerly in the French army.

BONIFACE, FRANCOIS, Jesuit missionary; sent to the Mohawks in 1668, 9, laboring there after 1673; d. at Quebec, Dec. 17, 1674.

BONKER, JOSEPH, b. in Marietta, O., Feb. 1790, and said to have been the fourth white male born in the north-west territory, after its organization; was chosen to serve in each house of the state leg., and was for many years asso. judge of the court of com. pleas; d. at Newport, Ohio, Jan. 6, 1860, a. 70.

BONNER, HENRY, an officer of the rev.; resided in Warren co., Ga.; d. Jan. 1, 1822, a. 98.

BONNETT, ISAAC, b. in New Rochelle, N. Y.; was a tory and left his property in N. Y. in 1783, on going to Annapolis Royal, N. S., where he d. 1838, a. 86. (*Sabine's Loyalists.*)

BONSALL, BENJAMIN S., marshal of the eastern dist. of Penn.; d. at Phila., Aug. 20, 1837, a. 40.

BOONE, ENOCH, d. in Meade co., Ky., March 8, 1862; b. in 1778, and was the first male white child born in Kentucky.

BOONE, RATLIFF, d. in La., Nov. 20, 1844, a. 63; b. in N. C., in 1781; was in cong. from Ind., from 1825 to 1827, and from 1829 to 1839.

BOONE, WILLIAM F., judge of the U. S. dist. court for New Mexico; d. at Philadelphia, Jan. 12, 1860.

BOOTH, B., secretary of the loyal refugees; issued a call for a meeting in N. Y., Sept. 1778, at which about 2000 were present.

BOOTH, DR. CHAUNCEY, physician and supt. of the McLean asylum for the insane; d. at Somerville, Mass., Jan. 12, 1858, a. 41; was a man of distinguished attainments and talents.

BOOTH, JAMES, chief justice of Delaware; d. in Newcastle, Delaware, March 29, 1855.

BOOTH, LEBBEUS, grad. at Union Coll. in 1813; was educated to the ministry at Princeton, but from his health failing he did not preach; was several years prin. of the Alb. Fem. Acad., and in 1824, established at Ballston, N. Y., a ladies' sem. which he conducted many years; d. Dec. 16, 1859, a. 70. (*Hist. Mag.*, iv, 61.)

BOOTH, THOMAS, d. in Burlington, N. J., May 29, 1843, a. 40; a prominent member of the society of Friends.

BOOTT, KIRK, a prominent and enterprising citizen of Lowell; d. April 11, 1831, a. 46; was b. in Boston, educated in Eng., and spent two years in the military school at Woolwich; returned about 1817, engaged in mercantile business, and a few years afterwards was called to superintend the erection of factories at Lowell, where he evinced great talent for business. (*Am. Almanac*, 1838, p. 314.)

BORDEN, ENOCH B., of Trenton, N. J., of the *State Gazette*; d. May 16, 1870.

BORDEN, JOHN, d. at Shrewsbury, N. J., Jan. 30, 1856, a. 95.

BORLAND, JOHN LINDALL, of Cambridge, Mass., son of John B., grad. at H. U. in 1772; entered the British army and became lt. col.; d. in England, Nov. 1825.

BOSOMWORTH, THOMAS, m. Mary Musgrove, alias Matthews, an Indian woman, and acquired claims to land in Ga. (*White's Hist. Ga.*, p. 21.)

BOSSEAU, JAMES, E., in 1782, was an ensign of infantry in the S. C. Loyalists.

BOSSIER, PETER E., d. in Washington, D. C., April 24, 1844; was a descendant of an old French family of La.; after serving ten years in the state sen., was elected a mem. of the 28th cong., but d. during his term.

BOSTON, POLLY, colored, d. in Maryland, April 25, 1859, a. 109.

BOSTWICK, ISAAC WELTON, land agt.; b. at Watertown, Ct., Mar. 6, 1776; settled in Turin, 1804, and the next year in Lowville, where he became agt. for Low, Harrison & Hoffman and Pierrepont, and held responsible trusts till late in life; was first surrogate in Lewis co., and a lawyer, but seldom practiced; d. Jan. 3, 1857, a. 81. (*Hough's Hist. Lewis Co. N. Y.*, p. 149, with portrait.)

BOSWORTH, ALFRED, one of the associate judges of the supreme court of R. I.; d. at Warren, R. I., June 10, 1862.

BOTELER, ALEXANDER R., he was mem. of the 36th cong. from the 8th dist. of Va., being the only successful *American* candidate from that state, and remained in cong. for some time after other mem. from Va. had resigned; participated in the bat. of Stone bridge with the rebels and was wounded; d. of lock jaw Aug. 1861; resided at Shepherdstown, Jefferson co., Va.

BOTHWELL, REV. DAVID E., b. in co. of Monaghan, Ireland; grad. at Glasgow, about his 28th year; studied theology under the pres. of Monaghan, and was licensed in 1787; came to Ga., in 1790, settled at Queensborough; d. at the house of Jared Irwin, Washington co., Ga., June 1801, a. 45. (*White's Hist. Ga.*, p. 503.)

BOTSFORD, AMOS, of Newtown, Ct.; became a loyalist, and rem. to New Brunswick, where he settled as a lawyer; in 1784, was elected to the house of assem., and was uniformly returned from Westmoreland co. through life; in 1792, was speaker; d. at St. John, in 1812, a. 69; his son William was appointed judge of vice-admir. of N. B., in 1803, and was long a mem. of the council and a judge of the sup. court. (*Sabine's Loyalists.*)

BOTTS, GEN. THOMAS H., d. in Fredericksburg, Va., June 11, 1854, a. 54; was a leading lawyer in Va.

BOUDINOT, ELIAS, a Cherokee, and a man of intelligence and talents; was murdered by Indians west of the Mississippi, June 10, 1839.

BOULDIN, THOMAS TYLER, mem. of cong. from Va.; d. in the Capitol at Washington, Feb. 11, 1834; was struck with paralysis as he was about speaking to the house; had been an able lawyer and judge, and resided in Charlotte co., Va.

BOULIGNY, DOMINIQUE, b. in La.; was a lawyer, and a senator in congress, from 1824 to 1829; d. 1833.

BOULIGNY, DON FRANCISCO, b. in Alicant, Spain, of noble parents, March 5, 1735; entered the army as a cadet at the age of 18; in 1762 went to Havana with his reg., and on the 24th of July arrived with the fleet at the mouth of the Miss.; Col. Bouligny, remained at N. O., at the head of his reg. until ordered to join the expedition of Galvez which took Mobile and Pensacola in 1780, 1; his bravery secured his prom. to the rank of brig. gen.; d. at N. O., Nov. 25, 1800, and was buried in the Cathedral of that city; he was greatly honored in La. (*B. F. French's Hist. Memoirs of La.*, p. 182.)

BOURK, WILLIAM, of N. C., a tory; was arrested March 1776, and placed in close confinement. (*Sabine's Loyalists.*)

BOURNE, SHEARJASUB, grad. at H. U., in 1764; was chief justice of the court of com. pleas for Suffolk co., Mass., and in cong. from 1791 to 1795; d. in 1806.

BOURNOUVILLE, DR. ANTHONY, a physician of Phila., Pa.; b. in 1798; d. in Philadelphia, Feb. 27, 1863.

BOUTELLE, TIMOTHY, LL.D., d. in Waterville, Me., Nov. 12, 1855, a. 77; was a native of Leominster, Mass., and grad. at Cambridge in 1800.

BOWDEN, REV. CHARLES, of N. Y.; was chaplain of the provincial cong. in 1775, and became a tory; was chap. of DeLancey's 1st batt.

BOWDEN, THOMAS, was in 1872 a maj. in De Lancey's 2d battalion, and at the peace went to England.

BOWDOIN, FRANKLIN W., d. in Henderson, Texas, June 6, 1857; b. in Ala.; was a rep. in cong. from that state in 1846-51; about 1852 rem. to Texas, and engaged in law practice; was a pres. elector in 1856.

BOWDOIN, GEORGE R. I., American lawyer at London; d. March 14, 1870, a. 61.

BOWDOIN, JAMES, of Boston; d. at Havana, Mar. 6, 1833, a. 38.

BOWDON, FRANKLIN W., b. in Ala.; was in cong. from 1846 to 1851; in 1852 rem. to Texas, and engaged in law practice; d. at Henderson, Texas, June 6, 1857.

BOWEN, BENJAMIN, b. in R. I.; rem. from Newport, R. I., to Fairfield, N. Y., in 1787, and in 1792, to Newport, N. Y., where he built mills; in 1798, was in assembly, and was 5 years a county judge; d. at an advanced age. (*Benton's Herkimer Co. N. Y.*, p. 301.)

BOWEN, CHARLES, lost on the steamer Belle Zane, on the Miss., 500 m. above N. O., Dec. 19, 1845, a. 35, with wife and oldest boy; b. in Charlestown, Mass., but lived most of his life in Boston; was many years pub. of the *North American Review*, the *American Almanac*, *The Token*, and many other works; in 1838, he rem. to Zanesville, O.; in 1840-1, was in the Ohio legislature, and for some years was actively engaged in politics.

BOWEN, COL. EPHRAIM, an officer of the revolution; d. at Providence, R. I., Sept. 1841, in his 89th year.

BOWEN, GEORGE T., prof. of chemistry in the University of Tenn.; he had while a student at Yale Coll. evinced a great talent for mineralogy and chemistry, and pub. several very creditable analyses; d. at Nashville, Tenn., Oct. 25, 1828, a. 28. (*Am. Jour. Sci. and Arts*, 1st series, xv, 403.)

BOWEN, HENRY, of Tryon (now Montgomery) co., N. Y., a neighbor of Johnson, and accompanied Sir John to Canada; was in several of the expeditions that ravaged the Mohawk valley; William B., of the same family, was also thus engaged; the family were from N. E., having emigrated to the Mohawk about 1728. (*Sabine's Loyalists.*)

BOWEN, W. W., a distinguished mem. of the Louisiana bar; d. at Opelousas, La., Oct. 1839.

BOWERS, JOHN M., d. in Cooperstown, N. Y., Feb. 24, 1846, a. 74; prominently concerned in land titles in Otsego co.

BOWIE, COL. JAMES, the man from whom bowie knives were named; b. in Burke co., Ga.; went in 1802 to La., and became noted for a terrible duel fight with Norris Wright and others, Sept. 19, 1827, on a bar of the Miss., in which he was wounded, and two men killed; was in the Texan army, showed great bravery on several occasions, and was killed with Col's Travis and Crocket, in the attack on the Alamo, March 6, 1836; was a son of Rezin P.; was long engaged in buying negroes of Lafitte, and smuggling them into La. (*Hist. Mag.*, ii, 249, iii, 24; *Texas Almanac*, 1857, p. 137.)

BOWIE REZIN P., d. at N. O., La., Jan. 17, 1841, a. 48; "well known in the south-west by his many deeds of valor in its early history among the Mexicans and savages."

BOWLES, ELD. CHARLES, a colored Free-Will Baptist minister of northern N. Y., and Vt.; b. in Boston in 1761; d at Lawrenceville, N. Y., March 16, 1843. (*Lewis's Life of Eld. C. Bowles.*)

BOWLS, WILLIAM, in 1782, was an ensign of Maryland Loyalists.

BOWMAN, JOSEPH, d. at New Braintree, Mass., Jan. 30, 1852, a. 80; was a native of that place, which he represented 14 years in the gen. court; was two years in the state sen., and 3 years of the gov. council; in the convention of 1820, and pres. of the Ware Bank for twenty years.

BOWNE, CHRISTOPHER, a soldier of the revolution; d. at Philadelphia, May 30, 1837, a. 107.

BOYD, COL., of Carolina, leader of a marauding band of tory robbers; while advancing to meet the royal army near Savannah, he met Col. Pickens, at the head of a large body of whigs, and fell with many of his men, in 1779. (*Sabine's Loyalists.*)

BOYD, DAVID, F. W. Bapt. preacher; several years in the Mass. leg. from Me.; a mem. of the Maine state conven.; d. at New Berwick, Me., Dec. 11, 1855, a. 74 y. 6 mo. (*F. W. Bap. Reg.* 1857, p. 87.)

BOYD, DR. GEORGE W., d. at the University of Va., Sept. 23, 1840; formerly curator of the lyceum of natural history at N. Y., and lately an assistant on the geological survey of Va.

BOYD, GORDON D., d. at N. O., April 8, 1850, a. 50; for many years a mem. of the house of representatives, and state senator in Mississippi.

BOYD, JOHN D., senator from Attala co., in the state senate of Miss.; d. at Jackson, Jan. 30, 1844, a. 44.

BOYD, JOHN I., merchant at Albany, son of James B., a Scotch emigrant; resided at Albany, and was interested in various public improvements; d. in N. Y., where he had gone on a visit July 13, 1856. (*Albany Evening Journal*, July 1856.)

BOYD, John, sheriff of St. Lawrence co., N. Y.; b. in N. Y. city, Aug. 2, 1772; settled at Hamilton (Waddington, N. Y)., in 1805; was sheriff from 1807 to 1811; d. July 17, 1833. (*Hough's Hist. St. Law. and Fr. Cos. N. Y.*, p. 585.)

BOYLE, John, judge of the U. S. court for the dist. of Ky.; was in cong. from 1805 to 1809, and also chief justice of Ky.; d. Jan. 28, 1834.

BOYLE, Junius J., commodore U. S. N.; d. at Norfolk, Va., Aug. 11, 1870.

BOYNTON, Seth, inventor; d. at Middleville, New York, March 31, 1870, aged 82.

BRACE, John P., a teacher eminent for his success in conducting ladies' seminaries, and afterwards editor of the *Hartford Courant*, d. in Litchfield, Conn., Oct. 18, 1872.

BRACE, Jonathan, mem. of cong. from Conn., in 1798 and 1800, and formerly chief judge of the Hartford co. court, and judge of probate; d. at Hartford, Conn., Aug. 26, 1837, a. 83.

BRACE, Rev. Joab, D.D., LL.D.; d. in Pittsfield, Mass., April 20, 1861, a. 80; was a Congregational minister and served fifty years in Newington, Connecticut.

BRACE, Thomas Kimberly, was b. in Glastonbury, Ct., Oct. 16, 1779; was for many years a prominent citizen of Hartford, Ct., and a mayor of that city from 1840 to 1843; d. at Hartford, Jan. 14, 1860.

BRACKET, Daniel, d. at New Market, N. H., April 4, 1837, a. 58. A short time before his death he weighed about 560 pounds.

BRACKET, James, d. in Rock Island, Ill., May 19, 1852, a. 70; b. in Greenland, N. H., March 31, 1783; grad. at D., in 1805; studied law and in 1808 began practice at Cherry Valley, N. Y. In old age he rem. to Illinois; was for a time surrogate of Otsego co., N. Y.

BRADBURY, George, b. in Portland (then Falmouth), in 1770; grad. at H. U., in 1789; settled as a lawyer in Portland, and in 1812 was elected to cong.; was again elected in 1814, and at the end of this term returned to practice until his death, Nov. 27, 1823.

BRADBURY, Jabez, a member of the executive council of Maine; d. of small pox at Hollis, Me., April 13, 1836, a. 43.

BRADBURY Theophilus, legislator and judge, of Newburyport, Mass.; grad. at H. U., in 1757, and settled at Falmouth (Portland), Me., in 1761; soon after the war begun returned to Newburyport; was several years in the leg. serving in both houses, and was in cong. in 1795–7; was then made associate just. of the supreme jud. court of Mass., and held this rank until his death Sept. 6, 1803, a. 66. (*Bradford's N. E. Biog.*)

BRADFORD, Andrew, a descendant of Gov. William Bradford, and a quartermaster in the revolution; d. at Duxbury, Mass., Jan. 1837, a. 91; his twin brother Peter, d. about two years before.

BRADFORD, Daniel, was a son of John Bradford, a pioneer printer of the west who established the *Kentucky Gazette* at Lexington, when the whole of the northwest territory was the home of savages; his son succeeded to the management of the paper and was long connected with public affairs in that state; d. at Lexington, July 14, 1849, of cholera. (*Stryker's Am. Reg.*, iii, 236.)

BRADFORD, CAPT. SAMUEL, an officer of the revolution; d. at Acworth, N. H., July 1833, a. 80.

BRADFORD, DUNSCOURT, d. in Paris, France, Dec. 5, 1837, a. 30; was vice consul of the United States, and formerly of N. Y.

BRADFORD, DR. GAMALIEL, d. at Bost., Mass., Oct. 22, 1839, a. 44.

BRADFORD, REV. JOHN MELANCTHON, b. an Danbury, Ct., May 15, 1781, son of Rev. Ebenezer B., the Cong. minister at that place; grad. at B. U.; studied theology with Rev. Dr. Green of Phil., and May 1805, was called to become pastor of the Ref. Prot. Dutch church at Albany; d. there in 1827; his son Alexander W. B., was many years surrogate in N. Y. (*Rogers's Hist. Discourse*, p. 40.)

BRADFORD, REV. WILLIAM H., a Presb.; d. at Homer, N. Y., April 1, 1861; was b. in Cooperstown in 1814; grad. at Hamilton Coll. and at the Theo. school at Auburn; had preached at Berkshire, N. Y., and for some years was connected with the *New York Evangelist*, of which for a time he was sole editor.

BRADFORD, THOMAS, LL.D., son of Thomas B.; b. in Phila. Sept. 11, 1781; became an eminent lawyer in that city, and d. there Oct. 25, 1851. (*Simpson's Eminent Philadelphians.*)

BRADISH, EBENEZER, a lawyer of Worcester, Mass.; grad. at H. U., in 1769; was a tory in 1774, and d. in 1818.

BRADLEE, JOSIAH, an honorable and successful merchant, and distinguished for his enlightened liberality and considerate charities; d. in Boston, Mass., Jan. 4, 1860, a. 56

BRADLEY, ABRAHAM, many years assistant post master general; d. at Washington, D. C., May 7, 1839.

BRADLEY, CYRUS PARKER, d. at Concord, N. H., in his 20th year, July 6, 1834; was remarkable for the precocity of his genius, and at the age of 16 edited the *Literary Gazette* at Concord.

BRADLEY, DAN., b. at Mount Carmel (since Haddam), Conn., June 10, 1767; grad. at Yale in 1789; became a pastor at Whitestown, N. Y., in 1792, and three years after settled in Marcellus, Onondaga co., then a wilderness; became a co. judge and prominent citizen; d. Sept. 19, 1838.

BRADLEY, DR. PHINEHAS, d. at Washington, D. C., Feb. 28, 1845, a. 75; many years Second Asst. P. M. Gen.; b. in Litchfield, Conn., July 17, 1769, and settled as a physician at Painted Post, N. Y.; about 1800 he relinquished his practice, and was appointed to an office in the gen. post office at Washington, which he held until Sept. 1829.

BRADLEY, EDWARD, d. Aug. 5, 1848, a. 40; a prominent citizen of Michigan.

BRADLEY, MRS. ANN, d. Jan. 8, 1840, at Danbury, N. H., a. 100.

BRADLEY, SAMUEL, d. at Saco, Me., June 26, 1849, a. 47; was a lawyer in extensive practice.

BRADSTREET, DR. EDWARD, d. in Beverly, Mass., Dec. 13, 1844; youngest son of Dr. B., of Newburyport; grad. at Harvard in 1844.

BRADY, GEN. WILLIAM, d. of cholera in Rutherford co. Tenn, July 23, 1835.

BRADY, WILLIAM V., ex-mayor of New York; d. March 31, 1870, aged 69.

BRAINE, JAMES H., shipping merchant; b. at Shelburne, N. S., in 1795; entered upon a seafaring life and rose to the post of capt. in a Liverpool packet before he was of age; in 1822 he m. and settled in N. Y., where he became an extensive flour dealer, and in 1832 a shipping merchant; d. Sept. 29, 1855, a. 61. (*New York Times*, Nov. 9, 1855.)

BRAINERD, LAWRENCE, at one time U. S senator of Vt.; d. at Montpelier, Vt., May 8, 1870, a. 86.

BRAINERD, REV. JOHN, missionary with the Indians; brother of Rev. David B.; grad. at Yale in 1746, and labored with the New Jersey Indians; d. March 21, 1781, a. 61.

BRAMAN, REV. ISAAC, b. in Norton, Mass., July 5, 1775; grad. at H. U., in 1794, and settled as a clergyman at New Rowley (now Georgetown), in 1797; the parish had been destitute of a minister for nine years, and he was the last of sixty-four candidates who preached there on probation; he remained at this place 61 years, being, towards the last, aided by a colleague; d. Dec. 26, 1858.

BRANCH, STEPHEN, formerly a prominent politician of R. I.; d. at Central Village, Ct., May 27, 1851.

BRANDON, GERARD C., for two terms gov. of Miss., d. Mar. 31, 1850.

BRANNAN, CHARLES, served the king in the rev., and on the peace went to St. John, N. B.; removed to Fredericton in 1785; d. there in 1828, a. 81.

BRANTLEY W. F., brig. gen. confederate army; assassinated at Winona, Miss., Nov. 2, 1870.

BRASHEARS, SAMUEL, an accomplished lawyer and scholar; d. at Philadelphia, Pa., Dec. 10, 1847.

BRATTLE, THOMAS, b. at Cambridge, Mass., 1742; grad. at Harv. in 1760; went to England in 1775, and was proscribed and banished in 1778; he labored to relieve the condition of prisoners in England; came to America in 1779, and landed in R. I.; the enactments against him in Mass., were rem. in 1784; d. Feb. 1801; he was humane, liberal and public spirited. (*Sabine's Loyalists.*)

BRAYTON, CHARLES, one of the judges of the sup. court of R. I.; d. at Warwick, R. I., Nov. 16, 1834.

BRAZEN, REV. John, D.D., pastor of the North Dutch church in Salem, Mass.; d. Feb. 26, 1846, a. 66; was b. in Worcester, Sept. 21, 1780; grad. at Cambridge, in 1813; was appointed Latin tutor in 1815, and Latin prof. in 1817, and held this office in Harv. Coll. till Nov. 14, 1820, when he was ordained in the church where he served till death; in 1829 he was elected one of the board of overseers of H. U.; was a member of the Am. Acad., and in 1836 was made D.D.; he wrote many articles for the *North American Review* and other publications. (*Am. Alm.* 1847, p. 330.)

BREARLY, COL. DAVID, d. at Dardanelles, Ark., Dec. 1837, a. 56; native of N. J., formerly of the army, and later, Indian agent; was an officer in the war 1812.

BRECK, REV. DANIEL, b. in Boston, Aug. 18, 1748; grad. at Princeton in 1774; served as chaplain in the rev., and was with Col. Porter's reg. in Canada; he was with the troops in the attack on Quebec; after the war he settled at Marietta, O.; d. at Hartland, Vt., Dec. 1845, a. 97;

was the father of Judge Daniel B., of the supreme court of Kentucky. (*Am. Almanac*, 1847, p. 323.)

BRECKINRIDGE, GEN. ROBERT, d. at Lexington, Ky., Sept. 1833, a. 78.

BRECKINRIDGE, JAMES D., d. at Louisville, Ky., May 1849; member of cong. from Kentucky, from 1821 to 1823.

BRECKINRIDGE, REV. JOHN, D.D., several years pres. of the Young Men's Colonization Soc.; formerly prof. pastoral theology in the Theol. Sem. at Princeton, and subsequently settled in the ministry at New Orleans; d. in Ky., Aug. 4, 1841.

BRECKNER, ROBERT H., d. near Jackson, Miss., Sept. 21, 1848, a. 45; was a native of Ky., and rem. to Miss., in 1824.

BREESE, THOMAS, purser in the U. S. navy; d. Oct. 11, 1846, at Cambridge, Mass.; b. in Newport, R. I.; was on the personal staff of Com. Perry, and in the battle of Lake Erie, where he assisted in firing the last gun on board the Lawrence.

BREHM, DIEDRICH, native of Germany, became lieut. in the 2d batt. of 60th regt. Feb. 21, 1756, and in 1759, acted as asst. engineer; he attended Maj. Rogers to Detroit in 1760, and went thence, it is said, to Michilimackinac; in 1774 he was capt., and March 19, 1783 became a maj. in the British army. (*Com. Wilson's Orderly Book*, 45.)

BRENT, DANIEL, U. S. consul at Paris, and agent for Am. claims; d. in Paris Jan. 31, 1841, in his 65th year.

BRENT, RICHARD, in cong. from Va., from 1795 to 1799, and from 1801 to 1803; was a sen. in cong. from 1809 to 1814; d. Dec. 30, 1814.

BRENT, WILLIAM, d. at Washington, D. C., Dec. 14, 1848, a. 73; clerk of the dist., circuit and criminal court.

BRENT, WILLIAM JR., of Alexandria, late chargè d' affaires to Buenos Ayres; d. May 1848.

BRENT WILLIAM L., a member of the 19th and 20th cong. from La.; d. at St. Martinsville, La., July 7, 1848.

BRENTON, SAMUEL, d. at Fort Wayne, Ind., March 29, 1857, a. 48; b. in Gallatin co., Ky.; was a minister from the age of 20 till 1848, when he was disabled by paralysis; he was then appointed regr. of the Fort Wayne land office; in 1851, and in 1855, he was elected to cong.; from 1853 to 1855, he was president of Fort Wayne College.

BRESSANI, FRANCOIS JOSEPH, Jesuit missionary; native of Rome; arrived in Canada Aug. 1640; prisoner with the Mohawks from April 30, to Aug. 19, 1644; left for Europe Nov. 2, 1650, and d. at Florence, Sept. 9, 1672; he wrote a history of Jesuit missions in Canada, pub. in 1653, and again at Montreal in 1852. (*Relation Abrégée par F. J. Bressani*, Montreal, ed. 1852: *Doc. Hist. N. Y.*, iv, 292.)

BREWERTON, GEORGE, of N. Y., commanded a N. Y. reg. in the French war, and the 2d batt. of De Lancey's Loyalist Corps in the rev.; d. in 1779.

BREWERTON, GEORGE AND JAMES, were ensigns in De Lancey's Corps; went to St. Johns, N. B.; were grantees of city lots and drew half pay.

BREWSTER, HENRY, a pioneer in the Genesee valley; settled in 1806 in Riga, N. Y., where he built the first house and church; he was prominent in religious affairs, and d. at LeRoy, N. Y., March 7, 1858. (*Rochester Democrat.*)

BRIAND, JEAN OLIVER, seventh R. C. Bp. of Quebec; b. in the parish of Plevin in Brittany; came to Quebec Aug. 17, 1741, as sec. of M. Pontbriand, whom he was chosen to succeed as Bp. Sept. 11, 1764; he visited England the same year; was consecrated Bp. May 16, 1766, and arrived at Quebec June 28, 1766; he chose a coadjutor in 1770 and resigned Nov. 29, 1784; d. June 25, 1794, a. 79 y., 5 m. (*Liste Chron. des Evêques et des Prêtres du Canada.*)

BRICE, NICHOLAS, during 34 years judge, and at the time of his death, senior and chief judge of Baltimore city court; d. at Baltimore, Md., May 8, 1851, a. 80.

BRIDGAM, JAMES, was an ensign in the Prince of Wales's American Volunteers in 1782.

BRIDGEN, EDWARD, of N. C., a tory; lost his estate by confiscation, but had it restored in 1785.

BRIDGHAM, EBENEZER, merchant of Boston; went to Halifax in 1776: was proscribed and banished in 1778; was dep. inspector gen. of loy. forces in 1782, and in 1783, was grantee of a lot in St. Johns, N. B.

BRIDGHAM, GEN. SAMUEL W., d. at Providence, R. I, Dec. 1840, a. 67; mayor of Providence from 1832 till the time of his death; was many years atty. gen. of R. I., and a long time chancellor of B. U.

BRIGGS, DAVID, an eminent attorney; formerly mayor of Fredericksburg, Va., and a counsellor at law; d. in Va., Nov. 5, 1836, a. 57.

BRIGHAM, CAPT. STEPHEN, a soldier of Bunker hill; d. at Vernon, N. Y., Oct. 11, 1849, a. 96.

BRIGHAM, ELIJAH, b, in Northborough, Mass.; grad. at Dart. in 1778; settled as a lawyer in Worcester, Mass., and from 1811 to 1816 was in cong.; was a justice of com. pleas in Worcester co., and some time a mem. of the sen. and ex. council; d. Feb. 22, 1816, at Washington city, a. 66. (*Bradford's N. E. Biog.*)

BRIGHAM, REV. JOHN C., D.D., Presb. clergyman, and 35 years cor. sec. of Am. Bible Soc.; d. in Brooklyn, N. Y. (E. D.), Aug. 10, 1862.

BRIMMER, GEORGE WATSON, d. at Florence, Italy, Sept. 1838; was of Boston; grad. at Harv. in 1803, and after some years in mercantile life, devoted much attention to the fine arts, and particularly to painting and architecture; he was a liberal patron of the cemetery of Mount Auburn, and the Boston Atheneum.

BRINCKERHOOF, GEN. HENRY R., d. in Huron co, O., April 30, 1844, a. 56; b. in Adams co., Pa., in 1788, and in early life settled in Cayuga co., N. Y.; in the war of 1812 he was capt. of a com. of vols. and distinguished himself at the battle of Queenston; emigrated to O. in 1837; was elected to cong. in 1843, and d. before the end of his term.

BRINLEY, GEORGE, merchant of Boston; a tory, was proscribed and banished in 1778; went to England in 1783, being then dep. com. gen.; in 1799 he was appointed com. gen. of his majesty's forces in British America; his son Thomas, lt. col. in the army, and qr. mr. gen. of British troops in the West Indies; d. there in 1805.

BRINSMADE, DR. THOMAS C., a distinguished physician of Troy, N. Y.; d. June 22, 1868, a. 66; b. June 16, 1802 at New Hartford, Litchfield co., Ct.; rem. to Lansingburgh, N. Y., in the fall of 1823, and to Troy in 1833. (*Transac, N. Y. State Med. Soc.*, 1869, p. 238.)

BRISBANE, JAMES, tory of Charleston, S. C.; congratulator of Cornwallis on the victory at Camden in 1780; lost his estate in 1782, and was banished.

BRISTED, CHARLES ASTOR, author; d. Jan. 15, 1874. (*Drake's Biog. Dict.*, 124.)

BRISTOL, WILLIAM, judge of the U. S. court for the dist. of Conn.; b. at Hamden, Ct.; grad. at Yale in 1798; became a distinguished mem. of the New Haven bar; was appointed a judge of the sup. court in 1819, and of the U. S. dist. court of Conn., in 1826; d. at New Haven, March 7, 1836, a. 57.

BRITTAIN, JAMES, of N. J., wished to remain neutral in the rev., but was plundered, escaped, joined Skinner with 70 men, and was in several battles; was once taken prisoner but escaped; in 1782 he was an ensign of the 18th batt. of N. J. vols., and at the peace a lieut.; in 1783 he went to St. Johns, N. B., and received a city lot and half pay; was a col. of N. B. militia, and at his death the oldest magistrate in Kings co.; d. at Greenwich, N. B., in 1838, a. 87; his widow d. in 1846, a. 94. (*Sabine's Loyalists.*)

BRITTAIN, JOSEPH, of N. J., br. of James B.; was an ensign in the N. J. vols.; was taken and escaped at the same time with his br.; went to St. Johns, N. B. in 1780; d. in 1830, a. 72; he received half pay.

BRITTAIN, WILLIAM, of N. J., br. of Jas. and Joseph B.: was in the king's service in the rev.; went to St. Johns, N. B., and d. about 1811. (*Sabine's Loyalists.*)

BRITTENNY, JOHN, a tory; went to N. B., and resided in King's co., till his death in 1846, in his 95th year.

BROAD, HEZEKIAH, revolutionary patriot; mem. of prov. cong. at Concord, Mass., 1774, and afterwards commissioner in the provincial army; he was a delegate to the Mass. const. convention at Cambridge in 1779, and d. at Natick, Mass., March 17, 1824, in his 66th year. (*Rogers's American Biog.*)

BROADDUS, REV. ANDREW, a Baptist divine; d. at Newtown, Va., Dec. 1, 1848, a. 78.

BROADNAX, GEN. WILLIAM H., d. at Petersburg, Va., Oct. 1834, of cholera, a. about 48; was a lawyer, and for several years a prominent mem. of the house of delegates; he favored a scheme of cautious abolition of slavery.

BROADUS, MAJ. EDWARD, represented Culpepper co., in the house of delegates, ten or twelve years; d. at the U. of Va., June 26, 1850. (*Stryker's Am. Reg.*, iv, 469.)

BROADUS, REV. ANDREW, a distinguished divine; d. at Newton, Va., Dec. 1, 1848; he was remarkable for his eloquence.

BROCK, DR. JOHN B., of the *Richmond Enquirer;* d. at Richmond, Va., April 27, 1870, a. 35.

BROCKENBRAUGH, WILLIAM H., d. at Tallahasse, Fla., June 1850, a. 37; was a senator under the territorial gov. of Fla., and at one time its pres.; was U. S. dist. atty. for the western dist. of the territory, and rep. in cong. from 1845 to 1847.

BROCKINGTON, JOHN JR., a tory of S. C.; held an office under the crown after the fall of Charleston, and lost his estate by confiscation.

BRODHEAD, THOMAS, M.D., reared and educated a physician in Ulster co., N. Y.; settled in Germantown, N. Y., in 1790, and soon after rem. to Clermont, N. Y., where he d. Nov. 11 ,1830, a. 65. (*Transac. N. Y. State Med. Soc.*, 1856, p. 177.)

BROGDAN, SAMUEL, a native of Philadelphia; d. at St. Anne La Perade, U. C., a. 107.

BROMFIELD, EDWARD JR., b. 1723; d. Aug. 18, 1746. (*Am. Hist. Record*, iii, 322.)

BRONSON, ETHEL, of Ct.; settled in Rutland, N. Y., as land agent; was in assem. in 1810, 4, 5; a county judge and pres. of Jeff. co. Bank, and d. in 1825. (*Hough's Hist. Jeff. Co. N. Y.*, p. 420.)

BRONSON, JOHN, d. at Walcott, Ct., Nov. 10, 1838, in his 104th year.

BROOKE, W. T. H., brig. gen., late of U. S. vols.; d. at Huntsville, Ala., July 19, 1870.

BROOKS, ALEXANDER S., lieut. col. U. S. A.; son of the late Gov. B., of Mass; was killed in consequence of the bursting of the boiler of the steam packet Dolphin, at St. Johns bar, Fla., Dec. 19, 1836, a. 54; he entered the army in 1808, with the rank of 1st lieut.

BROOKS, DR. PELATIAH, of Binghamton, N. Y.; d. March 2, 1864, a. 39. (*Transac. N. Y. State Med. Soc.* 1865, p. 302.)

BROOKS, ELEAZER, brig. gen. of the rev.; b. in Concord, Mass., 1726; rep. in gen. court in 1774, and continued 27 years in public life; was in the senate and council for some time; at the battle of White Plains he led a reg., and also in the second battle of Stillwater; d. at Lincoln, Mass., Nov. 9, 1806, a. 80. (*Rogers's Am. Biog.*)

BROOKS, FRANCIS J., d. March 3, 1851, a. 87; was 30 years judge of the court of appeals in Va., and had been an officer in the rev.; b. in Smithfield, near Fredericksburg, Aug. 27, 1763; practiced law in various places, and served in both houses of the state leg., before being chosen judge. (*Am. Almanac*, 1852, p. 332.)

BROOKS, HENRY, a Swede, said to be the last surviving officer of the Kane arctic expedition, in which he was 1st lieut.; d. at the Brooklyn navy yard, June 29, 1858, a. 45. (*Hist. Mag.*, ii, 251.)

BROOKS, JAMES, journalist, d. April 30, 1873, a. 66.

BROOKS, MICAH, b. at Cheshire, Ct., 1775; son of David B.; first visited the Genesee country in 1796, and settled at Bloomfield, Ontario co. in 1799; was about 20 years judge of the co.; located several important roads; served two campaigns as col. in the war of 1812, and represented several western counties with J. C. Spencer in the 14th congress; in 1821 he was in the state convention, and in 1824 was pres. elector; rem. about this time to Brooksgrove, in Mount Morris, and purchased a part of the tract which had been owned by Mary Jemison, "the white woman;" d. July 7, 1857, at Oramel, Allegany co., N. Y. (*Rochester Dem.*)

BROOKS, REV. EDWARD, grandson of Caleb B.; grad. at Harvard in 1757, and from 1758 to 1760 was librarian of that institution; was settled at N. Yarmouth, Mass., July 4, 1760, and in March 1769 asked a separation, when he returned to Medford, his native town; the line of march of the British April 19, 1775, led near his home and he was engaged in the battle of Concord; in 1777 he became a chaplain to the frigate Hancock; was taken prisoner, released and returned to Medford, where he d. May 6, 1781, a. 48; was the father of Peter C. Brooks.

BROUGH, JUDGE ——, presiding judge of the Hamilton co. court of com. pleas, and late editor of the *Inquirer;* d. at Cin., O., May 10, 1849.

BROUGHAM, MRS. JOHN, actress; d. at N. Y., May 4, 1870.

BROUWERE, JOHN H. J., a sculptor and artist; d. at Newport, R. I., Sept. 5, 1834.

BROWN, ANSON, mem. of cong. from N. Y., in 1839 and 1840; d. at Ballston, N. Y., June 1840.

BROWN, BEDFORD, d. in Tazewell co., N. C., Dec. 6, 1870, a. 75; was b. in Caswell co., N. C., in 1795, and elected to the house of commons of that state in 1815, in which office he served many years; was senator from N. C., in cong. from 1829 to 1841, and afterwards was elected to the state leg., but some years before his death retired to private life.

BROWN, CHARLES, proprietor of Tammany Hall, N. Y.; d. July 15, 1861, a. 45; was a native of Bradford, England.

BROWN, DANIEL, settled at Castine, Me.; was from Scotland, in his youth, and was an active tory; went to New Brunswick; d. at St. Stephen, March 1835, a. 91.

BROWN, DR. JAMES M., b. at Albany, Feb. 25, 1804; studied medicine with Dr. Chr. P. Yates, and was licensed by the Vt. acad. of med. in 1828; rem. in 1844 to Delphi, Ind.; d. Albany, May 23, 1844, a. 50. (*Munsell's Ann. Alb.*, ix, 109; *Annals Alb. Co. Med. Soc.*, i, 315.)

BROWN, GEN. SILAS, d. at Jackson, Miss., June 1839, a. 45; treasurer of Mississippi.

BROWN, HENRY, d. at Boston, O., Sept. 17, 1837, a. 104; was a soldier in the revolution.

BROWN, HUGH AND MALCOM, tories of S. C.; held offices under the crown after the fall of Charleston in 1780; lost their estates by confisc.

BROWN, JACOB, major in U. S. army; b. in Berkshire, co., Mass., 1788; served as a private in the war of 1812–5; became ensign of 11th infantry April 15, 1814, and 2d lieut. Sept. 1814; was retained, became capt. 1825, and maj. of 7th inf. Feb. 27, 1843; commanded at the fort op. Metamoras (now Brownsville, Texas); lost a leg by a shell from the enemy; d. May 6, 1846. (*Thorpe's Army of the Rio Grande*, p. 189.)

BROWN, JAMES, d at Phila., of apoplexy, April 7, 1835, a. 73; had been U. S. sen. from La., from 1812 to 1817, and from 1819 to 1824, having previously held state offices in that state; was appointed minister to France and remained 5 years, and settled in Phila., after his return.

BROWN, JAMES, d. in Watertown, Mass., March 10, 1856, a. 55; b. in Acton, Mass., in 1800; became a publisher in Boston and widely known as of the firm Little, Brown & Co.; his acquaintance with bibliography was equaled by few in the country; was a careful student of literature, fond of natural history, and a liberal patron of the soc. of natural hist., to which he gave a large part of his library. (*Am. Alm.*, 1856, p. 352.)

BROWN, JAMES JR., for many years second auditor of Va.; d. at Richmond, Va., Jan, 3, 1859.

BROWN, JEREMIAH, d. in Hartford, Conn., Aug. 15, 1852; b. in Granville, Mass.; was a merchant in early life at Hartford; was chosen state treas. in 1835, and annually thereafter until 1838, when he remained in the office as clerk, declining to again become a cand. for treas.

BROWN, JEREMIAH, formerly a mem. of the Penn. leg. and of the constitutional con.; a mem. of cong. in 1841–3, and one of the first asso. judges elected by the people; d. in Lancaster co., Pa., Mar. 2, 1858, a. 78.

BROWN, JOHN, a native of Ireland; d. at Mansfield, N. Y., June 22, 1836, a. 104.

BROWN JOHN CARTER, d. June 10, 1874, a. 77. (*See Bibliopolist and Am. Hist. Rec.*)

BROWN, JOHN R., d. in Morristown, N. J., March 27, 1843, a. 45; was a lawyer of excellent qualities.

BROWN, JOHN THOMPSON, several years a mem. of the Va. leg., and a very promising young man for his age; d. in Bedford co., Va., Nov. 20, 1836, a. 36.

BROWN, JOSEPH R., d. at N. Y., Nov. 9. 1870, while on business in that city; b. Jan. 5, 1805, in Hartford co., Ind.; went west about 1825; resided at Mendota; was a prom. mem. of the territorial leg.; was sec. of council in 1849 and 1851, and held various offices; was in the constitutional con. (democratic branch), and many years a journalist, pub. and Indian trader; in 1857 he established at Henderson. (*Collec. Minn. Hist. Soc.*, iii, 201.)

BROWN, MOSES, d. at Providence, R. I., Sept. 6, 1830, in his 98th year; b. in Providence, R. I., Sept. 1738, and was the youngest of four brothers, Nicholas, Joseph, John and Moses, all enterprising citizens, and largely engaged in commerce; at the age of 35 he became a Friend, and was noted for his philanthropy. (*Am. Alm.* 1838, p. 307.)

BROWN, MRS. MARY PORTER, d. at Constantinople, Turkey, March 28, 1862; was a sister of Com. David Porter, formerly American minister to Turkey.

BROWN, NICHOLAS, merchant of Providence, R. I.; b. April 4, 1760; grad. at the coll. of R. I. (since named from him Brown University), in 1786; was 50 years connected with this institution as treas. and trustee and gave most liberally for its endowment at various times; his total benefactions towards the coll. were nearly $100,000; the present name was given in 1789; Mr. B. inherited a large estate, became a merchant, was largely concerned in foreign trade in partnership with Thomas P. Ives, till the death of the latter in 1836, and evinced great capacity for business and strict integrity in his dealings; d. Oct. 27, 1841; in his will he gave $30,000 towards the erection of a lunatic asylum at Providence. (*Hunt's Lives of Am. Merchants*, i, 215; *Bradford's N. E. Biog.*)

BROWN, ORLANDO C., col. of the 1st Iowa reg. vol.; son of Capt. Geo. B., of Perch river, Jeff. co., N. Y.; emigrated to Muscatine, Iowa, about 1857 ; was engaged in merchandise, and was killed at the battle near Springfield, Mo, Aug. 10., 1861.

BROWN, REV. ISAAC V., D.D., d. in N. J., April 19, 1861 ; b. in N. J., Nov. 4, 1784 ; grad. at Princeton, and settled in Lawrenceville, N. Y., as a pastor, and classical teacher ; in 1833 he rem. to Mount Holly, N. J. ; he published several theological works and a number of tracts.

BROWN, REV. JOHN, D.D., d. at Hadley, Mass., March 22, 1840, a. 51 ; pastor of the Congregational church at that place ; b. in Brooklyn, Conn., in 1786 ; grad. at Dartmouth, in 1809 ; was two years tutor, 17 years pastor at Cazenovia, N. Y., 2 years at Pine street church Boston, and 8 years at Hadley.

BROWN, REV. THOMAS, b. in Oxford, Eng ; grad. at St. Allen's Hall ; came to America during the French war as chap., and in 1764 became rector of St. Peter's church, Albany ; rem. to Dorchester, Md., in 1773, and d. in 1784 ; his last surviving dau., Miss Eleanor B., d. in Alb. Nov. 18, 1859, a. 85. (*Hist. Mag.*, iv, 26.)

BROWN, STEPHEN W., b. in Williamstown, Mass. ; was several years a merchant in Salisbury, N. Y., and about 1830 settled at Little Falls, and became extensively engaged in manufactures ; in 1837 he was elected sheriff ; d. May 30, 1846, a. 49. (*Benton's Herkimer Co. N. Y.*, p. 300.)

BROWN, SUFAX, colored ; d. in Cumberland co., Va., a. 115 y. 7 m. and 5 d. ; was for many years a slave of the father of John Randolph, of Roanoke.

BROWN, THOMPSON S., civil engineer ; son of maj. Sam'l B., and nephew of Maj. Gen. Jacob B., was b. at Brownville, N. Y. ; grad. at West Point in 1825 ; was asst. prof. of math. a few months ; resigned in the army Oct. 31, 1836, and was chief of the Buf. & E. R. R. 1836–8 ; U. S. C. E. in the harbor improvements on Lake Erie in 1838–42 ; chief engineer on the W. Divis. of N. Y. & Erie R. R., to 1849, and then became a consulting engineer in the service of the Russian gov. on the St. Petersburg and Moscow R. R. ; d. at Naples, Italy, June 38, 1855 (?) a. 49.

BROWN, WILLIAM H., shipbuilder ; contractor of many vessels among which were the Atlantic and Baltic of the Collins line, the New World and Isaac Newton, on the Hudson, and several vessels for the Russian gov. ; d. at N. Y. Oct. 27, 1855, a. 52.

BROWN, WILLIAM J., b. in Ky., in 1805 ; emigrated to Ind. in 1821 ; was sec. of state, mem. of the leg. ; and from 1843 to 1845, and from 1849 to 1851, mem. of cong. ; was asst. P. M. under Polk's administration ; edited the *Indiana Sentinel* ; at the time of his death was special agt. of the P. O. department for Ill. and Ind. ; d. Indianapolis, Ind., Mar. 18, 1857.

BROWN, WILSON, d. at Cape Girardeau, Mo., Aug. 27, 1855, a. 57 ; b. in Md. ; rem. to Mo., in 1827, and represented Scott co., in the leg. in 1836 ; was auditor of the state from 1849 to 1853, and was then elected lieutenant governor.

BROWN, ZACHARIAH, a tory ; was lieut. in DeLancey's 3d battalion ; retired to N. B. ; rec. half pay, and d. in the co. of Sunbury, in 1817, a. 78.

BROWNE, FIELDING A., d. at Key West, Fla., March 2, 1852 ; one of the oldest res. of that place, and vice consul for France and Spain.

BROWNE, JOHN, sen. in cong. from Ky., from 1792 to 1805 ; d. at Frankfort, Ky., Aug. 28, 1837, a. 80.

BROWNELL, CHARLES FREDERICK, a prominent citizen of R. I.; b. in Providence, March 19, 1831 and d. in that city May 3, 1863.

BROWNELL, DR. CHARLES CLARENCE, d. at Egypt, May 20, 1862, while engaged in Mr. Petherick's expedition up the Nile; b. at East Haddam, Ct.; grad. at Trinity Coll., and several years a resident of Hartford, devoting himself to scientific pursuits.

BROWNSON, DR. NATHAN, revolutionary patriot in Ga.; a physician of Liberty co., Ga., and for a time surgeon of the Ga. brigade in the rev.; in 1781 he was speaker in the leg., and by that body was elected gov. of Ga.; in 1776-8, he was in the continental cong., and in 1788, speaker of the house of rep. of Ga., and pres. of the state sen. in 1789, 90, 91, and was in the conven. of 1789 for forming a state court; d. at Liberty co., Ga., Nov. 1796. (*White's Hist. Ga.*, p. 213.)

BROWNSON, ISAAC, d. at Greenfield, Conn., May 19, 1839, a. 77; he was a wealthy citizen of New York city.

BRUCE, DAVID, a tory of Charleston, S. C.; was an addresser of Sir Henry Clinton in 1780; was banished, and in 1782 his estate was confiscated.

BRUCE, JAMES, of Boston, Mass.; was a tory and banished; a capt. of this name commanded the ship Eleanor, which arrived with tea in Boston harbor, Dec. 1, 1773, which was soon after thrown overboard. (*Sabine's Loyalists.*)

BRUCE, REV. DAVID, Moravian missionary from Edinburgh, Scotland; came to America in 1741; d. at the Wechquaduach mission, near the line of Ct. and N. Y., July 9, 1749; a monument was placed to his memory by the Moravian Hist. Soc. Oct. 6, 1859. (*Moravians in N. Y. & Ct.*)

BRUEN, MATTHIAS, many years a resident of Perth Amboy, N. J., and formerly a merch. in N. Y.; d. at Alb., N. Y., June 29, 1846, a. 80.

BRUNEL, MARK ISAMBARD, b. at Hacqueville, France, and in his youth served in the French navy; came to America in 1793, and was with the first French surveyors of the Castorland tract on the Black river in 1793, and afterwards employed on a canal survey from the Hudson river to Lake Champlain, and in a cannon foundry and other enterprises in N. Y.; he went to England; became one of the most distinguished of engineers, and d. in London, Dec. 12, 1849, in his 81st year. (*Beamish's Memoir of Brunel; Chamber's Edinburgh Jour.*, xv, 38; *Precis Analyt. des Trav. de l'Acad. des Sci., Belles Lettres et Arts de Rouen* 1849–50, p. 67.)

BRUNNER, V. REV. FRANCIS DE SALES, a Benedictine, compelled by revolutions to forego convent life, established a convent in Switzerland; he subsequently formed a congregation of priests and another of sisters which he incorporated with the cong. of the Most Precious Blood, founded by the ven. Caspar de Bufalo; in 1844 he came to Am. and rem. his establishment to O., where it largely increased, the sisters being teachers, and the priests ministering in Stark, Anglaise and Seneca cos.; d. at Keldkirch, Voralberg, Austria, Dec. 29, 1859, a. 70.

BRUSH, CREAN, b. in Dublin, Ireland, about 1725; studied law, came to N. Y. about 1762; was several years asst. sec., and in 1771 rem. to Westminster, Vt., where he became clerk of Cumberland co.; he was afterwards surrogate, and in 1773 was elected to the gen. assem. of N. Y.;

he took an active part as a loyalist; was long imprisoned in Bost., but escaping in his wife's dress, fled to N. Y.; failing in any attempt to regain his property in Vt., and turned off with indifference by the authorities to whom he applied for redress, he committed suicide by shooting himself with a pistol, May 1778. (*Hall's Eastern Vermont*, p. 603, *with portrait*; *Sabine's Loyalists.*)

BRUYN, ANDREW D. W., b. in N. Y.; was in cong. from 1837 to 1838; d. at Ithaca, N. Y., July 1838.

BRYAN, COL. HENRY H., mem. of cong. from Tenn., from 1819 to 1823; d. in Montgomery co., Tenn., May 1835; was a native of Martin co., N. C.

BRYAN, JONATHAN, prominent in the early hist. of Ga.; with his son James he was sent to N. Y., and placed on board a prison ship; was exchanged, returned to Ga., and although 80, fought under Wayne; d. March 12, 1788. (*White's Hist. Ga.*, p. 366.)

BRYAN, NATHAN, a native of Jones co., N. C.; was a mem. of house of commons of that state; in cong. from 1795 to 1798; d. at Phila. 1798.

BRYMER, ALEXANDER, merch. of Bost., and a tory; was banished in 1778; a man of this name was sworn in as one of His Majesty's council of N. S.; d. at Halifax in 1809. (*Sabine's Loyalists.*)

BUCHANAN, JOHN, d. near Williamsport, Md., Nov. 4, 1844, in his 71st year; was 38 years a judge of the court of appeals of Md., and 21 years chief judge. (*Am. Alm.*, 1846, p. 313.)

BUCHANAN, THOMAS, of Wash. co., Md.; a jurist of ability; d. Sept. 29, 1848.

BUCHER, JOHN C., d. in Harrisburg, Pa., Oct. 26, 1851; was many years an asso. judge, and from 1831 to 1833, a mem. of cong.

BUCK AMOS, mem. of assem. from Lewis co., N. Y., in 1825 and 1843; d. Denmark, N. Y., July 11, 1855, a. 60.

BUCK, CAPT. THOMAS, d. June 4, 1842, at Front Royal, Warren co., Va., a. between 85 and 90; was an officer in the rev. war.

BUCK, CHESTER, formerly mem. of assem. from Lewis co., N. Y.; d. in Lowville, N. Y., July 3, 1847.

BUCK, DANIEL, an early settler of Vt., and mem. of cong. from that state from 1795 to 1797; d. in 1817.

BUCK, COL. DANIEL AZRO A., a son of the preceding; b. in Vt., in 1789; grad. at Middlebury in 1807, and at West Point in 1808, when he entered the army; resigned in 1811; reappointed capt. in 1813, and left in 1815; settled as a lawyer at Chelsea, Vt., and was 14 years in the leg., being half this time speaker; was state atty. from Orange co., 6 y., and in cong. from 1823 to 1825, and from 1827 to 1829; was afterwards connected with the Indian bureau of the war dept. at Washington, where he d. Dec. 24, 1841.

BUCK, HENRY, of S. C.; d. at Sar. Spgs., N. Y., Oct. 3, 1870, a. 70.

BUCKINGHAM, CALEB A., an atty. at law at Geneva, in Ill., and late of Cambridge, Mass.; d. at Chicago, Jan. 13, 1841, a. 26.

BUCKINGHAM, ELIAS, a tory of S. C.; held a commission under the crown after the fall of Charleston in 1780, and had his est. confis.

BUCKLE, THOMAS SEN., tory of Charleston, S. C.; was banished and his property confiscated.

BUCKLE, THOMAS JR., also a tory, and lost his property by confis.

BUCKLEY, CHARLES, a respected lawyer; d. at Berlin, Vt., April 24, 1836, a. 74.

BUCKLEY, DR. HENRY D., of N. Y. city; d. Jan. 4, 1872, a. 67.

BUCKNER, ALEXANDER, was sen. in cong. from Mo., from March 4, 1831, till his death in Mo., May 1833.

BUCKNER, RICHARD A., b. in 1763; was in cong. from Ky., from 1823 to 1829; d. at Greensburg, Ky., Dec. 8, 1847, a. 84.

BUDD, DR. DAVID, a physician of Turin, N. Y.; d. in that town Nov. 4, 1848. (*Hough's Hist. Lewis Co., N. Y.*, p. 246.)

BUEL, ALEXANDER HAMILTON, son of Roswell B., of Killingworth, Ct., who settled in Fairfield, N. Y., at an early period, and about 1800 began trade; d. in 1813 of an epidemic, a. 86: the son was b. July 14, 1801; conducted a large mercantile business at Fairfield; was elected to the 32d cong., and d. Washington, Jan. 31, 1853, a. 52. (*Benton's Herkimer Co. N. Y.*, p. 295 (with portrait).

BUEL, JESSE, journalist, politician and agriculturist; b. Coventry, Ct., Jan. 4, 1778; rem. at 12, to Rutland, Vt.; learned the printer's trade, and in 1797, with Mr. Moffit, began the *Troy Budget;* in 1801, he m., and with Mr. Joiner began at Poughkeepsie the *Guardian*, and afterwards with another the *Banner*. Failing he went to Kingston, N. Y., and published ten years the *Plebeian*; in 1813, he began at Albany the *Argus*, and in 1820, bought a farm on the sand barrens near Albany, upon which he afterward lived; his zeal and success in agricultural improvements were very remarkable; in 1834 he began the *Cultivator* (still published), and he took an active interest in agricultural societies and other movements of kindred object; in 1836, he was a candidate for gov., receiving 136,648 votes; he was in assem. in 1823, and many years a judge; d. at Danbury, Ct., Oct. 6, 1839, and interred at Albany. (*Griswold's Biog. Annual*, 1841, 37 (with portrait); *Munsell's Ann. Alb.*, vi, 201 (with portrait); *Am. Almanac* 1841, p. 275.)

BUFF, MICHAEL, d. in Oglethorpe co., Ga., May 28, 1839, a. 102; was a soldier under Gen. Forbes in 1758, and in the battles of Brandywine and Germantown.

BUFFUM, CAPT. SAMUEL, d. at Newport, R. I., Feb. 26, 1841, a. 86; was an officer on board the armed ship Protector in the rev. war.

BUFFUM, THOMAS, d. at Smithfield, R. I., June 17, 1852, a. 75; had been actively engaged in politics and held many offices of honor and trust; was a judge of the supreme court; had served in both houses of the leg. and was a mem. of the corporation of Brown University.

BULKLEY, JUSTUS R., pres. of N. Y. & New Haven R. R.; d. in Rye, N. Y., Dec. 30, 1862; became pres. of the road in 1854, and brought it out of the embarrassments from the Schuyler frauds.

BULL, GEORGE, b. in N. Y. city; was a lieut. cavalry in the Am. Legion under the traitor Arnold in 1782; settled on half pay in N. B., and d. at Woodstock, in 1838, a. 86.

BULL, HENRY, son of Henry Bull; a grandson of one of the first purchasers of R. I.; an early atty. gen. of that province; was b. Nov. 23, 1687; repeatedly chosen a mem. of the house of rep. of which in 1728–9 he was speaker; in 1728 he was one of a committee to revise the laws; d. Dec. 24, 1771, a. 84. (*Updike's Memoirs of the R. I. Bar*, p. 23.)

BULL, THOMAS, a soldier of the rev.; d. in Chester co., Pa., July 13, 1837, a. 94.

BULLFINCH, REV. STEPHEN G., D.D., d. at Cambridge, Mass., Oct. 13, 1870.

BULLOCK, RICHMOND, a ship owner and merch. of Providence, R. I.; once pres. of the town council of the marine soc. etc.; d. Aug. 22, 1849, a. 77; was a native of Seekonk, Mass., and d. very rich.

BULLOCK, RUFUS, formerly mem. of the state leg. of Mass., and of the constitutional convention; a successful manufacturer, and a liberal and honorable man; d. in Royalston, Mass.; Jan. 10, 1858, a. 78.

BULLOCK, WILLIAM B., d. in Savannah, Ga., March 6, 1852, a. 76; son of Archibald B., a patriot of the rev.; studied law with Judge Stephens, and was a prominent mem. of the bar as early as 1800; was a U. S. sen. in 1813, and in 1816 was chosen pres. of the bank of Ga., of which he was one of the founders, and held his office 27 years; in 1809 he was mayor of Savannah, and for some time was collector of the port.

BUNCKER, CAPT. ELISHA S., d. N. Y. city, Aug. 4, 1847, a. 75; was commander of the steamer Fulton, the first that ever made the passage around Point Judith, on a trip between N. Y. and Providence.

BUNN, JOHN, d. in Warren co., N. J., June 1836, a. 104.

BUNNER, RUDOLPH, mem. of cong. from N. Y. in 1827–9; d. at Otsego, N. Y., July 23, 1837, a. 58.

BUNTING, ROLAND, a loyalist; d. at Loch Lomond, N. B., in 1839, a. 100.

BURBANK, ELIJAH, d. in Brooklyn, N. Y., May 26, 1847, a. 85; was a paper maker, and made the paper for Isaiah Thomas at Worcester, for a nearly edition of the Bible at that place; in his youth he had served in the revolutionary war.

BURBECK, GEN. HENRY, d. at New London, Ct., Oct. 2, 1848, a. 94; was b. in Boston June 8, 1754, and spent the early part of his life in Castle William, now Fort Independence, Boston harbor; he served with distinction in the rev., and in the Indian wars of the west; in 1812–15 he commanded at N. Y., Newport and New Lond. (*Am. Alm.* 1850, p. 317.)

BURCH, REV. THOMAS, was connected with the ministry in the M. E. ch. for nearly 50 years; d. at Brooklyn, N. Y., Aug. 22, 1849, a. 81.

BURCH, ROBERT, b. in Killingly, Ct., Dec. 3, 1761; rem. to Berkshire co., Mass., and thence to Herkimer co., N. Y., where he settled, in Schuyler in 1799; in 1811–12 he was in assem.; d. June 26, 1830, in his 69th year. (*Benton's Herkimer Co., N. Y.*, p. 298.)

BURCHARD, PELEG, co. clerk Jeff. co., N. Y.; b. in Norwich, Ct., in 1790: settled early in Utica, and in 1809 in Watertown, N. Y., where he was a merchant; rem. to Brownville, failed in business, was elected co. clerk in 1828, and held 12 years; in 1843 he was appointed collector at Cape Vincent, and held two terms; d. there Feb. 2, 1851, a. 63; was a br. of Jedediah B., the celebrated revival preacher. (*Hough's Hist. Jeff. Co., N. Y.*, p. 428.)

BURCHARD, REV. JEDEDIAH, a noted and talented but eccentric revival preacher; d. at Adams, Jeff. co., N. Y., Oct. 1, 1864, a. 70.

BURCHE, SAMUEL, d. in Washington, D. C., Sept. 29, 1846, a. 50; was many years chief clerk in the clerk's office of the house of rep., and at the time of his death, a mem. of city council.

BURD, BENJAMIN, revolutionary patriot; in July 1775 (a. 21), he joined a rifle co., and in Oct. became lieut., leading in various skirmishes near Boston; was in the battle of Long Island, and as capt. in the 4th Pa. regt. fought in the battles of Trenton and Princeton; was conspicuously engaged through the war, and at its close settled on his paternal farm at Fort Littleton, and afterwards at Bedford, where he d. Oct. 5, 1823, in his 70th year. (*Rogers's Am. Biog.*)

BURD, GEORGE, in cong. from Pa. from 1831 to 1835; d. at Bedford, Pa., Jan. 13, 1844, a. 50.

BURDICK, DR. PHINEAS H., b. in De Ruyter, N. Y., June 3, 1800, and d. in Preble, N. Y., March 28, 1870. (*Transac. N. Y. State Med. Soc.*, 1871, p. 355.)

BURGEOIS, MARGARET, d. on Prince Edward's Island, Feb. 15, 1836, a. 110.

BURGESS, THOMAS, b. in Mass., but rem. to R. I. in 1796, where he was for several years chief just. of the court of com. pleas for Providence co., and from 1832 to 1853 judge of the municipal court; he acquired a large fortune by his profession, and d. May 18, 1856.

BURGESS, THOMAS MACKIE, second mayor of Providence, and re-elected annually for 12 years; d. at Prov., R. I., Oct. 17, 1856, a. 50; grad. at B. U., in 1822; studied law, and became a merchant.

BURGUIN, CAPT. JOHN HENRY K., 1st U. S. Dragoons; killed Feb. 7, 1847, in an action with the Pueblo Indians in their town near Taos, after having charged and driven them from their houses.

BURKE, REV. EDMOND, first vicar apostolic of N. S.; nominated July 4, 1817; d. at Halifax, Dec. 1, 1820, a. 67, and succeeded by Wm. Fraser. (*List Chron. des Evêques et des Prêtres du Canada.*)

BURLESON, GEN. EDWARD, d. at Austin, Texas, Dec. 26, 1851, a. 52; rem. to Texas from N. C. in 1830; was an active participant in the Texan struggle for independence.

BURNELL, BARKER, native of Nantucket; d. at Washington, D. C., June 15, 1843, a. 45; had served in both houses of the Mass. leg.; was a mem. of the constitutional conven., and of the conven. in 1840, which nominated Harrison for the pres.; was a rep. in cong. from 1841 till the time of his death. (*Am. Alm.*, 1844, p. 320.)

BURNET, DAVID S., b. at Newark, N. J., April 4, 1789; youngest son of Dr. Wm. B., a revolutionary surgeon; he aspired to a naval office but entered the counting house of Robinson & Hartshorne, in N. Y. in 1805; in 1806 was in Miranda's expedition as lt.; in 1808 he again joined Miranda at Caraccas, but the measure had failed; in 1817 he came to Natchitoches, lived a year with the Indians; went to Cin. and studied law; in 1826 he went to Texas; in 1833 he attended a con. at San Felipe; in 1834 was appointed by the state govt. judge of the municipality of Austin; in 1836 was elected pres. ad interim, and in Oct.

1836 was succeeded by Houston; became vice pres. under Lamar, and retired to a farm near San Jacinto. (*Texas Alm.*, 1857, p. 133.

BURNET, GEORGE WHITFIELD, b. in Newark, N. J. in 1772; grad. at Princeton in 1792; studied law and settled in Cincin. in 1796; he evinced early prominence in his profession, but d. at Chillicothe in May 1800. (*Campbell's Biog. Sketches*, p. 92.)

BURNET, ISAAC G., d. at Cin., O., March 11, 1856, a. 71; was a lawyer at Dayton and Cin.; was editor of the *Cincinnati Gazette*, mayor of the city several years, and clerk of the sup. court for Hamilton co.

BURNET, JAMES G., comedian; d. at Chicago, Ill., Mar. 20, 1870, a. 51.

BURNET, REV. MATHIAS, b. in N. J.; grad. at Princeton in 1769; settled at Jamaica, N. Y., in 1775, and remained through the war; in 1785 he was compelled to leave; he is said to have been the only Presb. minister of Queens co., who was a tory; became an Episcopal minister at Norwalk, Ct., and d. there in 1806.

BURNHAM, BENJAMIN, d. in Essex, Mass., April 14, 1847, a. 92; was a soldier in the revolution.

BURNHAM, DR. JOHN, a well known physician and politician; d. at Orland, Me., April 23, 1852, a. 80.

BURNHAM, JOHN, d. at Essex, Mass., April 16, 1847, a. 93; a soldier of the rev.; his wife Mehitable, d. April 16, 1847; they were both buried in one grave.

BURNS, ANTHONY, a colored Baptist preacher; d. in St. Catharine's C. W., July 27, 1862; his arrest and trial at Boston in 1854, as a fugitive slave attracted much notice at the time, and led to disturbances.

BURNS, TIMOTHY, d. in Wisconsin, Nov. 1853, a. 33; b. in Dublin, Ireland, in 1820; went to Wisconsin in 1837, and settled in Iowa co.; he held various public offices, and in 1851 was elected lieut. gov., which office he held till his death.

BURNSIDE, SAMUEL, d. in Worcester, Mass., July 29, 1850, a. 67; grad. at Dartmouth and was a lawyer.

BURNSIDE, THOMAS, one of the judges of the sup. court of Pa., and in cong. from 1815 to 1819; d. at Germantown, Pa., March 24, 1851.

BURR, HOWARD C., of the *N. Y. World;* d. at Washington, D. C., May 12, 1870.

BURR, THEODOSIA, dau. of Aaron Burr, vice pres.; lost her mother a. 11, in 1794, and became under her father's training one of the most polished women of her day, and the confidant of many of his plans and intrigues; she m. Joseph Allson, afterwards gov. of S. C., and was lost at sea on her passage from Charleston to N. Y. in 1812; gov. Allston d. at Charleston, Sept. 10, 1816, a. 38.

BURROUGHS JOHN, d. April 28, 1842, at Trenton, N. J., a. 89; he was a revolutionary soldier.

BURROUGHS, WILLIAM, d. at Germantown, Pa., March 24, 1861, a. 38; grad. at Yale, and studied law and divinity, and in 1853 was admitted to the bar in Phila.; he bequeathed $10,000 to the theological department of Yale College.

BURT, BENJAMIN, d. at Bellows Falls, Vt., June 1835, a. 95.

BURT, FRANCIS, gov. of Nebraska; d. at Bellevue in that territory, Oct. 18, 1854, a. about 45; was b. in Pendleton, S. C.; was appointed third auditor by Pres. Pierce, and resigned for the office in which he d., some two weeks after reaching the territory.

BURT, JAMES, rev. soldier; was in assem. from Orange co., N. Y., in 1798–9, 1800, 2, 3, 16, 21, 22, and in the state senate in 1823, 4, 5, 6; d. at Warwick, N. Y., March 17, 1852, in his 91st year.

BURT, WILLIAM, a tory of Charleston, S. C.; was banished and his estate confiscated.

BURTON, DR. CASPER VAN WIE, of Lansingburgh, N. Y.; d. Sept. 23, 1860, a. 50. (*Transac. N. Y. State Med. Soc.*, 1861, p. 275.)

BURTON, GEORGE, a lieut. in the British army; served in America in 1756–9.

BUSBEE, PERRIN, d. in Raleigh, N. C., Sept. 1853, a. 37; a lawyer, and reporter of the decisions of the sup. court, and pres. of the council of state.

BUSH, HORATIO N., d. in Harrisburg, N. Y., Oct. 1864; was a liberal benefactor of Lowville academy.

BUSH, MAJ. OLIVER, a militia officer of the war of 1812; d. in Turin, N. Y., April 9, 1844; was a native of Westfield, Mass.

BUSHE, DR. GEORGE MACARTNEY, a distinguished surgeon; d. in N. Y., April 17, 1836, a. 39.

BUSHNELL, DAVID, was a capt. in the rev., and contrived the submarine engines for blowing up British vessels above Phila., which floating down the tide, greatly alarmed the enemy and gave occasion for Hopkinson's ballad of the Battle of the Kegs; he went to Ga. about 1796, and became a teacher in Columbia co., having visited Europe and encountered heavy mercantile losses; he afterwards settled in Warrenton, Ga., and practiced under the name of Dr. Bush; d. a. 90, leaving legatees in Ct. (*White's Hist. Ga.*, p. 406.)

BUSHNELL, MRS. WILLIAM A., best known by her maiden name of Catharine Hays; b. in Limerick, Ireland, in 1820, and spent her early years in extreme poverty; her native vocal talent attracted notice, she was placed under instruction by the Bp. of Limerick, and in 1839 went to Paris, resolved to engage on the lyric stage; in 1841 she appeared in Milan, in 1845 in Marseilles, in 1846 in Vienna, and the next year in Venice; she sang in England with great success in 1849, and in 1851 came to America where she acquired distinguished eminence and visited many of the larger towns; in Cal. she attracted much notice, and afterwards she visited Australia and British India; in 1857 she m. W. A. Bushnell, of N. Y.; d. Aug. 1861 in Europe.

BUSKIRK, HENRY, a tory of N. Y.; went to N. S. in 1783, and was many years a magistrate in Kings co.; d. at Aylesford, N. S., in 1841.

BUSSEY, DAVID, d. in Lincolnville, Me., April 1840, a. 98, and his wife a. 102.

BUSTIN, THOMAS, of Va., a tory; joined the royal army at N. Y.; rem. to St. John, N. B., and d. there a. 90.

BUTLER, CHESTER, d. in Phila. Pa., Oct. 5, 1850, a. 52; was a mem. of cong. from Pa.; b. in Wilkesbarre, Pa., March 1798, and grandson of Col. B., who com. the American troops at the massacre of Wyoming;

grad. at Princeton in 1817; was admitted to the bar in 1820, and elected to congress in 1848.

BUTLER, COL. SAMUEL, d. at Marshall, Mich., March 23, 1847, a. 70; b. in Stillwater, N. Y., in 1777, and was driven with his family into Mass.; at the age of 14 he moved to Cherry Valley; at 22 to Deposit, N. Y., and in 1836 to Mich.; was capt. of a com. in the war of 1812.

BUTLER, CYRUS, one of the wealthiest citizens of R. I., and chief benefactor of the hospital for the insane at Providence, which bears his name; d. at Providence, Aug. 20, 1849, a. 82; he acquired his wealth as a merchant and ship owner.

BUTLER, JOHN, the celebrated huntsman; d. in Wake co., N. C., Jan. 19, 1836, supposed to be at least 110 years old.

BUTLER, JOSIAH, d. at Deerfield, N. H., Oct. 29, 1854, a. 74; grad. at Harv. in 1803; studied law and settled in Va., his native state, where he was chosen to the state leg.; was sheriff of Rockingham co., clerk of the courts, and in 1817, elected to cong. where he was continued 6 years; in 1825 he was appointed judge of the superior court of N. H., and continued till the court was abolished.

BUTLER, PIERCE, a distinguished lawyer, and for several years in the state leg.; d. at Louisville, Ky., Jan. 15, 1851.

BUTLER, REV. DAVID, d. July 4, 1842, at Troy, N. Y., a. 80; for many years pastor of St. Paul's church in Troy.

BUTLER, WALTER N., tory of the Mohawk valley; son of Col. John B., and like him of infamous memory; was taken and tried as a spy in 1777, but reprieved and escaped; he became a most vindictive scourge to the frontier settlements, especially in the Mohawk valley; in Oct. 1781, an expedition under Maj. Ross, fell upon the Johnstown settlements from the north, burning and destroying everything in their way; Butler was with this body, and was killed on the west Canada creek, Oct. 30, 1781, by a party under Col. Willett. (*Sabine's Loy.; Benton's Herk. Co., N. Y.*)

BUTTERFIELD, JUSTIN, formerly of Watertown, N. Y.; d. at Chicago, Ill., Oct. 1855; was commissioner of the Land office under Pres. Taylor, and for many years a prominent lawyer in Illinois.

BUTTERWORTH, MRS. CATHARINE, a native of Kildare, Ireland; d. at Dubuque, Iowa, Aug. 30, 1848, a. 114.

BUTTNER, REV. GOTTLIEB, a Moravian missionary; b. Dec. 29, 1716, in Silesia; went from Bethlehem, Pa., to Shekomeko, N. Y., in 1741, and d. there Feb. 23, 1745, a. 29; a monument was replaced over his grave Oct. 5, 1859, by a committee of the Moravian Hist. Soc. (*Moravians in N. Y. & Ct.*)

BYER, MRS. HANNAH, d. at Calais, Me., April 1836, a. 100.

BYLES, JAMES, d. at Oyster Bay, N. Y., Jan. 31, 1839, a. about 118 years; was a native of France, and a soldier under Gen. Wolf at the battle before Quebec.

BYLES, REV. MATHER JR., of Boston; grad. at Harv. in 1751; settled as minister at New London, Ct., and in 1768 was dismissed; was the same year made rector of Christ church, Boston, and in 1775 was compelled to abandon this charge; went to Halifax in 1776, and two years after was proscribed and banished; settled at St. John, N. B., was rector and chap., and d. in 1814. (*Sabine's Loyalists.*)

BYINGTON, HORATIO, d. in Stockbridge, Mass., Feb. 5, 1856, a. 58; was for several years a lawyer; a mem. of the leg., and judge of the court of com. pleas, which office he held till his death. (*Am. Alm.*, 1857, p. 351.)

BYRD, FRANCIS OTWAY, as capt. he served in Tripoli, and distinguished himself under Gen. Eaton in the battle of Derne; he served in the war of 1812–15, having entered as 2d lieut., 2d artillery, July 1812; was distinguished in Gaines's victory at Ft. Erie; was made brevet 1st lt.; for distinguished service in 1815, and was retained in the regular army till he resigned in 1818; he received from his native state, Va., a vote of thanks and a sword; rem. from Clark co., Va., to Baltimore in 1855, and d. there May 2, 1860, in his 70th year. (*Hist. Mag.*, iv, 189.)

BYRD, WILLIAM, b. March 28, 1674, to a large fortune in Va.; he was educated in England, studied law, was a fellow of the Royal Soc., and was appointed receiver gen. of his majesty's revenues in Va.; was thrice agent of the colony in England, and at the age of 37 became pres. of the council in Va.; d. Aug. 26, 1744, and was buried at Westover, Va.; he collected the finest private library which had then been formed in America. (*Campbell's Va.*)

BYRNE, BERNARD M., M.D., b. in Ireland; grad. at the University of Md.; was appointed asst. surgeon at Fortress Monroe, May 20, 1836, under Col. J. L. Gardner, and in the Mexican war was medical director for his dep. of the army; was in several battles, and bore Ringgold mortally wounded from the field; d. at Ft. Moultrie, S. C., where he had been 3 yr. attending physician, Sept. 1850. (*N. Y. Times*, Sep. 17, 1860.)

CABET, M., founder of the Icarian community at Nauvoo, d. at St. Louis, Mo., Nov. 9, 1856, of apoplexy, being about 69 years old.

CADWALLADER, DR. THOMAS, an eminent physician of Phila., son of John C., d. Nov. 14, 1779, a. 72. (*Simpson's Eminent Philadelphians.*)

CADY, DANIEL, justice of the Supreme Court of New York, b. in Columbia co., N. Y., April, 1773, read law in Florida, N. Y., was admitted in 1775, and soon removed to Johnstown, where he gained a wide reputation as an able lawyer. He was in assembly in 1809, 10, 11, 13, and in 1815, 17, was in congress. In 1847 he was elected a justice of the supreme court, for the term of 2 years, was reëlected in 1851, and resigned Jan. 1, 1855. He died Oct. 31, 1859, in his 87th year. Few lawyers have attained to greater merited distinction. (*Hist. Mag.*, iv, 25, *Alb. Eve. Jour.*, Nov. 1, 1859; *Raymond's Distin. Men. Colum. Co.*, p. 44; *Johnstown Independent*, Nov. 4, 1859.)

CAHILL, JERRY H., chancellor of Middle Tennessee since 1844; d. at his res. near Nashville, April 15, 1851. (*Stryker's Am. Reg.*, vi, 226.)

CALDWELL, ALEXANDER, judge of the U. S. court in the western district of Virginia; d. at Wheeling, Va., April 8, 1839.

CALDWELL, DAVID, son of Samuel C., succeeded his father in the office of clerk of the district court for eastern districts of Penn., of the U. S., till Oct. 6, 1831.

CALDWELL, FREDERICK, adjutant gen. of the Imperial Brazilian army; of Irish parentage; d. at Rio de Janeiro, April, 1873, a. 73.

CALDWELL, JAMES G., chancellor of South Carolina, an able jurist; d. near Columbia, S. C., March 11, 1850.

CALDWELL, JOSEPH P., d. in ——, N. C., Jan. 3, 1853; was member of congress from North Carolina, from 1849 till his death.

CALDWELL, MERRITT, prof. of metaphysics and political economy in Dickinson Coll., Carlisle, Pa.; d. at Portland, Me., June 6, 1848, a. 41.

CALDWELL, PHILIP, a soldier of the revolution; d. at Greece, Monroe co., N. Y., May 16, 1841, a. 86.

CALHOUN, ANDREW HAMILTON, formerly canal appraiser of state of N. Y.; clerk of the senate, and many years in the N. Y. custom house; d. at Brooklyn, N. Y., Dec. 17, 1874.

CALHOUN, DR. SAMUEL, prof. of materia medica in the Pennsylvania Medical College; d. at Philadelphia, Pa., April 7, 1841.

CALHOUN, JAMES L., governor of New Mexico; d. on the prairie near the line of Missouri, on his way from Washington to Santa Fe.

CALHOUN, John, formerly surveyor gen. of Kansas and Nebraska, and president of the Lecompton constitutional convention; d. at St. Joseph, Mo., Oct. 13, 1859.

CAMERON, CHARLES, surveyor and land agent, b. and educated in Scotland; emigrated at 18, with Col. Chas. Williamson in 1791, and was many years his surveyor, and from 1798 to 1805, agent at Lyons; built the first mill therein and was one of the first merchants at Canandaigua; he removed to Greene, N. Y., in 1821, and d. there in 1852, a. 80. (*Chenango American*, Jan., 1858.)

CAMERON, DUNCAN, d. near Raleigh, N. C., Jan. 3, 1853; formerly a judge of the superior court and afterwards for many years president of the Bank of the state of North Carolina, 1813.

CAMERON, WILLIAM, a cooper, of Charleston, S. C., a tory, was banished and his property confiscated.

CAMP, ABIATHER, father and son, tories of New Haven co., Ct.; went to St. John, N. B., in 1783, and received city lots, one of them d. in 1841, a. 84. (*Sabine's Loyalists.*)

CAMP, MAJ. JOHN G., d. in Washington, D. C., Feb. 21, 1855, a. 66; native of Virginia, and a prominent citizen of Sandusky, O.

CAMPBELL, ALEXANDER, became major of the Montgomery Highlanders; then the 62d, Jan. 7, 1757 was under Gen. Forbes in 1758, and Amherst in 1759, became lieut. col. of the 95th, Mar. 22, 1781; went on half pay in 1763; was lieut. gen. of St. George, Scotland, from 1774 to 1778; was again called into 1780; returned to half-pay in 1783, became a col. in the army in 1790, major gen., Oct., 1794, lieut. gen. Jan., 1801, and d. in 1804.

CAMPBELL, ALEXANDER, formerly of Albany, and a distinguished civil engineer; d. at sea on his way from Aspinwall to New Orleans, June 23, 1856; he was an engineer in the construction of railroads in South America.

CAMPBELL, ALLAN, son of Barcladine C.; came to America in 1756, as capt. in the 43d regiment, and in 1759, was appointed major for the campaign under Amherst; he was employed at the head of the grenadiers and rangers clearing the way for the army to the lakes; he became maj. in the army Aug. 15, 1762; went on half pay in 1763, having obtained a grant of 5000 acres at Crown Point; in 1770, he was a major of 36th

Foot in Jamaica; became lt. col., May, 1772; col. Nov. 17, 1780; maj. gen. in 1780; d. about 1797; his regiment did not serve in America in the revolution. (*Com. Wilson's Orderly Book*, 18.)

CAMPBELL, Anthony, native of Ireland; formerly a captain in the U. S. army, and afterwards marshal of the district of Mississippi; d. in Adams co., Miss., Sept., 1837, in his 74th year.

CAMPBELL, Archibald, removed from Voluntown, Ct., about 1750, to East Greenwich, R. I., as a lawyer; was elected in 1768, to the gen. assembly; d. Oct. 16, 1769, a. 41 years. (*W. Updike's Memoirs of the R. I. Bar*, p. 181.)

CAMPBELL, Brookins, d. in Washington, D. C., Dec. 24, 1853, a. 46; b. in Washington co., Tenn., in 1808; many years in the state legislature, and in 1845, speaker; was an officer in the quarter master's department in the Mexican war, and at the time of his death a member of congress from the 1st dist. of Tennessee.

CAMPBELL, Colin, ensign in De Lancey's 2d battalion (tory,) and q. m. of the corps; he was afterwards lieut.; his son Colin C., was sheriff of Charlotte co., New Brunswick. (*Sabine's Loyalists.*)

CAMPBELL, Colin, tory; settled as a lawyer at St. John, N. B., and d. there; his widow, who was a dau. of Bishop Seabury, d. in N.Y., in 1804.

CAMPBELL, Colin, tory; went from N. Y., to Shelburne, Nova Scotia, after the revolution, and lived 40 years; he was at one time collector of customs at St. Andrew, N. B.; d. in the co. of Annapolis, N. S., in 1834, a. 83.

CAMPBELL, Daniel, d. at Amherst, N. H., Oct. 7, 1838, a. 100; was long a magistrate.

CAMPBELL, Daniel, merchant; native of Ireland; acquired great wealth in Schenectady as a merchant, which he left to a Dr. Campbell of London, a nephew who resided several years in America. His estate was inherited by Daniel D. Schermerhorn, whose name was changed to Campbell by act of legislature in 1825; the latter was in the N. Y. state convention of 1846. (*Doc. Hist. N. Y.*, iv, 419.)

CAMPBELL, Donald and James, of N. C.; lieutenants in the N. C. loyalist volunteers in the revolution.

CAMPBELL, Donald, captain in the 3d battalion of N. Y. volunteers, loyalists.

CAMPBELL, Donald, of N. C.; a tory and ensign in the N. C. volunteers.

CAMPBELL, Donald, was appointed dep. q. m. gen. of the N. Y department with the rank of col., July 15, 1775; went to Canada; became obnoxious to the charge of cowardice, was court martialed and dismissed at Crown Point, July, 1776; his case was referred to congress who acquitted him and continued his pay and rank. (*Woodworth's Troy*, 57.)

CAMPBELL, Dugald, tory, and lieut. in the king's American regiment in the revolution.

CAMPBELL, Duncan G., came to Delhi co., Ga., in 1807 and took charge of a female school; he was several years in the legislature and was a com'r to negotiate a treaty with the Creeks at Indian Spring; he d. July 31, 1828.

CAMPBELL, Farquard, of N. C.; a man of wealth, education, and influence, and elected to provincial congress, in the revolution as a whig, but was suspected of holding communication with the enemy during the time he was in that body; in 1776, he was seized in his own house, while entertaining a party of loyalists, and he was afterwards banished, and his estate confiscated. (*Sabine's Loyalists.*)

CAMPBELL, George, a tory, and lieut. in the king's Am. regiment in the revolution.

CAMPBELL, George, native of Tyrone co., Ireland; emigrated to Philadelphia in 1765, and held various public offices, was in the legislature; and register of wills for Philadelphia; d. in 1810.

CAMPBELL, Jacob, only son of Archibald Campbell was b. in East Greenwich R. I., in 1760; graduated at the R. I. Coll., Sept. 1783, studied law and settled in his native town. Having but little practice he devoted a portion of his time to literature and published a volume of poetical essays and a number of essays in prose. He d. March 8, 1788, in his 28th year. (*W. Updike's Memoirs of the R. I. Bar*, p. 134.)

CAMPBELL, James, a prominent lawyer; d. at Nashville, Tenn., Aug. 20, 1849, a. 54.

CAMPBELL, John, a tory, and major in the second Am. regiment.

CAMPBELL, John, of Melford, Scotland, was lieut. in the 77th regt. served against Fort Duquesne in 1758, became captain in 1760, and continued in the army till 1770. (*Com. Wilson's Orderly Book*, 101.)

CAMPBELL, John, of N. C., captain of a tory force that encountered Col. Caswell in 1776, and was slain.

CAMPBELL, John, of Pa. was found guilty of supplying the enemy with provisions and sentenced to hard labor for one month. He was subsequently warned to appear and answer to charges of toryism.

CAMPBELL, John W., judge of the United States district court of Ohio; b. Feb. 23, 1782, near Miller's Iron Works, Augusta co., Va.; removed at 9 to Bourbon co., Ky., and a few years after to Ohio; he studied law with his uncle Thos. Wilson of Morgantown, Va., in 1808, was admitted to the Ohio bar and settled at West Union, Morgan co., where he became prosecuting attorney; he was elected to congress in 1816, and served 5 terms, his politics being opposed to Adams and in support of Jackson. In 1826, he removed to Brown co., O., and in 1828 was defeated as a candidate for governor. In March 1829, Pres. Jackson nominated him United States district judge for the state of Ohio, which office he held till death. In 1831 he settled in Columbus; he d. at Delaware, O., Sept. 24, 1833. (*Biog. Sketches with other Lit. Remains of the late John W. Campbell* by his wid. Columbus 1838 with portrait.)

CAMPBELL, Mrs. Maria, dau. of Gen. Wm. Hull; d. in Augusta, Ga., May 24, 1848. With a grandson of Gen. H.; she prepared his memoirs. (*White's Hist. Ga.*, p. 630.)

CAMPBELL, Peter, of Trenton, N. J., entered the royal service in the revolution, and was at the peace, captain in the N. J. volunteers; settled in the province of New Brunswick on half pay; and d. at Mangerville in 1822; he was buried at Fredericton. (*Sabine's Loyalists.*)

CAMPBELL, Robert, b. at Hackensack, N. J., July 5, 1846, a 82.

CAMPBELL, ROBERT, formerly lieut. gov. of N. Y.; d. at Bath, N. Y., July 13, 1870; was a lawyer, and many years a regent of the University.

CAMPBELL, THOMAS JEFFERSON, clerk of the house of representatives; d. at Washington, D. C., April 13, 1850; was a citizen of Tennessee, and a member of congress from that state from 1841 to 1843.

CAMPBELL, WALTER, was in 1782, a capt. in De Lancey's 2d battalion of loyalists and after the war settled at New Brunswick; he received half pay; d. at Musquash, N. B.

CAMPBELL, WILLIAM, a tory of N. C., lost his estate by confiscation in 1779.

CAMPBELL, WILLIAM, d. in Cherry Valley, N. Y., Oct. 27, 1844, a. 77; was oldest son of Col. C., of Cherry Valley, and the only member of his family who escaped death or captivity in the massacre of Nov., 1778; he was in assembly in 1816, '17 and '27, and recently surveyor general of New York; he was at the time of his death, one of the regents of the university. (*Am. Almanac*, 1844, p. 314.)

CAMPBELL, WILLIAM, of Pa., a tory; failed to appear upon a summons, and was attainted by order of the council, Oct. 30, 1778.

CAMPBELL, WILLIAM, of Worcester, Mass.; was sent away on account of tory principles; went from Boston to Halifax in 1776; was in N. Y., in 1783, but returned, and in 1786, removed to St. John, N. B; was mayor of St. John 20 years; d. 1823, a. 82; his widow Elizabeth d. in 1824, a. 84. (*Sabine's Loyalists.*)

CAMPEAU, JOSEPH, a wealthy citizen of Detroit; b. 1769; d. 1863; the last of the old French settlers of that place.

CAMPFIELD, REV. NATHAN P., d. at Bellows Falls, Vt., Sept., 1868, a. 30; pastor of the Presb. church at Cazenovia.

CANBY, EDWARD RICHARD SPRIGG, maj. gen. U. S. A.; murdered by Modoc Indians April 11, 1873, at the lava beds, Oregon, near Fort Klamath; b. in Ky., in 1819; settled in childhood in Ind., and grad. at West Point in 1839; served with honor in the Mexican war, and on the Union side in the rebellion.

CANBY, JOSEPH, of Pa., a loyalist; went to St. John, N. B., at the peace, and received a city lot; began business as a merchant; was member of an artillery co., in 1795; was killed in 1814, by falling from a wharf. (*Sabine's Loyalists.*)

CANDEE, DAVID, d. in Harwington, Conn., June, 1841; one of nine brothers, the average age of whom was about 81 years.

CANDLER, JOHN, JR., d. Aug., 1842, at Marblehead, Mass., a. 46; late pres. of the Grand Bank and Lafayette Insurance Company.

CANE, REV. ELIAS W., d. at Jamaica, N. Y., Nov. 10, 1840, a. 48.

CANER, REV. HENRY, D.D., grad. at Yale in 1724, and in 1727 went to England for ordination. He was several years minister at Norwalk and Fairfield, Ct., and in 1747, became rector of the 1st Ep. Ch., Boston, from which in 1776 he was driven to Halifax, N. S.; he went to England, and d. in 1792, a. 92. In 1778 he was proscribed and banished by Mass. (*Sabine's Loyalists.*)

CANFIELD, CAPT. AUGUSTUS, d. at Detroit, Mich., April 18, 1854; was a native of New Jersey; grad. at West Point, in 1822, and an officer of the corps of Topographical Engineers; was a son-in-law of Hon. Lewis Cass.

CANFIELD, JUDSON, formerly of Sharon, Conn.; d. at New York city, Feb., 1840, a. 81. He was several years a member of the council in Conn., and grad. at Yale in 1782.

CANFIELD, REV. SHERMAN B., D.D., long pastor of the 1st Pres. ch. at Syracuse, N. Y., and formerly of Cleveland, O.; d. at St. Louis, Mo., March 13, 1871, being on a visit to that place.

CANNON, E. A., d. in New Orleans, La., Sept. 14, 1849; judge of the second judicial dist. of Lousiania. He emigrated from France in 1815.

CAPE, BRIAN, a tory of S. C., held an office under the crown after the surrender of Charleston, and his estate was confiscated.

CAPERS, GABRIEL, of S. C., a tory, and office holder under the crown; he was a whig at first, and in 1775 a member of provincial congress; his estate was confiscated. (*Sabine's Loyalists.*)

CAPETON, HUGH, d. in Monroe co., Va., Feb. 9, 1847, a. 67; he was in congress from Va., from 1813 to 1815, having previously served for several years in the state legislature.

CARDEN, JOHN, entered the 17th regt., as ensign July 24, 1759, became lieut. April, 1767 and remained in the army till 1771; he served in America in the French war. (*Com. Wilson's Orderly Book*, 109.)

CAREY, COL. RICHARD, in the revolution an aid of Gen. Washington; d. in Cooperstown, N. Y.; Dec. 13, 1806.

CAREY, EDWARD L., d. in Philadelphia, Pa., June 16, 1845, a. 40; he was an enterprising publisher, and patron of the fine arts. (*Simpson's Eminent Philadelphians.*)

CAREY, GEORGE, b. in Md.; resided several years in Columbia co., Ga.; was in cong. from 1823 to 1827, removed to Upson, Ga., in 1834, and d. in 1844.

CAREY, JOHN L., late editor of the *Baltimore American*, and at the time of his death of the *New Orleans Daily Crescent;* d. at New Orleans, Dec. 14, 1852; he was author of several popular works on political economy.

CARHEIL, ETIENNE DE, jesuit missionary; arrived in Canada, Aug. 6, 1666; sent to Cayuga in 1668; absent in 1671, 2; returned and remained till 1684; d. at Quebec, July, 1726; said to have spoken the Iroquois better than his own language.

CARISIMO, DON JUAN ANDRES, native of Cadiz, and for the last ten years resident in Philadelphia; d. there Aug. 12, 1835; he was distinguished for his literary attainments.

CARLE, THOMAS. A tory of Dutchess co., N. Y.; went to St. John, N. B., in 1783 with his family.

CARLIN, THOMAS, d. near Carlington, Ill., Feb. 14, 1852; a. 60; was born in Kentucky, in 1790; and settled in Illinois, in 1812; was elected governor in 1838,and held this office four years.

CARLISLE, ABRAHAM, of Philadelphia, after the occupation of that city by the British, received a commission to guard the entrances and to grant passports; he was tried, sentenced and executed in 1778; in 1779 his estate was confiscated. (*Sabine's Loyalists.*)

CARLTON, REV. THOMAS, DD., d. at Elizabeth, N. J., April 16, 1870; city treasurer of Elizabeth at time of his death. Dr. Carlton was first appointed treas. of the missionary soc. in 1852, immediately after entering upon his work at the Book Concern; was regularly reëlected to the same office each successive year for 20 years, when he refused a reëlection in 1852 he was elected to the office of sen. agt. of the Meth. Book Concern in N. Y.; he held this office for 20 years, longer than it was ever held by any other man; at the time of Dr. Carlton's death he had served for 22 years on the board of managers of the miss. soc.

CARMACK, HON. SAMUEL W., d. in Jackson co., Fla., Dec. 18, 1849; a. 47; was b. in Davidson co., Tenn., Jan. 9, 1802; in 1838 removed to Florida on account of his health; in 1842, was appointed judge of the Apalachicola dist., and in 1846, judge of the southern dist., of Florida, but declined. (*Am. Almanac*, 1851, p. 307.)

CARMAN, RICHARD, a tory of N. Y.; went to St. John, N. B.; after the revolution was a granter in that city; and died in the county of York, N. B., in 1838; a. 71.

CARMAN, RICHARD F., d. at Carmansville, N. Y., July 13, 1867; a. 68.

CARNE, SAMUEL. A tory of S. C.; lost his estate and was banished in 1782.

CARPENTER, DR. WILLIAM M., d. at New Orleans, La., Oct. 4, 1848, a. 38; prof. of materia medica and therapeutics in the University of Louisiana.

CARPENTER, MRS. ELIZABETH, d. at Rehoboth, Mass., July 22, 1839; a. 101.

CARPENTER, SAMUEL, one of the greatest improvers and builders of Philadelphia, in an early day; d. in 1714. (*Simpson's Eminent Philadelphians.*)

CARPENTER, THOMAS, ensign in DeLancey's 3d battalion of loyalists, and an adjutant of the corps; he went to St. John, N. B.; was a grantee of that city and drew half pay.

CARPENTER, THOMAS FRANCIS, d. in Prov., R. I., July 14, 1859, a. 58; b. in Cranston, R. I., Feb. 21, 1796; grad. at Brown Uni. in 1818; became maj. gen. of state militia; declined election to civil office, and gained a high position at the Rhode Island bar.

CARPENTER, WILLET, a tory; settled in New Brunswick and d. at St. John, in 1833, a. 77.

CARR, BENJAMIN, professor of music; settled in Philadelphia in 1797; d. May 21, 1831, a. 62. (*Simpson's Eminent Philadelphians*, with portrait.)

CARR, DR. EDSON, of Canandaigua, N. Y.; d. Nov. 28, 1861, a. 60. (*Transac. N. Y. State Med. Soc.* 1862, p. 441.)

CARR, JOHN, member of congress from Indiana, from 1831 to 1837, and from 1839 to 1841; d. in Clarke co., Ind., Jan. 20, 1845.

CARR, PADDY, a Creek interpreter, half Irish, and brought up with civilized life; in 1826, he was interpreter to a delegation of Indians at Washington; he took sides with the U. S. in 1836; was guide and interpreter to Jessup, and when the Creeks revolted, marched to Florida at the head of 500 warriors; he owned 70 to 80 slaves, and lands and houses in 1837. (*White's Hist. Ga.*, p. 169, with portrait.)

CARR, PATRICK, a partizan in the revolution; lived and died in Jefferson co. Ga.; he is said to have destroyed a hundred tories, and to have been murdered long afterwards by their descendants.

CARRIGAN, ANDREW, commissioner of emigration at New York; d. Sept. 5, 1872, a. 68.

CARRINGTON, ABIJAH, d. in Milford, Conn., March 15, 1851, a. 72; grad. at Yale Coll. in 1800; was for several years a clergyman, but ill health required him to change; was afterwards a merchant; was a representative and a senator in the state legislature, and for two years comptroller of Connecticut.

CARRINGTON, GEN. EDWARD, d. in Providence, R. I., Dec. 24, 1843, a. 68, distinguished for his enterprise and liberality.

CARRINGTON, WILLIAM C., d. at Richmond, Va., Dec. 29, 1851, a. 30; editor of the *Richmond Times*, and distinguished for his attainments; was a native of Charlotte co., and educated at Hampden Sidney College; member elect to the state legislature.

CARROLL, ALEXANDER, many years editor of the *Charleston Courier;* d. in Charleston, S. C., August 22, 1856.

CARROLL, EDWARD, d. at New Brunswick, N. J., Aug. 30, 1840, a. 73.

CARSON, COL. JOHN, father of the late Samuel P. Carson, M. C., was a native of Ireland; settled at Pleasant Garden before the revolution, and served in that war; he was for a time in the gen. assembly; d. at Pleasant Garden, Burke co., N. C., April, 1841, in his 89th year. (*Am. Almanac*, 1842, p. 303.)

CARSON, COL. WILLIAM, d. in Warren co., Va., Dec. 21, 1865, a. 81; served in the revolution, and was a volunteer at Norfolk in the war of 1812; was many years a delegate in the legislature; was senator, and for three years a member of the executive council of Virginia.

CARSON, SAMUEL P., b. in Pleasant Garden, Burke co., N. C.; was several years in the legislature, and from 1825 to 1833, in congress; killed Dr. Robert B. Vance in a duel in 1827; removed to Arkansas; after the end of his term in congress; d. Nov. 1840.

CARTER, CAPT. LANDON N., d. at Norfolk, Va., Sept. 26, 1847; belonged to the U. S. marine corps., and from Virginia.

CARTER, CHARLES SHIRLEY, d. at Richmond, Va., Jan., 1840, a. 88; a lawyer and attorney of the state in the circuit court of Henrico co.; formerly a distinguished member of the state legislature.

CARTER, DR. WILLIAM V., of Cohoes, N. Y.; d. April 20, 1866, a. 54.

CARTER, GEN. WILLIAM B., d. in Carter co., Tenn., April 17, 1848, a. 56; he had served as state representative and senator; president of the constitutional convention, and from 1835 to 1841 in congress.

CARTER, ELIZABETH, d. in South Carolina, March 17, 1859, a. 101.

CARTER, JOHN, b. on Black river, Sumter dist., S. C., Sept. 10, 1792; grad. at the S. C. Coll., Columbia; studied law, and was in congress from South Carolina from 1822 to 1829; removed from Camden, S. C., to Georgetown, D. C., in 1836; d. June 20, 1850.

CARTER, JOHN C., commander U. S. N.; d. at Brooklyn, N. Y., Nov. 23, 1871, a. 60.

CARTER, NEHEMIAH, d. in Harrisburgh, N. Y., March 2, 1829, a. 87; was from Westfield, Mass.

CARTER, ROBERT, as pres. of the council succeeded Drysdale as acting gov. of Va., in 1726; he owned large estates between the Potomac and Rappahannock; speaker of the house of burgesses; treasurer of the colony, and many years one of the council; he lived at Corotoman, Lancaster co., Va., where he built a church; in Oct., 1727, he was succeeded by Gov. Wm. Gooch; from his large estate he was known as "King Carter."

CARTER, TIMOTHY J., d. at Washington, D. C., March 14, 1839; was member of congress from Maine, from 1837 till the day of his death.

CARTERET, PHILIP, brother of Sir George Carteret one of the proprieters of New Jersey; was appointed governor of that province Feb. 10, 1664, sailed in the ship Philip and arrived at Elizabethtown Point in August; he made Elizabethtown his seat and resided there; he married a daughter of Richard Smith of Smithtown L. I., April 1681; who survived him and inherited all his property; d. in December, 1682, in less than two months after resigning his authority into the hands of his successor. (*Coll. N. J. Hist. Soc.*, i, 84.)

CARTLAND, SAMUEL, d. in Exeter, N. H., Feb. 24, 1852, a. 58; was b. in Lee, N. H.; grad. at Dartmouth; was a lawyer, and served in both houses of the legislature; was president of the senate, judge of probate, and for a short time acting governor; was afterwards for some years a clerk in the treasury department at Washington, which office he relinquished in October, 1850.

CARTWRIGHT, REV. PETER, a venerable Methodist preacher; d. at Pleasant Plains, Ill., Sept. 25, 1872, a. 87.

CARY, DR. ZENAS, of Troy, N. Y.; d. May 11, 1862; b. in Putney, Vt., in 1787, and settled in Troy in 1822. (*Transac. N. Y. State Med. Soc.*, 1863, p. 389.)

CARY, GEORGE B., member of congress from the Petersburg district, Virginia, in 1842–3; d. in Southampton co., Va., March 5, 1850.

CARY, LEVI, member of congress from South Carolina from 1803 to 1807; d. Feb. 3, 1807.

CARY, THOMAS GREAVES, of Boston; d. July 3, 1859, at Nahant, Mass., a. 67; he was b. at Chelsea in 1791; grad. at Harvard in 1811; settled as a lawyer in Boston, but soon removed to Brattleboro, Vt., and in 1821 went to New York and engaged in the cotton trade; he was afterwards engaged in business in Boston, and was for many years pres. of the Hamilton and Appleton manufacturing cos., in Lowell; he was state senator from Suffolk several years, and much interested in matters of finance, literature and art, and a writer of merit on subjects of political economy, biography, etc. (*Am. Almanac*, 1860, p. 373.)

CASEY, JAMES, a tory of S. C., and officer under the crown after the surrender of Charleston in 1780; his estate was confiscated.

CASEY, SAMUEL, treasurer of the U. S.; appointed by Pres. Pierce, and holding this office at the time of his death, which occurred at Caseyville, Ky., Dec. 22, 1859, a. 70 years.

CASH, DR. MERRIT H., of Ridgebury, Orange co., N. Y.; d. April 26, 1861, a. 59. (*Transac. N. Y. State Med. Soc.*, 1862, p. 445.)

CASS, CHARLES L., d. Jan. 4, 1842, at Dresden, O., a. 54; served in the army through the whole of the war of 1812; in 1824 he was appointed Indian agent at Upper Sandusky, which office he held for six years.

CASS, MRS. ELIZABETH, wife of Hon. Lewis Cass; d. at Detroit, March 31, 1853, a. 65.

CASSADY, GEORGE, in congress, from New Jersey from 1821 to 1827; d. at Hackensack, N. J., Dec. 31, 1842, a. 58.

CASSELS, JAMES, of Georgetown, S. C.; a tory officer after the surrender of Charleston in 1780, and lost his estate by confiscation.

CASSIDY, WILLIAM, editor of the *Albany Argus*, and member of the constitutional commission of 1872; d. at Albany, Jan. 23, 1873; he was a prominent democratic politician, and a gentleman of cultivated literary tastes.

CASTANON, GONZALO, of the Havana *Voz de Cuba;* assassinated at Key West, Fla., Jan. 31, 1870.

CATHCART, GENERAL EARL, a distinguished officer, and in 1846, governor and commander in chief of Canada, Nova Scotia and New Brunswick; he d. in London, Eng., July 17, 1859.

CATHCART, REV. ROBERT, a Presbyterian minister; d. at York, Pa., Oct. 20, 1849; a. 90 years.

CATLANO, SALVADORE M., sailing master in the U. S. navy; d. in Washington, D. C., Jan. 4, 1846, a. 70; he was a native of Palermo, Sicily, and was admitted into the navy, as a reward of services, as a volunteer, to pilot Decatur into the harbor of Tripoli, when he set fire to the frigate Philadelphia, then in possession of the Tripolitans.

CATLIN, GEORGE S., b. in Litchfield co., Conn., in 1809, began law practice in 1830; was in congress from 1843 to 1845, and for several years in the state legislature, state's attorney and judge of the Windham county court; d. in Windham co., Conn., Nov. 26, 1851.

CATLIN, MARCUS, prof. of mathematics and astronomy in Hamilton College; d. in Clinton, N. Y., Oct. 11, 1849.

CATON, MRS., widow of Richard C., and eldest dau. of Charles Carroll of Carrollton; d. at Elkridge, Md., Nov., 1846. (*Am. Almanac*, 1848, p. 345.)

CATON, RICHARD, d. in Baltimore, Md., March 19, 1845, a. 83; native of Lancashire, Eng., and resident of Baltimore, 62 years; m. a dau. of Charles Carroll of Carrollton, and was father of the Marchioness of Wellesley, the Duchess of Leeds and Lady Stafford; he had for a long time the management of large landed estates, and was a zealous member of the Roman Catholic church.

CATTELL, JONATHAN, a veteran of the revolution and soldier of the battle of Princeton; d. at Woodbury, N. J., Sept. 19, 1849, a. 91 years.

CAUSEY, PETER F., ex-gov. of Delaware; d. at Milford, Delaware, Feb. 17, 1871.

CAVEDA, FREDERICO FERNANDEZ, a gen. of the Cuban insurgents; shot at Trinidad de Cuba, July 1871, a 39; was educated in the U. S., and was in the Union army in our late war.

CAZNEAU, ANDREW, of Boston, was a barrister and judge of admiralty, went to England in 1775, and held an honorable post at Bermuda;

in 1788 he returned to Boston where he died; he received $80,000 by his wife, a dau. of John Hammock; in 1790, his only dau. married Tho. Brewer, of Boston, who is supposed to have perished in 1812, in a voyage from the Cape of Good Hope to Sumatra; his widow resided at Eastport, Me. (*Sabine's Loyalists.*)

CELLINI, ROSA, opera singer; d. at N. Y., Dec. 20, 1869, a. 39.

CHACE, SHADRACH, a tory of Mass., proscribed and banished in 1778; in 1782, he was an ensign in De Lancey's Third battalion; he went to St. John, N. B., drew a city lot, and half pay, and d. in N. B., in 1829.

CHADBOURNE, THEODORE LINCOLN, lieut. 8th Regt. U. S. Infantry, b. at Eastport, Me.; cadet Sept., 1839, had been two years in the army and fell at the battle of Resaca de la Palma, May 9, 1846. (*Thorpe's Army of the Rio Grande*, p. 193.)

CHALMERS, GILBERT. A tory of Charleston, S. C., was banished and in 1782 his property was confiscated.

CHALMERS, JAMES, a tory of Md., a man of local influence, and commanded a corps of loyalists with the rank of lt. col.; he was in service in 1782. (*Sabine's Loyalists.*)

CHALONER, NIAYON, a tory from the states; settled in New Brunswick and was register of deeds and wills for King's co.; he d. at Kingston, N. B., in 1835.

CHALONER, WALTER, sheriff of Newport co., R. I., was a tory, and in N. Y., in 1782 as dep. commissary of prisoners; in 1783 he petitioned for lands in Nova Scotia; he sent to St. John, N. B., and d. there in 1796; his widow Ann d. in 1803. (*Sabine's Loyalists.*)

CHAMBERLAIN, ALFRED, late member of assembly from Otsego co.; d. at Richfield Springs, N. Y., Oct. 18, 1872.

CHAMBERLAIN, JOHN C., formerly a lawyer of Alstead, N. H., and from 1809 to 1811, a member of congress; d. at Utica, N. Y., Dec. 8, 1835, a. 62.

CHAMBERLAIN, PROF. WILLIAM, of Dartmouth Coll., d. at Peacham, Vt., July 18, 1838, a. 33 years.

CHAMBERLAYNE, DR. LEWIS W., d. near Richmond, Va., Jan. 28, 1854; was one of the founders of the Richmond Medical College, and from the first professor of therapeutics and materia medica.

CHAMBERS, A. B., editor of the *Missouri Republican* for many years; d. at St. Louis, Mo., May 22, 1854, a. 45.

CHAMBERS, COL. BENJAMIN, d. in Saline co., Mo., Aug. 27, 1840, a. 86; b. near Chambersburgh, Pa., and served in the revolution; he soon after removed to Indiana, and for the last thirty years had lived in Missouri, where he held various civil and military offices.

CHAMBERS, DAVID, d. in Cranberry, N. J.; Sept., 1842, a. 94; he was a soldier in the revolution.

CHAMBERS, ELD. HARRY, d. at Hillsboro', Scott co., Miss., Aug. 8, 1844, a. 83; native of N. C., and a preacher since 1812, in the Baptist church.

CHAMBERS, JOHN, d. near Paris, Ky., Sept. 21, 1852; was b. in New Jersey, in 1779, and emigrated to Kentucky at the age of 13; began law practice in Washington, Mason co.; served in the war of 1812, was an earnest partizan of Gen. Harrison, and after his election was appointed governor of Iowa Terr., where he acquired influence among discordant Indian tribes; was elected to congress in 1828, 1836 and 1840. (*Am. Almanac*, 1854, p. 326.)

CHAMPION, EPAPHRODITUS, member of congress from Conn., from 1807 to 1817; d. at East Haddam, Ct., Nov. 22, 1835, a. 78.

CHAMPNEYS, BENJAMIN, ex-mem. of the leg. of Penn.; d. at Lancaster, Pa., Aug. 9, 1871, a. 71.

CHANDLER, CHARLES PARSONS, b. at New Gloucester Me.; grad. at Bowdoin in 1822; was admitted to the bar at Portland, in 1825, and settled as a lawyer at Foxcroft, Me., in 1826; he filled many stations implying the confidence of his townsmen, and at the time of his death was senator elect; he d. Nov. 16, 1857, a. 56.

CHANDLER, DR. THOMAS K., acting passed asst. surg. U. S. N.; d. Feb. 1868; came from Fredonia, N. Y. in 1860, to Coll. of Physicians and Surgeons; grad. in 1862, and was in the naval service in the Miss. and Gulf squadrons till the close of the war; was afterwards assigned for duty at the Washington Naval Hospital.

CHANDLER, GEN. JOSEPH, d. in New York city, while on a visit to that place, Sept — 1846, a. 75; he was of Augusta, Me.; was collector of the Portland district for some years, and had been prominent in the affairs of that state; in the war of 1812 he was with Gen. Dearborn.

CHANDLER, JOHN, a native of Va.; served through the revolution under Greene and Sumpter, and shared the battles of Eutaw, Camden and Cowpens, he died near Jacksonville, Ala., Feb. 13, 1850, a. 104 years.

CHANDLER, JOHN, first son of Thomas Chandler; was b. at Woodstock, Ct., Mar. 4, 1736–7; removed with his father to Chester in 1763; held a commission of dedimus potestatem in Cumberland co., Vt., from July 17, 1766 to Apr. 14, 1772, and was county clerk from July 16, 1766 to Feb. 25, 1772, when he was removed for misconduct. (*Hall's Eastern Vermont*, p. 638.)

CHANDLER, NATHANIEL, a tory; d. at Portland, New Brunswick, in 1816.

CHANDLER, NATHANIEL, a tory of Worcester Mass.; son of Col. John C.; grad. at Harvard in 1768; began the practice of law, and in 1776 went to Halifax; in 1778, he was proscribed and banished; he returned and died at Worcester in 1801, a. 51. (*Sabine's Loyalists.*)

CHANDLER, PELEG, lawyer; d. at Bangor, Me., Jan., 1847, a. 73.

CHANDLER, RUFUS, of Worcester, Mass.; son of Col. John C.; was b. in 1747; grad. at Harvard in 1766, and became a tory; he went to Halifax in 1776; was proscribed and banished in 1778, and d. in London, Oct., 1823, a. 76.

CHANDLER, THOMAS, was born in Woodstock, Ct., July 23, 1709; removed to Walpole, N. H., and soon after to New Flamstead, now Chester, Vt.; in 1776, he became first judge of the inferior court of com. pleas, of Cumberland co., Vt.; a justice and surrogate, and in the revolution sympathized with the loyalists; he became impoverished in his old age and died a debtor in jail at Westminster, Vt., June 20, 1785. (*Hall's Eastern Vermont*, p. 633; *Sabine's Loyalists.*)

CHANDLER, THOMAS, JR., 2d son of T. C.; was born Sept. 23, 1740; served several years as clerk of Chester, Vt.; in March, 1778, was chosen first sec. of state of Vt., and soon after clerk of the house; in Oct. 1778, he was chosen speaker and afterwards served as member of council, representative and judge of the superior court, and com'r of sequestration; he subsequently became reduced to poverty, and died in obscurity. (*Hall's Eastern Vermont*, p. 638.)

CHANNING, WILLIAM b. in Newport, R. I., May 31, 1751; grad. at Nassau Hall in 1769; held many honorable offices; in 1777, was chosen attorney general of R. I., which office he held till 1787; d. at Newport, Sept 31, 1793; he was the father of the Rev. Wm. E. Channing of Boston, and Dr. E. T. Channing of Harvard University. (*W. Updike's Mem. of the R. I. Bar*, p. 94; *Bradford's N. E. Biog.*)

CHAPIN, DR. ——, emeritus professor of practice in the Pennsylvania Medical College; d. in Phila., 1853.

CHAPIN, JOHN, a native of Connecticut and a soldier of the French war, the revolution, and the war of 1812; d. at Ogdensburgh, N. Y., Nov., 1839, in his 101st year.

CHAPMAN, AUGUSTUS, pres. of the Oswegatchie Bank at Ogdensburgh; d. very suddenly at his residence in Morristown, N. Y., May 11, 1860.

CHAPMAN, DAN., b. in Ct.; settled on the Stone ridge, Herkimer Village, N. Y., as a merchant, but became a lawyer; in March, 1803, was appointed surrogate; removed in 1807; reäppointed in 1808, and held 'till Nov., 1816; in 1820, he removed to Oneida co.; returned to Herkimer, and finally to Montgomery, where he d. at an advanced age; he was a subaltern officer in the revolution. (*Benton's Herkimer Co. N. Y.*, p. 302.)

CHAPMAN, GEORGE A., an original proprietor of the *Indiannapolis State Sentinel* and a popular democratic editor; d. at Indianapolis, March 15, 1851, a. 44.

CHAPMAN, JOHN, a tory from the states; was a magistrate in New Brunswick; and d. at Dorchester, in that colony in 1833, a. 72.

CHAPMAN, JONATHAN, better known as Johnny Appleseed, an excentrict person well known half a century ago in the western country, said to have been b. in Boston; a devout Swedenborgian, barefooted and clad in rags, he wandered, on long journeys laden with a bag of apple seeds, planting them along the way. Sometimes he would stop a year or two; get a nursery started, and then sell out or abandon it, and renew his planting. A welcome guest everywhere, in the Indian wigwam and the settler's cabin; harmless — zealous and earnest in the work of his lifetime, this strange being in his way doubtless wrought more good to humanity than thousands who die rich; d. in Allen co., Ind., in the summer of 1847, a. 72.

CHAPMAN, JONATHAN, d. in Boston, Mass., May 25, 1848, a. 41; several years a mayor, and a man much esteemed.

CHAPMAN, REUBEN ATWATER, chief just. of the sup. court of Mass.; d. at Luzerne, Switzerland, June 28, 1873, a. 72.

CHAPMAN, REV. JEDEDIAH, b. at Chatham, Ct., in 1741; grad. at Yale in 1762; was soon after licensed to preach, and was ordained over a church in Orangedale, N. J., where he remained 'till about 1800; he then removed to Geneva, N. Y., as a missonary; he was installed over the Presb. church there with Rev. Henry Axtel, July 8, 1812; and d. May 22, 1813, a. 72. (*Hotchkin's Western N. Y.*, p. 264.)

CHAPMAN, SETH, president judge of the 8th judicial dist. of Pennsylvania; d. Dec. 5, 1835.

CHAPPELL, JOHN J., mem. of cong. from South Carolina, from 1813 to 1817; d. near Montgomery, Ala., May 23, 1871.

CHARDON, PETER, son of a Boston merchant, and descended from one of the French refugees after the revocation of the edict of Nantes; he grad. at Harvard in 1757; and d. at Charlotte Town in the West Indies, Oct., 1766; he was a lawyer, and on intimate terms with Rev. Edward Brooks, who named a son from him; the latter gave name to the town of Chandon Ohio.

CHARLTON, THOMAS U. P., a lawyer of note, published a life of Gen. James Jackson in 1808, and d. in Savannah, Ga.

CHASE, EDWARD J., U. S. marshall for the northern dist. of New York; d. at Lockport, N. Y., Oct. 14, 1862; b. in N. H., in 1809, and a brother of Salmon P. Chase, late chief justice of U. S.

CHASE, GEORGE M., b. in Vt., resided in Me., and was appointed consul at Lahania, in the Sandwich Islands, where he d. Dec. 5, 1855, a. about 50.

CHASE, HANNAH, widow of Stephen; d. in Unity, Me., June 21, 1845, a. 106 ys. 25 d.; b. in Swansea, May 27, 1739; left numerous descendants of whom about 130 walked in her funeral train. (*Am. Almanac*, 1846, p. 322.)

CHASE, LESLIE, grad. at West Point in 1838; served with distinction in the early part of the Mexican war and in 1847 was placed on duty in the war department as judge advocate of the army for which his early studies in law had fitted him; he d. at Smithsville, N. C., April 15, 1849. (*Stryker's Am. Reg.*, ii, 500.)

CHASE, MRS. HANNAH KITTY, widow of Judge Samuel Chase one of the signers of the declaration of independence; d. at Baltimore, Md., March 22, 1848, a. 93.

CHASE, REV. REUBEN, b. Plainfield, Ct., Dec., 1783; was a pioneer settler of Lowville, N. Y., and local preacher; d. there Feb. 1, 1871, a. 78. (*Northern Christian Advocate*, March 23, 1871.)

CHASE, SALMON P., chief just. of the sup. court of the U. S.; d. in Washington, May 7, 1873, a. 65.

CHASE, STEPHEN, prof. of mathematics in Dartmouth Coll., and a contributor to several religious periodicals; d. at Hanover, N. H., January 7, 1851, a. 37 years; he grad. at Dartmouth in 1832, and was professor from 1838.

CHASSANIS, PIERRE, a French speculator in New York lands, towards the close of the last century, and director of the "Compagnie de New York," or "Castorland company," on the Black river; d. in Paris. Oct. 28, 1803. (*Hough's Hist. Lewis Co.*, pp. 34–70.)

CHATTERTON, REV. BENJAMIN, F. W. Bap. preacher, b. in Acworth, N. H.; ordained Feb. 3, 1828, lived in Middlesex, Vt.; d. June 17, 1855, a. 77. (*F. W. Bap. Reg.*, 1857, p. 88.)

CHAUMONT, LE RAY DE, (see Le Ray.)

CHAUNCEY, LIEUT. CHARLES WOLCOTT, d. at Anton Lizardo, Aug. 10, 1847, in command of the U. S. steamer Spitfire.

CHEESEMAN, DR. JOHN C., d. in New York city Oct. 11, 1862, a. 75; was a medical professor and an eminent surgeon.

CHEEVER, COL. ABNER, d. at Lynn, Mass., Sept. 9, 1837, a. 81; was in the revolution, and a minute man at Lexington, in 1775.

CHEEVER, DR. ABIJAH, d. in Saugus, Mass., April 21, 1843, a. 84; grad. at Harvard in 1779; studied medicine with Dr. John Warren, and was several years in the medical department of the army and navy during the revolution; after the peace he settled in Boston, and acquired an extensive practice.

CHEEVER, SAMUEL, judge and agriculturist; d. at Waterford, N. Y., Sept. 25, 1874, a. 87.

CHERRY, WILLIAM W., d. at Jackson, N. C., May 2, 1845, in his 39th year; while attending the superior court for Northampton, co.; he was a distinguished advocate; twice in the state legislature; whig elector of president in 1840, and 1844, and at the time of his death a candidate for congress.

CHESTER, HENRY, a lawyer of Phila. associated with his brother-in law C. Chauncey; d. in Phila., July 26, 1848.

CHESTER, REV. JOHN, D.D., pastor of 2d Presb. ch. Albany; son of Col. John C.; b. at Wethersfield, Ct., Aug. 17, 1785; grad. at Yale in 1804; preached some time at Middletown, Ct., removed to Cooperstown, N. Y., and from 1810 to 1814, was pastor of a church at Hudson; in Dec. 1815, he was installed, over the 2d Presb. ch., Albany; d. at Phil'a., Jan. 12, 1829. (*Obituary Notices of Rev. J. C.*, Albany 1829, 8vo, pp. 84, with portrait; *Goodwin's Notes*, p. 17.)

CHETWOOD, JOHN J., d. at Elizabethtown, N. Y., Nov. 18, 1861; b. in 1800, was a lawyer; 14 years surrogate of Essex co., N. J., and identified with the great railroad enterprises of the state.

CHETWOOD, WILLIAM, b. in 1769; grad. at Princeton in 1792; admitted to the bar in 1798; served in the expedition to suppress the whiskey rebellion, and in the state council of N. J.; was in congress to fill a vacancy in Pres. Jackson's term, and d. Dec. 18, 1857.

CHEW, BENJAMIN, JR., b. Sept. 30, 1758, in Philadelphia, and d. near Germantown, Pa, April 30, 1844; was a lawyer, and practiced several years.

CHEW, DR. SAMUEL, d. Baltimore, Md., Dec. 26, 1863.

CHEW, JOSEPH, a magistrate of Tryon co., N. Y.; signed a declaration of loyalty in 1775; went to Canada in 1792, and was an officer under Sir John Johnson. (*Sabine's Loyalists.*)

CHEW, JOSEPH, a tory, of New London, Ct.; was com. in the royal service, and in 1777 was taken prisoner by the Whigs at Sag Harbor.

CHEW, ROBERT S., chief clerk of the state department in Washington; d. Aug. 3, 1873, a. 62.

CHEW, WILLIAM, lieut. in a corps of loyalists; settled in New Brunswick on half pay, and d. at Fredericton in 1812, a. 64.

CHEW, WILLIAM, was during a long period official interpreter at the Tuscarora village Lewiston, N. Y., of which tribe of Indians he was a member, and the grand sachem; d. Dec. 29, 1857.

CHICK, JOHN and JOHANNES, tories from Long Island, N. Y.; settled in New Brunswick in 1783, the latter, with a wife and two children.

CHILD, CAPT. ABRAHAM, an officer of the revolution; d. at Groton, Mass., Jan. 3, 1834, a. 92.

CHILD, WILLIAM, d. in Springfield, Mass., June 17, 1847, a. 59; was in the state senate in 1841, and had been previously in the house, and chairman of the county commissioners.

CHILDS, FRANCIS, was b. in Phila., Oct. 23, 1763; left early an orphan found friend and patron in John Jay who sent him to school at Esopus; he learned the printer's trade of Dunlap of Phila.; having obtained a press by the aid of Franklin he settled as a printer in New York, March 1, 1785, began the "*New York Daily Advertiser*," the first daily in N. Y., which he continued till 1795; he also printed the laws and journals of N. Y., several years; in 1796, he was appointed consul to Genoa but did not accept; he was afterwards several years an agent of government in France and Germany; he d. at Burlington, Vt., Aug. 17, 1830.

CHILDS, GEN. DAVID, d. at Maysville, Ky., Nov. 14, 1835, a. 68.

CHILDS, PERRY G., formerly in the Vermont state senate; d. at Cazenovia, N. Y., March 27, 1835.

CHILTON, GEORGE, emigrated from England in 1797, at the age of 30; and soon after settled in New York, as an instructor in chemistry, philosophy and astronomy; in 1803, he delivered a course of lectures on natural philosophy to a large class of ladies; in 1808, he began the manufacture of chrome yellow; and in 1811, established a manufactory of pigments of chrome from the ore; in 1822, he established himself as an analyst and chemist and maker and importer of apparatus; he was active in the pursuit and diffusion of science until his death Nov., 1836. (*Am. Jour. Sci. and Arts.* 1*st. Ser.*, xxxi, 421; *N. Y. American, Nov.* 17, 1836.)

CHILTON, REV. THOMAS, d. in Montgomery, Texas, Sept. 14, 1852; formerly of Kentucky and in 1819–20 in the state legislature; in 1824–5 clerk of senate; in 1827–31, and 1833–5 in congress from Hardin district; after leaving congress he became a clergyman, and preached in Kentucky, Alabama and Texas.

CHIPMAN, GEORGE, a tory, was sheriff 29 years in Nova Scotia; aud d. at Kentville, N. S., in 1838, a. 64.

CHIPMAN, JEFFREY, d. in Kalamazoo, Mich., Nov. 1, 1849, a. 60; b. in Rutland, Vt.; was many years a resident of Canandaigua, and was the magistrate before whom William Morgan was arraigned on a charge of larceny, when committed to the Ontario county jail, in the beginning of the anti masonic excitement of 1826–8.

CHIPMAN, JOHN, a tory from the states; d. at Cornwallis, Nova Scotia, in 1836, a. 91; he was "custos votulorum" of King's co.

CHIPMAN, WILLIAM ALLEN, a tory from the states; d. at Cornwallis, N. S., in 1845, a. 89.

CHISHOLM, MRS. MARY, d. in Albemarle co., Va., Oct. 27, 1839, a. 107.

CHISHOLM, REV. JAMES, d. in Portsmouth, Va., Sept. 15, 1855, a. 39; b. in Salem, Mass., in 1815; grad. at Cambridge in 1836; settled as rector of St. John's church in Portsmouth, in 1850, and resided till death; he remained during the fearful epidemic of 1855, to render aid to the sufferers, and fell a victim to the disease. (*Conrad's Memoir of Rev. J. Chisholm*, *Report of Portsmouth Relief Association*, p. 763.)

CHITTENDEN, NOAH, d. at Jericho, Vt., Jan. 8, 1835, a. 82.

CHITTENDEN, WILLIAM B., d. at Richmond, Va., Feb. 11, 1849, a. 51; pres. of the James river and Kanawha co., which office he held two or three years, after being its sec. from 1836; he was a native of N. Y.; grad. at Hampden, Sidney Coll., in 1824, and was some years a reporter for the press in New York; he returned to Richmond in the winter of 1834–5, and remained there till his death. (*Am. Almanac*, 1850, p. 325.)

CHITTI, LOUIS, an Italian exile, d. in New York, Sept. 1, 1853; secretary of finance to Murat; afterwards prof. of political economy at Brussels, and then a commissioner to the U. S., from the Belgian government. In the troubles in 1821, at Naples he was expelled from Italy, on account of his politics, and had since resided in this country.

CHOTEAU, PIERRE, one of the founders of St. Louis, and last survivor of the La Clede party; d. at St. Louis, Mo., July 9, 1849, in his 91st year.

CHOVET, DR. A., an eccentric physician of Philadelphia towards the close of the last century.

CHRISTIAN, JOHN B., d. in Williamsburg, Va., Feb. 21, 1856, a. 62; was one of the circuit and general court judges from 1836 to 1851, when a change of districts was made under which he was superseded; he was at the time of his death a visitor of the College of William and Mary.

CHRISTIAN, PHEBE (colored), d. in Ohio, March 20, 1859, a. 118.

CHRISTIE, CR., a tory of Md.; had his estate confiscated; after the revolution he recovered a portion of his debts. (*Sabine's Loyalists.*)

CHRISTIE, JAMES, JR., a merchant of Baltimore; was published as a tory in July, 1765. (*Sabine's Loyalists.*)

CHRISTIE, THOMAS, a tory of N. C.; had his property confiscated in 1779.

CHRISTY, GEORGE N. (See Harrington, George N.)

CHRYSTIE, JAMES, revolutionary officer; b. near Edinburgh, 1750; removed to Pa. in 1775; in 1776, entered the army, in which the next year he became captain; after Arnold's treason he was sent on an important errand to West Point, and brought important news for Washington. (*Rogers's Am. Biog.*)

CHUBB, JOHN, a tory of Phila., went to St. John, N. B., and was a grantee of that city, in 1795 he belonged to the Loyal Artil Co.; he d. in 1822, a. 69; his son Henry C., was proprietor of the *St. John Courier*.

CHURCH, DANIEL W., b. in Brattleboro, Vt.; was a millwright, and saw the beginnings of many places in northern N. Y.; was an adjutant in the reg. stationed at Ogdensburgh in the summer of 1812; d. in Morristown, N. Y., Jan. 7, 1857, in his 85th year. (*Hough's Hist. St. Lawrence and Franklin Cos.*, with portrait.)

CHURCH, JOHN B., came from England a few years before the revolution as a young adventurer and for several years lived in Boston as an underwriter; he was engaged in the commissary dep. through the war; m. a dau. of Gen. Schuyler. His business having been with the French army he with Jeremiah Wadsworth was compelled to visit France, where they remained 18 mo, he then removed to Berkshire near London, and in 1797, returned to N. Y.; he d. in London in 1816; his son John B., became a pioneer on the Genesee in 1803. (*Turners, Phelps & Gorham's Purchase*, p. 448.)

CHURCH, JOHN P., county clerk of Orleans co., N. Y.; d. at Albion, N. Y., Dec. 23, 1858. (*Orleans American*, Dec. 23, 1858.)

CHURCH, PHILIP, son of John B. C., and grandson of Gen. Schuyler, entered the army as capt. of 12th Infan., Jan. 8, 1796, was aid to his uncle Gen. Hamilton, but was disbanded in 1800; having about this time purchased a part of the Morris Reserve in Allegany co, he began its settlement and in 1803 went to reside on the Genesee, four miles from Angelica, at a place which he named Belvedere; he d. there Jan. 17, 1861, a. 83; he was an efficient advocate of the N. Y. & Erie R. R. (*Hist. Mag.*, v, 224; *Turners, Phelps & Gorham's Purchase*, p. 446.)

CHURCH, REV. JOHN H., D.D., d. June 13, 1840, at Pelham, N. H., a. 68; he was a Congregational minister.

CILLEY, JONATHAN, of Thomaston, Me., member of congress from Maine, and formerly speaker of the house in that state, killed in a duel at Bladensburg, Md., Feb. 21, 1839, by William J. Graves, member of congress from Kentucky; the weapons used were rifles, distance 80 yards.

CLAGETT, DR. HENRY, d. May 20, 1842, at Leesburgh, Va., a. 70, a distinguished practitioner of medicine.

CLAGHORN, JOHN W., d. in Phila., Oct. 17, 1869; b. in Mass., Aug. 25, 1789; came to Phila., and was partner in a large auction house.

CLAP, EBENEZER, d. in Bath, Me., Jan. 28, 1856, a. 77; was b. in Mansfield, Mass., in 1779; grad. at Harvard, in 1799; was admitted to the law in 1803, and began practice at Nantucket but soon removed to Bath; was a representative of his town in the Mass. legislature, and judge of the court of sessions; for 14 years was judge of the municipal court of Bath.

CLAPIER, LOUIS, an eminent shipping merchant of Philadelphia; b. in Marseilles, France, about 1763, and d. ——, 1838, in his 73d year.

CLAPP, EBENEZER, b. Aug. 25, 1771, son of Noah C.; grad. at Harvard in 1735, was 41 years clerk of Dorchester, and d. March 6, 1860. (*Hist. Mag.*, iv, 125.)

CLAPP, EZRA, a pioneer settler of Turin, N. Y.; d. in Westfield, Mass., his native town, June 17, 1838, a. 78.

CLAPP, JOHN MILTON, b. in Ohio; grad. at Yale in 1851; settled in South Carolina, and for many years was an editor of the *Charleston Mercury;* he d. Dec. 16, 1857, a. 47.

CLAPP, MRS. PHEBE, d. at Easthampton, Mass., Nov. 30, 1847, a. 97 y., 7 d. (*Am. Almanac*, 1849, p. 323.)

CLAPP, REV. DEXTER, d. at Salem, Mass., July 26, 1868, a. 52; grad. at Amherst, in 1839.

CLAPP, WASHINGTON, editor of the *Natick Times;* d. Aug. 5, 1868.

CLAPP, WILLIAM, d. at St. Albans, Vt., April 30, 1870, a. 59.

CLAREY, DANIEL, a tory of ninety-six, S. C.; held an office under the crown after the surrender of Charleston; his estate was confiscated.

CLARK, AARON, major, of New York; b. at Northampton, Mass.; removed to Middlebury, Vt.; grad. at Union Coll. in 1808; was private sec. to Gov. Tompkins; studied law with Erastus Root, at Delhi; went to Albany in 1814, was clerk of assembly, from 1815 to 1820 incl., and prepared a legislative manual, from which originated the present annual *Red Book* of the N. Y. legislature; he m. a dau. of Gen. Anthony Lamb; went to N. Y., was clerk in the N. R. Bank; was elected alderman in 1835, and in 1837, 8, was mayor of New York; he was for a time an extensive lottery and exchange dealer; director of the N. R. Bank, and the first pres. of the Merchant's Insurance Co.; he d. in Brooklyn, Aug. 3, 1861. (*N. Y. Eve. Post.*)

CLARK, ABRAHAM, signer of the Declaration of Independence; reared on a farm in Elizabethtown, N. J., where he was born Feb. 15, 1726; was a surveyor and lawyer, and held colonial offices several years; from 1776 to 1782, and in 1787-8, he was in continental congress, and he was a member of the convention that formed the U. S. constitution, under which he was again elected to congress, and from 1791 held till his death in the fall of 1794, in his 69th year.

CLARK, BENJAMIN, d. in New York city, March 2, 1840, in his 66th year; known as the "Quaker lawyer."

CLARK, CAPT. EBENEZER, d. at New Ipswich, N. H., Nov. 24, 1835, a. 82; he was a soldier of the revolution.

CLARK, CEPHAS, d. in West Turin, N. Y., Dec. 1, 1854, a. 91.

CLARK, DR. DARIUS, d. at Canton, N. Y., Jan. 23, 1871, a. 72; he was several years an inspector of state prisons.

CLARK, DR. ISRAEL, an eminent physician; d. at Clarksville, N. J., May 19, 1837, a. 78.

CLARK, DR. JOSEPH, of Stratford, Ct., fled to the British army in 1776; he went to New Brunswick with his family in 1783; settled in his profession at Mangerville on the St. John; was a judge of the court of com. pleas for Sunbury co., and in 1799, visited his friends in the U. S.; he d. at Mangerville in 1813, a. 78.

CLARK, ELISHA B., d. in March 1, 1842, in Patterson, N. J., a. 41; he was for several years a member of the house of assembly of N. J.

CLARK, GEN. MARSTON G., was b. in Lunenburg co., Va., Dec. 12, 1771, and was one of a family of 29 brothers and 2 sisters of the same parents; he went west, before coming of age, and acquired the confidence of his fellow citizens, whom he served in many stations, civil and military; he was with Gen. Wayne, and Gen. Harrison, and served in both houses of the Indiana legislature; he d. in that state, July 25, 1846, a. 74.

CLARK, GEORGE I. F., d. at St. Augustine, Fla., Oct. 20, 1836; he was a native of Florida, and for many years was lieut. gov., and surveyor general of the province of East Florida, under the Spanish government.

CLARK, HORACE F., a well known financier, and pres. of the Union Pacific R. R. Co., d. June 10, 1873, a 58.

CLARK, JABEZ, late chief justice of Windham county court; d. at Windham, Conn., Nov. 11, 1836; he was long a member of the bar, and had served during the revolution in the quarter master's department.

CLARK, JAMES, a tory of R. I., went to St. John, N. B., in 1783; was a grantee in that city; and d. in 1820, a. 90; his son James, d. in 1803, at St. John, a. 41.

CLARK, JOSEPH, son of Dr. Joseph, accompanied the family to N. B., and d. in N. Y., in 1828, while on a visit, a. 65.

CLARK, LOUIS GAYLORD, d. at Piermont-on-the-Hudson, Nov. 3, 1873. He was born at Otisco, Onondaga co., N. Y., in 1810; was a twin brother of Willis Gaylord Clark, well known as a writer of entertaining prose and pleasing verse, who d. in 1841; the two brothers were educated by their father; in 1834 Louis Gaylord took the editorial charge of *The Knickerbocker Magazine*, which had been established in December, 1832, by Charles Fenno Hoffman, who was succeeded in 1833 by the Rev. Timothy Flint. Mr. Clark edited *The Knickerbocker* for twenty-five years, and made hosts of friends by his management, in the course of which he became acquainted, either personally or by correspondence, with many of the best known writers in our own country, as well as with not a few of the English authors of note in his time. Mr. Clark's own contributions to *The Knickerbocker* were principally of a miscellaneous, gossiping, conversational character, and were to be found in the last pages of each number, under the headings "Editor's Table" and "Gossip with Readers and Correspondents." Mr. Clark's books were only his collected contributions to *The Knickerbocker*. The house in which he passed his later years and in which he died was dear to him, as having been bought with the proceeds of a volume, *The Knickerbocker Gallery*, made up of articles written for the purpose by his friends and by contributors to the magazine. (*N. Y. Tribune.*)

CLARK, MAJ. ARCHIBALD, d. at St. Marys, Ga., Dec. 26, 1848; was 34 years collector of that port, and prominently identified with the interests of that place.

CLARK, MAJ. JAMES W., d. in Tarboro, N. C., Jan., 1844, in his 65th year; b. in Bertie co., N. C.; educated at Princeton and settled in Edgecomb, where he resided about forty years; he served in both houses of the legislature both from Bertie and Edgecomb counties and was in congress in 1815 and 1816.

CLARK, NEHEMIAH, a tory and surgeon in the king's service; he went to St. John, N. B., received half pay, and d. at Douglas, N. B., in 1825, a. 86.

CLARK, REV. CHARLES, Baptist clergyman; b. Dec. 29, 1805; son of Elijah C., of Denmark, N. Y.; preached at Lowville, Watertown, Adams, and Rome, and d. at Rome, N. Y., Oct. 16, 1852. (*Hough's Hist. Lewis Co., N. Y.*, p. 170.)

CLARK, REV. JOSEPH S., D.D., b. in S. Plymouth, in 1800; grad. at Amherst and Andover; was pastor of the Congregational ch. in Strobridge, Mass., from 1832 to 1839, when he became sec. of the Mass. home missionary soc.; in 1857, he relinquished this office and became sec. and acting supt., of the cong. library asso.; he was the author of many historical and biographical sketches in the *Congregational Quarterly*; d. at West Trenton, Aug. 1861. (*Independent*, Aug. 29, 1861.)

CLARK, REV. WILLIAM, of Danvers, Mass.; son of Rev. Peter C.; grad. at Harvard in 1759; was Episcopal minister at Quincy, several years; went to England; drew a pension, and d. Nov., 1815.

CLARK, SAMUEL, b. at Lebanon, Ct., Feb. 28, 1777; was a merchant; represented Dover, Vt., and subsequently Brattleboro in gen. assem; was a member of the const. conven.; a justice and county judge; he d. at West Brattleboro, Vt., April 10, 1861. (*Hist. Mag.*, v, 224.)

CLARK, WILLIAM, d. in Dauphin co., Pa., April 28, 1851; was, prior to 1828, state treasurer of Pennsylvania, and in that year was appointed treasurer of the United States, and held office one year; from 1833 to 1837, he was a member of congress. (*Simpson's Eminent Philadelphians.*)

CLARKE, ALEXANDER, a loyalist from the states; d. at Waterborough, N. B., in 1825, a. 82; he was several years master armorer in the ordnance dep. at St. John.

CLARKE, AUGUSTINE, late treasurer of Vermont; d. at Burlington, Vt., June 17, 1841, a. 62.

CLARKE, ISAAC WINSLOW, a tory of Boston; he became commissary gen. of Lower Canada, and d. in 1822, after he had embarked for England; his dau. Susan, married Charles Richard Ogden; solicitor gen. of L. C. in 1829. (*Sabine's Loyalists.*)

CLARKE, JOHN HOPKINS, d. at Providence, R. I., Nov. 22, 1870, a. 79; was in the U. S. senate from R. I., in 1847–53.

CLARKE, LEMUEL, d. at Springfield, Mass., Aug. 22, 1840, a. 85; he served through the revolution.

CLARKE, MATTHEW ST. CLAIR, d. at Washington, D. C., May 6, 1852, a. 61, formerly clerk of the house of representatives.

CLARKE, RAY, d. near Oxford village, Chenango co., N. Y., May 6, 1847, a. 65; was formerly of East Greenwich, R. I., and grad. at Harvard in 1803.

CLARKE, REV. RICHARD SAMUEL, was Episcopal minister, 19 y. at New Milford, Ct., 25 y. at Gagetown, N. B., and 13 at St. Stephen, N. B.; he was the oldest missionary in the British colonies at his death, which occurred at St. Stephen, Oct. 6, 1824, a. 87. (*Sabine's Loyalists.*)

CLARKE, RICHARD, merchant of Boston; grad. at Harvard in 1729, he and his sons were consignees of the tea destroyed in Boston harbor early in the revolution; he was treated with severity by the whigs, went to England in 1775; Lord Chancellor Lyndhurst of Eng., was a grandson. (*Sabine's Loyalists.*)

CLARKE, WILLIAM, b. at N. Kingston, R. I.; entered the service of the crown, and was capt. in Col. Whiteman's regt. of loyal New Englanders; he settled in New Brunswick in 1783; was an alderman of St. John; d. there in 1804. (*Sabine's Loyalists.*)

CLARKE, WILLIAM WARNER, b. in Bristol, Vt., Aug. 19, 1826; grad. at Middletown, and was several years prin. of Gouverneur Wesleyan Sem.; in 1853, was called to the chair of mathematics in the Genesee Wes. Sem., at Lima, N. Y.; went to Baton Rouge, La., but a year after returned to Lima, and d. Dec. 19, 1869. (*Northern Christian Advocate*, March 24, 1870.)

CLARKSON, DR. GERARDUS, son of Matthew C. Clarkson a merchant of New York, who d. in 1779, was a popular practitioner of Philadelphia as early as 1774, and d. Sept. 19, 1790, a. 53.

CLAUS, DANIEL, tory, and attainted and banished Oct. 22, 1779, he was a son-in-law of Sir Wm. Johnson of Tryon co., N. Y.; served in the Indian dep.; withdrew to Canada, where his wife d. in 1801; his son William was dep. supt. gen. of Indian affairs in Canada. (*Sabine's Loyalists.*)

CLAY, REV. PORTER, last surviving full brother of Henry Clay and like him a selfmade man, d. at Camden, Ark., Feb. 16, 1850, in his 71st year. (*Stryker's Am. Reg.*, iv, 449.)

CLAY, THEODORE WYTHE, (lunatic son of Henry Clay); d. at Lexington, Ky., May 14, 1870, a. 68.

CLAYPOLE, DAVID C., d. in Philadelphia, Pa., about March 19, 1849, a. 92; was one of the proprietors of *Dunlap & Claypole's Daily Advertiser*, the first daily newspaper in the United States, first published as a daily in 1784. (*Simpson's Eminent Philadelphians.*)

CLAYTON, GEORGE R., d. at Milledgville, Ga., Nov., 1840; was 19 years treasurer of the state of Georgia, and afterwards cashier of the bank of that state.

CLEAVELAND, JESSE F., member of congress from Georgia, from 1836 to 1839, and subsequently a merchant at Charleston, S. C.; d. at Charleston, May 19, 1841.

CLELAND, JONAS, removed in early life to Warren, Herk. co., N. Y.; represented that county in assembly in 1814, 15, 19, 26, and was 40 years in succession a magistrate, and one year a judge; he was a successful merchant; d. at Warren, April 25, 1858.

CLEMENTS, PETER, a tory; entered the loyal service and at the close of the revolution was a captain in the king's Am. regt.; he went to St. John, N. B., in 1783; was a grantee of that city and drew half pay; he removed to York co., where he was a magistrate; d. on the St. John near Fredericton in 1833, a. 94. (*Sabine's Loyalists.*)

CLEVELAND, HANNAH, d. at Skaneateles, N. Y., June 14, 1861, a. 104 y. 7 mo.; b. at Northampton, Mass.; her two sisters with her own ages exceeded 300 years.

CLEVELAND, MASON, d. at Hampton, Conn., Sept. 13, 1852; was state sen. in 1842; comptroller of the state in 1846, and com. of the school fund in 1853; was 59 years old.

CLEVELAND, NEHEMIAH, for 53 years a practicing physician at Topsfield, Mass.; d. in that town Feb. 26, 1837; he was many years a magistrate, and for some time a member of the state senate.

CLEVELAND, WILLIAM, d. in Salem, Mass, July 30, 1842, a. 65; president of the Commercial Insurance Co.

CLEVELAND, WILLIAM CHARLES, prof. of civil eng. in Cornell University; d. at Ithaca, N. Y., Jan. 16, 1873; grad. at Lawrence Scientific Institute of Cambridge, Mass., where he resided and practiced his profession up to the time of being called to the place he occupied at the time of his death. His rare talents and knowledge in his profession attracted the attention of the university authorities at the beginning of selecting the faculty. Previous to this time he had never taught, but his connection with the university was successful in the extreme. He was a passionate lover of art, and the best influences of its study were stamped upon his daily life, and made him one of the pleasantest of men to associate with students, and to exert a refining influence upon them.

CLIFF, DEA. JOSEPH, of Marshfield, Mass.; d. April 6, 1849, a. 81.

CLIFFORD, JOHN, a lieut. in the revolution, d. in Bethlehem, N. J., Aug. 2, 1842, a. 94.

CLINCH, PETER, a tory; was in 1872 a lieut. in the Royal Fensible Americans, and adj. of the corps; he settled in New Brunswick on half pay; d. in the co. of Charlotte, N. B.

CLINTON, GEN. JAMES H., killed at Knoxville, Tenn., Sept. 27, 1871.

CLINTON, REV. ISAAC, first principal of Lowville Academy, N. Y.; b. at Milford, Ct., Jan. 21, 1759; served a little in the revolution; grad. at Yale in 1786; was installed over a Cong. ch. at Southwick, Mass., Jan. 30, 1788; in Aug., he lost five children within a week from disease; in 1807, he settled as pastor and teacher at Lowville, N. Y., and served many years; he was known as a writer upon Infant Baptism; d. at Lowville, N. Y., March 18, 1840. (*Lowville Acad. Semi-centen. Celebration*, p. 78; *Hough's Hist. Lewis Co.*, p. 164.)

CLITHERELL, DR. JAMES, a tory of S. C.; lost his estate in 1782, and was banished.

CLOPPER, GARRETT, was an ensign in the N. Y. volunteers (loyalists) in 1782, and a qr. mas. of the corps; he went to St. John, N. B., drew a city lot and half pay; was sergeant at arms, of the house of assembly, and a magistrate of York co.; d. in New Brunswick.

CLOPPER, JAMES, was a lieut. in a corps of loyalists, went to New Brunswick, drew half pay, and was a magistrate in York co.; d. at Fredericton in 1823, a. 67.

CLOUD, EZEKIEL, a revolutionary patriot; d. at Henry co., Ga., June 1850, a. 97 years.

CLUTTER, GEORGE W., first auditor of the state of Virginia; d. in Preston co., Va., July 16, 1857; he was a captain in the Mexican war.

CLYMER, GEORGE, inventor of the Columbian printing press, and formerly of Philadelphia; d. in London, Eng., Sept. 4, 1834, a. 80.

COATES, JOHN REYNELL, eldest son of Samuel C., and principally known as land agent to the Penn family; b. in Philadelphia, Nov. 22, 1777; d. Feb. 22, 1842. (*Simpson's Eminent Philadelphians.*)

COATES, SAMUEL, a distinguished merchant of Philadelphia; d. June 4, 1830, a. 81. (*Simpson's Eminent Philadelphians*, with portrait.)

COBB, GEORGE T., of N. J.; killed by railroad accident in Va., Aug. 6, 1870, a. 61.

COBB, THOMAS, d. in Jersey city, N. J., Feb. 17, 1845, a. 85; b. in Parsippany N. J., Jan. 16, 1760; served in the revolution, and during the last two years acted as captain. (*Am. Almanac*, 1846, p. 323.)

COBURN, MRS. BRIDGET H., d. in Bloomfield, Me., in her 100th year; she was formerly of Dracut, Mass.

COCHISE, an Indian of the Coyoteros, a branch of the Apache tribe; d. in Arizona, June, 1874. (*N. Y. Tribune* (s. w.), June 16, 1874.)

COCHRAN, DR. GEORGE, health officer of Brooklyn; d. Nov. 19, 1872, a. 40.

COCHRAN, MAJ. JAMES, d. at Oswego, N. Y., Nov. 7, 1848, a. 79; he was a member of congress from Montgomery co., N. Y., in 1797–9.

COCHRANE, COL. JAMES, served in the war of 1812, and was the captain of a volunteer rifle corps that rendered essential service in the protection of the ships built by Com. Perry until they were fitted out; he was elected to the Pa. house of representatives several years; and d. at Meadville, Pa., March 31, 1850, a. 73 years.

COCHRANE, RICHARD E., lieut. of 4th U. S. infantry, of Delaware; became 2d lt. 4th infantry, Sept. 18, 1838, and 1st lt. Dec. 1842; was killed among the advance troops, by a charge of Mexican cavalry, at Resaca de la Palma, May 9, 1846. (*Thorpe's Army of the Rio Grande*, p. 196.)

CODNER, JAMES, a tory; was an ensign in the 2d Am. regiment in 1782; went to St. John, N. B. in 1783 and drew a city lot; he was a magistrate and d. in 1821, a. 67.

COE, REV. JONAS, son of John C.; b. at New Hampstead, now Ramapo, N. Y., March 20, 1759; his father was an ardent patriot, and on one occasion took five sons with him to battle; he grad. at Queen's, now Rutger's Coll. in 1789; studied theology under Dr. Rodgers of N. Y.; was licensed to preach, Oct. 7, 1791 and June 25, 1793, was installed over the Presb. ch., then first formed at Lansingburgh and Troy; he settled in the former, but removed to Troy in 1802, and resided there until his death, July 21, 1822 in his 64th year. (*Woodworth's Troy*, 77.)

COFFEE, GEN. JOHN, representative in congress from Georgia; d. in Telfair co., Ga., Sept. 25, 1836.

COFFEE, JOHN, a negro slave, a. about 120 years; d. at Norfolk, Va., Jan. 2, 1836; he was a native of Africa, and was first sold at Barbadoes; he was brought to Norfolk about 1740, and lived there till his death.

COFFIN, CAPT. ALEXANDER, d. at Hudson, N. Y., Jan. 11, 1839; the last survivor of the original proprietors of Hudson city purchase in 1784; b. in Nantucket, in 1743; was mayor of Hudson in 1821–3, and held various other public offices.

COFFIN, COL. NATHANIEL, of Boston; a loyalist; after the revolution repaired to Canada; in 1812–15, he served against the U. S., and was for a number of years adj. gen. of the militia of N. C.; d. at Toronto, Aug. 12, 1846, a. 80.

COFFIN, ISAAC, during a long period he served as a town officer in various capacities, as a representative in the general court, as a senator of the commonwealth and for the last thirty-five years, as judge of probate for Nantucket county; d. Dec. 24, 1841, a. 78, at Nantucket.

COFFIN, JAMES HENRY, LL.D., prof. of mathematics and astronomy in Lafayette College; d. at Easton, Pa., Feb. 6, 1873, a. 67; was born Sept. 6, 1806, in Northampton, Mass.; was educated by the Rev. Moses Hillock of that state, and was graduated at Amherst, in 1838. His life was spent in teaching. While professor in Williams College, from 1838 till 1843, he advised and directed the building of Greylock Observatory, on Saddle mountain, the first combined self-registering anemometer and barometer being there placed by him, an improved duplicate of which he recently sent to the Brazilian government. Since 1846 he has been connected with Lafayette College. He was a member of the American Association for the Advancement of Science, and of the National Academy of Science. Shortly before his death he completed a revised and enlarged edition of the *Winds of the Northern Hemisphere*, published by the Smithsonian Institution in 1851. The most noteworthy of his other publications are *Solar and Lunar Eclipses*, and *A Discussion on the Meteoric Fireball.* As a private man his characteristics were kindness, integrity and honor.

COFFIN, JOHN, a Boston loyalist; was assist. commissary gen. in the British army, and d. at Quebec, in 1837, a. 78.

COFFIN, NATHANIEL, of Boston; grad. at Harvard in 1744, and when the revolution began was cashier of the customs at Boston; in 1776, he went to Halifax, and thence to England, where he d. before the peace, Admiral C., of the royal navy, was his son.

COFFIN, NATHANIEL JR., of Boston; son of the above; was a tory, and in 1783, went to Nova Scotia; he was afterwards 34 years collector of customs at the island of St. Kitts; d. in London in 1831, a. 83.

COFFIN, WILLIAM, three tories of this name of Boston are mentioned; at least two went to Halifax in 1776, and were proscribed and banished in 1778. (*Sabine's Loyalists.*)

COGGESWELL, JAMES, a loyalist; was in 1782, an officer in the superintendent dep. at N. Y.

COGSWELL, DR. MASON F., a prominent physician of Albany; d. Jan. 21, 1864, a. 54. (*Transac. N. Y. State Med. Soc.*, 1865, p. 286.)

COIT, JOSHUA, in New London, Conn., Oct. 7, 1758; grad. at Harvard in 1776; settled in New London as a lawyer; was in congress from 1793 to 1798, and served several years in the state legislature; d. at New London, Sept. 5, 1798.

COKE, RICHARD, JR., d. in Abington, Va., March 30, 1851; was a representative in congress from 1829 to 1833, and for many years a prominent member of the bar.

COLBURN, DANA P., prin. of the State Normal School, R. I.; b. at Dedham, Mass.. in 1822; was a grad. and teacher at the Normal School at Bridgewater; in 1852, became assistant to Prof. Greene at Prov., R. I., and in 1855, became principal of the State Normal School; he was the author of several arithmetics and other school books; d. Dec. 14, 1859, by being thrown from a carriage. (*Hist. Mag.*, iv, 60.)

COLBURN, WARREN, grad. at Harvard Coll., in 1820, and became the author of popular treatises upon arithmetic and algebra; d. at Lowell, Mass., Sept. 15, 1833, a. 40.

COLBY, ANTHONY, ex-gov. of N. H. (1846); d. at Concord, N. H., July 20, 1873, a. 80.

COLBY, HON. H. G. O., d. in New Bedford, Mass., a. 44; was judge of the court of common pleas from 1845 to 1847, and afterwards district attorney of the south district, and author of a work on practice.

COLCOCK, CHARLES J., d. at Charleston, S. C., Jan. 26, 1839; pres. of the State Bank of South Carolina, and formerly a judge of the court of appeals.

COLDEN, ALEXANDER, son of Lieut. Gov. C., of N. Y., was post master and successor to his father as surveyor gen.; he d. in 1774, a. 58.

COLDEN, DAVID, son of Lieut. Gov. C., of N. Y., was a tory, and attainted and banished Oct. 22, 1779; he went to England at the close of the war, and d. there July 10, 1784: his wife d. Aug., 1785; he was father of Cadwallader D. C., of N. Y. (*Sabine's Loyalists.*)

COLDEN, JOHN, a tory, was in 1782, capt. in the first battalion of N. J. volunteers.

COLDEN, THOMAS, was a captain of Penna. loyalists in the revolution.

COLE, DANIEL, d. at Adolphustown, E. C., July 5, 1856, in his 106th year; he was a native of Long Island.

COLE, DR. CORTLEY, of Philadelphia, a volunteer in the yellow fever epidemic at Portsmouth in the fall of 1855, fell a victim to the disease.

COLE, JOHN, a son of Elisha Cole, studied law with Daniel Updike, and began practice at Providence, R. I.; in 1763, he was elected an associate justice of the supreme court of the colony, and in 1764 was promoted to chief justice; in the following year he resigned and entered the gen. assembly of which, in 1767, he was speaker; in 1775, Mr. Cole was appointed advocate general in the maritime or vice admiralty court for R. I., which office he held till his death, Oct., 1777. (*W. Updike's Memoirs of the R. I. Bar*, p. 122.)

COLE, JOSEPH GREEN, d. in Paris, Me., Nov. 12, 1851; b. in Lincoln, Mass.; grad. at Harvard in 1822, and settled as a lawyer in Paris, was clerk of the house, representative in the state legislature, register of probate; clerk of the courts and judge of the western dist. court of Maine.

COLE, NATHAN W., d. at Burlington, N. J., July 18, 1848, a. 71; he had practiced medicine for fifty years at that place.

COLEMAN, CHAPMAN, d. in Louisville, Ky., July 21, 1850, son-in-law of Gov. Chittenden, and an influential citizen.

COLEMAN, DANIEL, at 12, he was employed to forward letters in the revolutionary army; in July 1794 he became capt. of militia in the 101st Pa. regt. and the next year was capt. in the 42d; he became col. and held that office through the war of 1812–15; d. at Danville, Va., June, 1860, a. 92. (*Hist. Mag.*, iv, 221.)

COLEMAN, DR. ANSON, d. at Rochester, N. Y., July 17, 1837.

COLEMAN, REV. HENRY, well known from his devotion to the study of agriculture; d. in England, Aug., 1849. (*Stryker's Am. Reg.*, iii, 240.)

COLEMAN, REV. JOHN, D.D., for 20 years rector of Trinity church, Southwark, Phila.; d. at St. Louis, Mo., Sept., 1869, a. 70.

COLEMAN, WILLIAM ATKINS, d. in New York, Jan. 27, 1850, a. 60; was for thirty years prominently connected with literature and art.

COLFAX, GEN. WILLIAMS, an officer of the revolution; d. at Pompton, N. J., Sept. 7, 1838, a. 84.

COLLET, MARK W., a distinguished cotton manufacturer; d. at Paterson, N. J., July 1, 1840.

COLLIER, COL. JAMES, a veteran of 1812; d. in Steubenville, O., July 20, 1873, a. 80.

COLLIER, ISAAC, a tory of Tryon co., N. Y.; in 1785 he signed a declaration of loyalty; his house is said to have been plundered by the whigs in 1778. (*Sabine's Loyalists.*)

COLLIER, JOHN A., an eminent lawyer; d. at Binghamton, N. Y., March 23, 1873, a. 80.

COLLIN, REV. NICHOLAS, of Upsal, sent to America, in 1771, appointed to Wicacoe in 1786; and d. in 1831, at the close of the Swedish mission in Philadelphia.

COLLINS, DR. WILLIAM, of Portsmouth, Va.; d. of yellow fever, Sept. 8, 1855; was formerly a member of the state legislature, and under Pres. Tyler first auditor in the treasury department.

COLLINS, ELA., dist. atty. and congressman; b. in Meriden, Ct., Feb. 14, 1786, son of Gen. Oliver; studied law in Whitestown; settled at Lowville, N. Y., in 1807; was many years dist. atty., of Lewis, Jeff. and St. Law. cos., holding in Lewis co., till 1840; he was in assembly in 1814, in the state convention of 1821, and in the 18th congress; d. at Lowville, Nov. 23, 1848. (*Hough's Hist. Lewis Co., N. Y.*, p. 152, with portrait.)

COLLINS, JONATHAN, judge; b. in Wallingford, Ct., May 3, 1775; served in the revolution, settled in Turin, N. Y., in 1796; was first judge of Lewis co., in 1809–15; and d. near Constableville, N. Y., Apr. 6, 1845, a. 90; he was presidential elector in 1820. (*Hough's Hist. Lewis Co., N. Y.*, p. 230, with portrait.)

COLLINS, OLIVER, brig. general, in the war of 1812–15; from Meriden settled in Oneida co., N. Y., at an early period, owned a fine farm at New Hartford and having served through the revolution, was appointed militia officer and commanded a brigade on the frontier in 1814; d. at New Hartford, N. Y., Aug. 14, 1838.

COLLINS, REV. ISAAC; d. at Baltimore, Md., May 26, 1870, a. 81.

COLLINS, ROBERT, one of the earliest settlers in Ky.; d. in that state, Oct. 11, 1833, a. 90.

COLLINS, THOMAS, of N. C.; a major in the loyalist force defeated by Col. Caswell in 1776; he was captured and confined.

COLLYER, THOMAS, an extensive ship builder; d. in New York city, Nov. 9, 1862.

COLSTON, EDWARD, d. in Berkeley co., Va., April 23, 1851, a. 63; was a distinguished citizen of Virginia, and held many public offices; was in congress from 1817 to 1819, and frequently served in the state legislature; was a long time one of the magistrates of his county, and for some time high sheriff. (*Stryker's Am. Reg.*, vi, 229.)

COLSTON, EDWIN, reporter for the N. Y. press, and formerly publisher of the *Northern Journal*, at Lowville, N. Y.; d. in Williamsburgh, N. Y., Oct. 11, 1857; b. in Carthage, N. Y., Nov. 8, 1824.

COLTON, DR. WALTER, b. at Long Meadow, Mass.; was many years a resident of Pompey, Onondaga co., N. Y., and a judge of the county court; rem. to Oswego, N. Y., and afterwards to Monroe, Mich., where he d. Sept. 27, 1834, a. 61.

COME, IMMANUEL, a colored man; d. at Claysville, Ky., May 15, 1851, a. 121.

COMIS, Ezra, a member of the Michigan house of representatives from Calhoun co.; d. at Detroit, Feb., 1837; he had been a member of the constitutional convention of 1835, and was of the first house of representatives under the state government.

COMLEY, Robert, of Penn., a tory; went to St. John, N. B., in 1783; d. at Lancaster, N. B., in 1838, a. 83.

COMMANDER, Thomas, a tory of S. C.; held an office under the crown after the surrender of Charleston in 1870, and his estate was confiscated.

COMSTOCK, Capt. Joseph J., of the Collins line of steamers; d. in New York city Aug. 16, 1868.

COMSTOCK, Rev. Oliver C., was a physician in Tompkins co., N. Y., and a representative in congress from 1813 to 1819; he gave up his seat to become a minister; was some years a chaplain in congress, and afterwards preached in New York, Illinois and Michigan; d. at Marshall, Mich., Jan. 11, 1860, a. 76.

CONANT, Dr. Abel Blood, b. in Lyme, N. H., Jan. 5, 1837; was a surgeon in a Kentucky regt. in the late war; d. Dec. 27, 1865, in New York city. (*Transac. N. Y. State Med. Soc.*, 1866, p. 345.)

CONANT, Dr. David S., b. at Lyme, N. H., Jan. 21, 1825; and d. Oct. 8, 1865, at New York city; he was a distinguished professor of anatomy and surgery. (*Transac. N. Y., State Med. Soc.*, 1866, p. 336.)

CONDICT, Benjamin, d. at Suckasunny, N. J., Oct. 29, 1839, a. 80; was a soldier of the revolution.

CONDIT, Joel W., many years a director of the Morris & Essex R. R., and vice pres., of the Mutual Benefit Life Ins. Co., a director in several banks and formerly in the N. J. legislature; d. at his residence in Newark, N. J., Sept. 12, 1860, in his 67th year. (*N. Y. Times*, Sept. 17, 1860.)

CONDY, Capt. Thomas Hollis, an officer of the revolution; d. at Pawtuxet, R. I., Aug. 29, 1833, a. 77.

CONE, Francis H., b. in Connecticut; grad. at Yale; studied law, and settled in Gainesboro, N. C., where he d. May 18, 1859, a. 61; he was judge of the Ocmulgee circuit from 1841 to 1845; and state senator in 1855–6.

CONEY, Samuel, ex-gov. of Me.; d. at Augusta, Me., Oct. 5, 1870.

CONGDON, Benjamin T., d. in New Bedford, Mass., April 6, 1851; for many years publisher of the *New Bedford Courier*, a paper devoted to the anti-masonic cause; he held various public offices under the state and federal governments, and was at the time of his death register of deeds for the county of Bristol.

CONKEY, Alexander, d. in Hardwick, Mass., Jan. 12, 1847; a. 93; was a soldier in the revolution and at Bunker hill, Saratoga and Bennington.

CONKLIN, Alfred, eminent jurist and author; b. at East Hampton, N. Y.. Oct. 12, 1789; d. Utica, Feb. 5, 1874.

CONKLIN, Sylvester, lieut. 4th N. Y. regt.; d. Dec. 7, 1778.

CONKLIN, Thomas L., a lawyer, d. in Martinsburgh, N. Y., June 30, 1851.

CONKLIN, TIMOTHY, a lieut. in the revolution, d. July 4, 1839; a. 96.

CONNELL, GEORGE, mem. of the Penn. senate from 1859 to 1871; d. at Phila., Pa., Oct. 26, 1871.

CONRAD, JOHN, d. in Philadelphia, May 9, 1857, a. 83; was a representative in congress from 1803 to 1815. (*Simpson's Eminent Philadelphians.*)

CONSTABLE, WILLIAM, merchant and extensive land proprietor in northern N. Y.; b. in Dublin, Jan. 1, 1752, engaged in trade in Schenectady and afterwards in N. Y., where he formed extensive commercial relations; after the revolution his business extended to India and China, and his trade with the West Indies was extensive; he early turned his attention to land speculations, and was a third owner of the great Macomb's purchase of northern N. Y., the most of which came into his hands; he was also interested in the ten towns on the St. Lawrence, and in Ohio, Kentucky, Virginia and Georgia; he d. in N. Y., May 22, 1802. (*Hough's Hist. Lewis Co., N. Y.*, p. 238, with portrait.)

CONSTABLE, WILLIAM JR., b. April 4, 1786, settled at Constableville, N. Y., and d. there May 28, 1821.

CONVERSE, WILLIAM M., of Franklin, Conn., d. July, 1872, at Norwich, Conn.; was a prom. democratic politician, and was for 12 years mem. from Conn. of the national democratic committee, and for 4 years a mem. of the national executive democratic committee.

CONWAY, EUSTACE, served several sessions in the house of delegates of Va., as a member from Spottsylvania, and was a member of the convention of 1850; elected judge to the eighth district but a painful disease, compelled him to retire from judicial life; he d. in Fredericksburgh, Va., May 20, 1857, a. 36.

CONWAY, WILLIAM B., d. at Burlington, Iowa, Nov. 6, 1839; secretary of the territory of Iowa, and a native of Delaware, was formerly a distinguished partizan editor of Pennsylvania, and a writer of poems, in which he acquired a considerable popularity.

CONYNGHAM, JOHN H., d. at Magnolia, Miss., Feb. 24, 1871, a. 67; was over 30 years judge of the court of com. pleas of Luzerne co., and a prom. mem. of the Protestant Episcopal church.

COOK, ATWATER, b. in Salisbury, N. Y., Dec. 17, 1795 was among the first in his section to turn attention to dairying; in 1831 and 1839 he was in assembly; he d. Feb. 14, 1853, at his home in Salisbury. (*Benton's Herkimer Co.*, p. 303.)

COOK, BATES, comptroller of the state of New York from 1840 to 1842; d. at Buffalo, N. Y., May 30, 1841.

COOK, DR. DANIEL, b. in Kingston, Mass., July 29, 1785; was a surgeon in the war of 1812; and d. at Maumee city, Ohio, March 22, 1863.

COOK, GEORGE AND JAMES, tories of Charleston, S. C., were banished and their estates confiscated.

COOK, JAMES M., N. Y. state sen., in 1848–51; comptroller of the state in 1854–5, and supt. of banking department in 1856–7; d. at Ballston Spa, N. Y., April 12, 1868; was a prom. banker and business man.

COOK, LOUIS, alias ATIATONHARONKWEN, St. Regis chief, and officer of the revolution; b. at Saratoga, about 1740, settled st Caughnawaga near Montreal, and in 1775 went to Boston to learn facts about the war; he was examined by a committee of the gen. court, appointed lieut. col., by Washington, and served with his Indians through the war, mostly on scouting parties; he removed to St. Regis, was a party to several treaties with that tribe, and in the war of 1812, again took up arms for the U. S.; he d. on the Niagara frontier during the war. (*Hough's Hist. St. Law and Fr. Cos., N. Y.*, p. 182.)

COOK, MRS. RACHAEL, d. in Albany, N. Y., Dec. 2, 1840, a. 100 years wanting 8 days.

COOK, WILLIAM H., settled in Norway, N. Y., in 1792, from Dutchess co.; became a farmer and merchant; was sheriff of Herkimer co. from 1802 to 1806, and in 1807; he was in the battle of Tippecanoe, Nov. 6, 1811, and d. at Vincennes, Ind. (*Benton's Herkimer Co. N. Y.*, p. 305.)

COOK, ZEBEDEE, b. in Newburyport, Mass., in 1786; removed to Boston in 1810 and became a merchant, and afterwards an insurance broker; in 1822, he became president of the Eagle Insurance co., and held five years; he was in 1835–9 in the Mass. legislature, and in 1838 became first president of the Mutual Safety Insurance co. of N. Y., and removed to that city; in 1857, he retired from business, and d. at Framingham, Mass., Jan. 24, 1858, a. 72.

COOKE, RT. REV. THOMAS R. C., bishop of Three Rivers, Canada; d. April 30, 1870, a. 78.

COOLEY, HORACE S., secretary of state of Illinois; d. at New Orleans March 31, 1850.

COOLEY, REV. TIMOTHY MATHER, b. in Granville, Mass., in 1774; grad. at Yale in 1792; studied theology there; was settled pastor at Granville, Feb. 3, 1796, and continued till 1854; he d. Dec. 14, 1859, at East Granville, Mass., a. 87. (*Hist. Mag.*, iv, 61; *Am. Almanac*, 1861, p. 387.)

COOLIDGE, JOSEPH, d. in Boston, Mass, Nov. 19, 1840, a. 67.

COOMBER, JOHN, a tory lieut. in the 2d battalion of N. J. vols.; settled in New Brunswick, in 1783, on half pay, and d. in 1827, a. 74.

COON, MICHAEL, soldier of the revolution; d. a. 105 y. 5 mo. 5d., at Phila., May, 1860. (*Hist. Mag.*, iv, 157.)

COOPER, DR. CHARLES DEKAY, sec. of state of N. Y.; son of Dr. Annanias C.; b. in Rhinebeck, N. Y. in 1769; studied with his father and Dr. Crosby, of N. Y.; evinced skill in surgery, and in 1792, settled in Albany; he soon became immersed in politics; in 1806 was judge of the county court, and in 1808, 9, 11, 12, was county clerk; he was also agent for paying Indian annuities, and in 1817 became sec. of state; he was a man of great physical strength and power of endurance; he d. Jan. 31, 1831, a. 63. (*Munsell's Ann. Alb.*, ix, 104.)

COOPER, DR. E. S., a distinguished surgeon, d. at San Francisco, Cal., Oct. 13, 1862; b. in Ohio in 1821; practiced in Peoria, Ill., and went to San Francisco in 1855, where he became professor of surgery in the University of the Pacific.

COOPER, JOHN, son of William C.; town clerk of Boston; was first sheriff of Washington co., Me., at its organization in 1790, and d. at Cooper, Me., Nov. 18, 1845, a. 80.

COOPER, Richard, was in 1782, an ensign in the 3d battalion of N. J. loyalist volunteers.

COOPER, Richard M., d. at Camden, N. J., March 10, 1843, a. 76; from 1820 to 1833, he was member of congress from New Jersey.

COOPER, Robert, a tory of S. C.; went to England, and was in London in 1779.

COOPER, Susan Augusta, widow of J. Fennimore Cooper; d. Jan. 20, 1852, a. 57.

COOPER, William, founder of Cooperstown, and father of James Fennimore Cooper the novelist; was prominently concerned in many public enterprises of his day, and a man of unusual ability, in whatever business he undertook; d. in Albany, Dec. 22, 1809, a. 55.

COOPER, William B., formerly governor of Delaware; d. near Laurel Hill, Del., April 27, 1849.

COPE, Herman, d. at Phila., March 20, 1869; b. in York, Pa., about 1789; was for many years agent for the U. S. Bank in Cin.; afterwards treas. of the bank of the U. S., under assignment, and for some years treas. of the gen. con. of the Prot. Epis. church.

COPE, Jasper, d. in Philadelphia, Pa., Jan. 13, 1856, a. 80; was of the society of Friends and very much respected; was the last of the three brothers Thomas, Israel and Jasper, prominent citizens of Philadelphia.

COPP, Rev. John B., F. W. Bap. preacher; b. at Lebanon, Me.; was ordained in 1835; taught at Corinna; went to St. Albans, Me., in 1836, and to Ashtabula, O., in 1847; d. at Flushing, Mich., Nov. 10, 1855, a. 44. (*F. W. Bap. Reg.*, 1857, p. 86.)

CORNELIUS, Lewis, d. at Milford, Pa., Sept. 27, 1841; his body weighed after death 645½ pounds.

CORNELL, Samuel, of Newbern, N. C.; was a member of the council of N. C., and evinced an early tendency to the loyal side in the revolution; he removed his family to N. Y., and his property was confiscated and sold; he had previously deeded his property to his children, but the confiscation act was found valid against these claims. (*Sabine's Loyalists.*)

CORNING, Erastus, b. in Norwich, Conn., Dec. 14, 1794; when 13 went to a store in Troy, N. Y., as clerk, and in 1814, to Albany, where from a subordinate place he came to be the head of a very extensive house in the hardware line, and largely concerned in iron works; was extensively concerned in railroads; first pres. of the Utica and Schenectady R. R., and after consolidation, was pres. of the N. Y. Central R. R.; was regent of the University from 1833 till death; state sen. in 1842–4, in cong. in 1857–9, and in the constitutional conv. of 1867; was much interested in benevolent and philanthropic enterprises; d. at Albany, Apr. 9, 1872, very wealthy.

CORNISH, E. J., b. in Connecticut in 1841; grad. at Amherst Coll., in 1845, and after 1856, was president of Jefferson College, Mississippi; d. May 17, 1859, a. 37, at Natchez, Miss.

CORNWALL, Daniel, was a lieut. of cavalry in the S. C. royalists in the revolution.

CORNWALL, John, was a tory of Westchester co., in the revolution.

CORNWALL, THOMAS, was a captain in the king's Am. regiment, in the revolution.

CORNWALL, WM., of Jamaica, N. Y.. was a tory in the revolution.

CORWIN, THOMAS, d. at Washington, Dec. 18, 1865; b. in Bourbon, Ky., July 29, 1794; rem. in childhood with his parents to Pendleton co., Ky., and from thence while young, to O., where he served in the leg., and in 1831 was elected to cong., and continued till 1840, when he was chosen gov. of O.; held that office 2 ys.; in 1845 was elected to the sen. from O.; in 1850 was made sec. of the treas., and in 1858 again chosen rep. in cong.; was at one time minister to Mexico.

CORYELL, GEORGE, a revolutionary soldier and at the close of the war removed to Alexandria, D. C.; he was in the battle of Monmouth and on terms of personal friendship with Washington; d. at Lambertville, N. J., Feb. 16, 1850, in the 91st year of his age.

COSKERY, V. REV. HENRY BENEDICT, vicar gen. and administrator of the arch diocese of Balt.; d. Feb. 27, 1872, a. 64.

COSSTELL, CHARLES M., assistant judge of the supreme court of S. C. adhered to the royal cause and went to England in the revolution.

COSTER, JOHN D., d. in New York city, Aug. 8, 1844, a. 82; was a merchant, and in early life a surgeon in the British army. (*Am. Almanac*, 1845, p. 314.)

COTES, DR. JOHN, of Batavia, N. Y.; d. Feb. 26, 1859, a. 64.

COTTEN, JAMES, a tory of N. C., lost his property by confiscation.

COTTON, DR. JOHN; d. at Marietta, O., May 2, 1847, a. 46.

COTTON, ROSSITER, register of deeds for the county of Plymouth, for a period of 48 years; d. at Plymouth, Aug. 12, 1837, a. 79; his father held the same office 33 years, and his grandfather 43 years making 124 years in succession.

COUGLE JAMES, of Pa., was a tory, was captain in the 1st battalion of N. J. vol.; went to New Brunswick in 1783; and d. at Sussex Vale in 1819, a. 73.

COULBOURNE, CHARLES, was a lieut. in the loyal Am. regiment and qr. mr. of the corps, during the revolution.

COULSON, JOHN, a tory of Anson co., N. C., and a man of influence; he was forced to make full confession or go to prison, and preferred the former. (*Sabine's Loyalists.*)

COULSTON, JAMES, journalist; d. in N. Y. city, July 23, 1873, a. 25.

COULTER, JOHN, d. in Stafford co., Va., Feb. 2, 1839; formerly a judge of the circuit court, and court of appeals of Virginia.

COULTER, RICHARD, d. in Westmoreland, Pa., April 20, 1852; a judge of the supreme court of Pensylvania.

COUPER, DR. JAMES, of Newcastle, Del.; d. Aug. 1865.

COUPER, John, b. at Lockumnoch, Renfrewshire, Scot., Mar. 9, 1759, removed to Ga., a. 16, in 1775; became a clerk, retired to Florida in the revolution; returned in 1783, and removed to Liberty co., and later to Glynn co. which he represented in assembly; in 1798 he was in the constitutional convention; he devoted great attention to the cultivation of sea island cotton; he d. in Glynn co., Ga., March, 1850, a. 91.

COURTENAY, JAMES G., d. at Charleston, S. C., Feb. 3, 1835, a. 32; he was during seven years an instructor in the college at that place.

COUTIER, JEAN, gov. of Surinam, from March 2, 1718, till his death in 1721.

COVENTRY, Dr. Alexander, of Utica, d. Dec. 9, 1831, a. 65.

COVENTRY, GEORGE, entered the British army as ensign of 55th foot, Dec. 25, 1755, and served in America in 1757 and 8; he was promoted to lieut., and May 5, 1759, became assist. dep. qr. mr. gen. to Amherst's army.

COVINGTON, ALEXANDER, d. at Warren City, Miss., Oct. 16, 1848, a. 71; b. in Prince George's City, Va., but for forty years a resident of Mississippi; he was in the Virginia legislature, and many years one of the judges of the county court, under the territorial government of Miss.

COWAN, JONATHAN, a pioneer of Watertown, and first mill owner at that place; b. July 12, 1760, in Gloucester, R. I.; and d. at Evans's Mills, N. Y., Nov. 27, 1870. (*New York Reformer*, Dec. 16, 1858.)

COWEN, ESEK, d. in Albany, N. Y., Feb. 11, 1844, a. 56; judge of the superior court of New York, and well known as reporter of the supreme court and court for the trial of impeachments and the correction of errors, and of other legal works.

COWLES, GEN. SOLOMON, an officer in the revolution; d. in Farmington, Conn., Nov. 25, 1846, a. 89.

COX, ALFRED, represented Washington county, Miss., in the house of representatives, and in the state senate for several years; d. Oct. 14, 1841, a. 40, at Vicksburgh, Miss.

COX, CLEMENT, a prominent member of the bar; d. at Georgetown, D. C., Jan., 1848.

COX, DANIEL, member of his majesty's council of N. J.; he was pres. of the board of refugees in N. Y., in 1779.

COX, JAMES, d. in Philadelphia, March —, 1834, a. 83; was a noted book collector; was a fashionable drawing-master; he finally transferred his books to the Philadelphia library, who gave him an annuity of $400, per an.; the number of books in his library exceeded 5,000. (*Simpson's Eminent Philadelphians.*)

COX, CAPT. JOHN, d. at Gosport, Va., Dec. 15, 1837, in his 85th year; was commissioned as captain in the naval service of Virginia in the revolution, and an earnest patriot of that day.

COX, JOHN, d. in Clarke co., Ala., Sept. 25, 1842, a. 78; b. in Essex co., Va., Oct. 19, 1764; settled in Alabama, in 1811. (*Am. Almanac*, 1844, p. 311.)

COX, COL. JOHN, d. in Georgetown, D. C., Dec. 14, 1849, a. 74; in the war of 1812, was inspector of the military of the district; was mayor of Georgetown twenty years in succession.

CRAIG, JOHN J., d. Jan. 9, 1839, at Staunton, Va., a. 36; was a lawyer, and a member of the legislature.

CRAIG, DR. PRESLEY H., surgeon in the army and medical director in the army under Gen. Taylor, in Mexico; d. at the barracks below

New Orleans, in Aug. 8, 1848; he was one of the oldest surgeons in the army.

CRAIN, DR. RUFUS, b. in Western, Worcester co., Mass.; studied with Dr. Ross of Colerain and settled in 1790 at Warren, N. Y., and acquired a large practice; he became a judge of the county court in 1817, and held several years; in 1828 he was a presidential elector; he d. in Warren, Sept. 18, 1846, at an advanced age. (*Benton's Herkimer Co. N. Y.*, p. 305.)

CRAMER, JOHN, d. at Watertown, N. Y., June 1, 1870, a. 92.

CRANCH, RICHARD, of Braintree, now Quincy, Mass.; self educated, a watchmaker and ingenious mechanic; he was a founder of the Am. Acad. of Arts and Sci., and was a state senator; he d. in 1800, a. 74. (*Bradford's N. E. Biog.*)

CRANDELL, DR. CHARLES MILFORD, d. at Belfast, Allegany co., N. Y., Oct. 4, 1867, a. 41; b. at Amity, N. Y., April 11, 1826, grad. at Castleton, Vt., in 1850; was in the assembly of New York, in 1864, 1865, and 1867. (*Transac. N. Y. State Med. Soc.*, 1868, p. 314.)

CRANE, JONATHAN, a tory; went to Nova Scotia, where he was a magistrate; his widow d. in Horton, N. S. in 1841, a. 88.

CRANNELL, BARTHOLOMEW, a public notary of N. Y., in 1782; he went to St. John, N. B., in 1783, and received a city lot; he began business as a merchant, and was in 1785, clerk of the common council.

CRARY, ISAAC E., d. in Michigan, May 8, 1854, was a delegate from the territory of Michigan in congress, in 1835, 1836, and representative from 1836 to 1841.

CRAWE, DR. ITHAMER B., was b. at Enfield, Ct., June 11, 1792, and in 1802 removed to Madison co., N. Y.; he began the study of medicine with Dr. Hastings, of Clinton, N. Y., and began to practice in 1822, in Watertown, N. Y.; he afterwards resided in Ogdensburgh, N. Y., and in Pontiac, Michigan, from whence in a few years he returned to Watertown; he was distinguished for his zealous researches in mineralogy and botany, and was drowned in Perch lake, Jeff. co., while on a botanical excursion, June 3, 1847. (*Hough's Hist. Jeff. Co. N. Y.*, 428; *Am. Jour. Sci. & Arts*, 2d ser., iv, 300.)

CRAWFORD, DAVID, a distinguished lawyer; d. at Mobile, Ala., Nov. 27, 1835.

CRAWFORD, GEORGE W., governor of Georgia; b. in Columbia co., Ga., Dec. 22, 1798; son of Peter C.; grad. at Princeton in 1820; studied law with Richard H. Wilde; was admitted in 1822, and opened an office at Augusta; in 1827 he became atty. gen., and held till 1831; in 1837, he was elected to the legislature, and continued till 1842; in 1843, he served a short term in congress, and the same year was elected governor, and continued till 1849, when he was appointed by Pres. Taylor, sec. of war; he resigned upon his death, and retired to private life; he was agent and attorney in pressing the Galphin Claim, the principal of which, was allowed during Polk's administration; upon entering the cabinet, he managed to procure a report in favor of the interest, and this enormous swindle was perfected. (*White's Hist. Ga.*, p. 245, with portrait.)

CRAWFORD, JOEL, b. in Richmond co., Ga., June 15, 1783; studied law, settled at Milledgeville; joined the army in 1813, under Gen. Floyd, and served as his aid through the war; he was in congress in 1817–21; in 1826 he removed to Hancock co., where he was elected state senator and held 3 years; in 1828, and 1831, he was defeated in elections for governor; he d. in Early co., Ga., April 2, 1858. (*White's Hist. Ga.*, p. 425.)

CRAWFORD, LORMAN, a native and prominent citizen of Georgetown dist., S. C.; d. at Mount Pleasant, Monroe co., Ala., Oct. 11, 1847.

CRAWFORD, MRS. MARY, d. at Castine, Maine, Feb. 20, 1836, a. 100 years and 5 months; she was the widow of Dr. William C., who was a chaplain and surgeon at Fort Point, in the revolution.

CRAWFORD, WILLIAM, d. near Mobile, Ala., April 28, 1849, a. 64; judge of the district court of the U. S.; native of Va., but a resident of Alabama, since 1810, where he filled various state and federal offices; was receiver of public moneys for lands; commissioner of claims under various treaties; state senator, U. S. dist. atty. and judge of the U. S. district court.

CREAGH, THOMAS B., a pioneer settler in Wilcox co., Ala.; d. in that county, March 30, 1842, a. 74.

CRENSHAW, B. MILLS, chief justice of Kentucky; d. May 5, 1857.

CRIPPEN, WILLIAM G., editor of *Cincinnati Times;* b. 1820, and d. May 23, 1863.

CROCKER, SAMUEL, d. in Taunton, Mass, April 3, 1853, a. 80; was county treasurer nearly 25 years; a member of the house, from 1809 to 1813, and of the state senate from 1813 to 1817; he was also state councillor, during the administration of Governor Brooks.

CROCKETT, JOHN W., son of the celebrated Davy Crockett; d. in Memphis, Tenn., Nov. 24, 1852; he was a member of congress from Tennessee from 1838 to 1843.

CROES, REV. JOHN, a son of Bishop Croes, of New Jersey; d. at Brooklyn 19th August, 1849, a. 63.

CROFT, JOHN, a revolutionary soldier; removed to Genoa, N. Y., about 1798, and to Locke in 1809; he was a native of Greenbush; he d. at Locke, N. Y., Dec. 24, 1857, a. 99.

CROGHAN, WILLIAM, revolutionary officer; emigrated from Ireland young; joined the army in 1776 as capt. of infantry in the Va. line, and was in the battles of Brandywine, Germantown and Monmouth; in 1779 he went south and shared the fortunes of the army under Gen. Lincoln at Charleston; in 1784 he removed to Kentucky; married a sister of Gen. Geo. Rogers Clarke, and resided at Locust Grove, Jefferson co., Ky., till his death, Sept. 1822, in his 70th year. (*Rogers's Am. Biog.*)

CROSBY, CLARKSON FLOYD, in 1845 was in the assembly and in 1848 was one of the presidential electors; in 1854, 5, he was in the state senate; he resided in Watervliet, N. Y.; he was a gentleman of brilliant talents, amiable, courteous and genial in his character; he d. at New York, Feb. 22, 1858, a. 41 years.

CROSBY, Oliver, d. in Atkinson, Me., July 30, 1851, a. 82; native of Billerica, Mass.; grad. at Harvard in 1795; studied law at Dover, N.

H., and practiced there nearly twenty-five years; in 1821, he relinquished the profession of law, and settled in Atkinson, where he was largely interested in lands.

CROSBY, WILLIAM, d. in Belfast, Me., March 31, 1852, a. 82; the oldest lawyer and judge in Maine, was b. in Billerica, Mass., in 1770; grad. at Harvard in 1794, and in 1802 settled in Belfast; was county attorney, till elected to the legislature; in 1808, was in the senate of Mass., and in 1812 was appointed judge of the circuit court, and held till it was reörganized; he then returned to practice and continued till 1831, when he withdrew wholly from public life.

CROSS, BENJAMIN, b. in Philadelphia, Sept. 15, 1786; educated at the University of Pennsylvania; devoted himself to music, of which he was a professor and performer; d. March 1, 1857. (*Simpson's Eminent Philadelphians*, with portrait.)

CROSS, ROBERT, b. at Newburyport in 1799; grad. at Harvard in 1819, and admitted to the Essex bar in 1823; he was in both houses of the Mass. legislature, and removed from his native state to Michigan, where from 1844 to 1849 he resided; he then returned to Mass.; settled in Lawrence, and d. there Nov. 9, 1859, a. 60.

CROSS, WILLIAM, a New York tory; went to Nova Scotia in 1783, and d. at Annapolis Royal in 1834, a. 83.

CROSWELL, DR. ANDREW, a grad. of Harvard College in 1798, and a skilful and successful physician; d. in Mercer, Me., June 4, 1858, a. 80.

CROSWELL, SHERMAN, son of Rev. Harry C., of New Haven; b. at Hudson, N. Y.; grad. at Yale in 1822; studied law, and was admitted in 1826; in 1826 he went to Albany; became associated with Edwin Croswell in the *Albany Argus*, and remained till 1855; he was many years legislative reporter, and prepared a manual of parliamentary rules, which has been received as authority, by the N. Y. legislature; he d. at New Haven, March 3, 1859, a. 56. (*Hist. Mag.* iii, 129.)

CROUSILLAT, LOUIS MARTIAL JACQUES, a prominent merchant of Philadelphia; b. July 1, 1757, in Salon, in the south of France; came to America in 1780; settled at Philadelphia, and d. July 12, 1836.

CROWE, C. C., ex-gov. of New Mexico; d. June 18, 1870.

CROWELL, COL. JOHNS, d. near Fort Mitchell, Ala., June 25, 1846; he was a delegate from the territory of Alabama, from 1817 to 1819, and first member of congress from that state, serving till 1821; he was soon after appointed an agent for the Creek Indians, then living in Alabama and Georgia, over whom, until their removal in 1836, he exerted considerable influence.

CROWELL, JOSEPH, capt. in the 1st battalion of N. J. volunteers; settled on half pay in New Brunswick, after the revolution, and d. at Carlton, N. B.

CROWNINSHIELD, EDWARD AUGUSTUS, b. in Salem, Mass., in 1817; grad. at Harvard in 1838; read law, but did not practice, and displayed great taste as a bibliographer; he collected a choice library, and d. in Boston, Feb. 20, 1859, a. 41.

CRUGER, HENRY, d. Feb. 5, 1780, St. James's square, Bristol, a. 76; formerly resided in New York city, where he was a member of assembly, and of the council.

CRUIKSHANK, Charles, became captain of the 2d N. Y. independent co. of foot, April 16, 1757, and served in 1759, at Ticonderoga.

CRUIKSHANK, Joseph, formerly a printer and bookseller at Philadelphia; d. in that city, Aug. 9, 1836, in his 90th year.

CRUMP, George P., an esteemed and active citizen of Vicksburg, Miss., and at the time of his death (June 1860, at the age of 45), he was physician to the city hospital; in the Mexican war, he was captain of one of the companies of the 1st Mississippi reg't.

CRUSER, William, late judge of the court of common pleas; d. near Princeton, N. J., Jan. 9, 1841, a. 53.

CULL, Rev. Hugh, d. near Richmond, Ind., Aug 30, 1862, in his 105th year; had lived there nearly 60 years.

CULLEN, Dr. John, long professor of the theory and practice of medicine, in the med. dep. of Hampden Sydney College, Va.; d. at Richmond, Va., Jan. 25, 1851, a. 53.

CULVER, Dr. Charles, d. at Ellington, Conn., Sept. 7, 1868, a. 21; house surgeon, Charity Hospital, Blackwell's island.

CUMMING, Alfred, of Georgia; d. Oct. 10, 1873, near Augusta, Ga.; was supt. of Indian affairs on the upper Mo., when in 1857 he was appointed gov. of Utah by President Buchanan; entered on that office at a critical time in the affairs of the territory; since their settlement at the Great Salt lake in 1848, the Mormons had been on bad terms with the federal authorities; Col. Steptoe who, in 1854, succeeded Brigham Young as gov. was deterred from entering on the duties of his office by the turbulent conduct of the Mormons, who continued their hostile acts until, in 1856, every U. S. officer, with the exception of an Indian supt., was forced to flee from the territory; it was during this condition of affairs that Mr. Cumming was appointed gov., and Judge Eckles of Ind. chief justice of Utah; a force of 2,500 men, under experienced officers, was sent to protect them in the discharge of their proper functions; the Mormons were greatly excited at the approach of these troops; Young, in his capacity of gov., issued a proclamation denouncing the army as a mob, and forbidding it to enter the territory, and calling the people of Utah to arms to repel its advance; the army, however, entered Utah, and, after being harassed by the Mormons, went into winter quarters near Fort Bridger; on Nov. 27, 1847, Gov. Cumming issued a proclamation declaring the territory to be in a state of rebellion; in the spring of 1858, however, by the intervention of Mr. Thos. L. Kane of Penn., who had gone to Utah by way of California, bearing letters from Pres. Buchanan, a good understanding was brought about between Gov. Cumming and the Mormon leaders; and toward the end of May an amnesty was offered to and accepted by the insurgents; the troops soon after entered Salt lake valley, and remained till May, 1860, when they were withdrawn from the territory. Gov. Cumming remained in office during Pres. Buchanan's administration, and was not afterward prominent in political affairs.

CUMMING, Rev. Alexander, son of Robert C., from Montrose, Scotland; b. at Freehold, N. Y., in 1726; studied theology with Rev. Wm. Tennent; was licensed in 1746 or 7; preached in New Brunswick, and in Oct. 1750, was ordained over the Presb. ch. of N. Y. city, and remained till Oct. 25, 1753; he was then called to the Old South ch., in Boston, as colleague of Dr. Sewall, where he d., Aug. 25, 1763. (*Miller's Life of J. Rodgers*, p. 104.)

CUMMINGS, DR. ISAAC, d. in N. Y., Dec. 17, 1869, a. 36; native of Mass., and house surgeon of the Demilt dispensary.

CUMMINGS, JOHN, was elected sheriff of Lycomming co., Pa., four times, the first in 1798; he was associate judge of that co. 17 years, and d. near Williamsport, June 3, 1850, at the a. of 84.

CUMMINGS, DR. MORGAN LEWIS, d. in Turin, N. Y., April 7, 1851.

CUMMINS, JOHN D., member of 30th congress from Ohio; d of cholera, at Milwaukee, Wis., Sept. 11, 1849.

CUNARD, EDWARD, bart.; b. Jan. 1, 1816; one of the proprietors of the Cunard line of steamships; d. at N. Y. April 6, 1869.

CUNLIFF, JOSEPH, a tory; was in 1782, a lt. in the 1st battalion of N. J. volunteers.

CUNNINGHAM, JOHN, was ensign in the loyal Am. regiment and adj. to the corps; he settled in N. B.; received half pay, and d. at Fredericton.

CUNNINGHAM, PATRICK, br. of Gen. Robert C.; in 1769 he was appointed dep. surveyor gen., of S. C.; removed to Charleston in 1776, and in 1780, was col.; his estate was confiscated in 1782; he went to Florida after the war; in 1785, he was restored to his rights in S. C., and his estate amerced 12 p. c., with certain personal disabilities for a term of years; he was elected to the legislature, but was led to resign soon after; he d. in 1714. (*Sabine's Loyalists.*)

CUNNINGHAM, THOMAS, was a lieut. in De Lancey's 1st battalion, and adj. of the corps; he went to St. John, N. B., and was one of the grantees of that city.

CUNNINGHAM, WALTER, of N. C.; a tory; lost his property in 1779, by confiscation; in 1782 there was an ensign of this name in the 2d Am. regiment of loyalists.

CUNNINGHAM, WILLIAM, of S. C., a tory known as Bloody Bill; early in the revolution served with the whigs; he changed sides, became a major, was engaged in many desperate struggles; his property was confiscated in 1782, and he withdrew to Florida after the war. (*Sabine's Loyalists.*)

CURRIE, ROSS, a lieut. in the Pa. loyalists and adj. of the corps; he settled in New Brunswick after the war, drew half pay, and practiced law; he d. in that province.

CURRY, JOHN, a loyalist, settled in New Brunswick after the war, and in 1792 was senior justice of com. pleas, in Charlotte co., in which co. he d.; his son Cadwallader C., was a merchant at Eastport, Me., and at Campo Bello, N. B. (*Sabine's Loyalists.*)

CURRY, OTWAY, d. in Marysville, O., Feb. 15, 1855, a. 51; a lawyer of respectable attainments, but better known as a literary man and poet.

CURTIS, CHARLES, of Scituate, Mass., grad. at Harvard in 1765; was driven to Boston as a tory; was proscribed in 1778, and d. in N. Y. previous to 1832. (*Sabine's Loyalists.*)

CURTIS, EDWARD, d. in New York, Aug. 3, 1856; a prominent lawyer and politician; b. in Vermont; grad. at Union Coll.; studied law, and began his political career in 1834, by entering the com. council of New York, where after a long contest he was elected president of the board of assistant aldermen; he was in congress from 1837 to 41; was appointed collector of New York by Gen. Harrison, and held this office nearly four years.

CURTIS, GEORGE, d. at Jacksonville, Fla., Jan. 14, 1856; b. in Worcester, Mass., Feb. 1796; came to Prov., R. I., at an early age; in 1819 became cashier of the Exchange Bank, and in Aug. 1835, treas. of the transportation co.; rem. to N. Y., and became cashier of the Bank of Commerce, and afterwards pres. of the Continental Bank; was in assem. in 1830, and a mem. of common council several years.

CURTIS, REV. HARVEY, D.D., pres. of Knox College, at Galesburg; d. there Sept. 18, 1862; b. in Adams, N. Y., in 1806; educated at Middlebury, Vt., and after preaching in various places with success, was appointed to the place in which he d. in 1858. (*National Almanac*, 1863, p. 629.)

CURTIS, HIRAM, inventor; d. at Albion, N. Y., May 18, 1870.

CURTIS, JAMES F., superintendent of the Boston and Worcester rail road; killed in a rail road car, at Boston, April 13, 1839.

CURTIS, DR. THOMAS, projector and editor of the *Encyclopedia Metropolitana*, and sole editor of Mr. Trigg's *London Encyclopedia;* perished Jan. 29, 1869, by the burning of the steamer North Carolina, in Chesapeake bay; he was of Limestone Springs, S. C., and 71 years of age.

CURTIS, WILLIAM, grand sec'y of the Grand Lodge of Pa.; d. at Phila., Dec. 27, 1859, a. 57.

CUSHING, JOHN P., d. in Watertown, Mass., April 17, 1862, a. 75; his vast wealth was used for the promotion of botanical science, and to confer pleasure on his fellow citizens.

CUSHING, COL. WASHINGTON, an officer of the war of 1812; d. at South Hingham, Mass., Aug. 24, 1849, in his 75th year.

CUSHMAN, JOHN PAINE, d. at Troy, N. Y., Sept. 16, 1848, a. 64; b. in Pomfret, Conn.; grad. at Yale in 1807, and settled at Troy; from 1817 to 1819 he served in congress, and in 1838, was appointed one of the circuit judges of the state of New York; he had previously been recorder of Troy; and was one of the regents of the University.

CUSHMAN, MINERVA, d. in Exeter, N. Y., March 1, 1842, a. 79; settled in Oswego co., in 1793. (*Am. Almanac*, 1843, p. 310.)

CUSHMAN, SAMUEL, judge of the police court of Portsmouth, N. H. and member of congress from 1835 to 1839; d. at Portsmouth, May 20, 1851, a. 68; he held several state offices at different times.

CUSICK, NICHOLAS, alias Kayhnatho, a Tuscarora chief; was b. at Oneida Res., June 15, 1756; served the Americans as lieut. in the war, 5 years, and at one time saved La Fayette's life; he d. at Tuscarora village near Niagara, Oct. 29, 1840, a. 82. (*Griswold's Biog. Annual*, 1841, 191.)

CUSTIS, JOHN PARKE, stepson of Gen. Washington; proved a wayward youth, married young to Miss Eleanor, dau. of Benedict Colvert, and had 4 children; Elizabeth Parke married Mr. Law; Martha Parke married Tho. Peters; Eleanor Parke married Laurence Lewis, a favorite nephew of Washington, and Geo. W. Parke, who was aid-de-camp of Washington at the siege of Yorktown. Was taken with a camp fever and d. at Elnathan in the fall of 1781. (*G. W. P. Custis's Recollec. & Priv. Mem. of Washington.*)

CUTHBERT, ALFRED, d. in Jasper co., Ga., 1856; representative in congress from Georgia, from 1814 to 1817, and again from 1821 to 1827, and senator in congress from 1825 to 1843.

CUTLER, EBENEZER, of Northborough, Mass.; a tory; he was allowed to join the British at Boston, without his effects, and he went with the army to Halifax; in 1778 he was proscribed and banished; he became prothonotary in Annapolis co., N. S., and d. at Annapolis Royal in 1831, at an advanced age. (*Sabine's Loyalists.*)

CUTLER, ELDRIDGE JEFFERSON, prof. of modern languages in Harv. Uni.; d, Dec. 27; b. in Holliston, Mass., and grad. at Harv. in 1853; taught several years, and was connected with the *New York Evening Post* and the *New York Tribune* in some editorial capacity for a short time; in 1865 received an appointment as asst. prof. of modern languages at Harv. Uni., but at the time of his death he had received a full professorship; in the first course of university lectures Prof. Cutler gave a series on Goethe, and the principles of criticism, and, had he lived, he would have continued them in the course for the coming year; he published a small volume of war poems a few years ago, which were very warmly received, both by the press and the public, and a poem called *Stella* was also published separately, not long since; although he wrote comparatively little for one who wrote so well, his contributions to the *Daily Advertiser* and the *North American Review* would make a very respectable volume; for some time he had written many of the book-notes in the quarterly just named.

CUTLER, LEVI, d. in Portland, Me., March 2, 1856, a. 83; b. in North Yarmouth, Me., in 1774; removed to Portland in 1806, and was mayor of that city from 1834 to 1841.

CUTLER, ROBERT CURRIE, d. at Livingston, Va., Oct. 31, 1846, a. 53; clerk of the circuit superior court of law and chancery, for Nelson co., and clerk or sec. to every public body in the county in which he served.

CUTTING, REV. LEONARD, b. near London in 1731; educated at Eton and Cambridge; came to America in 1750, and lived at New Brunswick, N. J.; in 1756, he became tutor and prof. in King's Coll., N. Y.; was ordained in Eng. in 1763, and in 1766 succeeded Rev. Mr. Seabury at Hempstead, where he taught a classical school; in 1784 he resigned, went south and d. sometime before 1803. (*Doc. Hist. N. Y.*, iii, 1063; *Sabine's Loyalists.*)

CUTTS, CHARLES, b. in Mass. in 1769; grad. at Harvard in 1790; was elected to the legislature in 1804, and then speaker of the house; was in the U. S. senate from New Hampshire, from 1810 to 1813, and served as secretary of the senate, from 1814 to 1825; he d. in Fairfax co., Va., Jan. 25, 1846, a. 76.

CUYLER, ABRAHAM C., of Albany, N. Y.; was authorized to raise 600 men, for the royal service, and in Nov. 1779, was recruiting at Jamaica; he was attainted and banished, Oct. 22, 1779; went to England in 1781; returned to America, and d. in Yorkfield, L. C., Feb. 5, 1810, a. 68; his son, Cornelius, was a major in the British service, and d. at Montreal in 1807.

CUYLER, BENJAMIN CLARK, D.D., an Episcopal clergyman; b. at Jamaica Plains, Mass., Feb. 6, 1798; d. at Brooklyn, N. Y., Feb. 10, 1863.

DABNEY, AUSTIN, a free colored soldier of the rev.; was a man of much sense, and acquired a large circle of friends; received a lot of land from the state of Ga., in Walton co.; acquired property; was a noted lover of horses and horse raising; a son was educated at Franklin Coll., and studied law; d. at Zebulon, Pike co., Ga., having many years drawn a pension. (*White's Hist. Ga.*, p. 584.)

DABNEY, FREDERIC, b. in Fayal, Aug. 2, 1809, and grad. at Harv. in 1828; returned to Fayal, and became a partner in the firm in which his father, for many years U. S. consul, was senior member; was greatly esteemed both by native and foreign residents; d. Dec. 29, 1857, a. 48.

DADE, GEN. LAWRENCE T., d. in Owensboro, Ky., March 25, 1842, a. 56; was a native of Orange co., Va.

DADE, PHILIP SLAUGHTER, d. in Dubuque, Iowa Ter., July 12, 1842, a. 28; was formely of King George co., Va.

DAKIN, FRANCIS ELIHU, p. in Utica, N. Y., Dec. 13, 1828; grad. in 1851 at Yale; went to Germany to complete his education, and became prof. of nat. phil., and chemistry at the State Normal School at Albany; resigned in Feb. 1854; d. at Freeport, Ill., Dec. 25, 1868.

DAKIN, SAMUEL DANA, b. in Jaffrey, N. H., July 16, 1802, and came with his parents to Oneida co., in 1815; grad. at Ham. Coll. in 1821; was associated for a time with Wm. J. Bacon, in editing a weekly paper; in 1826 he was admitted to the bar of Oneida co., and in 1839 he rem. to N. Y.; here he d. very suddenly of a disease of the heart, Jan. 26, 1853; at the time of his death he was known in the commercial world as one of the patentees of an improved floating dry dock, two of which were completed for the U. S. gov.; was the father of five sons, all of whom are graduates of Hamilton College.

DALLAS, JACOB A., artist; d. in N. Y. city, Sept. 9, 1857; b. in Phila., in 1825; rem. at the age of eight to Mo., and studied at Ames Coll; returned to Phila., and became an esteemed portrait painter, and resided the last eleven years at N. Y.; his talents were of a high order; was one of the chief illustrators of *Harper's*, *Putnam's*, *Frank Leslie's*, and other popular periodicals, while many larger volumes are wholly indebted to him for the engravings they contain. (*Simpson's Eminent Philadelphians.*)

DALLAS, TREVANION B., an eminent lawyer, and one of the judges of the dist. court for the county of Alleghany; d. at Pittsburg, Pa., April 7, 1841.

DALRYMPLE, JAMES A., register of wills in Calvert co., Md., and several ys. in the Md. leg.; d. near Prince Frederick, Md., Aug. 18, 1842.

DALTON, DR. EDWARD BARRY, d. at Santa Barbara, Cal., May 13, 1872, a. 36.

DALYELL, JAMES, was made lieut. in the 60th or Roy. Am. Regt. Jan. 15, 1756; obtained a comp. in the 2d batt. of royals, Sept. 13, 1760, and on the 31st of July, 1763, led a detachment against Pontiac, near Detroit; was killed in this engagement. (*Parkman's Conspiracy of Pontiac*, 275; *Coll. Hist. N. Y.*, vii, 547.)

DAMRELL, WILLIAM, S., b. in Portsmouth, N. H., Nov. 29, 1809; was in cong. from Mass. 1855 to 1859, and d. at Dedham, Mass., May 17, 1860; was a well known painter.

DAMUTH, GEORGE, a pioneer of Utica, being one of three settlers only who lived on its site in 1786; his lease, dated July 28, 1787, is the first lease or title of any kind obtained from the proprietors of the soil of which there is any knowledge.

DANA, JAMES, was b. at Ashburnham, Mass., May 20, 1780, and was the son of one of two Huguenot bros., who fled from France to England; at the age of 12, he rem. to Windsor, Vt., and about 10 years after started for the west, stopping a year at Schenectady, and in 1803 settling in Utica, where he afterwards resided; engaged in the saddlery and hardware business and followed the latter business with his son till 1850, when he retired; d. at Utica, Jan. 7, 1860. James D. Dana, of Yale Coll. is a son of this person.

DANA, DR. JOHN WHITE, son of Jas. Dana of Utica; b. March 28, 1817; attended medical lectures in N. Y.; d. of cholera in the city of N. Y., where he had commenced the practice of medicine, Aug. 27, 1849; his was the first body interred in Forest Hill cemetery, Utica.

DANE, JOSEPH, b. in Essex co., Mass.; grad. at Harv. in 1799; settled at Kennebunk, Me., early in this century; was chosen to the executive council of Mass. in 1817; was representative of York dist.; was in cong. from 1820 to 1823, and seven years in the state leg.; d. at Kennebunk, Me., May 1, 1858, a. 79. (*Hist. Mag.*, ii, 88; *Am. Alm.*, 1859, p. 353.)

DANFORTH, ASA, b. in Worcester, Mass., July 6, 1746; served in the rev.; became a pioneer and prominent settler in Onondaga co.; was a judge of the county court, supt. of the salt springs; mem. of assem. in 1801–2, and state sen. in 1803–6; was a maj. gen. of militia; d. at Onondaga Hollow, Sept. 2, 1818. (*Clark's Onondaga*, ii, 115.)

DANFORTH, SAMUEL, son of Rev. John D., of Dorchester, Mass.; grad. at Harv. in 1715; was several years pres. of the council, a judge, and in 1774, a mandamus councillor; was distinguished for his love of natural philosophy and chemistry; d. in 1777, a. 81.

DANFORTH, THOMAS, lawyer at Charlestown, Mass.; son of Hon. Sam'l D.; grad. at Harv. in 1762; was proscribed and banished as a tory, and was the only man in his town who sought British protection; went to Halifax in 1776; d. in London in 1825.

DANIELS, CONSTANS F., educated to the law, and many years connected with the press in South Carolina, in New York city and in New London, Ct., where he edited the *New London Chronicle*, and d. Oct. 20, 1858, a. 69.

DA-O-NE-HO-GA-WEH, a Seneca chief known as John Blacksmith, d. at Tonawanda, N. Y., April 14, 1851, a. 70; he was distinguished for the advocacy of the rights of his people and after the death of Red Jacket was the greatest of his tribe. (*Stryker's Am. Reg.*, vi, 225.)

DARBY, Ezra, mem. of cong. from New Jersey, from 1806, till his death, Jan. 28, 1808.

DARBY, John, became a maj. of the 17th regt. Sept. 21, 1756; served in 1758, at the seige of Louisburg; became lieut. col., May 14, 1759, and commanded a battalion of grenadiers in 1760; was adj. gen. at Martinico in 1762, and col. in the army in 1772; he left the British army in 1775. (*Com. Wilson's Orderly Book*, 61.)

DARGAN, George W., for a time commissioner of equity, for the Charleston dist.; was state senator in S. C., and was one of the chancellors of the state from 1847 till his death, June 12, 1859, a. 58.

DARLING, Sir Charles H., late governor of British Columbia; d. in London, Jan. 26, 1870; a. 61.

DARLINGTON, Isaac, president judge of the 15th judicial dist. of Pennsylvania, from 1821 till his death; d. at Westchester, Pa., April 27, 1839,in his 58th year; b. in Westtown, Chester co., Pa.; served in the state legislature, and as a volunteer in the war of 1812.

DARRACH, Lydia, a patriotic quaker lady of Philadelphia, who rendered service to the American cause in the revolution. (*Watson's Annals.*)

DARROW, Dr. William, a pioneer physician in northern part of Lowville, N. Y.; d. Jan. 8, 1815, a. 44; was from Hebron, N. Y., and served in assembly in 1812.

DAVEE, Thomas, b. in Plymouth, Mass., Nov. 9, 1797; removed to Maine; was bred a merchant; served 6 y. in the Maine legislature; was speaker; high sheriff of Somerset co., and in congress from 1837 to 1841; was many years a postmaster, and at the time of his death, Dec. 9, 1841, was senator elect to the state legislature.

DAVENPORT, Ashley, b. Feb. 12, 1794; was a state senator from Lewis and Jefferson cos., N. Y., in 1852, 3; a farmer and merchant, and d. at Copenhagen, Lewis co., N. Y., where he had long resided, Feb. 10, 1874.

DAVENPORT, Lieut. Hezekiah, Conn.; killed April 27, 1777.

DAVENPORT, John, of Stamford, Ct.; congressman 18 years; son of Abm. D.; b. Jan. 16, 1752; grad. at Yale 1770; was major of militia when the war began; was in congress from 1799 to 1817, (having succeeded his brother James); and d. Nov. 28, 1830; his wife d. in Brooklyn, N. Y., June 28, 1847, a. 93. (*Davenport Family*, p. 234.)

DAVENPORT, Rev. John, son of Rev. James D., b. at Freehold, N. J., Aug. 11, 1752; grad. at Princeton in 1769; was ordained at Mattituck, L. I., in 1775 and preached 2ys.; he lived at Bedford, N. Y., Deerfield, N. J., was dismissed on account of feeble health; and d. at Lysander, N. Y., July 13, 1825. (*Davenport Family*, p. 238.)

DAVENPORT, Thomas, in congress from Virginia, from 1825 to 1835; d. in Halifax co., Va., Nov. 1838.

DAVIDSON, Capt., d. at Lost Valley Creek, Pa., Jan. —1840, a. 88; belonged to the Pennsylvania line in the revolution, and was in several battles.

DAVIDSON, Hamilton, a tory from the states; d. in York co., N. Brunswick, in 1841, a. 92.

DAVIDSON, James, d. at Stockbridge, Mass., Nov. 27, 1840; was a major in the revolutionary war.

DAVIDSON, Lieut. Levi P., d. at Saratoga Springs, N. Y., June 27, 1842; he was of the 1st dragoons, U. S. A.; grad. at West Point in 1837; was a son of Dr. D. and brother of Lucretia and Margaret Davidson, noted for their early poetic talent.

DAVIDSON, William, b. in Mecklenburg co., N. C., Sept. 12, 1778; for many years a representative from Mecklenburg co., N. C. in the state senate, and a member of congress from that state in 1818–21; d. at Charlotte, N. C., Sept. 17, 1857, a. 79.

DAVIE, Col. G. W., several years a member of the state legislature of S. C.; d. at Chester, S. C., April 9, 1850.

DAVIES, Solomon B., of the firm of Davies & Warfield, Baltimore; d. in that city, June 25, 1860, in his 33d year.

DAVIS, Amos, member of congress from Kentucky; d. June 5, 1835, at Owingsville, Ky.

DAVIS, Gen. Aquila, of Warren, N. H.; d. at Cumberland, Me., of apoplexy, Feb. 27, 1835.

DAVIS, Charles B., d. at Washington, D. C., Oct. 3, 1839; a. 65.

DAVIS, Charles Mortimer, b. at Sennett, N. Y., July 6, 1838; grad., at Hamilton Coll., in 1861. Taught academy at Auburn, N. Y.; at the Oneida Seminary, and Cayuga Lake Acad., at Aurora; in April, 1864, became an assistant editor of the *Utica Morning Herald*, and d. at Sennett, Aug. 5, 1868. (*Regent's Report*, 1870, p. 598.)

DAVIS, Daniel, d. at Cambridge, Mass., Oct. 27, 1855, a. 73. He was for 32 years solicitor general of Massachusetts.

DAVIS, David, b. at Morristown, N. J., Oct., 1755; served as teamster through the revolution settled in Westchester co., and about 1830, went to Brooklyn; he died in indigence at Brooklyn, Nov. 11, 1858, nearly 105 years old. (*Hist. Mag.*, iii, 27.)

DAVIS, Frederick W., a practical chemist and metallurgist; d. at Boston, Dec. 12, 1854, a. 31 years; he received his chemical education with Prof. C. T. Jackson, and in 1847 was appointed supt. of the Revere Copper Cos., melting furnaces at Point Shirley. (*Am. Jour. Sci. and Arts.*, 2d ser., xix, 449.)

DAVIS, Garrett, U. S. senator and statesman of Kentucky; b. Sept. 10, 1801; d. at his home in Paris, Ky., Sept. 22, 1872. (*Drake's Dic. Am. Biog.*)

DAVIS, Capt. Isaac, Mass.; April 19, 1775, in revolution.

DAVIS, Isaac R., a conspicuous Philadelphia merchant and citizen; b. in 1809, in Montgomery co., Pa.; spent his life in Philadelphia and d. near that city, Feb. 4, 1857. (*Simpson's Eminent Philadelphians.*)

DAVIS, Gen. Jonathan, d. at Oxford, Mass., Aug. 3, 1838, a. 77; was for a long time a justice of the court of sessions, and sustained various other public offices.

DAVIS, Capt. Joseph, Penna.; killed in revolution, April 23, 1779.

DAVIS, Joseph, many years a state senator in Massachusetts; d. at Northboro, Mass., Oct. 23, 1843, a. 69.

DAVIS, Dr. Samuel H., prof. in the Jefferson Medical College, Phila.; d. March 2, 1872.

DAVIS, THOMAS, financier; b. in Plymouth, Mass., in 1758, engaged in the fishing trade and became well versed in mercantile affairs; he was chosen to the state senate, became president of an insurance co. in Boston, and held till his death in 1805, a. 48. (*Bradford's N. E. Biog.*)

DAVIS, RT. REV. THOMAS, D.D., P. E. bishop of South Carolina; d. at Camden, S. C., Dec. 2, 1872.

DAVIS, THOMAS KEMPER, son of Isaac P. Davis; b. in Boston; grad. at Harvard, in 1827; studied law, but having an ample fortune, devoted himself to, and became learned in English and classical literature; d. Oct. 13, 1853.

DAVIS, WARREN R., d. at Washington, D. C., Jan. 29, 1835; b. in S. C.; grad. at S. C. coll., in 1810; was solicitor for S. C. and from 1827 to 1835; a member of congress from South Carolina.

DAWKINS, GEORGE, of S. C., was in 1872, a capt. of cavalry in the S. C. Loyalists and his estate was confiscated.

DAWSON, DAVID, of Chester co., Pa., joined the royal army at Phila., went with it to N. Y., and was employed in passing counterfeit money. He was detected and executed in 1780.

DAWSON, GEN. JOHN B., d. at St. Francisville, La., June 26, 1845; member of congress from the 3d dist. of Louisiana.

DAWSON, JOSIAH, b. in Philadelphia, Sept. 1, 1772, was of the Society of Friends, and acquired a large property, after giving to his family, and friends, he bequeathed nearly $30,000 to the Friend's Asylum for the insane; $25,000 to the Westtown boarding school, and $11,000 to the Penna. Hosp., he left over $225,000 to his executors to be applied at their discretion to different charitable objects and benevolent institutions of the county of Philadelphia. (*Simpson's Eminent Philadelphians.*)

DAWSON, DR. ROBERT W., d. near New Madrid, Mo., April 6, 1843, in his 52d year; b. in Montgomery co., Md., and emigrated to Missouri, in 1812; where he engaged in practice of medicine; in 1815, was elected to the territorial legislature, and in 1820, aided in forming the first state consolidation, was chosen to the state senate in 1822, and continued by successive elections till 1836.

DAWSON, REV. WILLIAM, second pres. of William and Mary's Coll., Va., succeeded Pres. Blair in 1743, and held till his death in 1761; he was succeeded by Rev. Wm. Yates.

DAY, DAVID M., d. at Buffalo, N. Y., Dec. 12, 1839; a. 48; one of the publishers of the *Whig and Journal*, of that city.

DAY, ELKANAH, a physician of Westmoreland, Vt., was appointed a captain of rangers by the provincial congress of N. Y., but resigned Oct. 23, 1776; he was several years high sheriff of Windham co., and successively elected to both houses of the N. Y. legislature, from Cumberland co., before the erection of Vermont as a separate state. (*Hall's Eastern Vermont*, p. 640.)

DAY, DR. HORACE B., b. in West Schuyler, Herkimer co., January, 1819, graduated at Albany Medical College in 1844, and began practice of medicine. In 1849 he removed to Utica, where he pursued his profession until his death Aug. 23d, 1870.

DAY, MATTHIAS, d. in Newark, N. J., Dec. 29, 1844, a. 74; was for some time editor of a newspaper, and afterwards postmaster of Newark, which office he held 27 years.

DAYTON, AARON OGDEN, of Washington, D. C.; for 24 years fourth auditor of the treasury department; d. in Philadelphia, Oct. 4, 1858.

DAYTON, NATHAN, judge in the supreme court of New York; settled early in Niagara co.; held the office of first judge from March 1833 to Jan. 1836; was appointed circuit judge of 8th dist., Feb. 23, 1838; was elected county clerk in 1857, and d. April 26, 1859, in his 64th year; he resided at Lockport.

DEACON, CAPT. DAVID, of the U. S. navy; d. at Burlington, N. J., Jan. 22, 1840.

DEAN, GILBERT, d. at Poughkeepsie, N. Y., Oct. 12, 1870; b. in Dutchess co., educated at Yale; studied law, and was in congress in 1850–4, and a justice of the supreme court in 1864; he was a prominent lawyer and conspicuous in his management in the case of Mrs. Emma A. Cunningham, indicted in 1857 for the murder of Dr. Burdell in Bond st., N. Y.

DEAN, JACOB, of N. Y.; was a loyal declarator in 1775; became an inhabitant of New Brunswick, and d. at St. John, in 1818, a. 80.

DEAN, JAMES, was the eldest son of Hon. James Dean of Westmoreland, Oneida co., and was b. Dec. 19, 1787, in what was then Whitestown, Montgomery co.; was the first white male child born within the present limits of Oneida co.; having pursued his preparatory studies at the Hamilton Oneida Acad. he was graduated at Union Coll. in 1811 with the highest honor of his class; from 1813 to 1816 he was a tutor in Ham. Coll.; he studied law with Jonas Platt of Whitestown, and James Powers of Catskill, where he was admitted to the bar; he removed to New Hartford and subsequently to Utica, where he d. May 23, 1841, in his 53d year; he held for some years the office of judge of the county court; was treasurer of Ham. Coll. from 1825 to 1828; represented the county in the legislature, and was clerk of the county for a single term.

DEAN, JOHN, grad. at Hamilton College 1832, studied law in Utica; member of assembly 1846; d. 1863, a. 50.

DEAN, NICHOLAS, d. in New York city, Dec. 22, 1855, a. 64; was a prominent citizen and had held various offices of honor and trust; was president of the Croton Water Board, from 1849 to 1853, and afterwards was president of the Harlem rail road.

DE ANGELIS, PASCAL CHARLES JOSEPH, b. in the island of St. Eustatia, West Indies, Oct. 14, 1763; settled in Holland Patent, Oneida co. N. Y., in 1798; was one of the judges of the court of common pleas, of Oneida co., and president of Hobart Hall Academy; he d. Sept. 8, 1839, at Holland Patent. (*Utica Gospel Messenger, Sept.* 14, 1839; *Jones's Hist. Oneida co.*, pp. 466, 467, 468.)

DEARBORN, GREENLIEF, lt. col. U. S. A.; d. at Brattleborough, Vt., Aug. 9, 1846; entered the army as a lieut. of artillery in March, 1842, and served in the Seminole war.

DEAS, CAPT. EDWARD, of the 4th U. S. artillery was taken prisoner before the battles of 8th and 9th, of May; he was drowned from on board the steamer Yazoo, near Rio Grande city, May 6, 1849.

DEAS, HENRY, d. in Charleston, S. C., Dec. 2, 1846; late president of the senate of that state.

DE BEGNIS, SIGNOR, a celebrated musician; d. at New York, August, 1849.

DE BENNEVILLE, DR. GEORGE, b. in 1760, in Branditown in the 22d ward of Philadelphia; and d. at that place Dec. 17, 1850, in the house where he was b.; a. 90 years 1 month, rendered valuable services in the revolution. (*Simpson's Eminent Philadelphians.*)

DEBERRY, EDMUND, of N. C., member of congress, from 1829 to 1831, 1833 to 1845, and 1849 to 1851; d. in Montgomery co., N. C., Dec. 12, 1859.

DE BLAZMERE, PETER BOYLE, b. in Dublin, Apr. 26, 1783; entered the British, navy served as midshipman under Capt. Bligh, of the County, at the battle of Camperdown, was present at the mutiny of the nore, and emigrated to Canada in 1837; in 1858, he took a seat in the legislative council, and on the remodeling of the Toronto University, he was appointed chancellor, but subsequently resigned; he was also a member of the Anglican synod; d. at Yorkville near Toronto, C. W., Oct. 23, 1860. (*N. Y. Times*, Oct. 29, 1860.)

DEBLOIS, LEWIS, merchant of Boston, went with the British fleet to Halifax, in 1776, and in 1778 was proscribed and banished; he was in England in 1779 and 1784; and later a merchant in St. John, N. B.; where he d. in 1802. (*Sabine's Loyalists.*)

DE BOZE, LIEUT. COL. BARON, of Pulaski's Legion killed at Egg Harbor, N. J., 1778.

DEBRALER, JOHN, a revolutionary soldier; d. at Paris, Ky., Jan. 8, 1850, a. 99 years 6 months.

DE CAMP, JOHN, a soldier of the revolution; d. in New York city, Oct. 24, 1844, a. 84; was 27 years one of the inferior judges of New Jersey.

DEDERICK, STEWART J., a writer for the press; d. at Orange, N. J., June 3, 1874, a. 26; had been employed on *Scribner's Monthly*, and the *N. Y. Tribune.*

DEERING, DR. NICOLL H., of Utica, N. Y.; d. Dec. 19, 1867, a. 73. (*Transac. N. Y. State Med. Soc.* 1868, p. 307.)

DEETH, SYLVANUS G., bibliopolist, long resident at New Brunswick, N. J.; d. at Georgetown, D. C., Feb. 26, 1858. (*Am. Pub. Circular*, Mar. 6, 1858; *Hist. Mag.*, ii, 123.)

D'ESGLIS, LOUIS PHILIPPE MARIAUCHEAU, eighth R. C. bp. of Quebec; b. at Quebec, April 5, 1710; became priest Sept. 18, 1735; coadjutor of Quebec Sept., 1770, he succeeded M. Briand as bp. of Quebec, Nov. 29, 1785; and d. on the Isle of Orleans, June 4, 1788, a. 78 y. 2mo. (*Liste Chron. des Evêques et des Prêtres du Canada.*)

DE FOREST, HENRY ALFRED, M. D., missionary to Syria; b. in Watertown, Ct., May 1814; grad. at Yale in 1832; studied medicine and settled at Rochester, N. Y.; in five years married C. S. Saugeant and sailed for Beirut Syria, as a missonary; he founded a female seminary, acted at times as consul, and superintended the publication of books; he returned in 1854, and d. at Rochester, N. Y., Nov. 24, 1858. (*Hist. Mag.*, iii, 99.)

DE GAICOURIA, DOMINGO, Cuban patriot; garrotted at Havana May 7, 1870.

DE GRAFF, JOHN I., a member of the 20th and 25th congresses; d. at Schenectady, June 26, 1848.

DE GROOT, JACOB, d. at Bound Brook, N. J., July 22, 1843, a. 94; was many years a judge of com. pleas, for Somerset co.; his wife Rachel, d. July 10; they had been m. 59 years.

DE GROOT, WILLIAM, d. near Bound Brook, N. J., Aug. 28, 1840 a. 89; was an officer of the revolution.

DE HART, JACOB, aid-de-camp, Pa.; killed in the revolution, July 21, 1780.

D'HEU, JACQUES, Jesuit missionary, with the Onondagas in 1708, and the Senecas in 1709, said to have been drowned in 1728.

DEH-HE-WA-MIS. (See Jemison Mary.)

DEHUYNE, MAJOR GENERAL, d. July 25, 1780, at New York; a. 60, of the army of his serene highness, the landgrave of Hasse Cassel in the 42d year of his service. He had just returned from Charleston. (*Rivington's Gazette*, July 29.)

DEJIHNONDAWEHHOH, alias John Jemison, grandson of Mary J., "the white woman of Genesee," resided on the Buffalo Reservation till 1845, when he removed to Cattaraugus; he d. there Nov. 8, 1859. (*Hist. Mag.*, iv, 60.)

DEKAY, DR. JAMES E., was educated as a physician and studied in Edinburgh, Paris and Germany. His travels extended to Turkey and sketches of his travels were published in 1831–2. He devoted himself extensively to the study of natural history and he was appointed June 2, 1836, zoölogist to the geological survey of New York, the results of these labors were completed in 5 volumes, 4to, and confer upon him lasting honor. He died at his residence at Oyster Bay, N. Y., Nov. 21, 1851, at the age of 59 years; he married a daughter of Henry Eckford, the celebrated ship builder. (*Am. Jour. Sci. and Arts*, 2d ser., xiii, 300.)

DELAFIELD, BRIG. GEN. RICHARD, of the engineer corps, U. S. A., d. at Washington, D.C., Nov. 8, 1873; was born in New York city, and entered at West Point in 1814. He joined the engineer corps, and advanced through successive grades to the rank of major in 1838, when he was appointed superintendent of the Military Academy; an office he retained until 1845. During the Crimean war, acting under orders from Jefferson Davis, then secretary of war, he proceeded to Europe in company with Gen. McClellan and Major Mordecai, for the purpose of obtaining information in regard to the military service in general, and the changes which had been made in modern warfare. He made an elaborate report, accompanied by maps, giving an account of the siege operations at Sebastopol, and describing several great fortresses of continental Europe. This report, which made a large volume, was printed by order of congress. In 1856 Major Delafield was reäppointed superintendent at the Military Academy, and continued to hold that position until 1861. His advanced age unfitted him for service in the field during the civil war, but he gave the federal cause all the aid he could, and in 1864 was promoted to be brigadier-general. In 1865 he was commissioned major-general by brevet, and the year following retired from the service. The general was one of five brothers, all of whom have reached advanced years and attained prominence in various walks of life.

DELAMATER, JOHN, M.D., LL.D., b. Chatham, New York, April 18, 1787. His ancestors (De La Moitres) were Huguenots fleeing from France to Holland, intermarried with the Dutch, and came to the banks of the Hudson. He became a partner of Dr. Don at Chatham, at the age of 19 exhibiting great talents as a physician. In 1815 located at Sheffield, Berkshire co., Massachusetts. 1823, professor in Berkshire Medical Institute. 1827, prof. at Fairfield, N. York. 1836, prof. at Willoughby, Lake co. 1842, prof. at Cleveland Medical College. 1860, emeritus, lecturing occasionally for several years, always without notes. The lecture room was the glory and substance of his life. An incessant student, with a clear mind, a never failing memory; and a fluent use of language, it is doubtful if, as a college lecturer, he was surpassed, in the U. S. As a consulting physician, his opinions took the first rank, even after the infirmities of a long life prevented active practice. Benevolent, unostentatious, unselfish; he was an acknowledged genius, and a model Christian.

DELANCEY, JAMES, of Westchester co., N. Y., eldest son of chief justice and Lt. Gov. Jas. DeLancey, was educated at Corpus Christi Coll., Camb., rose to the rank of capt., in the royal army, and was aid to Abercrombie, in the campaign against Ticonderoga. He sold his commission soon after his father's death and became his chief heir. His wife was dau. of Chief Justice Allen, of Pa. He went to England in May, 1775, and settled at Bath, having served in gen. assembly in N. Y., from 1769 to 1775. He was attainted and banished Oct. 22, 1779. His son Charles D., was in the British navy and d. single. His son Jas. was lt. col., of 1st Dragoons. Capt. Jas. DeLancey was one of the com'rs for settling claims of loyalists to be adjusted by the British government.—(*Bolton's West Chester*, ii, 252; *Sabine's Loyalists.*)

DELANCEY, JOHN, son of Peter D.; his dau. Elizabeth, became the second wife of Gov. Yates, of N. Y.; he was in the N. Y. assembly in 1793–4–5.

DELANCEY, JOHN PETER, third son of Chief Justice DeLancey, b. July 15, 1753, and d. Jan. 31, 1828; his wife, a dau. of Col. Richard Floyd, d. May 7, 1820; his third son was Bp. Wm. H. DeLancey, of Western N. Y., who d. 5 Apl., 1865.

DELANCEY, OLIVER, third son of Peter D., held a commission in the British navy, but resigned on the approach of the revolution. He d. in West Chester co., Sept. 4, 1820, a. 70 years.

DELANCEY, OLIVER, JR., was educated in Europe and joined the 17th light dragoons, was captain of horse in the British army in 1776, became major of the 17th Regt. of Dragoons, and after André's death adj. gen., with the rank of lt. col. His brutal conduct is said to have caused the death of Gen. Woodhull taken prisoner in 1776. He subsequently rose to be a full general in the British army, and d. near the head of the army list, in 1820. He left one natural son who bore his name, and was killed in Egypt under Abercrombie. (*Sabin's Loyalists*, p. 254; *Bolton's West Chester*, ii, 254.)

DELANCEY, PETER, 3d son of Stephen De Lancey the emigrant of this family, was a man of wealth and influence in the colony of N. Y.

He married a dau. of Lt. Gov. Colden, resided in the borough of West Chester, which he represented in gen. assembly from 1750 to 1768.

DeLANCEY, Stephen, 2d son of Chief Justice DeLancey, resided at De Lanceytown, now the town of North Salem, West. co., N.Y., which he owned. He built the large house now the Academy at that place, in 1769 or 70, was a lay reader in the Episcopal church, and died in 1795 without issue.

DeLANCEY, Stephen, a French Huguenot fled to New York in 1686, married Anne, daughter of Stephanus Van Cortlandt, was an opulent merchant, and d. in 1741, upwards of 80, and worth £100,000 with large tracts of land in New York, West Chester and Ulster counties. His will is dated March 4, 1735. (*Bolton's West Chester*, ii, 252.)

DeLANCEY, Warren, of N. Y., was in 1780, a cornet of dragoons in the British service.

DELANO, Maj. Thomas, a pioneer in Watertown, d. N. Y., 1833. (*New York Reformer*, Dec. 15, 1859.)

DELANY, Sharp, b. in county of Monaghan, Ireland, was a druggist in Philadelphia before the revolution, and an active member of committees favoring independence, subscribed £5,000 to supply the army in 1780. Served in the state legislature, and was collector of the post of Philadelphia in Washington's administration. (*Simpson's Eminent Philadelphians.*)

DeLEON, David, M.D., formerly a medical officer in the army of the United States, was appointed to a responsible place in the medical department of the confederate army, and at the close of the late war returned to New Mexico, where he had long been stationed; d. Sept. 3, 1872.

DELESDERNIER, William, d. at Augusta, Me., Jan. 16, 1842; he was a member of the state senate from Aroostook co., and resided at Baileyville, Me.

DELEVAN, Col. Daniel E., of New York, local politician; d. at Danbury, Conn., March 30, 1870, a. 62.

DELLET, James, d. at Claiborne, Ala., Dec. 2d, 1848, a. 60; native of South Carolina, and one of the early graduates of the S. C. University, removed to Alabama in 1818; was frequently in the general assembly, and in congress from 1839 to 1841, and from 1843 to 1845.

DELLIUS, Rev. Godfreidus, early Dutch minister at Albany, came over in 1683, as a colleague of Dominie Schaats, and remained 16 y.; he sailed for Holland in 1699. (*Rogers's Hist. Discourse*, p. 16.)

DELMONICO, Constantine, caterer; d. at New York, June 11, 1870, a. 48.

DEMERITT, Gen. Samuel, d. at Lee, N. H., July 23, 1840, a. 58.

DEMING, Benjamin F., of Danville, Vt., member of congress in 1833; d. at Saratoga Springs July 11, 1834; was b. at Danville, Vt.; was clerk of his native county 16 years.

DEMURS, Rev. George W., an editor of the *Albany Evening Journal*; d. at Albany, May 25, 1870, a. 34.

DENANT, Pierre, R. C. bp. of Quebec, b. at Montreal July 20, 1843; became priest Jan. 27, 1767, coadjutor of Bp. Hubert, May 23, 1794, and bishop of Quebec, Sept. 4, 1797; he d. at Longueil, Jan. 17, 1806. (*Liste Chron. des Evêques et des Prêtres du Canada.*)

DENIO, HIRAM; a learned and distinguished judge; b. in Rome, N. Y., May 21st, 1799; pursued his academical course at Fairfield academy, and his legal studies partly in Rome, with Judge Hathaway, partly in Whitesboro with Storrs & White, and on their completion, in 1821, he formed a partnership with Wheeler Barnes of Rome; in July, 1826, moved to Utica and became a partner with Edmond A. Wetmore; May 7th, 1834, was appointed circuit judge, and on the 30th of October of the next year, became dist. attorney, and served nine years, his law partner at this time being Ward Hunt; on the 23d of June, 1853, was appointed to fill a vacancy in the court of appeals; twice afterwards was elected to the same position, closing his career in 1866. His decisions are accepted as standards and models. He was also bank com., a trustee of Ham. Coll., a manager of the N. Y. State Lunatic Asylum, and pres. of the Savings Bank of Utica; d. Nov. 5, 1871.

DENIO, JOHN, printer and editor, a relative of the above, d. at Albion, N. Y., March 30, 1859, a. 81; he was b. in Greenfield, Mass., and became the publisher of the *Gazette*, in 1800, the first paper printed there, on which he had served his apprenticeship; he removed to Albany in 1827, where he published the *Morning Chronicle;* he afterwards published papers in Rochester, Medina, and Albion; the tradition of his ancestor is, that he was in the expedition of Hertel de Rouville, which destroyed Deerfield in 1704; that being detained by an attachment formed in that vicinity, his father came from Canada, in pursuit of him, threatening to run him through with his sword if he did not return.

DENISON, REV. HENRY MANDEVILLE, rector of St. Peter's church, in Charleston, S. C.; d. there, Sept. 23, 1858; he was a native of Penn., and educated at the Episcopal Seminary in Virginia; settled at Greenville, S. C., then in Brooklyn, N. Y., and then in Louisville, Ky.

DENMAN, MATTHIAS, d. at Springfield, N. J., Jan. 24, 1841, a. 91; was one of the first owners of the land on which Cincinnati is built.

DENMEAD, ADAM, proprietor of Monument Iron Foundry, Baltimore;

DENNIS, CYRUS CURTIS, b. in Scipio, N. Y., May 6, 1806; d. in Auburn, June 1, 1866; was a manufacturer of iron work and machinery at Auburn; pres. of that village in 1840, 1, 2, and first mayor in 1848; became a carpet manufacturer, and supt. of railroads. (*Hall's Auburn.*)

DENNIS, LITTLETON P., member of congress in 1833 from Md.; d. at Washington, April 14, 1834; grad. at Yale in 1803.

DENNISON, DANIEL, of Ipswich, Mass.; counselor from 1650 to 1681, and major gen. of militia; was com'r for settling disputes in Maine and with the Dutch of Manhattan; d. in 1683. (*Bradford's M. E. Biog.*)

DENNY, HARMAR, d. Jan. 29, 1852, in Pittsburg, Pa., a. 58; grad. at Dickinson College; was a member of the Penn. legislature and in constitutional convention, and held various public offices in his native city.

DENNY, NATHANIEL PAINE, d. in Barre, Mass., Aug. 23, 1856, a. 85; his name was originally "Thomas Denny;" was b. in Leicester, Mass.; grad. at Harvard, in 1797; settled as a lawyer, and represented Leicester 11 years in the house, and in 1824–5 was in the senate; served many years as county com'r, and pres. of the Leicester Bank; from 1845 to June 1856 resided in Norwich, Conn.

DENT, GEN. LOUIS, d. at Washington, D. C., March 22, 1874; brother-in-law of Pres. Grant; was a lawyer, but drifted into southern politics during the reconstruction period, and in 1869 was nominated for governor of Mississippi by the national union republicans, a new party, organized on the basis of equal rights, general amnesty, and reconciliation; it was expected that he would receive the support of the administration in the canvass, but prior to his nomination President Grant wrote him to this effect: "I would regret to see you run for an office and be defeated by my act, but as matters now look, I must throw the weight of my influence in favor of the party opposed to you;" Judge Dent replied, defending the claims of his party, and asserting that their platform ought to be more acceptable to the people than that of the "bitter-enders," as his opponents were termed; although the democrats made no nomination, but gave their votes to Mr. Dent, he was badly beaten, receiving only 38,097 votes against 76,186 for Gov. Alcorn, the regular republican nominee; he withdrew after this from politics, and engaged in legal business of a general character at Washington, and was thenceforth a resident there.

DE PEYSTER, ABRAHAM, of N. Y., was a captain in the N. Y. loyalist volunteers and second in command at the battle of King's mountain in 1780, and surrendered after the death of Ferguson; went to St. John, N. B.; drew a city lot and half pay; was a treasurer of the colony and a col. of militia; d. there previous to 1799. (*Sabine's Loyalists.*)

DE PEYSTER, FREDERICK, of N. Y.; was a captain in the N. Y. loyalist volunteers in 1782; went to St. John, N. B., where he drew a city lot; in 1792 he was a magistrate of the co. of York; afterwards returned to the states. (*Sabine's Loyalists.*)

DE PEYSTER, JOHN, b. in N. Y., Jan. 14, 1693–4; moved to Albany, and married Anne Schuyler; he was recorder of Albany, from 1726 to 1728, and mayor from 1729 to 1731, and in 1732; in 1734 he became a com'r of Indian affairs, and in 1755, for paying the forces of Johnson's expedition. (*Munsell's Ann. Alb.*, vii, 312.)

DE PEYSTER, JOHN WATTS, JR., son of Gen. John W. De Peyster, died 12th of April, 1873, in N. Y. city. The deceased served during the early part of the rebellion as volunteer aid-de-camp on the staff of his cousin, Gen. Philip Kearney, and was especially commended for his gallantry at the battle of Williamsburg. At the battle of Chancellorsville he was chief of artillery of the second division, sixth corps, with the rank of major. For his gallantry on that and other occasions, on the recommendation of Major Gen. Hooker, he was promoted successively to be lieutenant colonel and colonel.

DEPUY, DR. CORNELIUS E., of New York; d. 1822, a. 30.

DERBY, RICHARD, JR., revolutionary patriot, merchant of Salem, Mass., took an active part in the revolution, was in several conventions and the provincial congress, a counselor and representative. (*Bradford's N. E. Biog.*)

DERBY, SAMUEL G., d. in Weston, Mass., Jan. 17, 1843, a. 76; formerly a merchant of Salem, and a graduate of Harvard in 1785.

DERING, DR. NICOLL HAVEN, b. on Shelter Island, January 1, 1794; was graduate at Yale College in 1813 and attended lectures at the College of Physicians and Surgeons of New York, taking his degree in 1817; the following year he was made health commissioner of the port of New York; after twenty years of practice in the metropolis, he retired to Rome in 1843, whence in 1847 he moved to Utica; died Dec. 19, 1867.

DE ROSSET, LEWIS H., of N. C., a member of the council, and took measures forbidding a whig convention in 1775; he was in communication with Gov. Martin after the royal authority had ceased.

DERRICK, WILLIAM S., d. in Washington, D. C., May 15, 1852, a. 50; b. in West Chester, Pa.; was a clerk in the department of state in 1827, and well versed in the Spanish and French languages.

DESMOND, DANIEL J., for many years consul for the Italian states; d. at Phila., July 29, 1849.

DE TOCQUEVILLE, ALEXIS C. H. CLAREL, was appointed in 1831 to visit the United States, on behalf of the French government to inspect our penitentiary systems; he wrote a work entitled *Democracy in America*, which has been widely read, and attracted great attention; he d. April, 1859, a. 53.

DE VEAUX, ANDREW JR., of Charleston, S. C., held an office under the crown after the fall of Charleston, in 1780, and lost his estate by confiscation.

DE VEAUX, JACOB, of S. C.; was banished, and in 1782, his estate was confiscated as a tory.

DE VEBER, GABRIEL, of N. Y.; entered the royal service; and in 1782 was lt. col. of the prince of Wales's Am. vols.; he settled in New Brunswick; was a grantee in St. John, drew half pay, and in 1792, was sheriff of the co. of Sudbury and col. of militia; d. there; his wife, a dau. of Dr. Nathaniel Hubbard of Stamford, Ct.; d. in King's co., N. B., in 1813.

DE VEBER, GABRIEL JR., of N. Y.; was in 1782, a lt. in De Lancey's 3d battalion; he went to St. John, N. B., after the revolution, was a grantee in that city and drew half pay; d. in New Brunswick.

DEVEREUX, JOHN CORISH, an early and leading merchant of Utica; b. at Enniscorthy, county of Wexford, Ireland, Aug. 5, 1775; he came to America, shortly before the outbreak of the rebellion of 1798; in 1802 he settled in Utica as a merchant, in which business he was uniformly successful and acquired a large property; he was prominent and influential in the community; he was president of the United States Branch Bank from its organization in Sept. 1830, and also of the Utica Savings Bank, of which he was one of the founders; he was mayor of the city in 1839 and 1840, being the first mayor elected by the people; aided by his brother Nicholas and a few others, he established St. John's, the first Catholic church of the place; of this and other charitable objects he was a munificent patron; d. Dec. 11, 1848.

DEVEREUX, JOHN CORISH JR., son of Thos. and adopted son of John C. Devereux of Utica; b. in Ireland Aug. 15, 1817; entered Yale in 1834, but left it for St. Mary's Coll., Maryland, intending to become a Catholic priest; this design he abandoned, studied law in Utica, and practiced in N. Y. city, where he d. Oct. 1861.

DEVEREUX, NICHOLAS, brother of John C., came to Utica, in 1806, and was at first a clerk and afterwards a partner of his brother John; acquired a large property and became an extensive land holder in Alleghany county, N. Y.; he took an active part in the organization of the Utica and Schenectady rail road company and in other public improvements; at the time of his death he was a director in the N. Y. Life Insurance and Trust company, the Utica Savings Bank and the Utica Steam

Woolen mills, and a manager of the N. Y. State Lunatic Asylum; he was a large benefactor to the Catholics of the state; he d. Dec. 29, 1855.

DEVEZAC, MAJ. AUGUSTE, was b. in St. Domingo in 1780, and was the son of a wealthy planter; he was educated at a military school in France and when his family fled to the U. S., he studied medicine in N. C. and practiced for sometime in Accomac co., Va.; he removed thence to New Orleans; studied law with Edward Livingston and became a celebrated pleader in criminal trials; he served under Jackson in the war; and in 1831, was appointed chargé to Holland where he remained sometime; in 1840, he was in the N. Y. assembly; d. at N. Y., Feb. 15, 1851, a. 70 years. (*Stryker's Am. Reg.*, vi, 213.)

DE VICO, FRANCIS, for some years a professor of astronomy in Rome, and supt. of the observatory, where he made great discoveries in astronomical science, and was honored with several gold medals, and other testimonials; in the political disturbances which followed; he came to the United States, and intended to accept the professorship of astronomy in Georgetown, D. C.; was on business in England connected with that college, and d. there Nov. 15, 1848.

DE VILLERS, LOUIS, d. at Ogdensburgh, N. Y., April 29, 1840, a. 83; native of Abbeville, France; came to America in 1783, having served as a lieutenant under Louis XVI.

DEVLIN, REV. FRANCIS, a Roman Catholic priest, fell a victim to the yellow fever at Portsmouth, Va., the autumn of 1855.

DEVOE, REV. DAVID, d. in Turin, N. Y., April 10, 1844, of apoplexy.

DEWEY, DANIEL NOBLE, b. in Williamstown; grad. at Yale in 1820, and engaged in the practice of law; he held many places of trust, civil and judicial, and was for many years sec. and treas. of Williams Coll.; d. in Williamstown, Jan. 14, 1859, a. 59.

DEWEY, MAJOR LEWIS F., d. at Jacksonville, Fla., Nov. 5, 1868; was from Lowville, N. Y., where he is buried. He had been in active service in the late war.

DEWEY, DR. ROYAL DWIGHT, b. in Westfield, Mass., Oct. 3, 1891; was a physician at Turin, N. Y., and d. there, Nov. 13, 1839; he held several public offices in that town.

DEWEY, TIMOTHY, civil engineer, native of N. E., and long resident in N. Y. city where he constructed the first gas works; he died at the residence of his son William in Lyme, N. Y., Nov. 18, 1853. (*Hough's Hist. Jeff. Co., N. Y.*, p. 429.)

DEWEY, DR. WALTER, d. in Collinsville, N. Y., Feb. 28, 1821; he was a pioneer in Turin, and built the first house in Turin village. (*Hough's Hist. Lewis Co.*, p. 208.)

DE WITT, CHARLES G., d. at Newbury, N. Y., April 12, 1839; late chargé d'affairs to Central America and member of congress in 1829–30.

DE WITT, JACOB H., b. in Ulster co., N. Y.; was in congress from New York from 1819 to 1821, and in N. Y. assembly in 1839 and 1847; d. at Kingston, N. Y., Jan. 30, 1857, a. 73.

DE WITT, REV. JOHN, native of Catskill, N. Y.; settled at Albany as colleague of the Rev. Melancthon Bradford of the R. P. D. church, in 1813; was a grad. of Nassau Hall in 1809; was elected prof. in the

Seminary at New Brunswick, and d. there Oct. 11, 1831, in his 42d year. (*Rogers's Hist. Discourse, R. P. D. Ch., Albany.*)

DE WITT, MOSES, b. in Deerpark, N. Y., Oct. 15, 1766, was a pioneer and prominent settler of Onondaga co., N. Y., a surveyor, and at the time of his death one of the most considerable landed proprietors of western New York; was surrogate of Herkimer co., and afterwards of Onondaga co.; many years a justice of the peace, judge of the county courts, and a prominent officer of militia; d. near Jamesville, Onondaga co., Aug. 15, 1794, a. 28. (*Clarke's Onondaga*, ii, 230.)

DE WITT, SIMEON, surveyor general of New York, b. Dec. 15, 1756, in Ulster co.; grad. with honors at Queen's (now Rutger's), Coll., joined the army, witnessed Burgoyne's defeat; and in 1775 was appointed assistant geographer to the army, and in 1780, succeeded Col. Robert Erskine as geographer; he was appointed surveyor gen. of the U. S., May 30, 1796, but declined; in 1784 he was appointed surveyor gen. of N. Y., and held by repeated appointments till his death, through a highly important period when most of the state lands were surveyed and sold; in 1798 he was elected a regent, in 1817 vice chancellor and in 1829 chancellor; he was a member of many learned societies, and author of numerous scientific notices and suggestions; he d. at Ithaca, N. Y., Dec. 3, 1834, a. 79. (*Rogers's Hist. Discourse*, p. 103; *Am. Jour. Sci. and Arts*, xxvii, 395; *Eulogium by Dr. T. Romeyn Beck.*)

DEWITT, REV. THOMAS, D.D., during 47 years one of the pastors of the Collegiate Ref. church, in N. Y. city; d. May 18, 1874, in his 83d year.

DEWOLF, WILLIAM HENRY, d. in New York city Nov. 19, 1853, a. 51; son of James D. of Rhode Island; b. at Bristol, R. I., May 15, 1802; served for a time in the navy; at the time of his death, was U. S. consul at Dundee, Scotland, to which office he was appointed by Pres. Pierce.

DEWOLFE, JAMES, d. in the city of New York, Dec. 21, 1837; late of Bristol, R. I. and U. S. senator in congress in 1821–5.

DEXTER, AARON, M.D., physician and chemist of Chelsea, Mass.; grad. at Harv. in 1776; was fond of professional and scientific studies especially chemistry, of which in 1783 he became the first professor in Harvard; d. in 1816. (*Bradford's N. E. Biog.*)

DEXTER, GEORGE, d. at Geneva, Switzerland, July 16, 1872; was of the American News Company; in the news business since 1843 in New York city.

DEXTER, S. NEWTON, contractor, manufacturer and banker; b. May 11th, 1785 in Providence, R. I., where his father, Andrew Dexter, had been the first manufacturer of cotton goods in the United States; entered Brown University, but soon left it, to engage in business in Boston; in 1815 he removed to Whitesboro, and two years later took and fulfilled a contract for building a section of the Erie canal; in 1824–9 he was engaged in constructing the Chesapeake and Delaware canal; returning to Whitesboro he became agent of the Oriskany Manufacturing Company; in 1832 assumed the charge of the Dexter Manufacturing Company near Oriskany; was also largely interested in manufactures elsewhere in the state of N. Y. and Elgin, Ill; a trustee of Hamilton College; for several years supported a professorship, giving the college in all about $32,000;

president of the bank of Whitestown from 1833 to 1853; in 1840 canal commissioner; in 1850 manager of the N. Y. State Lunatic Asylum; d. Nov. 18, 1862.

DIBBLE, REV. FREDERICK, b. at Stamford, Ct.; grad. at King's Coll., N. Y.; was a tory; went to New Brunswick, where he became rector of the Episc. ch. at Woodstock; d. there in 1826, a. 73; his widow d. in 1838, a. 83.

DIBBLE, HENRY, d. in Albany, N. Y., Feb. 20, 1840, a. 62; was a merchant.

DIBBLE, TYLER, lawyer at Stamford, Ct.; was in 1775, capt. of the 1st mil. co. of that place and a man of note; became a loyalist; in 1778 with 16 others was taken on L. I. by a party of whigs from Ct.; his property was confiscated; was deputy agent for the transportation of loyalists from N. Y. to New Brunswick; drew two city lots in St. John in 1784; some years after committed suicide. (*Sabine's Loyalists.*)

DIBBLE, WALTER, of Stamford, Ct.; settled at St. John, N. B. in 1784; d. at Sussex Vale in 1817, a. 53; was a tory from Ct.

DICK, JOHN, a loyalist from the states; settled in New Brunswick in 1783; d. at St. George in 1839, a. 95.

DICKENS, REV. JOHN, Meth. Ep., book agent; b. in London, joined the Methodists in 1774; traveled extensively during the revolution; was many years in charge of the book printing of the soc. at N. Y., and Phila.; where he d. of yellow fever, Sept. 27, 1798, a. 52. (*Lee's Hist. Meth.*, p. 253.)

DICKENSON, DR. L. L., d. at Colchester, Conn., Aug. 2, 1868.

DICKERSON, DAVID W., late a member of congress; d. in Franklin, Tenn., April 27, 1845.

DICKEY, JOHN, d. in Beaver co., Pa., March 14, 1853; was in congress from Washington and Beaver counties from 1843 to 1845, and from 1847 to 1849; at the time of his death, was U. S. marshal for the western district of Pennsylvania.

DICKINSON, CHARLES, a soldier of the revolution and for many years an alderman in the city of New York; d. at Tappan, N. Y., Aug. 21, 1836, a. 84.

DICKINSON, DAVID W., member of congress from Tenn., from 1833 to 1835, and from 1843 to 1845; d. at Franklin, Tenn., April 27, 1845.

DICKINSON, MAJOR, EDMUND B., Va.; killed at battle of Monmouth Va., June 28, 1778.

DICKINSON, JOHN, an eminent lawyer; d. in Caroline co., Va., Nov. —, 1835, a. about 48 years.

DICKINSON, JOHN D., b. in Middlesex co., Conn., in 1767; grad. at Yale in 1785, was in N. Y. assembly in 1817, from Rensselaer co., and in congress from 1819 to 1823, and from 1827 to 1831; d. at his home in Troy, N. Y., Jan. 28, 1841.

DICKINSON, RUDOLPHUS, of Lower Sandusky, O., a member of the 30th and 31st congresses; d. at Washington, March 12, 1849.

DICKINSON, REV. R. W., D.D., several years a pastor in N. Y. city; d. Aug. 16, 1874, in his 70th year.

DICKINSON, SAMUEL F., d. at Hudson, Ohio, April 22, 1838, a. 63; grad. at Dartmouth in 1795, and formerly a lawyer of Amherst, Mass.

DICKINSON, S. N., d. at Roxbury, Mass., Jan. 16, 1849, a. 47; was an enterprising printer.

DICKSON, DAVID, joined the revolution Feb., 1775, at Snow Camp on Reedy river; commanded a volunteer co., under Gen. Williamson in the Cherokee country in 1776; in 1777 he was stationed with a co. of minute men on the Ga. frontier, and in 1778 went to the attack upon Savannah; he returned to S. C., and d. in Fayette co., Ga., in 1830, a. 79; he was a militia general.

DICKSON, DAVID, of Jackson, Miss., d. at Little Rock, Ark., July 31, 1836; he was a member of congress from Mississippi.

DICKSON, JOHN, d. in Ohio, April 25, 1859, a. 110 years.

DICKSON, JOHN, member of the N. Y. assembly in 1829 and 1830; and of congress from New York in 1831–5; d. at West Bloomfield, Ontario co., N. Y., Feb. 22, 1852.

DICKSON, ROBERT, a loyalist, settled in Nova Scotia, was member of the house of assembly, and magistrate of the dist. of Colchester; he d. in 1835.

DICKSON, SAMUEL, member of congress from the Albany district in 1855–7; d. at his home in New Scotland, N. Y., May 3, 1858, from the effects of a spinal injury received while in the faithful discharge of his public duties at Albany; he was educated as a physician.

DICKSON, DR. SAMUEL HENRY, d. at New York city April 3, 1872.

DIGGES, DR. WILLIAM J., d. in Opelousas, La., Oct. 21, 1853, a. 34.

DILL, LIEUT. JAMES, Pa.; killed in the revolution Sept. 11, 1777.

DILL, COL. JOHN, b. in Shawangunk, Ulster co., N. Y., Nov. 27, 1757; served in the revolution; after the war was settled for a short time in N. Y., as a broker, and then at Middletown Point, N. J., as a merchant; in 1808, returned to Ulster co., and in 1813 settled in Onondaga co.; in 1828, made his home at Camillus where he d. Sept. 21, 1846. (*Clarke's Onondaga*, ii, 317.)

DILLARD, DR. THOMAS, surgeon U. S. A.; d. at Philadelphia, Pa., March 1, 1870, a. 70.

DILLET, JAMES, b. in S. C., was an early graduate of the university in that state; became a lawyer and settled in Alabama, in 1818, where he became judge of the circuit court, and was often in the legislature; was in congress from 1839 to 1841, and from 1843 to 1845; d. at Claiborne, Ala., Dec. 21, 1848, a. 60.

DILLON, ROBERT JAMES, d. in New York city, Nov. 26, 1872; was a prominent lawyer, and corporation council, under Mayors Westervelt and Wood; he took an active interest in the Irish Emigrant Soc., and was vice pres. of the Emigrant Saving Inst. Mr. D. was a patron of the fine arts, and his refined taste and appreciation of landscape scenery contributed in a great degree to the advancement of many of the delightful portions of the Central Park, in which he became especially interested before it was laid out, and for the establishment of which he labored assiduously before the legislature in 1856; and for the advancement of which he toiled with varying earnestness, as commissioner, from his appointment in 1857. After the disruption of the *ring*, and the resignation of Commissioners Sweeny and Hilton, he took renewed interest in all matters relating to the improvement of the Central Park and enterprises of a kindred nature; and as long as he was able to attend meetings of the commissioners maintained his interest in the enterprise.

DIMON, LIEUT. COL. DAVID, Conn.; killed in the revolution, Sept. 17, 1777.

DIMOND, FRANCIS M., several years U. S. consul at Vera Cruz, and afterwards lieut. gov. of R. I.; d. in Bristol, R. I., April 23, 1859, a. 63.

DINWIDDIE, REV. J. L., professor in the Theological Seminary at Allegany; d. at Baltimore, Jan. 11, 1849.

DISBOROUGH, DANIEL W., d. at New Brunswick, N. J., Sept. 10, 1837, a. 65; formerly cashier of the state bank at that place.

DISNEY, DAVID T., native of Maryland, but in 1820, removed to Cincinnati, and was repeatedly elected to each house of the legislature, and was thrice speaker in the senate; he was in congress, from 1849 to 1855; d. at Washington, March 14, 1857.

DIX, CHARLES TEMPLE, American artist of merit; and youngest son of Gov. Dix of New York; d. in Paris, March, 1873.

DIX, COL. ROGER S., a native of N. H., and brother of John A. Dix of N. Y.; was a son of Col. Timothy Dix, who lost his life in Wilkinson's expedition in 1813; he grad. at West Point in 1832, and at once volunteered to attend Gen. Scott on the Black Hawk expedition; after serving several years in the qr. m. department, he was appointed by Polk pay master in the army; he served with distinction in the Mexican war, and was brevetted lt. col. for his gallantry at Buena Vista; d. at Hillsboro, Pa., on his way from New Orleans to Washington, Jan. 7, 1849. (*Stryker's Am. Reg.*, ii, 252.)

DIXON, CHARLES, a loyalist, went to New Brunswick, near the close of the war; d. in 1817, a. 89.

DIXON, REV. DAVID R., teacher of grammar school in Utica, 1809–12; became first principal of Utica academy, 1816–18, during which time he studied divinity; was ordained as a Presbyterian minister and settled in Mexico, Otsego co.

DIXON, JAMES, ex-senator in congress from Connecticut; d. in Hartford, Conn., March 27, 1873, a. 58; b. in Enfield, Conn., Aug. 5, 1814; graduated at Williams College, Mass., in 1834, and adopted the profession of law. With natural tastes for politics and political life, he became prominent as a whig leader in the state very soon after entering upon the practice of his profession, and was always thereafter more devoted to politics and political controversies than to law. He was a member of the lower house of the Connecticut legislature in 1837, 1838, and 1844, and of the state senate in 1854, and took a leading position in all debates upon political questions. He represented the 1st (Hartford) district in congress from 1840 to 1849. During this time he was a constant contributor to the editorial columns of *The Hartford Courant*, then the leading organ of the whig party. In 1854, when the whigs carried the state, for the first time for several years, he was elected to the state senate; upon the expiration of Mr. Gillette's term, in 1856, Mr. Dixon was elected senator, and was reëlected in 1862; he attended the Philadelphia Johnson convention of 1866, and, with Senator Doolittle, was quite active in the effort to organize a Johnson party. This ending in failure he identified himself with the democratic party, who nominated him for reëlection in 1868, when they being in a minority in the legislature, the nomination was merely a compliment. The following year they nominated him for congress in the 1st district, but he was defeated by the late Hon. Julius L. Strong. Since then he has lived a very retired and quiet life at his residence, in Hartford, taking no part in politics and mingling but little in society.

DIXON, JOSEPH, a loyalist from the states; d. at Hampton, N. Brunswick in 1842, a. 92 y.

DIXON, MATTHIAS F., b. in Plainfield, Conn., in 1774; grad. at Brown Uni., in 1799; studied law, and settled in R. I., in 1802; in 1813 was elected to the general assembly, and continued by 34 successive elections, from 1839 to 1842; he was a senator in congress; d. at Washington, D. C., Jan. 29, 1842.

DIXON, THOMAS, d. at Boston, Mass., Sept. 15, 1849, a. 68; b. in Westminster, England, in 1781, removed early with his parents to the continent, and in the French revolution narrowly escaped death; came to America in 1816, and in 1822, settled in Boston; he was knight of several orders, and consul for the Netherlands, for the states of Mass., Me., N. H., and R. I.

DOBALDO, MANUEL, Mexican general and statesman; d. N. Y., June 19, 1865, a. 53 y.; late minister of foreign affairs of the Mexican republic, and governor of the state of Guanajuato.

DOBBS, EDWARD BRICE, a loyalist of N. C.; his property was confiscated in 1777.

DOBSON, CAPT. HENRY, Md.; killed in the revolution, Sept. 8, 1781.

DODD, REV. BETHEUL, first pastor of the united congregation of Whitesboro and old Fort Schuyler; b. in Bloomfield, N. J., 1767; grad. at Queen's, now Rutger's College in 1792, licensed the following year by the Presbytery of N. Y. and N. J.; he was settled at Whitesboro, Aug. 21, 1794; he d. April 11, 1804.

DODGE, SAMUEL, of Cleveland; native of New Hampshire; b. in 1776; came to northern Ohio, in 1797; and d. in 1855.

DOGGIT, JOHN, a tory of Middleborough, Mass.; went to New Brunswick and d. on the Island of Grand Menan in the Bay of Fundy in 1830, a. 70.

DOHERTY, JOHN, N. Y. state senator, b. Jan. 16, 1826, in N. Y.; became a lawyer, was elected by the democrats to the senate of 1858–9; d. at Albany, April 20, 1859. (*Murphy's Biog. of Legis.* 1858, p. 51.)

DOLAN, REV. JAMES, pastor of St. Patrick's R. C. church, Baltimore, Md.; d. Jan. 13, 1870.

DONALDSON, ALEXANDER, served in the British army as adj. and lieut. in the French war; became captain March, 1770, and major Dec. 1770, but his health not permitting him to serve he sold out. (*Com. Wilson's Orderly Book*, 98.)

DONALDSON, DR. MILES L., d. at Baltimore, Md., May 19, 1845, a. 28.

DONOVAN, ADJT. RICHARD, Md.; killed at Camden, Aug. 16, 1780.

DOOLEY, THOMAS., captain in the revolution; was killed in a skirmish with the Indians near the Ocanee river, Ga., July 22, 1776.

DOOLITTLE, DR. A. F., of Herkimer, N. Y.; d. ——— 1872.

DOOLITTLE, CHARLES H., b. in Herkimer, 1816, educated at Fairfield Academy, and at Amherst College, where he was graduated; studied law with Mr. Ford at Little Falls, and afterwards with Denio and Hunt at Utica, and was admitted to practice in 1839; in 1869, after thirty years of active duty as a practitioner at the bar, he was chosen justice of the Supreme Court; he was a learned lawyer and an excellent judge; in May 1874, he was lost at sea on his way to Europe.

DOOLITTLE, GEN. GEORGE, d. at Whitesboro, N. Y., Feb. 21, 1825, a. 65; b. in Middletown, Conn., emigrated in 1786, to Oneida co.; was a soldier of the revolution and much in public affairs; in 1811, he served Oneida co., in assembly. (*Jones's Oneida Co.*, p. 794.)

DOOLITTLE, HARVEY W., M. D., b. in 1789, reared at German Flats, N. Y.; and began practice in 1809, at Herkimer village; he was a member of the state med. soc.; d. in 1853. (*Tr. N. Y. St. Med. Soc.*, 1854, p. 92.)

DOOLITTLE, JESSE W., merchant of Utica, where he began in December, 1805, and continued in successful business nearly to the period of his death, Sept. 18, 1845.

DORCHESTER, ELIASAPH, printer, editor and teacher; b. in Farmington, Conn., 1780; learned the printing business in Utica of Thomas Walker, with whom in 1814–18 he was associated in the publication of the *Columbian Gazette;* established the *Oneida Observer* at Rome, in 1818, which he soon removed to Utica; during the years 1821–3 he filled the office of county clerk; his later years were chiefly spent as teacher of the public schools of Utica; d.

DORR, SAMUEL, d. in Boston, Mass., Dec. 18, 1845, a. 70; had been a representative and senator in the general court, and held many civil offices.

DORSEY, CLEMENT, associate judge of the first judicial dist. of Maryland; d. at Leonardstown, Md., Aug. 6, 1846, in his 69th year; filled many public stations in that state; from 1825 to 1831 was in congress.

DOSQUET, PIERRE HERMAN, fourth R. C. bp. of Quebec; b. at Lille, Flanders; came to Canada July, 1721; returned in 1823, was made bp. of Samos, *in partibus* and assistant of the pontifical throne; returned to Canada Aug., 1729; under authority from M. Mornay was confirmed as coadj. July 24, 1730; went to France in 1734; was made bp. of Quebec; returned the same year; resigned June 25, 1739; became vicar gen. of the archbp. of Paris; d. there March 4, 1777, a. 86. (*Liste Chron. des Evêques et des Prêtres du Canada.*)

DOTY, LOCKWOOD LYON, b. in Groveland, N. Y., May 16, 1827; was many years in the offices of canal appraiser and N. Y. state treasurer; deputy in the latter many years; priv. sec. to Gov. Morgan and for a short time, to Gov. Seymour; chief of bureau of mil. statistics (rank of col.), 1863–66; assessor internal rev. 6th dist. N. Y., 1869; editor of

Livingston Republican at Geneseo, 1869–70; treas. N. O., Mobile and Chatanooga R. R., 1870; pension agent N. Y., 1871–3; d. at Jersey City, Jan. 18, 1873; buried at Geneseo.

DOUGHERTY, THOMAS M., shot by an assassin near St. Louis, Mo., July 15, 1838; one of the judges of the St. Louis county court.

DOUGHTY, REV. JOHN, Episcopal; grad. at King's College in 1770; went to England; was ordained for the church at Peekskill; removed to Schenectady to which place he was appointed in 1773; in 1775 service was suspended and he was treated rudely; was twice taken prisoner; retired to Canada in 1777; was appointed chaplain of the royal regiment of N. Y.; remained at Montreal till Oct. 1781; went to England; returned to Canada June 12, 1784, having been appointed missionary at Sorel; resigned his mission in 1803, having for a short time in 1793, 4, been in charge of St. Anne's church, Brooklyn; his name was sometimes written Doty. (*Doc. Hist. N. Y.*, iv, 494.)

DOUGHTY, JOSEPH C., a leading citizen of Poughkeepsie, N. Y., d. there April 7, 1873; had been a prominent shipping merchant and freighter, and represented that district in the legislature.

DOUGLAS, ISAAC R., judge of the 13th circuit of Va.; d. of apoplexy at his residence near Charlestown, Va., Oct. 24, 1850, in his 61st year. (*Stryker's Am. Reg.*, v, 187.)

DOUGLAS, THOMAS, judge of supreme court Florida; b. at Wallingford, Ct., April 27, 1790; traded in Madison, Ind.; studied law, and was appointed U. S. dist. atty., for the E. dist. of Florida, in May, 1826, and held till a state government was formed; he was app. by the gov. judge of the circuit court for E. circuit, Sept. 27, 1845; and in 1853, he was elected judge of the supreme court; d. Sept. 11, 1855, a. 65 years. (*Autobiography of T. D.*, New York, 1856, 12mo, pp. 132, with portrait.)

DOUNIE, JOHN, a loyalist of Camden, S. C.; held office under the crown after the fall of Charleston, and his estate was confiscated.

DOUSMAN, COL. HERCULES, d. Sept. 12, 1868, at Prairie-du-chien, Wis.; b. at Michilimackinack in 1800, and prominently connected with the fur trade of the North West. (*Collec. Minn. Hist. Soc.*, iii, 192.)

DOVAN, JOSEPH M., b. in Phil.; grad. at the univ. of Pa.; studied law with David Paul Brown; was admitted April 3, 1824; practiced till 1820, when he became associate judge of the court of gen. sessions for Phila.; in 1837 he was in the constitutional convention; in 1843 he resumed his profession in which he greatly excelled, especially in the trial of criminal cases; d. June 6, 1859, in his 59th year. (*Hist. Mag.*, iii, 224.

DOVE, DAVID JAMES, a popular satirical poet; b. in England; settled in Philadelphia, as a schoolmaster before 1759; and was a teacher in the Phila. Acad., but disagreed with the trustees; and in 1762, became head master of a seminary at Germantown, but was not long retained. (*Simpson's Eminent Philadelphians.*)

DOW, REV. DANIEL, many years a trustee of Yale Coll., and one of the founders of the Theological Seminary at East Windsor; d. at Thompson, Ct., July 19, 1849, in the 77th year of his age; and the 51st of his pastoral relation with the 1st Cong. ch. of that place. (*Stryker's Am. Reg.*, iii, 237.)

DOWNER, Dr. Avery, d. at Preston, Ct., July — 1854, a. 91 y. 8mo.; b. at Preston, Nov. 17, 1762; admitted to practice in 1784; and was a witness of the massacre at Fort Griswold. (*Norwich Aurora*, July 19, 1854.)

DOWNS, Solomon U., d. at Orchard Springs, Ky., Aug. 14, 1854; collector of the port of New Orleans; and from 1847 to 1853, senator in congress for Louisiana.

DOXTATER, Peter, b. at German Flatts; prisoner with the Indians 3 y. and a soldier of the revolution; cong. granted him a pension in 1834; d. at Adams, N. Y., Dec. 1, 1842, a. 92.

DOXTATER, Robert B., engineer; b. at Adams, N. Y.; was many years a merchant; in 1849, became supt. of the Watertown and Rome R. R. and in 1853, of the Mich. Southern and N. Ind. R. R.; d. of apoplexy at Laporte, Ind., May 17, 1853, a. 39. (*Hough's Hist. Jeff. Co., N. Y.*, p. 429.)

DRAKE, Dr. Benjamin, of New York; d. Jan. 11, 1871, a. 65.

DRAKE, Rev. Benjamin M., D.D., was a native of North Carolina; removed to Kentucky when a child, and came to Mississippi, in 1822; d. in Jefferson city, Miss., May 8, 1860, a. 59.

DRAKE, Dr. Charles, of New York city; d. ——— 1832.

DRAKE, Francis, a loyalist from the states; d. at Queensbury, New Brunswick, in 1836, a. 81; he was several years in the service of the crown.

DRAKE, George K., lately a judge of the supreme court of Morris co., N. J.; d. in that state, May 6, 1837, a. 48.

DRAKE, Jeremiah, a loyalist, settled in New Brunswick, in 1783; d. at St. John, in 1846, a. 80.

DRAKE, John R., an early settler of Tioga co., N. Y.; was in congress, from 1817 to 1819; county judge in 1833; and in assembly, in 1834; d. March 21, 1857, at Owego, N. Y.

DRAKE, Capt. Joshua, an officer of the New York militia in the revolution; joined an expedition into the Indian country; and was killed in battle at Miami, Nov. 4, 1791.

DRAKE, Lieut. Thomas, Va.; killed in the revolution, Jan. 21, 1777.

DRAKE, Uriah, of N. Y., a loyalist, went to St. John, N.B.; was a grantee of that city; d. at Carlton, N. B., in 1832, a. 70.

DRAPER, Henry, director of English Opera comique and classical concerts; d. at Providence, R. I., Aug. 2, 1868.

DRAPER, James, a soldier of the revolution; d. in Warren co., Ga., a. 83; he was an early settler of Warren co.

DRAPER, Richard, printer and owner of the *Mass. Gazette, and Boston News Letter*, succeeded his father John D. in the business; he was government printer, and took a decided course in favor of the crown; he was a man of feeble health, and of delicate and gentle mind and manners; d. June 6, 1774, a. 47, without children; his wife Margaret, with the aid of John Howe continued his paper till the evacuation in 1776, went to Halifax and thence to England; where she d. about the close of the century; she drew a pension from the British government. (*Sabine's Loyalists.*)

DRAPER, SIMEON, SEN., was a soldier of the revolution for thirty years a member of the state legislature and a member of the state convention of Mass., in 1820, for revising the constitution; he long resided at Brookfield, Mass., and d. Dec. 28, 1848, a. 84; he was the father of Lorenzo D., formerly consul at Paris, and of Simeon D., of N. Y. city. (*Hunt's Biog. Panorama*, p. 294.)

DRAPER, WILLIAM, of Pontiac, Mich., d. at Mackinaw, Aug. 9, 1858; he was b. in Dedham, Mass., and grad. at Harvard, in 1803; he settled as a lawyer in Marlborough, Mass., and in 1832 removed to Nashua, N. H.; in 1833, he settled at Pontiac, Mich., where he afterwards resided.

DRAYTON, HENRI, a well known opera singer, d. in New York city, July 30, 1872; b. in Philadelphia, in 1822; finished his musical education in Paris, spent several years in Europe, engaged in his profession and in 1859 came with his wife to the United States; he was not only a good musician, but an actor of ability and earnestness, and the author of several plays and operas.

DRUMGOLE, GEORGE C., b. in Va.; bred a lawyer, and in congress from Virginia from 1835 to 1841, and from 1843 to 1847; d. April 28, 1847.

DRUMMOND, ALEXANDER, was in 1782, surgeon of the king's Am. regiment of loyalists.

DRUMMOND, JAMES, a loyalist, was one of the grantees of St. John, New Brunswick in 1783.

DRUMMOND, ROBERT, was major of the 2d battalion of New Jersey, loyalist volunteers in 1782.

DRURY, CALVIN, d. at Pittsford, Vt., Dec. 22, 1843, a. 78; was forty years a deacon in the Congregational church at that place.

DRY, WILLIAM, collector of customs and member of the royal council of N. C.; he sided for a time with the loyalists, and after the adoption of the constitution in 1776 was a member of the new council. (*Sabine's Loyalists.*)

DRYSDADE, HUGH, gov. of Va., succeeded Gov. Spotswood in Sept., 1722, and being a man of very ordinary talent, and chiefly anxious to retain place, yielded to party influences, and closed a weak administration by death in July, 1726.

DUANE, ANTHONY, from cong., in the co. of Galway, Ireland, was in youth a purser in the British navy, on the N. Y. station, resigned and settled as a merchant there, where he d. Aug. 14, 1747; his son Richard, d. at Kingston, Jamaica, in 1740, a midshipman, and Abraham d. at sea in 1767, a post captain in the British navy; his son James was afterwards mayor of N. Y., and a distinguished citizen. (*Doc. Hist. N. Y.*, 1064.)

DUANE, JAMES, eminent lawyer and statesman, b. in N. Y. city, Feb. 6, 1732–3, third son of Anthony D., studied law with Jas. Alexander, father of Lord Stirling, and was admitted to the supreme court, Aug. 3, 1754; he m. the eldest dau. of Robert Livingston, proprietor of the manor of L.; he became deeply engaged in law suits relating to the colonial boundaries, and in the Vermont controversy, was council for Trinity church, N. Y., and engaged in several contested election suits; in 1765, he began to settle Duanesburgh, N. Y., and in 1774 was chosen to continental congress where he remained till 1784, excepting a part of 1776–7, when he was serving in the state convention; he served in the state senate from 1783 to 1785 and from 1788 to 1790; was mayor of New York from Feb. 5, 1784 to Sept. 29, 1789, and in 1788 was in the state convention for adopting the U. S. constitution; in 1789, he was appointed U. S. dist. judge for N. Y., by Washington, without his previous knowledge; he resigned Apr. 8, 1794, retired to Duanesburgh, where he d. Feb. 1, 1797. (*Doc. Hist. N. Y.*, iv, 10, 61; *Munsell's Hist. Series*, v, 169; *Sargent's Loyalist Poetry*, 157.)

DU BOIS, REV. GAULTHERUS, of the Dutch Ref. ch., N. Y.; b. in 1671 at Streef-Kerk, Holland; was educated at Amsterdam and Leyden, and was examined before the classis of Amsterdam, July 1, 1697; he was settled at New York, in Oct. 1699, a. 28, and served regularly till Sept. 29, 1751; d. Oct. 1751. (*Doc. Hist. N. Y.*, iii, p. 537.)

DU BOIS, PETER, of Ulster co., N. Y.; lost his property by confiscation and was banished in 1779; he is thought to have been the Col. D. of a loyalist corps under Sir John Johnson. (*Sabine's Loyalists.*)

DUBOSE, WILLIAM, d. at St. Stephen's parish, S. C., Feb. 24, 1855, a. 67; b. in that place; grad. at Yale, in 1807; was a planter, and avoided public life but served as state senator, and in 1836, was chosen lieut. gov., for 2 years.

DUBOURG, WILLIAM LOUIS VALENTINE, D.D., archbishop of Besançon, Fr., and formerly bp. of New Orleans; b. Feb. 14, 1766, at Cape Francois, St. Domingo; educated in Sulpitian Seminary, Paris; was driven by the revolution to Bordeaux, and to Spain, from whence he sailed to Baltimore, in 1794; in 1796, he was sent to the coll. at Georgetown, as pres.; thence in 2 y. to Havana, and in 1799, to Baltimore; in 1802, he sailed to New Orleans, with the design of teaching, but returned again to Balt., and devoted several years to active labors in teaching clerical duties and the founding of Catholic institutions; in 1812, he was appointed administrator apostolic, of New Orleans, took an active part in encouraging resistance to the British in Jan. 1815, and sailed soon after for Europe; he was consecrated bp. of N. O. by the pope, Sept. 24, 1815; he became a resident of New Orleans, in 1823, having tarried in St. Louis, until then; he sailed for France, June 1826, to enter upon the diocese of Montauban, and Feb. 1833, the archdiocese of Besançon; d. Dec. 12, 1833, a. 65. (*Metropolitan Cath. Almanac*, 1839, p. 50, with portrait.)

DUCATEL, JULIUS TIMOLEON, was b. at Baltimore, June 6, 1796; and was the eldest son of Eome Ducatel a pharmaceutist of that city; he was educated at Saint Mary's College, and after his course of study engaged in his father's business but finding that this pursuit was not congenial to his mind his father indulged him with ample opportunities for study in Paris, from whence he returned in 1822, with an intimate acquaintance with the sciences of chemistry and geology; he was appointed not long after as a professor of natural philosophy in the Mechanics Institute of Baltimore, and then as professor of chemistry and geology in the university of Maryland, in both which he acquired much reputation; in 1830, he was elected to the chair of chemistry in the medical department of the University; in 1832, he was appointed with J. H. Alexander upon a survey for a new map of the state in connection with a geological survey, which was suspended in 1841, from want of funds by the state;

during these labors he was appointed a professor in St. John's Coll., which he resigned in 1838 or 9, to devote himself more exclusively to geology; in 1843 he accompanied Nicollet on a geological tour to the upper Mississippi, and in 1846, he visited the Lake Superior region; he returned from the journeys with impaired health; and d. at Baltimore, April 23, 1849; he was the author of a manual of toxicology, and for some time editor of the *Baltimore Times.* (*Am. Jour. Sci. & Arts*, 2d Ser., viii, 146.)

DUCHÉ, Anthony, ancestor of Rev. Jacob D., and one of Penn's emigrants. (*Simpson's Eminent Philadelphians.*)

DUCHÉ, Thomas Spence, b. in Philadelphia, about 1766; was a painter, and his father being a tory clergyman, removed to England, where he enjoyed the instructions of Benj. West. He painted a portrait of Bishop Seabury, which was engraved by Sharpe.

DUCKINFIELD, Sir Nathaniel, baronet, a member of the council in N. C.; lost his estate by confiscation in 1779.

Du COUDRAY, Gen. Holstein, H. L. V., formerly a distinguished officer under Napoleon; after the dethronement of the emperor he came to America, and resided some years in New York, and for eight years in Albany, where he d. April 23, 1839; he was the author of a *Life of Gen. Lafayette.*

DUDLEY, David, d. at Roxbury, Mass., April 21, 1841, a. 54; late president of the Traders' Bank in Boston.

DUDLEY, Edward B., d. November —, 1855, at Wilmington, N. C.; was in congress from 1829 to 1831; and in 1836 was elected governor for 4 years; afterwards became president of the Wilmington and Raleigh (now Weldon) rail road co.

DUDLEY, Major Samuel E., Col. Warren's regt. and scalped in invasion of Niagara frontier, Dec. 30, 1813.

DUFF, James, actor, d. at Brooklyn, July 22, 1870.

DUFFIELD, Edward, was a clock and watch maker of Philadelphia; executed the first medals ever struck in the province of Pennsylvania; was a friend and executor of Dr. Franklin. (*Simpson's Eminent Philadelphians.*)

DUGAN, Thomas, d. at Columbia, S. C., Oct., 1839; for the last twenty years a member of the South Carolina legislature.

DULANEY, Walter, was in 1782 a major of the Md. loyalists.

DULANEY, William H., a lawyer; d. at Richmond, Va., May 2, 1870.

DULANY, Lloyd, of Annapolis, Md.; took a bold stand against the whigs; became a refugee; went to England; in 1779 addressed the king; was a lawyer.

DULCE, Domingo, formerly captain general of Cuba; d. at Madrid, Nov. 23, 1869; was sent to Cuba in 1860; was succeeded by Gen. de Rodas.

DUMAN, J. N., d. at New Orleans, La., March 25, 1841; formerly a judge of the city court.

DUMAS, Hippolite, d. at Washington, D. C., July, 1841, a. 52; native of France; formerly a captain of the U. S. engineers.

DUNBAR, CAPT. JOSEPH, d. at New Bedford, Mass., July 20, 1841, a. 54.

DUNCAN, ALEXANDER, d. in Cincinnati, O., March 2, 1852; member of congress from 1837 to 1841, and from 1843 to 1845.

DUNCAN, DANIEL, b. in Penn. July 22, 1806; removed to Newark, Ohio; was elected to the 30th congress; d. at Washington, D. C., May 18, 1849.

DUNCAN, COL. JAMES, b. in Orange co., N. Y. in 1814; grad. at West Point in 1835; served in the Seminole war; was highly distinguished in Mexico, as commander of light artillery; for these services he was promoted to the office of captain and colonel and in 1849 to the office of inspector general; d. at Mobile, July 3, 1849. (*Stryker's Am. Reg.*, iii, 234.)

DUNCAN, CAPT. RICHARD, a partizan tory officer of the revolution; formerly of Schenectady; d. there in Feb. 1819; was for a time member of the executive council of Upper Canada.

DUNCAN, THOMAS, a lawyer of Philadelphia; was appointed a judge of the supreme court in March, 1817, and held till his death, Nov. 16, 1827.

DUNHAM, CYRUS L., member of congress from Indiana, from 1849 to 1855; d. at Valley Farm, Ind., Oct. 25, 1856.

DUNHAM, DANIEL, soldier of the revolution; d. at Mexico, Oswego co., March 31, 1860, a. 98; was at Bunker hill, Camden, Yorktown, and the crossing of the Delaware. (*Hist. Mag.*, iv, 125.)

DUNLAP, MAJ. ALEXANDER, d. in Jackson, Fla., Nov. 10, 1853, a. 67; b. in Ky.; volunteered as a private in the war of 1812; a prisoner; was promoted to a captain; in the Mexican war was major.

DUNLAP, JOHN, a loyalist of N. C.; lost his property by confiscation in 1779.

DUNN, GEORGE G., was bred to the bar and reached a high position as a lawyer; was in congress from the 6th dist. of Indiana in 1847–9; d. at Bedford, Lawrence co., Ind., Sept. 4, 1857, a. 44.

DUNN, JOHN, a loyalist of N. Y.; was one of the founders of St. Andrew, New Brunswick; for many years was comptroller of customs at that port; d. April 14, 1829, a. 76. (*Sabine's Loyalists.*)

DUNN, REV. JOHN P., pastor of St. John's R. C. church, Phila.; d. Dec. 28, 1869.

DUNN, JOSIAH, d. in Portland, Me., Feb. 3, 1843, a. 65; late sheriff and for many years a representative in the legislature of Mass.; senator and counselor from Oxford county.

DUNN, OSCAR J., lieut. gov. of Louisiana (colored); d. at New Orleans, La., Nov. 22, 1871.

DUNN, CAPT. PETER, Va.; killed in the revolution, Sept. 16, 1777.

DUNTON, WILLIAM, d. in Northampton co., Va., June 1, 1835, a. 60.

DUPERRON, FRANCOIS, jesuit missionary; arrived in Canada in 1640; returned to France in 1650; was missionary at Onondaga from 1651 to 1658; went again to France in 1658, and to Canada in 1665; d. at Ft. St. Louis, Chambly, Nov. 10, 1665.

DUPONT, GIDEON JR., of Charleston, S. C.; was a loyalist, and was banished; in 1782 his property was confiscated.

DUPREE, COL., mortally wounded by the hand of his son-in-law, Graves himself being the assailant, in Hinds co., Mississippi, June 8, 1850. (*Stryker's Am. Reg.*, iv., 466.)

DUPUY, CHARLES H., prof. of the French language; d. at Baltimore, Md., 1869, a. about 51; was a prominent free mason.

DURALL, LIEUT. EDWARD, Md., killed in revolution at Camden, N. J., Aug. 16, 1780.

DURANG, CHARLES, an actor and author, d. at Philadelphia, Pa., Feb. 15, 1870, a. 70; b. in Phila., son of John D., an actor of Hallam's Am. co., at the old S. st. theatre in 1785; was a dancer, and had been ballet master in almost every theatre in the United States; wrote a hist. of the Phila. stage from 1752 to 1854, for the *Philadelphia Despatch.*

DURANT, CHARLES P., d. in Jersey city, March 2, 1873, a. 68; was the author of several books of a scientific character; he made the first balloon ascension in America, in 1833, from the battery, New York; subsequently he made 14 aerial voyages, on one occasion descending into the Atlantic ocean, and at another time landing on the steamer Independence in Chesapeake bay; he was the author of a valuable work on the shells and sea-weeds of New York harbor, for which he received a medal from the government; his latest book was on astronomy, which has as yet only been printed for private circulation among scientific men; he was a gentleman of wealth, and was the owner of Kepler market, Jersey city.

D'URBAN, SIR BENJAMIN, entered the British army in 1793; served in the peninsular and French wars, and at the time of his death was commander of the British forces in North America; he d. at Montreal, May 25, 1848, a. 72. (*Stryker's Am. Reg.*, ii, 503.)

DURELL, DANIEL M., b. in Mass.; grad. at Dartmouth, in 1794; was in congress from 1808 to 1809, and d. in 1841, a. 71.

DURHAM, EARL OF (John George Lambton), formerly governor general of Canada; d. at Cowes, Eng., July 28, 1840, a. 48; he was the eldest son of Wm. Henry Lambton, of Lambton castle, in the county of Durham, and by the death of his father at the age of 5 years he succeeded to a large estate; on his majority, he was elected to parliament, and in 1828, was raised to the peerage; he went out as governor of Canada in 1838, but finding himself not so well supported in the measures as he expected, he returned home the same year, and afterwards published his report on Canada, which was highly commended. (*Am. Alm.*, 1842, p. 289.)

DURRIN, NOAH, an aged Methodist Episcopal minister; d. in Lowville, N. Y., Jan. —, 1853.

DURYEE, REV. PHILIP, d. at Morristown, N. J., in the 76th year of age and the 52d of his ministry, Feb. 27, 1850.

DUTTON, GEORGE, musician and music dealer, being the first who sold musical instruments in Utica, whither he came about 1822.

DUTTON, JOHN, a native of New Haven, Ct., and late of La.; d. in Mexico, June 18, 1850.

DUY, ALBERT W., b. in Philadelphia April 9, 1823; was early a subject of religious impressions and grad. at the Theological Seminary of

Virginia; was ordained in July, 1845; settled over St. Ann's church, Brooklyn, N. Y., but d. April 13, 1846, at his father's house in Philadelphia. (*Simpson's Eminent Philadelphians.*)

DWIGHT, REV. HENRY, b. June 25, 1783, in Springfield, Mass.; was the youngest of four brothers, all of whom have occupied conspicuous positions as bankers; grad. at Yale Coll.; engaged for a time in mercantile pursuits; these he abandoned to devote his life to the Christian ministry; his professional studies were begun with Rev. Dr. Dwight of New Haven, and finished at Princeton Theolog. Sem.; from Feb. 1813 to Oct. 1817 held the pastorate of the Pres. ch. in Utica; the failure of his voice compelled his return to secular business; removed to Geneva and established the Geneva Bank, of which he was pres. until the expiration of its charter in 1853; was 15 years a trustee of Ham. Coll.; thirty a trustee of Auburn Theolog. Sem.; one of the first directors; twenty years pres. of the Am. Home Missionary Society; d. at Geneva, Sept. 6, 1857.

DWIGHT, HENRY W., d. in New York city, Feb. 21, 1845; was in congress in 1821 to 1831.

DWIGHT, THOMAS, grad. at Harvard in 1778; was in congress from Mass. from 1803 to 1805; d. in 1819.

DYCKMAN, COL. GEORGE W., d. in New York, May 21, 1868; was in the Mexican war which he entered as a captain, and at the close of the war was brevetted lieut. col. for bravery and meritorious conduct; was register of New York; in the late rebellion entered the 1st N. Y. vols. as lieut. col. and succeeded to the colonelcy.

DYE, LIEUT. JONATHAN, Va.; killed in battle Sept. 11, 1777.

DYER, CHARLES JR., passed midshipman in the navy; drowned at Pensacola, Fla., Aug. 23, 1850, in attempting to save the crew of a vessel in distress.

DYER, JOHN J., native of Pendleton co., Va.; was appointed by Pres. Polk in 1846 judge of the Iowa district; d. at Woodstock, Va., in July, 1855, a. 46.

DYER, WYNDHAM D. M., British consul at Baltimore; d. there April 23, 1859.

DYSON, DAVID, an English naturalist, who made large collections of natural history in the U. S. and Central America; d. at Rusholme, Eng., Dec. 10, 1856.

EAKIN, CONSTANT M., d. in Philadelphia, Oct. 2, 1869, a. 75; b. in France; grad. at West Point, in 1817, and after 20 y. service in the corps of topographical engineers, obtained the rank of major; was largely concerned in organizing the U. S. coast survey; resigned in 1850, and was engaged in civil engineering till the war; in 1862, although at the advanced age of 62, became colonel in the Pennsylvania volunteers.

EARLE, CALEB, d. in Providence, R. I., July 13, 1851, a. 80; was several years in the legislature, was formerly lieutenant governor and twice an elector of president, viz., in 1824 and 1828.

EARLL, JONAS, JR., d. in Syracuse, N. Y., Oct., 1846, a. 60; was canal commissioner from 1842 to 1846; was in assembly from Onondaga co., in 1820–1, and in the state senate in 1823–6.

EARLY, RT. REV. JOHN, D.D., oldest bishop of the Meth. Episc. church south; d. at Lynchburg, Va., Nov. 5, 1873; he was b. in Virginia in 1785; joined the conference of that state and became an itinerant minister; he filled successively the offices of secretary of conference, presiding elder, and delegate of the general conference. At the general conference of 1846 — the first held by the separately organized church of the South — he was appointed book agent, and held that office until elected bishop, in 1854.

EASBY, WILLIAM, late commissioner of public buildings; d. at Washington, D. C., July 29, 1854.

EAST, BRIG. GEN. WELLINGTON H., d. at Bloomsburg, Pa., Nov. 5, 1871.

EASTERBROOKS, JAMES, a loyalist, was an early settler in New Brunswick; a magistrate and member of the house of assembly for many years; d. at Sackville, N. B., in 1842, a. 85.

EASTMAN, BENJAMIN C., d. in Platteville, Wis., Feb. 5, 1856; was from 1851 to 1855 a representative in congress from Wisconsin.

EASTMAN, MAJ. ELBRIDGE GEORGE, b. in Bridgewater, N. H., in 1813, and resided in Concord; was some years in office in Washington, but about 1840, removed to Knoxville, Tenn., and established the *Argus;* afterwards was for many years principal editor of the *Union and American;* he was for a time, sec. of the house of representatives of Tenn., and of the Agricultural Bureau of that state; d. Nov. 23, 1859, a. 46.

EASTMAN, DR. ELI, a pioneer settler of Adams, N. Y.; d. Sept. 6, 1844, a. 77.

EASTMAN, REV. ORNAN, sec. Am. Tract Soc.; d. in New York, April 24, 1874, in his 78th year.

EASTON, GILES C., merchant, at Lowville, N. Y.; d. Feb. 19, 1860.

EASTON, JOHN, attorney-gen. of R. I. many years, and deputy governor, in 1674–5; d. at Newport, Dec. 18, 1705; he left a manuscript account of Philip's Indian war, which was first printed at Albany, in 1858.

EASTON, RUFUS, established and edited at Whitesboro, in 1794, the *Western Centinel,* the first paper started in Oneida county; he was a lawyer by profession; he removed about 1808 to St. Louis, Miss., and became a representative of that territory in the U. S. congress, about 1814.

EASTON, WILLIAM L., a successful merchant, and in early life a printer; b. in Hancock, Mass., March 13, 1806; d. at Lowville, N. Y., where he spent most of his life, March 7, 1865; was much concerned with politics, and surrogate of Lewis county, N. Y., in 1840–1844.

EATON, REV. ASA, b. at Plaiston, N. C., July 25, 1778; grad. at Harvard, in 1803; was rector of Christ church Boston, 1805–1825, and for 8 years a city missionary; from 1837 to 1841, he was connected with a literary institution in New Jersey, and afterwards with the Church of the Advent in Boston, where he d. March 24, 1858.

EATON, EBENEZER, printer, from Worcester, Mass., and a brother of General Eaton, who afterwards distinguished himself in the war with Tripoli; in coöperation with his brother-in-law, Thomas Walker, he set up at Rome, N. Y., in Aug. 1799, the *Columbian Patriotic Gazette,* which was the first paper of the place, and the third in the county of Oneida; he left the paper and the village at the end of eighteen months.

EATON, GEORGE W., LL.D., pres. of Madison University and Hamilton Theological Seminary; b. near Huntington, Pa., July 3, 1804; removed when an infant to Ohio; and grad. at Union Coll., in 1829; was one year tutor, and then became principal of the Union Academy at Belleville, N. Y.; in 1831, removed to Georgetown College, Ky., and in 1833, became prof. of mathematics in what was then known as the Hamilton Lit. and Theol. Inst., at Hamilton, N. Y., and since 1846, Madison University; in 1856, became pres.; d. Aug. 3, 1872. (*Regents' Report*, 1873, p. 633.)

EATON, REV. ISAAC, settled in Hopewell, N. J., in 1748; and remained pastor of the Baptist church at that place till his death, July 4, 1772, in his 47th year.

EATON, JOHN H., senator from Tennessee, from 1818 to 1829; sec. of war under Gen. Jackson from 1829 to 1831; governor of the territory of Florida, from 1834 to 1836; and minister to Spain from 1836 to 1840; d. in Washington, D. C., Nov. 17, 1856, a. 70.

EATON, SAMUEL A., a journalist, d. at Richmond, Va., April 27, 1870.

EATON, TIMOTHY DWIGHT, son of Prof. Amos Eaton of Troy, adjunct prof. in the Rensselaer school; d. Nov. 14, 1828, at Troy, a. 21 years; he had evinced much enthusiam in natural history. (*Am. Jour. Sci. and Arts*, 1st ser., xv, 404.)

EATON, MAJ. —— Ga., killed at Augusta, Ga., May 21, 1781.

ECCLES, JOHN DICKS, d. near Fayetteville, N. C., a. 64; b. at Fayetteville, N. C., March 29, 1892; grad. at Yale in 1715; studied law and became an eloquent lawyer and orator, was several years a member of the house of commons, in the general assembly and was noted for his wit and eloquence.

ECHOLLS, R. M., pres. of the senate of Ga., lived in Ware co.; d. in Mexico and was brought home for burial.

ECKFELDT, JACOB R., chief assayer of the U. S. mint at Phila.; d. Aug. 9, 1872, a. 70; had been forty years employed in the mint, and was a son of Adam E., who was appointed chief coiner in 1794.

ECKHARD, GEORGE B., d, in Charleston, S. C., Feb. 11, 1845, a. 51, judge of the city court of Charleston, S. C.

EDDY, JAMES, gen. supt. of Am. telegraph co.; b. at Ithaca, N. Y.; was a pioneer in the telegraph business and built the first line from Boston, east to Calais, Me.; he d. at Burlington, Vt., Aug. 23, 1858; a. about 40. (*Hist. Mag.*, ii, 315.)

EDDY, NORMAN S., secretary of state of Indiana; d. at Indianapolis, Ind., Jan. 28, 1872.

EDDY, ZACHARIAH, a native of Middleborough, Mass.; d. in that town Feb. 14, 1860; a. 79; he graduated at Brown University in 1779, was a lawyer, and a diligent student of New England history.

EDES, PETER, printer, d. at Bangor, Me., March 29, 1840, a. 85; son of the editor and publisher of the *Boston Gazette*, at the period of the revolution.

EDGAR, WILLIAM, d. May 22, 1845, a. 77, at Rahway, N. J.; he had served frequently in the state legislature, and for the last 14 y. was pres. of the bank of Rahway.

EDMOND, William, b. in South Britain, Conn., Sept. 28, 1755; grad. at Yale in 1773; was a volunteer soldier in the revolution, and received a wound at the burning of Danbury, which made him lame for life; was a lawyer; a member of the legislature; one of the council; a judge of the supreme court, and from 1798 to 1801, member of congress; d. at Newton, Conn., Aug. 1, 1838.

EDMONDS, Hiram Augustus, M.D., b. in Ridgefield, Ct., Sept. 21, 1824; was several years a teacher at Southport; grad. at Alb. Med. Coll., in 1853, and settled in Albany, where he d. April 13, 1857. (*Munsell's Ann. Alb.*, ix, 112.)

EDMONDS, John Worth, an eminent lawyer, jurist, legal writer and spiritualist; b. in Hudson, N. Y., and d. there in 1873. (*Drake's Dict. Am. Biog.*)

EDSALL, Joseph, a pioneer settler of Madrid, N. Y.; b. in Vernon, Sussex co., N. J., in 1763; d. in Madrid, in 1844.

EDSON, Capt. Alvin, d. on board the U. S. frigate Raritan, on her passage from Havana to Norfolk, July 15, 1847; was distinguished at the siege of Vera Cruz, and other operations in the gulf; was native of Vermont, and entered the marine corps in 1822.

EDSON, Dr. Josiah, of Bridgewater, Mass., and known by the two most infamous appellations of *Rescinder* and *Mandamus Councillor;* he was driven from home in 1774; went in 1776 to Halifax, and thence to N. Y., where, or on L. I., he d. soon after; he had grad. at Harvard in 1730, was a col. of militia, and in most respects a useful citizen. (*Sabine's Loyalists.*)

EDWARDS, Maj. Benjamin W., d. at Clinton, Miss., Aug. 18, 1838, was a candidate for the office of governor at the time of his death.

EDWARDS, Evan, major in the American army, originally a Baptist and designed for the ministry, he imbibed the spirit of the times; entered the revolution at the beginning, and was one of the defenders of Ft. Washington where he was taken prisoner; he was afterwards an aid to Gen. C. Lee, and received a third of his estate.

EDWARDS, George C., b. in Stockbridge, Mass., Sept. 28, 1787; d. at Bath, Steuben co., N. Y., Nov. 18, 1837; was an able lawyer, and from 1826 to 1838, first judge of Steuben co.

EDWARDS, Henry P., one of the justices of the supreme court of the state of New York, for the 1st dist.; d. Feb. 16, 1855.

EDWARDS, John, d. in Chester, Pa., June 25, 1843; was a member of the last two congresses (1839–1843).

EDWARDS, Lyman, of New Jersey, d. Aug. 12, 1870.

EDWARDS, Col. Munroe, b. in Danville, Ky., 1808; a noted forger and swindler; d. in Sing Sing prison, Jan., 1847; he was largely concerned in business in the south west, and aided the Texan revolution.

EGAN, Dr. Michael, first Roman Catholic bishop of Philadelphia; d. in that city, July 22, 1814, in his 53d year; was consecrated bishop, Oct. 10, 1810.

EGAN, Dr. William D., d. in the co. of Derry, Ireland, came young to America, taught schools in Canada, N. Y., and Va.; began medical practice in Mississippi, in 1832, went thence to Chicago, and by a series of successful operations in real estate acquired great wealth; he was elected recorder of Cook co., in 1843, and held 4 years; in 1852 he was in the state legislature, and in 1856, was a candidate for lieut. gov.; he d. at Chicago, Ill., Oct. 28, 1860. (*N. Y. Times*, Nov. 2, 1860).

EICHELBERGER, REV. LEWIS, b. in Pa., removed in early life to Winchester, Va., and was several years editor of the *Winchester Virginian*, and afterwards prof. in Lexington Coll. S. C.; he was a Lutheran divine, and d. Sept. 17, 1859; a. about 60. (*Hist. Mag.*, iii, 354).

EIGHTS, JONATHAN M.D., of Albany; b. in Albany, Nov. 26, 1773; began medical practice in 1795, near Albany; went to Canajoharie in 1797, and in May, 1810, again settled in Albany, and gained a large practice; he d. Aug. 10, 1848. (*Tr. N. Y. St. Med. Soc.*, 1857, p. 42; *Munsell's Ann. Alb.*, ix, 99).

ELD, LT. HENRY, JR., a naval officer of high standing, and a member of the exploring expedition under Capt. Wilkes, in 1838–42; d. in March 12, 1850, of yellow fever at sea, on board the Ohio, soon after leaving Rio Janeiro; he was a son of Henry Eld, of New Haven, Ct. (*Am. Jour. Sci. and Arts*, 2d Ser., x, 137.)

ELHOLM, AUGUSTUS CHRISTIAN GEORGE, b. in the Duchy of Holstein, Denmark, came to America early in the revolution and served in the dragoons, rendering important services in Georgia, under Gov. Telfair; he became adj. gen. of Ga., and planned a system of defense against the Indians; when Geo. Mathers was gov. a collision occurred with Elholm who was court martialed and cashiered; he had a grandiloquent style of expression and writing; his death occurred at Augusta, Ga., in 1799. (*White's Hist. Ga.*, p. 628.)

ELIAS, DOMINGO, sec. of state of Peru, under Gen. Castilla; d. at Lima, Dec. 4, 1867, a. 62.

ELIOT, THOMAS D., ex-member of congress; d. at New Bedford, Mass., June 14, 1870, a. 64.

ELL, THOMAS, African, d. in Somerset co., N. J., May 1, 1842, a. 104, as nearly as could be ascertained.

ELLERY, CHRISTOPHER, grad. at Yale, in 1787; was senator in congress, from R. I., from 1801 to 1805, and in 1806 was appointed commissioner of loans; was appointed collector at Newport, in 1828; and d. in 1840.

ELLERY, JOHN GRAEM, was educated at Hamilton Coll., N. Y., engaged in geology and mineralogy as the great study of his life, completed his studies in the Royal Academy of Mines in Freiberg, Saxony, and while engaged in a geological survey of North Carolina, sickened and d. at Gold Hill, N. C., June 2, 1855. (*Am. Jour. Sci. & Arts 2d* ser., xx, 296.)

ELLICE, RT. HON. EDWARD, English statesman; d. Sept. 16, 1863, at his summer residence at Ardochy in Scotland, a. 81; he was the owner of extensive estates in Canada, and at Ticonderoga, Little Falls, and elsewhere in the state of New York, and was largely concerned in mercantile affairs, and in British politics. (*Alb. Eve. Journal*, Oct. 12, 1863.)

ELLIOT, ANDREW, collector of customs in N. Y., from 1764 to the revolution; in 1774, he seized some arms and was threatened with tar and feathers; he continued in office under the British, and in 1782, was lieut. gov., receiver gen. of quit rents supt. gen. of police, and chief of the superintendent dep. estate in 1777; in 1780, he was one of the three comr's sent to save Andre; his estate was confiscated after the war. (*Sabine's Loyalists.*)

ELLIOT, JOEL M., major in U. S. army; killed in battle with the Cheyennes and Arapahoes, on the Washita river, near Antelope Hill, Indian territory, 1869.

ELLIOT, JOHN, grad. at Yale in 1794; resided in Sunbury, Liberty co., Ga.; was a senator in congress from 1819 to 1825; and d. in 1827.

ELLIOTT, JAMES GURNSEY, b. at Catskill, N. Y.; grad. at Hamilton Coll., in 1823; d. in N. Y. city, Feb. 14, 1862.

ELLIS, CALEB, b. at Walpole, N. H.; grad. at Harvard, in 1793; was admitted to the bar, and settled at Claremont, N. H.; was in congress from 1805, to 1809; a member of the council, and in 1811, was elected to the state senate; in 1812, was presidential elector, and in 1813, became a judge of the supreme court of N. H., in which office he continued till his death, May 9, 1816, a. 49.

ELLIS, ELIZABETH E., wife of Rev. Geo. E. E., pastor of the Harvard church, Charlestown, Mass.; d. April 8, 1842, a. 27.

ELLIS, HARVEY W. d. near Fairfield, Pickens co., Ala., Nov. 12, 1842; was of Tuscaloosa, Ala., and 41 years old; native of Fayette co., Ky., and in 1802 settled as a lawyer in Alabama; was several times in the general assembly. (*Am. Almanac*, 1844, p. 311.)

ELLIS, HENRY, colonial gov. of Georgia; b. in 1720, was sent as agent of parliament, on an exploring expedition to find a new passage to the Pacific in 1746, and his report gained him a fellowship in the royal society; he was appointed lieut. gov. of Ga., Aug. 15, 1756, and arrived Feb. 16, 1757; he found the colony distracted and defenseless, but evinced great firmness and decision, and was so successful that he was appointed governor-in-chief of the colony, May 17, 1758; in Nov. 1759 his failing health induced him to solicit a recall, and he left Nov. 2, 1760, amid the sincere regrets of the people; he was afterwards, for 2½ years, gov. of Nova Scotia; he was compelled by ill health to visit France and Naples; d. in 1805, over 85 years of age. (*White's Hist. Ga.*, p. 185.)

ELLIS, REV. JOSEPH S., d. in Harvard, Mass., June 19, 1842; pastor of the Meth. Epis. ch., a. 31, and the 10th of his ministry.

ELLIS, LYMAN, early proprietor of Ellisburgh, N. Y., which is named from him; was from Troy, N. Y., and d. in Ellisburgh, March 31, 1847.

ELLIS, MORREL, brother of the above; d. in Utica in 1806, a. 46.

ELLIS, CAPT. PAUL, Mass.; killed at Monmouth, June 28, 1778.

ELLISON, HENRY, settled from N. E., in Herkimer, N. Y., several miles north of the village; was many years engaged in farming and tanning, and in 1836 was a presidential elector; he d. about 1850. (*Benton's Herkimer Co., N. Y.*, p. 308.)

ELLWELL, MRS. MEHETABELL, d. at Saco, Me., a. 100.

ELMER, DANIEL, d. at Bridgeton, N. J., July 3, 1847, a. 64; late a judge of the supreme court of New Jersey, and a member of the constitutional convention of 1844.

ELMER, JOHN EDGAR, b. at Unionville, N. Y., Jan. 17, 1848; grad. at Ham. Coll. in 1870; d. at Morehead, Minn., May 27, 1874.

ELSEFFER, JOHN, d. at Redhook, N. Y., Feb. 18, 1873, a. 74 y. 5 m. 24d.

ELY, SUMNER, M.D., was b. at Lyme, Ct., May 22, 1787; and grad. at Yale Coll., in 1804; he studied medicine with Dr. Tho. Brodhead of Clermont, N. Y,. and in 1809, took a diploma from the Greene co. med. soc.; he settled in practice at Clarksville, Otsego co., N. Y., where he afterwards resided; in 1840, he became president of the State medical soc., and March 14, 1843, a fellow of the Coll. of Physicians and Surgeons of the University of N. Y.; in 1836, he was in assembly, and in 1839, he was elected to the state senate for four years; he d. Feb. 3, 1857. (*Tr. N. Y. State Med. Soc.*, 1858, p. 23, with portrait.)

ELY, WILLIAM, grad. at Yale, in 1787; was in congress from Mass., from 1805 to 15; d. in 1817.

ELY, WILLIAM M., late member of assembly from Broome co.; d. at Binghamton, N. Y., Feb. 6, 1872, a. 53.

ELZEY, ARNOLD, ex-confederate brig. gen., at Baltimore, Md.; d. Feb. 21, 1871, a. 55; b. in Maryland, in 1816; grad. at West Point; served in the Florida and Mexican wars, and resigned to join the southern cause at the beginning of the late war.

EMANUEL, DAVID, governor of Georgia; settled in Ga., about 1770, in Burke co., served in the revolution; was captured by loyalists, sentenced to be shot, but the gun missed its aim and he fled, nearly naked; he was many years in the legislature; was pres. of the senate and in 1801, gov.; d. in 1808, a. 64. (*White's Hist. Ga.*, p. 221.)

EMATHLA, TUSTENNUGGEE, a Creek warrior, was full blooded and b. on the Tallapoosa in 1793; he attached himself to the party wishing to emigrate; and in the Florida war rendered important services; he perished with 236 of his nation, on board the steamer Monmouth with four of his children. (*White's Hist. Ga.*, p. 174, with portrait.)

EMERSON, ARTHUR, d. at Portsmouth, Va., June 7, 1842, a. 65; pres. of board of trustees of that place, and senior warden of Trinity church parish.

EMERSON, BENJAMIN D., one of the compilers of *Emerson's Arithmetic;* d. Oct. 1872, at Jamaica Plains, Mass.; he bequeathed a quarter of a million of dollars to public objects, among which was over $100,000 to Dartmouth College.

EMERSON, ELIHU, d. in Leicester, Mass., Oct. 31, 1873, a. 102 y. 3mo.

EMERSON, FREDERICK, an eminent instructor, and author of a valuable treatise on arithmetic extensively used in the schools; d. in Boston, Mass., April 26, 1857, a. 68.

EMERSON, RUTH, mother of Ralph Waldo Emerson; d. at Concord, Mass., Nov. 16, 1853, a. 83.

EMERY, JOHN A., d. in Exter, N. H., Oct. 25, 1842, a. 25, member of senior class of Harvard College.

EMLEN, DR. SAMUEL, b. in Chester co., Pa., March 6, 1789; grad. at the university of Penn., and continued his medical studies in England and France; was one of the physicians of the Phila. dispensary, and afterwards a manager, and the secretary; was connected with other charities, and in 1819, sec. of the board of health in an epidemic of yellow fever; became sec. of the Coll. of Physicians, and in 1825, a physician to the Penn. Hosp.; d. April 17, 1828. (*Simpson's Eminent Philadelphians.*)

EMMETT, ROBERT, d. at New Rochelle, N. Y., Feb. 15, 1873; son of Thomas Addis E., leader of the United Irishmen of 1798; who came to the United States in 1798; was a lawyer, and through life took an active interest in Irish affairs.

EMMETT, THOMAS ADDIS, an eminent lawyer of New York; d. at Astoria, Aug. 12, 1863; a. 63; he was a nephew of the Irish patriot, Robert Emmett.

EMORY, GEN. THOMAS, d. at Old Point Comfort, Va., Aug. 24, 1842; he was of Queen Annes co., Md.; had often served in the house of delegates and senate of Md., and had filled many other public offices.

ENGLE, PHILIP H., d. at St. Louis, Mo., Feb. 16, 1844; late judge of the circuit court of St. Louis.

ENGS, GEORGE, d. Dec. 16, 1846, at Newport, R. I., a. 60; was an enterprising merchant, and several times lieut. gov. of the state.

ENNIS, WILLIAM, a member of the bar; d. at Newport, R. I., June 7, 1849; a. 47.

ENO, ENISGN MARTIN, Conn.; killed in revolution, Oct. 11, 1780.

ENOS, DR. DE WITT C., of Brooklyn, b. in De Ruyter, N. Y., March 17, 1820; settled as a physician in Brooklyn about 1849, and d. there, ——, 1868. (*Transac. N. Y. State Med. Soc.*, 1868, p. 262.)

ENSTON, WILLIAM, a millionaire, d. in Charleston, S. C., March 23, 1860; being childless he gave his vast estate to the city of Charleston, for public purposes. (*Vincent's Semi An. Register*, p. 205.)

EPPES, LIEUT. COL. FRANCIS, Va., killed in battle of Long Island, Aug. 27, 1776.

ERVING, JOHN, of Boston, loyalist in 1775.

ERVING, JOHN JR., grad. at Harvard in 1747; in 1760 signed the Boston memorial, but in 1774 was a mandamus councillor; he fled to Halifax in 1776, and thence to England; he was proscribed and banished in 1778; and in 1779 his estate was confiscated; he d. in Eng., in 1816, a. 89; his wife was a dau. of Gov. Shirley, and the wife of Gov. Bowdoin was his sister. (*Sabine's Loyalists.*)

ERWIN, JAMES, member of congress from South Carolina, from 1817 to 1821; d. at Darlington C. H., S. C., Oct., 1838.

ESKIDGE, REV. VERNON, of the Meth. Epis. church, a victim of the yellow fever at Portsmouth, Va., in the autumn of 1855; was. b. Oct. 26, 1801, in Westmorland co., Va., and had been a traveling preacher since 1827.

ESSELSTYN, RICHARD M., merchant and co. clerk; b. at Claverack, N. Y., May 22, 1778; in 1801 came to Chaumont, N. Y., as surveyor, and soon settled in trade at Cape Vincent, N. Y.; he was clerk of Jeff. co. in 1813–15; and d. at Utica, Oct. 2, 1822. (*Hough's Hist. Jeff. Co., N. Y.*, p. 430.)

EUSTACE, Thomas, of Charleston, S. C., a tory, was banished in 1782, and his property confiscated.

EUSTIS, George, ex-congressman from Louisiana, and confederate envoy to France; d. at Cannes, France, March 15, 1872.

EVANS, Albert S., of San Francisco, Cal., lost on steam ship Missouri, Oct., 1872, a. 45; native of New England, and many years a resident of California; was invited by Mr. Seward to accompany him in his journey through Mexico, and wrote a book entitled *Our Sister Republic*, was an elegant writer; contributed much to the press, and was for many years editor of the *Alta California;* more recently, he was agent at San Francisco, for the associated press.

EVANS, Dr. Cadwallader, an original member of the Am. Phil. Soc.; d. 1773, a. 57.

EVANS, Charles, d. at Pensacola, Fla., Jan. 31, 1856; was formerly mayor of the city; judge of probate; representative in the state legislature and marshal of the United States for the western district of Florida.

EVANS, David E., for thirty years connected with the agency of the Holland Land Co.; was elected to the state senate in 1818, and to congress in 1826, but he resigned the latter before taking his seat; he d. at Batavia, May 17, 1850. (*Stryker's Am. Reg.*, iv, 464; *Turner's Holland Land Co.*, p. 442.)

EVANS, Ethni, a pioneer of Jefferson co., N. Y., and millwright from Hinsdale, N. H.; removed to Jeff. co., N. Y., about 1802, and d. Feb. 22, 1832, a. 62; the village of Evans's Mills, N. Y., is named from him.

EVANS, Joel, of Phila.; a loyalist merchant; lost his estate by confiscation in the revolution.

EVANS, William B., a successful Philadelphia publisher; d. Oct. 8, 1874, a. 40; he had charge of the publications of the Presbyterian board for some years, and bore an excellent reputation for strict integrity in business, and amiability in private life. (*Publisher's Weekly.*)

EVERETT, Meletiah, a lawyer, and in early life a federalist in politics; he was in the senate of Mass., and acted with the whigs and free soilers in later times; he long resided at Wrentham, Mass., where he died Dec. 26, 1858, a. 82. (*Hist. Mag.*, iii, 93.)

EVERITT, George, was a qr. mr. in the king's service in the revolution; went to New Brunswick in 1783, and d. at Fredericton in 1829, a. 70.

EVERHEART, Lawrence, b. in Middletown valley, Frederick co., Md., May 6, 1755; entered the army as a soldier, in Aug, 1776; was in the battle of Long Island; escaped at the surrender of Ft. Washington, and returned home in the spring of 1777; he again enlisted in 1778, under Col. W. Washington, and served faithfully in the south as sergeant, and was present at the surrender of Yorktown; he returned to agriculture in his native valley, and some years after became a Methodist preacher; he d. in 1839. (*Papers relating to the Md. Line*, pub. by the Seventy-Six Soc., 1857, p. 42.)

EVERTS, Dr. Franklin, of Oswego; d. Feb. 12, 1864, a. 36. (*Transac. N. Y. State Med. Soc.*, 1864, p. 441.)

EWELL, Richard S., a confederate general; d. in Maury co., Tenn., Jan. 25, 1872.

EWING, Maj. Henry, of the *St. Louis Daily Times;* d. in that city, June 13, 1873, a. 31.

EWING, John, b. at sea on a voyage of his parents from Ireland to Baltimore; bred a merchant, served in both houses of the Indiana legislature, and was in congress from 1833 to 1835, and from 1837 to 1839; d. suddenly at Vincennes, in the winter of 1857.

EWING, John Presbury, d. at Mammoth Cave, Ky., Sept. 27, 1854; son of Judge E., of the court of appeals; a representative in congress from the dist. of Kentucky; was one of the most brilliant and promising young men of the state.

EWING, Samuel, d. at Philadelphia, Feb., 1825; was a well known literary writer. (*Simpson's Eminent Philadelphians.*)

EYRE, William, British army engineer; became major of the 44th foot, Jan. 7, 1756; and built Ft. Wm. Henry on Lake George; in Jan., 1758, he was commissioned engineer in ordinary and in July, Lt. col. in the army; in July, 1759, he became chief engineer of the army, and laid out a plan for a new fort at Ticonderoga; he accompanied Amherst from Oswego to Montreal, in 1760; and remained in America till 1764, when he was drowned on his passage to Ireland. (*Com. Wilson's Orderly Book*, 27.)

EYRE, Sir William, major general in British army, formerly commander of the English forces in Canada, and one of the heroes of the Crimean wars; d. in Warwickshire, Eng., Sept. 8, 1859, a. 53.

FAEY, Ensign Joseph, N. H.; killed in the revolution, Sept. 19, 1777.

FAGAN, Rev. Peter C., d. in Brooklyn, N. Y., May 25, 1868, a. 35, pastor of St. Patrick's church (R. C.).

FAILE, Edward G., an eminent agriculturist, and ex-president of the N. Y. state agricultural society; d. April 20, 1864, in the 66th year of his age, was formerly engaged in commercial pursuits.

FAILE, Thomas Hall, d. at Nice, France, Jan. 13, 1873, a. 70.

FAIRBANKS, Charles B., of Boston, Mass.; d. Sept. 3, 1859, a. 32; he was a young man of ability and promise, and had acquired a considerable literary reputation.

FAIRBANKS, Jason, b. Sept. 5, 1785, at Mendon, Mass., son of Samuel; learned the trade of saddle and harness maker, settled at Newport, N. Y., in 1807; but in 1808, removed to Watertown, N. Y., where he afterwards resided; he there engaged very extensively in business, having a tannery, saddle and harness shop, and merchandize with several business connections at other places; in the course of his large mechanical operations he had more than 500 apprentices, at different times, of whom 365 served out their time, and at least 350 proved to be respectable citizens; in 1815, he was bondsman with Perley Keyes, for the honesty of Samuel Whittlesey, paymaster of drafted militia, who professed to have been robbed of some $30,000 of public moneys; by watching, eaves-dropping, cross questioning and inquiry, they became convinced that W. and his wife had stolen the money, and by enticing him into a by-place, and almost drowning him, compelled him to confess; the wife at once committed suicide upon learning that a disclosure had been made; the money was found quilted into a pair of drawers, with a kind of *will*, or directions to the children as to how it should be divided among them; Mr. Fairbanks was for some years sheriff of Jefferson co., and remained in full enjoyment of health and mental powers till near his death, which occurred January 10, 1875, at Watertown, N. Y. (*Hough's Hist. of Jefferson Co.*, with portrait.)

FAIRCHILD, JAMES M., a loyalist, went to New Brunswick in 1783; and d. at St. John, in 1807.

FAIRCHILD, MORTON, brevet major in the Mexican war, native of Troy, and orderly serg. of the Troy citizen's guard; served in every battle in the Mexican war except that of Molino del Rey, and at Cerro Gordo led his regiment with great bravery; he d. in N. Y., Aug. 3, 1860, a. 54; a few years since a committee of the com. council of N. Y., awarded him a gold snuff box, left in the will of Gen. Jackson, to the man, a citizen of New York, who should evince the greatest bravery in the first foreign war.

FAIRCHILD, ROBERT, formerly a judge; d. at Stratford, Ct., July —, 1835, a. 66.

FAIRFAX, CHARLES SNOWDEN, d. at Baltimore, Md., April 4, 1869, a. 40; was clerk of the supreme court of California, and a prominent democratic politician.

FAIRFAX, GEORGE WILLIAM, great grandson of Thomas, 4th lord Fairfax and son of Hon. Col. Wm. F., who was lt. of the co. of Fairfax, collector of customs of S. Potomac, and pres. of the Va. council; he was educated in Va., was an early companion of Washington, and an associate land surveyor; he m. dau. of Col. Carey of Hampton, was a member of council and lived at Belvoir; he went to England in 1773, and remained; he settled at Bath, and d. in 1787, a. 63; a part of his estate in Va., was confiscated. (*Sabine's Loyalists.*)

FAIRFIELD, GEORGE J., U. S. consul; d. at Buenos Ayres, S. A.; only brother of the late John F., of Maine.

FAIRLIE, JAMES, entered the revolution in 1775, or 1776, was first made lt. in the 1st N. Y., reg't. under Col. McDougall, and afterwrds under Col. Philip Van Cortlandt; he was present at the capture of Burgoyne and in 1778 was appointed aid to Steuben in which capacity he served in the battle of Monmouth; he was taken prisoner in Va., was exchanged, joined the army at Newburgh and served till peace; he was in assembly in 1798–9, 1809, and in convention in 1821; d. in N. Y. city Oct. 10, or 11, 1830.

FAIRMAN, GIDEON, b. in Newtown, Conn., June 26, 1774; was apprenticed to a firm of jewelers and engravers in Albany, and in 1810, settled in Philadelphia, as one of a firm of bank note engravers; was a captain, and then a colonel of militia and volunteers in the war 1812; in 1819, became a partner with Jacob Perkins, and went to England where he resided three years; d. April 18, 1827.

FANNIN, W. B., d. at Montgomery, Ala., Dec. 8, 1868; was many years a member of the Georgia legislature.

FANNING, JOHN, was in commission under the crown, after the fall of Charleston, S. C., in 1780, and his estate was confiscated.

FARDO, JOHN GEORGE, of S. C.; held a royal commission, after the fall of Charleston, and lost his estates by confiscation.

FARIBAULT, BARTHOLOMEW, b. in Paris; became a lawyer and was appointed military secretary to the French army in Canada; after the English conquest, he retired to private life at Berthier, Canada, and held the office of notary till his death in 1801.

FARIBAULT, JEAN BAPTISTE, son of the above; was b. at Berthier, Canada, in 1774; became a trader in the north west, and identified with some of the pioneer events of Minnesota; he resided at the place now called Mendota, and d. Aug. 20, 1860, a. 87. (*Collections Minn. Hist. Soc.*, iii, part 2, p. 168.)

FARLEY, CAPT. CALEB, d. at Hollis, N. H., April, 1833, a. 102.

FARLEY, GEORGE FREDERICK, d. in Groton, Mass., Nov. 8, 1855, a. 62; b. in Dunstable, Mass., April 5, 1793; grad. at Harvard in 1816; studied law, and was admitted to the bar in New Hampshire in 1820; practiced at New Ipswich, N. H., till 1831, when he removed to Groton; was one of the most eminent and successful lawyers in Middlesex county.

FARLIN, DUDLEY, d. at Warrensburg, N. Y., Sept. 27, 1837; member of congress in 1835–7.

FARMER, JOHN W. a well known compiler of several valuable maps of Michigan and Wisconsin; d. in Detroit, March 24, 1859.

FARMER, W. W., d. at Baton Rouge, La., Oct. 29, 1854, a. 48; was a native of Louisiana, and at the time of his death lieutenant governor.

FARNHAM, JOHN FAY, a native of Mass.; grad. at Harvard Coll., in 1811, was a lawyer of distinction and sec. of the Indiana hist. soc.; he d. at Salem, Ind., July 10, 1833, of cholera, a. 42.

FARNHAM, NOAH LANE, col. of the N. Y. Fire Zouaves, son of Geo. W. F., a merchant tailor of N. Y. city; was b. in New Haven, Ct., June 6, 1829; went to N. Y., with his parents in 1833; received an academic education at Cheshire, Ct., and at 16 became a clerk with S. M. Berkley & Co. of N. Y.; at 18 he joined the city guard, a crack regiment, and at 20 the engine co., No. 42, and soon after the hook and ladder co., No. 1, of which he became foreman; he introduced several new forms, and practiced his men in climbing, jumping, and other athletic feats; in 1856 he became assist. engineer of the N. Y. fire dep.; joined the 7th regt. in 1857, and became 1st lt. of co. B.; on the visit of Col. Ellsworth of Chicago to N. Y., Farnham escorted the co. to West Point, when the corps of Fire Zouaves was formed in April, 1861, he became second in command, and on Ellsworth's death became col.; he was wounded at Stone bridge, and d. at Washington, Aug. 16, 1861. (*N. Y. Eve. Post.*)

FARNSWORTH, OLIVER, b. in Woodstock, Vt., served an apprenticeship to printing at Windsor came to Newport, R. I., and was editor of the *R. I. Republican*, till 1805; he returned to Vt., thence went to Cincinnati, O., where he established the first printing office and in 1857 returned to Newport; he d. at Newport, Oct. 23, 1859, in his 84th year. (*Hist. Mag.*, iii, 384.)

FARNSWORTH, WILLIAM, settled at Sheboygan, Wisconsin, as a trapper and Indian trader in 1818, and in 1835 returned and bought half the village interest, of which he sold a sixteenth for $30,000 to the N. Y. & Erie transportation co., and another sixteenth for $25,000; he resided there subsequently and perished on the steamer Lady Elgin on Lake Michigan, Sept. 7, 1860; his body was recovered.

FARNUM, MAJ. GEN. J. EGBERT, late of U. S. vols.; d. at New York, May 16, 1870, a. 46; b. in Pendleton, N. J.; entered the military service in 1847, as sergeant major, and served through the Mexican war; was colonel of the 70th N. Y. vols., in the late war, wounded at Spottsylvania, and promoted to brig. gen. of vols.

FARNUM, CAPT. JOSEPH, d. at Concord, N. H., Nov. 1, 1837, a. 97; was a soldier of the French and revolutionary wars.

FARQUHAR, WILLIAM, became major of the 18th or Gen. Amherst's regt., Mar. 12, 1754; served against Rochefort in 1757, and at the siege of Louisbourg in 1758; he commanded the 44th regt. as lieut. col. at the siege of Fort Niagara in 1759.

FARR, LEVI, M.D., b. in Pittsfield, Mass., July 22, 1787; studied with his br. Jonas, of Minden, N. Y., was licensed in 1806 and settled the next year at Greene, Chenango co., N. Y., where he d. July 18, 1859, (*Tr. N. Y. St. Med. Soc.*, 1850, p. 174.)

FARRAR, PRESTON W., speaker of the house of representatives of Louisiana; d. at Baton Rouge, March 7, 1850, a. 44; he was a grad. of Transylvania University; removed to Mississippi in 1827 and served with credit in both houses of the legislature.

FARRAR, WILLIAM, a tory of Va., went to England, and in 1779 was an addresser of the king.

FARWELL, LEVI, d. at East Brookfield, Mass., May 27, 1844, a. 60, was of Cambridge, steward of Harvard Coll;

FAULKNER, CAPT. DANIEL P., an early property holder and spirited citizen of Dansville, acquired the name of Captain Dan, and from him the present village of Dansville, Livingston co., N. Y., is named.

FAXTON, CHARLES O., of the *Louisville Journal;* d. at Clarksville, Tenn., Jan. 28, 1870, a. 45.

FAY, CYRUS M., teacher; removed from Saratoga co., to Lowville, N. Y., having grad. at Union coll. in 1831, and was 3 y. a principal of the academy there; he taught 16 years in Buffalo, went to California and d. on his return, at San Juan Nicaragua, Dec. 12, 1850, a. 45. (*Lowville Acad. Semi-Cent. Celeb.*, p. 81).

FAY, DR. JONAS, a native of Vermont, he practiced medicine in Cazenovia, N. Y., as early as 1802; in the year 1810 he was the first president of the village; he moved to Utica and became a lumber dealer.

FAY, NAHUM, d. at Northborough, Mass., Nov. 16, 1841; was for more than forty years an instructer of youth, and he served his fellow citizens in various other offices.

FAY, SAMUEL PHILLIPS PRESCOTT, d. at Cambridge, Mass., May 18, 1856, a. 78; b. in Cambridge, Mass., in 1778; grad. at Harvard in 1798; studied law, was a member of the Massachusetts legislature; of the executive council in 1818 and 1819, and of the convention in 1820; in May, 1821, was appointed judge of probate for Middlesex co., and held this office 35 years.

FEETER, WILLIAM, b. at Stone Arabia, N. Y., Feb. 2, 1756; was a soldier of the revolution and served in Tryon co.; he was afterwards col. of militia, settled in Glen's Purchase, Little Falls, N. Y., and d. May 5, 1844, a. 88. (*Benton's Herkimer Co.*, p. 420).

FELIX, ELIZABETH RACHEL, a noted actress and singer, well known in the United States; d. in Cannes, France, Jan. 5, 1858; a. 57.

FELLOWS, ENSIGN DAVID, Conn., killed in the revolution, Dec. 10, 1779.

FENTON, COL. NATHANIEL, b. in Mansfield, Ct.; served in the revolution, and settled in Otsego co., N. Y., in 1791; he represented Otsego co. in assembly, in 1815 and 1818, and Chautauque co., in 1828; he d. in Jamestown, N. Y., Jan. 25, 1846, a. 82.

FENTON, William M., ex-lieut. gov. of Michigan; d. at Flint, Mich., May 13, 1871; was col. in the 8th Mich. vols. in the late war, till his resignation, March 15, 1863.

FENWICK, RT. REV. BENEDICT JOSEPH, R. C. bp. of Boston; b. near Leonardstown, Md., Sept. 3, 1782; studied at the Georgetown Coll. and was called to teach some of the higher classes in that institution; in 1805 he entered the seminary of St. Sulpice, Balt., and the next year became a novitiate of the S. J. in Georgetown Coll.; he was ordained priest in 1807, and began labor in N. Y. city, where on the death of Rt. Rev. Dr. Concannon, he became administrator of that diocese; in 1817 he became pres. of Georgetown Coll.; in 1818 was sent as vicar general to S. C.; in 1822 returned to Georgetown, and May 10, 1825, was appointed by the pope to the see of Boston; having erected an Ursuline school at Charlestown, it was occupied July 17, 1826, and in Nov. following a convent at that place, which were destroyed by a mob in 1834; he closed an active life Aug. 11, 1846, a. 65. (*Metropolitan Cath. Almanac*, 1850, p. 57; *Am. Almanac* 1847, p. 335.)

FENWICK, RT. REV. EDWARD, first R. C. Bp. of Cincinnati; b. in St. Mary's co., Md., in 1768; was educated at the Dominican Coll. of Bornheim, near Antwerp, Belgium, and labored some years as professor and procurator; the French army broke up this establishment, but he was released, and he undertook to found his order in America; he was sent as a missionary to the west in 1805; founded a house of his order in Washington co., Ky.; he was consecrated bp. of Cincinnati, Jan. 13, 1822; went to Rome; was liberally assisted with funds and spent many years in zealous labors throughout the west, and in founding churches, schools, and religious houses; he d. at Canton, O., Sept. 25, 1832. (*Metropolitan Cath. Almanac*, 1848, p. 58.)

FENWICKE, THOMAS, of S. C.; was an office holder after the fall of Charleston, under British authority in 1780, and lost his estate by confiscation.

FERGUSON, JOSIAH, a captain in the revolution; d. at Princeton, N. J., March 16, 1836, a. 80 years.

FERNALL, BENJAMIN C., teacher; d. in Portland, Me., Nov. 12, 1868, a. 67.

FERRIS, BENJAMIN, d. at Wilmington, Del., Nov. 10, 1867; author of *Early Settlements on the Delaware;* was a watchmaker; lived several years in Philadelphia, and was a long time clerk of the Phila. Yearly Meeting of Friends.

FERRIS, CHARLES G., member of 23d and 27th congresses from New York city; d. at New York, June 4, 1848.

FERRIS, Rev. Isaac, pastor of the 2d R. P. D. church of Albany from Oct. 1824 to 1836, when he was elected chancellor of the University of New York, and removed to New York city; d. in Roselle, N. J., June 16, 1873, a. 75.

FERRIS, Joseph, a tory of Stamford, Ct., raised a company and was capt. in Col. Butler's rangers; he was taken prisoner but escaped, and after the war went to Newfoundland, and thence removed to New Brunswick; he lived for a time at Eastport, Me., after it was captured by the British in the war of 1812, but returned to N. B.; and d. at Indian island, in 1832, a. 92; he enjoyed half pay 53 y. (*Sabine's Loyalists.*)

FERRY, Heman, a merchant in Remsen, N. Y., whence he removed to Utica; was in 1838 one of the first board of directors of the Bank of Central New York; he was b. in Granby, Mass., Aug. 4, 1786; d. in Utica, March 31, 1856.

FERRY, Rev. William M., founder of the city of Grand Haven, Mich.; b. at Granby, Mass., Sept. 8, 1796; grad. at Union Coll.; was ordained as a minister of the Presb. ch., in 1822; went to Mich., in 1834, and settled at Grand Haven, where he d. Dec. 30, 1866.

FETTERMAN, W. W., an eminent member of the Pittsburg bar; d. at Pittsburg, Pa., Dec. 12, 1838.

FIDLER, Rev. Daniel, d. in Pemberton, Burlington co., N. J., Aug. 21, 1842, a. 71; was 53 years a Methodist minister.

FIELD, Rev. Alpheus, d. at Argentine, Genesee co., Mich., Feb. 4, 1861, a. 72; many years a resident of Jefferson co., N. Y.

FIELD, Barnum, grad. at Brown University in 1821, established the *Independent Inquirer* at Providence, and after some time spent in the printing business at Providence, removed to Boston and labored 25 years as a teacher with great ability and success; he d. at Boston, May 7, 1851, master of the Franklin school.

FIELD, Jonathan E., d. in Stockbridge, Mass., April 23, 1869, formerly president of the Massachusetts senate.

FILLMORE, Miss Abby, dau. of ex-Pres. Millard F.; d. at Aurora, N. Y., July 26, 1854, a. 22.

FILLMORE, Mrs. Abigal, wife of ex-President Millard F.; d. in Washington, D. C., March 30, 1853, a. 55.

FILLMORE, Millard, president of the United States from the death of Pres. Taylor, July 9, 1850, to the end of his term; d. at Buffalo, March 8, 1874.

FILTER, Daniel, formerly high sheriff of Philadelphia; d. in that city, Oct. 4, 1849.

FINCKE, Andrew A., d. at Little Falls, N. Y., May 22, 1871, in the 89th year of his age, son of Major Andrew Fincke of the revolutionary army.

FISCHER, Charles, d. at Hillsborough, Miss., May 7, 1849, a. 58; was many years in the state legislature of North Carolina, of which he was several times chosen speaker, and a member of congress.

FISHER, Dea. Elijah, d. in Livermore, Me., Jan. 28, 1842, a. 85; a revolutionary soldier and a native of Attleborough, Mass.

FISHER, Rev. George H., D.D., a native of New Jersey, a grad. of Rutgers college and the Theolog'l Sem. of New Brunswick; was for several years pastor of the Broome st. Reformed Dutch church in N. Y., whence he went in 1855 to take charge of the Reformed church of Utica; after his resignation of the pastorate of the latter in Sept., 1859, he had no settled charge; in 1849 he was pres. of the general synod of the Reformed Dutch church; he d. at Hackensack, N. J., Nov. 23d, 1872, in his 69th year.

FISHER, John, of Orangeburg, S. C., held a commission under the crown; was banished, and lost his estate under the act of 1782; he was a colonel.

FISHER, Miers, b. in Philadelphia, June, 1748, of quaker parents, and became a lawyer; was member of the city council from 1789 to 1791, and in the latter year, a member of the house of representatives of the state, was many years a director of the Bank of North America, and of the Insurance Company of Pennsylvania; d. March 14, 1819, in his 72d year. (*Simpson's Eminent Philadelphians.*)

FISHER, Rev. Samuel Ware, D.D., LL.D., a preacher of eloquence and power, a faithful pastor and a liberal minded and influential college president; the son of an eminent Presb. minister, he was b. in Morristown, N. J., April 5, 1814; was grad. at Yale college in 1835 and pursued his theolog'l studies at Princeton and at Union Theolog'l Sem.; grad. in 1839; from April of that year to Oct., 1843, he was minister of the Presb. church in West Bloomfield, N. J.; from 1843 to 1847 of the Fourth church of Albany, N. Y.; and from 1849 to 1858 of the Second church of Cincinnati, Ohio; in July 1858 he was appointed president of Ham. Coll.; after a service of 8 ys. he was again solicited to engage in pastoral work, and assumed the care of Westminster church in Utica, Nov. 15, 1867, but resigned on account of ill health in Jan., 1871. He d. in Cincinnati, Jan. 18, 1874. He was moderator of the new school general assembly in 1857, and was one of the committee of conference which reported the plan of reunion of the two schools in 1869; he published the *Three Great Temptations*, and a volume of *Sermons and Addresses*. (*Memorial of Rev. S. W. Fisher*, with portrait.)

FISHER, Turner, of Boston, son of Wilfred F., followed the British to Halifax in 1776, entered the navy and became sailing master; after the war he m. Esther the dau. of Ezekiel Foster of Machias, Me., and settled in N. B.; his son Wilfred has a magistrate of the island of Grand Menan, N. B., where his wife d. Nov. 1844, a. 88.

FISHER, Wilfred, a Boston loyalist, went to Halifax in 1776; and was with a corps of light horse; died before the peace; he was proscribed and banished in 1778, and his estate confiscated; his son Wilfred, a whig and shipmaster, was captured by the British, carried to N. Y., and died there in prison.

FISKE, Dr. Caleb; d. at Scituate. R. I., Sept. 1834; a. 65.

FISKE, Dr. Joseph; d. at Lexington, Mass., Sept. 25, 1837, a. 85; served in revolutionary war, as a surgeon.

FISKE, Josiah J., d. at Sturbridge, Mass., Aug. 15, 1838, a. 50; was of Wrentham, and for several years a state senator.

FISKE, Samuel, d. at Claremont, N. H., Dec. 30, 1834; a. 65.

FITCH, Mrs. Abigal, d. in Lebanon Ct., March 17, 1842, a. 88.

FITCH, Eleazer, 2d son of John F., of Norwich, Ct.; b. Aug. 27, 1726; commanded the 4th Ct. regt., at the battle of Ticonderoga, and down to 1760.

FITCH, Rev. Eleazer T., D.D., ex-professor of divinity at Yale Coll.; d. at New Haven, Conn., Jan. 31, 1871, a. 80; was appointed pastor of the Yale Coll. church, and prof. of divinity in 1817, and held the latter office 35 years.

FITCH, Elisha, d. at Pensacola, Fla., Oct. 22, 1839; prof. of mathematics in the navy; on board the Levant; was formerly of Connecticut.

FITCH, Jeremiah G., d. at Orono, Me., Feb. 25, 1845, a. 35; grad. at Harvard in 1831; had formerly resided in Boston.

FITCH, Joseph, d. at Geneva, O., Jan. 13, 1841, in his 100th year.

FITZGERALD, Edward H., b. in Va.; entered the army as 2d lieut. of 6th infantry Oct. 26, 1839; was assist. qr. mr., with rank of captain when the Mexican war began; was aid to Gen. Pierce, in the valley of Mexico; capt. of 9th inf. Sept. 1847; brevet major for gallantry at Chapultepec, and was in every battle on Gen. Scott's line from the surrender of Vera Cruz to the fall of Mexico; he served several years in New Mexico and California; and d. in Cal., June 9, 1860. (*Hist. Mag.*, iv, 125.)

FITZGERALD, Thomas H., d. in Niles, Mich., March 25, 1855; served in the war of 1812, under Gen. Harrison; in 1848–9, was senator from Michigan by governor's appointment.

FITZHUGH, Thomas, d. in Fauquier co., Va., Nov. 23, 1843, a. 81; was for many years presiding judge of the county court.

FITZHUGH, Col. William, d. in Livingston co., N. Y., Dec. 27, 1839, in his 79th year; formerly of Maryland; was a lieut. of dragoons at the siege of Yorktown, in the revolutionary war. (*Turner's Phelps and Gorham Purchase*, p. 364.)

FITZPATRICK, Thomas, d. in Washington, D. C., Feb. 8, 1854, a. about 70 years; was agent for the upper Arkansas and Platte Indians, and a valued servant of the Indian department, having much influence with the Indian tribes of the great plains.

FLAGG, Azariah C., ex-secretary of state, d. in New York city, Nov. 24, 1873, a. 83; began public life as editor of a newspaper at Plattsburg, N. Y., and published the *Plattsburg Republican* from 1813 till 1826; was in assembly in 1823–4; secretary of state in 1826–38; and comptroller of the state in 1842–7; was afterwards comptroller of the city of New York.

FLAGG, Major Ebenezer, R. I.; killed by tories under Col. Delancy, in West Chester co., N. Y., May 13, 1781.

FLANDERS, Charles, of the New Hampshire bar; d. at Plainfield, N. H., April 15, 1860, a. 72; author of *Life and Times of the Chief Justices of the United States*, and of two legal works.

FLANDRAU, Thomas Hunt, a skillful jury lawyer, was of Huguenot descent, and b. in New Rochelle, Sept. 8, 1801, whence he removed with his father's family to Utica; he graduated at Ham. Coll., in 1819, and read law with Judge Nathan Williams of Utica; soon after his admission to the bar, he was for about two years a law partner of Aaron Burr in

N. Y.; he practiced law several years at Waterville, N. Y., and afterwards at Whitesboro and at Utica; his death occurred October 2d, 1854.

FLEESON, PLUNKETT, b. in Philadelphia, Pa.; d. in 1791; was much concerned in local charities and was long a magistrate; was among the early contributors to the Pennsylvania hospital, and a director of that institution. (*Simpson's Eminent Philadelphians.*)

FLEET, MISS ANN, last of the name long connected with the printing business in Boston; she d. July, 1860, a. 89; her grandfather Thomas T. came in 1712; was a printer and the putative father of *Mother Goose's Melodies.* His paper, the *Eve. Post,* was continued by his sons Thomas and John till April 24, 1775; and their other business till 1808. (*Hist. Mag.*, iv, 286; *Thomas's Hist. Printing,* 2d ed., i, 104; ii, 49.)

FLEMING, BENJAMIN, d. at Erie, Pa.; May 9, 1870, a. 88; supposed to be the last survivor of the crew of Com. Perry's fleet of the battle of Lake Erie.

FLEMING JOHN, printer at Boston, and a loyalist; was proscribed and banished under the act of 1778; he was a partner of Mein, and some of the books they printed have a London imprint; in 1767, they began the *Boston Chronicle,* which in 1768, became tory, and extremely abusive to the whigs; Mein left the country, and the paper (the first *Boston Semi Weekly*), was suspended in 1770. Fleming went to Eng., in 1773, and came to the U. S. but once after, subsequent to 1790, as the agent of a commercial house; he d. in France, where he had lived several years. (*Sabine's Loyalists.*)

FLEMING, JOHN, late president of the Mechanics' Bank; d. in New York city May 7, 1837; he was found dead in bed, and according to the coroner's verdict, died of *mental excitement.*

FLETCHALL, THOMAS, of S. C.; col. of a considerable body of loyalists during the difficulties with the Cunninghams in 1775; and signed a truce as agreed upon between the whigs and loyalists; after the fall of Charleston in 1780, he held office, and in 1782, his estate was confiscated; he was a man of considerable influence before the war. (*Sabine's Loyalists.*)

FLETCHER, ANDREW J., of Tennessee; d. July 16, 1870, a. 51.

FLETCHER, GEN. ISAAC, d. at Lyndon, Vt., Oct., 19, 1842; formerly in the Vermont legislature, and in congress from 1837 to 1841.

FLETCHER, JONATHAN EMERSON, b. in Hartford, Vt.; went to Ohio when young and settled at Muscatine, Iowa, in 1838; In 1846, was appointed Indian agent to the Winnebagoes and held 11 years; residing during this time at Port Atkinson, Iowa, and Long Prairie and Blue Earth, Minn.; returned to Muscatine in 1858; and d. April 6, 1872.

FLETCHER, SAMUEL, was b. at Grafton, Mass., in 1728; served in the French and revolutionary wars; In 1776, he was chosen qr. mr., and soon after captain; he served as major, brig. gen. and maj. gen.; represented Townshend, Vt., in gen. assembly at its first session; was chosen councilor and in 1782, a judge of the supreme court, but refused to serve; from 1788 to 1806, he was high sheriff of Windham co., and in 1778, 83, 4, 6, a judge of the county court; he d. Sept. 15, 1814, a. nearly 70 y. (*Hall's Eastern Vermont,* p. 640.)

FLEWELLEN, CAPT. WILLIAM, an officer of the revolution; d. Sept. 23, 1834, in Carroll co., Tenn., a. 81.

FLEWELLING, ABEL, a New York tory, settled in New Brunswick, and drew a lot at St. John; he was a magistrate, and d. at Mangerville in 1814, a. 68; Morris F., of N. Y., also went to St. John. (*Sabine's Loyalists.*)

FLINT, COL. DANIEL, d. at Reading, Mass., June 5, 1838, a. 78.

FLOYD, BENJAMIN, loyalist, 3d son of Richard F. 3d, b. Dec. 4, 1740; was a col. of militia, and lived on the paternal estate of Setauket; he made himself conspicuous in 1775, by circulating a petition for the support of the royal authority; he d. Dec. 27, 1820, a. 80.

FLOYD, DAVID RICHARD. (See Jones, David Richard Floyd.)

FLOYD, CHARLES A., d. at Comac, Long Island, Feb. 20, 1873, in his 82d year.

FLOYD, JOHN, son of Charles F., of Va., who settled in Beaufort dist., S. C. John F. was b. there Oct. 3, 1769; was apprenticed to a carpenter; removed in 1791 or 1792 to Ga., and settled at the mouth of St. Illa river Camden co.; where he became a boat builder, and acquired wealth; he was often in the legislature, and, in 1827–9 was in congress; he became brig. gen., and afterwards major gen. of militia; during the war of 1812–15 he was engaged against the Creeks; and led at the battle of Chalibbee; he d. June 24, 1824. (*White's Hist. Ga.*, p. 289.)

FLOYD, MATTHEW, of S. C., was in commission under the crown after the fall of Charleston in 1780, and his estate was confiscated.

FLOYD, RICHARD, 1st common ancestor of the name on Long Island, N. Y., came from Wales, and settled at Setauket, L. I., in 1656, where he acquired a considerable landed estate; he was one of the 55 original proprietors of Brookhaven, and d. about 1700. (*Thompson's Long Island*, ii, 431.)

FLOYD, RICHARD 2d, son of Richard F., the first settler of the name; was b. at Brookhaven N. Y., May 12, 1665; married a dau. of Matthias Nicoll, sec. of the colony, Sept. 10, 1686; was many years a judge and col of Suffolk co., and d. Feb. 28, 1728; he had 5 daughters, and 2 sons. (*Thompson's Long Island*, ii, 431.)

FLOYD, RICHARD, 3d, eldest son of Col. Richard F., second of the name in America; b. in Brookhaven, N. Y., Dec. 29, 1703, inherited the family estate at Setauket, and was also a county judge and colonel, and d. April 21, 1771; his children were Richard, Elizabeth, John, Margaret, Gilbert, Wm., Samuel, Mary and Anne. (*Thompson's Long Island*, ii, 431.)

FLOYD, RICHARD 4th, loyalist; b. at Mastic, N Y., Feb. 26, 1731; eldest son of Hon. Richard Floyd 3d; he married Arrabella, dau. of David Jones of Queens co., N. Y.; he was attainted and banished, Oct. 22, 1779, and he d. at St. John, N. B., in 1792; the farm called Paterquas, was sold by the com's of forfeited estates, Aug. 5, 1784, to Benj. Floyd his brother; his children were Elizabeth (who married John Peter DeLancey, father of Bp. D. of Western N. Y.) Anne Willet, and David Richard. (*Sabine's Loyalists; Thompson's Long Island*, ii, 432.)

FLOYD, COL. RUSH, of Va; brother of the secretary of war; d. at Washington, D. C., Feb. 15, 1860.

FLOYD, DR. W. P., of Virginia; accidentally killed in Tazewell co., Dec. 21, 1871.

FOGG, WILLIAM, noted for his fondness for local historical investigation; b. in Eliot, Me.; lived on the farm which had belonged to his family since 1680, a period of four generations, and d. Sept. 18, 1859, a. 69; he left in ms. a hist. of Kittery, Me. (*Hist. Mag.*, iii, 354.)

FOISSIN, ELIAS, held office under the crown in S. C., after the fall of Charleston, in 1780, and his estate was confiscated.

FOLKER, JOHN, a loyalist; was qr. mr. of the 2d battalion of N. J. volunteers in the revolution.

FOLLETT, TIMOTHY, a grad. of the University of Vermont, in 1810; was in early life a lawyer and afterwards a successful merchant, and the pioneer and first president of the Rutland and Burlington rail road; d. at Burlington, Vt., Oct. 12, 1857, a. 66.

FOLLIOT, GEORGE, a merchant of N. Y.; was elected to the provincial congress in 1775, but declined serving; he was also one of the committee of 100, but refused to serve; he was attainted and banished, Oct. 22, 1779.

FOLSOM, CAPT. JOSEPH L., d. at San José mission, Cal., July 19, 1855, a. 38; b. in Strafford co., N. H., May 19, 1817; grad. at West Point in 1840, and served in Florida; was soon after appointed assistant instructor of tactics at West Point; arrived in California in March, 1847, as assist. qr. mr. in the 7th N. Y. vols., and was the first collector of customs of San Francisco; is said to have been the richest man in that city.

FONDA, ALEXANDER G., b. in Schenectady, Aug. 17, 1785; grad at Union Coll. in 1804, and began practice in 1806, at Schenectady, where he continued many years. (*Munsell's Ann. Alb.*, ix, 97.)

FOOTE, COL. ENOS, d. June 20, 1840, at Southwick, Mass.; a. 68; had held many public offices.

FOOTE, MOSES, b. Aug. 4, 1734, in Waterbury, Conn.; d. in Clinton, N. Y., Feb. 9, 1819; a. 84.

FOOTE, MOSES, a captain in the army of the revolution; in 1787, he led a colony of seven or eight families from Plymouth, to begin the settlement of Clinton, Oneida co., N. Y., which was his place of residence until his death.

FOOTE, STILLMAN, pioneer settler of Canton, N. Y., in 1801; b. at Simsbury, Ct., Sept. 10, 1783; d. May 12, 1831. (*Hough's Hist. St. Law. and Fr. Cos. N. Y.*, p. 589).

FOOTE, DR. THOMAS MOSES, only son of Moses F.; b. Aug. 9, 1808, graduated at Ham. Coll. in 1825, and completed a course of medical studies at Fairfield; in 1836, he became editor of the *Buffalo Commercial Advertiser* and soon a proprietor; in 1849 he was appointed minister to Bogota, under President Harrison, and on his return in 1850, became one of the editors of the *Albany State Register;* soon after he was appointed minister to Vienna, under President Fillmore, but held the post only one year; at the time of his death, at Buffalo, Feb. 20, 1858, a. 49; he was still connected with the *Commercial Advertiser;* a man of extensive reading, a good writer and an entertaining talker.

FORBES, ALEXANDER S., had been to Mexico for the bodies of Lt. Col. Baxter, of N. Y., Capts. Pearson and Barclay, Lieuts. Gallagher and Chandler, of N. Y., and Capt. Van Olinda, of Albany; while returning home he d. at New Orleans, June 29, 1848.

FORBES, CAPT. JOHN, S. C., killed at battle of Guilford, March 15, 1781.

FORBES, REV. REVES, LL.D., native of Bridgewater, Mass., graduated at Harvard in 1762, and settled as pastor in Raynham where he d. in 1798, a. 57; he was employed to lecture on astronomy and nat. philosophy at Brown University. (*Bradford's N. E. Biog.*)

FORBES, WILLIAM C., many years a theatrical manager at the south; d. April 14, 1868.

FORCE, REV. JAMES G., a graduate of Princeton and a soldier of the revolution; d. at Sandystown, N. J., July 3, 1849, in the 84th year of his age and the 57th of his ministry. (*Stryker's Am. Reg.*, iii, 233.)

FORD, LT. COL. BENJAMIN, Md., killed in battle at Hobkirk's hill, April 25, 1781.

FORD, DAVID, militia colonel in war of 1812; b. in N. J.; was an officer in the expedition into Western Pa., in 1794; settled in Morristown, N. Y., as agent in 1804, and d. at Ogdensburgh, Nov. 6, 1835, a. 75; he was brother of Judge David F. (*Hough's Hist. St. Law. & Fr. Cos. N. Y.*, p. 589.)

FORD, JOHN, loyalist of N. J.; fled to Staten Island, and remained several years; in 1783 he was commissioned to take charge of a company of loyalists, emigrating to Nova Scotia, and settled at St. John, N. B., where he received a city lot; he went thence to Hampton, and d. in 1823, a. 77.

FORD, NATHAN, pioneer agent and settler at Ogdensburgh, and judge; b. at Morristown, N. J., Dec. 8, 1763; settled at the mouth of the Oswegatchie in 1726, as agent of Samuel Ogden; was 1st judge of St. Lawrence co., from 1802 to 1821, and d. April, 1829; he was a man of great originality and energy. (*Hough's Hist. St. Law. & Fr. Cos. N. Y.*, p. 589, with portrait.)

FORD, SIMEON, settled in Herkimer co., from Berkshire co., Mass., before 1797, as a lawyer, and some years partner of Gaylord Griswold; he became dist. atty., June 10, 1818, and held till May, 1823, and again in 1836; in 1821, and 1822 he was in assembly; in 1824 he was appointed engineer at the Syracuse Salt Springs and held till 1826; lived 5 y. in Rochester, returned to Herkimer in 1832, and in 1836 settled in Cleveland, O.; he was prosecuting attorney from this time till his death, Oct. 12, 1839, a. 63. (*Benton's Herkimer Co., N. Y.*, p. 311.)

FORD, THOMAS, d. at Washington, D. C., Feb. 29, 1868, in his 55th year; had been lieut. gov. of Ohio, and commanded a brigade at Harper's Ferry during Lee's invasion.

FORD, VIRGINIA, (colored), d. in Washington, June 22, 1859, a. 120 years.

FORMAN, JOSHUA, b. in Pleasant Valley, Dutchess co., N. Y., Sept. 6, 1777; grad. at Union Coll., and studied law; in 1800 settled in Onondaga valley, N. Y., and became a prominent lawyer; in 1803, became a law partner with Wm. H. Sabin; took an active interest in the Erie canal, and was elected to assembly, where he became a leading advocate of that measure; was first judge of Onondaga co.; was one of the founders of the city of Syracuse, where he settled in 1819; in 1829–30, he bought of the state of North Carolina some 300,000 acres of land in Rutherford co.; and took up his residence there; where he d. Aug. 7, 1849, a. 72. (*Clark's Onondaga Co.*, ii, 69–83; *Leavenworth Genealogy*, p. 357, each with a portrait.)

FORMAN, Dr. Samuel, d. at Freehold, N, J., Dec. 11, 1845, a. 81; he was for 40 years an elder of the Presbyterian church at that place.

FORNEY, Daniel M., b. in Lincoln co., N. C., May 1784; was a major of the state line in the war of 1812; in congress from 1815 to 1818; and in 1820 was a comr. to treat with Creek Indians; from 1823 to 1826 was in the state legislature; in 1834, removed to Lowndes co., Ala., and d. there Oct. 1847.

FORNEY, Peter, b. in Lincoln co., N. C., April 1756; served in the revolution, and in the state legislature several years; was in congress from 1813 to 1815; and d. Feb. 1, 1834.

FORREST, Edwin, a celebrated tragedian; d. in Philadelphia, Dec. 12, 1872, a. 66. (*Drake's Am. Biog.*)

FORRESTER, George Peabody, a loyalist from the states; d. at Hampton, King's co., New Brunswick, in 1840, a. 83.

FORRESTER, Joseph, a loyalist, and a grantee of St. John, N. B.; he d. while in Boston, in 1804, a. 46.

FORSYTH, Oliver, a revolutionary soldier; d. in Greig, N. Y., Feb. 24, 1838, a. 76; was in the battle of Stonington.

FORSYTH, Robert, U. S. marshal for Ga., appointed by Washington, Sept. 26, 1789; and killed by one Beverly Allen while endeavoring to serve a process at Augusta, in 1794; he was the father of John F. the statesman.

FORT, Arthur, was a soldier of the revolution, one of the committee of safety of Ga.; resided 75 years in Ga., and d. in Twiggs co., a. 85 y. (*White's Hist. Ga.*, p. 657.)

FORT, George F., ex-gov. of New Jersey; d. at Egypt, N. J., April 23, 1872, a. 63.

FORT, Dr. Tomlinson, d. in Milledgeville, Ga., May 11, 1859, a. 72; he was a member of the state legislature; was in congress from Ga., from 1827 to 1829; and president of the Central Bank of Georgia, from 1832, till his death.

FOSS, Archibald C., d. at Clarens, Switzerland, April, 1870; a Methodist minister, in 1861, was prof. at the Wesleyan University; had been pastor at Morrisania, N. Y. city, Tarrytown and Poughkeepsie.

FOSSIT, Thomas, a distinguished merchant of Phila.; d. at that city, March 28, 1836, in his 60th year.

FOSTER, Rev. Charles G., of the Tennessee conference; b. Sept., 16, 1820, d. Oct. 26, 1853. (*Deems's Annals of Southern Methodism*, p. 347.)

FOSTER, Ensign Ebenezer, Mass., killed in the revolution, Oct. 19, 1777.

FOSTER, EDWARD, and EDWARD JR., loyalists of Boston; blacksmiths; went to Halifax in 1776, and was proscribed and banished in 1778; they d. at Union Me.; the father d. July, 17, 1822; a. 72. (*Sabin Loyalists; Sibley's Hist.* of *Union*, p. 333.)

FOSTER, EPHRAIM H., d. at Nashville, Tenn.; Sept. 4, 1854; entered public life at an early age, and in 1829, was speaker of the house of representatives of Tennessee; in 1837, was elected to the U. S. senate; resigned in 1839, from having received instructions from the legislature which he could not obey; and in 1843, was elected to fill out the remainder of a term; in 1845, was unsuccessful candidate for governor.

FOSTER, FREDERICK, a loyalist from the states; settled in New Brunswick; and d. on the island of Grand Menan in 1834, a. 74.

FOSTER, HERMAN TEN EYCK, d. at Lakeland, on the east shore of Seneca lake, N. Y., Feb. 9, 1869; b. in the city of New York, March 1, 1822; grad. at Columbia Coll., and settled as a farmer; took much interest in agricultural pursuits. (*Memorial of H. T. E. F. by A. B. Conger*, 1870.)

FOSTER, ISAAC, patriot and surgeon of the revolution; native of Charlestown Mass.; grad. at Harvard in 1758; studied medicine abroad and settled in his native town; he was a delegate to the co. convention, and prov. cong.; early in 1775, was appointed a surgeon and served professionally in camp and hospital till 1780; he d. in Feb. 1781 a. 45, of health impaired by intense service in discharge of duty. (*Bradford's N. E. Biog.*)

FOSTER, JUDGE JABEZ, b. Aug. 1, 1777, at Lebanon, Ct.; removed to Lewis co., and soon after to Jefferson co., N. Y.; he engaged largely in trade; was many years a county judge, and d. at Monroe, Mich., Dec. 10, 1847. (*Hough's Hist. Jeff. Co. N. Y.*, p. 430.)

FOSTER, T. HERON, d. at Pittsburg, Pa., April 21, 1868; b. at Greensburg, Va., in 1822; was a printer and established the *Pittsburg Dispatch*, in 1846.

FOSTER, NATHANIEL, celebrated hunter in northern New York; b. in 1767; settled at Salisbury N. Y.; in 1834, he was tried for the murder of an Indian but acquitted; he died in Ava, N. Y., March, 1841, a. 74. (*J. R. Simms's Trappers of N. Y.*, p. 175–252.)

FOSTER, R. C., recorder of Nashville; d. at that place, Dec. 27, 1871.

FOSTER, THEODORE, U. S. senator from R. I.; son of Jedediah F.; grad. at the coll. of R. I. in 1740; acquired a large legal practice in R. I. and was several years one of the overseers of the college; he was U. S. senator from 1790 to 1803. (*Bradford's N. E. Biog.*)

FOSTER, THOMAS F., b. in Greensborough, Ga., Nov. 23, 1790; grad. at Franklin Coll. in 1812; studied law at Litchfield, Conn., and was admitted to the bar in 1816; was many years in the Georgia legislature, and in congress from 1829 to 1835, and from 1841 to 1843; d. in 1847.

FOSTER, WILLIAM, was appointed lieut. col. of 1st royals, Dec. 24, 1755, and served at the siege of Louisburg in 1758; he served in 1759, on Lake Champlain; became a col. in the army in Feb., 1762, and is found on the army lists till 1768.

FOSTER, LIEUT. COL. WILLIAM, of 4th U. S. infantry, d. at Baton Rouge, La., Nov. 26, 1839.

FOSTER, WILLIAM B., a prominent citizen of Philadelphia; vice pres. of the Penn. rail road, and formerly a civil engineer in the construction of that road; d. at Philadelphia, March 4, 1860, a. about 50; was elected a member of the state canal board, and served 3 y., ending Jan., 1847; was formerly a member of the select council from the 9th ward.

FOULKE, WILLIAM, d. in Philadelphia, Pa., Aug. 30, 1775, in his 67th year. (*Simpson's Eminent Philadelphians.*)

FOWLE, REV. ROBERT, d. at Holderness, N. H., Oct. 16, 1847; rector of Trinity church in that town, and one of its earliest inhabitants; had officiated as a lay reader to the parish before his ordination; was admitted to the ministry by Bishop Seabury, Dec. 13, 1789.

FOWLE, WILLIAM, a merchant of Alexandria, Va.; d. Jan. 8, 1860.

FOWLER, CALEB, of White Plains, N. Y., a loyalist, and in 1775 denounced the whigs and their deeds; entered the royal service and became captain in the loyal Am. regt.; he went to N. B.; drew half pay, and d. near Fredericton.

FOWLER, REV. HENRY, d. at Vineyard Haven, Mass., Aug., 1872; he was about 48 years old, and was born in Stockbridge, Mass., and was graduated at Williams College; he afterward edited *Holden's Magazine* and other journals in this city, and was the proprietor of *The Chicago Tribune* in its early days, before it had achieved its present prosperity, and become a power in the north-west; he studied theology in the Rochester Theological Seminary, and subsequently became professor of political economy in the university of that city; fourteen years before his death he was chosen pastor of the Central Presbyterian church in Auburn, N. Y., and during his ministration, caused by his individual exertions the erection of two churches for his congregation; last year his health had grown so delicate and his eyesight so defective that he resigned his charge, but only too late, to seek rest and recuperation; the Rev. Mr. Fowler, was the author of several works, among them *The American Pulpit*, which has had a large sale.

FOWLER, CAPT. JOHN, a soldier of the revolution who attained the rank of captain; member of congress from 1797 to 1807; d. at Lexington, Ky., Aug. 22, 1840, a. 85.

FOWLER, REV. JOHN W., at first studied law, and afterward a course of theology; was settled as a Presbyterian minister in Binghamton, N. Y., whence he went in May, 1836, to the charge of the First Presbyterian church of Utica; for gross immorality he was deposed in June, 1841; he was an eloquent public speaker and did effective service for Henry Clay in 1844; he established a law school at Saratoga, which he afterwards removed to Poughkeepsie; he d. at the latter place July 1st, 1873.

FOWLER, ROBERT, a leading merchant and prominent politician; d. at Baltimore, Md., March 3, 1874; he held the office of state treasurer from 1862 to 1870, and was a member of the present Maryland house of delegates. During the war he was a strong unionist and as a business man was largely identified with the commercial interests of the state.

FOWLER, SAMUEL, b. in N. J., in 1776; d. in Sussex co., N. J., Feb. 21, 1844, a. 65; was a distinguished physician, and a member of congress from New Jersey, from 1833 so 1837.

FOWLER, CAPT. SOLOMON, killed in the attack upon a picket guard at Horseneck, Ct., May 22, 1780; buried May 26, in the burying ground at Hunt's Point; he was a loyalist. (*Rivington's Royal Gazette*, June 3.)

FOWLER, THEODOSIUS, of New York, an officer of the revolution, and former owner of the town of Fowler, St. Lawrence co., N. Y., and other lands in northern New York.

FOX, JABEZ, removed from Ct. to Herk. co., N. Y., about 1810; was admitted to the bar Jan. 1813; settled in Herkimer and then at Little Falls where he was elected co. clerk in 1822, for 3 years; he d. at Herkimer, Jan. 1825, a. 35.

FOX, DR. JAMES L., for many years a physician at Cooperstown, N. Y.; d. in that village, Jan. 16, 1857.

FRANCIS, REV. AMZI, d. at Bridgehampton, N. Y., Oct. 18, 1844, a. 52; pastor of Presb. church.

FRANCIS, EBENEZER, financier, (only son of Col. Ebenezer F., who was killed at Hubbardton, Vt., July, 1777.) He came to Boston, Jan., 1787; became a large ship owner, and acquired a large fortune, estimated from 3½ to 4 millions; he was known in financial circles as a large dealer and operator in negotiable paper and stocks; he d. at Boston, Sept. 21, 1858, in his 83d year. (*Hist. Mag.*, ii, 347; *Am. Almanac*, 1858, p. 369.)

FRANCIS, GILBERT Y., d. at New Orleans, of yellow fever, Nov., 1839, formerly of Va.; his life was romantic and eventful; though a man of defective education his great energy of character and extensive travels, which extended to the four quarters of the globe, made him a most entertaining companion. (*Am. Almanac*, 1841, p. 278.)

FRANCIS, TENCH, many years agent of the Penn family in Pennsylvania, and first cashier of the Bank of North America, in which office he d. In 1780 he subscribed £5000 for supplying the American army with provisions.

FRANK, ANDREW (col'd), d. at Johnstown, R. I., Dec. 15, 1834, a. 104.

FRANK, JOHN, son of Conrad F., a patentee of Staley's 3d tract in Herkimer co.; he was many years a judge of the Herkimer co. court, served actively in the revolution and d. in German Flats, about 1836, in old age; his house was nearly opposite Herkimer village near Ft. Herkimer. (*Benton's Herkimer Co., N. Y.*, p. 309.)

FRANKLAND, SIR CHARLES HENRY, colonial collector at Boston; b. in 1716; inherited a baronetcy in 1747; resided several years in Boston; 1757, was consul general to Portugal; d. at Bath, Eng., Jan. 11, 1768, a. 51 y. 8 m. (*Mason's Life of.*)

FRANKLIN, MESHACK, d. in Surry co., N. C., Dec. 18, 1839, a. 67; was in congress from North Carolina in 1807–15.

FRANKLIN, WALTER, president, judge of the court of common pleas of Lancaster co.; d. at Lancaster, Feb. 7, 1836.

FRANKLIN, WALTER S., d. at Lancaster, Pa., Sept. 30, 1838; was of York co., Pa., clerk of the house of representatives of the United States.

FRANKLIN, WILLIAM TEMPLE, grandson of Dr. Benjamin F., and for some years his secretary; he edited the papers of his illustrious relative; d. at Paris, in May, 1823.

FRARY, Dr. Robert G., of Hudson, N. Y., d. Dec. 29, 1862, a. 69. (*Transac. N. Y. State Med. Soc.*, 1864, p. 435.)

FRAZER, Maj. Donald, U. S. A.; d. at Brooklyn, N. Y., March 6, 1860; served in the war of 1812; was near Gen. Pike when mortally wounded at York, N. C.; was a superior partizan officer.

FRAZER, Dr. James, a loyalist of S. C.; held an office under the crown; lost his estate under the act of 1782; a man of this name d. at Charleston in 1803.

FRAZER, John, a loyalist; was b. in Scotland; settled in N. Y. before the revolution; went to Nova Scotia; d. at Shelburne, in 1840, a. 88.

FRAZER, Lewis, a loyalist; settled in Nova Scotia in 1783; d. in Kings co. in 1835, a. 72.

FRAZER, John W., prof. in the University of Penn. at Philadelphia; d. Oct. 13, 1872, a. 63.

FRAZER, Thomas, a loyalist; was a major of the S. Car. loyalists

FRAZIER, William C., d. at Milwaukee, Wis., Oct. 18, 1838, a. 62; associate judge of the court of the territory of Wisconsin.

FREDET, Rev. Pierre, D.D., prof. in St. Mary's R. C. Seminary, Balt., about 1801, at Sehasat, Fr.; educated at Clermont; became a member of the soc. of St. Sulpice; came to Balt. in 1831; till his death was attached to St. Mary's Seminary in that city; was a diligent and thorough student and voluminous writer; d. Jan. 1, 1856. (*Metropolitan Cath. Almanac*, 1857, p. 43.)

FREEDLEY, John, b. in Norristown, Pa., May 22, 1793; was admitted to the bar in 1820; engaged in business of various kinds with success; was in congress from 1847 to 1851; d. Dec. 8, 1851.

FREEMAN, Enoch, patriot of the revolution; native of Eastham on Cape Cod; grad. at Harv. in 1729; was a delegate to a co. convention in Maine in 1774; was chosen to preside; was a delegate to the prov. conven. at Concord in 1774; with Jedediah Preble was employed in 1775 in preparing defenses for Falmouth and other points in Maine; was col. of a regt. till declining health prevented. (*Bradford's N. E. Biog.*)

FREEMAN, Rev. Evan E., of the N. C. conference M. E. ch. south; b. in Granville co., N. C., Aug. 15, 1820; d. in Pittsylvania co., Va., April 8, 1859.

FREEMAN, Rev. Joshua, d. at Adams Centre, N. Y., Feb. 14, 1860, (*N. Y. Reformer*, March 8, 1860.)

FREEMAN, Russell, of Sandwich, Mass.; d. in Boston, Mass., Jan. 19, 1842, a. 59; formerly collector of the port of New Bedford, and at several times in the state legislature, and of the executive counsel.

FREEMAN, Samuel, revolutionary patriot of Falmouth, Me.; was secretary of the Cumberland convention in 1774, and delegate to the 2d and 3d prov. cong. of Mass., where he was also, in the latter, secretary; he was clerk to the representatives in 1775; and served in many public trusts; he was an active friend of Bowdoin College, and a member of its board of trustees; d. at Portland, June, 1831, a. 88. (*Bradford's N. E. Biog.*)

FREEMAN, COL. WILLIAM H., of the U. S. marine corps; d. in Westboro, Mass., March, 1845, a. about 50; he entered the service in 1812, and was present in the action of the Constitution with the Java; and in that with the Cyane and Levant.

FRELINGHUYSEN, REV. JOHANNES, son of Rev. Jacobus Theodorus F., pastor at Raritan, N. J., from 1750, till his death in 1754, a. 28.

FRELINGHUYSEN, REV. THEODORUS, pastor of the R. P. Dutch church, Albany, from 1745; he took passage for Holland in 1760, and is said to have been lost overboard on the passage. (*Rogers's Hist. Discourse, R. P. D. Ch., Albany; Munsell's Hist. Coll. Albany*, i, p. 2.)

FRENCH, ABEL, of Albany; was in assembly from Oneida co., N. Y., (the part now Lewis co.), in 1799, 1801, 2, 3, and from Albany co. in 1810; d. in Albany Nov. 17, 1843, a. 78. (*Hough's Hist. Lewis Co.*, p. 84.)

FRENCH, MAJ. BENJAMIN B.; d. at Washington, D. C., Aug. 12, 1870; b. in N. H., went to Washington about 1830; was reading clerk in the house of representatives for several years, and clerk from Jan. 1847 to Dec. 1847; was afterwards com'r of pub. buildings and grounds; was a prominent free mason.

FRENCH, BENJAMIN VINTON, for many years a merchant in Boston, and well known for his skill in agriculture and horticulture; he d. in Dorchester, Mass., April 11, 1870, a. 68.

FRENCH, DANIEL, formerly attorney general of New Hampshire; d. at Chester, N. H., Oct. 16, 1840, a. 72.

FRENCH, GEORGE, (colored); d. at Poughkeepsie, N. Y., Sept. 7, 1868, a. 106.

FRENCH, JAMES, was in 1782, a captain in De Lancey's 1st battalion of loyalists; he went to St. John, N. B., in 1783, and drew a city lot and half pay; he was several years a magistrate in York co., and d. there in 1820, a. 75.

FRENCH, JOSEPH, of Jamaica, N. Y., was elected to the provincial congress of 1775, but refused to serve; in 1777 he contributed to a loyalist fund, and in 1780 he was an addresser of Gov. Robertson. (*Sabine's Loyalists.*)

FRENCH, RALPH HILL, d. in Manchester, N. H., Oct. 31, 1855; b. in Marblehead, Mass., Jan. 31, 1776; grad. at Harvard in 1796; practiced law in Essex county and was for twenty years register of deeds for that county.

FRENCH, SAMUEL T., d. at Concord, N. H., Feb., 1840, a. 38; weighed 430 lbs.

FRENCH, STEPHEN, d. May 22, 1842, in Prince William co., Va., a. 82; was in the revolutionary war.

FRENCH, THOMAS, a loyalist of N. Y., was in 1782 a captain in De Lancey's 1st battalion.

FRENCH, V. B., d. at Dorchester, Mass., April 11, 1860, a. 69; from 1812 to 1836 was a merchant in Boston and afterwards devoted to agricultural pursuits; in 1843, was one of the governor's council. (*Vincent's Semi An. Register*, p. 278.)

FREY, BARENT, a tory of N. Y., was in the royal service with Brant and a band of tories and Indians, ravaging the Mohawk valley.

FREY, HENDRICK, a loyalist of N. Y., served as a major in the revolution. (*Sabine's Loyalists.*)

FREY, PHILIP R., a tory of Tryon co., N. Y., entered the royal service as ensign in the 8th regt., was in the battle of Wyoming, and d. at Palatine, N. Y., in 1823; his son Samuel C., settled in Canada, and furnished for Wm. L. Stone particulars of the Wyoming massacre for the *Life of Brant.* (*Sabine's Loyalists.*)

FRICK, HENRY, d. in Washington, D. C., March 1, 1844, a. 48; member of congress from Pennsylvania; educated as a printer; became an editor, and served three sessions in the state legislature before being chosen to congress.

FRICK, WILLIAM, d. at Warm Sulphur Springs, Va., July 29, 1855; judge of the superior court of Baltimore.

FRINK, NATHAN, b. in Pomfret, Ct., entered the British service and was a capt. of cavalry in the Am. Legion, and aid to Arnold after his treason; he went to St. John, N. B., and a few years after to St. Andrew; finally moved to St. Stephen, and d. there Dec. 4, 1817, a. 60. He had been educated for the bar, and in New Brunswick was a merchant and shipowner, and for more than 30 y. a magistrate in Charlotte co.; he was nearly related to several prominent whig families in the United States. (*Sabine's Loyalists.*)

FRISBY, JAMES, was a captain in the Md. Loyalists in the revolution.

FROST, REV. BARZILLAI, b. in Effingham, N. H., grad. at Harvard, in 1830, studied theology at Cambridge; was instructor of undergraduates for 2 years, and settled at Concord, Mass., in 1837; he remained there till Oct., 1857, and d. there, Dec. 8, 1858; a. 54.

FROST, REV. JOHN, from March 1813, he was for many successive years minister of the Presbyterian church of Whitesboro; a useful and respected minister.

FROTHINGHAM, JOSEPH, d. in Salem, Mass., Aug. 12, 1846, a. 75; a shoe manufacturer, in which business he acquired a very handsome estate. (*Am. Almanac*, 1847, p. 335.)

FRY, JOSEPH, captain of the filibustering steamer Virginius; was executed at Santiago de Cuba, Nov. 7, 1873, with 36 of the crew, and on the next day 12 more Cuban passengers were shot; he was a son of Major Fry of the United States army, who died in Florida during the Seminole Indian war. Young Fry was appointed a midshipman in the navy in 1841, and after the formation of the school at Annapolis studied there for nearly a year, and was graduated a passed midshipman; he married the daughter of Capt. Sands of the United States army; in 1847 Fry fought a duel near Washington, with Midshipman Brown of Mississippi; but after drawing his antagonist's fire generously refused to return it. He served for 20 years in the American navy, and his record during that time is a good one; when Louisiana, his native state, seceded, he threw up his lieutenant's commission, and went south; he was given a command in the rebel army, their navy not being sufficiently large to furnish commissions to all the naval officers who seceded, and served during the war in the south-west; he is charged with having allowed his command on one occasion to fire on our sailors, who had leaped overboard to escape the scalding water and steam from the boiler, which had been penetrated by a rebel shot; this is denied by Capt. Fry's friends; all agreed that he was a brave man.

FRY, WILLIAM, b. in 1777; with Robert Walsh, he established the *National Gazette*, of Philadelphia, which acquired great prominence, and was connected with that paper till 1849; d. at Philadelphia, Aug. 31, 1855, in his 78th year. (*Simpson's Eminent Philadelphians.*)

FRY, WILLIAM H., d. in Philadelphia, Pa., Aug. 31, 1855, a. 78, was founder of the *National Gazette.*

FRYE, PETER, a loyalist of Salem, Mass.; he grad. at Harvard in 1744, was in the gen. court, and in 1768 was a rescinder; he was a judge of com. pleas, regr. of probate, and col. of Essex co. militia; he d. in England, Feb., 1820, a. 97. His dau. m. Dr. Peter Oliver, a loyalist of Mass., and afterwards Sir John Knight of the British navy; she d. at her seat near London in 1839.

FULLER, AZARIAH, a revolutionary soldier; native of Fitchburg, Mass.; d. at Hingham, Mass., March 1846, a. 82; he entered the army at the age of 16, and served in Capt. Bradford's company.

FULLER, BENJAMIN, native of Ireland; became the most eminent ship-broker of his time, at Philadelphia; acquired a handsome fortune, and d. unm.; in 1780, he subscribed £2,000 to supply the American army with provisions. (*Simpson's Eminent Philadelphians.*)

FULLER, GEORGE, a S. C. loyalist, lost his estate by confiscation in the revolution.

FULLER, HENRY HOLTON, b. at Princetown, Mass., July 1, 1790; son of Rev. Timothy F.; grad. at Harvard in 1811, taught at Exeter, N. H.; studied law at Litchfield, Ct., and was admitted to practice Sept. 19, 1815, at Boston; he was several times a representative in the state legislature, and in 1832, aided in starting the *Boston Atlas* and held an interest in it till 1835; he was instrumental in effecting several useful public improvements and was long a laborious and successful member of the Suffolk bar. (*Livingston's Biographical Sketches*, p. 121.)

FULLER, PERRY, a prominent politician; d. at Washington, D. C., Jan. 11, 1871, a. 44; was active in promoting the free state party operations in Kansas in the troubles preceding the late war, and held several offices in the territories; in 1868, was appointed collector of customs at New Orleans, by Pres. Johnson.

FULLER, PHILO C., d. at Rose Hill, near Geneva, N. Y., Aug. 1855; was in assembly in 1829 and 1830; in the state senate in 1831–2; and in congress from 1833 to 1837; in 1840, was appointed assits. post master general, from which office he was removed by Pres. Tyler; went to Mich., but returned, and became comptroller of the city of New York.

FULLER, REV. SAMUEL, d. at Rensselaerville, N. Y., April 9, 1842; founder and first pastor of Trinity church at that place, in his 75th year, and the 50th year of his ministry. (*Two Sermons by his son Rev Samuel Fuller on the death of S. F.*, Andover, Mass., 1843.)

FULLER, SAMUEL W., of the Chicago bar; d. Oct. 25, 1873; he was one of the oldest and ablest lawyers of that city.

FULLER, SILAS, M.D., was distinguished as a surveyor in the war of 1812–15; practiced in eastern Ct., till 1834, when he succeeded Dr. Todd, as sup't of the Retreat for the Insane at Hartford, where he held till 1839; he was several years pres. of the Ct. State Med. Soc.; and d. at Hartford, Nov. 1847, a. 73. (*Am. Jour. Insanity*, iv, 279.)

FULLER, WILLIAM A., d. in Ontario co., N. Y., Nov. 10, 1868, a. 64 y.; was justice of the peace 38 years, and associate justice of the county court.

FULLER, WILLIAM S., an American statesman; b. in Cecil co., Md., 1795; settled in Arkansas, where he was appointed first secretary; in 1835–6, was governor and from 1836 to the end of life, U. S. senator; d. near Black Rock, Ark., Aug. 15, 1844.

FULLERTON, DAVID, d. at Greencastle, Pa., Feb. 1, 1843, a. 72; was several years in the state legislature and from 1819 to 1820 in congress.

FULTON, JOHN H., a member of the 23d congress; d. at Abingdon, Va., Jan. 28, 1836.

FURMAN, GABRIEL, d. in New York city, July 23, 1844; member of assembly in 1796 and 1814, and state senator from 1839 to 1842.

FYFFE, DR. CHARLES, held an office in S. C., after the fall of Charleston in 1780, and his estate was confiscated.

GABEL, JOHN, a loyalist; settled in New Brunswick, and d. at St. John, in 1816, a. 84.

GAGNA, GEN. ANTONIO, was 52 years in the Mexican service, and was governor of St. Juan d'Ulloa, when bombarded by the French; he adhered to Iturbide during all his vicissitudes, and was brave, benevolent and courtly; he d. at Puebla, Mexico, June 24, 1848.

GAINES, MAJ. AUGUSTUS W., U. S. A. paymaster; d. at Fort Smith, Arkansas, Feb. 19, 1860. (*Vincent's Semi-An. Register*, p. 120.)

GAIR, S. S., d. at Liverpool, Eng., Feb. 13, 1847; native of Boston; was the chief manager in the Liverpool house, and one of the partners of the firm of Baring Brothers & Co.

GAITHER, GEN. WILLIAM LINGAN, of Montgomery co., Md.; formerly a prominent politician of that state and for many years in the house of delegates and state senate; d. at Berkeley Springs, Aug. 2, 1858.

GALBRAITH, BENJAMIN, an eminent lawyer in New York city; d. May 9, 1871.

GALBRAITH, JOHN, was a native of Penna.; member of congress from that state in 1833–7, and from 1839 to 41; d. at Erie, Pa., June 15, 1860, being at the time judge of the 6th judicial dist. of the state.

GALE, REV. GEORGE WASHINGTON, entered Union College from Greenbush, N. Y.; grad. in 1814; then pursued theological studies at Princeton; became pastor of Presbyterian church in Adams, N. Y. (1832), whence he removed to Whitesboro (1828?); was principal of the Oneida Institute; about 1834 (?) he headed a colony which settled Galesburg, Ill., which place was named from him and there he resided until his death, 1866; founded Knox College at Galesburg; was a professor therein.

GALE, SAMUEL, member of gen. assembly from Orange co., N. Y., from 1750 to 1759 and from 1769 to 75; was regarded as a loyalist and is alluded to in *McFingal*.

GALE, DR. SAMUEL, a pioneer physician at Troy, N. Y.; 5th son of John G., of Goshen, N. Y.; b. March 3, 1743; resided at Killingworth, Ct., till 1787; settled at Troy in that year; d. Jan. 1799; four of his sons were merchants. (*Woodworth's Troy*, 48.)

GALE, SAMUEL, b. in Hampshire, Eng., Oct. 14, 1747; came to America as paymaster in the army about 1770; settled in Westminster, Vt., became a clerk of the court; bore a conspicuous part as a loyalist in the Westminster massacre; was imprisoned the next day; in March following was sent to Northampton, where he was released; went to N. Y.; was soon after seized and again imprisoned, but at length released on parole; removed to Quebec; was appointed provincial secretary; d. at Farnham, Canada, June 26, 1826. (*Hall's Eastern Vermont*, p. 643; *Sabine's Loyalists.*)

GALES, WESTON B., editor of the *Raleigh Register*, N. C.; d. at Petersburg, Va., July 19, 1848, in his 47th year.

GALLAGHER, REV. JAMES, a Universalist clergyman; d. at Hamilton, O., July 11, 1857.

GALLATIN, MRS. HANNAH, a daughter of James Nicholson; first on the list of American port captains; widow of the Hon. Albert Gallatin; d. at New York, May 25, 1849, in her 83d year. (*Stryker's Am. Reg.*, ii, 504.)

GALLUP, ALBERT, d. Nov. 1851, in Providence, R. I.; sheriff of the county of Albany in 1831–4; a representative to the 25th congress from the Albany district and collector of Providence during Mr. Polk's administration.

GALLUP, ELIAS, formerly sheriff of Lewis co., N. Y.; d. in Harrisburgh, N. Y., Oct. 25, 1864, a. 64.

GALLUP, ROBERT, last survivor of the Ft. Griswold massacre in the revolution; d. at Greene, N. Y., May 19, 1858, a. 98.

GALT, PATRICK, lieut. col. U. S. A., a native of Williamsburgh, Va., entered the army in the war of 1812; he d. in the service at Phila., Jan. 12, 1848.

GALUSHA, REV. ELON, minister of the Baptist church in Whitsboro from May, 1816, to the spring of 1831; afterwards in charge of the Baptist church in Utica; an esteemed and successful preacher.

GAMBEL, DR. WILLIAM, an enterprising explorer and naturalist of Philadelphia; he left for California in 1849 by the overland route and d. Dec. 13, 1849; his favorite sciences were botany and ornithology. (*Am. Jour. Sci. and Arts*, 2d ser., xi, 143.)

GAMBLE, COL. JOHN M., of the United States marine corps; d. at Brooklyn, N. Y., Sept. 11, 1836.

GAMBLE, DAVID, of the 8th Pa. regt. in the revolution; in 1778 he deserted, was tried, found to have counterfeit continental money in his possession and sentenced to suffer death.

GAMBLE, LIEUT. PETER, U. S. navy; killed Sept. 11, 1814, in naval battle before Plattsburg.

GAMBLE, ROGER L., d. Dec. 20, 1847, was a member of congress from Georgia from 1833 to 1835, and from 1841 to 1843, and afterwards a judge of the superior court of that state.

GAMMEL, ELIZABETH, d. in Georgia, Sept. 28, 1859, a. 115.

GANNETT, BENJAMIN, husband of Deborah Gannett the woman soldier of the revolution; d. Feb., 1837, a. 80; at the time of his death a bill was pending in congress for giving him a pension in consideration of the military services of his wife.

GANNETT, DEBORAH, heroine soldier in the revolution; enlisted and served in male apparel through the war, under the name of Robert Shurtlieff; discharged a soldier's duty faithfully, and was discharged unsuspected and unblemished; m. Benj. Gannett, Apr. 9, 1784; was long a pensioner of Massachusetts, and of the U. S., and d. April 9, 1827; her maiden name was Deborah Sampson. (*Memoir Dedham, Mass.*, 1797, 12 mo., pp. 258, with port.; *Women of the Revolution, by E. F. Ellet; Hist. Mag.*, ii, 339.)

GANNON, MARY, (Mrs. Stephenson), comic actress; b. at N. Y., Oct. 8, 1829, and d. Feb. 22, 1868; m. Geo. W. Stephenson, a lawyer, and after his death, resumed her maiden name.

GANSEVOORT, LEONARD, br. of Gen. Peter G.; was a patriot of the revolution, and much of his life devoted to commercial pursuits at Albany; he was pres. of the state const. conven. of 1777, and 1st judge of Albany co., from Mar. 19, 1794, to Feb. 7, 1797; the latter part of his life was spent at Whitehall, N. Y. (*Rogers's Hist. Discourse*, p. 102.)

GANSEVOORT, TEN EYCK, M. D., son of Conrad G. of Alb.; b. at Minden, N. Y., Jan. 5, 1803; grad. at Union Coll. in 1822, and at the Univ. of Pa. in 1825; practiced in Albany and in Bath, N. Y., where he gained reputation as a surgeon; he d. in Sept., 1842, a. 40. (*Munsell's Ann. Alb.*, ix, 111.)

GANSON, JOHN, b. in Leroy, N. Y.; grad. at Harvard in 1839; removed to Buffalo, at the age of 30; was a prominent lawyer, and in 1862–3, a state senator; d. at Buffalo, Sept., 1874, a. 57.

GANTT, ROBERT, d. in Greenville, S. C., Oct. 18, 1850, a. 85; was appointed to the bench of the general sessions and common pleas of South Carolina in 1815, and discharged the duties of this office till 1842, when he resigned.

GANYARD, JAMES, b. at Killingsworth, Conn., Jan. 14, 1772; removed to Bristol, Ontario co., in 1793; and in 1811 to Granger, Ohio, where he d. Dec. 20, 1844.

GARDEN, BENJAMIN, of S. C.; was a loyalist, but in 1775 a member of provincial congress; his estate was amerced 12 p. c. in 1782.

GARDEN, LIEUT. JAMES, royal Newfoundland regt.; killed in action on Lake Erie, Sept. 10, 1813.

GARDEN, WILLIAM, a loyalist; was employed under the crown after the revolution, and d. in York co., New Brunswick in 1812, a. 63, holding at that time the office of assist. dep. qr. mr. gen. of the garrison at Fredericton, N. B.

GARDINER, CHARLES K., formerly col. in the U. S. army; d. at Washington, D. C., Nov. 1, 1869, a. 82; b. in N. J.; entered the army as ensign in 1808; adj. gen. under Brown in 1812; adj. gen. of U. S. from 1815 to 1818, when he resigned; was 1st assist. p. m gen. under Jackson; auditor of the treasury under Van Buren; p. m. at Washington under Polk; surveyor gen. of Oregon under Pierce; was the author of a dictionary of the army, and other military works.

GARDINER, DAVID, killed on board the steamer Princeton by accident, Feb. 28, 1844, a. 55; resided in New York; from 1824 to 1827 state senator.

GARDINER, FERDINAND, many years U. S. consul at Port Praya; d. May 6, 1847.

GARDINER, JAMES B., editor of the *Ohio Free Enquirer;* d. at Marion, O., of apoplexy, April 13, 1837.

GARDINER, JETHRO, d. at Dorchester, Mass., May 25, 1838 (colored), supposed to be over 100 years old.

GARDINER, VALENTINE, entered the British army in 1755; became a major in 1776; served in the southern states in the revolution; presumed to have d. about 1781. (*Wilson's Orderly Book*, 192.)

GARDNER, EDWIN L., of Nashville, Tenn.; a prominent merchant; d. June 18, 1860.

GARDNER, FRANCIS, formerly of Walpole; member of congress from New Hampshire from 1807 to 1809; d. at Roxbury, Mass., June 25, 1833, a. 63.

GARDNER, DR. HENRY, b. in Boston, Aug. 2, 1779; grad. at Harvard in 1798; studied medicine, but having inherited a large amount of property did not practice; was a member of the constitutional convention of 1820 from Dorchester; in the state legislature from 1822 to 24; in the senate from Norfolk co. from 1825 to 27; d. in Boston, June 19, 1858.

GARDNER, JOHN, a soldier of the revolution; d. at Lower Bethel, Pa., April 1, 1850, a. 104 years.

GARLAND, JOHN, first lieut. on board a British vessel in battle of Lake Erie, Sept. 10, 1813.

GARNIER, JULIEN, Jesuit missionary, b. in 1643, arrived in Canada, Oct. 27, 1662; was ordained April, 1666; sent to the Mohawks, May 17, 1668, passed to Onondaga and thence to Seneca; on the mission till 1683; he appears to have been sent to the Cantons in 1702. (*Doc. Hist. N. Y.*, iv, 292.)

GARRETT, COL. HENRY A., d. in Adams co., Miss., Feb. 12, 1844, a. about 38; a lawyer by profession.

GARRETTSON, REV. FREEBORN, an itinerant Methodist minister; began to preach in 1775; and d. in New York city, Sept. 27, 1827, a. 76.

GARRETSON, JOHN, a soldier of the revolutionary war; d. in Somerset co., N. J., Aug. 1, 1842, a. 70.

GARRISON, JOHN, a loyalist, settled in New Brunswick and was several years in the house of assembly; he d. on the St. John in 1810; Joseph G., d. at Deer Island, N. B., in 1819, a. 50.

GARROTT, WILLIAM, d. in Warren co., N. B., about Jan. 1834, a. 105 years.

GARROW, NATHANIEL, marshal of the U. S. dist. court for the northern dist. of New York; b. in Barnstable, Mass., April 26, 1780; d. at Auburn, N. Y., March 3, 1841. (*Hall's Hist Auburn*, p. 540.)

GARTH, WILLIAM, was several years prof. of mathematics in the Georgetown College; settled on a farm near Paris, Bourbon co., Ky., and perished on the Lady Elgin on Lake Michigan, Sept. 7, 1860. (*N. Y. Times*, Sept. 14, 1860.)

GARTLAND, Rt. Rev. Francois Xavier, Roman Catholic bishop, of the diocese of Georgia; d. of yellow fever Sept. 20, 1854, during an epidemic, in which he refused to leave his people and the post of duty.

GARYAN-WAH-GAH, or Corn Planter; a celebrated Indian chief; friendly to the Americans in the revolution; d. at the Seneca Reservation, Pa., Feb. 17, 1836.

GASTON, William, d. at Newark, N. J., Sept. 12, 1837; a merchant of Savannah, Ga.

GATLIFF, Capt. Charles, d. in Whitley co., Ky., June 30, 1838, a. about 90; was an early adventurer in Kentucky; appointed a captain of Martin's Station in 1780; served in most of the campaigns in Kentucky.

GAULTIER, Rev. Lucien, first Catholic priest of St. Paul; b. in the department of Ardechen, France in 1811; was ordained at Dubuque, Jan. 5, 1840; soon entered on his duties at Fort Snelling; in 1848 he returned to France, but returned to Prairie du Chien where he d. Feb. 21, 1866. (*Collec. Minn. Hist. Soc.*, iii. 221.)

GAVIT, John E., son of Joseph G., b. in N. Y. city, Oct. 29, 1817; learned the transfer branch of bank note engraving with Burton, Durand, and Edmonds; settled in Albany in 1838; in the employment of Hall, Packard & Cushman, bank note engravers; in 1840 on the retirement of C, became partner; successful competitor for engraving part of *Nat. Hist. of N. Y. Survey;* the firm failing in 1841, he started business for himself; many years did an extensive business in engraving at Albany; in 1859 went to N. Y. having been instrumental in establishing the American Bank Note Co. by consolidation of many interests, of which his was one; became general supt. in the new company; vice pres. in 1864; in 1866 succeeded G. W. Hatch as president, which office he held till his death at Stockbridge, Mass., Aug. 25, 1874. Mr. G. was an active and energetic man, devotedly attached to the study of natural history; a skillful microscopist; a proficient in minute dissections, and the preparation of objects of which he left a large and valuable collection; took an early interest in telegraph; was well versed in the sciences upon which it depends; in short his active mind appeared to grasp and comprehend almost any science that he took in hand. Although eminently successful in the business he had chosen, there were many of his friends who would have wished that his early education and subsequent studies had been exclusively given to science, in which he evinced especial talents, and might have won the highest fame as an original investigator and pioneer discoverer; his later studies related to the microscopic fauna of the north-eastern coast, and Bay of Fundy, and facts concerning the gulf stream in its influence upon deposits; from a great number of facts which he had accumulated he was deducing a theory which would have been published in a year or two had his life been spared; was pres. of the N. Y. Microscopical Soc.; a member of the Bailey Club, whose specialty relates to microscopy.

GAY, Allen, revolutionary soldier; entered the army at 16, as his father's substitute; was attached to Gen. Greene's army; served at the battle of Eutau Springs, where he took 5 prisoners; removed to Ga. after the war; d. in Columbia co., a. 82. (*White's Hist. Ga.*, p. 414.)

GAY, Ebenezer, d. in Hingham, Mass., Feb. 11, 1842, a. 71; grad. at Harvard in 1789; studied law with Gov. Gore; two years in the state

Massachusetts; was offered the office of judge of the court of com. pleas, but declined.

GAY, GEORGE, d. at Andover, Mass., Nov. 9, 1843, a. 53; grad. at Harvard in 1810; soon after his admission to the bar removed from Dedham, his native town, to Boston, where he remained in practice till his death.

GAY, MRS. LYDIA, d. at Natick, Mass., April 12, 1837, a. 103; her hair which had been white with age, was turning to its original color, black.

GAY, DR. MARTIN, was b. at Boston, Feb. 16, 1803; was the eldest son of Ebenezer Gay; grad. at Harvard in 1823; received a medical diploma in 1826; was one of the founders of the Boston soc. of nat. hist.; particularly occupied in mineralogy and chemistry in the intervals of his professional engagements; d. at Boston, January 12, 1850. (*Am. Jour. Sci. and Arts*, 2d ser., ix, 305; *Stryker's Am. Reg.*, iv., 444.)

GAY, SAMUEL, son of Martin Gay; b. in Boston; grad. at Harvard in 1775; left the country soon after the revolution began and settled in New Brunswick; he was there in assembly; several years a magistrate, and chief justice of com. pleas; he d. at Ft. Cumberland, N. B., Jan. 21, 1847, a. 93. (*Sabine's Loyalists.*)

GAY, MAJ. SETH, a native of Mass.; removed to Gardiner, Me., in 1783; he was present at the battle of Lexington, and although a lad of but fifteen, he was one of the first to give notice of the approach of the British; he was town clerk of Gardiner 41 years, and postmaster a quarter of a century, and d. in that town, Jan. 30, 1851, a. 89.

GAYLORD, CAPT. ENOCH, a revolutionary soldier; d. at Triangle, N. Y., Nov. 7, 1857, a. 94.

GAYLORD, WYLLYS, b. in Bristol, Conn., in 1792; removed in 1802 with his father to Otisco, N. Y.; with slender opportunities for education, he evinced a fine taste for literature, and self taught, became an effective writer and contributed to the magazines; d. at Howell Hill, Camillus, N. Y., March 27, 1844, in his 51st year. (*Clark's Onondaga*, ii, 339.)

GEAKE, SAMUEL, a whig soldier; taken prisoner and induced to become a spy; he was arrested in 1778, tried and condemned to death, and confessed his crime, but was spared for the information he possessed concerning Hammell, formerly brigade major to Gen. James Clinton. (*Sabine's Loyalists.*)

GEARY, JOHN WHITE, ex-gov. of Pennsylvania; d. at Harrisburg, Pa., Feb. 8, 1873; he was b. Dec. 30, 1819, in Westmoreland co., Pa., and after spending some years in commercial pursuits, he became a civil engineer and surveyed rail road lines in Kentucky; on the outbreak of the Mexican war he promptly responded to the call for volunteers, and organized a company, which he named the American Highlanders, afterward incorporated in the 2d Pennsylvania regiment, of which Geary was made lieutenant colonel; he joined, with this regiment, the army of Gen. Scott at Vera Cruz, and served with marked distinction in the advance upon and capture of the Mexican capital; President Polk recognized his services by appointing him postmaster of San Francisco, and mail agent for the Pacific coast. Col. Geary arrived in California in April, 1849, and during the three years which he spent in the young state, he held successively several important judicial and municipal offices, including the mayoralty of San Francisco; he took an active part in establishing order and promoting the prosperity of the golden state, displaying considerable executive ability. After spending three years at farming in his native county, he was appointed in 1856, governor of the territory of Kansas, then disturbed by the free soil and pro-slavery conflicts; he held this position about six months, when he tendered his resignation to President Buchanan, who had just come into power. Gov. Geary returned to his Pennsylvania farm, and was residing there when the war for the union began; he promptly tendered his services, and received the commission of colonel of the 28th regiment of Pennsylvania volunteers, which he had organized within a month; henceforth he was one of the most active and prominent soldiers of the war; he was in command in several minor engagements in the Shenandoah valley in the fall of 1861; in April, 1862, he received the commission of brigadier general, and, with his brigade, the second of the first division of Gen. Banks's corps, served in the Cedar mountain campaign; he was severely wounded at the battle of Cedar mountain, and was disabled for active service until December, when he was again in the field, and captured Winchester from the confederates; in 1863 he was promoted to a major generalship and placed in command of the second division of the twelfth army corps; in this capacity he served in the great battles of Fredericksburg, Chancellorsville, and Gettysburg, and in 1864 was ordered to Tennessee to join Gen. Sherman; assuming command of the second division of the twentieth corps, he joined in the "march to the sea," participating prominently in several of the principal engagements; addressing his troops, in 1864, at Savannah, of which he had been appointed military governor, he enumerated their battles as follows: Rich mountain, Carrick's Ford, Winchester, Port Republic, Bolivar, Cedar mountain, Second Bull Run, Antietam, Chancellorsville, Gettysburg, Wauhatchie, Lookout mountain, Missionary Ridge, Ringgold, Mill Creek Gap, Resaca, New Hope Church, Pine hill, Muddy creek, Nove's creek, Kolb's Farm, Kenesaw, Peach Tree creek, Atlanta, and Savannah; following the fortunes of Sherman, he served in the Carolina campaigns, and witnessed the surrender of Johnson, his military career terminating only with the close of the war.

In March, 1866, the republican state convention of Pennsylvania nominated him for governor, and after an animated contest with Heister Clymer, the democratic nominee, he was elected by a majority of 17,178; he was reëlected three years later by a reduced majority, over Asa Packer, and retired from his official duties as recently as the 20th ult., when Gen. Hartranft came into office. (*N. Y. Tribune.*)

GEDDES, JAMES, b. near Carlisle, Pa., July 22, 1763; when a young man, in 1793, went to Onondaga, and engaged in salt making; settled in Camillus; became a surveyor and was one of the engineers of the Erie canal, of which he was an early and earnest advocate; was in assembly in 1804, and 1822, and in congress in 1813–15; was engaged in canal surveys in Ohio, Pennsylvania and the south and west; in 1809, became an associate justice, and in 1812, a judge of the Onondaga co. court; d. Aug. 19, 1838. (*Clark's Onondaga*, ii, 45, with a portrait.)

GEDNEY, DR. ELEAZAR, a skillful dentist; settled at Utica, some time prior to 1824; he removed thence to Orange, N. Y.; in 1828 he received the honorary degree of M. D., from the regents of the state.

GEER, SAMUEL, a revolutionary soldier; d. at Fredonia, N. Y., March 31, 1860, in his 97th year; b. at Preston, near New London, Conn.; removed in 1787 to Paris, Oneida co., and in 1806 to Chautauque co., N. Y.; was a volunteer in the war of 1812.

GEFFRARD, CHARLES CLODOMIR FABRE, colonel in the Haytien army, and son of the president of Hayti; d. in Port au Prince, Hayti, Jan. 28, 1859.

GEIGER, JACOB, of S. C., a loyalist and office-holder under the crown after the surrender of Charleston; his estate was confiscated.

GELBARDT, DR. LEON, a volunteer physician from Richmond, Va., in the yellow fever epidemic at Portsmouth, Va., in the autumn of 1855; fell a victim to the disease.

GEORGE, CAPT., civil and war chief of the Onondaga nation of Indians; d. on the Onondaga reservation, nine miles south of Syracuse, Sept. 24, 1873, a. 78. Capt. George was with Gen. Scott at Lundy's Lane, and was bearer of dispatches to the Onondagas for reinforcements; in late years he was the recognized head of the remnants of the six nations.

GERHART, ANDREW, member of the general assembly of Ohio from Richland county; d. at his residence in Bellville, O., Nov. 24, 1868, a. 36; b. in Cumberland co., Penn.; settled in Richland co., twenty years before his death.

GERRARD, GEN. JAMES, d. in Bourbon co., Ky., Sept. 1, 1838, a 64; was many years a member of the legislature of Kentucky, and an officer of militia in the war of 1812; was a distinguished agriculturist.

GERRISH, MOSES, grad. at Harvard in 1762, and in the revolution was in the commissary dep. of the royal army. With Thos. Ross and one Jones he undertook to found a settlement on the island of Grand Menan, N. B., but failed; he was many years a magistrate, and d. in 1730, a. 80. (*Sabine's Loyalists.*)

GERSTNER, FRANCIS ANTHONY CHEV. DE, of Vienna, a distinguished Austrian engineer, d. at Philadelphia, Pa., April 12, 1840, a. 44; b. in Prague, Bohemia, April 17, 1796, and educated under his father who was a distinguished mathematician and founder of the Polytechnic School at Prague; at 21, was appointed prof. of practical geometry at the Polytechnic School of Vienna, and held 6 years; pub. an elaborate work on practical mechanics in 3 vols., 4to; after a visit to England, he obtained a charter for a rail road from Budweis on the Moldau, to Lintz, on the Danube, and began work at his own risk; it was finished by a company, in 1832; is 130 miles long, and the first executed on the continent of Europe; in 1834, he went to Russia, and in 1837 opened a rail road from St. Petersburg to Zarskoe-Selo and Pawlowsky; having made repeated visits to England, and having traveled through Germany, Belgium, Holland and France, he put in execution a favorite plan of visiting the United States, where he arrived in Nov., 1838; was everywhere received with due attention, and visited various parts of the country, examining with great care the public works, particularly the rail roads, and collected a great mass of information which it was his intention to publish. (*Am. Almanac*, 1841, p. 290. The Almanac of 1840 has an article by him on American and Belgian railroads. *Griswold's Biog. Annual*, 1841, p. 136.)

GETMAN, MARGERET, d. at Phila., May 21, 1834, a. 108; she was a native of Frankfort, Germany, and had lived 70 years in Phila.

GETTIS, JAMES, d. at Tampa, Fla., Dec. 14, 1867; had been a member of the legislature, and district judge.

GHOLSON, JAMES H., b. in Va; grad. at Princeton, in 1820, was circuit judge in Va.; and a member of the 23d congress (1833–5); d. at Brunswick, Va., July 2, 1848, a. 50.

GIBBENS, EDWARD, of Pa., was in 1778 ordered to appear and stand trial for treason, or have his estate confiscated.

GIBBON, DR. J. H., d. in Baltimore, Md. Dec. 16, 1868, a. 74; was a native of Philadelphia, but had lived south many years, and was the father of Maj. Gen. J. H. Gibbon.

GIBBS, DAVID, d. at Norwalk, O., March 16, 1840, a. 51; was an early settler of Huron co., and many years clerk of the court of common pleas.

GIBBS, JOHN W., of Charleston, S. C., a loyalist, was banished in 1782, and his estate confiscated.

GIBB, THOMAS, was in 1782, a surgeon of the N. Y. loyalist volunteers.

GIBBS, ZACHARIAH, of S. C.; held office under the crown in the revolution, and his estate was confiscated.

GIBSON, ABRAHAM P., d. in London, Eng., Nov. 30, 1852; was many years consul of the U. S., at St. Petersburg.

GIBSON, HENRY B., native of Washington co., N. Y.; in 1803, he was a clerk in Utica; in 1809, teller of the Manhattan Branch Bank of that place, and three years later of the Bank of Utica; after carrying on for six years a successful mercantile business in N. Y., he was appointed in February, 1820, cashier of the Ontario Bank at Cannandaigua; this post he held until the expiration of the charter Jan., 1856, having acquired reputation as a banker, and amassed a large property; his death occurred Nov. 20th, 1863, at the age of 81.

GIBSON, JAMES, d. in Philadelphia, Pa., July 8, 1856, a. 87; oldest member of the Philadelphia bar, having been admitted in Sept., 1791.

GIFFORD, ARCHER, a respectable lawyer of New Jersey; d. at Newark, N. J., May 12, 1859, a. 64.

GILBERT, BENJAMIN J., a native of Brookfield, Mass.; graduated at Yale Coll., in 1786; and settled as a lawyer at Hanover, N. H.; he maintained a highly respectable standing in his profession during more than a quarter of a century; and d. Jan. 1, 1850, a. 85. (*Stryker's Am. Reg.*, iv, 440.)

GILBERT, BRADFORD, of Freetown, Mass., br. of Tho. F. jr.; was proscribed and banished in 1778; settled in New Brunswick, in 1783; and received a lot in St. John; in 1803, he was an alderman; he d. in 1814, a. 68.

GILBERT, FRANCIS, a loyalist, and naval officer of New Brunswick; d. at St. John, in 1821, a. 82.

GILBERT, DAVID, d. in Mansfield, Mass., Sept. 12, 1842, a. 71; counselor at law and a graduate of Harvard, in 1797.

GILBERT, ELISHA M., leather dealer of Utica, an efficient and prosperous business man; he was president of the Michigan Southern rail road, a director of the First National Bank of Utica, and of the Central Bank of New York, a trustee in other public enterprises; he d. March 16, 1868, a. 61.

GILBERT, Ezekiel, b. in Middletown, Conn., in 1755; grad. at Yale in 1778; was in congress in 1793–7, and in assembly in 1799, 1800 and 1801; for thirty years before his death he was deprived of active usefulness by paralysis; and d. at his home in Hudson, N. Y., in July, 1841; he was a lawyer by profession.

GILBERT, Marinus W., many years a merchant at Watertown, N. Y.; held several important town and county offices, was interested in a privateering enterprise on the St. Lawrence in the war; and d. June 7, 1833, a. 53. (*Hough's Hist. Jeff. Co. N. Y.*, p. 430.)

GILBERT, Perez, of Freetown, Mass., was proscribed and banished as a tory; settled in New Brunswick with his father and brothers and d. there.

GILBERT, Samuel, of Berkley, Mass., br. of Thos. G., and went with him to Halifax, in 1776; in 1778 he was proscribed and banished; he settled in New Brunswick, but finally returned to the U. S.

GILBERT, Stephen F., member of assembly from Steuben co., N. Y., in 1873; d. at Hornellsville, N. Y., June 14, 1874.

GILBERT, Sylvester, in 1756, in Hebron, Conn; grad. at Dartmouth in 1775; studied law, and was admitted to practice law in 1777, at Hebron; in 1780, was in gen. assem; in 1788, state's attorney, for Tolland co., and held this office 21 y.; in 1807, became chief judge of the county court and judge of probate, and held till 1825, except a term in congress in 1818–9; in 1810, was teacher of a law school, and contin. 7 y.; in 1826, in the legislature, and speaker; had been elected to that office 30 times; d. Jan. 1846.

GILBERT, Thomas, of Berkley, Mass., son of Francis G., fled to Boston in 1775, but did not accompany his father to Halifax; he was proscribed and banished in 1778; was an active loyalist, and settled in New Brunswick, where he d. on the river St. John.

GILBERT, Thomas, of Freetown, Mass., a loyalist; was in 1745, a captain in the siege of Louisburg, and in 1755, a lieut. col. under Brig. Gen. Ruggles at Crown Point. After the death of Col. Ephraim Williams he succeeded to the command of his regiment; in the revolution he was an early and decided tory, and at the time in the legislature and a col. of militia; he raised 300 loyalists, was bitterly denounced by the provincial congress, fled to Boston, in May, 1775, went to Halifax, in 1776, was proscribed and banished in 1778, and continued with the army but not in commission through the war; in 1783, he settled in Nova Scotia, and later in New Brunswick, where he d. in 1796, a. 82. (*Sabine's Loyalists.*)

GILCHRIST, Edward, surgeon in the navy; resident physician at Chelsea hospital; d. at Boston, Nov. 7, 1860, a. 57.

GILCHRIST, John, d. in Charlton, Saratoga co., N. Y., May 4, 1849, a. 75; b. in Scotland, and emigrated to America when 15 ys. old; was three times elected to assembly and was 9 years one of the judges of the court of common pleas.

GILCHRIST, Robert B., d. in Charleston, S. C., May 1, 1856; judge of the U. S. district court of South Carolina.

GILES, JOHN, of Salisbury, d. in Stanley co., N. C., while on his circuit, March 2, 1846; he grad. at the University of N. C., in 1808, studied law, and was a member of the bar for more than thirty years; in 1829 he was elected to congress, but resigned before taking his seat, on account of ill health; he was a member of the N. C. constitutional convention of 1835.

GILLESPIE, WILLIAM, d. at Belleville, O., March, 1841, a. 104; was a colonel in the rebel army in Ireland in 1768–9; came to America in 1770, and served in our revolution.

GILLET, REV. MOSES, first minister of Congregational church of Rome, N. Y.; he grad. at Yale in 1804, and began his labors in Rome two years later; until Oct., 1837 he devoted himself faithfully and effectively to the duties of his pastorate; during this time 807 members were added to the church; he d. in 1848.

GILLIS, THOMAS H., a native of Somerset co., Md., was born in 1768, and in 1798 was appointed chief clerk to the navy, accountant as he was then called, now fourth auditor of the treasury; he removed to Washington in 1800 and continued in the same office until age and infirmities compelled him to resign in June, 1850; he d. at Washington, Feb. 25, 1851, a. 83.

GILLIAM, ALBERT M. b. at Lynchburg, Va., was consul in Mexico under Tyler, and author of *Travels in Mexico;* he was ed'r of the *Dover Intelligencer of Tenn.*, and d. suddenly Sept. 13, 1859. (*Hist. Mag.*, iii, 353.)

GILLILAND, WILLIAM, was b. near the city of Armagh, Ireland, of respectable parents; at an early age he emigrated to New York and formed a mercantile partnership with a merchant of wealth named Phagan, whose daughter he m. 8th Feb., 1755; he purchased largely soldier's grants issued under the royal ordinances of 1763; he located these extensively in the environs of Lake Champlain with the purpose of establishing a baronial domain. He was the pioneer settler of the Champlain valley; introduced a colony in May, 1765, and erected, on the banks of the Bouquet river, the first civilized habitation between Crown Point and the Canada line; this was the scene of Burgoyne's famous Indian treaty; the colony at the opening of the war was prosperous and populous, but during its progress was entirely destroyed and Gilliland fell from large wealth into indigence, and disordered in mind wandered into the forest and perished from exposure and starvation 2d Feb., 1796, at the age of 62. Mr. Gilliland was an eminent actor in the early history of the region, and was prominently engaged with Skeene and others in the project of forming a new province (*Munsell's Series Local Hist.*, vol. I; *Watson's Pioneer Hist. of the Champlain Valley.*)

GILMAN, PETER, son of Maj. John G., was b. in 1704, commanded a regiment in the French war, was a speaker of assembly and a member of the council of N. H., and d. in 1788, a. 84; he resided at Gilmanton. (*Sabine's Loyalists.*)

GILMAN, R. C., member of congress from North Carolina; d. at Oxford, N. C., Oct. 17, 1870.

GILMER, JOHN A., d. in Greensboro, N. C., May 21, 1868; he was b. in 1805, educated for the law, and admitted to the bar in 1832; he was a member of the state senate of North Carolina from 1846 to 1856, and was elected a representative to the 25th congress, serving as a member of the committee of elections; in 1855 he was the whig candidate for governor of his state, but was defeated; he was reëlected to the 26th congress, and made chairman of the committee of elections; during the rebellion he was a member of the Confederate states congress.

GILMOR, ROBERT, a banker and merchant of high social standing and distinguished for his fondness for mineralogy; d. at his residence in Baltimore, Md., Nov. 30, 1848, at the age of 74. (*Am. Jour. Sci. and Arts*, 2d ser., vii, 142.)

GILMORE, ADDISON, d. in Waterton, Mass., Jan. 10, 1850, a. 47; was b. in Windsor co., Vt., and came to Boston about twenty-five years before his death, and engaged in various business with success, became interested in rail roads, and president of the Western rail road, which office he held till his death.

GILMORE, THOMAS, first printer at Quebec, with Wm. Brown, about 1765–74. (*Thomas's Hist. Printing*, i, 362; ii, 183, 2d ed.)

GILPIN, JOSHUA, son of Thomas G., b. in Philadelphia, Pa., Nov. 8, 1765, became a lawyer, but devoted himself to the care of his family estates, which were large, and located in Pennsylvania, Delaware, Maryland and Virginia; was in Europe from 1795 to 1801; was prominently concerned in promoting the construction of the Chesapeake and Delaware canal, and d. in his 75th year. (*Simpson's Eminent Philadelphians.*)

GILPIN, THOMAS, b. March 18, 1728; on coming of age, settled on a farm near the Susquehannah, but afterwards on the Brandywine, near Wilmington, Del., where he became owner of mills; went to England, and soon after his return, in 1753, settled at the head of tide water on Chester river on the eastern shore of Maryland, where he founded the town of Millington; m. in 1764, and settled in Philadelphia. He was of the society of Friends, and incurred the displeasure of the patriotic party, and with others was removed to Winchester, Va., under charges of disloyalty to the revolutionary cause; he d. there March 2, 1778. (*Simpson's Eminent Philadelphians.*)

GILPIN, THOMAS 2d, son of Thomas G., b. in Philadelphia, Sept. 10, 1776; and d. in that city, March 3, 1853; became an extensive manufacturer on the Brandywine, where he had woolen, cotton and paper mills, and in 1817, succeeded in making paper by machinery, in a continuous sheet; his mills were destroyed by a flood, in 1822; afterwards resided in Philadelphia and resumed commercial business, in connection with literary pursuits. (*Simpson's Eminent Philadelphians.*)

GILPIN, THOMAS W., d. at Belfast, Ireland, Jan. 9, 1848; consul of the U. S., at that post.

GILSEY, PETER, d. in New York city, April 10, 1873; an alderman. He was b. on May 22, 1811, at Hobro, in the province of Jutland, Denmark, and after receiving a fair education, emigrated to America in 1827.

GIRTY, SIMON, among the most infamous of tories and most cruel of partizan brigands in the revolution; in 1778 he was a prisoner at Pittsburg, but escaped; in 1778 he went through the Indian country to Detroit, inciting the Indians to murder, and in 1782 witnessed the torture of Col. Crawford; the same year he assisted in driving away the Moravians from among the Wyandots, and in 1791 was with the enemy against St. Clair. In 1793, he acted as interpreter at a treaty, and was very insolent and false to his duty, and the failure of the negotiation was ascribed to him. (*Sabine's Loyalists.*)

GIST, Dr. W. R., a young physician of much promise; d. at Jackson, Miss., Feb. 12, 1849.

GITTINGS, Maj. Thomas, d. at his residence, Hills and Dales, Montgomery co., Md., Dec. 1, 1847, a. 62; was 10 years a member of the Maryland legislature, from that county.

GLASCOCK, Thomas, served as lieut., under Pulaski at the siege of Savannah; was col. in the Indian wars, and became general of militia; he d. in Richmond co., Ga., a. 54. (*White's Hist. Ga.*, p. 628.)

GLASCOCK, Gen. Thomas, was in the Indian wars of the west, and in congress from Georgia, from 1836 to 1839; d. at Decatur, Ga., May 9, 1841.

GLASS, James W., artist and engineer; son of an English merchant at Cadiz; spent his early life in England and the U. S. in engineering, and was connected with the coast survey and fortification service as a draftsman; he studied painting with Huntington, in 1845, and excelled in wild, stirring scenes, in which horses could be introduced; in 1847 he went to England, where he painted several years and acquired notoriety; he returned in 1855, and d. by his own hand, Dec. 22, 1855. (*Crayon*, Jan., 1856.)

GLEN, Henry, a delegate in the N. Y. provincial congress; served 3 years in assembly and 8 years in congress (1793–1801); d. at Schenectady, Jan. 6, 1814, a. 74.

GLEN, John, a loyalist of S. C.; lost his estate by confiscation, in 1782, and he was banished.

GLEN, William, of Charleston, S. C.; a loyalist; was banished and estate confiscated; he went to England.

GLEN, John, judge of the U. S. district court of Maryland; d. at Baltimore, Md., July 8, 1853.

GLENNY, William, lieut. 2d N. Y. regt.; killed in the revolution, Oct. 30, 1781.

GLONINGER, John, d. at Lebanon, Pa., Jan. 22, 1836, a. 77; he was many years an associate judge.

GLOVER, Rev. Joseph, projector of the first printing in America; he sailed for Massachusetts in 1638, but d. on the voyage.

GLOVER, P. G., d. Oct. 16, in Missouri; for many years treasurer of the state.

GLOVER, Rev. Solomon, d. in Newton, Ct., July 26, 1842, a. 92; he was the oldest Universalist clergyman in the United States.

GLYNN, James, commodore in U. S. navy; d. at New Haven, Conn., May 13, 1871; was 56 years in service.

GOBERT, Jacques Benjamin, formerly vice consul of France in Savannah, Ga.; d. a. 80, in Jefferson co., Ga.

GODARD, M., aeronaut; d. June 25, 1855, at New Orleans.

GODDARD, Dr. Giles, first to establish a printing press in Providence, R. I.; he afterwards settled in Philadelphia and Baltimore, but returned to Rhode Island, and d. near Providence, Dec. 23, 1817.

GODDARD, WILLIAM, son of Giles G.; a p. m. of New London, Ct.; was bred a printer, and started the first paper at Providence, R. I., in 1762; he soon went to N. Y., and with John Holt published the *N. Y. Gazette and Post Boy.* After the repeal of the stamp act in 1766, he went to Phila., and with Galloway and Wharton, issued the *Pa. Chronicle;* the firm fell to quarrelling and Goddard went to Balt., started another paper, and engaged in a plan to establish a line of post riders from N. H. to Ga. in opposition to the p. o. of the crown, and was entirely successful, but failing to succeed Franklin as p. m. gen., resigned in disgust, and returned to Balt., where his paper had meanwhile been conducted by his sister. He excited the whigs against him so greatly, March, 1777, that he was forced to claim protection from the assembly; he was repeatedly mobbed, but continued variously employed upon the paper, until 1797 when he sold and retired to a farm in Johnston, R. I., where he d. in 1817, a. 77; he was a bosom friend and an heir of Gen. Chas. Lee. (*Sabine's Loyalists.*)

GOFF, DUELL, formerly a judge of Lewis co., N. Y.; d. at Houseville, N. Y., Sept 8, 1852.

GOFFE, JOHN, b. in 1701, probably at Boston; settled near Manchester N. H.; removed to Bedford, Hillsboro co., N. H., and in 1746 to 1755, was a captain in service; in 1757 he served against Crown Point, as lieut. col., and in Col. Munroe's surrender, lost 80 men by massacre; in Amherst's campaign he was second to Col. Lovewell, and in 1760 led 800 provincials to Montreal under Haviland; in 1768 he was col. of the 9th N. H. regt.; he was a patentee of Amherst; was a representative from 1767 to 1775; a judge of probate from 1771 to 1776; he was a warm patriot of the revolution, and d. Oct. 20, 1781; he gave name to Goffetown, N. H. (*Com. Wilson's Orderly Book*, 58.)

GOGGIN, WILLIAM, d. at Richmond, Va., Jan. 4, 1870, a. 63; b. in Bedford co., May 31, 1807; was admitted to the bar in 1828, and practised in several of the circuit and district courts of the state of Va.; in 1836 was in the legislature; elected to congress in 1839, 1841, 1843, and 1847; was afterwards a visitor to West Point, and in later years engaged in his profession, in connection with agricultural pursuits.

GOIN, THOMAS, d. in New York, March 14, 1847; was acting master in the U. S. navy, and founder of the naval apprenticeship system.

GOING, REV. JONATHAN, D.D., d. in Granville, O., Nov. 9, 1844; president of Granville College.

GOLD, THEODORE SEDGWICK, son of Thomas R.; was graduated at Hamilton College in 1816, and twelve years later one of its trustees; he was a merchant of Utica, and in 1837, mayor of that city; he d. 1863, a. 67.

GOLD, THOMAS RUGGLES, a leading lawyer and public man of Oneida co., N Y.; b. at Cornwall, Conn., 1764, and graduated at Yale College in 1786; about 1792 he settled in Whitesboro, N. Y.; he obtained much influence and held several offices; he was state senator 1796 to 1800; district attorney, 1798, member of council of appointments, 1800; member of assembly 1808, and representative of congress 1809–13, and again 1815–17; he d. Oct. 25, 1827. (*Jones's Oneida Co.*, p. 795.)

GOLDEN, DAVID V. W., b. in Beekmantown, N. Y.; in 1792 removed to Niskayuna, N. Y., as a merchant, and in 1798 settled in Columbia,

Herk. co., N. Y., where he traded till his death, Feb. 11, 1814, a. 41; he was several years a county judge. (*Benton's Herkimer Co., N. Y.*, p. 314.)

GOLDSBOROUGH, ROBERT H., senator in congress, from Md., from 1813 to 1819, and from 1835 to 1837; d. at New Easton, Md., Oct. 5, 1836.

GOLDSMID, JOHN L., b. near London, Nov. 1789; entered the British army in his youth and served many years as an officer in Spain and the East Indies; after traveling extensively, and experiencing great vicissitudes in finance, he settled at Champion, N. Y., about 1830 and a few years after at Watertown, where he died Dec. 8, 1853, a. 64. (*Hough's Hist. Jeff. Co., N. Y.*, p. 430.)

GOLDSMITH, REV. BENJAMIN, Presb. minister, in the town of Riverhead, N. Y.; d. Nov. 19, 1810, a. 75. (*Prime's Hist. L. I.*, p. 155.)

GOLL, PIERRE FREDERICK, one of Napoleon's body guard; d. at Newark, N. J., May 18, 1860, a. 71. (*Vincent's Semi-An. Reg.*, p. 418.)

GOOD, DAVID, a loyalist, went to New Brunswick, in 1783; and d. at King's Clear, co. of York, in 1842, a. 95; leaving a very large number of descendants.

GOODE, WILLIAM O., many years a member of the Virginia house of delegates; once a speaker of that house; a member of convention in 1829, and since 1855, in congress and a member elect at the time of his death, July 3, 1859.

GOODHUE JONATHAN, merchant, b. at Salem, Mass., June 21, 1783; son of Benjamin G.; entered a counting house, and went to China as supercargo, in 1803–5; made a second voyage in 1805–6; and settled in N. Y., in Nov., 1807. His commercial transactions gradually expanded, and extended to various parts of Europe, the East Indies, South America and Mexico, and he was known as a man of integrity, and benevolence, with a strict regard for the rights of others, and a simplicity and humility of manners quite in contrast with many persons having much less of substantial wealth and worth; he d. Nov. 24, 1848. (*Hunt's Lives of Am. Merchants*, i, 345.)

GOODMAN, ALFRED T., b. of English parents, Washington, Pa., Dec. 15, 1845; d. Cleveland, O., Dec. 20, 1871; grad. of Cleveland High School 1863, taking the lead in all the studies; the superintendent said of him, "his capacity to acquire knowledge was remarkable, and his industry kept pace with his capacity." 1864 a private in the 150th regiment Ohio nat. guards; present at the attack on Fort Saunders, Washington; reporter and asst. ed. *Patriot and Union*, Harrisburgh, Pa. 1868, secretary W. R. and Northern Ohio Historical Society, Cleveland, O.; an indefatigable searcher after historical books and especially Mss.; author of *Notices of the Governors and Supreme Judges of Ohio; Notice of Col. Wm. Crawford and of Genl. Harmar's Campaign of* 1790; edited *Capt. Trent's Journal of* 1752, from the Mss., 1871; engaged upon a Life of Genl. St. Clair, nearly finished when cut down by quick consumption, his rare powers only partially developed.

GOODRICH, DR. ABEL, d. Jan. 12, 1841, at Merrimack, N. H.

GOODRICH, REV. CHAUNCEY ENOCH, son of Dr. Enoch Goodrich; he was b. near Troy, N. Y., Sept. 19, 1801; he graduated at Union College in 1825, and at Princetown Theological Seminary in 1828. He held pastorates in Salisbury, Herkimer co., in Butternuts and Fly Creek, Otsego county, and again in Herkimer county, at Winfield. Removing to Utica with broken health in 1841, he became a market gardener; for sixteen years he devoted himself to the improvement of the potato, renewing the seed with tubers obtained from Chili, and thus producing several new and valuable varieties; he furnished for different agricultural journals as many as one hundred and thirty papers on various topics. For the last nineteen years of his life he acted also as chaplain of the N. Y. State Lunatic Asylum; his death took place May 11, 1864.

GOODRICH, ELIZUR, lawyer of Utica, trustee of Ham. Coll., 1828–33; returned to Hartford, Conn., whence he came; d. 1868.

GOODRICH, LIEUT. EZEKIEL, Mass., killed in the revolution, Oct. 7, 1777.

GOODRICH, LEVI., an enterprising citizen of Pittsfield, Mass.; d. at that place Aug. 8, 1868, a. 84.

GOODRICH, REV. W. H., LL.D., b. at N. Haven, Conn., Jan. 19, 1824; d. Lausanne, Switzerland, July 11, 1874; at Yale from primary to theological departments and tutor, 1850; a licensed Pres. minister, traveling in Europe; pastor at Bristol, Conn., and Binghamton, N. Y.; assistant pastor 1st Pres. church, Cleveland, July, 1858; afterwards pastor, then the sole male representative of five generations. He was a finished scholar; occasionally a poet; a pleasing, logical, and earnest preacher. Probably no man of our times possessed more of the qualifications of a successful minister, and pastor, though many have possessed some of them in a higher degree; a well balanced and rounded character, attractive manners, a good judge of men and measures, he enjoyed the respect and affection of a large church and society, in a large and growing city, until his death. In the rebellion he took firm patriotic ground, laboring in the field on the sanitary and Christian commissions; another distinguished pastor has spoken of him as distinguished for "sanctified common sense."

GOODSELL, JONAS PLATT, son of Dr. Thomas, was an engineer much employed on the Erie canal, and in November, 1865, was appointed state engineer.

GOODSELL, LIVINGSTON, another son of Dr. Thomas; grad. at Ham. Coll., in 1838, studied law and began its practice in Cayuga co., but d. young.

GOODSELL, DR. THOMAS, b. June, 1775 at Washington, Litchfield county, Conn.; attended medical lectures at the University of Pennsylvania, and was licensed in 1809; practiced at Woodbridge and New Haven, Conn., at Whitesboro, N. Y., but for a longer period at Utica. Received honorary degree of M. D., at Yale Coll., in 1822, and from the regents of the state of N. Y., in 1842; in 1827 was appointed to the chair of materia medica in Pittsfield Medical School. Was much interested in agricultural pursuits, and secretary of the first Oneida County Agricultural Society. He d. Jan. 12, 1864, a. 89.

GOODWIN, REV. DANIEL L., for 30 y. pastor of the Prot. Epis. ch., Wilkinsonville, Mass.; d. Dec. 25, 1867.

GOODWIN, HENRY, a native of Boston, began the practice of law at Taunton; removed to Newport and was elected attorney general of R. I., in 1787–8; he d. at Bristol, on a visit to Gov. Bradford, May 31, 1789. (*W. Updike's Memoirs of the R. I. Bar*, p. 90.)

GOODHUE, JONATHAN, d. in New York city, Nov. 24, 1848, a. 65; native of Salem, Mass., and an opulent merchant.

GOODLOE, W. C., formerly judge of the Lexington dist., Ky.; d. at Lexington, Aug. 14, 1870.

GOODMAN, JOHN, b. in Germantown, Pa., in 1763; was in the revolution; in 1803–6, in the state legislature, and was then appointed a justice of the peace, and in 1809 a notary public in Philadelphia; in the war of 1812, was colonel of the 42d regiment of Pa. militia; in 1822, became prothonotary of the district court. (*Simpson's Em. Philadelphians.*)

GOODRICH, LEVI, d. at Pittsfield, Mass., Aug. 8, 1868; rail road contractor on the Harlem road; built the Pittsfield and North Adams rail road, and on various other public enterprises.

GOODWIN, HENRY C., b. in De Ruyter, Madison co., N. Y., June 25, 1824; was admitted to the bar in 1846, was dist. atty. of Madison co., 1848 to 1850 inclusive; he was in the 33d and 35th congresses and d. at Hamilton, N. Y., Nov. 12, 1860.

GOODWIN, CAPT. NATHANIEL, Conn., killed in the revolution, May 1, 1777.

GORDON, DR. ALEXANDER, of Norfolk, Va., in Feb., 1775, was censured by a whig committee for importing medicines contrary to continental asso.; he went to Eng., and was an addresser of the king in July, 1779.

GORDON, ANTHONY, Jesuit missionary, founded the mission at St. Regis, in 1760; his health failing, he returned in 1775 to Caughnawaga near Montreal, where he d. July 29, 1779.

GORDON, ARCHIBALD, became capt. June 9, 1740, was wounded at Ticonderoga, July 8, 1758 and July 16, became major of the regt.; in 1760 he accompanied Amherst into Canada, and in 1762 served at Martinico and Havana, where it is thought he d.

GORDON, CHARLES, lawyer of Cecil co., Md., was declared a public enemy to the whigs in 1775. (*Sabine's Loyalists.*)

GORDON, CHARLES, lawyer at St. George, Del., a loyalist, was required to submit to a trial for treason or lose his estate, during the revolution.

GORDON, LORD GORDON, a noted swindler, shot himself at Fort Garry, Manitoba, Aug. 1, 1874, while under arrest, in his room. The *New York Tribune* speaking of him says: "Gordon Gordon, whose singular career has closed so sadly, came to this country about three years ago, representing that he was authorized to act for the English shareholders of the Erie railway company; his statement received general credence and secured him the countenance of leading capitalists; he went west, and after sojourning some time in Minnesota returned to this city, and stated that he was Lord Gordon; that he intended settling part of his Scotch tenantry on lands in the west, where on account of his health he would be compelled to reside; having procured by false pretences a large sum of money from the late Horace F. Clark, and also victimized Jay Gould, he decamped from New York and settled in Manitoba; he resided in the latter province undisturbed until, at the instance of the executors of the Clark estate, he was arrested near the frontier; the Canadian authorities, however, interfered, placed his captors in jail for exercising unlawful authority on British soil, and allowed Gordon to escape; he was supposed to have gone to British Columbia, but he appears to have returned soon to Manitoba, where his grand schemes of colonization bewildered the settlers; in appearance Gordon was gentlemanly and pleasing; he had the bearing of a man who had moved in good society, and spoke intelligently on current topics of the day; he affected to be on intimate terms with the British nobility, and among other things, stated that his cousin was to have married the wealthy Marquis of Bute, but the match was broken off. He lived extravagantly in this city, and professed to have unlimited means at his control; his address and ingenuity were such that if well applied he might have earned a fair livelihood and been generally respected."

GORDON, GEN. JAMES, was in early life an Indian trader at Detroit and Schenectady, and was b. at Killead, county Antrim, Ireland, in 1793; was on active service as colonel of militia, in what is now Saratoga co., N. Y., in the revolution; was in assembly in 1778, 9, 80, 1, 4, 6, 7, 8, 9, 90; in congress from 1791 to 1795, and in the state senate, from 1797 to 1804; was for some time county judge, and the first supervisor of Ballston; he d. at Ballston, N. Y., Jan. 17, 1810. (*Albany Gazette*, Jan. 29, 1810.)

GORDON, HARRY, of Pa., was attainted in 1781 and his estate sold in 1780, on account of loyal principles. (*Sabine's Loyalists.*)

GORDON, JAMES, of S. C., a loyalist, held an office under the crown after the fall of Charleston and lost his estate by confiscation.

GORDON, J. WRIGHT, d. in Pernambuco, S. A., Dec., 1853; formerly lieut. gov. of Michigan, was accidentally killed by a fall from a balcony.

GORDON, NANCY, widow of David Gordon d. Feb. 19, 1851, a. 90 y.; having had 163 descendants of whom 114 survived her.

GORDON, THOMAS K., last chief justice of S. C., under the crown; he was a loyalist, and was allowed to leave the country.

GORDON, WILLIAM F., member of congress from Va., 1829 to 1835, and said to be the first one to propose the sub-treasury scheme of Pres. Jackson's day; d. in Albemarle co., Va., July 21, 1858.

GORDON, WILLIAM W., d. at Savannah, Ga., March, 1842; he was much interested in the internal improvements of his state.

GORE, ASA A., last survivor of the Wyoming massacre, having been carried away when a child in his mother's arms; he d. at Preston, Ct., Dec. 1, 1859. (*Hist. Mag.*, iv, 29.)

GORHAM, NATHANIEL, JR., son of the great land proprietor of western New York; settled in Canandaigua, N. Y. in 1789; was an early supervisor, county judge, and pres. of the Ontario Bank, from its organization till his death in 1826, a. 62.

GORHAM, WILLIAM, d. in the parish of Iberville, La., Jan., 1845; was a native of Barnstable, Mass., and had resided in Louisiana for more than 30 years.

GORUM, NATHANIEL, a tory, went to New Brunswick in 1783, and d. at Kingston, N. B., Feb. 9, 1846, a. 94, leaving numerous descendants.

GOUGE, JOSEPH, a soldier of the revolution, and native of Virginia; d. in Gwinnett co., Ga., Jan. 24, 1838, in his 109th year.

GOULD, CAPT. BENJAMIN, d. at Newburyport, Mass., May 27, 1841, a. 90; was an officer of the revolution, and an officer of the guard at West Point, on the night when the treachery of Arnold was discovered.

GOULD, DAVID, surgeon, Va.; d. in the revolution, July 12, 1781.

GOULD, REV. DANIEL, d. in Rumford, Me., May 21, 1842, a. 90; he was two years in the revolutionary war, and left to enter Harvard Coll., where he graduated in 1782.

GOULD, GEORGE, d. at Troy, N. Y., Dec. 6, 1868; b. in Litchfield, Conn., in 1807; practiced law in New York city for many years; was elected mayor of Troy in 1852, and elected one of the judges of the supreme court of New York in 1855 and 1863.

GOULD, JACOB, b. in Essex co., Mass., 1794; settled in Rochester, N. Y.; in 1816, was major gen. of militia; collector of the port; pres. of the Rochester City Bank, and U. S. marshal for the northern dist. of N. Y.; d. at Rochester, Nov. 18, 1867.

GOURGAS, FRANCIS R., d. in Concord, Mass., July 12, 1853, a. 41, represented Concord in the state legislature in 1841–2, and in the senate in 1843, was one of the executive council in 1852, and at the time of his death, was a member of the state constitutional convention.

GOURLAY, MRS. ANN, d. in Charleston, S. C., March, 1846, a. 99. (*Am. Almanac*, 1847, p. 336.)

GOVE, CHARLES FREDERICK, d. at Nashua, N. H., Oct. 21, 1856, a. 63; he was b. in Goffstown, N. H., May 13, 1793; grad. at Dartmouth, in 1817; practiced law in his native town from 1820 to 1839, and then removed to Nashua; he was in the state legislature in 1830–34; senator and president of the senate in 1835; solicitor of Hillsborough co., from 1834 to 1837; attorney general from 1837 to 1842; circuit judge of com. pleas from 1842 to 1848 and for many years after 1848, superintendent of the Lowell and Nashua rail road.

GOVE, JESSE, d. in Rutland, Vt., April 30, 1842, a. 60; he grad. at Middlebury in 1805, and held the office of clerk of the U. S. circuit and district courts in Vermont, from 1810 till the time of his death.

GOYER, JAN DE, Dutch gov. of Surinam from April 15, 1707, till his death in 1715.

GRACIE, ARCHIBALD, b. in Dumfries, Scot., in 1756, received a mercantile education of a high order in Liverpool, came to America soon after the revolution; m. a sister of Moses Rogers of N. Y., and settled in Va., where in 1796 he was ranked among the first merchants for credit and capital; he removed to N. Y., engaged extensively in commerce, and his transactions amounted to millions; his opinion was sought with confidence, and his reputation for honor and credit stood high; the restrictive system and the war swept away his fortune. He was made pres. of an insurance co., and was again ruined; he d. April 11, 1829, in his 74th year. (*Hunt's Am. Merchants*, i, 467.)

GRAEFF, GEORGE, a revolutionary officer; marched from Lancaster, Pa., in 1776, as lt., and was soon promoted to captain; he served at the battle of Long Island and d. at Lancaster, Nov. 13, 1823, in 68th year. (*Rogers's Am. Biog.*)

GRAFF, FREDERICK, August 27, 1775; was in early life a carpenter in Philadelphia, became a draftsman under Mr. Latrobe, and in 1799 aided in erecting the first water works in Philadelphia; was afterwards a distinguished engineer in various public works, and d. April 13, 1847. (*Simpson's Eminent Philadelphians.*)

GRAHAM, CHARLES, d. in New York city, Feb. 12, 1838, a distinguished lawyer and citizen.

GRAHAM, CHARLES J., d. at Newark, N. J., April 27, 1840, a. 58; many years cashier of the State Bank in Newark.

GRAHAM, GORDON, became ensign in 43d Highlanders, May, 1740, served in Flanders, and shared in the defeat at Fontenoy in 1745; in 1756, he came to America with a company, and in 1757 was at the surrender of Ft. Wm. Henry; in 1758, he was wounded before Ticonderoga. He succeeded as major July 17, 1758, and was with Amherst in 1759–60; he served in the West Indies, became lieut. col. in 1763, and in 1763, returned to N. Y., and defeated the western Indians at Bushy Run; he d. about 1771. (*Com. Wilson's Orderly Book*, 14.)

GRAHAM, JAMES, b. in Lincoln co., N. C., Jan., 1793; grad. at the N. C. Univ., in 1814; studied law, and practiced with success some years; was 4 y. in the state legislature, and from 1833 to 1843, and from 1845 to 1847, in congress; he spent the close of his life in agricultural pursuits, and d. Sept., 1851.

GRAHAM, CAPT. JOHN, of the 1st N. Y. regiment, was promoted to major, and commanded for a time at Fort Stanwix; he d. May, 7, 1832.

GRAHAM, MAJ. RICHARD, b. in Va., and in the war of 1812, aid to Gen. Harrison; afterwards Indian agent in Mo., till 1829; he was one of the com'rs to establish the boundaries of Illinois, and in the later years of his life, having gained an ample fortune, retired to private life; he d. in St. Louis co., Mo., July 27, 1857, a. 77.

GRAHAM, WILLIAM, d. near Valonia, Ind., in 1857, a. 76; he was a member of the first constitutional convention of Indiana, and served many years in both houses of the legislature; in 1837, he was elected to congress, and at the end of his term retired to private life.

GRANGER, REV. JAMES NATHANIEL, D.D., studied theology at Hamilton, N. Y., preached in N. Y., state; in 1842 became pastor of a Baptist church in Providence, and d. there Jan. 5, 1857, a. 42.

GRANGER, JOHN A., d. at Canandaigua, N. Y., May 26, 1870, a. 75.

GRANGER, MRS. MINDWELL, mother of Hon. Francis G., and of Hon. John A. G., of Canandaigua; d. April 17, 1860, a. 99.

GRANGER, RALPH, d. in Cleveland, O., Dec. 7, 1843, a. about 50; native of Suffield, Conn.; grad. at Yale in 1810, and several times a member of the Ohio senate.

GRANT, DR. ASAHEL, studied medicine in Utica, and became a member of the Oneida County Medical Society in 1832; in 1835 he embarked as a missionary among the Nestorians of Persia; d. at Mosul, 1844; is the author of a *History of the Nestorians.*

GRANT, DANIEL, native of Gillespie, Scotland; came to America before the revolution and in 1783 went to St. Andrew, N. B., where he d., Jan., 1834, a. 82.

GRANT, FRANCIS, served in Flanders and became a major in the 42d Highlanders; he became lt. col. in 1755, and came the next year to America; he was in the battle before Ticonderoga, July 8, 1758, and in 1759–60, was with Amherst, and commanded the van in the descent of the St. Lawrence; in 1761 he led an army against the Cherokees, and in 1762 was brig. gen. in the expedition against Martinico; he became that year a col. in the army, and afterwards commanded the 90th light infantry. He was at the seige of Havana, and went on half pay at the peace of 1763; in 1768 he became col. of the 63d, in 1770, major gen., in 1777, lieut. gen., and early in 1782 he died. (*Com. Wilson's Orderly Book*, p. 3.)

GRANT, JESSE R., father of President Grant, and post master at Covington, Ky.; d. in that city, June 29, 1873, a. 79.

GRANT, JOHN, JR., held the office of 1st judge of Oswego co., from 1820 to 1828, and was for some time collector at the port of Oswego; he died at that place, May 26, 1850, about 60 years of age. (*Stryker's Am. Reg.*, iv, 464.)

GRANT, DR. WILLIAM HENRY, b. at East River, Nova Scotia, Dec. 22, 1811; came to Philadelphia in 1836, to attend medical lectures, and grad. in 1839; was demonstrator of anatomy, and a professor in the Pennsylvania College; he d. March 28, 1852. (*Simpson's Eminent Philadelphians*, with portrait.)

GRATZ, HYMAN, d. Jan. 27, 1857, in Philadelphia, where he had been for many years a merchant, a. 81; was many years president of the Penn. Insurance Co., and pres. of the Pa. Acad. of the Fine Arts. (*Simpson's Eminent Philadelphians.*)

GRAVES, JOHN, revolutionary officer, b. in Culpepper co., Va.; entered the revolution in 1776 as lieut. in the 8th Va. regt., and retired with the rank of major; he was in the battles of Brandywine, Germantown, and Monmouth, and at the siege of Yorktown. Upon the peace he settled in Ga., and in 1786, commanded a regiment against the Creeks; he d. in Wilkes co., Ga., in his 77th year. (*White's Hist. Ga.*, p. 683.)

GRAVES, JOHN, b. in Dutchess co., N. Y.; removed to Russia, N. Y., in 1795; in 1813 and 1824 he was in assembly; in 1829 he became sheriff of Herkimer co., and held one term; he d. at Gravesville, N. Y., Feb. 16, 1855, a. 76. (*Benton's Herkimer Co., N. Y.*, p. 320.)

GRAVES, DR. JOHN W., d. at Lowell, Mass., Nov. 28, 1873, native of N. H.

GRAVES, LEWIS, member of the New York assembly in 1808 and 1810; judge and supervisor, in Lewis co., N. Y.; d. in Denmark, N. Y., May 10, 1816, a. 61; his widow d. in 1852.

GRAVES, REV. MATTHEW, from England, missionary of S. P. G., at New London, from 1745 to 1778, when he adhered to the royal cause and was violently deposed; he remained in great penury several years, and d. in N. Y., March 29, 1780; his brother John was minister at Providence, R. I., where he d. Nov., 1785. (*Doc. Hist. N. Y.*, iv, 486.)

GRAVES, DR. ROSEWELL, d. at New York city, Oct. 28, 1837.

GRAVES, WILLIAM T., d. at Louisville, Ky., Sept. 27, 1848, a. 43; was in congress from Kentucky from 1827 to 1841.

GRAY, MRS. ELIZABETH S., d. in Boston, Mass., Aug. 15, 1842, a. 33; dau. of the late Joseph White, Jr., of Salem.

GRAY, GEORGE, was an active friend of the revolution at Philadelphia, and a member of the convention for amending the constitution; was in the legislature of Pennsylvania, and speaker of the house; d. 1800. (*Simpson's Eminent Philadelphians.*)

GRAY, LIEUT. HUGH, Mass., killed in the revolution, Aug. 3, 1777.

GRAY, JAMES, a lieut. in the British army at Albany in 1756.

GRAY, REV. JEDUTHAN, a pioneer Baptist preacher in Chenango co., N. Y.; settled in Greene, N. Y.; from Berkshire co., Mass., in 1806; labored over a large district till his death at Sugar Grove, Pa., in 1830, a. 75. (*Chenango American*, Jan., 1858.)

GRAY, JOHN, an original member of the N. Y. Typographical Soc.; early friend of the Sunday school movement; d. at New York, April 18, 1850, at an advanced age. (*Stryker's Am. Reg.*, iv, 458.)

GRAY, JOHN, b. at Boston in 1793; grad. at Brown Univ. in 1823; studied law in Ct.; settled in Brooklyn, Windham co., Ct; edited for a time, the *Windham Co. Telegraph;* afterwards removed to Newburyport, Mass., where he was a bookseller, and to Worcester, where he was librarian of the Y. M. Lyceum; d. in Worcester, Nov. 21, 1859, a. 61.

GRAY, LIZZY, d. a. 127 years, on the farm of D. E. T. Mines, Edgefield, S. C., Sept. 1860; was an African. (*N. Y. Times*, Sept. 20, 1860.)

GRAY, NINIAN EDWARDS, native of Ky.; grad. at Yale in 1831; studied law in Lexington and became eminent in his profession; served in both branches of the legislature; was a member of the constitutional convention of 1850; many years prosecuting attorney and a judge of the circuit court; d. at Hopkinsville, Ky., Nov. 18, 1859, a. 51.

GRAY, WILLIAM, a tory of Westchester co., N. Y.; settled in New Brunswick; was a magistrate; d. in 1824, a. 96. A man of this name was a capt. in the N. Y loyalist volunteers in the revolution.

GRAY, WILLIAM, chief and interpreter at the Indian village of St. Regis upon the St. Lawrence; was stolen from Cambridge, N. Y., a. 17; was adopted and lived with the Indians; in 1812 was taken prisoner by the British; d. in jail at Quebec. (*Hough's Hist. St. Law. and Fr. Cos. N. Y.*, p. 198.)

GRAY, WILLIAM, a wealthy tobacconist of Richmond, Va.; d. in that city, Nov. 28, 1873, a. 75.

GRAY, CAPT., of the British quarter master general's department; killed in battle of Sacket's Harbor, May 29, 1813.

GRAYHILL, HENRY, b. at Lancaster, Pa.; removed to S. C.; was active in the revolution; was a surveyor; clerk of the court; four times in the Ga. legislature; 42 y. a resident of that state; d. in Hancock co., Ga., a. 82. (*White's Hist. Ga.*, p. 492.)

GRAYSON, PETER W., d. by suicide at Bean's Station, Tenn., July, 1838; minister plenipotentiary from Texas to the United States; a native of Kentucky.

GRAYSON, COL. SPENCE M., a distinguished lawyer; d. in Mississippi, Aug. 8, 1839, a. 37.

GREANER, WILLIAM, d. in Richmond, Va., Dec. 30, 1858, a. 75; native of Baltimore; a soldier in the war of 1812; since 1815, a tobacco manufacturer; during the war his factory was used as a prison, under the name of Castle Thunder.

GREELEY, HORACE, founder of the *New York Tribune;* one of the most distinguished journalists of his age; a writer of great eminence; late candidate for president of the United States; d. in Westchester co., N. Y., Nov. 29, 1872.

GREELEY, John, last surviving brother of Horace G.; d. at Londonderry, N. H., May 16, 1872, a. 88 y. 5 m. 5 d. His father, Zaccheus G., d. about 20 y. before, a. 94; his brother Zaccheus at Wayne, Erie co., Pa., Dec. 18, 1868, a. 86.

GREELEY, Col. Joseph, d. at Hudson, N. H., May 12, 1840, a. 81; was a soldier of the revolution; wounded at the battle of Bunker hill.

GREELEY, Philip, d. at Havana, Cuba, March 15, 1854, a. 48; b. in Portland, Me.; many years in business in Boston; collector of the port of Boston and Charlestown under Presidents Taylor and Fillmore; by his suggestion to the government, a notorious system of false entries at several of the large ports was broken up.

GREEN, Dr. Abel, of Paine's Hollow, Herk. co., N. Y.; d. 1862.

GREEN, Rev. Beriah, a preacher of anti-slavery and temperance; remarkable for clearness and force of logic, and fearless and persistent zeal; b. at Preston, Conn., March 24th, 1795; grad. at Middlebury, 1819; entered the ministry in 1824; pastor at Brandon, Vt., and Kennebunk, Me.; in 1830 was made prof. of sacred lit. in Western Reserve Coll., O. His strong denunciations of slavery caused opposition which led to his resignation in 1833; became pres. of the Oneida Inst., a manual labor school at Whitesboro, N. Y., until 1839; in 1838 separated from the Presb. church of Whitesboro, of which he was the pastor, and with a few anti-slavery adherents, formed a Congregational church; to this church, though much reduced in numbers, he ministered until his death, May 4, 1874, having no sympathy with the war that put an end to slavery, because humanity, he argued, should have effected a bloodless reform.

GREEN, Rev. Caleb, a Baptist minister; d. at Stillwater, N. Y., April 16, 1841, a. about 78.

GREEN, Isaiah L., b. in Massachusetts; grad. at Harvard in 1781; was in congress from Mass. in 1805 to 1809; from 1811 to 1813; from the Barnstable district; d. in 1841.

GREEN, Capt. James Jr., U. S. A. of the 2d artillery; d. at Fort Columbus, N. Y. harbor, Aug. 17, 1842.

GREEN, James S., b. in Fauquier co., Va., Feb. 28, 1817; 1836 with no fortune but a common English education, removed to Alabama; a year later to Missouri; was admitted to the bar in 1840; was in the convention of 1845; elected to congress in 1846 and 1848; in 1853, was appointed chargé d' affaires, and afterwards minister resident at Bogota, New Granada; was elected to congress in 1856, but before taking his seat was chosen to the U. S. senate; d. at St. Louis, Mo., Jan. 17, 1870, a. 63.

GREEN, Lester, M. D., b. in Middlebury, Schoharie co., N. Y., Feb. 18, 1797; removed to Trenton, N. Y. in 1803; studied with Dr. L. Guiteau; grad. at Fairfield in 1821; settled at Little Falls, N. Y.; d. Feb. 7, 1849. (*Tr. N. Y. St. Med. Soc.*, 1851, p. 199.)

GREEN, Matthew D., a prominent sporting character; d. at New York, Feb. 8, 1870, a. 58.

GREEN, Samuel, d. in Washington, D. C., March 22, 1850; was formerly judge of the supreme court of New Hampshire; for fifteen years a clerk in the treasury department.

GREEN, SAMUEL, b. in New London, Ct.; became a printer; published the *New London Gazette*, and *The Register*, an annual statistical volume; d. at Hartford, Sept. 6, 1859, a. 91, being at the time, the oldest printer in the state.

GREEN, THOMAS, first printer in Hartford, Ct., 1764; d. 1812, a. 73.

GREEN, TIMOTHY, son of Samuel jr.; early printer at Boston; removed in 1714 to New London, Ct.

GREEN, COL. THOMAS I., d. in Warren co., Miss., March 5, 1845, a. about 40; was formerly a member of the state senate.

GREEN, TIMOTHY B., d. at Whitehall, near Savannah, Ga., March 16, 1840; a member of the New York bar; one of the managers of the American Bible Society.

GREENE, ALPHEUS S., native of R. I.; settled in Jeff. co., N. Y., in 1812; was in assembly in 1827–8; was a co. judge; a member of the convention in 1846; eleven years p. m. at Watertown; d. in the Lunatic Asylum, Utica, Feb. 25, 1851, a. 64. (*Hough's Hist. Jeff. Co., N. Y.*, p. 430.)

GREENE, BENJAMIN F., one of the judges of the supreme court of New York, for the 8th judicial dis.; d. in Fredonia, Aug. 7, 1860, a. 39.

GREENE, CHARLES WINSTON, b. in Norwich, Ct., July 3, 1783, and removed with his father's family, when young, to Boston; grad. at Harvard in 1802, and was for some years a merchant in Boston; meeting reverses, he established a school at Jamaica Plain, where he taught for more than twenty years, with great success; he removed to East Greenwich and continued to teach till within a year of his death, which occurred Dec. 24, 1857, a. 74. (*Am. Almanac*, 1859, p. 348.)

GREENE, NATHANIEL RAY, son of Gen. N. G., of the revolution; b. Jan. 11, 1780; he died at Greensdale, R. I., June 11, 1859; his elder and only brother was drowned in the Savannah river, in 1792. (*Hist. Mag*, iii, 255.)

GREENE, REV. SAMUEL, d. at Boston, Nov. 20, 1834, a. 42.

GREENE, SAMUEL, formerly judge of the supreme court of New Hampshire, and clerk in the U. S. treasury department during the last 15 years; d. at Washington, D. C., March 22, 1851.

GREENLAW, CHARLES, of Castine, Me.; a loyalist; went to St. Andrew, New Brunswick, and d. in 1811, a. 68.

GREENLAW, EBENEZER, of Castine, Me.; a loyalist; went to St. Andrew, N. B., and d. in 1810, a. 70.

GREENLAW, JONATHAN, of Castine, Me.; went to St. Andrew, N. B., in 1783, and d. in 1818, a. 80; his six sons were whigs; Wm., the only one who served in the revolution, d. at Deer Island, Me., in 1838, a. 87.

GREENLEAF, BENJAMIN, patriot of the revolution, and judge; b. at Newburyport, Mass.; grad. at Harvard in 1751; became a patriot in the war, and wrote in its defense; he was representative several years before, and in Oct., 1774, became of the executive council and committee of safety; in 1775, 6, he was again in the council, and afterwards was judge in the court of com. pleas for Essex co., in which office he continued many years; he d. in 1799. (*Bradford's N. E. Biog.*)

GREENLEAF, Daniel, d. at Jackson, Miss., March, 1839, a. about 40; late district attorney for the 1st dist. of Mississippi.

GREENLEAF, Samuel, d. in Boston, Mass., Nov. 16, 1845, a. 77; he was a merchant of excellent reputation.

GREENLEAF, Thomas, d. in Quincy, Mass., Jan. 5, 1854, a. 80; grad. at Harvard in 1784, and for more than six years the sole survivor of his class.

GREENLY, Mrs. (colored), d. in Pa., Dec. 25, 1859, a. 110.

GREENWOOD, Samuel, of Boston, was a tory, and went to Halifax in 1776 where he d.; his son Samuel d. there in 1832, a. 57.

GREENWOOD, William, of Charleston, S. C., a loyalist, was banished in 1782, and his property confiscated.

GREENWOOD, Holmes, a revolutionary soldier, and survivor of the Jersey prison ship captives; d. at Providence, R. I., April 9, 1860, a. 95. (*Vincent's Semi-An. Register*, p. 271.)

GREER, Maj. David B., secretary of state of Arkansas; d. at Little Rock, Aug. 28, 1859.

GREGG, Frederick, of New Hanover, N. C., a loyalist, lost his estate by confiscation in 1779.

GREGOR, John, was an ensign and lieut. in the French war, went on half pay in 1783; entered active service in the English army Aug. 27, 1775, and March 22, 1780, became captain; he served through the war and d. Dec., 1782.

GREGORY, Benjamin, of S. C., was in office under the crown after the surrender of Charleston, in 1780, and his estate was confiscated.

GREGORY, J., gov. of the Bahamas; d. July 30, 1854.

GREGORY, Matthew, a lieutenant of the revolution and last survivor of the New York Cincinnati; d. at Albany, N. Y., June 4, 1848, in his 91st year. (*Munsell's Annals of Albany, passim.*)

GREGORY, William, an assistant judge of the superior court of S. C., under the crown, and was allowed to leave the country in the revolution. (*Sabine's Loyalists.*)

GREIG, John, prominent land agent and financier; b. at Moffat, Scotland, Aug. 6, 1779; came to Canandaigua, N. Y., in 1800, as a lawyer; became agent of the Hornby and Colquhoun estate in 1806; pres. of the Ontario Bank in 1820; regent of the University in 1825; member of congress in 1841 and was for many years president of the Ontario Co. Ag. Soc.; he d. at Canandaigua, April 9, 1858. The town of Greig, Lewis co., N. Y., was named from him. (*Hough's Hist. Lewis Co., N. Y.*, p. 101; *Turner's Phelps and Gorham Purchase*, p. 282.)

GREINER, John, author of the Log Cabin, and other songs, popular during the political campaign; d. at Toledo, Ohio, May 13, 1871, a. 60; the songs known as *Old Zip Coon*, and *Tippecanoe and Tyler too*, were of his production.

GRENVILLE, Sir Richard, kinsman and associate of Sir Walter Raleigh in the early settlement of Va.; he was killed in 1791, in an action with the Spanish fleet near the Azores.

GRESHAM, ALEXANDER, served in the revolution, and in 1812–15 as a silver-gray; he d. Feb. 23, 1823, in Greene co., Ga., a. 70. (*White's Hist. Ga.*, p. 478.)

GRIDLEY, DR. T. J., d. in Amherst, Mass., March 10, 1852, a. 65; grad. at Yale in 1808 and formerly a member of the executive council of Massachusetts.

GRIDLEY, ORRIN, a merchant and influential citizen of Clinton, N. Y.; b. Aug. 30, 1786; was a captain in the war of 1812; in 1845 he established the Kirkland Bank of Clinton; was a trustee of Hamilton College from 1834 until his death April 3, 1847.

GRIDLEY, PHILO, LL.D., b. at Paris, N. Y., Sept. 16, 1796; grad. at Hamilton College in 1816; studied law in Onondaga and in Waterville, and practiced in the latter place, and afterwards in Hamilton. After serving some time as district attorney of Madison county, he was in July, 1838, elected circuit judge of the fifth judicial district, and the following year removed to Utica. After the adoption of the state constitution of 1846 he was elected judge of the supreme court for six years, serving the last year of his term as judge of the court of appeals. After another short term on the bench of the supreme court, he resumed practice, his health much shattered by successive paralytic attacks; he d. Aug. 16, 1864. He presided at the trial of Alexander McLeod, upon the issues of which was thought to depend the question of war with England. His acuteness, vigor and despatch joined with his untiring industry gave him the soubriquet of "steam boat judge."

GRIDLEY, REV. WAYNE, son of preceding; b. Nov. 12, 1811; grad. from Hamilton in 1836; studied at Andover Seminary and was ordained a missionary but was prevented from fulfilling his purpose. In February, 1840 he became pastor of the Congregational church at Clinton, but at the end of five years he was obliged by ill health to relinquish his charge; he d. Nov. 23, 1846.

GREIRSON, GEORGE, of Warsaw, S. C., held an office under the crown after the surrender of Charleston in 1780, and lost his estate by confiscation.

GRIERSON, JAMES, native of Scotland, settled in the colonies before the revolution, served in the royal army, and in 1783 went to Nova Scotia, where he d. in 1846, a. 105; he was a pensioner more than sixty years.

GRIFFIN, CAPT. DAVID, d. at Ogdensburgh, N. Y., April 2, 1840, in his 75th year, settled at that place in 1800.

GRIFFIN, EBENEZER, an eminent counselor and advocate; b. at Cherry Valley, N. Y., July 29, 1789; he removed in his youth with his father's family to Clinton; he was two years in Union College, but did not remain to graduate, and in 1818, received the degree of A.M. from Hamilton College; he studied law and was admitted to the bar in 1811; having practiced eight years in Clinton, and six in Utica, (until 1825,) and after brief residences in New York, in Rochester, and again in N. Y., he finally settled in Rochester in 1842; his practice was still more ubiquitous, for his reputation extended throughout the state, and was equaled by that of few lawyers at the bar. He d. Jan. 22d, 1861.

GRIFFIN, JOHN K., member of congress from South Carolina, from 1831 to 1841; d. at Milton, S. C., Aug. 1, 1841.

GRIFFIN, NATHANIEL, b. in Windham co., Conn., Oct. 11, 1761; settled in 1790 on a farm of 315 acres bought of Pres. Washington and Gov. Clinton, in present town of Kirkland, N. Y., and d. there Dec. 26, 1836.

GRIFFIN, MAJ. THOMAS, second in command at the battle of Hampton, and member of congress from Virginia, in 1803–5; d. at Yorktown, Va., Oct. 7, 1836.

GRIFFITH, REV. DAVID, D.D., went to Eng. for orders in 1770, became missionary to Gloucester, N. J.; moved to Va. In 1776, was appointed chaplain and surgeon to 3d Va. battalion, and settled as pastor at Fairfax, Va.; he was elected bishop of Va., in 1786, but was never consecrated owing to his inability to visit England; he resigned his pastoral charge in 1789; and d. at Phila., Aug. 3, 1789. (*Doc. Hist. N. Y.*, iv, 440.)

GRIGGS, JOSEPH, d. at Brimfield, Mass., Aug. 26, 1840, a. 91; was an officer in the revolution.

GRIMES, JAMES W., ex-senator from Iowa; d. at Burlington, Iowa, Feb. 7, 1872, a. 55.

GRIMES, CAPT. WILLIAM, Va., killed in the revolution, Aug. 1, 1777.

GRINNELL, CORNELIUS, d. at Ryde, Isle of Wight, Aug. 10, 1869, a. about 40; he succeeded his father Henry Grinnell, late of the firm of Grinnell, Minturn & Co.; established the house of Grinnell & Co. in London, about 1859, and was pres. of the N. Y. Packet Line, v. pres. of the Liverpool and London Insurance Co., and was engaged in other mercantile enterprises.

GRINNELL, MICHAEL, d. in Clinton tp., Pa., Feb., 1858, a. 106.

GRISCOM, DR. JOHN H., a prominent writer and engaged in various educational and benevolent movements; d. in New York city, April 28, 1874, in the 65th year of his age.

GRISWOLD, CHESTER, b. in 1779; son of Simeon G., of Pittsfield, Mass.; removed to Nassau, Rens. co., N. Y., in 1804, and to Troy in 1810, but returned to Nassau, where he died Sept., 1860, a. 81; he was in assembly in 1823–31–35; many years supervisor, and p. m.; he was father of Hon. John A. G., and Mrs. Isaac B. Heartt, of Troy.

GRISWOLD, ELIHU, b. Aug. 17, 1756; removed from Windsor, Ct., early in the settlement of Herkimer co., N. Y.; he was county clerk from April 6, 1804, to Feb., 1810, and in 1811, was again appointed and held till his death, Jan. 12, 1812, a. 55. (*Benton's Herkimer Co.*, p. 317.)

GRISWOLD, GAYLORD, b. in Windsor, Ct.; settled in Herkimer, N. Y., soon after it was formed, as a lawyer, and was an energetic politician; he was in assembly in 1797 and 1798, and in congress in 1803–5, and d. in Herkimer, March 1, 1809, a. 41, leaving a fine estate. (*Benton's Herkimer Co., N. Y.*, p. 314.)

GRISWOLD, GEORGE, was b. at Lyme, Ct.; began business with his brother Nathaniel, in N. Y., as a merchant, in 1794, and long maintained an honorable and conspicuous place among the merchants of that city, and as a man noted for his benevolence and charity. He was a whig elector in 1848, but held no other public office, and d. Sept. 5, 1859, on Staten Island, a. 83.

GRISWOLD, JOAB, b. in Goshen, Ct., June 29, 1769; settled early in Herkimer co.; was an active federalist; was appointed co. clerk in March, 1798, and held 6 y.; the office and records were burned the night before he was to deliver possession to his successor, perhaps by accident. He was a lawyer and farmer, and lived at Herkimer. (*Benton's Herkimer Co., N. Y.*, p. 316.)

GRISWOLD, JOHN, d. at Hyde Park, N. Y., Aug. 4, 1856, a. 74; native of Lyme, Conn., and a prominent merchant of New York.

GRISWOLD, JOHN A., d. at Troy, N. Y., Oct. 31, 1872; b. in Nassau, N. Y., in 1822; went to Troy at the age of 17, and in a few years went into business as a druggist; but became interested in the iron manufactures, and a partner in the Rensselaer Iron Co.; in this field of enterprise he was eminently successful; his business expanded from year to year, until not many years ago, by the consolidation of his works with those of Mr. Corning, he became the principal partner in one of the largest iron establishments of the country, owning a rolling-mill and Bessemer steel works in Troy and blast furnaces at Fort Edward and on the Hudson; he was also, with his partners, the owner of an iron mine at Lake Champlain, and, besides, was largely interested in several local companies. In 1856 he was elected mayor of Troy; was an active union man in the war, and assisted in raising the 30th, 125th, and 169th regiments of New York volunteers, as well as the Black Horse Cavalry and the 21st New York or Griswold Light Cavalry. Mr. Griswold also rendered effective aid to the union cause by building, at great pecuniary risk, the celebrated Monitor, which rendered such effective service in its conflict with the Merrimac in Hampton Roads. Besides this vessel, Mr. Griswold and his partners displayed great energy and patriotic confidence in meeting the demands of the naval service at critical periods during the war.

In October, 1863, Mr. Griswold, at that time a democrat, was nominated as a candidate for representative in congress, and although the district (the XVth) was strongly republican, he was elected by a majority of 1,287 votes. He soon afterward joined the republican party, and was reëlected by large majorities in 1864 and 1866. He served on the naval committee, and, on returning to Washington for the third term, was placed on the committee of ways and means. In 1868, he was republican candidate for governor, but was defeated by Mr. Hoffman.

GRISWOLD, MARY, d. at Goshen, N. Y., Jan., 1840, a. 100.

GRISWOLD, SETH, a loyalist, settled in New Brunswick in 1783, and d. at Queensbury, York co., in 1838, a. 81.

GRISWOLD, REV. WHITING, rector of St. John's church, St. Louis, Mo.; d. of cholera, Aug., 1848, while devoting his energies to the care of the sick. (*Stryker's Am. Reg.*, iii, 238.)

GROSS, EZRA C., b. in Windsor co., Vt.; grad. at the University of Vermont, in 1806; was in congress from Essex co., N. Y., in 1819–21, was in assembly in 1828, and 1829 but d. before the close of his second year; he lived at Keeseville, N. Y.

GROSVENOR, COL. THOMAS W., prosecuting attorney at Chicago Ill.; shot Oct. 20, 1871.

GROUT, John, was b. in Lunenburgh, Mass., June 13, 1731, settled in Windsor, Vt.; became a land agent, but siding with the loyalists, met with many difficulties and in 1777 removed to Canada; he was attainted by the laws of Vermont. He became somewhat eminent as a lawyer and his end was as tragic as his life was turbulent and unhappy; he was murdered for money known to be in his possession, but the facts were not ascertained until years after when they were confessed on the gallows by a convicted murderer. (*Hall's Eastern Vermont*, p. 650.)

GROVER, Talleyrand, prof. in Del. Coll., son of Dr. John G., of Bethel, Del.; grad. atBowdoin; in 1843 was made prof. of modern languages and rhetoric in Deleware Coll., Newark, N. Y., and afterwards prof. of ancient languages; he d. at Stockholm, Sweden, June 4, 1859. (*Hist. Mag.*, iii, 352.)

GROVER, Thomas D., acquired a large fortune in Phila., and spent much in acts of benevolence to the poor and in aiding worthy young men; he d. at west Phila., March 8, 1849, a. 60. (*Stryker's Am. Reg.*, ii, 496.)

GRUYER, William de, Dutch gov. of Surinam, from Oct. 23, 1706, till his death in 1707.

GUERARD, David, a loyalist of S. C., lost his estate by confiscation in the revolution.

GUERLIS, Francois Vaillant de, Jesuit missionary, arrived in Canada before 1674; succeeded Boniface among the Mohawks about 1674; accompanied the expedition against the Senecas in 1687; on the 31st of Dec., 1687, sent to New York, and in 1703–4 to the Senecas.

GUEST, John, an enterprising merchant of Philadelphia; b. May 11, 1768, and d. in St. Domingo in 1817, whither he had gone for health, and on business. (*Simpson's Eminent Philadelphians.*)

GUEST, William, a loyalist of Tiger River, S. C., was in commission under the crown after the fall of Charleston, in 1783, and his estate was confiscated.

GUIDICINI, Giuseppe, artist and architect; d. at N. Y., Jan. 8, 1868; b. at Bologna, Italy, in 1812; came to America in 1832; was scenic artist, and decorated many theatres; was especially successful as a fresco painter.

GUILD, Benjamin, died at Boston, Mass., March 30, 1858, a. 72; he was b. in Boston, May 8, 1785; grad. at Harvard in 1804; studied law, and practiced in Boston; he was, for over thirty years, an active member of the Mass. Soc. for the Promotion of Agriculture, and for a time its corresponding secretary.

GUILFORD, Nathan, d. in Cincinnati, O., Dec. 18, 1854, a. 68; b. in Spencer, Mass., July 19, 1786; grad. at Yale in 1812, and settled as a lawyer in Cincinnati in 1815; was eminent in his profession, and conspicuous for his efforts in promoting the cause of popular education.

GUION, James, d. at Staten Island, N. Y., March 8, 1846, a. 68; he represented Richmond co., in assembly in 1811, 2, 3, 4, and West Chester co. in 1819, and was a member of congress in 1820–21.

GUION, John J., d. in Vicksburg, Miss., June 26, 1855, a. 54; was a son of the late Major Isaac G. of the army, and b. in Natchez, in 1801; at the time of his death, was judge of the 3d judicial district, to which office he had been elected for nearly 2 years; was formerly judge of the criminal court of Adams county; state senator, and as president of the senate, governor *pro tem*, from Feb. 3, 1851, to Nov. 3, 1851, on Gov. Quitman's resignation.

GUION, JOHN W., d. at Newbern, N. C., July 17, 1840, a. 58; cashier of the Merchants' Bank at Newbern.

GUITEAU, CALVIN. This and the two following were sons of Dr. Francis Guiteau of Pittsfield, Mass., who all settled in Oneida county, N. Y. *Calvin* resided in Deerfield, and was much employed as a surveyor in the central part of the state, from a period at least as early as 1795. *Francis* was a physician in Deerfield in 1792, and the first supervisor of the town; in 1801 he took up his residence in Utica, and until 1814 was actively engaged there in the practice of his profession; afterwards at Whitesboro, where he died about 1822.

GUITEAU, LUTHER, M.D., b. in Lanesboro, Mass., in 1778; studied with Dr. Buel of Sheffield, Mass., and settled in Trenton, N. Y., in 1802, where he practiced extensively and with great success; he d. Feb. 12, 1850. (*Tr. N. Y. St. Med. Soc.*, 1851, p. 187; *Jones's Hist. Oneida Co.*, p. 472.)

GUNN, JAMES, U. S. senator from Georgia, from 1799 to 1801; d. at Louisville in that state, July 30, 1801.

GURLEY, HENRY H., b. in Lebanon, Conn., in 1787; grad. at Williams Coll.; studied law, and settled in Louisiana; was U. S. judge of the dist. court of La.; and in congress from 1823 to 1831; d. in 1832.

GURLEY, RALPH R., D.D., a well known Presbyterian clergyman of Washington, D. C., d. July 30, 1872, a. 75; he was sec. of the Am. Colonization Soc.

GURNEY, NATHAN, formerly a member of the Massachusetts senate, and many years an alderman of Boston; d. in that city January 12, 1850, a. 81.

GUSTIN, LYDIA, d. at Marlow, N. H., July 20, 1847, a. 101 y. 20 d.; her maiden name was Mack; she was b. at Lyme, N. Y., June 25, 1746. (*Hunt's Biog. Panorama*, p. 479.)

GUSTINE, AMOS, d. in Lost Creek Valley, Pa., March 3, 1844; was in congress from 1841 to 1843, from Pennsylvania.

GUTHRIE, JAMES, d. in Louisville, Ky., March, 1869; b. near Bardstown, Ky.; educated at the Bardstown acad.; became a trader to New Orleans; studied law, and was appointed prosecuting attorney for Nelson co., Ky., in 1820; was a member of one or the other house of the state legislature 15 years; secretary of the U. S. treasury from 1853 to 1857; and U. S. senator from 1865 to 1868, when he resigned.

GUYON, JAMES, was in the N. Y. assembly from Richmond co., in 1811, 12, 13, 14, 19; and in congress from 1819 to 1821; d. on Staten Island, N. Y., March 8, 1846.

GWINAP, DR. JABEZ, d. in Oxford, Warren co., N. J., June 1, 1843, a. 72; was for fifty years an active and successful practitioner.

GWINN, CAPT. JOHN, entered the U. S. naval service in 1809; he was a native of Md., and d. at Palermo, on board of the U. S. frigate Constitution of the Mediterranean squadron Sept. 4, 1849.

GWINN, WILLIAM, major in the revolution, settled in Pa., from Ireland in 1772, and entered the staff dep. of the army in 1776 under Gen. Mifflin. He rem. to Md., after the war, and set. on a farm. He d. at Monkton Mills, Balt co., Md., Oct. 1, 1819, a. 70. (*Rogers's Am. Biog.*)

GWYNN, COL. SAMUEL, d. at New Orleans, La., Dec. 1838, a. about 45; cashier of the Union Bank of Mississippi.

GWYNN, WILLIAM, d. in Hartford, Md., Aug. 14, 1854, a. 80; was of Baltimore, and formerly editor of the *Baltimore Gazette;* the oldest lawyer of Maryland.

HABERSHAM, RICHARD W., d. in Habersham co., Ga., Dec. 2, 1842, a. 56; a representative in congress from Georgia; b. at Savannah in 1786; grad. at Princeton in 1805; studied law, and served in various offices of the federal and state governments; was elected to congress in 1838 and 1840.

HACKETT, JAMES H., a distinguished comic actor; b. in N. Y., at the close of the last century; was prepared for Columbia Coll., and for a brief period a student there; a fit of sickness suspended his studies and he became a clerk with a wholesale grocer; in 1820 he began mercantile business at Utica, but after a successful career of four years he removed to N. Y.; ill-judged speculations soon wrought his financial ruin, and in March, 1826, he went upon the stage. As an actor of broad comedy, he was a great favorite both in this country and in Europe, which he three times visited professionally; he was one of the first to introduce the Yankee type of the American character; was admired in his impersonation of Sir John Falstaff, of Monsieur Mallet, the irritable Frenchman, &c., &c.; Organically a humorist and a mimic, he showed great versatility in the expression of his ludicrous conceptions; he d. about 1871.

HACKLEY, AARON, moved from Wallingford, Conn., with the family of his father, Aaron Hackley, to Salisbury, N. Y., in 1795; grad. at Williams Coll., and then studied law, setting up in practice at Herkimer; in 1812 he was county clerk, in 1814–15, in assembly, and in 1818 in congress; in 1828 he was dist. att.; he resided afterward some years at Utica, and for a shorter time in N. Y., where he d.

HACKLEY, REV. CHARLES W., professor of Columbia Coll. (*See Appleton's Annual Cyclopædia* for 1861.)

HACKLEY, PHILO M., b. in Wallingford, Ct., Oct., 1776; settled in Salisbury, N. Y., with his father, Aaron H., in 1795, and removed to Herkimer where he became a merchant; he was federal in politics. In 1807 he was surrogate, in 1810 sheriff and in 1820 member of assembly; he resided several years at Little Falls, and went thence to Auburn, N. Y., about 1839; five years after he removed to Allegan, Michigan, where he d. Oct. 24, 1849, a. 73. (*Benton's Herkimer Co. N. Y.*, p. 337.)

HADLEY, HENRY H., prof. of Hebrew in the Union Theological Seminary, N. Y.; b. July 19, 1826; d. in Washington, D. C., Aug. 1, 1861, of disease contracted in the service of the U. S. Sanitary Commission; he was a son of Prof. James Hadley of Geneva, N. Y.

HADLEY, DR. JAMES, d. at Buffalo, N. Y., Oct. 17, 1869, a. 84; was a long time professor in the Fairfield and Geneva Medical Colls.; b. in Weare, N. H., July 5, 1785; grad. at Dartmouth in 1809. (*Transac. N. Y. State Med. Soc.*, 1871, p. 345.)

HADLEY, JAMES, prof. at Yale Coll.; was b. in Fairfield, Herkimer co., N. Y., March 30, 1821; his father, Dr. James Hadley, was for many years professor of chemistry in the Medical Coll. at Fairfield, and afterward held the same chair in the Medical Coll. at Geneva, N. Y.; he entered in September, 1840, the junior class at Yale, and was grad. in 1842; he continued his studies at the coll., except when for a brief period he acted as tutor in Middlebury Coll., Vermont; and in 1845 joined the Yale Faculty as assistant professor in Greek. In 1851, ex-President Woolsey resigned the professorship of Greek, and Prof. Hadley was appointed to that chair; in 1860, the professor published a *Greek Grammar for Schools and Colleges* founded on a similar work by Prof. George Curtius, in Germany; and in 1869, an abridgment under the name of *Elements of the Greek Language.* Prof. Hadley contributed articles to various scientific and literary periodicals, especially to *The New Englander.* He was an active member of the American Oriental Society, and was the president thereof at the time of his death. Beside his varied linguistic attainments, he was well versed in civil law, and his course of lectures on that subject was included in the curriculum of the Yale Law School, and was also delivered at Harvard; he attained excellence in whatever branch of study he pursued, and possessed wise, discriminating judgment, which gave great weight to his opinions; his private character was pure and amiable, and he was deservedly held in esteem by the faculty and students. He d. in New Haven, Nov. 14, 1872.

HAGA, GODFREY, b. at Isinger in Wirtemburg, Nov. 30, 1747; came to Philadelphia as a redemptioner, and became an importing merchant, and acquired a large estate; he withdrew from active business in 1814, and d. Feb. 7, 1825, a. 77. (*Simpson's Eminent Philadelphians.*)

HAGADORN, DR. STEPHEN, of Cohocton, N. Y.; d. Aug. 1, 1863, a. 52.

HAGEDORN, CLAMOR F., many years consul for several German states at Philadelphia, d. Feb. 25, 1868; native of Bremen, where b. May 23, 1773; came to America when a young man, and was engaged in commercial business.

HAGAMAN, JOHN I., b. at Nine Partners, Dutchess co., N. Y., March 21, 1792; removed in childhood to Lodi, N. Y., and in 1821 settled in Auburn; was a builder; settled in Lodi in 1843, and d. Oct., 1853. (*Hall's Auburn*, p. 568.)

HAGAN, THEODORE, one of the ablest musical critics and representatives in the country; d. Dec. 27, 1871, a. 42.

HAGNER, THOMAS H., d. March, 1848; b. in Maryland and son of third auditor of U. S. treasury; had resided eight or nine years in Florida and was a lawyer.

HAIGHT, GEN. NICHOLAS, d. in New York city, Aug., 1854; was an active officer of the war of 1812.

HAIGHT, THOMAS G., d. at Colt's Neck, Monmouth co., N. J., Sept. 2, 1847, a. 52; was formerly speaker of the house of assembly, and a member of the constitutional convention of 1844.

HAIL, MRS. CATHARINE, d. at Flat Creek, Lancaster dist., S. C., in her 102d year; native of Virginia.

HAILE, LEVI, asso. justice sup. court, R. I., b. at Warren, R. I., in 1797, and resided there through life; he grad. at Brown Uni., in 1821; studied law, was in gen. assem., from 1824 to 1835 when he became associate justice of the supreme court and held till his death July 14, 1854. (*Prov. Journal*, July 17, 1854.)

HAILE, WILLIAM, a member of congress from Mississippi, in 1826–8; d. near Woodville, Miss., March 7, 1837, a. about 40.

HAIT, TRUEMAN, d. at Palmyra, N. Y., Feb. 6, 1838.

HAJAONGUEH, alias TWO GUNS, head chief of the Senecas, and step son of Red Jacket, served through the war of 1812–15, and was in the battles of Bridgewater and Chippewa; he possessed great influence with his people; and d. June 17, 1855, a. 75 y. (*Buff. Com. Adv.*, June 19, 1855.)

HALE, ALBERT M., d. at Cape Island, N. J., July 14, 1838; a prominent merchant of Philadelphia.

HALE, ALEXANDER, d. in Pensacola, Fla., Aug. 23, 1850, a. 21; assistant engineer in the U. S. service; grad. at Harvard, in 1848; he lost his life in assisting the crew of a vessel in distress.

HALE, CYRUS K., sec. of the Mass. Life Insurance Co.; d. June 5, 1874, in Boston; he was a son of the late Rev. B. Hale former president of Geneva College, N. Y.

HALE, JOHN P., d. in Dover, N. H., Nov. 19, 1873, a. 67; many years a senator in congress from New Hampshire and afterwards U. S. minister to Spain. (*Drake's Am. Biog.*)

HALE, MOSES, M.D., of Troy, N. Y.; b. June 12, 1780, son of Moses H., of Alstead, N. H., settled in practice at Troy, N. Y., in 1804, where he resided till his death, Jan. 3, 1837; his widow d. in 1853; his son, Richard Hale, M.D., d. in 1849, a. 41. (*Tr. N. Y. St. Med. Soc.*, 1857, p. 73.)

HALE, SAMUEL, native of Mass., and one of the first settlers of Oneida co., N. Y.; d. in Southport, Wis. Terr., Aug. 25, 1842.

HALE, WILLIAM, d. at Mobile, Ala., Nov. 17, 1844, a. 55; native of Albany, N. Y., but for 20 years a resident of Mobile.

HALE, WILLIAM, d. at Dover, N. H., Nov. 8, 1848, a. 84; was a member of congress in 1810–11, and from 1813 to 1817.

HALL, BOLLING, member of congress from Georgia, from 1811 to 1817; d. near Montgomery, Ala., March 25, 1836, a. 67.

HALL, CALDWELL BRIG. GEN. R., late of U. S. vols.; d. at Newton, N. J., May 30, 1870, a. 31.

HALL, REV. DANIEL, Presb. minister at Sag Harbor; for the last six years at Shelter Island, N. Y.; d. April 12, 1812.

HALL, EBENEZER L., d. at Bartlett, N. H., Nov. 18, 1834, a. 74; was 5 years in the revolutionary war; a judge of probate 18 years.

HALL, DR. EDMUND H., of Auburn, N. Y.; d. April 28, 1871; b. in Keene, N. H., Feb. 28, 1821; educated at Keene; grad. at the Harvard Medical School; settled at Hoosick, N. Y.; in 1858 in Auburn where he took charge as medical superintendent of the asylum for insane convicts. (*Transactions N. Y. State Med. Soc.*, 1872, p. 333.)

HALL, JOHN, d. at Perrysburgh, Ohio, Jan., 1840; native of Connecticut; lieutenant in the revolution.

HALL, JOHN B., editor and proprietor of the *Catskill Recorder;* d. at Catskill, Oct. 1, 1874, a. 47; served in the constitutional commission of 1872–3, in place of Wm. Cassidy, deceased.

HALL, JOSEPH, grad. at Harvard in 1781; formerly judge of probate in Suffolk co.; d. April 14, 1848, a. 87.

HALL, LANCELOT, a lieut. in the English army in the French war; became lieutenant May 28, 1768; capt. Aug. 31, 1770; left the 55th regt. in 1783.

HALL, LOT, was b. in Yarmouth, Mass., in 1757, enlisted in May, 1775, in the naval service of S. C.; became a lieut., captured a vessel, and attempted to reach home with the prize; the prisoners mutinied, took command and sailed to Glasgow; he was discharged in 1777, attempted to return, was captured but exchanged and reached Phila., in Jan., 1778; he studied law, moved to Vermont in 1782, and settled in Westminster. He was several years in gen. assembly, a presidential elector in 1792, and in 1800 he was constituted a fellow of Middlebury Coll. From 1794 to 1801 he was a judge of the supreme court. He d. May 17, 1809; his widow survived till Feb. 21, 1843. (*Hall's Eastern Vermont*, p. 658.)

HALL DR. MARSHALL, a physician of eminence who visited the United States in 1853–4, and published a little work entitled, *The Two-fold Slavery of the United States;* he d. at Brighton, Eng., Aug. 4, 1857.

HALL, NATHAN K., formerly M. C., p. m. gen., and for many years before his death, judge of the U. S. district court for the northern dist. of N. Y., d. at Buffalo, March, 1874.

HALL, MAJ. NATHANIEL NYE, a gallant officer in the war of 1812, and 15, aid to Gen. Gaines at the attack on Fort Erie; he d. in New York, May 2, 1850. (*Stryker's Am. Reg.*, iv, 463).

HALL, PRIMUS (colored) a revolutionary pensioner, d. in Boston, March 22, 1842, a. 84; he was fond of relating revolutionary incidents and had been attached to the quartermaster general's department.

HALL, RICHARD, d. at Francestown, N. H., Oct. 18, 1834, a. 92.

HALL, DR. THOMAS H., d. at Tarborough, N. C., June 30, 1853, a. 80; was in congress from the 3d dist. of N. C., from 1817 to 1825, and from 1827 to 1835.

HALLET, SAMUEL, was in 1782, a capt. in DeLancey's 2d battalion of loyalists; he retired on half pay in 1783, settled in St. John, N. B., and drew a city lot. In 1792 he was a vestryman of the Episcopal church and d. before 1804.

HALLET, GEORGE, d. in Roxbury, Mass., Sept. 13, 1847; a. 64; was an eminent merchant of Boston.

HALLET, DANIEL, was in 1782, a lieut. in DeLancey's 2d battalion of loyalists; he went to St. John, N. B., where he was a grantee; he d. in York co., N. B., in 1827, a. 76.

HALLET, COL. WILLIAM R., of Mobile, Ala.; d. in New York city, June 5, 1860; was nearly thirty years president of the Bank of Mobile, and a successful merchant and banker.

HALLETT, BENJAMIN, was b. in 1760; served 3 years on board the Frigate Dean and in the land forces, and was a member of the legislature and magistrate; he d. at Barnstable, Mass., Jan. 14, 1850. (*Stryker's Am. Reg.*, iv, 443).

HALLETT, STEPHEN, b. in Salisbury, N. Y., in 1787; son of Maj. Jonathan H., of the revolution; in 1820 he settled in Fairfield, N. Y., as a merchant; in 1821, he became sheriff of Herkimer, and held till 1826; he d. at Fairfield, Nov. 19, 1827, a. 40. (*Benton's Herkimer Co. N. Y.*, p. 336.)

HALLETT, WILLIAM PAXSON, for several years clerk of the supreme court of New York; d. in New York city, Oct. 26, 1848.

HALLIBURTON, REV. WILLIAM, was chaplain of the royals, from May 22, 1787, to March 27, 1765, and served in America.

HALLOWAY, RANSOM, of Beekman, Dutchess co., N. Y., a member of the 31st congress; d. at Mount Pleasant, Prince George co., Md., April 6, 1851.

HALLOWELL, BENJAMIN, loyalist com'r of customs at Boston, Mass., was proscribed and banished in 1778 and included in the conspiracy act of 1779; he went to Halifax in 1776, and thence to England; he afterwards settled in Canada, the township of Manchester, N. S., was granted to him, and a number of loyalists went there and settled. (*Sabine's Loyalists.*)

HALLOWELL, JOHN, settled at Darby, now Delaware co., Pa., in 1682, from Nottinghamshire, Eng.

HALLOWELL, JOHN, a descendant of the above, b. in Philadelphia, Sept. 10, 1768; became a lawyer, and in 1815 a member of the house, in the state legislature; was appointed to the court of com. pleas in 1820, and in 1825 became a judge of the district court, which office he held till November, 1832; he d. Jan. 7, 1839, having been some years afflicted with paralysis. (*Simpson's Eminent Philadelphians.*)

HALSTED, JOB S., d. at Newton, N. J., April 13, 1844; was a member of the New Jersey bar for nearly fifty years.

HALSTEAD, OLIVER, law bookseller; d. at Moristown, N. J., July 24, 1857.

HAMBLETON, SAMUEL, senior purser in the U. S. navy; d. in Talbot co., Md., Jan. 18, 1851, a. 73 years; was purser on board the Lawrence in the battle of Lake Erie; served with Com. Perry at the last gun fired from that brig.; was desperately wounded by a discharge which dismantled the gun and left the vessel powerless.

HAMBLIN, MAJ. GEN. JOSEPH E., late of the U. S. vols.; d. at New York, July 4, 1870.

HAMERSLEY, DR. WILLIAM, senior consulting physician at the New York Hospital; formerly prof. of the theory and practice of physic in the College of Physicians and Surgeons; d. in New York city, Feb. 8, 1837, a. 72.

HAMILTON, ARCHIBALD, of Queens co., N. Y.; an active loyalist and aid-de-camp of Gen. Robertson; in 1780, his house in Flushing was burned with its contents; commanded the militia of Queens co., and had 17 companies. (*Sabine's Loyalists.*)

HAMILTON, CLAUDE, actor; d. at Washington, D. C., July 12, 1847.

HAMILTON, CORNELIUS S., member of congress for the 8th dist. of Ohio; killed by his son (a maniac), Dec. 22, 1867, a. about 50; had been several times in the legislature.

HAMILTON, FREDERICK, became major of the 2d battalion of 1st Royals, March 7, 1757; served at Louisburgh in 1758, and against the Cherokees in 1760; retired from the army Nov. 24, 1776.

HAMILTON, JAMES, b. in Philadelphia; in 1741, became prothonotary; in 1747, lieut. gov. of Pennsylvania; resigned in 1754; in 1759, being then in England, again accepted this office, and held till 1763, retaining, however, a place in the council. He d. soon after the revolution, at an advanced age.

HAMILTON, JOHN, of S. C.; accepted a military appointment under the crown; became lieut. col. of N. C. volunteers in the revolution; his estate was confiscated in 1779. (*Sabine's Loyalists.*)

HAMILTON, JOHN, d. in Washington co., Penn., Aug. 31, 1837, a. 84; formerly high sheriff of that county; member of congress in 1805–7.

HAMILTON, LOUIS M., capt. 7th U. S. cavalry, killed Nov. 31, 1868, in an engagement with Black Kettler's band of Cheyenne Indians; was b. in N. Y.; entered the army as 2d lieut., in 1862, and served through the war.

HAMILTON, PAUL, SEN., of Charleston, S. C.; was banished in 1782, and his estate confiscated.

HAMILTON, WILLLAM, b. in Philadelphia, and a man of great wealth; he owned the site of the city of Lancaster and valuable property in and around Philadelphia; was a botanist; in the revolution was suspected of disloyalty to the popular cause, and tried for treason, but acquitted; he d. about 1824, at Woodlands, Philadelphia. (*Simpson's Eminent Philadelphians; Sabine's Loyalists.*)

HAMILTON, COL. WILLIAM S., youngest son of Alexander H., and four years old at his father's death; grad. at West Point at the age of 21; went to Illinois; became a surveyor of public lands, and held various public offices; removed to Wisconsin and thence to California; d. in Sacramento, Aug. 7, 1850.

HAMLIN, WILLIAM D., b. in Conn. in 1805; about 1822 he removed to Utica, N. Y., and began business as a wagon maker; from small beginnings he built up a large and lucrative business, and d. March 3d, 1873, leaving an ample estate; was pres. of the Utica Water Works Co.; vice pres. and director of the Second National Bank, of that city.

HAMMEL, JOHN, was a surgeon of the 3d battalion of N. J. volunteer loyalists in the revolution.

HAMMIT, REV. WILLIAM, founder of the Primitive Methodists; of Irish birth; was a Meth. Ep. preacher in the W. I.; came to Charleston, S. C., in 1791; withdrew and founded a sect which he styled Primitive Methodists; he died May, 14, 1803. (*Lee's Hist. Meth.*, p. 206.)

HAMMOND, LIEUT. BENJAMIN, Pa.; killed in the revolution, Feb. 20, 1778.

HAMMOND, SAMUEL, son of Charles H., was b. in Richmond co., Va., Sept. 21, 1757; served against the Indians under the order of Gov. Dunmore, and in the revolution as captain, major and col.; served actively in the south, and evinced great bravery; he resided several years in Savannah, which he represented in assembly, and was surveyor gen. of Ga., and state com'r; in 1793 he commanded on the Indian frontiers; in 1803–5 was in congress, and resided 20 y. in the territory of Missouri, where he was appointed to the legislative council in 1813, and became receiver of public moneys in 1815; he fell into habits of speculation, became heavily involved in debt to the U. S.; returned to Charleston and was arrested, but settled up; he removed to Varellofarm, on Horse creek, 3 miles below Augusta, Ga.; in 1827 he was elected surveyor gen. of S. C., and in 1831 sec. of state, residing occasionally at Charleston and Columbia, until 1835; he then retired to Varello, and d. Sept. 11, 1842, a. 85. (*White's Hist. Ga.*, p. 624, with portrait.)

HAMMOND, Rev. John, a native of England; b. about 1740; was in 1795 minister of the Baptist church of Schuyler, N. Y.; he lived afterwards for the most part in Utica, and d. Aug., 1819; he was also a land surveyor, as were his sons Calvin, Worden and John D., all of whom were much employed in this capacity in New York and Ohio.

HAMMONS, Joseph, member of congress from New Hampshire from 1829 to 1833; d. at Farmington, N. H., April 1836.

HANCOCK, Dr. R. C., d. in De Soto co., Mississippi, Feb. 1857, a. 56; he had been for several years a representative in the state legislature.

HAND, Capt. David, a soldier of the revolution; d. at Sag Harbor, N. Y., Feb. 29, 1840, a. 81.

HAND, John, a loyalist from N. J., settled in St. John, N. B., in 1783.

HAND, Joseph W., d. in Washington, D. C., May 25, 1843, a. 52; chief clerk in the patent offi., b. in Madison, Conn., grad. at Yale, in 1813.

HANDY, Lieut. Levin, U. S. N.; d. on board the U. S. frigate Constellation at Hong Kong, China, Sept., 1842, a. 29.

HANFORD, Thomas, of Ct., was a loyalist, and settled in St. John, N. B., after the revolution; he there became an eminent merchant; and d. at St. John, in 1826, a. 73.

HANNA, Gen. Robert, a member of the Indiana Constitutional Convention of 1846; d. at Indianapolis, Ind., Nov. 19, 1858.

HANNA, Rev. William, first presb. minister in Albany; educated at Dr. Finley's Acad., Nottingham, Md.; attended at Princeton Coll., and in 1759, grad. at Kings Coll., N. Y. He was licensed to preach May 28, 1760, and settled in Albany in 1762, and preached 5 y.; he then went to Schenectady, and settled as a lawyer in May 1767; in 1772, he received holy orders from the bp. of London. (*Doc. Hist. N. Y.*, iv, 373.)

HANSINFRANTS, Mrs. Catharine, d. in New York city, a. 102.

HARALSON, Hugh A., b. in Greene co., Ga., Nov. 13, 1805; grad. at the University of Georgia, in 1825; studied law and by special act was admitted to practice before of age, was many years in the Georgia legislature; was in congress from 1843 to 1851, and d. at his residence Oct., 1854.

HARDEE, Gen. William J., of Selma, Ala.; d. Nov. 6, 1873, at Wytheville, Va.; entered the military academy at West Point from Georgia in 1834, and joined the second dragoons in 1838. He attained the rank of captain in 1844, and was appointed major by brevet in March, 1847 for gallant conduct in the combat at Medelin, near Vera Cruz, during the Mexican war. He also behaved creditably at San Augustine and El Molina del Rey, and was rewarded with the rank of lieutenant colonel by brevet. His compilation of *Infantry Tactics* was adopted by the war department for the United States regular army, and continued to be the standard authority until superceded during the war by that of Casey. At the outbreak of the civil war he went over to the confederates, and attained eventually command of one of the three corps forming Braggs's army of 45,000 men. His corps began the fighting at Stone river, and shared in the subsequent disasters which befell his commander's forces. During Sherman's campaign Gen. Hardee was driven, step by step, into Savannah, which he held at the head of 15,000 men, but promptly abandoned just as Gen. Slocum was ready to attack him. He retreated to Charleston, but finding himself flanked by the advance of the federal troops and the fall of Columbia, he caused the cotton warehouses and the arsenals to be fired, and hastily retreated. He finally joined the forces of Gen. Jo. Johnston, and surrendered with them. After the war Gen. Hardee lived in comparative retirement. He frankly accepted the results of the conflict, and labored to restore good feeling between the once hostile sections.—*N. Y. Tribune.*

HARDEN, SAMUEL, d. at Baltimore, Md., Feb. 9, 1841, a. 65.

HARDENBERGH, REV. JAMES BRUYN, D.D., d. at New York, Jan. 22, 1870, a. 70; b. in New York state June 28, 1800; grad. at Union coll., and at the sem. of the R. P. D. ch., at New Brunswick, and was pastor at New Brunswick; N. J.; of Orchard st. ch., N. Y. city; at Rhinebeck, N. Y., and Phila. and at the Franklin st. church and mission church in N. Y. city.

HARDENBURGH, CORNELIUS L., was a lawyer, and for several years prosecutor of the pleas for Somerset co., N. J., and in 1836–7, in the New Jersey legislature; for more than forty years, he was a trustee of Rutgers Coll., and d. at New Brunswick, July 17, 1860, a. 70.

HARDENBURGH, JACOB, d. in Albany April 29, 1874, a. 49.

HARDIN, BENJAMIN, b. in Westmoreland co., Pa., and in congress from Kentucky from 1815 to 1817, from 1819 to 1823, and from 1833 to 1837; d. at Bardstown, Ky., Sept. 24, 1852.

HARDING, FISHER AMES, one of the editors of the *Detroit Daily Advertiser*, d. at Detroit, Mich., Aug. 4, 1846; he was b. in Dover, Mass., in 1811; grad. at Harvard in 1833, and settled at Chicago as a lawyer in 1835; in 1837 he went to Detroit, and formed a law partnership with Fletcher Webster; in 1841, he was elected to the state legislature, and the same year became associated with Morgan Bates in the *Advertiser*, with which he continued (with about a year interval) till his death.

HARDING, WILLIAM, went to St. John, N. B., in 1783 as a loyalist, and was a grantee of that city; he d. there in 1818, a. 73.

HARDMAN, CAPT. JOHN, Md., killed in the revolution Sept. 1, 1780.

HARDY, ELIAS, a loyalist; settled at St. John, N. B., and practiced law; the traitor Arnold sued him for slander in saying that A. had burned his own warehouse; was fined two shillings and six pence; in 1792 was a member of the house of assembly; d. at St. John before 1800.

HARE, EDWARD, of Charleston, S. C.; a loyalist; was banished, and in 1782 his estate was confiscated.

HARE, HENRY, a tory lieut.; engaged with Brant and Johnson in the Mohawk valley in the revolution; was seized and hung at Canajoharie, N. Y., in 1779, while Gen. Jas. Clinton was stopping at that place on his way to join Sullivan's expedition.

HARE, MICHAEL, of Bedford co., Pa.; a loyalist; was ordered to stand trial for treason or suffer banishment and confiscation in 1778.

HARKER, JOSEPH, member of the New Jersey legislature from the second dist. of Gloucester co.; d. at Mullica Hill, N. J., Jan. 27, 1860.

HARKNESS, ANTHONY, b. in Rhode Island in 1793; became a machinist at Paterson, N. J.; went to Cincinnati in 1820; established a shop for building engines, and afterwards locomotives, which business he continued till 1851, when he retired with a large fortune; d. in Cincinnati, O., May 10, 1858.

HARLAN, CARTER B., sec. of state of Ohio; d. at Philadelphia, Ohio, June 10, 1840.

HARMANSON, JOHN H., d. in New Orleans, La., Oct. 25, 1850, a. 47; b. in Norfolk, Va., Jan., 1803; removed to Louisiana when 8 years old; became a lawyer, but finally a planter; entered the state senate in 1844; in Nov., 1845, was elected to congress and again in 1847 and 1849; was actively engaged in securing land grants for levees on the banks of the Mississippi.

HARMON, ELIAS, d. Sept. 18, 1851, in Mantua, Portage co., Ohio, a. 78; b. in Connecticut; removed to Ohio in 1799; settled on a farm in Mantua; was county treasurer in 1806; in the legislature in 1810, 11, 12; associate judge for Portage co., for 21 years, attending every court but one during that period.

HARPER, COL. CHARLES CARROLL, d. near Paris, France, June 23, 1837, in his 36th year; was of Baltimore; son of the late Robert Goodloe Harper; late secretary of the American legation at Paris.

HARPER, FRANCIS J., elected to congress from Pennsylvania, but d. before taking his seat, March 18, 1837, a. 38.

HARPER, JOHN, a militia colonel of New York, in revolution, and a pioneer settler in Tryon co.; d. at Harpersfield, Delaware co., N. Y., Nov. 20, 1811.

HARPER, JOSEPH W., of the house of Harper Brothers; d. at Brooklyn, N. Y., Feb. 15, 1870, a. 70; b. at Newtown, N. Y., in 1801, served as an apprentice of his brother with whom he became a partner.

HARPER, KENTON, editor of *Stanton Spectator*, d. in Stanton, Va., Dec. 25, 1867, a. 60; had been mayor and pres. of a bank, and member of the legislature, was agent in the Indian Territory under Fillmore, and in the late war commanded confederate militia at Harper's Ferry.

HARRINGTON, ALFRED W., d. at Chicago, Dec. 31, 1867, b. in N. C.; had been a Methodist preacher, lawyer, legislator in Arkansas and judge in Texas; in 1857, resumed law practice in Chicago.

HARRINGTON, GEORGE N., well known as George N. Christy, Ethiopian comic vocalist; d. in New York city, May 12, 1868, a. 40.

HARRINGTON, Isaac R., mayor of Buffalo, N. Y., in 1841, and since 1847 postmaster; d. in that city Aug. 10, 1851.

HARRINGTON, Jonathan, d. in Lexington, Mass., March 26, 1854, a. 85; was a fifer for the Minute men who assembled at Lexington Green, April 19, 1775, and said to be the last survior of that battle.

HARRIOT, Dr. Hampton, d. April 2, 1868, in New York city.

HARRIS, Dr. Augustus, b. in Rensselaer co., July 17, 1776, son of Dr. Nicholas H., with whom he studied medicine; he settled in Bethlehem, N. Y., in 1803, and in 1817, in Van Buren, N. Y., where he practiced till 1821. (*Tr. N. Y. St. Med. Soc.*, 1857, p. 33; *Munsell's Ann. Alb.*, ix, 97.)

HARRIS, Charles, b. in Eng., educated in France, came to Ga., in 1788, settled in Savannah and became eminent as a lawyer; he d. March 17, 1827.

HARRIS, Ezekiel. A soldier of the revolution, d. in Wilkes co., Ga., a. 71.

HARRIS, Francis H., lieut. col. in the revolution, son of Francis H., of Ga., was in college in England when the revolution began; returned, became capt. in the continental army, and soon after commanded a battallion; he was taken prisoner at Briar Creek, and served in the battles of Camden and Eutaw; he d. in 1782, and was buried at the High hills of Santee. (*White's Hist. Ga.*, p. 365, with portrait.)

HARRIS, Horatio J., U. S. dist. atty. for southern dist., of Mississippi, and member of the city council of Vicksburgh; d. in Newark, O., Oct. 25, 1859; he was formerly auditor of public accounts in the state of Indiana.

HARRIS, Lieut. John, Conn., d. in the revolution, Dec. 7, 1777.

HARRIS, Sampson W., d. in Washington, D.C., April 1, 1857, a. 48. Since 1847 he had been a representative from the state of Alabama.

HARRIS, Gen. W. P., d. at Gallatin, Miss., May 17, 1845, a. 50; formerly a receiver of public moneys at Columbus, Miss.; and a member of the Mississippi legislature.

HARRIS, William R., one the judges of the supreme court of Tennessee; d. June 26, 1858, at Memphis, Tenn.

HARRIS, W. S., commander in the U. S. navy; drowned by the swamping of a boat on the bar of Tuspan, May 15, 1848.

HARRISON, Albert G., d. at Fulton, Mo., Sept. 7, 1839; was a member of congress; and was again elected to the 26th congress; b. in Kentucky; a lawyer by profession and had resided in Missouri the last twelve years.

HARRISON, Charles, was a captain in the 2d battalion of N. J. volunteers (loyalists,) and after the revolution went to St. John, N. B., and drew a lot and half pay; he was lt. col. of militia in N. B.; he was a relative of President Harrison.

HARRISON, Eliphalet Porter, d. in Boston Oct. 7, 1856, a. 74; he was a native of Walpole, Mass., and for more than half a century a merchant; prominent in the affairs of his town, and five years a representative in the state legislature.

HARRISON, Lieut. JAMES, Va., killed in the revolution, Oct. 7, 1777.

HARRISON, JAMES, a lieut. in the 2d battalion of N. J. loyalist Volun., and went to St. John, N. B., where he drew a lot in 1783.

HARRISON, JOHN and S., tories and captains of loyalist troops, in the state of South Carolina.

HANDY, JOHN HARREY, merchant of New Hartford and of Utica, N. Y.; b. in Waterbury, Conn., Nov. 21, 1785; d. at Utica, July 12, 1833.

HARRIS, DANIEL, sergeant, Capt. Wm. B. Hamlin's co., killed in invasion of Niagara frontier, Dec. 30, 1813.

HARRISON, DR. J. P., a professor in the Ohio Medical Coll.; d. at Cincinnati of cholera, Aug. 27, 1849.

HARRISON, LT. MONTGOMERY P., a grandson of President Harrison, was shot by the Indians near the Colorado river, Texas, Oct. 7, 1849.

HARRISON, ROBERT MONROE, U. S. consul at Kingston, Jamaica; d. May 24, 1858, a. 90 years; he was a native of Virginia, and cousin of President Harrison.

HARRISON, THOMAS, d. at Greenville dist., S. C., July 21, 1837, a. 47; lately comptroller general of South Carolina.

HART, ELI, an enterprising merchant of New York city, and at times the largest holder of flour in the United States; acquired an ample fortune and retired some two or three years before his death, which occurred Jan., 1846, at the age of 65 years.

HART, ELI, son of Thomas; was a prosperous merchant in New York city; d. in 1843.

HART, ELISHA, d. May 30, 1842, a. 83; at New Haven, Conn., formerly of Saybrook, Conn.

HART, EPHRAIM, b. in Farmington, Dec. 27, 1774; in 1801 he succeeded his father as a merchant, but in 1817 removed to Utica where he continued in mercantile pursuits. During the years 1817–23, he represented his district in the state senate. Was a friend of DeWitt Clinton, and a firm supporter of the Erie canal; director of Utica Bank from its organization; he d. at St. Augustine, Fla., Feb. 14, 1839.

HART, DR. ERASTUS L., d. at Elmira, N. Y., Oct. 22, 1871, a. 84.

HART, LEVI, many years a judge of the county court of Lewis co., N. Y., and in 1818, a mem. of assembly; d. in Turin, Dec. 30. 1834, a. 61.

HART, ORSON B., d. at Jacksonville, Fla., March 18, 1874; was appointed associate justice of the supreme court of Florida by Gov. Reed in 1868, and held that position until he became governor in 1873. He was the republican nominee for the latter office, and received at the election in November, 1872, 17,603 votes, against 16,004 for Bloxham, the democratic candidate. In his first message he urged the legislature to improve the election laws and adopt a sound financial policy. Lieut. Gov. Marcellus B. Stearns succeeded him by virtue of his office.

HART, ROSWELL, son of Thomas, merchant at Rochester, N. Y.; d. in 1824.

HART, STEPHEN, a pioneer of Turin, N. Y.; d. in that town Aug. 13, 1857, a. 91.

HART, THOMAS, a native of Farmington, Conn., he settled about 1790 in Clinton, N. Y.; was a farmer and merchant. County judge, 1801–2; member of assembly 1806; d. about 1809.

HART, TRUMAN, son of Thomas; was a lawyer; lived at Palmyra, Wayne co., N. Y.; was a member of assembly from Ontario county in 1820–21; a state senator in 1826–9; d. in Palmyra, 1838.

HARTMAN, JOHN ADAM, b. in Edenkoben, Germany, Sept. 1743; settled on the Upper Mohawk; served through the revolution; d. April 5, 1836, in his 93d year. He was reputed an inveterate hater and killer of Indians. (*Benton's Herkimer Co.*, p. 409.)

HARTSHORN, RICHARD, d. near Rahway, N. J., Nov., 1836, a. 87; belonged to the society of Friends.

HARTWELL, MAJ. DAVID, d. in West Bridgewater, Mass., April 1, 1844, a. 89; served in the revolution; was a pensioner.

HARTWELL, REV. JESSE, D.D., b. in New Marlborough, Mass., in 1794; grad. at Brown U. in 1819; taught school; studied theology; preached and taught at the south; in 1855, became president of Mt. Lebanon University; d. at Mt. Lebanon, La., Sept. 16, 1859, a. 65.

HARTWICK, REV. JOHN CHRISTOPHER, a Lutheran, b. in Saxe Gotha, Jan. 6, 1714; pastor at Frederick, Md.; chaplain in the revolution; missionary to the Palatines of Albany and Dutchess co.; resided in New York, and at Rhinebeck; became proprietor of a valuable tract of land in Otsego co., and was founder of Hartwick Seminary; d. July 16, 1796. (*Hartwick Seminary Semi Centennial.*)

HARVEY, HENRY L., formerly of Champion, N. Y., and of Watertown, N. Y., where he published the *Watertown Register;* afterwards published a paper at Erie, Pa.; was last, a clerk in the navy department at Washington, D. C., where he d. Oct. 20, 1859, a. 55.

HARVEY, SUSANNA, d. in Rhode Island, Aug. 17, 1859, a. 100 years.

HARVEY, SIR THOMAS (vice admiral in British navy); d. in Bermuda, May 28, 1840, a. 65; was commander in chief in the West Indies and North America.

HARVEY, WILLIAM, a member of the Canadian parliament for East Elgin; d. at Aylmer, Canada, June 13, 1874.

HARVIE, JAQUELIN B., d. in Richmond, Va., Feb. 8, 1856, a. 67; had held various honorable stations in civil life, and at the time of his death, was major general of the 4th div. of Virginia militia.

HASBROUCK, DR. DAVID, was son of Gen. Joseph Hasbrouck of Shawangunk, Ulster co., N. Y.; he pursued his medical studies here and in N. Y., and in 1804 settled at Utica; there he practiced medicine and sold drugs until about 1815, when he returned to Ulster county; he d. in Schenectady.

HASBROUCK, JONATHAN, descendant of a Huguenot settler of New Paltz, N. Y.; removed to Newburgh in 1853 and at the beginning of the revolution was a militia colonel. (*Munsell's Hist. Series*, v, 160.)

HASBROUCK, LOUIS, first clerk of St. Lawrence co., N. Y.; b. at New Paltz, N. Y., Apr. 22, 1777, settled at Ogdensburgh as co. clerk in 1802, and held till 1817; he d. Aug. 20, 1834, while holding the office of state senator. (*Hough's Hist. St. Law. & Fr. Cos*, p. 594.)

HASBROUCK, Dr. Moses Cantine, of Nyack, N. Y.; b. in Marbletown, N. Y., Nov. 23, 1808, and d. Oct. 28, 1870. (*Transac. N. Y. State Med. Soc.* 1872, p. 354.)

HASCALL, Asa, legislator and dist. atty; from Essex co., Vt.; settled at Malone, N. Y., in 1815, as a lawyer; was in assembly in 1825, 6, 35, 9, and dist. atty. of Franklin co. from 1818 till 1841; he d. at Malone Jan. 5, 1852, a. 66. (*Hough's Hist. St. Law. & Fr. Cos, N. Y.* p. 593.)

HASELL, James, one of the council of N. C., advised prompt measures against the whigs early in the revolution, and for a time acted as governor, being president of the council; he was also temporarily chief justice of the colony.

HASEY, Benjamin, oldest lawyer in Maine; d. at Topsham, where he had lived 37 years; March 24, 1851, a. 79 years; was b. in Lebanon, York co., Me., July 5, 1771; and never married.

HASSELBAUGH, Nicholas, first printer in Baltimore, Md.; he was lost at sea, and in 1773, his printing materials were bought by Wm. Goddard.

HASSLER, Marianne, widow of F. R. Hassler, first supt. of U. S. coast survey; d. at Miller's Place, Suffolk co., Feb. 25, 1858, a. 87 years.

HASLETT, Capt. John, Del.; killed in battle of Princeton, Jan. 3, 1777.

HASTINGS, C. C. P., d. at Mendon, Mass., Sept. 25, 1848.

HASTINGS, Eurotas Parmelee, b. July 20, 1791; was a banker in Geneva, N. Y., and in Detroit, Mich.; was president of the Bank of Michigan until its close; was sometime auditor general of the state of Michigan; d. June 1, 1866.

HASTINGS, Maj. John, d. at Cambridge, Mass., Feb. 16, 1839, a. 85; grad. at Harvard in 1772; entered the army as captain in 1775, and served during the whole war.

HASTINGS, John, d. in Columbus, Ohio, Dec. 29, 1854; was in congress from Ohio, from 1839 to 1843.

HASTINGS, Joseph Stacy, of N. H.; grad. at Harvard in 1762; was ordained at North Hampton in 1767, and having embraced the Sandemanian faith left the ministerial office in 1774. He went to Halifax in 1776, but returned to Boston and kept a grocery; he d. in 1807, on a journey to Vt.

HASTINGS, Orlando, b. March 7, 1789; was a lawyer of good standing in Geneseo and in Rochester, N. Y.; was dist. attorney of Livingston county in 1824, and member of assembly in 1853; d. March 19, 1861.

HASTINGS, Seth, grad. at Harvard in 1782; was in congress from Mass., from 1801 to 1807, and d. in 1831.

HASTINGS, Dr. Seth, b. Aug. 23, 1780; removed with his father's family from Washington, Litchfield co., Conn., to Clinton, N. Y., Feb., 1797; practiced medicine in Clinton from 1801 to 1851, when he was disabled by a paralytic attack; d. March 26, 1861.

HASTINGS, Thomas, Dr. Music, b. Oct. 15, 1784; from 1806 or 7, he was a teacher of sacred music in Central New York; in 1817–18 he lived in Troy; in 1823 he moved to Utica and was editor of the *Western*

Recorder; thence in 1832 he removed to New York, where he d., May 15, 1872; between the years 1819 and 1860 he published upwards of twenty collections of sacred music, besides editing 7 or 8 others; of the 600 hymns and versions of the psalms, which he composed, 200 are current in this country and in Great Britain; he received the degree, Doctor Musicae, from New York University.

HASTINGS, WILLIAM SODEN, d. at the Sulphur Springs, Va., June 17, 1842; he was frequently in the Mass. legislature, and from 1837 to 1842 in congress. (*Am. Almanac*, 1843, p. 315.)

HATCH, CHRISTOPHER, of Boston, was proscribed and banished as a tory in 1778, became a capt. in the loyal Am. regt., was wounded, retired upon half pay, drew a city lot and settled in St. John, N. B., and afterwards in St. Andrew, N. B., as a merchant; he was a magistrate and col. of militia, and d. in 1819, a. 70; his son Harrison Hatch, has been a prominent officer in N. B. (*Sabine's Loyalists.*)

HATCH, JAMES LEWIS, assist. ed'r of *Charleston Mercury*, b. in Oxford co., Me., grad. at Bowdoin Coll. in 1854, became a contributor for N. E. journals, went to S. C. for his health, was engaged upon the *Standard*, and in 1857 upon the *Courier.* He d. of yellow fever, at Charleston, S. C., Sept. 25, 1858. (*Hist. Mag.*, ii, 348.)

HATCH, DEA. JOEL, of Marshfield, Mass.; d. April 5, 1849, a. 79.

HATHAWAY, BENONI, revolutionary officer of New Jersey, led a company under Brig. Gen. Winds, in a night attack on Elizabethtown in Dec., 1777, was severely wounded but recovered; he d. at Newark, April 19, 1823, in his 70th year. (*Rogers's Am. Biog.*)

HATHAWAY, JAY, son of Joshua; was for many years post master at Rome, N. Y.

HATHAWAY, JOSHUA, b. in Suffield, Conn., Aug. 13, 1761; he was present with his father and brothers at the battle of Bennington. In 1787 he grad. at Yale College. He became a lawyer and settled in Rome, N. Y., where in 1798, he was justice of the peace. He was surrogate during the years 1808–13, 1815–19, 1821–27, and judge of county court 1821 and 1828–33. In the war of 1812, he was appointed quarter master general of the N. Y. state militia, and was in command at Sackett's Harbor. He had the honor of removing the first shovelful of earth when ground was broken for the construction of the Erie canal July 4, 1817; he d. Dec. 8, 1836.

HATHAWAY, ELNATHAN PIERCE, grad. at Brown University in 1818, studied law, and was a member of the state legislature of Mass., and of the convention of 1853, for revising the constitution; he d. Jan. 23, 1858, at Freetown, Mass. He was for some years commissionary of insolvency for Bristol county.

HATHAWAY, JOSHUA, judge of the court of common pleas in the county of Oneida; d. at Rome, N. Y., Dec. 8, 1836.

HAUN, HENRY P. was a native of Scott co., Ky.; and was admitted to the bar in 1839, was prosecuting attorney of Scott co., and in 1845 removed to Iowa; in 1846 he was a member of the constitutional convention of that state; in 1849, he emigrated to California, and became a county judge in 1850; he was appointed senator in place of Mr. Broderick, and d. at Marysville, Cal., May 6, 1860.

HAUVERMAN, ADAM, d. in Antwerp, N. Y., Aug. 8, 1860, a. 102; b. in 1758, was a captive in Canada in his childhood.

HAVEN, JONATHAN NICOLL, member of the New York assembly from Suffolk co. from 1786 to 1795, and in congress from 1795 to 1799, but d. before the end of his second term; resided at Shelter island, N. Y.

HAVILAND, EBENEZER, surgeon's mate, 2d N. Y. regiment; d. June 28, 1781.

HAVIS, MAJ. THOMAS, d. July 31, 1841, at Franklin co., Miss.; was formerly a member of legislature of that state.

HAWES, ALBERT G., member of congress from Kentucky, from 1831 to 1837; d. in Davis co., Ky., April 14, 1849.

HAWES, DR. AYLETT, d. in Culpeper co., Va., Aug. 31, 1833, in his 65th year; he was a noted philanthropist, and at his death manumitted all his slaves, 110 in number, and made provision for their removal to Liberia.

HAWES, PRINCE, an honorable merchant, of Boston; d. Aug. 2, 1859, a. 69.

HAWKINS, JOSEPH, settled in Henderson, N. Y., in 1810, was a prominent business man, and largely concerned in lake trade; he was in congress in 1829–31, and d. April 20, 1832, a. 50. (*Hough's Hist. Jeff. Co., N. Y.*, p. 43.)

HAWKINS, CAPT. MOSES, Va., killed in the revolution at Germantown, Oct. 4, 1777.

HAWKINS, NATHAN, revolutionary patriot of R. I., early entered the revolution at the head of a volunteer corps, served in several engagements, and settled at Charlestown, Mass., as a farmer, where he d. Oct. 3, 1817, in his 69th year. (*Rogers's Am. Biog.*)

HAWLEY, JESSE, d. at Lockport, N. Y., Jan. 10, 1842; one of the projectors of the Erie canal; a member of assembly from Genesee co., in 1821, and for several years a collector of the port of Genesee.

HAWLEY, JOEL EDWIN M.D., son of Rev. Stephen H., b. in Bethany, Ct., Sept. 14, 1802; educated at West Point, studied medicine with Dr. Reed of Charlotte co., Va., and Dr. Ives of New Haven, and grad. at the Yale Med. School in 1829; he settled at Ithaca, N. Y., was elected prof. of surgery at Geneva, Dec. 1853, and held till April, 1855. He d. at Ithaca, Aug. 1, 1859, a. 57. (*Tr. N. Y. St. Med. Soc.*, 1860, p. 173.)

HAYES, CATHARINE (see Bushnell, Mrs. William A.).

HAYDEN, CHESTER, b. near Rome, Oneida co., N. Y., studied law in Rome; was member of assembly from Oswego county in 1825; removed to Utica, and was first judge of Oneida co., 1830–40, and again 1843–6; he removed to Saratoga, where he was connected with a law school, and afterwards to Cleveland Ohio; d. about 1868.

HAYES, JOHN E., d. Sept. 17, 1868, at Savannah; proprietor of the *Savannah Republican.*

HAYES, WILLIAM R., U. S. consul at Barbadoes; d. at that place, July 13, 1852.

HAYNE, William E., d. in Charleston, S. C., Nov. 24, 1844; was a distinguished citizen, and had discharged the duties of several important offices, was a son of Mr. Hayne, martyr in the revolution.

HAYNES, Aaron, d. in Princeton, Mass., Feb. 16, 1842, a. 83; he served in the revolutionary war.

HAYNES, Col. Thomas, d. at Savannah, Ga., Jan. 5, 1842, a. 55; native of Va., but resident of Georgia from childhood; was many years in the state legislature and state treasurer, in which last office he died.

HAYS, Col. Andrew, d. at Jackson, Miss., Sept. 10, 1843, a. about 60, an eminent lawyer, formerly of Tennessee.

HAYWARD, Dr. Joshua Henshaw, son of Dr. Lemuel H.; was b. in Boston, Feb. 6, 1797; grad. at Harvard in 1818; studied medicine and visited Europe to complete his education. He soon left his profession, was for a time in the drug business, and afterwards a portrait painter; he d. in Boston, Dec. 2, 1856, a. 59.

HAYWOOD, William H., d. in Raleigh, N. C., Oct. 5, 1852, was an eminent lawyer, and a senator in congress from 1843 to 1845.

HAZARD, Benjamin, d. March, 1841, a. 69, at Newport, R. I., was an eminent lawyer, and for more than thirty years in succession a member of the legislature of Rhode Island, and for several years speaker of the house.

HAZARD, Nathaniel, b. in Newport, R. I., was in congress from 1819 to 1821, and d. Dec. 17, 1820, a. 47.

HAZELWOOD, John, of Phila., was employed to construct fire rafts for the defense of the Delaware, in the revolution, with the rank of captain; he was sent to the Hudson on business relating to the obstruction of navigation; he was raised to the rank of commodore Oct. 7, 1777, and rendered efficient aid at the attack on Ft. Mercer, Oct. 21, 1777; he was presented by congress with a sword. (*Munsell's Hist. Series*, v, 19.)

HEARD, Stephen, acting governor of Georgia in the revolution, was an active revolutionary officer; he had emigrated from Ireland to Va., during the French war and he served as captain under Washington in that war; during a part of the time that Ga. was overrun by the British he was president of the executive council; he was chief justice of the superior court and a trustee of the acad., at Washington, Ga.; he d. Nov. 15, 1815. (*White's Hist. Ga.*, p. 212.)

HEARNE, Edward L., ex-judge, d. Jan. 27, 1870, at Far Rockaway, N. Y., a. 65.

HEATH, James P., b. in Delaware, Dec. 21, 1777, served in the war of 1812; in 1838, was wrecked on the steamer Pulaski; was in congress from Maryland, from 1833 to 1835, and d. at Georgetown, D. C., June 12, 1854.

HEATH, Upton S., d. in Baltimore, Md., Feb. 21, 1852; judge of the U. S. district court of Maryland.

HEATHCOTE, Caleb, son of Gilbert H., mayor of Chester, Eng., and brother of Sir Gilbert H., founder and 1st pres. of Bank of Eng., and ld. mayor of London, in 1711; he came to N. Y. in 1692, bought large tracts of land in Westchester co., which were erected March 21, 1701, into the manor of Scarsdale. He was judge of Westchester and col. of militia, first mayor of Westchester, a councillor, and from 1715 to 1721, receiver general of customs for all North America; he was many years vestryman of Trinity church; he died in 1721. (*Bolton's Hist. Westchester Co.*, ii, 102; *Doc. Hist. N. Y.*, iv, 1039.)

HEATON, DAVID, member of congress from North Carolina, d. at Washington, D.C., June 25, 1870; b. in Hamilton, O., March 10, 1823; became a lawyer, was in the state senate of Ohio, and in 1847, removed to Minnesota, where he was three times elected to the state senate; was appointed third auditor of the treasury, but declined; became pres. of the National Bank at Newbern in the fall of 1865, was elected to congress in April, 1868, and reëlected; was a republican politician and author of the Platform adopted at Raleigh in 1867.

HEDDEN, JAMES, an active officer of the New Jersey militia, during the revolution; d. at Newark, N. J., May 18, 1838, a. 83.

HEDGE, BARNABAS, d. at Boston, Mass., July 12, 1840, a. 73; was a merchant of Plymouth, Mass., of wealth and eminence.

HEENAN, JOHN CARMEL, pugilist; d. of consumption in Wyoming Territory, Oct. 26, 1873; b. in West Troy, N. Y. in 1834; in 1849, went to California and there acquired the title of "the Benecia boy" by which he was afterwards known in sporting circles; in 1858, was defeated by John Morrissey at Long Point, Canada; his great fight was with Tom Sayers in England, in 1860.

HEILMAN, JULIUS F., brevet lieut. col. U. S. A.; d. at Fort Duane, June 27, 1836.

HEISTER, GEN. GABRIEL, formerly surveyor gen. of Tennessee; d. at Pittsburg, Pa., Sept. 14, 1834, a. 56.

HEISTER, ISAAC E., ex-member of congress, d. at Lancaster, Pa., Feb. 6, 1871; b. in Lancaster co.; grad. at Yale in 1842; admitted to the bar; deputy atty. gen. for Lancaster co. in 1848; in congress from 1853 to 1855.

HEISTER, WILLIAM, d. Oct. 14, 1853, in Pennsylvania, a. 62; was for many years an active politician and leading antimason; member of congress from 1831 to 1837; and a delegate in the constitutional convention.

HELM, JOHN, pioneer and surveyor, b. Nov. 29, 1761, in Prince William co., Va., son of Thomas H.; the family settled at what is now Louisville, Ky., in 1780; and soon after at Elizabethtown, Ky. He served with courage and success in the Indian wars, escaping many dangers; and continued actively employed mostly as a surveyor through life; he was many years surveyor of Washington co., and a local judge; d. at Elizabethtown, Apr. 3, 1840, a. 51. (*Griswold's Biog. Annual*, 1841, 247.)

HELME, ROUSE J., a son of James Helme; was elected dep. sec. to the gen. assem. of R. I. Oct. 1776; clerk of the council of war Feb. 1777; one of a committee to draft a form of government Sept., '77; and to other important committees in the war; he was several times elected to the gen. assembly of R. I., from New Shoreham; d. Oct. 13, 1789, in his 46th year. (*W. Updike's Memoirs of the R. I. Bar*, p. 110.)

HELMS, WILLIAM, an officer of the revolution; member of congress from New Jersey from 1801 to 1811; removed to Tennessee, and d. at an advanced age.

HEMBEL, DR. WILLIAM, b. in Philadelphia, Sept. 24, 1764; studied medicine and served in the medical department of the army; his favorite study was chemistry; he was pres. of the Academy of Natural Sciences, of Philadelphia, until he resigned in 1849; d. June 12, 1851, a. 87, a batchellor.

HEMPHILL, REV. ANDREW, d. at Hereford, Md., Sept., 1837, a. 60; was an eminent Methodist minister.

HENDERSON, DR. FREDERICK B., b. Feb. 7, 1807 in New England; studied medicine, and before he was of age, commenced practice in Floyd, Oneida co., N. Y.; thence in 1833 he removed to Whitesboro, and was successful, both as a medical practitioner and in other business affairs; was president of the bank of Whitestown; d. July 1, 1863.

HENDERSON, GEN. JOHN, a lawyer by profession; senator from Mississippi, from 1839 to 1845, and during the latter part of his life in the practice of law in Louisiana; d. at Pass Christian in 1857, a. 62.

HENDERSON, SAMUEL J., a member of the bar; d. at Phila., June 21, 1850.

HENDERSON, THOMAS, d. at the Virginia Military Institute, Aug. 11, 1854, a. 85; Surgeon in the U. S. army, was well known as a practitioner of medicine in Washington and Georgetown, D. C., before entering the army in 1833.

HENDRICKS, CAPT. JOHN, Penna., killed in the revolution, Dec. 31, 1775.

HENLEY, MAJ. ——, aid to Gen. Heath; killed at Montressor's Island, Sept. 24, 1776.

HENNEGAN, BENJAMIN K., d. in Marion dist., S. C., Jan. 10, 1855, was lieut. gov. of S. C., in 1838, and on the death of Gov. Noble, in April, 1840, he became governor for the residue of the term ending in December of that year.

HENNON, ALFRED, a lawyer, d. at New Orleans, La., Jan. 25, 1870, a. 84.

HENRY, EDWARD W., commander in U. S. navy; d. at Piedmont, N. Y., March 8, 1873.

HENRY, HUGH H., U. S. marshal for Vermont; d. at Chester, Va., Dec. 18, 1869.

HENRY, JOHN CAMPBELLS, member of the governor's council under the old constitution and for many years judge of the orphan's court of Dorchester co., Md.; d. near Cambridge, Md., April 1, 1857, a. 69.

HENRY, LOUIS D., lawyer; and several times in the N. C. house of commons, of which he was one year the speaker; d. at Raleigh, N. C., June 12, 1846, a. 55; he was one of the com'rs to settle the claims of American citizens under the treaty with Spain, and in 1842, was democratic candidate for governor.

HENRY, THOMAS, of Beaver co., Pa.; d. July 27, 1849; was a representative from that district, for three successive congresses (1837–1843); b. in Ireland, and came in early childhood with his parents, and settled in the west in 1787.

HENRY, a slave, d. in Woodford co., Ky., Oct. 24, 1846, a. 112.

HENSHAW, JOSEPH, revolutionary patriot, of Leicester; grad. at Harvard, in 1748; served in county convention and provincial congress and in 1775, was made col. but failed to raise a regiment; he was employed in collecting military stores for the army for sometime; he d. in 1794. (*Bradford's N. E. Biog.*)

HENTZ, PROF. NICHOLAS M., entomologist, of French birth was many years employed as a teacher, first with Geo. Bancroft at Northampton, Mass., and afterwards at Cincinnati, O., and Chapel Hill, N. C., as prof. of belle-lettres; he was early devoted to the study of natural history especially to the crachnida and insects, concerning which he published several valuable papers; he d. at the residence of his son Dr. Charles A. Hentz, at Marianna, Florida, Nov. 25, 1856; his wife, Mrs. Caroline Lee Hentz, was known in literature. (*Am. Jour. Sci. & Arts*, 2d ser., xxiii, 148.)

HERBERT, REV. HARDY, early Methodist preacher; b. in N. C., raised in S. C., preached 6 y.; and d. Nov. 20, 1794, a. 25; he was a young man of genius and a pleasant speaker. (*Lee's Hist. Meth.*, p. 225.)

HEREFORD, JOHN, d. in Mason co., Va., June 13, 1846, in his 89th year; he was b. in Fairfax co., Va.; was raised in Leesburg, Loudon co., and was many years a magistrate of that county; he had served in the revolution and was adjutant under Col. John Alexander, of the Loudon militia, Col. Dabny of the Louisa militia, and Col. Geo. West, of the Loudon militia, the latter serving at the siege of Yorktown.

HERKIMER, JOHN, son of George and nephew of Gen. Nicholas H., inherited the general's home estate and held it till about 1814; he was in assembly in 1800–4–6, and several years a judge of Montgomery and Herkimer cos, his residence having been set off in the town of Danube, in 1817 from the former to the latter. He was a major in Col. Mill's regt. in 1813, and served at the battle of Sackett's Harbor; he was in earlier days a republican and afterwards anti-Clintonian; in 1823–5, he was in congress; he d. in Danube, N. Y., a. 73, leaving no male issue. (*Benton's Herkimer Co., N. Y.*, p. 170.)

HERRICK, ANSON, editor of *N. Y. Sunday Atlas*, b. in Lewiston, Me., in 1812; went to New York in 1836, and a partner in establishing the *Atlas* in 1836; was an alderman, naval store keeper, and in 1862, elected to congress; d. at N. Y., Feb. 6, 1868.

HERRICK, EBENEZER, member of congress from Maine, from 1821 to 1827; d. at Lewiston, Me., May 7, 1839.

HERRICK, MRS. RACHEL, d. at Hopkinton, N. H., Jan., 1837, a. 103.

HERRICK, RICHARD P., b. in 1791, and a member of congress from New York from 1845 till his death, which occurred at Washington, June 20, 1846. In 1839, he represented Rens. co., in the New York assembly.

HERRICK, SAMUEL, b. in Dutchess co., N. Y., April 14, 1779; settled as a lawyer at Zanesville, O., and was appointed collector of taxes, and afterwards prosecuting attorney, and U. S. dist atty.; was in congress from 1817 to 1821, and in 1829 again dist. atty.; d. Dec., 1851.

HERRICK, STEPHEN, d. Nov. 3, 1841, at Randolph, Vt., a. 82, a revolutionary soldier and a prisoner of war for nine months on board the memorable Jersey prison ship in New York harbor. He was a lineal descendant of Sir William Herrick, of Ball Manor England.

HERSEY, EBEH, d. at Hingham, Mass., a. 97, Dec. 27, 1836.

HESEY, REUBEN, a soldier of the revolution; d. at Hingham, Mass., Nov., 1845, a. 88; he was the 4th in descent from William H., who d. in Hingham, March 22, 1657–8, and his ancestors were of remarkable longevity; his father d. at 82; his grandfather at 84, and his great grandfather at 81.

HESTON, EDWARD, was an officer of the revolution, and at its close a lieut. colonel; served for some years in the Pennsylvania legislature, and was a judge of the court of common pleas of Philadelphia; for the last fifteen years of life, he was a farmer; d. in Hestonville, Philadelphia co., Pa., March 14, 1834, a. 79; of which about 60 were spent on the patrimonial estate. (*Simpson's Eminent Philadelphians.*)

HETH, JOYCE, a blind negress, d. Feb. 22, 1836, very old, she had been exhibited by Mr. Barnum as the "nurse of Gen. Washington," but a post mortem examination showed that she was less than a hundred.

HETZEL, CAPT. ABRAHAM B., assist. quarter master U. S. A.; d. at Louisville, Ky., July 20, 1847.

HEWETT, RANDALL, a native of Canaan, Ct., at the age of 16; joined the army in 1776 and went on the expedition to Canada; he d. at Seneca Falls, N. Y., May 2, 1850, a. 90.

HEWSON, JOHN, a revolutionary patriot; d. at Philadelphia, Pa., Jan. 1, 1860; b. in England in 1756; was a calico printer. (*Vincent's Semi An. Register*, p. 5.)

HIBBARD, HARRY, d. at Somerville, N. H., July 30, 1872. He was b. in Vermont, and grad. at Dartmouth Coll. in 1835. After having been successively assistant clerk and clerk of the house in the New Hampshire legislature, he was elected a member of the house, and was speaker in 1844 and 1845. He was a member of the state senate from 1846 to 1849, officiating two years as president. In 1849, Mr. Hibbard, who was a democrat, was elected in the IVth cong. dist. of New Hampshire a representative in congress by a large majority over his whig opponent, and served in all three terms.

HICKCOX, AUGUSTUS, an early settler in Utica, N. Y., and a capt. in the war of 1812–15; d. at Brooklyn, May 3, 1861.

HICKEY, THOMAS M., late judge of the circuit court of Kentucky; d. at Lexington, Ky., Dec. 29, 1842; was a distinguished lawyer.

HICKS, CAPT. SAMUEL, d. at Warren, R. I., a. 88. He was an officer of the revolution.

HICKS, SAMUEL, d. at New York, Oct. 12, 1837, was a member of the society of Friends, and a prominent merchant.

HICKS, ZACHARIAH, d. in Boston, Mass, May 11, 1842, a. 87; he was a revolutionary soldier and was once a representative in the state legislature.

HIGBEE, REV. EDWARD, of Trinity church, New York city; d. Dec. 10, 1871.

HIGBY, AMOS, many years town clerk in Turin, Lewis co., N. Y.; resigned when he could be no longer *unanimously* elected; and d. in that town, Feb. 17, 1858, a. 63.

HIGBY, REV. JEREMIAH, d. in Turin, N. Y., Jan. 1850, a. 84; b. in Middletown; formerly preached at Enfield, Conn.

HIGBY, ZACCHEUS, d. in ——, Illinois, Sept. 14, 1861, a. 98; he was a pioneer settler of West Turin, N. Y., where he spent most of his life.

HIGGINS, JOHN, a lieut. in the Mass. regt. in the Mexican war; and acting adjutant of that regiment on its return in 1848; d. at Boston, Mass., Feb. 17, 1850, a. 28 years.

HIGINBOTHAM, SANDS, b. in Rensselaer co. in 1790; he removed with his parents to central New York; his youth was passed in Utica as a student and a clerk; in 1810 he began as a merchant in Vernon; and after a successful business of 24 years, moved to the site of the present village of Oneida; where he had previously purchased several hundred acres; shortly afterward the Syracuse and Utica R. R. company located their road through his farm and made there an important station; under his fostering care the place grew during his life-time to be a thriving and beautiful village. He was a man of high standing in his vicinity though he declined any political office; for thirty years he was a trustee of Hamilton Coll.; his death took place in Sept., 1868.

HILDEBRAND, PETER, d. at New Holland, Lancaster co., Pa., Nov. 1832, a. 103 years.

HILDRETH, REV. HOSEA, cor. sec. of the Massachusetts Tem. Soc.; d. at Sterling, Mass., July 10, 1835; he was b. at Chelmsford, Mass., in 1782; grad. at Harvard in 1805; was some years prof. of mathematics at Philip's Academy, Exeter, and 8 years Cong., minister at Gloucester.

HILDRETH, WILLIAM, a distinguished agriculturist; d. at Phelps, N. Y., Nov., 1839, a. 56.

HILL, ISAAC, was b. near Cambridge, Mass., April 6, 1788, and removed at the age of 10 to Ashburnham, Mass.; in 1802 he was apprenticed to Joseph Carling of the *Amherst Cabinet* as a printer, and in 1809, he went to Concord and published the *Am. Patriot*, soon changed to the *N. H. Patriot*, a paper which long enjoyed an extensive patronage and great credit; he was chosen to the N. H. legislature and served in both houses; he entered the U. S. senate in 1831; in 1836 was chosen governor of New Hampshire and repeatedly reëlected until 1839 when he retired to private life. In 1840, he was appointed by Van Buren subtreasurer at Boston but was the next year removed by the whigs. He established *Hill's N. H. Patriot* with two of his sons, but in 1847 this was united with the old *Patriot*. During ten years he edited the *Farmer's Monthly Visitor*. He d. at Washington, D. C., March 22, 1851, a. 63 years. (*Stryker's Am. Reg.*, vi., 220).

HILL, DR. JOHN, d. in Wilmington, N. C., May 9, 1847, a. 51; president of the Bank of Cape Fear; grad. at the University of North Carolina.

HILL, MARK LANGDON, d. in Phipsburg, Me., Nov. 26, 1842, in his 71st year; from 1792 to the end of life almost constantly in public office, was at various times in the two houses of the Mass. legislature; a judge of com. pleas; member of congress from 1819 to 1821; post master at Phipsburg, Me.; collector at Bath, and in various town and county offices; was an overseer of Bowdoin Coll., till 1821, when he became a trustee and during 49 years attended every meeting except one. (*Am. Almanac*, 1844, p. 312).

HILL, NICHOLAS JR., reporter to sup. court and court of errors in New York; b. in Florida, Montgomery co., N. Y., in 1805, and studied law; he assisted Esek Cowen in preparing some of his Reports in sup. court and court of errors, and from Jan., 1841 to Dec., 1844, reported the decisions of that court, in 7 vols.; he settled in Albany, and in 1843 formed a partnership known as Hill, Cagger & Porter; he d. May 1, 1859, a. 53. (*Alb. M. Express*, May 2, 1859; *Memoir by a Committee of the Bar of New York City; with Portrait.*)

HILL, RICHARD, b. in Maryland, bred a mariner and afterwards settled in Philadelphia; was 25 y. a member of the governor's council, several times speaker of assembly, and for several years first commissioner of property; he was for the last 10 years of life a judge; was an influential member of the society of Friends, and a member of the Philadelphia city council in 1708, 9, and mayor in 1710, 15, 16, 17; d. in Phila., Sept. 9, 1729.

HILL, SIMON, a soldier of 1812, and one of the Marine corps; d. April 18, 1860. (*Vincent's Semi. An. Register*, p. 306).

HILLARD, CAPT. MINER, of Danby, Vermont, d. at that place Feb. 28, 1846; a. 82 y. 11 mo.; he was a revolutionary patriot.

HILLARD, REV. TIMOTHY, b. at Kensington, N. H., graduated at Harvard in 1764, and was tutor from 1768 to 1771; he was ordained at Barnstable and in 1784 at Cambridge, over the 1st Cong. ch., and d. in 1790. Several of his sermons were published. (*Bradford's N. E. Biog.*)

HILLARD, TIMOTHY, grad. at Yale, in 1793; was several years rector of the Episcopal church in Portland, Me., and d. in Claremont, N. H., Jan. 2, 1842.

HILLHOUSE, AUGUSTUS LUCAS, son of James H., of New Haven, grad. at Yale in 1810; soon went to Europe, and resided most of his life in retirement near Paris; he was a scholar of uncommon endowments, and translated Michaux's great work on the forest trees of America; he d. March 14, 1859, a. 67. (*Hist. Mag.*, iii, 193; *Am. Alm.*, 1860, p. 375.)

HILLHOUSE, MRS., of Wilke's co., Ga., upon the death of her husband in 1804, took charge of his paper, the *Monitor and Impartial Observer*, and conducted it several years; she was printer to the legislature of Ga. for a time.

HILTON, LIEUT. WILLIAM, N. C.; killed in the revolution, July 15, 1779.

HINCKLEY, EDWARD, of the Baltimore bar; d. June 30, 1854, in Washington, D. C.

HINCKLEY, SYLVANUS, d. at Barnstable, Mass., Aug. 1, 1841, a. 94; was a revolutionary pensioner.

HINDS, GEN. THOMAS, a distinguished officer in the battle of New Orleans; b. about 1775; was in congress from Mississippi, from 1828 to 1831; d. in Jefferson co., Miss., Aug. 23, 1840.

HINCKLEY, JOHN GODDARD, b. in Buckland, Mass., Aug. 27, 1809; grad at Hamilton in 1834; was one of the founders of the Westfield Academy, and d. March 6, 1869.

HINCKLEY, REV. ORRAMEL S., d. at Natchez, Miss., Sept. 13, 1837; prof. of languages in Oakland College; grad. at Dartmouth, in 1819.

HINDS, REV. WILLIAM PRESCOD, b. in Barbadoes, June 3, 1795; educated in England, was a minister in Barbadoes, and about 1834, settled in Phil.; where he d. Jan. 23, 1859. (*Simpson's Eminent Philadelphians.*)

HINES, RICHARD, d. Nov. 10, 1851, at Raleigh, N. C., a. 58; served his country both in the state and national councils.

HINMAN, BENJAMIN, a native of Southbury, Conn., served some years in the army of the revolution as capt., commissary, wagon master, and aid to Gen. Greene; soon after the war he settled in Little Falls and afterwards near Trenton, whence in 1797, he removed to Utica, and d. April 7, 1821.

HINMAN, JOEL, ex-chief justice of Connecticut; d. at Cheshire, Conn., Feb. 21, 1870, a. 68.

HINMAN, JOHN EDWARD, b .at Little Falls, June 2, 1789; in the war of 1812, was qr. m. of the 134 militia; several years deputy sheriff of Oneida, co.; in 1821, appointed sheriff, and elected in 1822, and 1828; in 1851, 1852 and 1854, he was mayor of Utica; d. Aug. 12, 1873.

HINMAN, ROBINSON S., d. in New Haven, Conn., Nov. 10, 1843, a. 42; clerk of the state senate. and of the superior and county courts; general of a brigade of militia and judge of the court of probate for the district of New Haven.

HIROSAWA, N. KENZO, a young Japanese nobleman pursuing studies in the Polytechnic Institute Brooklyn; d. April 9, 1873. (*N. Y. Tribune* s. w., April 15, 1873.)

HITCHCOCK, HENRY, president of the Alabama Life and Trust Company; d. at Mobile, Ala., of yellow fever, Aug. 11, 1839, a. 48.

HITCHCOCK, LUKE, a prominent citizen of Onedia, Madison co., N. Y., member of assembly in 1841; well known as a canal contractor and prominent politician, formerly of the democratic, and afterwards of the republican school; d. April 30, 1860.

HITCHCOCK, DR. MARCUS, physician and druggist at Utica, from 1803 to 1829, during which time he was also P. M.; b. in New Haven, Conn., and d. at Terre Haute, Ind., where his latter years were passed.

HOA, ALBERT, d. in New Orleans, La., Feb. 14, 1844, a. 38; prominent as a lawyer, and had served in the state councils.

HOAG, TRUMAN H., member of congress from Ohio; d. at Washington, D. C., Feb., 3, 1870.

HOBAN, JAMES, U. S. dist. attorney for the dist. of Columbia; d. at Washington, Jan. 19, 1846, a. 38; he was a native of Washington, and had raised himself by his talents to a place of distinction.

HOBART, NATHANIEL P., from 1836 to 1838, auditor general of Pennsylvania; d. at Pottstown, Pa.. July 3, 1860, a. 70.

HOBBS, WILLIAM, d. in North Berwick, Me., March 16, 1848, a. 81; for some twelve or fifteen years a member of the Massachusetts legislature, and also of the legislature of Maine after the separation; was a delegate to the Maine convention of 1820.

HOBSON, JULIUS A., an old citizen of Richmond, Va.; 10 y. city collector, killed by the falling of the floor of the court of appeals in the Capitol building, April 20, 1870.

HOCKLEY, COL. G. W., a native of Pa., resided some time in Tennessee, and removed to Texas in 1835; he commanded the artillery and acted as Gen. Houston's aid, at the battle of San Jacinto; was sec. of war under Houston, and sec. of the navy, under Lamar; in 1843 he went with Col. S. M. Williams to Mexico, on an unsuccessful mission. He d. at Corpus Christi, Texas, June 6, 1851. (*Am. Almanac*, 1852, p. 338.)

HOCKNELL, JOHN, early Shaker leader; b. in Cheshire, Eng.; joined the Methodists, became a follower of the Wardley's, and of Mother Ann, and d. Feb. 27, 1799, a. 76. (*Evans's Shaker's Compendium*, p. 181.)

HODGE, DR. HUGH L., d. in Philadelphia, Feb. 26, 1873; he was educated at Princeton College and the University of Pensylvania, and in 1835 succeeded to the chair of Prof. Dewees at the latter institution, retaining it until 1863, when the burdens of age compelled him to resign. He wrote two medical works, and was a devoted and useful member of the Presbyterian church.

HODGES, WILLIAM D., d. at Richmond, Va., Feb. 26, 1840, a. 28; a member of the house of delegates.

HOFFMAN, DR. WILLIAM, d. at West Farms, N. Y., March 16, 1833, a. 52.

HOFFMAN, COL. WILLIAM, of the army; d. at Corpus Christi, Texas, Nov. 26, 1845; he entered the army in 1813, and was retained in 1815, serving with the army through life.

HOGAN, DR JAMES, d. June 7, 1843, at Vicksburg, Miss.; b. in Ireland, and about 38 years old; resided sometime in Essex co., Va., where he taught school, and practiced medicine; removed to Washington, and was a reporter for the *Telegraph;* thence to Philadelphia, and when the plan of a Washington monument was started, he became an agent, to obtain subscriptions; settled in Vicksburg, and became an editor; was killed in the street, in a fight with D. W. Adams, one of the political party that Dr. Hogan had attacked. (*Am. Almanac*, 1844, p. 324.)

HOGAN, MICHAEL, founder of Hogansburg, N. Y., and formerly a merchant in New York; d. at Washington, D. C., March 26, 1833, a. 68. He had for several years, held the office of consul for the U. S., at Valparaiso, Chili.

HOGEBOOM, HENRY, b. in Columbia co., N. Y.; grad. at Yale, and was admitted to the bar in 1830, at Hudson, where he acquired an eminent position; he held the office of master in chancery, from 1831; was a county judge, and in 1831, member of assembly; in 1857, was elected a justice of the supreme court, for the third judicial district, and was chosen to a second term, but d. before its close, at Hudson, N. Y., Sept., 1872.

HOGG, DR. THOMAS T., a young physician; d. at Port Gibson, Miss., Aug. 28, 1840.

HOGG, WILLIAM, d. at Brownsville, Pa., Jan. 28, 1841, in his 86th year, leaving an estate, valued at a million; more than fifty years before, he came to Brownsville, poor, and established himself in trade.

HOLBIRD, WILLIAM S., d. in Winsted, Conn., May 22, 1855; was a prominent lawyer of Litchfield co. U. S. attorney for Connecticut from 1833 to 1840; and lieut. gov. of the state in 1842–3.

HOLBROOK, E. D., delegate from Idaho in congress; assassinated at Idaho city, June 18, 1870.

HOLBROOK, JOSIAH, d. near Lynchburgh, Va., June, 17, 1854, a. about 65; b. in Derby, Conn.; grad. at Yale in 1810, and devoted himself to the cause of popular education; was very successful in diffusing among the young a love of mineralogy and geology, and in establishing village lyceums; prompting exchanges, and introducing school apparatus; was killed by falling into Black creek, while on a geological excursion.

HOLBY, JOHN M., of Lyons, N. Y., a member of the 30th congress; d. at Florida, March, 1848.

HOLDEN, LEVI, revolutionary officer, served through the war, during 3 years of which he was an officer in Washington's Life Guard and lived in his family; he d. at Newark, N. J., April 19, 1823, in his 70th year. (*Rogers's Am. Biog.*)

HOLE-IN-THE-DAY, a Chippewa chief, assassinated June 29, 1868; he owned a large amount of property in Minn. (estimated at $2,000,000), and resided at Crow-Wing. During the Indian war of 1861–3, he exerted his influence to preserve the peace, and with some success.

HOLGATE, JACOB, b. June 10, 1767; d. Sept. 18, 1832, in Philadelphia; was several years in the state legislature, and an influential republican politician of the old school; was democratic candidate for governor of Penn., but not elected. (*Simpson's Eminent Philadelphians.*)

HOLLAND, CORNELIUS, member of congress from 1831 to 1833; d. at Lewiston, Me., June 3, 1870, a. 87; was a member of the constitutional convention of 1820; several years in the state legislature; and in 1831–3 in congress.

HOLLAND, PARK, d. in Bangor, Me., May 22, 1844, a. 91; was an officer of the revolution and a pioneer in the settlement of Eastern Maine.

HOLLAND, CAPT. THOMAS, Del., killed at Germantown, Oct. 4, 1777.

HOLLAND, DR. WILLIAM, formerly editor of the *N. Y. Standard*, and of the *N. Y. Times;* d. at Washington, D. C., Nov. 1839.

HOLLEY, JOHN M., d. at Jacksonville, Fla., March 8, 1848; member of 30th congress from the Seneca and Wayne district, N. Y.

HOLLEY, MYRON, canal commissioner in N. Y., b. in Salisbury, Ct., Apr. 29, 1779; was in the N. Y. assembly in 1816, and 1821; was canal com'r from 1816 to his death Mar. 4, 1841, at Rochester, and gave his personal attention to the construction of several canals. A monument was erected over his grave June 13, 1844, by admirers of his anti-slavery principles.

HOLLIDAY, LIEUT. JAMES, Penna.; killed in the revolution at Brandywine, Sept. 11, 1777.

HOLLINGSWORTH, HENRY, son of Valentine, one of the first settlers under Penn. in 1682, assisted in surveying the city of Philadelphia; in 1695, he represented Newcastle co. in assembly, and was sheriff of Chester county. Afterwards was deputy master of the rolls, and prothonotary of the court of common pleas. He removed to Maryland, settled at Elkton, and was a surveyor of Cecil county, under Lord Baltimore.

HOLLINGSWORTH, LEVI, b. in Elkton, Md., Nov. 29, 1739; and d. in Philadelphia, Pa., March 24, 1824, was an enterprising merchant, and prominent in public affairs. (*Simpson's Eminent Philadelphians.*)

HOLLINGSWORTH, VALENTINE, one of William Penn's emigrants in 1682; was a member of assembly, for Newcastle co., in 1683, and several succeeding years, and one of the first grand jurors empaneled in the province.

HOLLINGSWORTH, ZEBULON, pres. of the court of Cecil co., Maryland, and one of the nine magistrates of that county, in colonial times. He d. at Elkton, Md., where his father Henry, was one of the first settlers.

HOLLISTER, FREDERICK, merchant and manufacturer at Utica; b. in Berkshire co., Mass., about 1810, went to Utica from Buffalo in 1831, at first as a clerk, but soon as a partner in a wholesale drug and grocery store. Enlarging his operations, he bought and built cotton factories at Checkerville and Clayville, and expended at the two places over a million of dollars. Was endowed with wonderful enterprise, but his failure was as signal as his enterprise was great, his obligations amounting to $1,800,000. d. in New York, Dec. 16, 1863, where he was living as a broker.

HOLMAN, GEN. SILAS, d. at Bolton, Mass., May 1847, a. 86, was connected with the state legislature twenty or thirty years, as a member of the house, or of the senate.

HOLMES, ABRAHAM, d. at Rochester, Mass., Sept., 1839, a. 86; one of the last three survivors of the delegates of the Massachusetts convention of 1788.

HOLMES, DAVID, surgeon, Conn., d. in the revolutionary service, March 20, 1779.

HOLMES, REV. HENRY S., of the northern N. Y. conference, M. E. church, b. in Richland, N. Y., Mar. 10, 1829, and d. at Vienna, N. Y., Aug 18, 1872. (*Northern Christian Advocate*, Nov. 7, 1872.)

HOLMES, HOPKINS, editor of the *Athens Banner*, and a member of congress from Georgia from 1836 to 1839; d. at Columbus, Ga., March 31, 1859, a. 59.

HOLMES, JAMES, was made a captain in the 27th or Inniskilling regiment, Feb. 2, 1757, and acted as major of light infantry in 1759. In 1760 he accompanied Gen. Haviland's expedition to Montreal. In 1771 his name was dropped from the army lists.

HOLMES, OWEN, d. at Wilmington, N. C., June 6, 1840, in his 45th year, was an eminent lawyer, and active politician.

HOLSEY, ROBERT D., masonic writer; d. at New York, March 12, 1870, a. 54.

HOLT, DAVID, settled in Herkimer co., in 1805 from Hudson, N. Y., and began printing a paper and continued several years. He was many years P.M. at Herkimer, a collector of direct tax, and a county judge. He published a paper at Herkimer and Little Falls, went to Albany and thence to Wisconsin. (*Benton's Herkimer Co., N. Y.*, p. 321.)

HOLT, JOHN E., nearly 20 years mayor of Norfolk, Va.; d. in that borough, Oct. 13, 1832.

HONYMAN, JAMES, a son of Rev. Jas. H., of Newport, was elected attorney general of R. I., in May, 1732, and annually until May, 1741. He then became king's atty., for Newport co., and a com'r for settling the boundary of Mass. In 1756, he was elected first senator and continued till 1764. He was soon after appointed by the crown, advocate gen. of the court of vice admiralty in the colony which office he held till the revolution, when he resigned his commission to the assembly. He d. at Newport, Jan. 15, 1778, a. 67, while the British held possession of the Island. (*W. Updike's Memoirs of the R. I. Bar*, p. 27.)

HOOD, WASHINGTON, capt. U. S. topographical engineer corps; d. at Bedford Springs, Pa., July 17, 1840, a. 33.

HOOKER, DR. CHARLES, of New Haven, Ct., d. March 19, 1863, a. 64.

HOOKER, EDWARDS, b. in Farmington, Ct.; grad. at Yale in 1835, studied law, but engaged in agriculture; and filled various civil offices in his native town, where he d. May 5, 1846, a. 61.

HOOKER, ZIBEON, d. at Newton, Mass., Dec., 1840; was in the revolution in which he became a lieutenant.

HOOKS, CHARLES, b. in Bertie co., N. C.; was many years in the state legislature and in congress in 1816–17; and in 1819–25, removed to Alabama, and d. in 1851.

HOOPS, ADAM, pioneer surveyor and settler at Hamilton, now Olean, N. Y.; was from Philadelphia, and had served in the revolution; he was unmarried; and d. in West Chester, Pa., in 1835 or 1836. (*Turner's Phelps & Gorham Purchase*, p. 243.)

HOOVER, JONAH D., ex-marshall of the District of Columbia, d. at Washington, D. C., June 4, 1870, a. 48; was marshal under Pierce, and prominent in political affairs.

HOPE, REV. MATTHEW B., prof. at Princeton; was appointed prof. of belles lettres in 1847; and d. Dec. 17, 1859. (*Hist. Mag.*, iv, 61.)

HOPES, CAPT. ROBERT, Pa., killed at Brandywine, Sept. 11, 1777.

HOPKINS, BENJAMIN F., member of congress; d. at Madison, Wis., Jan. 1, 1870; b. in Washington co., N. Y., April 22, 1829, went to Wisconsin; was private secretary to the governor, in 1856–7; in the state legislature in 1865; and state senate in 1862–3; was member of the 40th congress, and reëlected.

HOPKINS, HENRY, settled at Herkimer, N. Y., at an early day in trade; became sheriff in 1813, and held 2 years; was in assembly in 1816; he d. Nov., 1827; in politics he was republican. (*Benton's Herkimer Co. N. Y.*, p. 339.)

HOPKINS, JAMES D., d. at Portland, Me., June, 1840; an old and eminent lawyer.

HOPKINS, JAMES G., a lawyer of Ogdensburgh, N. Y.; d. at Saratoga Springs, July 6, 1860, in his 60th year; was formerly county clerk of St. Lawrence co., and state senator in 1840–44.

HOPKINS, JESSE, b. at Waterbury, Ct., 1766, evinced a taste for literature, and engaged in manufactures. After spending five years in the W. I. he became a land agent for Wm. Henderson in Jeff. co., and settled in 1805. He was visionary and unfortunate, and d. at Henderson, N. Y., a. 71. (*Hough's Hist. Jeff. Co., N. Y.*, p. 432, with portrait.)

HOPKINS, JOHN, d. at New Market, N. H., July 3, 1842, a. 52; he was of Portsmouth, and had been recently inspector of customs at that place.

HOPKINS, JOSHUA, d. in Orleans, Mass., March 19, 1842, a. 88; he had been a whaler on the coast of Greenland, in early life, and served in the revolutionary war.

HOPKINS, COL. MARK, of Great Barrington, Mass.; d. at White Plains, N. Y., Oct. 26, 1776, a. 36.

HOPKINS, ROSWELL, pioneer of Hopkinton, N. Y., and co. sec. state of Vt.; b. at Amenia, N. Y., May, 1757. Served in the revolution, was ten years sec. state of Vt., settled in St. Law. co., N. Y., 1802. Was in assembly in 1810–1–2–3, and d. at Chazy, N. Y., Sept. 5, 1829, a. 73. (*Hough's Hist. St. Law. and Fr. Cos. N. Y.*, p. 595.)

HOPKINS, SAMUEL M., d. at Geneva, N. Y., Oct. 8, 1837, was an eminent lawyer; grad. at Yale in 1791, and a member of congress in 1813–15.

HOPKINS, CAPT. WEIGH, Sheldon's horse, killed in the revolution, July 15, 1779.

HOPKINSON, THOMAS, d. in Cambridge, Mass., Nov. 17, 1856, a. 52; he was b. in New Sharon, Me., Aug. 25, 1804; grad. at Harvard, in 1830, and settled as a lawyer in Lowell. He was chosen to each house of the legislature, and in 1848, was appointed judge of com. pleas but the next year resigned to become president of the Boston and Worcester R. R. which office he held till his death. He removed to Boston in 1849, and to Cambridge in 1855. In 1853, he was a member of the constitutional convention. (*Am. Almanac*, 1858, p. 348.)

HOPOETHLEYOHOLO, a Creek chief, principal councillor of great influence and friendly to the U. S., in the troubles of 1836, in which he received the rank of colonel. He was opposed to emigration to the last. In 1834 or 5 he bought lands in Texas, but lost them through the jealousy of the Mexicans. (*White's Hist. Ga.*, p. 165, with portrait.)

HOPPEL, JOHN ADAM, d. at Philadelphia, Pa., Aug. 11, 1836, in his 101st year. He was a native of New Jersey.

HOPPER, JASPER, b. in New York city, June 10, 1770, entered the office of secretary of state as a clerk, at the age of 18, and in 1821 became deputy sec. state, and held till 1802, when he removed to Onondaga co., where he was county clerk from 1810 till 1818, was census marshal in 1810, resided at Onondaga Hollow 19 ys., and d. at that place June 30, 1848, a. 79. (*Clarke's Onondaga*, ii, 124, with a portrait.)

HORN, CHARLES E., a musical composer d. at Boston, Mass., Oct. 26, 1849, a. 63.

HORNBECK, John W., d. at Allentown, Penna., Jan. 16, 1848, member of congress from Lehigh and Bucks dist., Pennsylvania.

HORTON, REV. AZARIAH, d. March 27, 1777, a. 62; b. at Southold, N. Y., was a missionary to the Indians of Long Island, removed to South Hanover, N. J., and was 25 years pastor. (*Prime's Hist. L. I.*, p. 104.)

HORTON, HIRAM, judge, agent, etc., b. at Springfield, Mass., removed to Brandon, Vt., was dep. sec. state of Vt., and in 1808 settled at Malone, N. Y., where he built mills, and held the offices of co. treasurer, 1st judge, land agent, etc. He d. in 1834, a. 64. (*Hough's Hist. St. Law. & Fr. Cos, N. Y.*, p. 596.)

HORTON, DR. WILLIAM, distinguished for his researches in the science of mineralogy and assistant to Prof. L. C. Beck in the mineralogical survey of New York. He d. at Craigville, Orange co., N. Y., in the spring of 1846. (*Am. Jour. Sci. and Arts,* 2d ser., i, 152.)

HOSKINS, Charles, 1st lieut. 4th infantry, killed in battle of Monterey, Mex., Sept. 21, 1846, a. 33; b. in Edenton, N. C.; grad. at West Point in 1836, and at once entered the army and joined a company in the Cherokee country. In 1839, removed to Port Gibson, Ark.; went to Corpus Christi in 1845, and did good service in the battles of Palo Alto, and Resaca de la Palma.

HOSMER, John, d. Oct. 5, 1780, on Long Island a merchant of N. Y.

HOSMER, Rufus, d. at Boston, Mass., Aug. 20, 1839, a. 61; was of Stow, Mass., a member of the Executive Council.

HOSMER, Dr. Timothy, b. in Hartford, Conn., in Sept., 1745, settled as a physician in Farmington, Conn., and was a surgeon in the revolution, settled in Avon, N. Y., in 1792, and d. there Nov. 29, 1815. (*Turner's Holland Purchase*, p. 376.)

HOTCHKIN, Rev. Beriah, b. in Guilford, Ct., March 27, 1752 (o. s.) learned the trade of a tanner and shoemaker; in 1780 removed to Cornwall, Ct., studied theology and Aug. 17, 1785, was ordained and installed pastor of a Congregational church in Guilford. In 1789, he was settled at Greenville, Greene co., N. Y., where he remained till 1824, when he removed to western N. Y., preached at Wheeler and Pulteney, Steuben co., and in 1827 went to reside with a son at Prattsburgh where he d. Jan. 28, 1829. (*Hotchkin's Western N. Y.*, p. 283).

HOUGH, Rev. Alfred, son of Levi, b. in West Turin, N. Y., Feb. 23, 1803, grad. at Yale in 1830, and at Andover in 1833; was ordained a Presbyterian minister and settled at Vernon Centre, N. Y.; d. at Philadelphia, May 2, 1838, while attending General Synod.

HOUGH, David, son of David H., b. in Norwich, Conn., March 13, 1753, was a ship carpenter and employed in building the ships of Arnold's fleet on Lake Champlain, and the frigate Confederacy, at Norwich; in 1778 settled in Lebanon, N. H.; was many years in the state legislature; justice of the peace; col. of militia, and delegate in convention for forming constitution. In July, 1798, was appointed a commissioner of valuation, and was in congress from New Hampshire in 1803–7; d. at Lebanon, N. H., April 18, 1831.

HOUGH, Horatio Gates, physician, b. in Meriden, Ct., Jan. 5, 1778, removed with his parents to Southwick, Mass., in 1787, and in 1797, settled in Constableville, N. Y.; early in 1805 he removed to Martinsburgh, N. Y., and d. Sept. 3, 1830; he was the first physician who settled in Lewis co. His widow, Mrs. Martha H., afterwards m. Judge Ichabod Parsons, of Denmark, N. Y., and d. in Martinsburgh, N. Y., Aug. 20, 1874, a. nearly 87.

HOUGH, John, son of David; b. Dec. 28, 1757, in Bozrah, Conn., served in the revolution, and settled in his native town, where he was a justice of the peace, and col. of militia; removed in 1816 to Unadilla, N. Y., and d. there Nov. 19, 1832.

HOUGH, Rev. John, b. Aug. 17, 1783; son of Walter H., grad. at Middlebury Coll., Vt., and was a professor in that college 27 years; d. July 17, 1861, at Fort Wayne, Ind.

HOUGH, RICHARDSON HARMAN, b. in Warrensburg, N. Y., July 15, 1806, settled as a farmer and lumber dealer (making a specialty of birdseye maple), at West Leyden, N. Y., was in assembly from Lewis co., in 1860; d. at West Leyden, Aug. 26, 1871.

HOUGH, WILLIAM, common ancestor of nearly all of this name of New England origin, was b. in Cheshire co., England, in 1619 emigrated in the party of Rev. Blinman, in 1640; settled first at Green's Harbor near Plymouth; then at Gloucester, Mass., and finally at New London, Conn., where he d. Aug. 10, 1683.

HOUGH, WILLIAM JARVIS, b. March 20, 1795, at Eaton, Madison co., N. Y.; settled as a lawyer in Cazenovia; was in assembly in 1835–6, and in congress in 1845–7; removed to Syracuse, N. Y., and d. there Oct, 4, 1869.

HOUGHTON, J. DUNBAR, many years principal of an academy at Belleville, Jeff. co., N. Y., and at Oneida, N. Y.; d. at Carthage, N. Y., Oct., 1874.

HOUGHTON, LEVI, for many years one of the wealthiest men, and most extensive ship owners, in Maine, and an unostentatious, but liberal contributor to the various benevolent enterprises of his day; d. at Bath, Me., Dec. 22, 1857, a. 74.

HOUNSFIELD, EZRA, a Sheffield cutler; came to N. Y., about 1800, and became part owner of the town of Hounsfield, N. Y., named from him; d. about 1817 in the city of New York.

HOUSE, ANSON, a lawyer, of Rochester, N. Y.; d. at that place, Aug. 15, 1864, a 75.

HOUSE, JAMES, brevet brig. gen. U. S. A., col. of the 4th artillery; d. at Georgetown, D. C., Nov. 17, 1834.

HOUSEL, CAPT. WILLIAM, served five years in the army, and was on the Canada frontier, where he was taken prisoner, and confined at Quebec; d. at Louisburgh, Pa., June 8, 1850, a. 61. (*Stryker's Am. Reg.*, iv, 466.)

HOUSTON, DR. JOHN A., d. in New York, Sept. 17, 1849, a. 33; formerly official reporter for the senate of the U. S., and at one time conductor of a medical periodical.

HOUSTON, ROBERT, emigrated from Abbeville dist., S. C., to Knox co., Tenn., in 1790; was first sheriff of that co., and several years secretary of state; in the war of 1812, he was paymaster in East Tennessee; he d. April 2, 1834, in his 69th year.

HOW, REV. THOMAS Y., b. in Princeton, N. J., grad. at Princeton in 1794; studied law, and was selected by Hamilton, as his mil. sec., in the expected war with France; he made a tour with him, through N. E., and settled early at Brownville, N. Y.; he returned to N. Y., practiced for a while, and became an Episcopal clergyman, but was prevented from continuing, by an incident, which caused much feeling at the time. He spent many years in lecturing, and d. at Brownville, N. Y., May 9, 1855, in his 79th year.

HOWARD, BENJAMIN C., compiler of *Howard's U. S. Supreme Court Reports*, d. at Baltimore, Md., March 6, 1872, a. 81.

HOWARD, DANIEL, formerly a judge of the county court, d. at West Bridgewater, Mass., Aug. 1833, a. 85 years.

HOWARD, GEORGE, formerly governor of Maryland, d. in Anne Arundel co., Md., Aug. 2, 1846.

HOWARD, JAMES, an actor and vocalist; d. in Philadelphia, Pa., 1848.

HOWARD, JOHN, d. in Fayette co., Ky., Nov. 1, 1834, a. 103. He served in the rev., and was a member of the Presb. church over 80 years.

HOWARD, JOHN, d. in Springfield, Oct. 23, 1849, a. 58.

HOWARD, DR. SAMUEL L., d. at Princeton, N. J., Nov. 1, 1835, a. 48.

HOWARD, TILGHMAN A., b. near Pickensville, S. C., Nov. 14, 1797. Removed to Tennessee; became a lawyer, served in the legislature, and was a Jackson elector at his first election, was in congress from Indiana, in 1839–41. Removed to Indiana; became U. S. dist. atty., and in 1844, became chargé d'affaires to Texas. He d. in that republic, Aug. 16, 1844.

HOWARD, WILLIAM, became adj. of the 17th Foot Dec. 12, 1746, capt. 2, 1756, served in America in the French war, and left the army in 1767.

HOWARD, DR. WILLIAM of the U. S. topographical engineers, d. at Baltimore, Md., Aug. 25, 1834.

HOWE, GEN. HEZEKIAH, d. at New Haven, Conn., May, 1838, a. 63; was a well known bookseller.

HOWE, JOSEPH, lieut. gov. of Nova Scotia; d. at Halifax, N. S., June 1, 1863, a. 68.

HOWE, REV. SAMUEL B., D.D., for 30 y. pastor of the 1st Ref. Prot. Dutch church, at New Brunswick, N. J.; d. at that place, March 1, 1868, in his 79th year.

HOWE, SOLOMON, surgeon, Conn.; d. in the rev. service, June 10, 1778.

HOWELL, ARTHUR, by trade a tanner and currier, and a prominent member of the society of Friends among whom he was a preacher; d. Jan. 26, 1816, in his 68th year. (*Simpson's Eminent Philadelphians.*)

HOWELL, NATHANIEL W., b. in Blooming Grove, Orange co., N. Y.; grad. at Princeton in 1788, studied law at Goshen, N. Y., taught 3 y. at Wand's Bridge, Ulster co., N. Y., and was admitted to practice in the supreme court in May, 1794. In May, 1795, opened an office in Union, near Binghamton, N. Y., and in 1795, removed to Canandaigua, where he resided till his death and held many offices; was assist. atty. gen.; member of assembly in 1804, in congress from 1813 to 1815, and first judge of Ontario county from 1819 to 1833; d. at Canandaigua, Oct. 10, 1851, a. 81. (*Turner's Phelps and Gorham Purchase*, p. 179.)

HOWLAND, BENJAMIN, senator in congress from Rhode Island, from 1804 to 1809; d. May, 1821.

HOWLAND, GARDINER, G., d. Nov. 9, 1851, in New York. An eminent and successful merchant, and a useful and energetic member of the charitable institutions of his city.

HOWLAND, SAMUEL S., d. in Rome, Italy, Feb. 9, 1853; senior partner in the house of Howland and Aspinwall, of New York.

HOWLE, DR. THOMAS PARKE, of Richmond, was a volunteer physician in the epidemic at Portsmouth, Va., in the fall of 1855, and fell a victim to the disease.

HOWLEY, Richard, governor of Georgia; was a lawyer; was a member from Liberty co., in the legislature, and was elected gov., Jan. 4, 1780. When the state was overrun by the enemy, a council was held, and the state officers retreated to N. C., barely escaping capture on the way; in 1780–1, he was in continental cong., and while there strenuously opposed a proposition for conceding Ga. to the British. (*White's Hist. Ga.*, p. 211.)

HOXIE, Joseph, politician; d. at Westerly, R. I., Aug. 18, 1870, a. 75.

HOXSIE, Stephen, d. at Leonardsville, N. Y., Oct. 6, 1836, in his 102d year; was of the society of Friends.

HOYT, David P., b. in Danbury, Conn., Nov. 17, 1778; settled in Utica, as a tanner and currier, in 1803; was a man of enterprise; member of assembly, 1819; d. June 3d, 1828.

HOYT, Dolly E., missionary, b. in Danbury, Ct., Apr. 27, 1797; undertook a mission to the Osage nation, as a member of the Union Missionary family, and d. on the Arkansas river, on her way thither, July 20, 1820, a. 23. (*Memoirs of D. E. H., Danbury*, 1828, 18mo, pp. 108.)

HOYT, John C., b. in Danbury, Conn.; came to Utica, in 1798; was a merchant tailor, an active man and a participant in all the enterprises designed to improve the place; he d., 1820.

HOYT, John P., sergeant Capt. Warner's co.; killed in invasion of Niagara frontier, Dec. 30, 1813.

HUBBARD, David E., d. at Glastonbury, Conn., Feb. 20, 1860, a. 63; was formerly much engaged in public affairs, and was a member of the constitutional convention of 1818. (*Vincent's Semi-An. Reg.*, p. 121.)

HUBBARD, Rev. Henry Clarke, d. at South Kingston, R. I., May 9, 1841, a. 73; was a Baptist minister, and d. suddenly in his pulpit.

HUBBARD, Noadiah, the pioneer settler of Champion, and a prominent citizen of Jefferson co., N. Y.; b. in Middletown, N. Y., Oct. 11, 1764; d. in Champion, June 12, 1859. (*Hough's Hist. Jefferson Co.*)

HUBBARD, Rev. Robert, an early minister in Western N. Y.; b. in Shelburne, Mass.; grad. at Williams Coll. in 1803, studied law, practiced a few years, and became a Presbyterian preacher. He settled in Allegany co., and d. at Canisteo, N. Y., May 24, 1840, a. 57. (*Hotchkin's Western N. Y.*, p. 96.)

HUBBARD, Thomas H., native of Connecticut, and grad. at Yale; settled as a lawyer at Hamilton, N. Y., was a surrogate in Madison co., 10 years, and in 1823, settled in Utica. He was in congress from 1817 to 1819, and from 1821 to 1823. In 1812, 1844 and 1852, he was a presidential elector. He d. in Utica, N. Y., May 22, 1857, a. 76.

HUBBARD, Thomas Hill, son of Rev. Bela Hubbard of Trinity church, New Haven, Conn., in 1781, and grad. at Yale, in 1799; pursued legal studies with John Woodworth of Troy, and settled about 1804, in Hamilton, N. Y. He was the first surrogate of the county and served from 1806 to 1816. For two years thereafter he was prosecuting attorney of the district, composed of Madison, Oneida and Herkimer counties. In 1821–3 he represented his district in congress. Receiving the appointment of clerk of the court of chancery, he moved to Utica in 1823, and soon after received that of clerk of the supreme court. He was thrice elector of pres. voting for Madison, Polk and Pierce. He d. May 21st, 1827.

HUBBELL, FERDINAND WAKEMAN, b. in Philadelphia, Pa., May 4, 1801; was a prominent lawyer, and d. Aug., 1852. (*Simpson's Eminent Philadelphians.*)

HUBBELL, FREDERICK A., for twenty years a member of the Clinton county bar; d. at Champlain, N. Y., April 25, 1853.

HUBERT, JEAN FRANCOIS, ninth R. C. bp., of Quebec, b. at Quebec, Feb. 3, 1739, became priest, July 20, 1766, coadjutor Nov. 30, 1784; succeeded D'Esglis as bp. June 12, 1788, and resigned Sept. 1, 1797. He d. at Quebec, Oct. 17, 1797. (*Liste Chron. des Evêques et des Prêtres du Canada.*)

HUBLEY, EDWARD B., d. in Philadelphia, Pa., Feb. 23, 1856; was in congress from 1835 to 1839, was from New York, and in the assembly of that state in 1841.

HUDSON, WILLIAM, a Quaker and one of the first settlers of Philadelphia, acquired a large property as a tanner, and dealer in real estate, and d. in 1742. (*Simpson's Eminent Philadelphians.*)

HUDSON, WILLIAM HENRY, was b. in Prince Edward co., Va., in 1808; grad. at Yale in 1827, and became a professor in a college in Va., in Lagrange co., Tenn., and in the University of Alabama. In 1841, he became a prof. of mathematics in the University of Mo., at Columbia, and held till 1856, when he was chosen president of this college; d. June 14, 1859, a. 52.

HUFTY, JOSEPH, engraver and stationer; d. at Philadelphia, Pa., May, 13, 1860.

HUGER, DANIEL ELLIOTT, d. in Charleston, S. C., Aug., 1854; a distinguished citizen of South Carolina; was for half a century identified with the public service of his state, as a member of the legislature, senator, and from 1843 to 1846, senator in congress.

HUGHES, CHRISTOPHER, d, in Baltimore, Md., Sept. 18, 1849; was for many years in public life, as charge to Sweden, and afterwards as minister to Holland.

HUGHES, CAPT. ELIAS, d. near Utica, Licking co., Ohio, Feb. 22, 1845, a. 90; took an active part in the Indian wars that harassed the new settlements of the west.

HUGHES, GEORGE W., d. at West River, Md., Dec. 3, 1871; b. in 1806; partly educated at West Point; served in the Mexican war, and remained an engineer officer; was afterwards minister to the Hague; pres. of the Northern Central R. R., and from 1861 to 1863 member of congress.

HUGHES, JEREMIAH, d. at Baltimore, Md., Nov. 27, 1848, a. 65; was many years editor of the *Annapolis Republican;* printer to the state, and a member of the legislature; after the death of Mr. Niles, he became the editor and proprietor of *Niles's Register*, which he conducted until within a few months of his death.

HUGHES, MAJ. PETER, a deserving officer of the revolution; commanded at Ft. Schuyler for a time; d. at Cayuga, N. Y., Dec. 1816, a. 65.

HUGHES, SARAH W., d, in Mississippi, July 16, 1859, a. 113 years.

HUGUENIN, GEN. DANIEL, d. in Kenosha, Wis., June 1874, a. 59; was an officer in the war of 1812, and from 1825 to 1827, a member of congress from Oswego, N. Y.; afterwards U. S. marshal for the territory of Wisconsin.

HUIDEKOPER, HARM. JOHN, d. in Meadville, Pa., May, 1854, a. 78; b. in Holland, and at an early age entered the service of the Holland Land Co., which owned large landed estates, and had an office at Meadville, until he bought the company's interests in that part of the state. He was a man of wealth and education and the founder of a Theological Institute and Unitarian church at Meadville.

HULBERT, COL. JOHN W., b. on Alford, Mass., in 1775; grad. at Harvard in 1795, was a lawyer at Pittsfield, Mass., and in 1805, was in the legislature. In 1814 was elected to congress, went to Auburn, N. Y., in 1817; was in assembly in 1825, and d. at Auburn, Oct. 19, 1831. (*Hall's Auburn*, p. 573.)

HULL, DR. AMOS G., settled in New Hartford, N. Y., as early as 1798. Continued in practice at New Hartford until 1812 and at Utica until 1821, when he removed to New York. Was the first president of Oneida County Medical Society, of repute as a surgeon, and inventor of the hernial truss known by his name.

HULL, REV. HOPE, b. in Md., in 1763, was admitted as a traveling minister in the Methodist Ch., in 1785, and went to Ga., in 1788. He drew crowded audiences and left deep impressions. He ceased to travel about 1796, established a classical school at Washington, Wilkes co., settled at Athens in 1803, and was one of the trustees of the State University; he d. Oct. 1, 1818; his son Asbury H., has held many offices, and Dr. Henry H., was a prof. in the university. (*White's Hist. Ga.*, p. 393.)

HULL, DR. LAURENS, of Angelica, N. Y.; d. June 27, 1865, a. 86.

HULL, DR. MARSHALL, an eminent physician, visited the U. S. in 1853–4, and lectured with success. He made many important discoveries in medicine, and d. in Brighton, Eng., Aug. 11, 1858, a. 67.

HUME, LIEUT. ALEXANDER, S. C., killed in the attack on Savannah, Oct. 9, 1779.

HUMPHREY, CHARLES, of Ithaca, N. Y., was in assem. in 1834–5–6 and 42 and 1835–6, was speaker. He was afterwards clerk of the supreme court; he d. at Albany, N. Y., April 18, 1850, in his 59th year. (*Stryker's Am. Reg.*, iv, 458.)

HUMPHREY, ISAAC, was the first to make known the value of the gold discoveries in California; b. in Ga., and a gold miner when the discoveries of nuggets at Sutter's mill were made he reported them as gold, the first authentic information that was received on the subject; d. at Victoria, Dec. 1, 1867.

HUMPHREY, JOHN, an original patentee of Mass., in 1628, and one of 1st board of assistants, came over in 1634, settled at Lynn. His wife was sister to the Earl of Lincoln and to Lady Arbella the wife of Isaac Johnson. He was unfortunate in commercial speculation suffering in property and character. (*Bradford's N. E. Biog.; Young's Chron. Mass.*, p. 106.)

HUMPHREY, MICAH, an early settler of Harrisburgh, N. Y., d. in that town, Nov. 16, 1847, a. 81.

HUMPHREY, WILLIAM, M.D., son of John H., b. at Albany, Feb. 2, 1796; grad. at Union Coll. in 1813, studied medicine with Dr. Eights and grad. at the Coll. of Ph. and Sur., in 1819. He practiced till his death, at Albany, Mar. 12, 1829, a. 31. (*Munsell's Ann. Alb.*, ix, 105.)

HUMPHREYS, JOSHUA, d. in Delaware co., Pa., Jan. 12, 1838, in his 67th year; formerly of Philadelphia, and a distinguished ship builder; one of the society of Friends; the frigate United States was built under his direction, and the Constitution, President, Congress and Constellation from his drawings. (*Simpson's Eminent Philadelphians.*)

HUMPHREYS, SAMUEL, chief naval contractor of the U. S. navy; d. Aug. 16, 1846, a. 68.

HUMPHRIES, CAPT. JOHN, Va., killed in the revolution, at Quebec, Dec. 31, 1775.

HUNGERFORD, ORVILLE, merchant and banker; b. in Farmington, Ct., Oct. 20, 1790; settled in Watertown, N. Y.; and was long a successful merchant and banker; he was in congress in 1843–7; a candidate for state comptroller in 1847; and pres. of the Watertown and Rome R. R.; he d. at Watertown, April 6, 1851. (*Hough's Hist. Jeff. Co., N. Y.*, p. 435, with portrait; *Watertown Jeffersonian*, Apr. 12, 1851.)

HUNSICKER, HENRY, of the Mennonist society, d. at Shippack, Pa., July 8, 1836; he was a preacher 54 years.

HUNT, ALVAH, for many years an enterprising merchant in Greene N. Y.; removed to Brooklyn, and died there Oct. 23, 1858, a. 60 y.; he was in the state senate from Chenango co., in 1839, '40, '1,'2; and state treasurer in 1848, '9, '50, '51.

HUNT, ALVIN, many years an editor at Watertown, N. Y., where he resided over thirty years; d. March, 1859, a. about 64. (*New York Reformer*, March 24, 1859.)

HUNT, BENJAMIN FANEUIL, of Charleston, S. C.; d. in New York city, Dec. 6, 1854, a. 62; b. in Watertown, Mass., Feb. 29, 1792; grad. at Harvard in 1810, and in the fall of that year settled in Charleston; studied law, and was admitted to the bar in 1812, became a distinguished lawyer; was many years in the legislature of South Carolina.

HUNT, JAMES B., of Pontiac Mich.; d. in Washington, D. C. Aug. 15, 1857; he was a native of New York; was many years law partner with Michael Hoffman; removed to Michigan at about the time of her admission to the Union, and was chosen to several offices of trust, and from 1843 to 1847, was in congress.

HUNT, JONATHAN, member in congress from Vt.; d. at Washington, D. C., May 14, 1832; he entered congress from Brattleboro, in 1827; and grad. at Dartmouth, in 1807.

HUNT, MONTGOMERY, son of Ward Hunt, was b. at Mt. Pleasant, Westchester co.; grad. at Columbia Coll., about the year 1792, and was then placed as clerk in the Bank of America; was sent, in 1808, to Utica, to inaugurate a branch of the Manhattan Bank. From this he was transferred in 1812, to the cashiership of the Bank of Utica, and continued to occupy this post until Dec. 30, 1834, when he res.; d. at St. Cruz, 5th Jan., 1837. He was considerably interested in political affairs, but held no office, save that of presidential elector, in 1816, voting for Mr. Munroe. He was also grand master of the Utica lodge of Masons.

HUNT, JOSIAH, d. May 24, 1841, at Phila.; was a soldier in the rev.

HUNT, SAMUEL, was a captain in Sir Wm. Johnson's campaign in 1755, and active in the French and revolutionary wars; he settled in Charlestown, N. H., in 1759, and in 1775 was a member of the committee of safety; he was in convention, at Concord and Walpole; was appointed sheriff, and held till his death in 1799. (*Coll. N. H. Hist. Soc.*, iv, 128.)

HUNT, SANFORD, father of Gov. Washington Hunt, b. in Coventry, Ct., Apr. 17, 1777; was a merchant clerk, from 16 to 21, and in June, 1798, settled at Batavia, near Windham, Greene co., N. Y., where he remained about 20 y., as a merchant; in 1818 he removed to Hunt's Hollow, Livingston co., N. Y., and d. there June 7, 1849. (*Hunt's Biog. Panorama*, p. 254.)

HUNT, WALTER, a distinguished inventor, but without the faculty of profiting from his own genius; spent his early life in Lewis co., N. Y., and d. in New York city, June, 1859.

HUNT, WILLIAM, d. in Md., in 1772, a. 113. (*Kirby's Museum*, ii, 280.)

HUNTER, GEN. ALEXANDER, d. at Washington, D. C., Jan. 21, 1849, a. 59; late marshal of the District of Columbia.

HUNTER, EDMUND P., d. at Berkley Springs, Va., Sept. 9, 1859; was a lawyer, and for some time a member of the state legislature.

HUNTER, DR. EDWIN, of Brooklyn; a volunteer, in the yellow fever epidemic, at Portsmouth, Va., in the autumn of 1855, fell a victim to the disease.

HUNTER, H. C., lieut. in U. S. navy; son of Wm. H., assist. sec. state; d. at Barcelona, Spain, Sept. 30, 1873.

HUNTER, ROBERT, colonial gov. of N. Y., son of James H. a lawyer; was apprenticed to an apothecary; left for the army and rose to the rank of maj. gen.; in 1707, was appointed lt. gov. of Va., but was captured by a French privateer and carried back; in June 1710, he became gov. of N. Y., and held till 1719; on the death of the Duke of Portland, he was appointed gov. of Jamacia; he d. there in March, 1834. (*Doc. Hist. N. Y.*, iii, 457.)

HUNTER, WILLIAM L., d. in Newport R. I., Dec. 3, 1849, a. 75; grad. at Brown U., in 1791; studied law, and was admitted to the bar at Newport, at the age of 21; In 1799, was in the legislature, and after, at various times till 1811, when he was chosen senator in congress, where he remained till 1821. In 1834, was appointed chargé to Brazil, and continued as minister, till 1844, when he returned to Newport, and resided till his death. (*Am. Almanac*, 1851, p. 308.)

HUNTINGTON, DR. ABEL, b. in Norwich, Conn.; removed at an early age to Easthampton, L. I., and was sixty years a practicing physician; was in congress from 1833 to 1837; collector at Sag Harbor under Polk, and member of the constitutional convention of 1846; d. May 18, 1858, a. 82, at East Hampton, N. Y.

HUNTINGTON, ASAHEL, b. in Topsfield, Mass., July 23, 1798; grad. at Yale, in 1819; became a lawyer, settled in Salem, Mass., and was county and afterwards district attorney. At the instigation of enemies, charges of malfeasance in office were made against him, but a committee of the legislature, after careful investigation, wholly exonerated him from them; and in 1845, he resigned the office of district attorney, which he had held since 1832; in 1851, he was appointed clerk of the courts of Essex co.; in 1853, was delegate in the state constitutional convention, and in 1854, mayor of Salem, He d. 1871.

HUNTINGTON, GEORGE, judge of common pleas in 1798, and in assem. in 1810, '11, '12, '18, '20, and '21; collector of the Western Inland Navig. Co., from the opening of their work until the opening of the Erie canal. Agreed on all other matters, he and his brother were opposed in political sentiments, and both were candidates for the office of lieut. governor; he d. Sept. 23d, 1841, in his 72d year.

HUNTINGTON, HENRY, b. in Norwich, Conn.; removed with his brother George, to Rome, N. Y., before 1798; they became country merchants and each acquired a large property, Henry at the time of his death being the wealthiest man in the county; he had a high standing in community, and filled several important offices; was a member of the constitutional convention of 1801, and 1821; a member of the state senate 1805–7, and of the council of appointment in 1806; presidential elector in 1808; and a member of assembly in 1816–17. From the year 1812 until his death he was president of the Bank of Utica, going from Rome to Utica twice a week to attend to the affairs of the bank; he was also one of the first board of trustees of Hamilton College. He d. Oct. 15, 1846, a. 80.

HUNTINGTON, HEZEKIAH, d. in Middletown, Conn., May 27, 1842, a. 83; for many years attorney for the district court of Connecticut.

HUNTINGTON, SAMUEL G., d. at Troy, N. Y., July 5, 1854; was from Middletown, Conn.; removed to Waterford and practiced law, and afterwards settled in Troy; was a judge of com. pleas under Gov. De-Witt Clinton.

HUNTINGTON, WILLIAM, a pioneer settler of Watertown, N. Y., b. in Tolland, Ct., removed to N. H., in 1785; and to Watertown in 1804; d. May 11, 1842, a. 85.

HUNTLING, REV. NATHANIEL, second Presb. pastor at East Hampton, N. Y.; d. Sept. 21, 1753, a. 80 or more. (*Prime's Hist. L. I.*, p. 176.)

HURD, JOSEPH, formerly of Charleston, Mass., an eminent merchant; d. in Portsmouth, N. H., Aug. 14, 1842, a. 89.

HURD, JOSEPH, b. in Concord or Lincoln, Mass.; grad. at Harvard in 1797, and became a merchant in this country and England; after 1812 he settled on a farm, and was successfully employed in a patent for refining sugar, which yielded him a large profit; he willed $5,000 to each of the states of Maine, New Hampshire, Vermont and Massachusetts, the income of which, was to be applied in promoting the manufacture and refining of sugar; d. in Malden, Mass., March 19, 1857.

HURLBURT, KELLOGG, d. Oct. 19, 1847, a. 64; a distinguished citizen of Oneida co., N. Y., and a native of Richmond, Mass.

HURLEY, REV. MICHAEL, D.D., an eminent Catholic clergyman; d. in Philadelphia, May 15, 1837, a 57.

HUSON, CALVIN, JR., grad. at Geneva Coll., in 1845; studied law with Wm. H. Seward, at Auburn; was admitted to practice in 1847, sett. at Rochester, and was dist. atty. for Monroe co., from 1857 to 1860; he was captured at Stone Bridge, taken prisoner to Richmond, and d. in Oct., 1861.

HUSSEY, JOSIAH, magistrate at Nantucket, Mass.; d. Nov., 1839, a. 71.

HUSTON, CAPT. ALEXANDER, Pa.; killed at Brandywine, Sept. 11, 1777.

HUSTON, ELI, a distinguished lawyer; d. at Natchez, Miss., June 13, 1835.

HUSTON, GEN. FELIX, native of Kentucky; d. near Natchez, Miss., Feb. 25, 1857, a. 53; he went to Natchez about 1828, and began law practice with his brother Eli; he was for a time in the Texas war of independence, but returned to La., and engaged in planting, taking little part in politics, except with his pen, with which he evinced eminent abilities.

HUTCHINS, SOLOMON, d. at Wakefield, N. H., Aug. 3, 1846, a. 86; he was with John Paul Jones, on board the Bon Homme Richard in the action with the Serapis, and in other exploits of the revolution.

HUTCHINS, THOMAS, capt. 60th Royal regiment of foot, 1762, from New Jersey; engineer to Col. Bouquet's expedition against the Indians, on the Ohio, 1763, and Muskingum, 1764; conceived a plan for military settlements in the Indian country, 1765, with surveys, in sections of a mile square; early in the revolution, a captain in the confederate service; arrested in London, and his property confiscated in 1778; reached Charleston, S. C., and appointed geographer to the United States; 1786–7, executed the first surveys of public lands in the U. S., among hostile Indians in Ohio, next west of the Pa. line; d. in office at Pittsburg, 1788; buried in the cemetery of the 1st Pres. church, with no stone or monument. The simple system of surveys into townships and sections, by north and south, and east and west lines, adopted in the surveys of the U. S. lands, and practiced to this time, had never been tried, and probably never thought of before. He was a man of genius, science, and patriotism. (*C. W.*)

HUTCHINSON, ANDERSON, formerly judge of the supreme court of the republic of Texas; d. at Jackson, Miss., Dec. 31, 1852.

HUTCHINSON, ANDREW B., vocalist, son of Jesse H. of Milford, N. H., and one of a well known family of vocalists; d. at the Lunatic Asylum, S. Boston, Oct., 1860, a. 52.

HUTCHINSON, ELI, of Catskill; d. at Albany, N. Y., Oct. 3, 1842, a. 63; was a man of large wealth.

HUTCHINSON, HOLMES, an engineer in the construction of the Erie canal, and in the location and defining of numerous tracts of land in Central and Western N. Y.; was active and influential in the construction of the Syracuse and Oswego rail road, and long its president; b. in Columbus, O., Feb., 1695. His residence was in Utica, where he was many years director of the Bank of Utica, and where he d. Feb. 21, 1865, in his 70th year.

HUTCHINSON, DR. JAMES, b. in Wakefield township, Bucks co., Pa., Jan. 29, 1752, and fell a victim to the yellow fever in Philadelphia Sept. 5, 1793. He was partly educated in Europe; was a surgeon in the revolution, and conspicuous for his talent and learning. (*Simpson's Eminent Philadelphians*, with portrait.)

HUTCHINSON, REV. SYLVESTER, d. at Hightstown, N. J., Dec., 1840, a. 55; a minister of the Methodist Episcopal church.

HUTCHINSON, Titus, grad. at Nassau Hall, N. J., in 1796, and for many years was an eminent lawyer of Vermont, and for several years chief justice of that state; he d. at Woodstock, Vt., Aug. 24, 1857, a. 86.

HUXFORD, William, d. in Brooks, Me., July 9, 1842, a. 87; was from Martha's Vineyard, and had lived in Oneida co., N. Y., but resided in Brooks, Me., for many years; in the revolution in the navy.

HUYLER, John, ex member of congress, murdered at Hackensack, N. J., Jan. 9, 1870, a. 61.

HYBART, Thomas L.,d. near Fayetteville, N. C., Jan. 1, 1847; was a member of the bar.

HYDE, Dr. Williams of Stonington, Conn., an eminent physician; d. Sept. 25, 1873.

IDE, Rev. George B., d.d., pastor of the First Baptist church in Springfield, Mass.; d. April 16, 1872, a. 66.

IDE, Dr. W. E., d. in New York city, April 15, 1873. Dr. Ide resided in Columbus, O., for over twenty years; was a man of large resources, which he used with great benefaction, and of a masculine, cultured mind. He contributed much to the advancement of Columbus, by his public spirit, and to its social life by his genial disposition. He was b. in Kirby, Vermont, and was 57 years of age.

IMLAY, William H., an enterprising and successful merchant; d. in Hartford, Ct., Sept. 4, 1858, a. 78.

INCHES, Henderson, b. in Boston, Feb. 7, 1774; grad. at Harvard in 1792, and became an intelligent and successful merchant; d. in Boston, Sept. 9, 1857, a. 83.

INGE, Zebulon Montgomery Pike, lieut. 2d U. S. dragoons of Alabama, cadet in 1834, and made 2d lt., July 1, 1838, and 1st lt. May 1, 1841; he fell at the battle of Resaca de la Palma, in a charge at the head of dragoons. (*Thorpe's Army of the Rio Grande*, p. 195.)

INGERSOLL, John, clerk of the courts of the county of Hampden; d. at Springfield, Mass., Dec. 26, 1840, a. 41.

INGERSOLL, Capt. Jonathan, d. at Windsor, Vt., July, 1840, a. 89, formerly of Salem, Mass.

INGERSOLL, Ralph I., a prominent lawyer of New Haven; d. Aug. 26, 1872, a. 84, served in the state legislature many years; was in congress from 1825 to 1833; at one time state attorney, and for two years minister to Russia.

INGERSOLL, William J., d. at Mobile, Ala., Oct. 6, 1839, was cashier of the Bank of Mobile.

INGLIS, Rt. Rev. John, bishop of Nova Scotia, d. in N. S., Oct. 27, 1850; he was the son of the Rt. Rev. Charles Inglis first bp. of N. S., was educated at King's Coll., Windsor and consecrated in 1825; he was in his 73d year. (*Stryker's Am. Reg.*, v, 187.)

INGHAM, Miss Marietta, b. in Saybrook, Conn., in 1800; d. in LeRoy, N. Y., June, 1867. In 1835, she founded the Ingham Collegiate Institute which in 1857, received a university charter. (*Regent's Report*, 1868, p. 708.)

INGHAM, Samuel D., d. at Trenton, N. J., June 5, 1860, in his 81st year; b. in Buck's co., Pa., Sept. 16, 1779, became a lawyer, and in

1805–6–7, was elected to the legislature; was in congress from 1813 to 1818, and from 1822 to 1829. When he was appointed secretary of the treasury, resigned with others of Jackson's cabinet. In 1856, he favored Fremont's election.

INGRAHAM, JOSEPH W., a member of the board of education; d. at Boston, Mass., Aug., 28, 1848.

INMAN, WILLIAM, land agent, b. in Somersetshire, Eng., and when young a clerk of Lord Pultney. Came to America in 1792, as agent of Patrick Colquhoun for the town of Leyden, and the Brantingham tract in Lewis co.; lived many years in Whitestown, afterwards in N. Y., as a merchant and d. in Leyden, N. Y., Feb. 14, 1843, a. 81. His principal had cause to regret placing confidence in him. Henry I., the painter, John I., the editor and writer, and Wm., captain in the U. S. navy, were his sons. (*Hough's Hist. Lewis Co. N. Y.*, p. 124.)

ION, JACOB BOND, b. in South Carolina; grad. at Yale in 1803, entered the army in 1811 and served till 1815. He was retained on the peace establishment, and was placed in charge of the fortifications at Charleston and Savannah. He was many years president of the state senate, a member of the convention of 1832, which passed the nullification ordinance; he d. at Charleston, July 17, 1859, a. 77.

IRELAND, WILLIAM H., prominent politician, d. in N. Y., Aug. 1849.

IRISH, GEORGE, judge of the first judicial district of Mississippi; d. at Port Gibson, Sept. 17, 1836, a. about 45.

IRVIN, SAMUEL A., collector of internal revenue at Chicago; d. Oct. 11, 1874, a. 50; b. in Gettysburg, Pa., in 1824; was a lawyer many years in Chicago; corporation council four years.

IRVING, WALTER, d. at Natchez, Miss., July, 1839, a. about 67; native of Ireland, one of the longest residents at Natchez.

IRVINE, ANDREW, revolutionary officer of Irish birth, and brother of Gen. Wm. J.; entered the army as lt. marched with his br. to Canada, served under Wayne, and participated in movements prior to the massacre of Paoli, where he was wounded; he served in the northern campaigns and at the South serving actively and honorably through the war; he d. at Carlisle, Pa., May, 4, 1789. (*Rogers's Am. Biog.*)

IRVINE, GEN. CALLENDER, d. at Phila. Oct. 9, 1841, a. 67; commissary general of purchases of the U. S. army.

IRVINE, WILLIAM W., representative in Ohio legislature, and judge of the supreme court of that state, for some years; was in congress from that state from 1829 to 1833; d. at Lancaster, O., April, 1842.

IRVING, EBENEZER, eldest brother who survived Washington I.; d. at Sunnyside, Tarrytown, N. Y., Aug. 22, 1868; b. in 1775; was his brother's business agent.

IRWIN, COL. ALEXANDER J., receiver of the land office at Green Bay; d. in Brown co., Wis., June 1847, a. 45; was an old resident of the territory, and for many years member of the legislative council.

IRWIN, DOUGLASS S., 1st lieut. 3d U. S. infantry; killed in battle of Monterey, Sept. 21, 1846; educated at West Point, and served in the Florida war.

IRWIN, JAMES, member of congress from S. C., in 1817–21; d. at Darlington, C. H., S. C., Oct. 1838.

IRWIN, WILLIAM W., member of Congress from Pennsylvania from 1841 to 1843; and chargé d' affaires to Denmark from 1843 to 1847; d. in Pittsburgh, Pa., Sept. 15, 1856.

ITABORABY, VISCONTE DE, prime minister of Brazil, d. at Rio Janeiro, Jan. 8, 1872, a. 68.

IVES, ELI, M.D., prof. in Yale Medical School, New Haven; b. in Windsor, Ct., in 1770; grad. at Yale in 1798, with honors; studied medicine and in 1802, was admitted to practice; in 1813, he became prof. of materia medica and botany in the Yale Med. Sch., in 1829, prof. of theory and practice, and in 1852, of materia medica and therapeutics, in 1853 he became emeritus prof.; his death occurred Oct. 7, 1861, a. 84. (*N. Y. Eve. Post*, Oct. 8, 1861.)

IVES, JOHN, an officer of the revolution, and pioneer settler of Turin, N. Y.; d. in that town, March 13, 1828, a. 66; his wife d. Feb. 12, 1841. (*Hough's Hist. Lewis Co.*, p. 228.)

IVES, LEVI, father of the late Bishop Levi S. Ives, committed suicide by drowning in Turin, N. Y., June 19, 1815.

IVES, MOSES BROWN, grad. at Brown Uni., in 1812; studied law at Litchfield, Ct., and became a merchant in Providence, R. I., where he d. Aug. 7, 1857, a. 63. He was an active promoter and liberal benefactor of learning, philanthropy and religion, and was for 35 years trustee of Brown University and for 32 years its treasurer.

IVES, DR. TITUS, a pioneer of Watertown, Jeff. co., N. Y.; d. Feb. 12, 1847, a. 69.

JACK, JAMES, b. in Pa., settled in Charlotte, N. C., and took an active part in the revolution. He afterwards settled in Ga., and d. Jan. 18, 1823 in Elbert co., Ga., a. 84. (*White's Hist. Ga.*, p. 447.)

JACK, SAMUEL, a revolutionary soldier, d. in Wilkes co., Ga., a. 65; he was a col. of militia.

JACKSON, GEN. C. M., ex-speaker of the house of representatives of Georgia; d. Feb. 26, 1860, at Augusta, Ga.

JACKSON, ELIZABETH WILLING, sister of Richard Willing, and widow of Major Wm. Jackson, aid and sec. of Washington. He was chosen to deliver the funeral oration upon Washington at Phila., and many years conducted a daily paper. His wid. d. Aug. 5, 1858 in her 93d y. (*Hist. Mag.*, ii, 283.)

JACKSON, COL. EPHRAIM, Mass., killed in the revolution, Dec. 19, 1777.

JACKSON, GEORGE W., son of Richard J., from Feb., 1836 to July, 1838 was proprietor of the *Providence Journal* and marshal of R. I., under Fillmore; he d. at Prov. Oct., 1860, a. 55.

JACKSON, ISAAC RAND, d. in Copenhagen, Denmark, July 27, 1843; chargé d'affaires at the court of Denmark.

JACKSON, JOSEPH W., d. at Savannah, Ga., Sept. 28, 1854; he was frequently a member of the city council, and had been a mayor; was a member repeatedly of each house of the legislature, and was in congress from 1850 to 1853.

JACKSON, COL. PHILIP, N. J.; killed at the battle of Long Island, Aug. 27, 1776.

JACKSON, DR. SAMUEL, d. at Philadelphia, Pa., April 6, 1872, a. 85.

JACOBS, PHEBE ANN, a black woman; d. at Brunswick, Me., March 3, 1850, at an advanced age; she was remarkably honored at her funeral, by the attendance of many eminent persons, on account of her Christian virtues. (*Stryker's Am. Reg.*, iv, 452.)

JACQUES, COL. SAMUEL, a well known agriculturist; d. in Somerville, Mass., March 27, 1859, a. 82.

JACQUETT, MAJ. PETER, d. on the banks of the Christiana, in Delaware, Sept., 1834, in his 80th year; he was appointed, Jan., 1775, lieut. in the Delaware regiment, and was engaged in thirty battles of the war.

JAMES, AMOS, d. in Stephentown, Feb. 9, 1845, a. 84; was one of the party who captured Gen. Prescott on Rhode Island, and brought him over to the American camp.

JAMES, JOHN, revolutionary officer of S. C.; b. in Ireland in 1732; came an infant with his parents, to S. C., and settled at what is now Kings-Tree, Williamsburg. In 1776, as captain of militia, he marched to the defense of Charleston; he served nearly through the war, as major, and was reduced from comparative wealth to poverty; he retired to his farm, and d. in 1791. (*Rogers's Am. Biog.*)

JAMESON, GEORGE W., comedian; d. at Yonkers, N. Y., Oct. 1868.

JAMIESON, W. L., comedian, son of Geo. J., actor; d. at New York, Nov. 9, 1868, in his 33d year.

JANSEN, HENRY, member of assembly from Sullivan and Ulster counties, New York in 1812, 1813, and delegate from these counties in the constitutional convention of 1821; d. suddenly in the hall of the Capitol, Sept. 14, 1821.

JARNAGIN, SPENCER, U. S. senator from Tennessee from 1845 to 1847; d. at Memphis, Tenn., June 24, 1851; b. in Granger co., Tenn.; grad. at Greenville Coll. in 1813, and was admitted to the bar in 1817.

JARRATT, REV. DEVEREUX, b. in New Kent co., Va., Jan., 1733, of obscure parents, received a slender education but by application acquired sufficient to teach in Albermarle co., Va. He studied Latin and in 1763, took orders in the Episcopal church, in England. While abroad he heard Wesley preach. After his return to Va., he gained celebrity as a preacher and spent part of his time in itinerant preaching, going hundreds of miles in every direction. He was in the habit of speaking in the open air, and was by some considered a Methodist, although he never broke off from the church of England. His sermons were published in several volumes. (*Campbell's Va.*)

JARVIS, SAMUEL, a loyalist from Stamford, Ct.; d. Sept. 1, 1780, at New York city, a. 60; he was many years recorder in Stamford. About a year before his death he was stripped, and landed from a whale boat at Matinicook Point. (*Rivington's Gazette*, Sept. 6.)

JARVIS, WILLIAM, was b. in Boston; became consul of U. S. at Lisbon in the time of Jefferson, and in 1810, returned and settled in Wethersfield, as a farmer. He did much to improve the growth of wool in the U. S., and imported from Spain over 3,500 fine wooled sheep; he d. at Wethersfield, Ct., Oct. 21, 1859, a. 89.

JARVIS, WILLIAM C., of Charlestown, Mass.; d. at Weathersfield, Vt., Oct. 3, 1836; he was formerly speaker of the house of representatives of Mass.

JEANDELL, DR. WILLIAM D., publisher and journalist; d. at Wilmington, Del., Dec. 12, 1870, a. 52.

JEMISON, JOHN. (*See* Dejihnondawehhoh.)

JEMISON, MARY, alias DEHHEWAMIS, the white woman of the Genesee; b. on the voyage of her parents to America, in 1742 or 3. Her father's family was attacked by French and Indians in the spring of 1755, at Marsh Creek, Pa., was saved while the rest were murdered, and grew up among the Indians. She was twice m. and bore eight children, and lived many years at Gardeau reservation on the Genesee, containing 17,927 acres given to her at the council of Big Tree, by the chiefs. The Seneca reservations were sold in 1825, and in 1831, she removed to Buffalo creek, where she d. Sept. 19, 1833, a. 91. She witnessed many cruelties among the Indians, and only confessed her origin and history in old age; three daughters d. nearly at the same time in 1839, a. 69, 63, and 58, and one of her sons, was the murderer of another. (*Life of M. J. by Ja's E. Seaver*, 4th ed., N. Y. and Auburn, 1856, pp. 312.)

JENKINS, CHARLES J., b. in Beaufort dist., S. C., Jan. 6, 1805; settled in Jeff. co., Ga., in Jan., 1816; grad. at Union Coll., N. Y., in 1822, studied law in Ga. and settled at Saundersville, Ga. In 1825 he removed to Augusta, and was elected to the assembly in 1830; in 1831, was elected atty. gen. of Ga., was again returned to the legislature in 1836, and annually till 1852, except in 1842; in 1840, 3, 5, 7, he was speaker; in 1850, he was offered the post of sec. of the interior but declined; he was afterwards beaten in an election for governor 510 votes.

JENKINS, CHARLES MONTGOMERY, and JENKINS, HIRAM TUTTLE, sons of Timothy and his partners in the law. The former was b. Sept. 21st, 1830, the latter April 8, 1833; they entered Hamilton College together, grad. in 1852, and were admitted to the bar in 1854; the health of the former began early to decline; he spent the winter of 1855–6, in Nassau, New Providence, and d. the 21st Dec., following. Hiram T. was in 1859, elected district attorney of Oneida county, was reëlected without opposition in 1862, and in 1865, was again elected, having been placed in nomination by both parties; he d. July 29, 1868.

JENKINS, DAVID T., col. 146 regt. N. Y. state vols., was the son of J. Whipple Jenkins, brother of Timothy; he was educated at the Rensselaer Institute in Troy, studied law, and was gaining repute in his profession when the war commenced. He joined the 146th regt. as adjutant, and became successively major, lieut. col. and col.; he was killed at the battle of the Wilderness, May 5, 1864.

JENKINS, JOHN J., d. near Port Tobacco, Md., Jan. 2, 1845, a. 57; judge of the orphan's court in Charles co. (*Am Almanac*, 1846, p. 327.)

JENKINS, TIMOTHY, was b. in Barre, Mass., in 1799; where he was educated to the law and admitted to the bar; he began practice at Oneida Castle, Oneida co., N. Y., where he resided the remainder of his life; from 1840 to 1845, he held the office of district attorney for Oneida co.; and he was elected to the 29th, 30th, and 32d congresses; the republican nomination for judge of the court of appeals was tendered to him with much unanimity, in 1857, and he received 175,325 votes for that office, while Mr. Denio his opponent received 196,016. He d. at Martinsburgh, N. Y., after a brief illness on the 29th of Dec., 1859; he had gone thither to attend court, and by a singular coincidence d. at the place where nearly a year previous he narrowly escaped alive from a burning hotel; he was distinguished for his sound learning, acute penetration and forensic abilities. (*N. Y. Eve. Post*, Dec. 24, 1859; *Hist. Mag.*, iv, 61; *Alb. Eve. Jour.*, Dec. 27, 1859.)

JENKS, Greenville T., of Brooklyn, a lawyer; d. at Saratoga Springs, Aug. 14, 1870.

JENNESS, Richard, ex-mayor of Portsmouth, N. H., d. Feb. 3, 1872, a. 73.

JENNINGS, Chester, b. in Connecticut, and for many years a successful hotel keeper in New York city; d. at the Astor House, N. Y., Jan. 25, 1854; leaving his estate to his sister Mrs. Otis Warren, of Leyden, N. Y.

JENNINGS, Henry, founder of an immense estate in New Jersey; came to America towards the close of the 17th century; and settled in Burlington, N. J.; he d. in Phila. 1707, leaving a son Isaac, who left a son and four daughters; the latter married Lippincott, Price, Flanagan and Burrough; the estate early in this century was valued at forty millions. (*Hist. Mag.*, i, 158.)

JEROME, Rev. Charles, b. in Pompey, Onondaga co., N. Y., Jan. 2d, 1815; grad. at Hamilton, in 1839; studied theology at Auburn and at New Haven; spent twenty years of service in the ministry at Oxford Bergen, Ellicottville and Fenton, N. Y.; in 1861 he removed to Clinton, and d. May 31, 1873.

JEROME, Rev. William, b. in Burlington, Conn.; d. Jan. 14, 1871, at Rome, N. Y., a. 61. (*Northern New York Advocate*, March 16, 1871.)

JESSOP, Dr. Robert, formerly of Ireland, d. at Mount Erie, Ill., Oct. 30, 1867, in his 67th year.

JEWELL, Dr. Wilson, physician and author, d. at Philadelphia, Nov. 4, 1867, a. 67.

JEWETT, Freeborn G., judge of the court of appeals, settled at Skaneateles, N. Y., about 1815, as a lawyer, became surrogate of Onondaga co., Feb. 11, 1824, and held till 1831. In 1826 he was in assembly, and in 1831–3 was in congress, but declined reëlection, and March 5, 1845, he was appointed a puisne justice of the supreme court, and held about two years. In 1847 he was elected judge of the court of appeals, drew the term of 2 years; was reëlected in 1849 but resigned in 1853. He d. at Skaneateles, Jan. 27, 1858, a. 68. (*Syracuse Standard*, Jan. 28, 1858; *Auburn D. Amer.*, Jan. 30.)

JOHNSON, Alexander Bryan, A.M., son of Bryan, an eminent banker; b. at Gosport, Eng., May 29, 1786. Removed to Utica in 1801. Was in business with his father until 1809; studied law and was admitted as a counselor, but never practiced. In 1816 he became a banker at first as cashier and secretary of the Utica Insurance Company, a banking institution whose charter he procured, and afterwards as president of the Ontario Branch Bank of Utica. The latter position he occupied from Sept., 1819 until July, 1857. He d. Sept. 9, 1867. Besides a volume of political papers made up of newspaper contributions, he was the author of several works relating chiefly to his philosophy of human knowledge, viz.: "The Philosophy of Human Knowledge, or a Treatise on Language," "The meaning of Words Analyzed." "The Physiology of the Senses," "Deep Sea Soundings, or the Ultimate Analysis of Human Knowledge," etc., also "Religion in its Relation to the Present Life" and "Papers in Banking."

JOHNSON, COL. AMES, d. at Redfield, N. Y.; Dec. 7, 1858, a. nearly 100 years, b. at Middletown, Conn., Sept. 16th, 1860; and served in the revolution.

JOHNSON, AMOS, b. in Middletown, Ct., Sept. 16, 1760; served in the revolution; settled early at Redfield, N. Y., and d. there Dec. 7, 1858, in his 99th year.

JOHNSON, AUGUSTUS, was b. at Amboy, N. J., about 1730; came to R. I., young; studied law with Matthew Robinson and settled in Newport in the practice. In May 1757, he was appointed attorney General and held 9 years. In 1765, he accepted the office of stamp master, against the entreaties of his friends and was compelled by the mob to resign; while the British held Newport in the war he had several civil appointments, and in 1779, he withdrew with the enemy to N. Y., and his property was confiscated. He received a pension from the British government until his death. The town of Johnson R. I., was named from him in 1759. (*W. Updike's Memorial of R. I. Bar*, p. 65.)

JOHNSON BENJAMIN PIERCE, b. Nov. 30, 1793, in Canaan, N. Y.; grad. in 1813, at Union Coll.; studied law and settled in Rome, N. Y. was in Assembly in 1827, 8, 9; took a deep interest in agricultural affairs. Published with Elon Comstock at Rome the *Central New York Farmer*. In 1845 became cor. sec. of the State Agricultural Soc.; and in 1845 its president; traveled in England and in 1847 entered upon the duties of corresponding sec. of the State Agricultural Soc., and held till his death, which occurred at Albany, April 12, 1869. (*Memorial by Gen. M. R. Patrick*, 1870.)

JOHNSON, BRYAN, b. in England 1740; removed to Old Ft. Schuyler (now Utica), July 4, 1797. Was a prominent and sucessful merchant; retired in 1809, and d. April 12, 1824.

JOHNSON, DR. DANIEL, killed in a duel with Thomas F. Jones at Bladensburg, Md., Feb. 2, 1846.

JOHNSON, EDWARD, a pioneer of Turin, N. Y.; d. in Martinsburgh, N. Y., March 19, 1851, at an advanced age.

JOHNSON, EDWARD a confederate general, d. at Richmond, Va., March 2, 1873. He was b. May 12, 1816, in Virginia, and was graduated in 1838 at West Point, with Gens. Beauregard, Hardee, and others of the confederate service, and Gen. McDowell of the United States army. He was appointed second lieutenant in the 6th regiment of infantry and served with credit in the Seminole and Mexican wars, attaining the rank of brevet major, and receiving a valuable sword from his native state; in 1861 he resigned his commission and joined the confederate service, attaining in a short time the rank of brigadier-general. Just before the Gettysburg campaign he was assigned to the command of Stonewall

Jackson's old division, and took part in the fighting in the Shenandoah Valley, in the Wilderness, and in Tennessee, where he was made prisoner and confined in Fort Adams until the close of the war. Since the war he was engaged in farming and mercantile pursuits.

JOHNSON, FRANCIS, revolutionary colonel, sheriff of Phila.; b. in Pa., left the law to join Wayne's regiment and upon his promotion commanded 5th Pa. regt., with which he was present in many engagements; he held several offices of trust, and became high sheriff of Phila. co. He d. in Phila., Feb. 22, 1815, in his 67th year. (*Rogers's Am. Biog.; Simpson's Eminent Philadelphians.*)

JOHNSON, FRANCIS, one of the oldest members of the bar in Louisville, Ky.; d. in that city May 14, 1842.

JOHNSON, G., a well known citizen of Mobile, Ala.; d. Aug. 28, 1873, on board the steamer Yazoo, after leaving Philadelphia for New Orleans.

JOHNSON, JEROMUS, d. in Goshen, N. Y., Sept. 7, 1846; was a representative in congress from the city of New York, from Brooklyn, from 1825 to 1829.

JOHNSON, JOHN, b. in Pa., in 1775, accompanied Wayne's army to the west in 1793, was long an Indian agent and made the Wyandot treaty in 1841–2; he was pres. of the Ohio Hist. Soc. at the time of his death, which occurred at Washington, D. C., Feb., 1861. (*Hist. Mag.*, v, 128.)

JOHNSON, REV. JOHN BARENT, b. at Brooklyn, N. Y., March 3, 1769, son of Barent G.; grad. at Columbia Coll. about 1792; was licensed by the Classis of N. Y., April 21, 1775, and June 5, 1796, was ordained as colleague pastor at the R. P. D. Ch. Albany. In 1802, he was called to Brooklyn, where he d. Aug. 29, 1803. He was a man of great eloquence, and preached a funeral discourse on death of Washington before the N. Y., legislature. (*Rogers's Hist. Discourse*, p. 35; *Munsell's Annals.*)

JOHNSON, ELD. JOHN F., brother of Richard M. Johnson, was once judge of the court of appeals in Kentucky, and member of congress from 1821 to 1825. He was afterwards for thirty years preacher of the gospel without a salary, and d. in Lexington, Mo., Dec., 18, 1857.

JOHNSON, CAPT. J. H., of the *Louisville Courier*, d. at Louisville, Ky., May, 12, 1870, a. 39.

JOHNSON, JOHN MERCER, member of the dominion parliament; d. Nov. 9, 1868, a. 50; b. in Liverpool; had been solicitor gen.; p. m. gen. and atty. gen. and speaker of the house.

JOHNSON, JOSEPH, a revolutionary soldier; d. in Wilkes co., Ga., a. 98.

JOHNSON, COL. JOSEPH E., d. at St. Francisville, La., Dec., 21, 1838, late president of the senate of Louisania.

JOHNSON, LAWRENCE, type founder and stereotyper in Philadelphia; d. April 26, 1860, a. about 60. (*Vincent's Semi An. Reg.*, pp. 333, 345.)

JOHNSON, MARMADUKE, early printer in Cambridge, Mass. He undertook to print the Indian Bible translated by the Rev. John Eliot, but was dismissed before the end of the work. (*See Thomas's Hist. Printing.*)

JOHNSON, NOADIAH, d. at Albany, N. Y., April 4, 1839; a member of the New York senate from Delaware co., and member of congress in 1833–5.

JOHNSON, OSGOOD, late principal of the Phillips Academy at Andover, Mass ; d. in that town, May 9, 1837, in his 34th year; grad. at Dartmouth in 1828, and became principal at Andover in 1832.

JOHNSON, SAMUEL, LL.D., third pres. of Columbia Coll., son of Samuel J., 1st pres. C. Coll., grad. at Yale in 1744, studied law, and in 1784 was elected to congress; was appointed pres. of Columbia Coll. Nov. 12, 1787, and held till July 16, 1800, when he resigned from old age and returned to Stratford, Ct., where he d. a. 93, nearly twenty years after leaving N. Y.; while pres. he was first senator for Ct., in congress. (*Moore's Hist. Columbia Coll.*)

JOHNSON, WILLIAM COST, d. at Washington, D. C., April 15, 1860; b. in Maryland in 1806, served several years in the state legislature and from 1837 to 1843, in congress. Was again in the state legislature, and in the convention for revising the constitution. (*Vincent's Semi-An. Register*, p. 294.)

JOHNSON, WILLIAM, H. d. at Cambridge city, Ind., April 28, 1839; judge of the Wayne criminal circuit court, at the time of his death, and a prominent lawyer of Indiana.

JOHNSON, WM. R., a native of North Carolina; resided mostly in Virginia. He was styled the "Napoleon of the Turf;" he d. at Mobile Ala., Feb. 10, 1849, a. 70 y. (*Stryker's Am. Reg.*)

JOHNSON, COL. WITTER, a patriot of the revolution; d. at Sidney Plains, N. Y.; Nov. 4, 1839, a. 86; was a lieut. in Col. Willet's regiment and was an active officer on the frontiers.

JOHNSTON, CHARLES C., member of the 22d congress from Va.; d. at Washington June 18, 1832.

JOHNSTON, EDWARD W., d. at St. Louis Mo., Dec. 9, 1867; in his 68th year; b. in Va., and had been a prof. of history and belles letters in the Uni. of S. C., and editor or asssociate editor of the *Richmond Whig, National Intelligencer, N. Y. Times, St. Louis Intelligencer and Leader.*

JOHNSTON, JAMES, first printer in Georgia, (1762); d. Oct. 1808, a. 70.

JOHNSTON, WILLIAM F., ex-gov. of Pennsylvania; d. at Pittsburg, Pa., Oct. 25, 1872.

JOHNSTON, WILLIAM S., judge of the parish of Rapides, La.; d. at Alexandria, La., Sept. 20, 1839, a. 24.

JOHNY APPLESEED. (*See Chapman, Jonathan.*)

JONES, AARON, pugilist, and trainer of Heenan in his fight with Sayres, in England; d. Feb. 16, 1869, at Leavenworth, Kan.

JONES, REV. DABNEY, prominent temperance lecturer in Georgia; settled on Shoal creek, Ga., in 1828; preached the first sermon at Newnan, and began lecturing in 1832. From that time to 1847, he lectured at most of the superior courts of Ga. (*White's Hist. Ga.*, p. 414.)

JONES, DR. DANIEL T., of Baldwinsville, N. Y.; d. March 29, 1861, a. 60.

JONES, DAVID R. FLOYD, in assembly from New York in 1841–2–3, and from Queens co., in 1857; in the state senate in 1844–5–6–7; secretary of state in 1860–1, and lieut. gov. of N. Y., in 1863–4; d. at South Oyster Bay, N. Y., Jan. 9, 1871.

JONES, COL. DE GARMO, d. in Detroit, Mich., Nov. 14, 1846, a. 59; was a member of the territorial council before the admission of Michigan as a state, and afterwards member of the city council, mayor, and state senator.

JONES, ELEAZER, d. at Worcester, Mass., April 14, 1843, a. 89; grad. at Harvard in 1778.

JONES, JAMES, b. in Md., went young to Ga., settled at Savannah as a lawyer; was often in the legislature, and was in cong. in 1799–1801; he d. at Washington, Jan. 12, 1801.

JONES, GEN. JAMES J., of New York city; d. in Basle, Switzerland, Sept. 4, 1858; he was active in the concerns of the charitable institutions of New York city.

JONES, JOEL, d. in Farmington, Me., Feb. 4, 1860, in his 77th year.

JONES, JOHN COFFIN, b. at Newbury, Mass., grad. at Harvard in 1768, and settled as a merchant at Boston; he was incidentally concerned in politics; in 1788 was in the gen. court and in the state senate; his commercial knowledge led to his appointment to a convention of states for increasing the powers of congress, which led to the fed. convention of 1787; he d. in 1829. (*Bradford's N. E. Biog.*)

JONES, JOHN H., d. at Leicester, Livingston co., N. Y., Jan. 4, 1856, a. 85; was youngest brother of Capt. Horatio Jones, Indian interpreter of former times and a pioneer settler of Livingston co., of which in 1821 he was judge. (*Genesee Republican.*)

JONES, REV. J. H., D.D., d. in Philadelphia, Dec. 22, 1868, a. 68; was pastor of the 6th Presb. ch. from 1840 to 1860, and after that, was supt. of the society for relief of superannuated clergymen.

JONES, J. M., d. Dec. 14, 1851, in San Jose, Cal., United States district judge for the southern district of California; was a native of Scott county, Ky., but resided several years in New Orleans where he practiced his profession of the law before going to California; was a member of the convention which formed the state constitution.

JONES, RANDAL, b. in Columbia co., Ga., Aug. 19, 1786; went in 1810, to Wilkinson co., Miss. ter.; in 1812 entered the army as a volunteer, and in 1814 became captain; he went to the Sabine in 1814, engaged in Indian trade in Texas, shared largely in the rough vicissitudes of that country, and was concerned with Lafitte; he was elected to the consultation, served in the Ayuntamiento; and was at the Bradburn affair in 1835; he resided many years in Fort Bend co., Tex. (*Texas Almanac*, 1857, p. 137.)

JONES, STEPHEN, d. in Ashby, Mass, April 30, 1842, a. 66; formerly a member of the general court of Massachusetts.

JONES, SYBIL, wife of Eli Jones, of China, Me.; d. Dec. 4, 1874. During 40 years she was a popular preacher in the society of Friends, of which her husband was also a distinguished member; she visited with him the new republic of Liberia, and afterward traveled in Europe, whence they made two temporary tours to Egypt and the Holy Land. Mrs. Jones preached eloquently, and found attentive hearers among her co-religionists, both at home and abroad.

JONES, WALTER RESTORED, financier, son of John Jones, b. at Cold Spring, N. Y., April 15, 1793; prominent in all benevolent objects, and many years pres. of the Atlantic Mutual Insurance Co., N. Y.; d. April 7, 1855, a. 62. The first Atlantic Ins. Co. of which he was v. pres, ended in 1826; in 1829 with J. L. Hale, he started the second, with $350,000 capital; in 1842 it was reorganized on the mutual plan, and under his presidency, grew into great favor; for 10 y., from Jan., 1844, its annual average was over 33 p. c., and in $11\frac{1}{2}$ y., its business profits were $6,092,-571; he was concerned in manufactures and whaling at Cold Spring, Suffolk co.; the Life Saving Benevolent Asso., found in him a zealous friend, and the life boat stations on the coast were the result of these efforts. (*Hunt's Lives of Am. Merchants*, i, 415.)

JONES, William Carey, son-in-law of Thomas H. Benton, and a prominent lawyer of San Francisco, Cal.; d. Nov. 5, 1867.

JOSE, Louis D., commonly called Old Portuguese Joe; burned in a hotel of which he kept the bar, at New Orleans, La., Nov. 1, 1842, a. about 70; was captain of the Maintop, on board of Com. McDonough's ship Saratoga, in the naval battle before Plattsburg; the flag being shot away, he mounted the rigging, and nailed the flag to the mast, for which the public thanks of the commodore were given when the fight was over.

JOSSLYN, Dr. Charles, settled in Greene, N. Y., in 1805, where he was physician 25 years; p. m. 20 years, and for a long time co. judge and magistrate; d. in Windsor, N. Y., in 1856. (*Chenango American*, Jan. 1858.)

JOUOTT, Capt. Mathew, Va., d. Nov. 15, 1775.

JOURDAN, John, supt. of N. Y. police; d. at New York, Oct. 10, 1870, a. 39.

JOYNER, Col. Andrew, d. in Halifax co., N. S., Sept. 20, 1856, a 71; he was an officer in the war of 1812, and served in both houses of the general assembly, being several times speaker of the senate.

JOYNES, Thomas R. Sen., a lawyer and member of the Virginia state constitutional convention of 1829–30; d. in Accomac co., Va., Sept. 12, 1858, a. 69.

JUAREZ, Gen. Don Benito, president of the republic of Mexico; d. July 22, 1872.

JUDD, Rev. Bethel, b. at Watertown, Ct., in 1776; grad. at Yale in 1797; was ordained deacon by Bp. Moore in 1798; was rector of St. James ch. New London, Ct., 15 y.; a pioneer of the Ep. ch. in N. C., and a missionary at St. Augustine, Fl. He was an early president of St. John's Coll. Annapolis, and d. at Wilmington, Del., April 18, 1858. (*Hist. Mag.* ii, 215.)

JUDD, CHAUNCEY, was abducted by a gang of tories from Naugatuck, Ct., in 1778; narrowly escaped being murdered; was conveyed to Long Island, rescued by his friends, and d. at Waterbury, Ct., in 1823, a. 53. (*Hist. Mag.* iii, 263.)

JUDD, Dr. G. P., at Honolulu, Sandwich Islands, July 12, 1873; he was b. at Paris, New York state, in 1803; when he was 25 years of age he went to the Sandwich Islands as physician to the American Mission. Twelve years afterward he accompanied Commodore Wilkes in an exploring tour through the islands; in 1842, Dr. Judd resigned his position in the Mission and became recorder and interpreter to King Kamehameha III; in the following year, finding the government was resolved to abrogate laws for the maintenance of moral order, he dissolved his connection with the government; but he was soon called by the king to constitute a ministry; in this ministry he selected for himself the department of the interior. In 1849, when the Princes Liholiho and Lot made their journey to Europe to reärrange the relations with foreign powers, they were accompanied by Dr. Judd. His official career lasted about ten years, during the most eventful period in the history of the island; the influence which he exerted was most beneficial for the country of his adoption.

JUDD, PHILIP, serjeant in Capt. Peck's co., killed in invasion of the Niagara frontier, Dec. 30, 1813.

JUDD, SYLVLSTER, for many years editor and part proprietor of the *Hampshire Gazette;* d. at Northampton, Mass., April 18, 1860, a. 71.

JUDSON, ANDREW T., d. in Hartford, Conn. March 17, 1853, a. 67; U. S. district judge for Connecticut; b. at Eastford, Conn., Nov. 29, 1784; was admitted to the bar in 1806, and removed to Montipelier, Vt.; returned to his native town, and in 1809, settled permanently in Canterbury. In 1819, was made U. S. attorney for Windham co., and held for 14 y.; served in both houses of the legislature, was in congress from 1835 to 1839, and was then chosen district judge, and held this office till his death.

JUDSON, DAVID C., b. in Washington, Ct., in 1786; settled in St. Lawrence co., N. Y., in 1808; was employed for a time in teaching and afterwards as deputy sheriff and sheriff; in 1818, he served in assembly, and in 1822 in the state senate, his term being cut short by the adoption of a new constitution. He was one of the county judges from 1829 to 1840, and many years a trustee of Ogdensburgh village; he was prominent in public affairs, acquired a very large estate, and was liberal in aiding various objects of local improvement; he died at Ogdensburgh, N. Y., May, 5, 1875, in his 89th year. (*Notice and Portrait in Hough's Hist. St. Law. and Franklin Cos.*)

JULIAND, JOSEPH, b. at Lyons, France, Jan. 17, 1749, entered the mercantile marine and made several voyages as captain of a vessel. He settled in Greenfield, Mass., in 1788, and in 1798 joined a French colony at Greene on the Chenango, where he d. Oct. 13, 1821. (*Chenango American*, Dec., 1857.)

JULICK, ABRAM J., d. at Cranberry, N. J., Feb. 25, 1842, a. 87; a revolutionary soldier.

KAIGHN, JOSEPH, d. in Gloucester co., N. J., Feb. 23, 1841, a. 67; was of the society of Friends, and for several years in the legislature of New Jersey.

KALBFLEISCH, MARTIN, ex-mayor of Brooklyn, N. Y.; d. in that city, Feb. 12, 1873, a. 69. (*See Stiles's Brooklyn*, with portrait.)

KANE, ELIAS, navy agent, formerly a prominent merchant of New York; d. at Washington, D. C., Oct. 3, 1840, in his 65th year.

KANE, ELIAS K., senator from Illinois in congress; d. at Washington, D. C., Dec. 12, 1835; b. in New York, went in early life to Tennessee, and finally settled at Kaskaskia, Ill., in 1815; was in the convention of 1818 for preparing a state constitution and became first secretary of state; was afterwards in the legislature and from 1825 till his death, in the federal senate.

KANE, JOHN K., b. in Albany, May 16, 1795; d. Feb. 21, 1858, in Philadelphia, grad. at Yale, and became a lawyer and prominent in public affairs; was a distinguished politician of the democratic school; in 1845, was appointed attorney general of the state, and in 1846, became judge of the U. S. district court, for the eastern dist. of Pennsylvania. (*Simpson's Eminent Philadelphians*, with portrait.)

KANE, DR. JOSEPH, a practitioner in Philadelphia; d. March 3, 1860.

KASEY, REV. RICHARD, F. W. Bap. preacher; b. in Levant, Me., 1795, joined the Methodists in 1822, and the Bap. in 1837; he preached in Maine many years, and d. at Cox Creek, Iowa, Aug. 12, 1855, a. 60. (*F. W. Bap. Reg.*, 1857, p. 89.)

KAUFMAN, DAVID S., member of congress from Texas; d. at Washington, Jan. 31, 1851, aged 38 years; he was a native of Cumberland, Pa.; grad. at Princeton Coll. in 1833, studied law with Gen. Quitman at Natchez, and settled at Nacogdoches, Texas, in 1837, and in 1838 was elected to the Texan congress, of which he was twice chosen speaker; in 1843 he was a member of the senate, and after the adjournment of the Texan congress in 1845, was appointed chargé to the U. S; he was one of the first members elected from Texas to the congress of the U. S. (*Stryker's Am. Reg.*, vi, 212; *Am. Almanac*, 1852, p. 399.)

KAY, JAMES, d. in Philadelphia, Pa., April 22, 1856, in his 52d year; native of England, became an extensive publisher in Philadelphia, especially in the departments of law and medicine. (*Simpson's Eminent Philadelphians.*)

KEAN, CHARLES JOHN, tragedian; visited the U. S. in 1830, 1839, 1845, and 1863; d. in London, Eng., Jan. 21, 1868.

KEAN, JAMES, d. in Pa., Aug. 20, 1859, a. 105 y.

KEATING, JOHN, d. in Philadelphia, Pa., May 19, 1856, a. 96; b. in France, came to America with some thirty noble French families, after the death of Louis XVI, and settled at Asylum, near Towanda, Pa., was grandson of Jeffries K., who raised a troop of horse during the siege of Limerick.

KEELER, REV. EZRA, D.D., pres. of Wittenberg Coll., Springfield, Ohio; d. Jan. 3, 1849.

KEENE, LAURA, a well known actress, d. at Mount Clair, N. J.; Nov. 6, 1873, a. 43.

KEENE, COL. RICHARD R., of New Orleans, d. at St. Louis, Mo., Sept., 1839; b. in Maryland; grad. at Princeton, in 1795; was U. S. attorney for the territory of Orleans, and afterwards passed several years in Spain, during the war with Bonaparte; where he bore the title of colonel in the Spanish service.

KEEP, HENRY, d. in New York city, July 30, 1869; b. in Adams, Jeff. co., N. Y., June 22, 1818; was in boyhood a canal driver; became an exchange broker at 19; established several banks, under general banking law of New York, and in 1854, went to New York, where he became extensively engaged in stock speculation and the management of rail roads; became an important stockholder and president of the Cleveland & Toledo, Michigan Southern, N. Y. Central, and Chicago and Northwestern rail roads, all of which under his management prospered; buried at Watertown, N. Y.

30

KEESE, Theodore, a native of New York and most of his life a resident of that city, and a successful merchant; removed to Cooperstown, N. Y., and d. there Sept. 27, 1858, a. 58. (*Livermore's Cooperstown*, p. 165.)

KELL, Dr. Thomas, d. at Baltimore, Md., March 8, 1846, in his 74th year; he was a native of Baltimore, and began law practice in August, 1796; was attorney gen. of Md., in 1824, and until appointed a judge of the Baltimore county court in 1827; in 1833, he was appointed clerk of Baltimore co., and held till 1845.

KELLER, Charles Theodore, ll.d., editor of *Die Freie Presse*, Philadelphia, d. in that city, Nov. 1, 1870, a. 68; b. in 1807, in Altdorf, Saxony.

KELLEY, Alfred, b. Middletown, Conn., Nov. 7, 1789; d. Columbus, O., Dec. 2d, 1863; emigrated from Lowville, N. Y., to Cleveland, O., 1810; admitted to the bar and made prosecuting att'y, Cuyahoga co., O., on the day of his majority; member of Ohio legislature, 1814–22–36–44 and 1857; com'r to survey and construct the Ohio canal 1822–30, with double the number of locks in the Erie canal, it was built at a cost of $4,000 per mile less, and also below the estimates; his pay was three dollars per day. As state fund commissioner in 1840–44, when the party in power proposed to repudiate the bonded debt of Ohio, acting in connection with the late Gov. Brough, his opponent in politics, the public credit was saved; he raised half a million on his personal responsibility for state purposes; in 1819, originated a bill to abolish imprisonment for debt; in 1844, another to establish the State Bank of Ohio; in Ohio he was best known as the father of the Ohio canal.

KELLOGG, Daniel, b. in Williamstown, Mass., April 19, 1780; was admitted to the bar in 1800, settled at Auburn, in 1802, and at Skaneateles in 1803; in 1813 was appointed dist. attorney for four counties, and held for three years; in 1818 was elected pres. of the Bank of Auburn, and held till his death, which occurred at Skaneateles May 4, 1836. (*Clark's Onondaga* ii, 300, with a portrait.)

KELLOGG, L. C., ex-judge supreme court of Vermont; d. at Benson, Vt., Nov. 26, 1871, a. 55.

KELLOGG, Spencer, b. at Williamstown, Mass., Sept. 19, 1786, removed with his parents to Otsego co., N. Y., in 1794; was a merchant at Plainfield, from 1813, and at Utica from 1825; in 1841 was mayor of Utica; d. Dec. 31, 1871.

KELLUM, John, an eminent architect of New York; d. at Hempstead, N. Y., July 25, 1871.

KELLY, Daniel, judge, b. in Norwich, Ct., Nov. 27, 1775; was a pioneer settler and mill owner at Lowville, N. Y., in 1798, and first judge of Lewis co., from 1805 to 1809; he moved to Cleveland, O., in 1814, and was p. m., and co. treas.; he d. there Aug. 7, 1831, a. 79. Alfred, Irad, Datas and Thomas Kelly of Ohio were his sons. (*Hough's Hist. of Lewis Co. N. Y.*, p. 144.)

KELLY, James, ex-post master of New York city, from 1863 to 1869; d. Jan. 10, 1871, a. 59.

KELLY, MICHAEL J., journalist, d. in New York city, Jan. 27, 1873, a. 32.

KELLY, WILLIAM, a wealthy and distinguished citizen of Rhinebeck, N. Y.; formerly a merchant of the city of New York, and afterwards an agriculturist, and prominently connected with the State Agricultural Soc.; was state senator in 1856–7, and democratic candidate for governor in 1860; trustee of several colleges and benevolent institutions, in the welfare of which he took much interest; d. at Forbay, England, Jan. 14, 1872. (*Historical Record*, i, 238; *Regent's Report*, 1873, p. 643.)

KELSEY, EBER, a pioneer millwright from Killingworth, Ct., to Lewis co., N. Y.; d. at Cape Vincent, N. Y., Aug. 18, 1839, a. 76.

KEMBAL, REV. HEBER C., a mormon leader; b. in 1801; embraced the mormon faith in 1832, and remained an active member of this church through all its vicissitudes till his death at Salt Lake city, June 23, 1868; he was uneducated, coarse, cunning and revengeful, and an especial advocate of polygamy.

KEMBLE, REV. DAVID T., senior pastor of the first church in Ipswich, Mass.; d. Feb. 3, 1860, in his 78th year, and the 54th of his ministry.

KENAN, COL. THOMAS, b. in Duplin co., N. C., in 1771; in 1799, was in house of commons, and served in state senate in 1804; was in congress from North Carolina from 1805 to 1811; removed to Alabama and served for many years in the legislature; d. near Selma, Ala., Oct. 22, 1843.

KENDALL, REV. JAMES, D.D., was b. in Sterling, Mass., in 1769; grad. at Harv., in 1796; was a teacher in Phillips Academy in Andover; studied theology; was a tutor of Greek in Harvard, in 1798–9; was ordained in Plymouth in 1800, and sole pastor of the society for 48 years, when a colleague was settled with him; he published fifteen sermons at different times; d. at Plymouth, Mass., March 17, 1859, a. 89.

KENDALL, JAMES BROWN, a young man of excellent character and great promise; grad. at Harvard in 1854; taught at Portsmouth, N. H., studied law, and had just settled at Worcester; d. in Framingham, Mass., Oct. 9, 1859, a. 25.

KENDALL, JONAS, d. in Leominster, Mass., Oct. 22, 1844, a. 87, was 13 years in one or the other branch of the legislature, and in 1819–21, in congress.

KENDALL, JOSEPH G., d. at Worcester, Mass., Oct. 2, 1847, son of Jonas K. of Leominster, Mass.; grad. at Harvard in 1810; tutor there from 1812 to 19; from 1829 to 1833, in congress from the northern dist. of Worcester co., was afterwards clerk of the courts.

KENNARD, NATHANIEL, patriot of the revolution, volunteered in a Massachusetts regiment one year, was captured on a privateer and held 2½ years in prison, was sent to France in a cartel, and served with Paul Jones on the Bon Homme Richard; he was sent on a prize to France, was again captured, escaped in Jamaica; he returned to America just before the peace, continued a shipmaster till 1812 when he was appointed to command a revenue cutter through the war; he was then made inspector of the customs at Portsmouth, till his death June 24, 1823, a. 68 y. (*Rogers's Am. Biog.*)

KENNEDY, ANDREW, b. in Ohio, in 1810, had no advantages for education in his youth, but afterwards studied law, and was in the Indiana, state senate, and from 1841 to 1847 in congress; d. at Muncietown, Ind., Dec. 31, 1847.

KENNEDY, DAVID, was captain in the British army in 1747, served under Lord Loudon in 1757, and Abercrombie in 1758; in 1759, he was sent to St. Francis with a flag of truce, and detained, this brought down a severe chastisement to the Indians; he soon after sold out. (*Com. Wilson's Orderly Book*, 34.)

KENNEDY, JOHN, one of the associate brothers of the Supreme Court of Pennsylvania; d. at Philadelphia, Pa., Aug. 1848, a. 71.

KENNEDY, JOHN A., ex-supt. of New York Metropolitan Police, in the city of New York; d. in that city June 30, 1873, a. 70.

KENNEDY, MRS. MARGARET, a pioneer of Monroe co., N. Y.; d. at West Webster, N. Y., June, 1860, a. 97; widow of Robert K., who in 1805 refused to purchase land where the city of Rochester now stands.

KENNEDY, SAMUEL, surgeon, Penn., killed in the revolution, June 28, 1778.

KENSETT, JOHN FREDERICK, artist; d. Dec. 14, 1872, in New York city; b. in Cheshire, Conn., March 22, 1818; and was apprenticed to his uncle, Alfred Daggett, an engraver of bank-note vignettes. The young artist experimented with oil colors in his spare hours, and in 1840 went to England to study painting. On his arrival in London he became known to Durand, Casilear, and Rossiter, and shared their studies. For five years he studied oil-painting, supporting himself by engraving. At the end of this time he exhibited a view of Windsor Castle in the exhibition of the society of British artists, at the rooms in Suffolk-st., Pall Mall East. It is the custom of this association to have a lottery at a guinea a head, and the holders of the two lucky numbers are allowed to choose a picture each as a prize. The winner of the first prize on this occasion selected Kensett's picture, which was admitted by every one to be the best landscape painting in the collection. A sketching tour down the Rhine, over the Alps, among the Italian lakes, yielding abundant fruit in a well-filled portfolio, and upon his arrival at Rome he began to paint with earnestness and power. In 1848 he sent to the Academy of Design his landscape View on the Anio, and a fanciful sketch, entitled The Shrine. He was unanimously elected associate, and the following year was made Academician. In 1850 he returned to New-York, and began a series of landscapes of the mountain, river, and lake scenery of New-York and the Eastern States, with marine views, which found eager purchasers. There is scarcely an American art collection of note that is not graced by one of his pictures. In 1859 he was appointed a member of the national art commission, and engaged to superintend the ornamentation of the national capitol. His works were highly esteemed in France, Belgium, and England, as well as in this country.

KENT, REV. BENJAMIN, was b. in what is now Somerville, Mass.; in 1794; grad. at Harvard in 1820; settled as a pastor at Duxbury, Mass., in 1826, and in 1833, removed to Roxbury, where he taught a private school for young ladies several years; he was afterwards librarian of the Roxbury Atheneum, and d. Aug. 6, 1859, a. 65.

KENT, JACOB, d. at Caldwell, N. J., June 2, 1840, a. 87; a soldier of the revolution, leaving 268 descendants.

KENTNER, JOHN P., a pioneer settler of Turin, N. Y.; d. in that town, Nov. 11, 1836, a. 86.

KENYON, REV. WILLIAM COLGROVE, b. in Hopkinton, R. I., Oct. 14, 1812; did not graduate, but received the degree of A.M., from Union College in 1844; became a teacher at Alfred, N. Y., and in 1857, became president of Alfred University; was compelled to suspend labors by sickness; went to Europe; and d. in London, June 7, 1867. (*Regent's Report*, 1868, p. 712.)

KERR, REV. GEORGE, b. about 1815 in the north of Ireland, of Scotch ancestry, removed at nine to Canada and thence to Plattsburgh, N. Y.; and to Windham, and Hunter, N. Y.; grad. at Williams Coll.; and at the Union Theological Sem. N. Y, in 1844; became prin. of the Delaware Lit. Inst. at Franklin, N. Y.; and remained 16 y.; in 1860 became prof. of Math., in the Ag. Coll., at Ovid till it closed; was then prin. of the Jefferson Co. Inst. at Watertown, N. Y., 2 y.; and at Cooperstown Seminary; d. Feb. 27, 1867, a. 52. (*Regent's Report*, 1868, p. 709.)

KERR, JOHN LEEDS, d. at Easton, Md., Feb. 21, 1844, a. 64, late U. S. senator, and a leading member of the bar of the eastern shore; b. at Greenbury Point near Annapolis, Jan. 15, 1780; grad. at St John's Coll. in 1799; studied law, and was in cong. from Maryland from 1825 to 1829, and from 1831 to 1833; was in the U. S. senate 1841 to 1843; before entering congress he was the agent of Maryland in the prosecution of militia claims against the United States.

KETCHAM, HIRAM, d. at New York, Sept. 16, 1870. a. 78.

KETCHUM, GEORGE H., of the Cincinnati bar; d. May 17, 1858, at Cincinnati, O.

KEY, EDMUND, many years one of the judges of the circuit court of Maryland; d. in Prince George's co., Md., Feb. 19, 1857, a. 86.

KEY, JOHN, first b. white child of Philadelphia, in 1682, in a cave at N. W. cor. of Vine and Water st.; he d. July, 1767, resided in Chester co. (*Simpson's Eminent Philadelphians.*)

KEYES, EDWARD L., edited for many years a paper at Dedham, Mass., and served in the state senate, and as a member of the executive council; he d. in Somerville, Mass., June 6, 1859.

KEYES, JOHN, d. in Concord, Mass., Aug. 29, 1844, a. 57; b. in Westford, 1789; grad. at Dartmouth in 1809; was admitted to the Middlesex bar in 1812, and practiced at Concord till his death; he was a delegate to the convention of 1820; a representative from Concord in general court, in 1822–3, and in 1823–30 in the state senate, afterwards again a representative, and for a time speaker.

KEYES, PERLEY, state senator, b. at Ackworth, N. H., Feb. 24, 1774; settled at Watertown, N. Y., in 1808 and in 1815, with Jason Fairbanks evinced great shrewdness and enterprise in recovering money stolen by paymaster Whittlesey; he was sheriff in 1808–12; and very influential in the senate where he served in 1814–7 and 1824–7, and in 1816 was one of the council of appointment; he d. at Watertown, May 13, 1834. (*Hough's Hist. Jeff. Co. N. Y.*, p. 436.)

KEYES, Samuel Whitney, d. in Highgate, Vt., Feb. 18, 1851, a. 66; was an enterprising merchant.

KEYSER, Elhanon W., d. in Philadelphia, Pa., Feb. 17, 1860; was an active member of the historical, agricultural, and other local societies. (*Vincent's Semi-An. Register*, p. 115.)

KEYSER, Rev. Peter, descended from one of the early settlers of Pennsylvania, who came from Amsterdam in 1688, via. N. Y.; was a clergyman, and active in various public charities; d. in Germantown where he was b. May 21, 1849, a. 83. (*Simpson's Emineni Philadelphians*, with portraits.)

KIBBY, Epaphras, d. at Mobile, Ala., Sept. 15, 1839, a. 27; one of the editors of the *Mobile Register*.

KILGOUR, Charles J., judge of the county court of Montgomery co. Md.; was killed about twenty miles from his residence at Rockville, Md. Aug. 1837, by being thrown from his carriage.

KILGOUR, John, a native of England, and for many years engaged in banking in Cincinnati, O.; d. April 18, 1858, a. 60.

KILHAN, Thomas, a pioneer settler from Westfield Mass., to Turin, N. Y.; d. April 25, 1825, a. 73, from an opiate given in over dose by a drunken physician, his wife Mary d. March 18, 1845, a. 93.

KIMBALL, Rev. David Tenney, was b. in Bradford, Mass., in 1782; grad. at Harvard in 1803, and was settled at Ipswich, in 1806, where he filled the pastoral office for nearly forty years, without a colleague; he d. there Feb. 3, 1860, a. 77.

KIMBALL, Rev. Reuel, installed as pastor of Presb. ch. Leyden, N. Y., 1817; and pastor till 1826, d. at East Hampton, Mass., Oct. 1, 1847, a. 67.

KIMBALL, Richard, was constructor of the Middlesex canal, and was consulted by Gov. Clinton of N. Y., in the beginning of the N. Y. canals, parts of which he personally directed; he died at Mount Lebanon, N. H., Feb. 12, 1860, in his 92d year; he was engaged in the construction of the Middlesex canal, Mass. (*Hist. Mag.* iv, 127.)

KINDELTON, Rev. Adam, Founder of the Catholic Association for the relief of destitute male orphans; d. at New Orleans, La., Oct. 14, 1837.

KING, Adam, member of congress from Pennsylvania, from 1827, to 1833; d. May 1835.

KING, Alexander, ex-member of state senate of Pennsylvania in 1847–50; d. at Bedford, Pa., Jan. 10, 1871, a. 76; was elected judge of the 16th judicial district, in 1864.

KING, Austin A., ex-governor of Missouri, d. April 22, 1870, at St. Louis, Mo., a. 70.

KING, Daniel Putnam, d. July 25, 1850, in Danvers, Mass., a. 50; grad. at Harvard in 1823; served several years in the Massachusetts legislature, and in 1843 was elected to congress, where he was continued till his death. (*Am. Almanac*, 1851, p. 316.)

KING, Gen. Edward, a distinguished lawyer, and formerly speaker of the house of representatives of Ohio, d. at Cincinnati, O., Feb. 6, 1836.

KING, REV. GEORGE, (S. J.), b. at Laurel, Del., ordained priest in 1835, and sent to eastern Md., where he labored 20 y.; in 1855, he removed to Newtown, Md., and d. in Balt., June 20, 1856. (*Metropolitan Cath. Almanac*, 1857, p. 299.)

KING, HENRY, b. in Hampden co., Mass., July 6, 1790, an elder br. of T. Butler King of Ga.; in 1810 began to study law under W. H. Brainerd, of New London, Ct.; went to Wilkesbarre, Pa., in 1812, was admitted to the bar, and settled at Allentown, Pa.; in 1825 he was elected to the state senate, and again in 1829; he was in congress from 1831 to 1835, and to his influence is largely due a reform securing a more equal appointment of cadets at West Point; he was deeply interested in reforms in prison discipline and the result of his system at Moyamensing, Pa., led to an invitation for assistance by the Prussian government; he was a whig, a warm friend to the public canals and railways, and opposed to the incurring of heavy public debts; he d. at Allentown, Pa., July 13, 1861. (*N. Y. Eve. Post.*)

KING, JOHN, member of congress from New York, in 1831–3; d. at New Lebanon, N. Y., Sept. 1, 1838, a. 63.

KING, JOHN GLEN, d. in Salem, Mass., July 26, 1857; a. 70; he was b. in Salem, March 19, 1787; grad. at Harvard in 1807, studied law and became eminent in his profession; he served in both branches of the legislature and in the executive council, and held several offices of trust in his native city, where he d. July 26, 1857. (*Am. Almanac*, 1858, p. 356.)

KING, JOHN W., in 1838 and 1839, was speaker of the house of representatives, of Mississippi; d. at Brandon, Miss., Mar 18, 1859, a. 49.

KING, MILES, d. in Norfolk, Va., Dec. 8, 1849, a. 63, was an officer in Ott's Norfolk light artillery when it was in service in 1812; was in gen. assem., and in 1816, was made naval agent, which office he filled for eleven years; was again elected to the legislature, and afterwards for 13 successive years mayor of Norfolk.

KING, REV. SAMUEL, d. in Southampton, N. Y., Nov. 29, 1833, in his 42d year.

KING, GEN. THOMAS D., elder brother of the late William R. King, vice pres. of U. S.; d. at Tuscaloosa, Ala., Feb. 24, 1854, a. 74; b. Sept. 22, 1779, in Duplin co., N. C., and educated in Univ. of N. C.; while yet young, frequently elected to the legislature in which he served in both houses; in 1812 was major of the 43d regt. and held till peace; lived many years in retirement, and was fond of literary pursuits.

KING, WALTER, b. in Norwich, Conn., and son of the Presbyterian minister of that town; grad. at Yale College in 1805, and soon removed to Utica; pursued the study of law with Erastus Clark and became his partner; he remained in practice until 1832, when in consequence of ill health, he engaged in farming in Marcy; he d. 1852, he was an able biblical scholar, and the author of a *Harmony of the Gospels.*

KINGMAN, ENSIGN EDWARD, Mass., killed in the revolution Sept. 26, 1777.

KINGSBURY, JAMES, d. at Newburg, N. Y., Dec. 12, 1847, a. 80; was one of the very first settlers of the western reserve, having landed at Connaut in the summer of 1796 and settled at Newburg the same season;

was a territorial judge, and a member of the legislature of Ohio at an early day. (*Whittlesey's Cleveland*, pp. 262–273.)

KINGSBURY, R., a lieut. in British army, killed at battle of Plattsburg, Sept. 6, 1814.

KINGSBURY, SAMUEL, a prominent citizen of Brockport, Monroe co., N. Y.; d. Dec., 1855.

KINGSLEY, ELIJAH, a soldier of the French and revolutionary wars; d. at Bernardstown, Mass., Oct. 30, 1839, a. 98.

KINGSLEY, LEWIS, ex-judge and deputy naval officer of New York; d. in Brooklyn, N. Y., Feb. 7, 1872, a. 46.

KINGSLEY, MARTIN, b. in Bridgewater, Mass., June 2, 1754; grad. at Harvard in 1778; studied medicine; served some in the revolution, and was in the convention for forming the constitution of his native state; was in the legislature about 30 years, and at different periods in the council; was judge of com. pleas, judge of probate, and in congress from 1819 to 1821; d. at Roxbury, Mass., June 20, 1835.

KINGSLEY, RUFUS, d. at Hartford, Susquehannah co., Pa., a. 84; he was a drummer in the revolution, and served in this capacity through the war.

KINNICUTT, THOMAS, b. in Warren, R. I., Nov. 30, 1800; grad. at Brown U., in 1822, settled in law at Worcester, Mass., in 1825, and for several years in the state legislature, being in 1842, speaker of the house; in 1838, 9, he was senator; in 1848 he was appointed judge of probate for Worcester co., and held this office till his death, Jan. 22, 1858. (*Am. Almanac*, 1859, p. 355.)

KINTZING, ABRAHAM, of the house of Pratt & Kintzing, of Philadelphia; was b. in 1763, first settled in Winchester, Va., but returned and became an importing merchant of extensive business; d. June, 1835, a. 72. (*Simpson's Eminent Philadelphians.*)

KIP, ISAAC L., many years assistant register of the court of chancery in the state of New York; d. in New York city, Jan. 20, 1837, a. 70.

KIRK, REV. EDWARD N., D.D., d. at Boston, March 27, 1874, a. 72; was b. here in 1802, and after graduation at the Princeton College in 1820, he entered a New York office, where he remained eighteen months; he then became a member of the Theological School at Princeton, and after four years of study received an appointment from the board of commissioners for foreign missions; his ministerial labors began at Albany, where he was invited to take charge of a pulpit for a few months; at the expiration of this engagement a new Presbyterian church was organized, of which, in 1828, he became pastor; here his ministrations were continued for nine years; his health demanding a change, he resigned his pastoral charge and visited Europe, preaching regularly in Paris for one year; on his return he preached as an evangelist, with great popularity and usefulness in several Eastern cities, and then became pastor of the Mount Vernon church in Boston, retaining that charge until 1871, when the infirmities of age compelled him to abandon the active care of his church.

KIRKLAND, MRS. CAROLINE MATILDA (Stansbury), wife of William, was b. January, 1801; she was a successful authoress; among other works she wrote, under the name of Mrs. Mary Clavers, *A New Home, Who'll Follow?*, *Forest Life*, and *Western Clearings*; upon settling in New

York, she undertook the education of young ladies; was next editress of the *Union Magazine*, and, after a visit to Europe, wrote *Holidays Abroad*, *Personal Memoirs of George Washington*, and several other works; she d. April 5, 1864.

KIRKLAND, GEORGE WHITFIELD, son of Rev. Samuel and twin brother with Rev. John Thornton Kirkland, pres. Harvard College, merchant of Clinton, N. Y.; b. 1771, d. at Port au Prince, April 21, 1810.

KIRKLAND, JOSEPH, b. in Norwich, Conn., Jan. 18, 1770; grad. at Yale College in 1790, and pursued legal studies; in 1794 he removed to New Hartford, Oneida co., N. Y., and engaged in practice, removing in 1813 to Utica; in 1804 and 5, he was a member of the assembly, and again in 1818, 1820, '21, and '25; in Feb., 1813, he was appointed district attorney of the 6th district; in 1821–3 he was a representative in congress; he was the first mayor of Utica, and served as such during the years 1832, '34, and '35; he d. Feb. 2, 1844.

KIRKLAND, LIEUT. NATHANIEL, Conn.; killed in the revolution, Oct. 12, 1777.

KIRKLAND, REV. SAMUEL, missionary to the Oneidas and Senecas, and his son *Rev. John Thornton Kirkland*, president of Harvard College, may be found in all the dictionaries; d. March 28, 1808, a. 66.

KIRKLAND, WILLIAM, son of Joseph, was b. in New Hartford, Feb. 6, 1802, grad. at Hamilton College and was tutor and professor of Latin in that institution; he lived subsequently in Seneca co., in Michigan and in New York city, and was for the most part engaged in teaching; d. 1846.

KIRKPATRICK, JOHN, b. Glasgow, Scotland, 1819, only son of an invalid machinist, with whom he worked in the shop; 1842, having lost his father and married, emigrated to a new farm near Port Stanley, Canada, on account of his connection with the Chartists; an ardent student in natural history and chemistry between the hours of labor; removed to Cleveland, O., 1843, employed as a machinist until 1856; collected full specimens of entomology; secretary of the Cleveland Academy of Natural Science; asst. editor of the *Ohio Farmer;* 1863, joined the volunteers for 100 days, and on his return made commissioner of drafts. 1866, superintendent of city infirmary; studied mental diseases, botany, and conchology; member of the city council of Cleveland attaked by chronic laryngitis d. at Cleveland, suddenly Dec. 4, 1869. An earnest, energetic, thoughtful, self-taught man of genius, cut down in the fullness of his mental activity.

KIRKPATRICK, DR. WILLIAM, b. in Amwell, Huntingdon co., N. J., Nov. 1768, son of Rev. William K., a Presb.; grad. at Princeton; studied medicine with Dr. Rush, and began practice of medicine at Whitesboro, N. Y., in 1795; in 1806, removed to Salina and became supt. of Salt Springs, while living in Oneida co.; was in congress in 1807–9; in politics was a republican, as then called; was a man of literary tastes; d. of cholera at Salina, Sept. 2, 1832. (*Clark's Onondaga*, ii, 39.)

KIRTLAND, REV. ORLANDO L., b. in Durham, N. Y., May 15, 1801, several years a Presbyterian pastor at Morristown, and at Springville, N. J.; d. at Morristown, N. J., May 23, 1874.

KIRTLAND, WILLIAM A., sole survivor from the wreck of the Charles Lawrence, which foundered at sea in 1865 and of the S. S. Varuna, that foundered off the coast of Florida, in 1870; d. at West Brook, Conn., Jan. 24, 1872, a. 25.

KITE, JOHN, d. at Baltimore, Md., Sept. 18, 1870, a. 108, was a teamster in the revolution, and many years sergeant at arms for the Baltimore city council.

KITTS, JOHN, revolutionary veteran; d. at Baltimore, Md., Sept. 19, 1870, a. 108.

KNAPP, DR. FREDERICK A., d. at Smithville, Jeff. co., N. Y., Feb. 14, 1860, a. 37. (*N. Y. Reformer*, March 1, 1860.)

KNAPP, COL. JARED, d. at Copenhagen, N. Y., March 29, 1854, a. 73.

KNICKERBACKER, HERMAN, b. July 27, 1779, studied law with John V. Henry, and John Bird, began practice and adopted federal politics, and was in congress in 1807–9; in 1816 he was in assembly and was many years a co. judge and supervisor; he was popularly known as the Prince of Schaghticoke, and distinguished for his courteous manners, generous hospitality and ready wit; he d. at Schaghticoke, in 1855. (*Woodworth's Troy; Munsell's Notes*, 91.)

KNIGHT, DR. JONATHAN, d. at New Haven, Conn., Aug. 24, 1864, a. 75.

KNIGHT, JONATHAN, b. in Bucks co., Pa., Nov. 22, 1787; removed in 1801, to E. Bethlehem, Washington co., was mostly self educated, and became a surveyor; was 3 y. county com'r; in 1827 was employed on the national road between Cumberland and Wheeling, and through Ohio and Indiana; in 1822, was elected to the legislature, and served 6 y.; in 1828 visited England to acquire a thorough knowledge of engineering and was chief engineer on the Balt. and Ohio R. R.; was in congress from 1855 to 1857 and d. in Washington co., Pa., Nov. 22, 1858, a. 69.

KNIGHT, MARY, a sister of Gen. Worrell, and devoted friend of the suffering at Valley Forge in the revolution; d. at Rahway, N. J., of cholera, July, 1849, at the age of 90. (*Stryker's Am. Reg.*, iii, 233.)

KNIGHT, SAMUEL, was commissioned as a lawyer June, 1772, and was present at the affray at Westminster, Vermont, March 13, 1775; he was with four others declared guilty of death at the inquest upon the body of Wm. French; he fled to Boston, and thence to N. Y., but returned to Brattleboro a year after; he favored the N. Y. claims as long as there was hope, when he became a supporter of the Vermont government; he was 1st judge of Windham co., 4 years, and presided as chief justice of the state from 1789 to 1793. (*Hall's Eastern Vermont*, p. 673.)

KNOWER, BENJAMIN, d. at Watervliet, N. Y., Aug. 23, 1839, a. 64; was more than forty years a mechanic and then a merchant of Albany.

KNOULTON, CALVIN, son of Luke Knoulton; grad. at Dartmouth Coll. in 1788; studied law, and d. Jan. 20, 1800, a. 34. (*Hall's Eastern Vermont*, p. 676.)

KNOWLTON, LUKE, a native of Shrewsbury, Mass., removed to Newfane, Vt., in 1772 where he was town clerk 16 y.; representative in gen. assem. in 1784, 8, 9, a member of the council 1790 to 1800, a member of the constitutional convention in 1793, and a judge of Windham co., from 1787 to 1793; he took an active part in settling the Vermont controversy; he d. Dec. 12, 1810, a. 73. (*Hall's Eastern Vermont*, p. 675.)

KNOX, Rev. John, d.d., b. in Adams co., Pa., June 17, 1790, licensed to preach June, 1815, ordained colleague pastor of the Reformed Prot. Dutch church in the city of New York, July 16, 1816, and d. in that city, Jan. 8, 1858. (*Knox Memorial Volume*, with portrait.)

KOHL, Johann George, a distinguished German archæolgist, and author of numerous books describing his travels, d. in Bremen, Germany, June 6, 1871, a. 63; he prepared for the Maine Historical Society, a volume of documents relating to the early discoveries of that coast, of great merit.

KOSSUTH, Emilié Zalavasky, sister of Louis Kossuth, the Hungarian patriot; d. at Brooklyn, N. Y., June 29, 1860, a. 43.

KOZTA, Martin, a Hungarian refugee whose rescue from the Austrian authorities in 1853 by Commodore Ingraham occasioned much diplomatic correspondence; d. near the city of Guatemala, May 25, 1858.

KRAITSER, Prof. Dr. Charles, a Polish exile, came to America in 1833 devoted himself to teaching, and in 1842, was appointed prof. of modern languages in the Univ. of Va.; he published several remarkable works on philology and lectured extensively on the subject; he d. at Morrisania, N. Y., May 7, 1860, a. 56. (*Hist. Mag.*, iv, 189.)

KRAMER, Allen, banker, d. at Pittsburg, Pa., Nov. 8, 1869.

KRAUSE, David, d. at Norristown, Pa., June 13, 1871, a. 73, was president judge of the 7th judicial dist. of Pennsylvania, in 1845–51.

KREPPS, Gen. Solomon G., senator of Pa.; d. of cholera at Brownsville, Pa., July 14, 1833.

KUHN, Jacob, for fifty years messenger of the general court of Massachusetts; d. at Boston, Sept. 22, 1835.

KUPER, Henry George, British consul in Baltimore; d. in that city of suffocation in a burning building, Dec. 7, 1856.

LACOSTE, Felix, consul general of France for the United States; d. Nov. 14, 1853, at New York city.

LACY, Thomas J., a member of the bar, and formerly a judge of the Arkansas supreme court; d. at New Orleans, La., Jan. 11, 1849.

La FRENIÈRE, Nicholas Chauvin de, attorney general of Louisiana was b. in 1736; and became an ardent advocate of French supremacy in that colony as opposed to Spain, and his eloquent and fearless appeals made him the object of great regard by the people; his eloquence has been compared to Patrick Henry's, and his speech before the superior council is regarded as a master piece of eloquence and logic; upon the arrival of a Spanish fleet in July 1769, he was seized with a few others, tried and condemned; and on the 25th of October, 1769, he was shot with his compatriots, by a file of Spanish grenadiers in the yard fronting the barracks. (*B. V. French's Hist. Memoirs of La.* p. 183.)

LaGAUDE, Pierre Paul Frs. de, Sulpitian missionary; arrived in Canada, May 1755; succeeded Picquet at Oswegatchie in 1760, and d. at Montreal April 4, 1784.

LAIDLEY, Joseph, chemist, b. in Ireland, came to Phila., in his youth; grad. at the College of Pharmacy in that city in 1850; he secured a place with Adie & Gray of Richmond; was several years with them, and then engaged in business on his own account; he engaged in the preparation of detonating powder for the rebel army at Richmond, Va., in the summer of 1861, and was killed by an accidental explosion, Aug., 1861.

LAIDLIE, REV. ARCHIBALD, D.D., b. in Scotland, accepted a call to the Dutch ch. of Flushing in Zealand where he lived 4 y. and came to N. Y. in 1764; he was the first minister of the Dutch ch. in America who officiated in English; he d. at Redhook, N. Y., in 1778; an exile on account of the war. (*Miller's Life of Rev. J. Rogers*, p. 136.)

LAKE, WILLIAM HUME, d. at Toronto, Canada, Nov. 15, 1871; was many years prof. of law, in the University of Toronto; and for many years chancellor of the court of chancery of Canada.

LAMAR, JOHN, soldier of the revolution, served bravely as a partisan under Marion and Pickens; was at Eutaw, Cowpens, the siege of Augusta and in other engagements, and was twice wounded; he removed to Ga. and d. in Jones co. (*White's Hist. Ga.*, p. 506.)

LAMAR, JOSE, ex-president of Peru; d. at Cartago, Central America, Nov. 15, 1830.

LAMAR, L. Q. C., judge of the Oakmulgee circuit, d. in Georgia, July 4, 1834, a. 32 years.

LAMAR, MAJOR MARION, Penn.; killed Sept. 21, 1777.

LAMB, JOHN, d. at Washington, D. C., Sept. 20, 1837, a. 62; chief clerk in the office of first comptroller in the treasury.

LAMBDIN, REV. WILLIAM, of Memphis conference; b. in Talbot co., Md., June 4, 1784, and d. at Paris, Tenn., May 22, 1854. (*Deems's Annals of Southern Methodism*, p. 348.)

LAMBERVILLE, JACQUES DE, Jesuit missionary; arrived in Canada June 21, 1673; among the Mohawks in 1675–8; subsequently at Onondaga, which he left in 1686; at Montreal in 1700; with the Iroquois in 1703, and at Onondaga in Sept., 1708; he was at Cayuga in 1709, whence he fled on the breaking out of war; he d. Sept. 16, 1718.

LAMBERVILLE, JEAN DE, Jesuit missionary, arrived in Canada about 1671; at Onondaga in 1671, 2; left and sent to Niagara in 1687; at Laprairie in 1690 and in France in 1699.

LAMBORN, JOSIAH, d. in Whitehall, N. Y., March 21, 1847; attorney general of Illinois.

LAMBTON, JOHN GEORGE. (*See Durham, Earl of.*)

LANE, AMOS, member of the Indiana legislature and in one session speaker, was a lawyer of eminence and in congress from Louisiana from 1833 to 1837; d. at Lawrensburg, Ind., in 1850.

LANE, DERICK, son of Matthias L.; b. at Bedminster, N. J., April 30, 1755; served as lieut. and capt. of N. J. troops in the revolution and was in several battles; he settled in Troy, N. Y., as a merchant at an early day, was several years loan com'r for Rensselaer co., and in 1808–9 was in assembly; he d. March 26, 1831. (*Woodworth's Troy.*, 38.)

LANE, REV. D. HOWE, D.D., d. at Granville, O., Nov. 10, 1870, a. 65.

LANE, GILBERT COOKE, b. March 18, 1828; grad. at Middlebury in 1853; evinced talent as a poet, and especially as a classical scholar; he had nearly finished a commentary on Herodotus; he d. at Cornwall, Vt., Nov. 10, 1858. (*Hist. Mag.*, ii, 368.)

LANG, ANDREW J., b. at Palmyra, Maine, in 1831; grad. at Union Coll.; taught academies at Fort Plain, N. Y., at Essex, Conn., and at Waverly, N. Y.; d. at Waverly, Aug. 22, 1870. (*Regent's Report*, 1872, p. 699.)

LANG, ROBERT U., senior editor of the *New York Gazette;* d. in the city of New York, July, 1837.

LANGLEY, WILLIAM, d. at Hawley, Mass., July 8, 1836, a. 92; he was a year in the French war, and five years in the revolution.

LANIER, CAPT. EDWARD, U. S. N., d. at Baltimore, Md., March 20, 1872.

LANSING, ABRAHAM G., brother of Chancellor L., b. in Albany, saw some revolutionary service, and settled as a lawyer in Albany; he was surrogate from Mar. 13, 1787, to April 12, 1808, and d. in 1834, a. 77. (*Rogers's Hist. Discourse*, p. 111.)

LANSING, BARENT BLEECKER, son of Col. Gerrit G. Lansing of the army of the revolution; b. in Argyle, N. Y., Jan. 17, 1793; merchant in Utica, 1813 to 1830; in 1831–2 bookkeeper of U. S. Branch Bank of Utioa; in 1835 cashier of Bank of Belleville, N. J.; in 1837 cashier of Oneida Bank of Utica; d. Dec. 3, 1853.

LANSING, DIRCK C., D.D., b. in Lansingburg, N. Y., March 3, 1785; grad. at Yale, was licensed to preach in 1806; was settled at Onondaga, and Auburn; and in 1829 at Utica, where he was pastor of the 2d Presb. ch. and in 1833 went to New York; in 1856 removed to Walnut Hill near Cincinnati, and d. there, March 19, 1857. (*Thompson's Funeral Discourse*, with portrait.)

LANSING, GERRIT Y., LL.D., a prominent lawyer and citizen of Albany, d. in that city Jan. 3, 1862; was judge of the State court of probates from 1816 until the office was abolished in 1823; was chosen a regent of the University in 1829; and for the last twelve years was chancellor of the regents; and from 1831 to 1837, was in congress.

LANSING, JOHN JR., chief justice and chancellor of N. Y.; son of Gerrit L. b. in Albany Jan. 30, 1754; studied law with Robert Yates (chief justice) at Alb. and Jas. Duane at N. Y.; in 1776, 7, he was mil. sec. to Gen. Schuyler; he settled at Albany, was in assembly in 1780–1, to '84, and in 1786, 7–9, being speaker in 1786, 9; in 1786, was appointed mayor of Albany; in 1787 he was appointed to congress; he was in the convention that formed the U. S. const., but being opposed to its provisions withdrew; and in 1788, in the N. Y. state conven. voted against its adoption; he served on several state commissions, and Feb. 15, 1798, was appointed chief justice of N. Y., and Oct 21, 1801, became chancellor; in 1817, became a regent, in 1824 was pres. elector, and secretary of the electoral college. He d. Dec. 12, 1829, in his 76th year. (*Street's Council of Revision* p. 159; *Rogers's Hist. Discourse*, p. 104.)

LANSING, RICHARD R., son of Col. Gerrit G., grad. at Union Coll. 1808, studied law and practiced in Utica; was clerk of northern district of N. Y., 1818 to (about) 1827; removed to the city of New York and became a wine merchant; thence went to Detroit and dealt in lands; he gave the name to Lansing, capital of Michigan, d. 1854.

LANSING, SANDERS, b. in Albany June, 17, 1766; bro. of John L., chief justice; he was educated to the law, and and appointed register in chancery; in 1820, he settled at Little Falls, N. Y., in a land agency; was in the state convention of 1821; was a county judge until 1828, and held several other legal officers; he finally settled in Manheim, N. Y., and d. there Sept. 19, 1850, in his 85th year. (*Benton's Herkimer Co. N. Y.*, p. 340.)

LAPHAM, SENECA, d. at Mount Tabor, Ohio, Dec. 30, 1853, a. 70.

LAPORTE, COUNT DE, d. near Tully, Lewis co., Mo., July 30, 1858; well known as a teacher of French, and formerly instructor in French at Harvard.

LARDNER, DR. DIONYSIUS, professor of natural philosophy and astronomy in the University of London, and editor of the *Cabinet Cyclopedia;* in 1840, he visited the United States, and lectured with success; he d. in Paris, April 29, 1859, a. 66.

LARKIN, THOMAS O., b. at Charlestown, Mass., Sept. 16, 1802; arrived in California April, 1832, was appointed U. S. consul at Monterey, in 1844, and was of great service to the U. S. during the Mexican war; he d. at San Francisco, Oct 27, 1858, a. 56 years. (*Hist. Mag.*, iii, 26.)

LARKINS, REV. JOHN, one of the ministers of the R. C. ch. of St. Francis Xavier, 16th st., N. Y.; d. suddenly Dec. 11, 1858. (*Hist. Mag.*, iii, 28; *Tribune*, Dec. 14, 1858.)

LARNED, GEN. CHARLES, d. of cholera at Detroit, Aug. 13, 1834.

LARNED, JAMES, chief clerk in the office of first comptroller of the treasury; d. near Frederick, Md., Aug. 1, 1849. (*Stryker's Am. Reg.*, iii, 238.)

LARNED, SAMUEL, d. in Providence, R. I., 1847; many years a merchant at Cadiz, Spain, where he was U. S. consul; in 1823, was appointed sec. of legation to Chili, and in 1829, chargé d'affaires, to the confederated republics of Peru and Bolivia; was recalled in 1837, at his own request and retired to domestic life.

LA ROCHE-HERON, HENRY DE COURCY DE, b. at Brest, France, in 1820; came to the U. S. in 1845; was engaged in mercantile affairs and was a contributor to the *Univers* and *Ami de la Religion*, of France, and to periodicals in this country; he wrote a sketch of the female convents of Canada, in 1855, and *The Cath. Ch. in the U. S.*, in 1856; he returned and d. at Cannes, dep. of Var, France, May 14, 1861. (*Hist. Mag.* v, 224.)

LA ROCHE, DR. RÉNÉ, d. in Philadelphia, Pa., June 6, 1819, in his 65th year; b. in St. Domingo in 1755; educated in France, and fled to America, from the massacres of 1793; was skilled in his profession, but of feeble health, and of mild and retiring habits. (*Simpson's Em. Phila.*)

LARRABEE, WILLIAM C., native of Maine, and formerly supt. of public instruction, in Indiana; d. at Greencastle, Ind., May 5, 1859, a. 59.

LARRANAGA, VINCENTE ANTONIO, Spanish consul at Charleston, S. C.; d. at that place, Aug. 19, 1860.

LATHROP, ISAAC, of Plymouth, grad. at Harvard in 1726; was a representative and one of the council, and some years a justice of the court of com. pleas; he d. at Plymouth in 1750, a. 42. (*Bradford's N. E. Biog.*)

LATHROP, Rev. John, D.D., native of Norwich, Ct., grad. at Princeton in 1763; studied theology with Rev. Eleazer Wheelock and in 1768, was ordained over the 2d Cong. ch. in Boston where he labored till his d. in 1816. (*Bradford's N. E. Biog.*)

LATHROP, John Hiram, LL.D., an eminent educator; b. in Sherburne, N. Y., Jan. 22d, 1799; entered Hamilton Coll. in 1814, but grad. at Yale in 1819; was four years tutor of Yale, during which he studied law and was admitted to the bar; was engaged two years in teaching in Vermont and in Maine; from 1828 to 1840, professor of Hamilton Coll. holding successively the chairs of mathematics and nat. philos., of ethics and political economy, and of law, history &c.; in 1840 he became president of the University of Missouri, in 1848 chancellor of that of Wisconsin, and in 1859 president of that of Indiana; in 1860 he returned to the University of Missouri, at first as professor of English literature, but at the time of his death Aug. 2d, 1866, he was again its president.

LATHROP, Samuel, b. in Hampden co., Mass., in 1771; grad. at Yale in 1792; studied law, and gained a high position at the bar; was in congress from Mass. from 1818 to 1826, and d. in W. Springfield, July 1, 1846.

LATOUR, Anthony, d. at Utica, N. Y., Oct. 8, 1839, in his 87th year; was a soldier of the revolution and a native of France; he came to America with Lafayette.

LATTIMORE, William, b. in Norfolk, Va., Feb. 9, 1774; studied medicine and removed to Mississippi ter.; was a delegate in congress from 1803 to 1807, and from 1813 to 1817, was in the convention that formed the first state constitution, and d. April 3, 1843.

L'AUBE RIVIERE, Francois Louis de Pourroy de, fifth R. C. bp. of Quebec; b. at Attigny, Fr.; priest of Sorbonne, when chosen in 1739 to succeed M. Dosquet, which was confirmed the same year; he was consecrated bp. of Quebec, Dec. 21, 1739; he arrived at Quebec, Aug. 8, 1740, and d. the 20th of the same month, a. 29. (*Liste Chron. des Evêques et des Prêtres du Canada.*)

LAURENS, Lieut. Col. John, S. C.; killed in a skirmish on the Combahee, Aug. 27, 1781.

LAW, Maj. James O., d. in Baltimore, Md., June 2, 1847; was formerly mayor of the city, and held various other offices.

LAW, Lyman, b. in New London, Conn., Aug. 19, 1870; grad. at Yale in 1791; studied law with his father Richard, (who was in continental congress) and practiced law at New London; served in the state legislature, and was speaker; was in congress from 1811 to 1817, and d. at New London, Feb. 3, 1842.

LAW, Thomas, a native of England, son of Dr. Edmund Law, formerly bp. of Carlisle, and a brother of the late Lord Ellenborough; d. at Washington, D. C., July, 1834, a. 78 years.

LAWLER, Rev. Joab, b. in N. C., June 12, 1796; was a Baptist minister; in 1826 was in the Alabama legislature, and continued till 1831, when he was chosen to the state senate; in 1852 was made receiver of public moneys for the Coosa land dist., and held till 1855; in 1833 was made treasurer of the University of Alabama; was in congress from 1835 to 1838, and d. at Washington, D. C., May 8, 1838.

LAWLOR, John, d. April 18, 1869, a. 59; b. in Canada; in 1848 founded the Philadelphia *Sunday Dispatch*, with which paper he was connected till his death.

LAWRASON, Samuel C., a surgeon in the navy, on board the Germantown sloop of war; d. at Pensacola, July 14, 1849. (*Stryker's Am. Reg.*, iii, 236.)

LAWRENCE, Alexander H., d. in Washington, D. C., March 16, 1857, a. 46; he was b. in New Hampshire, grad. at Dartmouth, and opened a boy's school at Washington in 1834; was appointed a clerk in the General Land office in 1836, and studied law; in 1845 he was removed and began his practice, in which he acquired honorable success.

LAWRENCE, Dr. Ebenezer, d. in Pepperell, Mass., June 14, 1856, a. 86; b. in that place in 1770; grad. at Harvard in 1795, and first settled in Hampton, N. H., where he practiced 51 years; about five years before his death, he returned to his native town.

LAWRENCER, Isaac, d. in New York city, July 12, 1841, a. 74; late pres. of the branch of the U. S. Bank in that city.

LAWRENCE, Rev. James, b. in Richmond, Ky., March 12, 1821; d. Oct. 16, 1853. (*Deems's Annals of Southern Methodism*, p. 344.)

LAWRENCE, John L., one of the secretaries at the treaty of Ghent; a member of assembly in 1816–7, and of the senate in 1848, 9, and of the constitutional convention of 1821; d. of cholera at New York, July 23, 1849; he was at the time of his death, city comptroller. (*Stryker's Am. Reg.*, iii, 237.)

LAWRENCE, Joseph, b. in Pa., in 1788; was 9 y. in state legislature, 1 y. state treasurer, and from 1825 to 1829, and from 1841 till his death, April 17, 1842, a member of congress; d. at Washington, D. C.

LAWRENCE, Philip K, judge of the U. S. dist. court, for the eastern dist. of Louisiana; d. at New Orleans, May 19, 1841.

LAWRENCE, William A., d. at Harrisburg, Pa., April 22, 1860; was late speaker of the house of representatives of Pennsylvania.

LAWRIE, Gawen, deputy governor of New Jersey, was one of the assignees of Edward Byllinge (the purchaser of West Jersey from Lord Berkley), who in 1676 placed the whole of that province in their hands for the benefit of his creditors; he resided at Elizabethtown until his death in the autumn of 1687, having surrendered the government to his successor, in October, 1686. (*Coll. N. J. Hist. Soc.*, i, 126.)

LAWSON, Alexander, b. in Lanark, Scotland, in 1773, became a self-taught engraver, and at the age of 20 settled in Philadelphia; his plates for Alexander Wilson the ornithologist, form his chief work.

LAWSON, Fabius M., formerly treasurer of the state of Virginia; d. in Goochland co., Va., Oct. 1, 1857, a. 51.

LAWSON, Dr. Thomas G., an Englishman, came to Sodus Point, N. Y., and resided some years; he returned to England and d. there in 1833.

LAWTON, Charles W., d. at Red Sulphur Springs, Va., Aug. 7, 1838; native of England, and a merchant of Charleston, S. C.

LEA, Col. Luke, a native of Tenn., distinguished himself under Jackson in the Indian wars in Florida; was in congress from East Tenn., from 1833 to 1837, and for 30 years discharged faithfully the duties of cashier of the state bank, and register of the state land office of Tenn.; in 1849 he was appointed Indian agent at Ft. Leavenworth; and d. near Westport, Mo., June 17, 1851. (*Am. Almanac*, 1852, p. 340.)

LEAKE, JOHN G., son of Robert Leake, d. in N. Y., a bachelor, June 2, 1827, leaving an estate valued at $400,000, and an informal will, bequeathing his estate to Robert Watts upon condition of his taking the surname of Leake; if he did not, or died before 21, he gave funds for an orphan asylum in N. Y. city; this Watts died soon after becoming of age, and before changing his name; his father released his interest, in behalf of the asylum which bears the name of the Leake and Watts Orphan Asylum; the will was contested, and found valid so far as concerned the personal estate, but the real estate escheated to the state and $85,754.49, was paid into the treasury Jan. 1842; James Hay and others have since set up claims as heirs but without success. (*N. Y. Assem. Doc.* 87, 1850; do 93, 1854, etc.)

LEAKE, ROBERT, b. about 1710, at Calder in Lanarkshire, Scotland, joined the horse guards in 1741, and was wounded at the battle of Dettingen, in 1743; in 1745 he was lieut. of an independent co.; in Feb. 1747, was appointed commissary at Cape Breton; and in 1849 returned to England on half pay; in 1754 he was commissary of provision to Braddock, and served in America till 1763; he resided in N. Y. till his death Dec. 8, 1773.

LEAKIN, SHEPPARD C., d. near Baltimore, Md., Nov. 20, 1867, in his 78th year; commanded a troop at the battle of North Point; was mayor of Balt. in 1842, and for some years editor of the *Balt. Daily Chron.*

LEAMING, THOMAS, b. Aug. 20, 1748; rendered good service to his country in the revolution, as a lawyer, a soldier and a merchant, was a prominent delegate to the convention that formed the constitution of Pennsylvania, and d. of yellow fever in 1797. (*Simpson's Eminent Philadelphians.*)

LEAR, W. W., major 3d U. S. infantry; d. Oct. 31, 1846, at Monterey, of wounds received in the battle of Sept. 21st.

LEARNED, EDWARD D., d. at Jackson, Miss., Sept. 27, 1837, in his 39th year; native of Maine; grad. at Bowdoin.

LEAVENWORTH, REV. MARK, b. in Stratford, Conn.; grad. at Yale in 1737; was chaplain in a Connecticut regiment in 1760, and went to Canada, settled at Waterbury, Conn., and d. Aug. 20, 1797, in the 86th year of his age, and the 58th of his ministry.

LEAVENWORTH, THOMAS, common ancestor of most of those of this name in the United States; b. in England; d. in Woodbury, Conn., Aug. 3, 1683.

LEAVITT, REV. JOSHUA, D.D., b. at Heath, Mass., Sept., 1794; grad. at Yale in 1814; taught for a while, studied law, and opened an office in Putney, Vt.; soon afterwards, he went to New Haven and entered the Theological Seminary. Settled as pastor in Stratford, Conn., where he remained four years; in 1819, while a student of law in Heath, Dr. Leavitt organized one of the first Sunday schools in western Massachusetts, embracing not only the children, but the entire congregation, all of whom were arranged in classes for religious study. An earnest revival resulted, and the school grew into one of the strongest churches in the region. He early became interested in the improvement of the public schools. Before he entered the Theological Seminary, he prepared a new reading book, called *Easy Lessons in Reading*, which met with an extensive sale. Dr. Leavitt was among the first to perceive the evils of intemperance, and exerted all his influence against it, and when the American Temperance Society was formed, he became its first sec., was one of its traveling agents, and spent several months in lecturing in New Haven, Northampton, and towns in that neighborhood, in many places delivering the first temperance lecture the people there had ever heard. In 1828 he came to this city as secretary of the American Seamen's Friend Society and editor of *The Sailor's Magazine*, and he has ever since been engaged in editorial work. The society, under his management, became popular and useful. He established chapels in Canton, the Sandwich Islands, Havre, New Orleans, and other domestic and foreign ports. At this time, too, he aided in starting the first city temperance society, and became its first secretary. Perceiving early the advantage of having a combined hymn and tune book for use in revival and social meetings, nothing of the kind then existing, he, in company with an excellent young musician, set about making one, which was published under the name of *The Christian Lyre.* This has always been considered one of the best of its kind. Dr. Leavitt, in 1831, became editor and proprietor of the *The Evangelist*, which had been started a year before, during which time he had frequently assisted in its editorial work. He went to work earnestly, and soon made his paper one of the most powerful in the land; it was the organ of the more liberal religious movements, and was outspoken on the subjects of temperance and slavery. It early became noted for doctrinal discussions, in which he was completely at home, possessing a keen argumentative mind, and a thorough knowledge of the intricacies of theological contests. Dr. Leavitt bore a conspicuous part in the early anti-slavery conflict, and his denunciation of slavery during the time of the excitement attending the formation of the first abolition societies and the robbery of the mails at Charleston cost his paper its circulation in the south and a large portion in the north, and it seemed as though it would have to suspend. To bring up its circulation again he then undertook the difficult feat of reporting in full Finney's revival lectures, which, though not a shorthand reporter, he accomplished so successfully that his subscribers came back by hundreds, till his list reached 12,000. These reports were afterward published in book form, and sold to the extent of over a hundred thousand copies. The financial crash of 1837 compelled him, while erecting a new building, to sell out *The Evangelist*, which thenceforward became thoroughly Presbyterian, and lost almost entirely the strong anti-slavery character which Dr. Leavitt had given it. Dr. Leavitt's correspondence with Cobden and his *Memoir on Wheat*, setting forth the unlimited capacity of our western territory for the growth and exportation of wheat, were very instrumental in procuring the repeal of the English corn laws During his visit to England he also became much interested in Sir Rowland Hill's system of cheap postage, which he advocated for adoption in this country, both through the newspapers and before the congress committee; he d. in New York, Jan. 16, 1873.

LE COUTEULX, LOUIS STEPHEN, b. at Rouen, Fr., Aug. 24, 1756; came to America in 1786 on business, and remained; lived first in Trenton,

N. J.; then in Bucks co., Pa.; was a farmer and imported the first Merino sheep into the U. S. from Spain in 1789; traveled extensively; was arrested at Ft. George in 1800 on suspicion of being a French spy, and kept in prison at Quebec till 1802; went to Buffalo, N. Y., in 1804; became county clerk of Niagara co., and agent of the Holland Land Co., and in 1812 removed to Albany; was sergeant at arms in the senate, and in convention of 1821; returned to Buffalo, and d. Oct. 16, 1839; the city of Buffalo is largely indebted to him for his public benefactions. (*Turner's Holland Land Co.*, p. 501, with portrait.)

LEDERER, BARON LOUIS, consul general for the Austrian states, d. at New York, Dec. 22, 1845; he had long resided in this country and was distinguished for his mineralogical researches; his collection of foreign minerals was purchased by the University of Michigan. (*Am. Jour. Sci. & Arts*, 1st ser., xliv, 216.)

LE DUC, MARY P., d. near St. Louis, Mo., Aug. 15, 1842, a. 70, was b. near St. Denis, France, and settled at St. Louis near the close of the last century; he was secretary of the province under the Spanish government of Louisiana, and held till it was ceded to the U. S. and afterwards till Missouri became a state; he was in the constitutional convention in 1820, and judge of the county court of St. Louis co., many years.

LEDYARD, JOHN DENISE, son of Col. Benjamin Ledyard of the revolutionary army; b. at Middletown Point, N. J., June 10th, 1793, but was removed the following year with his father and family to Aurora, N. Y.; in 1798 he became an inmate with his brother-in-law, Col. Lincklaen of Cazenovia; he grad. at Union College in 1812, studied law, and then joined Col. Lincklaen in the agency and purchase of the unsold lands of the Holland Land Company lying in Madison and Chenango counties; after the death of Col. L., in 1822, he had the sole management and in 1844 the ownership of these lands; he was president of the third Great Western Turnpike Company, first president of the Madison County Agricultural Society, a trustee of Hamilton College, and foremost in every project for the improvement of his town and neighborhood; his death occurred Jan. 7, 1874.

LEE, DR. CHARLES A., of Peekskill, N. Y.; d. Feb. 14, 1872, a. 71.

LEE, EDMUND L., d. in Alexandria, D. C., May 30, 1843, a. 71, was several times mayor, and many years clerk of the U. S. district court.

LEE, EDWARD G., confederate brig. gen.; d. in Virginia, Aug. 27, 1870.

LEE, EZRA, captain in the revolution, was often employed upon secret and dangerous service, and made an unsuccessful attempt to blow up the ship Asia in New York harbor, with a submarine engine called the *Marine Turtle*, made by David Bushnell of Saybrook. Capt. Lee d. at Lyme, Ct., Oct. 29, 1821, a. 72. (*Rogers's Am. Biog.*)

LEE, GIDEON, b. in Amherst, Mass., April 27, 1778, became a tanner, began business at Worthington, Mass., and spent his first earnings in educating himself at the Westfield Academy; he was extremely industrious, but having lost all by a fire, made a voyage to St. Mary's Fla., where his constitution was permanently injured by fever, and was wrecked on his return; he settled in N. Y., where from nothing he became successful and eminent, as a leather dealer; in 1823 he was in assembly, in 1833 was mayor, and in 1857 in congress; in 1840 he was elected to the electoral college; he removed to Geneva, N. Y., bought and improved a beautiful estate, and d. Aug. 21, 1841, in his 64th y. (*Hunt's Lives of Am. Merchants*, i, 401; *Am. Almanac*, 1842, p. 310.)

LEE, DR. JAMES, of Mechanicville, N. Y., d. April 13, 1866, a. 47; b. at Fishkill, N. Y., Nov. 15, 1818. (*Transac. N. Y. State Med. Soc.*, 1864, p. 466.)

LEE, JAY ELEN, b. in Sweden, N. Y., Dec. 27 1833; grad. at Ham. Coll. 1858, was a capt. N. Y. Independent Battery in 1861–3; N. Y. military agent in Wash. in 1865–8; d. at St. Paul, Minn., Oct. 10, 1873.

LEE, LUDWELL, second son Richard Henry Lee, d. at Belmont, Loudon co., Va., March 25, 1836, a. 76.

LEE, MRS. MARY CUSTIS, widow of Gen. Robert D. Lee, and only dau. of Geo. W. P. Custis, formerly of the Arlington house near Washington, D. C., d. at Lexington, Va., Nov. 6, 1873, aged about 67; her grandfather, Col. John Parke Custis, was a son of Martha Custis, afterwards the wife of George Washington; Mrs. Lee was a woman of strong intellectual powers, and persistently favored the Confederate cause; she was in Richmond during the war, and when the contest was over, accompanied her husband to Lexington, where she resided until her death; she had been an invalid for about ten years, suffering from a rheumatic affection; the funeral took place on Saturday in the Memorial Church in Lexington; her three sons, W. H. F. Lee, Custis Lee, Robert E. Lee, and her daughter, were present, besides a large number of friends.

LEE, DR. MOSES A., prof. of materia medica and pharmacy in the Berkshire Medical Inst.; d. at Pittsfield, Mass., June 16, 1842, in his 36th year.

LEE, RICHARD BLAND, eminent for his literary ability and member of congress from Va., from 1789 to 1795; he was judge of the orphan's court at Washington, at the time of his death, which occurred in 1827.

LEE, ROBERT, d. in Rahway, N. J., March 14, 1842, a. 57.

LEE, THOMAS, member of the council of Va., and as pres. succeeded Gov. Gooch in the administration in Aug., 1749, but d. a few days after; his sons, Philip Ludwell, Richard Henry, Thomas L., Arthur, Francis Lightfoot, and William, were public characters; they were natives of Westmoreland co. (*Campbell's Va.*)

LEE, THOMAS, merchant, b. in Beverley, Mass., Oct. 11, 1779; d. in Boston, Dec. 14, 1867; was of the firm of Lee & Cabot; in 1865, presented the statue of Alexander Hamilton to Boston, and in 1866, a fountain.

LEE, WILLIAM, br. of Ann Lee founder of Shakers, b. in Manchester, Eng., and in 1740, adopted the Shaker faith, and d. July 21, 1784. (*Evans's Shakers' Compendium*, p. 156.)

LEE, WILLIAM L., chief justice of the Sandwich Islands; b. at Sandy Hill, N. Y., Feb. 25, 1821; began the practice of law at Troy, N. Y., in 1844, but threatened with consumption started soon after for Oregon; he arrived at Honolulu on his way, Oct. 12, 1846, was invited to remain, accepted the office of presiding judge of the old court of Oahu, and after the organization of the judiciary in 1847, was appointed chief justice of the superior court of law and equity; in 1852 he was appointed chief justice of the supreme court and chancellor of the kingdom; in 1855 upon revisiting the U. S., he was made minister to the U. S., and negotiated a treaty at Washington; he d. at his home in Honolulu, May 28, 1857.

LEE, T. COLLINS, judge of the superior court of Balt.; son of Richard Bland Lee, grad. in a Va. Coll., read law with Wm. Wirt, and settled in Baltimore; he was appointed U. S. dist. atty. by Tyler, and continued through Fillmore's term; in Nov., 1855, he was elected judge of the sup. court of Balt., and held till near the time of his death, which occurred Dec. 26, 1859. (*Hist. Mag.*, iv, 29.)

LEECH, WILLIAM A., d. in Philadelphia, July 20, 1870; b. in that city; entered at West Point; afterwards studied law, served in the 17th Pa. regt. as major, and in the 9th as lieut. col. in the late war; was in prison at Richmond, Salisbury and Danville; was brevetted brig. gen.; in 1867, was elected register of wills at Philadelphia.

LEEDS, HENRY H., auctioneer at New York; d. March 12, 1870, a. 69; b. in New London, Conn., and came to New York in 1801; in 1847, became auctioneer with A. B. Minor.

LEESUG, MISS CATHARINE, an actress, who excelled in the line of comedy; in 1819, while at the height of her popularity, she m. Mr. James Hackett, and left the stage; she resumed her profession in 1826, and made her last appearance at her husband's benefit at the National Theatre in Leonard st., N. Y.; she d. at Jamaica, L. I., Dec. 4, 1845, a. 47.

LEET, ISAAC, d. in Washington, Pa., June 10, 1844, a. 42; M. C. from 1829 to 1831, and for several years in the state senate.

LEGG, REV. JUDSON L., d. in Speedsville, N. Y., Aug. 30, 1871, a. 43. (*Northern Christian Advocate*, Oct. 5, 1871.)

LEHMAN, WILLIAM, b. in Philadelphia, Pa., Sept. 14, 1779; d. at Harrisburg, Pa., March 29, 1829; studied medicine but did not practice, and became a druggist in Philadelphia; was elected to the legislature, in 1814, and annually after for 15 years. (*Simpson's Em. Philadelphians.*)

LEIGH, WILLIAM, d. July 19, 1871, a. 84; was judge of the circuit court, from 1830 to 1857.

LEIPER, GEORGE G., d. at Lapidea, Pa., Nov. 17, 1868, in the 83d year of his age; b. in Philadelphia; was in congress from 1829 to 1831, from Pennsylvania; was identified with the building of the first rail road in the U. S., in 1809, from the Leiper quarries, Delaware co., to Ridley creek, one mile in length.

LEIPER, THOMAS, native of Scotland, settled first in Virginia, and then in Philadelphia; was a prominent democratic politician, but accepted no offices, other than as director of the banks of Philadelphia, and of the U. S.; com'r for defense of the city; was a liberal giver for the public good, and d. July, 1825. (*Simpson's Em. Philadelphians*, with portrait.)

LEITCH, MAJOR ANDREW, Va., k. at Harlem Plains, Sept. 28, 1776.

LELAND, AARON LARKIN, b. in Sherborn, Mass., in 1813; grad. at Harvard in 1835; studied medicine, and settled in Pontiac, Mich.; removed to Detroit, in 1847, and continued to practice medicine till his death, Nov. 14, 1858.

LELAND, JOHN D., d. in Fayette, Mo., June 6, 1847; was judge of the 2d judicial circuit of Missouri, seven years before his death, and a native of Virginia.

LELAND, SIMEON, a prominent and successful hotel proprietor, in New York city; d. at New Rochelle, N. Y., Aug. 3, 1872, a. 56.

LEMERCIER, FRANCOIS JOSEPH, Jesuit missionary; arrived in Canada, July 20, 1635; superior, from 1653 to 1656; sent to Onondaga, May 17, of that year, and remained till March 20, 1658; he died in the West Indies.

LEMON, LIEUT. JAMES, Pa., killed Sept. 11, 1777, at Brandywine.

LEMUS, SENOR C. JOSÉ MORALES, Cuban agent in the United States; d. at Brooklyn, N. Y., June 28, 1870.

LENNARD, THOMAS B., brevet maj. of corps of topographical engineers of U. S. army; d. at Phila., April 24, 1851, a. 41.

LENOX, ROBERT, d. in New York city, Dec. 13, 1839, a. 80; native of Scotland, but for sixty years a resident of New York, and one of the most enterprising and wealthy of the merchants of that city.

LENT, JAMES, JR., member of congress from Newtown, Queens co., N. Y.; d. at Washington, D. C., Feb. 22, 1833.

LEONARD, JAMES HARVEY, merchant; b. in West Springfield, Mass., Sept. 22, 1780; settled in Lowville, N. Y., in 1804, and continued in business, till 1839; he was many years p. m.; he d. at Syracuse, Mar. 14, 1845. (*Hough's Hist. Lewis Co. N. Y.*, p. 150, with portrait.)

LEONARD, JAMES LOREN, youngest son of James Harvey Leonard; was b. at Lowville, June 5, 1821, and d. in that town, Jan. 25, 1867; he acquired a considerable estate, became president and sole owner of the Bank of Lowville, and was a liberal benefactor of the Lowville Academy and other public objects.

LEONARD, JONATHAN, late of Canton, Mass.; d. at Covington, Ky., Oct. 20, 1839, a. 76; was a prominent member of the society of Friends.

LE RAY, JAMES DONATIEN (de Chaumont), land proprietor in northern N. Y.; b. Nov. 13, 1760, at Chaumont, France; son of a commissary of the Am. fleet and host of B. Franklin, when living at Passy, Fr.; he came to America in 1785, returned in 1790, and in 1808, made a permanent settlement at Le Raysville, Jeff. co.; he had been many years concerned in the Company of N. Y., a Parisian land speculation, and in the Antwerp Company, of Holland, and finally became owner of much of their lands in Jefferson and Lewis cos., N. Y.; in 1812, he was employed to negotiate a foreign loan, but without success; in 1823, he encountered heavy pecuniary difficulties, and in 1832, returned to France, but in 1836 revisited America; he d. in France, Dec. 31, 1840, a. 80; he was the first president of the State Ag. Soc., in 1832, and took a zealous interest in all public improvements. (*Hough's Hist. Jefferson Co. N. Y.*, p. 441, with portrait.)

LESESNE, J. W., a judge in the Alabama courts, and a native of South Carolina; was drowned in Mobile bay, Ala., Oct. 16, 1856.

LETTERMAN, DR. JONATHAN, formerly medical director of the army of the Potomac; d. at San Francisco, Cal., March 17, 1872.

LEVIN, LEWIS C., d. March 14, 1860, at Philadelphia, Pa.; b. in Charleston, S. C., Nov. 10, 1808; grad. at Columbia Coll., S. C., became a lawyer, and practiced in Md., La., Ky., and Pa.; was in congress from Pa., from 1845 to 1847, and from 1847 to 1851; was an active politician and one of the founders of the American party. (*Vincent's Semi-An. Register*, p. 183.)

LEVINGS, REV. DR., financial secretary of the American Bible Society; d, at Cincinnati, Ohio, Jan. 10, 1849, a. about 53.

LEWIS, ADDIN, d. April 7, 1842, a. 62; was b. in Stonington, Conn., grad. at Yale in 1803, and was for a time instructor in the University of Georgia, and afterwards collector at Mobile; he was afterwards post master, president of a bank, mayor of Mobile, and for several of the last years of his life a resident of Mobile.

LEWIS, ALFRED J., recorder of the third municipality of New Orleans; d. at that place Oct. 23, 1842, a. 32.

LEWIS, MAJ. LAWRENCE, of Wood Lawn, Va., a nephew of Gen. Washington; d. at Arlington House near Washington, Nov. 30, 1839, a. 73.

LEWIS, MORDECAI, b. in Philadelphia, Sept. 21, 1748; and d. March 13, 1799; was extensively engaged in foreign trade at Philadelphia, and spent some years in Europe; was a director of the Bank of North America, of the Philadelphia Contributionship for the insurance of houses from loss by fire, of the Phila. Library Company, and treasurer of the Pennsylvania Hospital. (*Simpson's Eminent Philadelphians.*)

LEWIS, CAPT. ROBERT, Conn., killed March 22, 1777.

LEWIS, REV. STEPHEN, F. W. Bap. preacher, ordained in Whitfield, Me., Nov. 7, 1834, and spent much of his life in Windsor; he d. at Augusta, Me., March 15, 1856, a. 77. (*F. W. Bap. Reg.*, 1857, p. 88.)

LEWIS, LIEUT. WILLIAM, Va., killed Sept. 14, 1779.

LEWIS, WILLIAM, b. in Chester co., Penn., in 1751; studied law, and for some time president of the council and recorder of Philadelphia; was a member of the legislature, and a leading federalist; in 1789 was in the convention that revised the constitution; became U. S. dist. attorney and afterwards district judge, but soon after returned to the bar; d. Aug. 15, 1819. (*Wharton's State Trials; Simpson's Eminent Philadelphians.*)

LIEBER, FRANCIS, publicist and professor in the law school of Columbia Coll.; d. in New York city, Oct. 14, 1872, a. 72. (*Drake's Am. Biog.*)

LIGHTFOOT, ROBERT, was b. in London in 1716; grad. at Oxford, studied law in the Inner Temple, was appointed judge of vice admiralty in the southern district of the Am. colonies, and came to Newport; he d. at Plainfield, Ct., in 1794, where he had settled. (*W. Updike's Memoirs of the R. I. Bar*, p. 246.)

LILLIE, JOHN, officer of the revolution; b. at Boston about 1752, entered the army as lt. of artillery, and on the peace held the rank of captain, having served actively and honorably; he was appointed chief officer at West Point in 1799, and d. soon after. (*Bradford's N. E. Biog.*)

LILLIE, JOHN SWEETSER, for thirty years pension clerk in the loan office; d. at Boston, Mass., Aug. 16, 1842, a. 76.

LINCKLAEN, JAN VAN, was b. in Amsterdam, Holland, Dec. 24, 1768; educated for the most part under a private tutor in Switzerland, he entered the Dutch navy at the age of 14 years, served therein several years; in 1790 he came to this country under the patronage of Mr.

Stadnitski of Amsterdam, the principal director of the Holland Land Company's affairs in America; in 1792 he penetrated the wilderness of Central New York, and surveyed the land subsequently purchased by this company, and the following year, as their agent, he began the settlement of Cazenovia, N. Y.; becoming the joint purchaser of the unsold lands belonging to this company in Madison and Chenango counties he devoted the remainder of his life, which terminated Feb. 9th, 1822, to promote their occupation and improvement.

LINCOLN, CAPT. GEORGE, 8th U. S. infantry, killed in battle of Buena Vista, Feb. 23, 1847; b. in Worcester, Mass.; entered the army in 1837, and was brevetted for honorable services at the battle of Resaca de la Palma.

LINDLEY, ELEAZER, officer in the *Jersey Blues* in the revolution, explored the Genesee country in 1790, and bought tp. 1, 2d r., Phelps and Gorham's purchase, and settled with forty persons; this tract is now the town of Lindley, N. Y.; he d. in 1792 while attending the legislature at N. Y. city. (*McMaster's Hist. Steuben Co., N. Y.*, p. 79.)

LINDSEY, AARON, d. Dec., 1841, at Jackson, Miss., a. 28, formerly secretary of state and senator; was a ready political writer, and distinguished himself as a newspaper editor.

LINDSEY, HENRY, d. in New Bedford, Mass., Oct. 27, 1853; was editor of the *New Bedford Whalemen's Shipping Lists.*

LINGARD, JAMES W., formerly manager of the Bowery Theatre, N. Y.; d. July 6, 1870, a. 47.

LINNARD, THOMAS B., brevet major of the corps of topographical engineers, U. S. A.; d. at Philadelphia, Pa., April 24, 1851, a. 41.

LINTON, WILLIAM C., of Terre Haute, Ind.; one of the canal fund com'rs of Indiana; d. at Philadelphia, Pa., Jan. 31, 1835.

LIPSCOMB, DR. DABNEY, d. in Columbus, Miss., June 22, 1850, a. 56; president of the state senate.

LISTON, SIR ROBERT, first minister from Great Britain to the United States after the acknowledgment of independence, and late minister to Constantinople; d. at Edinburg, Scotland, July 15, 1836, in his 94th year. (*Am. Almanac*, 1838, p. 295.)

LITTLE, CHARLES C., d. at Cambridge, Mass., Aug. 9, 1769; b. at Kennebunk, Me., 1799; brought up a bookseller, and about 1829, formed with James Brown, the partnership of Little, Brown & Co., having bought out the old firm of Hillard and Gray, of Boston.

LITTLEFIELD, EDWARD B., president of the Planter's Bank, of Tenn., and a native of Newport, R. I.; d. at Nashville, Tenn., Feb. 18, 1836.

LIVINGSTON, HENRY A., a grandson of Philip Livingston, and son of a R. P. D. clergyman; was in assembly in 1827, and in senate in 1838–41; d. at Poughkeepsie, N. Y., June, 1849. (*Stryker's Am. Reg.*, ii, 505.)

LIVINGSTON, JOHN W., d. in New York city, April 11, 1860; was in the army in early life, and served in the war of 1812; became marshal of the northern dist. of New York, and took up his residence at Skaneateles; after residing there 21 years, removed to New York city; he retired to private life.

LIVINGSTON, MORTIMER, shipping merchant and financier; son of Maturin L., and grandson of Gov. Lewis; he became concerned in the shipping business in N. Y., with Bolton & Fox, proprietors of a line of N. Y. and Havre packets; upon Bolton's death, the firm was known as Fox & Livingston, and later as Mortimer L., alone; he was pres. of the U. S. mail, N. Y. and Havre Steam Packet Line, and director in several financial institutions at the time of his death, which occurred Aug. 24, 1857, a. about 49, at his home on Staten Island.

LIVINGSTON, COL. PETER R., son of Robert L., 3d prop'r of the manor of Livingston, b. May 8, 1737, was in the gen. assem. of N. Y., 1761 to 1769, and in 1774; was chosen pres. of the provincial convention in 1776, and chairman of the committee of safety; he was in assembly in 1780–1; and d. Nov. 15, 1794, a. 57; his sister Mary m. James Duane. (*Doc. Hist. N. Y.*, iv, 448.)

LIVINGSTON, PETER R., a native of Dutchess co., a man of fine fancy and great declamatory power, who filled many stations in the state and national governments; was a member of the New York assembly in 1823, and speaker of the house, and of the state senate from 1821 to 3, and from 1826 to 9; d. at Rhinebeck, Jan. 19, 1847, a. 81.

LIVINGSTON, PHILIP, second prop'r of manor of Livingston, b. in Albany, 1686, attended his uncle Col. Vetch, to Quebec in 1705, served at Port Royal in 1710, and served on a perilous mission to Quebec; he was admitted to the bar at N. Y., Dec. 31, 1719, and in 1720 was made com'r of Indian affairs; in 1721, succeeded his father as sec. of that board and clerk of Albany; he was appointed councillor in May, 1725, and in 1726 again visited Canada; he served on various commissions for settling boundaries, and d. in N. Y., Feb., 1749; his daughter Sarah m. Lord Stirling of the revolution. (*Munsell's An. Alb.*, vii, 311.)

LIVINGSTON, PHILIP CORTLANDT, son of Lt. Gilbert Ja's L., of Poughkeepsie; b. Nov. 17, 1790; was a midshipman on board the Chesapeak, and was killed in the action with the Shannon, June 1, 1813, a. 22.

LOCKE, FRANCIS, colored, killed at Charlotte, S. C., Sept. 25, 1780.

LOCKE, FRANCIS, b. in Rowan co., N. C., Oct. 31, 1766; elected a judge of the superior court in 1803, and having resigned, was chosen senator in cong. from North Carolina, for the years 1814–15; d. Jan., 1823.

LOCKE, RICHARD ADAMS, formerly editor and journalist of New York, d. at Staten Island, Feb. 16, 1871, a. 71; was author of the *Moon Hoax*, and other sensational stories; was editor of *The N. Y. Sun*, *The New Era*, and other journals.

LOCKHART, JAMES, member of congress elect from the first congressional dist. of Indiana; d. at Evansville, Ind., Sept. 7, 1857.

LOCKWOOD, JOHN DAVENPORT, b. in Stamford, Ct., evinced an early maturity of talent, became a student in Yale in 1844; and d. suddenly Dec. 20, 1844. (*Memoirs of J. D. L., by his Father.*)

LOCKWOOD, LE GRAND, of the banking house of Lockwood & Co., New York; d. Feb. 24, 1872, a. 52.

LOGAN, WILLIAM, b. in Harrodsburg, Ky., Dec. 8, 1776; was in the state constitutional convention of 1779; practiced law, and was several years in the legislature, and speaker; was twice chosen judge of the court of appeals; was a senator in congress in 1819–20, and d. Aug. 8, 1822.

LOMAX, MAJ. MANN P., of the U. S. ordnance corps; d. at Watertown, Mass., March 27, 1842, a. 55; he was a native of Virginia.

LONGNECKER, HENRY C., d. at Lehigh, Pa., Sept. 18, 1872, a. 49; was a soldier of the Mexican war; member of congress in 1858–61; colonel of the 9th Pa. regt., in 1861, 2, 3, and judge of Lehigh co., from 1867.

LONGSTREITH, MOSES, b. in Philadelphia, Dec., 1800; became a merchant, and in 1835, became a farmer in White Marsh township, 12 m. from Philadelphia; was for a time, associate judge of the courts in the county of Montgomery, and in 1847, was elected canal commissioner; was a democratic candidate for governor, but was defeated; d. at his farm residence, April 26, 1855. (*Simpson's Eminent Philadelphians.*)

LOOKER, OTHNIEL, d. in Palestine, Ill., July 23, 1845, a. 87; b. in N. J., Oct. 6, 1757; served in the revolution, emigrated to Hamilton co., O., in 1804, and was chosen to the senate of Ohio, in 1813; was afterwards speaker of the senate, and after the resignation of Gov. Meigs, in 1814, became acting governor of Ohio; was associate judge of Hamilton court of com. pleas, for the term of 7 years.

LOOMIS, COL. GUSTAVUS, U. S. A., d. at Stratford, Conn., March 5, 1872.

LOOSEY, CHEVALIER C. F. DE, Austrian consul general at New York, d. July 21, 1870, a. 60.

LORD, CHARLES B., judge of the circuit court, St. Louis, Mo.; d. Nov. 16, 1868.

LORD, FREDERICK WILLIAM, of Greenport, L. I.; d. in N. Y. city, May 24, 1860, a. 59; he was b. in Lyme, Ct.; grad. at Yale in 1810; studied medicine, and lived at Lyme, from 1828 to 1830, when he removed to Sag Harbor, N. Y., and practiced till 1846; he was in congress from New York in 1847–9.

LORD, JAMES COOPER, d. at New York, Feb. 9, 1869; was noted for his efforts in philanthropic enterprises.

LORD, JOSEPH, of Putney, Vt., was 2d judge of the inferior court of C. P., in Cumberland co., Vt., from 1766 till the revolution; he stood high in the confidence of government. (*Hall's Eastern Vermont*, p. 677.)

LORD, RUFUS L., banker, d. in New York, May 15, 1869, a. 83; b. in Franklin, Conn.; began life as a clerk in a dry goods store in that state; came to N. Y., in 1805, and began business which he continued till 1832; was the victim of a noted bond robbery.

LORD, GEN., a Cuban minister of war; d. at Los Guiros, Cuba, May 29, 1870.

LORILLARD, JACOB, b. in N. Y., in 1774, was self taught and self made, was apprenticed to a tobacconist, and spent his life in this business evincing great capacity, and acquiring a large estate; he was distinguished for his benevolence and activity in various societies and organizations for charitable and religious objects, and the promotion of the public welfare; he was many years a vestryman of Trinity church, and in 1812–13, was in assembly. (*Hunt's Lives of Am. Merchants*, i, 391.)

LORIMER, GEORGE S. F., a member of the house of delegates; d. in Essex co., Va., Nov., 1839.

LORING, REV. BAILEY, was b. in Pembroke, Mass.; grad. at Brown University in 1807, and was settled over the first church in Andover, in 1810; he d. there May 5, 1860, a. 73.

LORING, COL. BENJAMIN, a merchant of the old school; wealthy, liberal and charitable; a prominent member, and at one time an officer of the Mass. Charitable Mechanic's Assoc.; the Loring theological library was given to Harvard Coll. library, and he made donations to his native town, Hingham, Mass.; d. at Boston, Dec. 23, 1859, a, 83.

LORING, F. W., author, killed near Wickenburg, Arizona Ter., Nov. 5, 1871.

LORING, ISAAC, d. at Port Gibson, Miss., June 18, 1843; b. in Sunbury, Mass.; removed to Marietta, O., in 1787, where he was for some time acting as commissary in the army under Gen. Wayne; in 1803, removed to Claiborne co., Miss., then just formed, and built the first framed house at Port Gibson; was the 3d grand master of Free Masons in Miss.

LOTHROP, JOHN H., b. in New Haven Conn., May 15th, 1769; he grad. at Yale in 1787; he studied law at Middletown, and after a brief residence in Georgia removed to Oneida county, N. Y., in 1795 or 6; in 1803 he became editor of *The Whitestown Gazette and Cato's Patrol*, which name he changed to *Utica Patriot;* in 1811 he disposed of the paper and removed to New Hartford to practice his profession; in 1816 he was appointed cashier of the Ontario Branch Bank and returned to Utica to live; this employment and a partial connection with the paper occupied him until his death, June 15, 1829; he was trustee of Hamilton College, and clerk of the board from 1812 until his death.

LOTHROP, CAPTAIN JOHN THORNTON KIRKLAND, b. in New Hartford, Dec. 25, 1813; he attended school at Northampton, Mass., and while visiting at Boston, became enamored of the sea; between 1827 and 1835, he made several voyages in merchant vessels; in the latter year he entered the Texan service, was captured by the Mexicans and imprisoned; on his release, he was placed in command of a vessel, and in 1842, was assigned to the defence of Galveston; in 1843, after the exhibition of great bravery in different actions, and in command of different ships, he was ordered by President Houston, to take command of the fleet; he refused to supersede Commodore Moore, and while attending as a witness, on the trial of the latter, he d., Sept. 15, 1844.

LOUDON, JANE (colored), d. at New London, Conn., April, 1841, a. 108.

LOUIS, DR. VINCENT BERNARD SYLVESTER, d. at the navy hospital near Norfolk, Va., Aug. 15, 1854; surgeon of the French government steamer Chinese.

LOVETT, JOHN, b. in Ct.; grad. at Yale in 1782; attempted to establish a school at Albany; studied law, and went to Ft. Miller as tutor in the family of Col. Duer, and land agent; he removed thence to Lansingburg; in 1800, 1, was in assembly, and in 1807, settled in Albany; in 1812, he became military sec. to Gen. Van Rensselaer, and suffered a permanent injury to his hearing, by a cannon at Queenston; he was elected to the 13th cong.; he bought the Twelve Mile Square tract, at the mouth of the Maumee, where he began the settlement of Perrysburg, and was one of the owners of the first steamboat on Lake Erie; he d. at Fort Meigs, O., Aug., 1818, a. 53. (*Munsell's An. Alb.*, x, 351; *Woodworth's Troy.*)

LOVETT, JOHN, a member of assembly from Schoharie co., in 1856, and a prominent business man; d. at Esperance, N. Y., April 23, 1859, a. 40.

LOVEWELL, ZACHEUS, b. at Dunstable, N. H., July 24, 1701; succeeded Col. Blanchard, in April, 1758, in command of the N. H. regt.; was ordered to join Gen. Prideaux, at Niagara, July 23, 1759, and d. April 12, 1772, a. 72. (*Fox's Hist. of Dunstable*, 247.)

LOW, ISAAC, a prominent New York merchant, of the city of New York; was in the first provincial congress of N. Y., but when the question of separation from England, came up, he sided with the mother country, and he was attainted and banished in 1779; withdrew to England in 1783, and d. in 1791.

LOW, NICHOLAS, merchant in N. Y., and proprietor of lands in northern N. Y.; b. near New Brunswick, N. J., March 30, 1739; 5th son of Cornelius L.; became a prominent merchant, before the revolution, and in 1788, 9, was in assembly; he was also member of the convention for adopting the U. S. constitution; he built the Sans Souci Hotel, and a cotton factory at Ballston, before the war of 1812, and having with Harrison, Hoffman, and Henderson, bought a large and valuable tract in Jefferson and Lewis cos., in 1796, withdrew himself from other business, in later years, and attended only to its settlement; he d. Nov. 15, 1826, a. 83; the town of Lowville, N. Y., bears his name; he was proprietor also of Adams, and Watertown, N. Y.; his son Cornelius, d. in N. Y., June 30, 1849, a. 54, and Nicholas in 1849. (*Hough's Hist. Lewis Co.*, p. 135, with portrait.)

LOWE, GEN. JOSEPH, a public spirited citizen of Concord, N. H; d. Aug. 28, 1859, a. 70.

LOWERY, JOHN M., d. at Crawfordville, Miss., July 18, 1856, a. 41; b. in S. C., in 1814; educated at Columbia College, and settled in Mississippi in 1840; became one of the most successful planters in that state.

LOZIER, MRS. CHARLOTTE DENHAM, M.D., d. at New York, Jan. 4, 1870, a. 36; b. in Milburn, N. J., in 1844; grad. at the N. J. State Normal School; studied medicine and surgery in Philadelphia and New York, and practiced with great success; after her graduation, she m. Dr. Abraham H. Lozier.

LUCAS, FIELDING, d. in Baltimore, Md., March 12, 1854, a. 72; a much esteemed citizen.

LUCAS, LIEUT. THOMAS, Penn., killed Oct. 4, 1777, at Germantown.

LUCKEY, REV. SAMUEL, D.D., b. in Rensselaerville, N. Y., April 4, 1791; became a Methodist Episcopal minister in Lower Canada, and afterwards at Troy, N. Y.; in 1832, became principal of the Genesee Wesleyan Seminary at Lima, N. Y.; in 1847, was chosen a regent of the University of the state of New York; d. 1869.

LUDLAM, PROVIDENCE, senator from Cumberland co., in the N. J. senate; d. at Bridgeton, N. J., Jan. 20, 1868; was county clerk from 1857 to 1862, and senator from 1862 till his death.

LUDLOW, CAPT. CHARLES, formerly of the U. S. navy; d. at New Windsor, N. Y., Oct. 20, 1839.

LUDLOW, C. D., captain of the steamer Ariel was killed in a storm, Dec., 1858, and buried at N. Y.

LUDWICK, CHRISTOPHER, b. in Germany in 1720; in early life served in the Austrian army against the Turks; was afterwards in the Prussian service, and after peace entered an Indiaman and went to India under Boscawen; he afterwards made many voyages, from 1745 to 1752 from London to Holland, Ireland, and the West Indies as a sailor, and in 1753, came with a small venture to Philadelphia; became a baker of gingerbread, grew into influence, aided in the revolution, and in 1777, was appointed baker general to the army. (*Simpson's Eminent Philadelphians.*)

LUFBOROUGH, NATHAN, d. at Milton, Md., Dec. 7, 1848, a. 76; formerly chief clerk in the office of the comptroller of the treasury.

LUFF, EDMUND, b. in England, first preacher at Sackett's Harbor, N. Y.; d. at that place in 1822.

LUKENS, ISAIAH, an eminent philosophical artist and vice pres. of Franklin Inst.; d. at Philadelphia Nov. 13, 1846, a. 69. (*Am. Jour. Sci. & Arts*, 2d ser., iii, 144.)

LUMPKIN, JOHN HENRY, judge and M. C., b. in Oglethorpe co., Ga., June 13, 1812, was educated at Franklin and Yale Colleges but did not graduate, was sec. in the exec. dep. of Ga., studied law and was admitted in 1834; in 1838 was solicitor gen. of the Cherokee circuit; for a time in the legislature, and from 1843 to 1849 in congress; he was 3 y. judge of the Cherokee circuit court, and a judge of the supreme court of Ga.; he d. in Rome, Ga., July 9, 1860. (*Hist. Mag.*, iv, 284.)

LUMSDEN, FRANCIS ASBURY, journalist, b. in N. C., was early apprenticed to Joseph Gales, printer at Raleigh; spent 9 y. on the *Nat. Intelligencer* at Washington; went to New Orleans, and in 1837 with Mr. Kendall began the *N. O. Picayune*, with which he was connected till his death; he was an editor of superior ability, and of much influence in the southern states; he perished with his family on the steamer Lady Elgin on Lake Michigan, Sept. 7, 1860; his body was recovered, and buried at New Orleans, Oct. 18, 1860. (*N. O. Picayune*, Sept. 16, 1860.)

LUNDY, REV. FRANCIS JONES, D.C.L., d. at Newburg, N. Y., April 7, 1868, in his 54th year.

LUSH, STEPHEN, private sec. of Gov. George Clinton, member of assembly from Albany co., in 1792–3, 1803–5–6, and state senator in 1801–2; d. in Albany April 15, 1825.

LUTZ, COL. NICHOLAS, of the Penn. Flying camp; captured on Long Island, Aug. 27, 1776; exchanged Sept. 10, 1799, and returned to Reading, Pa., where he d.

LYDIUS, REV. JOHANNES, Dutch minister at Albany, began in 1703, labored to instruct the Indians, and d. March 1, 1710; his son John Henry L., was a prominent Indian trader, who retired to England in 1776 and d. near London in 1791, a. 98. (*Rogers's Hist. Discourse*, p. 19.)

LYDNOR, FORTUNATUS, d. at Lynchburg, Va., June 7, 1840, a. 51; cashier of the branch of the Bank of Virginia.

LYFORD, FIFIELD, d. in Cabot, Vt., April 15, 1846, a. 84; he was b. in Exeter, N. H., and served in the revolution.

LYLE, DAVID M., chief engineer of the Philadelphia fire department, d. Nov. 23, 1867, in his 50th year.

LYMAN, HANNAH W., first lady principal of Vassar College; b. in Northampton, Mass., in 1816; began to teach at an early age, and after filling subordinate stations in various places, went, in 1839, to Montreal, and opened a school for young ladies, which proved quite successful; she was called in 1865, from thence to fill the place in which she d., at Poughkeepsie, N. Y., Feb. 21, 1871. (*Regents' Report*, 1872, p. 694.)

LYMAN, JOSEPH H., journalist, d. at Richmond Hill, L. I., Jan. 28, 1872, a. 47.

LYMAN, SAMUEL PHELPS, b. May, 1804, at Siloam, Madison co., N. Y., and educated in the academy at Hamilton; he studied law at Peterboro and at Utica, and was admitted to practice in 1826; after a few years of devotion to his profession, and to the editing of the *Elucidator*, he turned his attention to the building of rail roads; he was attached to the N. Y. and Erie road, at a time when a small portion of it was completed, and when the work was suspended for want of capital; by a series of letters to the *Commercial Advertiser*, and by other means, he commended it to public notice, and essentially aided in its construction; in 1836 he was its general superintendent; he was also rail road commissioner of the state; he projected the iron cars, now in use, and as superintendent of the company engaged in their manufacture, was completing a few details, regarding their construction, when he d., at Cold Spring, N. Y., Sept. 30, 1869.

LYNCH, JAMES, ex-sheriff of New York co.; d. at Manhattanville, N. Y., Jan. 22, 1851, a. 51.

LYNCH, JAMES, d. near Rhinebeck, N. Y., Oct, 3, 1853, a. 67; son of the elder Dominick Lynch; began law practice at Rome, N. Y., but removed to Utica, and was in assembly in 1823; in 1826, removed to New York, and afterwards appointed a judge of the marine court, in which office he remained till his death; was an early and active member of the American Institute.

LYNCH, REV. WILLIAM R., d. at Augusta, Ga., Feb. 25, 1871; long a member of the Wyoming conference, N. Y. (*Northern Christian Advocate*, March 23, 1871.)

LYND, CORNELIUS, an officer of the revolution; d. at Williamstown, Vt., Feb. 21, 1836, a. 84.

LYON, CALEB, land agent, b. at East Windsor, Ct.; in 1761, removed to Greenfield, Mass., and was a pioneer agent and settler at Walworth and North Penfield, N. Y., and in 1819, removed to the town of Greig, N. Y., where in 1823 he began improvement at Lyonsdale; he was in assembly in 1824, and d. suddenly, Sept. 15, 1835; he was father of Hon. Lyman R. L., of Lyon's Falls, and of Caleb Lyon, of Lyonsdale. (*Hough's Hist. Lewis Co. N. Y.*, p. 109, with portrait.)

LYON, CHITTENDEN, member of congress from Kentucky, from 1827 to 1835; d. in Caldwell co., Ky., in Nov., 1842.

LYON, LUCIUS, b. in Vt.; removed when a young man to Michigan, and was several years a surveyor; was delegate in congress in 1833–4–5, and senator from Michigan, from 1836 to 1840; was in congress from 1843 to 1845, and afterwards was surveyor general in the north west; d. at Detroit, Sept. 25, 1851.

LYON, MATTHEW, b. in Ireland, about 1746, settled in Vt., and was in congress from 1799 to 1801; he removed to Ky., and was in congress in 1803 to 11; was a victim of the sedition law, passed in the term of the elder Adams, and was imprisoned in Vermont in 1798–9; having served in both houses of the Kentucky legislature, he d. Aug. 1, 1822, at Spadra Bluff on the Arkansas river near Little Rock, nine years after, his remains were conveyed to Eddyville, Lyon co., Ky., and reinterred with kindred. (*Hist. Mag.*, iii, 23; *Address by Pliny H. White before the Vermont Hist. Soc.*, Oct. 29, 1858.)

LYON, N. W., a revolutionary soldier, d. at Easton, Conn., April 18, 1860, in his 101st year.

LYON, Patrick, b. in London about 1779; landed in Philadelphia, Nov. 25, 1793; was an eminent locksmith, and his reputation as such led to a groundless charge of robbery of the Bank of Pennsylvania in 1798; he sued his accusers, and recovered $12,000; he lived to a ripe old age, and d. in Philadelphia, where he was highly esteemed and greatly trusted. (*Simpson's Eminent Philadelphians.*)

LYON, Robert, was the second son of Wolfe Lyon of London, and came to New York in 1844, where he was several years concerned in commercial affairs; he founded the *Asmonean*, a Jewish paper, Oct. 26, 1849, and continued to conduct this journal till his death, which occurred at New York March 10, 1858, a. 49. (*Hist. Mag.*, ii, 155.)

LYONS, William T., of New York city, d. March, 1871, giving his estate valued at $40,000 to $50,000, to the missionary soc. of the Meth. Epis. church.

LYTTLE, Robert T., a distinguished public speaker, and member of congress from Ohio from 1833 to 1835; d. in New Orleans, Dec. 21, 1839.

MACALESTER, Charles, an eminent Philadelphia merchant, b. at Campbelltown in Argyleshire, Scotland, April 5, 1765, and d. at Willow Grove near Philadelphia, Aug. 27, 1832; was extensively engaged in foreign commerce.

McALLISTER, John, b. in Feb., 1753, in Glasgow, Scotland; came to America in 1775, settled in Philadelphia as a turner; first making walking canes as a specialty, and afterwards whips; in 1799 he went into manufacture of spectacles; he d. May 12, 1830.

McALPINE, George, d. at Grand Gulf, Miss., April 6, 1841, in his 94th year; was from Glasgow, Scotland, and came to America before the revolution.

McARTHUR, Rev. John, formerly professor in the Miami University, O.; d. at Indianapolis, Aug. 19, 1849.

McARTHUR, William P., lieut. commanding U. S. N., assistant in the coast survey, and commander of the surveying schooner Ewing; d. at Panama, Dec. 23, 1850.

McCABE, Rev. Bernard, burned to death while in bed, at Malone, N. Y., Nov. 24, 1857; was Catholic priest at that place.

McCAFEE, Col. Morgan, d. in Rankin co., Miss., 1857, about 53 years of age; he was for several years in the state legislature, where he held an influential position.

McCALL, Dr. John b. in Hebron, Washington co., N. Y., Dec. 25, 1787; tended medical lectures, at Columbia College, in 1810, '11 and '12; was appointed surgeon's mate of U. S. army, and attached to the 13th regiment; he was soon promoted to a surgeoncy, and remained with the army until

July, 1815, having been present in the battle of Queenston, at the capture of Fort George, and at French Mills; he settled in Deerfield, N. Y., but in 1818, moved to Utica, continuing in active practice until his death, Oct. 5, 1867; he was president of both County and State Medical Societies; received the honorary degree of M.D., from Geneva College, and was elected mem. of the College of Physicians and Surgeons, of New York.

McCARTER, ROBERT H., judge of the court of errors and appeals in New Jersey; d. at Newton, N. J., March, 1851, a. 57.

McCAULEY, LT. NATHANIEL, N. H., killed in the rev. Aug. 30, 1779.

McCAULEY, MRS. SARAH, sister of Singleton Mercer, d. in Philadelphia, Pa., April, 1860; was painfully prominent, some years ago, as being the person injured by Hutchinson Heberton, who was hunted down and shot by S. M., her brother, as he was crossing the ferry. (*Vincent's Semi-An. Register*, p. 306.)

McCAY, CHARLES F., d. at Apalachicola, Fla., Dec. 24, 1852; prof. of math., astron., and civil engineering, in the University of Georgia.

McCHESNEY, ROBERT, formerly a judge, d. at Cranberry, N. J., May 11, 1835, a. 77.

McCHESNEY, ROBERT, physician, from Troy, N. Y.; removed in 1810 to Madrid, N. Y.; d. May, 1824, a. 36. (*Hough's Hist. St. Law. and Fr. Cos., N. Y.*, p. 599.)

McCLARY, MAJ. ANDREW, N. H., killed at Bunker hill, June 17, 1775.

McCLEARY, GEN. JAMES, member of congress from Louisiana; d. in New York city, Nov. 5, 1871.

McCLEARY, SAMUEL F., d. in Boston, Mass., Jan. 12, 1855, a. 75; b. in Boston, April 28, 1780; was admitted to the bar in 1808; was a warm federalist; appointed assist. clerk of the state senate in 1810–1, and clerk in 1813, and annually after till 1822, when he became city clerk, and continued till 1852.

McCLELLAN, DR. JOHN, b. June 22, 1773, in Colerain, Mass., studied medicine with Dr. Hyde of Guilford, N. H., settled in Seneca co., N. Y., in 1796, and the next year in Livingston, N. Y.; in 1842 he removed to Hudson and practiced till 1853; he d. there Oct. 18, 1855, a. 83. (*Tr. N. Y. St. Med. Soc.*, 1857, p. 79.)

McCLELLAN, SAMUEL, b. Sept. 21, 1800, at Woodstock, Conn., of Scotch descent; grad. at the Yale Med. School, and settled in Philadelphia; was demonstrator of anatomy at the Jefferson Medical College, and afterwards professor of obstetrics; he finally returned to practice, and d. Jan. 4, 1853. (*Simpson's Eminent Philadelphians*, with portrait.)

McCLELLAN, SAMUEL, M.D., b. June 13, 1787, in Colerain, Mass., studied medicine and practised with his br. John of Livingston, N. Y., and in 1813 removed to Schodack near Nassau, N. Y., and d. April 8, 1855; he was extensively known as a surgeon, and private teacher of medicine. (*Tr. N. Y. St. Med. Soc.*, 1857, p. 51.)

McCLELLAND, DR. SAMUEL, of Philadelphia; an eminent physician; d. in that city, Jan. 4, 1854, a. 53.

McCLELLAND, DR. WILLIAM, b. in Galloway, Scot., in 1769; educated in Edinburg, and settled at Albany, as a physician, where he d. Jan. 29, 1812; he was first pres. of the N. Y. Med. Soc. (*Tr. N. Y. St. Med. Soc.*, 1857, p. 29; *Munsell's An. Alb.*, ix, 93.)

McCLENACHAN, Blair, b. in Ireland; was in business in Philadelphia before the revolution, and in that war engaged in privateering, in which he was very successful; he subscribed £10,000, in 1780, to supply the army; he afterwards engaged extensively in mercantile operations, was a ship owner on a large scale, and d. in Philadelphia, at an advanced age. (*Simpson's Eminent Philadelphians.*)

McCLINTOCK, Nathaniel, revolutionary officer of New Hampshire; b. March 21, 1757; grad. at Harvard in 1775; joined the revolution, as lieut., and was soon made adjutant in Col. Poor's reg't, and promoted to the rank of brigade major; from difficulties concerning rank, he tendered his resignation, after honorable service at Trenton, Ticonderoga, and elsewhere; in 1779, he returned home, engaged in privateering in the ship Gen. Sullivan, of 20 guns, Captain Manning, and having taken a ship of war from the enemy, engaged in a cruise in company, as second to Lt. Broadstreet in command; in 1780, he was killed in an engagement with two vessels of superior force. (*Rogers's Am. Biog.*)

McCLUNG, Col. Alexander R., d. in Jackson, Miss., March 23, 1855, a. about 43; b. in Kentucky, settled in Miss., served in the Mexican war, and gained the rank of lieut. colonel; was appointed chargé d'affaires to Bolivia, by Pres. Taylor, and resigned about two years before his death.

McCLURE, Charles, formerly secretary of the commonwealth of Pennsylvania, and superintendent of schools; d. in Pittsburg, Pa., Jan. 10, 1846. He was a lawyer by profession.

McCLURE, David, d. in Philadelphia, Pa., April 13, 1842, a. 58; prof. of mathematics in the U. S. Navy.

McCLURE, Gen. George, b. in Ireland in 1770; became a carpenter; emigrated in 1790; was a pioneer in Capt. Williamson's settlement at Bath, N. Y.; moved in 1800 to Dansville and kept store, and in 1801 bought the Cold Spring Mill site between Bath and Crooked lake, where he built mills and did a heavy business in trade. In 1814 he removed to Bath; in 1816 was made sheriff of Steuben co., and in 1823, 4, 7 was in assembly; moved to Elgin, Ill., in 1834, and died Aug. 16, 1851. He commanded the militia on the Niagara frontier in 1813, 14, and his wanton destruction of Newark, U. C., provoked a heavy retribution from the enemy in Dec. 1813. (*McMaster's Hist. of Steuben Co. N. Y.*, p. 113.)

McCOLME, John, was appointed surgeon of 2d battalion of royalists, May 1, 1744, and his name was continued till June 1767; he served in the French war.

MACOMB, Harriet Balch, widow of Maj. Gen. Alexander McC.; d. in Washington, D.C., May 23, 1869, a. 86.

MACOMB, William H., commodore in the U. S. navy, d. at Phila. Aug., 1872; was a son of Major Gen. Alexander Macomb, formerly commander in chief of the army.

McCONNELL, Felix G., member of congress from Alabama, d. by suicide in Washington, Sept., 1846, under the effect of intemperance, a. 36; was a native of Lincoln co., Tenn., and in 1824 he removed to Talladega, Ala., where his family resided at the time of his death.

34

McCOOK, Gen. Edwin S., territorial secretary of Dakota; was shot at Yanktown, D. T., by P. P. Wintermute, a banker of that place, Sept. 11, 1873; was the fifth son of Gen. Daniel McCook of Ohio.

McCORMICK, Daniel, a native of Ireland; settled as a merchant in New York before the revolution, and afterwards was largely concerned with Alexander Macomb, Wm. Constable and others, in land speculations in Northern New York; d. at N. Y. Jan. 31, 1834, a. 92; was the last occupant of a first class dwelling on Wall street, since wholly devoted to business.

McCORMICK, James, Sr., d. at Harrisburg, Pa., Jan. 19, 1870, a. 69; was originally a lawyer; at the time of his death, although he had been blind several years, he was president of the Dauphin Deposit Bank, and Harrisburg Bridge Co., and was interested in several manufacturing establishments.

McCORMICK, James, a revolutionary soldier, d. Jan. 23, 1860, a. 103 y. 6 mo. 14 d.; b. in Cumberland co., Pa., July 9, 1756.

McCORNISH, Rev. Andrew T., d. at Washington, D. C., April 27, 1841; was 23 years minister of the first Episcopal church formed in Washington.

McCOY, Gen. Robert, d. at Wheeling, Va., June 7, 1849; formerly of Carlisle, Pa.; prothonotary of Cumberland co., brig. gen. of militia, canal commissioner, and representative in congress.

McCRACKEN, Joseph, a militia officer in Charlotte (now Washington) co., N. Y., in the rev.; mem. of assembly in 1783, 6, 9; d. at Salem, N. Y., May 1825, in his 89th year.

McCULLOUGH, Col. William, d. at Asbury, N. J., Feb. 9, 1840, a. 81.

McCUNN, John H., recently a judge of the superior court of N. Y. city; removed from office upon proof of official misconduct and d. in N. Y. city, July 6, 1872, a few days after his disgrace; was one of the currupt men who for a time controlled public affairs in N. Y. city.

McDEARMON, James H., d. at Jefferson City, Mo., March, 1848; auditor of public accounts of Missouri, and a native of Virginia.

McDERMOTT, Rev. John, formerly of Mechanicville, N. Y.; d. at New York, Jan. 16, 1860, at St. Joseph's Hosp., Phila.; was a student in the College of St. Charles Borromeo; ordained by Archbishop Hughes, in 1854.

McDERWENT, James, a rev. soldier, d. in Richmond co., Ohio, Jan. 1860, a. 101. (*Vincent's Semi-An. Reg.*, p 77.)

McDONALD, Charles J., gov. of Ga., b. in S. C.; removed young to Ga., and settled in Hancock co., where he entered the school of Rev. Nathan S. S. Beman; grad at Columbia Coll., S. C.; studied law with Joel Crawford, and was admitted to the bar in 1817; soon gained a large practice. In 1822, he was elected solicitor gen., of the Flint circuit, and in 1825, he became its judge; and resigned the office of brig.-gen. which he then held. In 1830, he was elected from Bibb co., to the legislature, and in 1834, and 1837, to the state senate; in 1839, he was elected gov., and held till 1843; the financial embarrassments of the country which happened during his term, were met with ability, and he forbade the treasurer from paying the legislature their salaries until certain needful taxes and appropriations were passed; he also encountered Indian hostilities, and was engaged in a controversy with Gov. Seward of New York. (*White's Hist. Ga.*, p. 239, with portrait.)

MACDONALD, JAMES, M.D., b. at White Plains, N. Y., July 18, 1803; son of Dr. Archibald M., a Scotch surgeon, in the British army; studied with Isaac Hulse, since navy surgeon; completed his medical studies with Dr. Hosack, and grad. at the Coll. of Ph. and Sur., N. Y., in 1825; was appointed resident physician of Bloomingdale Asylum for the insane; resigned in 1830, engaged in general practice; in 1831 was sent to Europe by the gov'r of N. Y. Hospital, to examine foreign asylums; he returned Oct., 1832, and remained in charge of Bloomingdale till the fall of 1837; after some years spent in practice, he in June, 1841, with his brother Allan M., opened a private asylum at Murray Hill, N. Y., and in 1846, removed to an elegant and spacious edifice (Sanford Hall) in Flushing, N. Y.; d. May 5, 1849. (*Am. Jour. Insanity*, vi, 71.)

MACDONALD, JOHN SANFIELD, member of the government of Ontario, Canada; d. June 1, 1872.

McDONALD, MICHAEL, a pioneer settler of Ballston, N. Y.; d. June 28, 1823, a. 93.

McDONALD, MOSES, b. in Limerick, Me., April 8, 1815; practiced law from 1837 to 1845; was in the Me. legislature in 1841, 2; speaker in 1845; treasurer of the state in 1848, 9; in congress in 1851–5, and collector of Portland and Falmouth in 1857; d. at Saco, Me., Oct. 18, 1869.

McDONELL, ALEXANDER, first R. C. bp. of Kingston, U. C.; b. July 17, 1762; appointed auxiliary of the bishop of Quebec, for U. C., Dec. 31, 1820; Upper Canada having been erected into a bishoprick by Pope Leo XII, Jan. 17, 1826, he was appointed bishop of Kingston. (*Liste Chron. des Evêques et des Prêtres du Canada.*)

McDONNEL, PETER, a prominent merchant and citizen of Troy, N. Y.; d. Feb. 8, 1860.

McDONOUGH, CHARLES S., capt. U. S. navy, eldest son of Com. McDonough, b. in Conn., in 1819; after a brief stay at Hamilton College, he was appointed to the navy April 8, 1835; he saw repeated service in the Mediterranean, on the coast of Africa and in the Pacific, and was afterwards employed on the receiving ships at New York and at Portsmouth; d. at Montclair, N. J., Dec. 2, 1871, having been for some time in failing health.

McDOWELL, DR. JOHN D., d. at St. Louis, Mo., July 8, 1868, a. 64.

McDOWELL, JOSEPH N., M.D., an eminent surgeon in the West; d. at St. Louis, Mo., Sept. 28, 1868, a. 63.

McDOWELL, MAJ. THOMAS, of the turf, d. at Hanover, Va., Oct. 26, 1870, a. 72.

McDUFFIE, WILLIAM, b. in Philadelphia, Pa., May 29, 1847; grad. at Hamilton College in 1873; d. in Phil., June 2, 1874.

McELROY, JOHN, d. at Warren, O., Feb. 18, 1841, a. 83; native of Ireland, and a soldier in the revolution.

McEWEN, Rev. Abel, d.d., pastor of the 1st Congregational ch., New London, Ct.; grad. at Yale Coll. in 1801; d. at New London, Sept. 7, 1860, a. 80. (*N. Y. Times*, Sept. 17, 1860.)

McFADDEN, ——, d. at Embden, Me., Nov. 18, 1840, in his 101st y.

McFARLAND, Rev. James, b. Feb. 22, 1813, in Mechlenburg co., N. C., and d., July 17, 1854, at Memphis, Tenn. (*Deems's Annals of Southern Methodism*, p. 349.)

McFARLANE, Judge ——, editor of the *Harrisburg Key Stone*, d. at Hollidaysburg, Pa., Sept. 27, 1852.

McFEELY, Col. George, d. in Carlisle, Pa., Jan. 19, 1854, a. 74; appointed by Madison, lieut. col. of 16th U. S. infantry, March 14, 1812; commanded at Ft. Niagara, which he defended in a severe attack, Nov. 21, 1813; was honorably engaged in various battles on the northern frontier, and continued till the army was reduced in 1815.

McGARY, James, second officer of the brig Advance in Dr. Kane's arctic expedition, d. at Boston suddenly, Sept. 2, 1857, a. 36.

McGELDART, John, d. at Jackson, Miss., Nov., 1838, a. about 47; was an eminent lawyer.

McGILL, Rt. Rev, John, R. C. bishop of Richmond, Va., d. Jan. 14, 1872, a. 62.

McGILLIVRAY, Lachlin, a Scotchman, came to S. C. in 1735; m. Sehoy a Creek woman: was a loyalist and lost his estate by confiscation; his son Alexander was a man of great influence with the Creeks. (*Sabine's Loyalists; White's Hist. Ga.*, p. 154.)

McGINTY, E. P., d. in Nashville, Tenn., Sept. 21, 1855; was many years connected with the press of Tennessee; at the time of his death, editor of the *True Whig*, at Nashville.

McGIRTH, Daniel, settled in what is now Bullock co., Ga., from Kershaw dist., S. C., during the revolution, and was an active partisan on the patriot side, acting as a scout, and in procuring intelligence; he owned a favorite mare which an officer coveted, an altercation arose, and he was sentenced to be whipped for words used by him; he escaped from prison after one whipping, mounted his favorite mare and rode off, denouncing vengeance upon his late friends; he proved true to his word, and was a scourge of the country; he fled to Florida, was arrested by the Spaniards, lodged 5 years in a dungeon at St. Augustine where his health was ruined; he finally returned to Sumter dist., S. C., and d. there. (*White's Hist. Ga.*, p. 281.)

McGREGOR, Rev. David, b. in Ireland, son of Rev. Jas. M. (Presb.); came to Mass., in 1718, and soon settled near Haverhill, N. H., which he and his associates called New Londonderry; he labored in the ministry there till his death Mar. 5, 1729.

McGREGOR, Rev. David, son of the above, came to America, a. 8; was ordained in 1735, and was the second Presb. minister, at Londonderry, N. H., where he d. May 30, 1777, a. 67. (*Miller's Life of J. Rodgers*, p. 112.)

McGREGOR, Sir Evan John Murray, governor and commander in-chief of Barbadoes, St. Vincent, Grenada, Tobago, St. Lucia and Trinidad; d. at Barbadoes, June 14, 1841, a. 56; he served in the British army many years, in Spain and the East Indies.

McGREGOR, GEN. JOHN, d. July 3, 1835, at Jefferson, Rutherford co., Tenn.

McGROARTY, GEN. STEPHEN JUDSON, d. at Cincinnati, O., Jan. 4, 1870; b. in Ireland, came when young to America; studied law, and at the beginning of the late war, raised the 61st Ohio regiment, and fought in West Virginia and in the army of the Potomac, was made brevet brig. gen.

McGUIRE, REV. EDWARD C., D.D., rector of St. George's church, Fredericksburg, Va., d. Oct. 8, 1858; b. in Winchester, Va., July 26, 1793. (*Sketch of the Life and Labors of Rev. E. C. McG.*, New York, 1859.)

McHENRY, ALEXANDER R., d. in Philadelphia, Pa., April 11, 1874; was nearly 20 years engaged in the exportation of breadstuffs, petroleum, and provisions; did a large business as ship-broker.

MACHIN, THOMAS, b. in Staffordshire, Eng., March 20, 1744; was employed on the construction of the Duke of Bridgewater's canal, and came to America in 1772, to examine a copper mine in N. J.; settled in Boston; helped destroy the tea, and fought at Bunker hill as lieut. of artillery, and was wounded; in 1776 he was employed in placing chains across the Hudson in the highlands, and in Oct., 1777, was wounded at Ft. Montgomery; in 1779 he went with Col. Van Schaick's reg. to Onondaga, and with Sullivan to the Genesee, acting as engineer; in 1781 was employed in laying out the works at Yorktown, and in 1783 settled at New Grange, Ulster co.; built mills west of Newburgh, and coined copper money for states; in 1793 was made capt.; in 1797 removed to Mohawk, N. Y., where he practiced surveying, and d. April 3, 1819, a. 72. (*Simms's Hist. Schoharie Co.*)

MACHIN, THOMAS, son of the preceding, was a capt. in the war of 1812; d. in Albany, May, 1875, in his 90th year.

MACILVAINE, CHARLES PETIT, bishop of Ohio, d. in Florence, Italy, March, 1873; was b. in Burlington, N. J., June 18, 1798. His father, Joseph MacIlvaine, was a leading lawyer and U. S. senator from N. J. at the time of his death, in 1826. He was graduated in 1816 at Princeton; was admitted to deacon's orders July 4, 1820, by Bishop White, and, having labored in Christ Church, Georgetown, Md., he received, two years later, priest's orders from Bp. Kemp of Maryland; in 1825, he became prof. of ethics and chaplain in the U. S. Military Academy at West Point; in 1827, he became rector of St. Ann's Church, Brooklyn, N. Y., where he remained until 1832, when he was consecrated bp. of O. Bishop MacIlvaine was a large contributor to theological literature. His *Lectures on the Evidences of Christianity*, delivered in N. Y. University, in 1831, were published by request of the council, and have gone through many editions. During the early part of the controversy arising out of the Oxford tracts, appeared his *Oxford Divinity Compared with that of the Romish and Anglican Churches*, which the *Edinburgh Review* recommended as one of the best "confutations of the Oxford school." In 1854 he published a volume of sermons entitled *The Truth and the Life*. He also compiled two volumes of *Select Family and Parish Sermons*, and wrote several other works of a minor character. In 1853, the degree of D.C.L. was conferred on him by the University of Oxford, and in 1858 that of LL.D. by the University of Cambridge. The deceased was distinguished for the soundness and clearness of his evangelical views and for the expository character of his preaching.

MACILVANE, JAMES, b. in N. J.; grad. at Princeton in 1818; senator in congress from N. J. from 1823 to 1826; d. Aug. 18, 1826.

McINTOSH, CAPT. ENEAS, captain and paymaster in the 71st regiment in Georgia (British); d. Nov. 1779.

McINTOSH, JAMES S., b. June 19, 1787, in Liberty co., Ga.; entered the army Nov. 13, 1812, as 2d lt. of rifles; was distinguished at Sandy Creek, Black Rock and elsewhere; was retained in 1815; became capt. in 1817, maj. in 1827, lt. col. in 1839, and col. in 1846, for gallantry at at Palo Alto and R. de la Palma, where he was dangerously wounded; he commanded a brigade under Worth in the battle of Cherabusco, and led in the storming of El Molina Sept. 8, 1847, in which he was mortally wounded, and d. Sept. 26, 1847.

McINTYRE, ALEXANDER, a soldier of 1812; and long a resident of Washington, D. C., d. there Jan. 24, 1860.

McINTYRE, ARCHIBALD, comptroller of New York state; b. in Kenmore, Scot.; came to America before the revolution, a. 4 y; settled in Broadalbin, N. Y., and attained to wealth and distinction; was in assembly in 1798, 9, 1800, 1, 2, 4; in 1806 was appointed comptroller, and held till 1811, and was a short time in the state senate in 1822; was many years in charge of the state lotteries, with John B. Yates, and amassed a large fortune; in 1828 and 1840 he was a presidential elector; late in life he was concerned in an iron manufactory in Essex co., N. Y.; d. in Albany, May 5, 1858, a. 86. (*Hist. Mag.*, ii, 217.)

MACK, ELISHA, d. in Salem, Mass., Dec. 9, 1852, a. 69; judge of the police court at that place.

McKAVETT, HENRY, capt. in 8th infantry; killed in battle of Monterey; was of Irish parentage; left an orphan, and reared in an orphan asylum in the city of New York, to which he bequeathed all his property.

MACKAY, COL. ENEAS, deputy quarter master general of the army; d. at St. Louis, Mo., June 3, 1850.

McKAY, JAMES, b. in Bladen co., N. C. in 1793; bred to the law, and from 1815 to 1831 in the state senate; for a time U. S. district attorney; in congress from 1831 to 1849; d. at Goldsboro, N. C., Sept. 14, 1853.

MACKAY, JOHN, a retired ship master; became a partner of Jonas Chickering of Boston in the manufacture of pianofortes in 1830, and was exceedingly prospered; in 1841 he sailed for South America for a cargo of beautiful and costly woods, and was never heard from, his vessel having probably foundered at sea.

McKEAN, HENRY SWASEY, d. in Boston, May 17, 1857, a. 47; was b. in Boston, Feb. 9, 1810; grad. at Harvard in 1828; was tutor of Latin from 1830 to 1835, and then studied engineering; from July 1842 to May 1845, he was librarian of the Mercantile Library of N. Y. city, and afterwards assistant engineer on the Boston Waterworks.

McKEAN, SAMUEL, d. in McKean co., Pa., June 23, 1840; member of congress from Pennsylvania, in 1823–9, and U. S. senator in 1836–9.

McKEENE, DR. JAMES, d. at Topsham, Me., Nov. 28, 1873, a. 76; was a member of the medical profession fifty years, and was a medical professor at Bowdoin Coll., fourteen years.

McKENNEY, WILLIAM E., commander in the U. S. navy; d. at the navy yard, Brooklyn, N. Y., Aug. 24, 1839.

McKIM, ISAAC, a wealthy merchant of Baltimore; in congress from Maryland, from 1823 to 1825, and again from 1835 to 1838; d. in Washington, D. C., April 1, 1838.

McKIM, JAMES MILLER, an old-time abolitionist of Pennsylvania; d. at West Orange, N. J., June 13, 1874; b. in 1810; was educated at Dickinson and Princeton Colleges, and preached for a year; in 1832 engaged in anti-slavery discussions, and in 1836, left the pulpit to devote his energies to the cause of emancipation. (*N. Y. Semi-weekly Tribune*, June 16, 1874.)

McKIMM, ALEXANDER, d. at Baltimore, Md., Jan. 18, 1832, a. 84.

McKINNEY, JOHN M., U. S. judge, Florida; d. in N. Y., at Quarantine, Oct. 13, 1871.

McKINNEY, MORDECAI, d. at Harrisburg, Pa., Dec. 17, 1867; was a lawyer, and widely known for many treatises and books of reference prepared and edited by him.

McKINSTRY, COL. John, a militia officer of the revolution, was repeatedly in the service and severely wounded; served in the Mohawk valley; settled on a farm in Livingston, Columbia co., N. Y.; twice elected to assembly, and d. June 9, 1822, a. 77. (*Alb. Gazette*, June 18, 1822; *Stone's Life of Brant*, i, 155; p. 490.)

McKIZZICK, COL. JAMES, Cherokee agent; d. at Ft. Gibson, Jan. 12, 1848.

McKNIGHT, CALVIN, first judge of Jefferson co., N. Y.; settled early in Watertown, N. Y.; was magistrate, and in 1829 became first judge, holding till 1840; was in assembly in 1820 and 1834; removed to western N. Y., and thence to Guilford, Ct., where he d. Oct. 25, 1855.

McKNIGHT, JOHN L., d. at Bordentown, N. J., Nov. 30, 1868, in his 71st year; was one of the originators of the Camden and Amboy rail road, and the heaviest stockholder in that and the joint companies, at the time of his death.

McLAIN, ENSIGN ROBERT A., Penn.; killed in the revolution Sept. 27, 1777.

MACLAY, REV. ARCHIBALD, a Baptist preacher, d. in New York city, May 2, 1860. (*Vincent's Semi-An. Register*, p. 363.)

McLEAN, FERGUS, father of John McL., judge of the U. S. supreme court; d. at Clear Creek, Warren co., O., Feb. 1837, a. about 91; one of the pioneers of the settlement of the Miami valley, having removed to that region in 1797.

McLEAN, John, d. at Shawneetown, Ill., Oct. 4, 1830; a member of congress from Ill., in 1818, 19; senator in congress from 1824 to 1825, and from 1829 till his death.

McLEAN, JOHN, judge, native of Washington co., N. Y., grad. at Union Coll. in 1815; admitted to the bar in 1818; became master and examiner in chancery; was in the state senate from 1829 to 1832, and in 1837; was appointed first judge of Washington co., March 18, 1835, and held till 1847; appointed a regent, April 8, 1845, and held till his death, which occurred at his home in Salem, N. Y., December 5, 1858. (*Hist. Mag.*, iii, 28.)

McLEAN, WILLIAM, native of N. J., d. at Cincinnati, O., Oct. 12, 1839; in congress from Ohio, in 1823-9; was a brother of Judge McL. of the supreme court.

McLELLAN, BRYCE, formerly a judge; d. at Bloomfield, Me., Sept. 29, 1836, a. 74.

McLENE, JEREMIAH, of Columbus, O.; d. at Washington, D. C., March 19, 1837, a. 70; member of congress in 1833–7, and for twenty-one years secretary of state of Ohio.

McLEOD, JOHN, d. in Washington city, Dec. 26, 1846, a. 80; a native of Ireland, but for more than 40 years a successful teacher in Washington.

McLEOD, REV. JOHN N., for 46 years pastor of the 1st Reformed Presbyterian church, N. Y. city; d. April 27, 1874, in his 68th year.

McLEON, DR. DAVID CAMDEN, d. at Santa Fé, New Mexico, Sept. 3, 1872, a. about 50; b. in S. C.; entered the army as assistant surgeon, and went through the Seminole war, and for some years was stationed on the western frontiers; was in the Mexican war, where he displayed great energy and hardihood; in the late war was at the head of the confederate medical department, and after the war went to Mexico, and after a year's residence to New Mexico, where he had been stationed many years and owned property.

McMAHON, JOHN D. L., lawyer and historian of Maryland; d. at Cumberland, Md., June 15, 1871, a. 71.

McMAHON, WILLIAM, d. at Cumberland, Md., Sept. 2, 1841, a. 81.

McMICKEN, MAJ. ISAAC S., U. S. consul at Acapulco, Mexico; d. June, 1860, together with nearly the whole of the American residents, by yellow fever. (*Vincent's Semi-An. Register*, p. 618.)

McMULLEN, GEORGE, superintendent of the Ohio Institution for the Blind; d. at Columbus, O., July, 1852.

McMYERS, CAPT. ANDREW, N. J.; k. at Germantown, Oct. 4, 1777.

McNAIRY, DR. BOYD, a skillful medical practitioner; d. at Nashville, Tenn., Nov. 2, 1856, a. 73.

McNAIRY, John, late judge of the circuit court of the U. S. for the district of Tenn.; d. near Nashville, Tenn., Nov. 12, 1837, a. 75; held this office 45 years.

McNAUGHTON, DR. JAMES, b. in Perthshire, Scotland, in 1787; grad. at the medical dept. of the University of Edinburgh in 1816, and came to America in 1817; settled at Albany; was 20 years a prof. in the Fairfield Med. Coll., and from 1840 till his death prof. in the Albany Med. Coll.; was an eminent medical practitioner at Albany, and d. in Paris, France, June 12, 1874, while on a journey in Europe.

McNEIL, ELIHU M., was a member of N. Y. assembly in 1842 and 1846, and of the constitutional convention from Jefferson co.; d. at his residence in Smithville, Jefferson co., N. Y., Jan. 9, 1858, a. 60.

McNUTT, J. H. W., a distinguished member of the Ohio senate; d. in Preble co., O., Sept. 29, 1837.

MACOMBER, WILSON, d. in Westport, Me., March 3, 1843, a. 93 y 10 m.

McPHERSON, MRS. CELESTIA, wife of Samuel C. McP., and dau. of the late Joseph Edelen, of Prince George's co., Md., d. in Grand Coteau, La., March 13, 1852.

McPHERSON, JOHN, aid-de-camp to Gen. Montgomery; killed at Quebec, Dec. 31, 1775.

McPHETERS, DR. JAMES A., d. at Natchez, Miss., May 20, 1847.

MACRAE, SAMUEL, brevet lieut. col., quarter master U. S. A.; d. at St. Louis, Mo., July 14, 1849, a. 48; served in the Fl. and Mexican wars, and received a brevet appointment for services on the Rio Grande.

MACREADY, WILLIAM CHARLES, English actor well known in Am., and engaged at the Astor Place Opera House in N. Y. city when that place was attacked by a mob, May 10, 1849; retired from the stage soon after, and d. at Weston-Super-Mare, England, April 29, 1873, a. 73.

MACREE, LT. COL. SAMUEL, a graduate of West Point; served in the Black Hawk, Florida and Mexican wars; d. at St. Louis, Mo., July 15, 1849, in his 49th year. (*Striker's Am. Reg.*, iii, 236.)

MACRERY, DR. ANDREW, d. at Louisville, Ky., Sept. 14, 1843; b. in Delaware, Dec. 27, 1775, and removed to near Natchez in 1803.

McROBERTS, SAMUEL, d. in Cincinnati, O., March 27, 1843, a. about 40; a senator in congress from Illinois, from 1841 to the time of his death.

McSHERRY, JAMES, d. at Littlestown, Penn., Feb. 3, 1849; was twenty years in the legislature, and one of the delegates in constitutional convention; represented a district of Pennsylvania in congress.

McSHERRY, REV. WILLIAM, d. at Georgetown, Ky., Dec. 17, 1839; pres. of Georgetown College.

McTAVISH, JOHN, d. in Baltimore, Md., June 21, 1852, a. 64; for the last sixteen years British consul at that place.

McVEAN, CHARLES, district attorney of the U. S. district court, for the southern district of New York; d. at New York city, Dec. 20, 1848, a. 46; b. in Johnstown, N. Y.; educated as a lawyer, and practiced with success in Montgomery co., until he removed to New York city in 1839; at the age of 30 he was elected to congress; from the early part of 1844, until appointed U. S. dist. attorney, he was surrogate of New York county.

McWHIR, REV. WILLIAM, D.D., b. in Ireland in 1759; grad. at Belfast, and was licensed by the Presbytery of that place; came to Alexandria, Va., in 1783; was 10 years at the head of an academy; went to Sunbury, Ga., in 1793, and established an acad.; he excelled as a classical teacher; about 1823, 4, he organized the first Presbyterian church in Florida at St. Augustine; he never was settled as a pastor; was eminently benevolent and at the age of 90 became a voluntary colporteur of the Am. Tract Soc.; d. in Liberty co., Ga., in his 92d year, Feb. 3, 1851. (*White's Hist. Ga.*, p. 532, with portrait.)

McWILLIAMS, DR. ALEXANDER, a native of St. Mary's co., Md.; entered the navy in 1801, and having served in the Tripolitan war, resigned in 1806, and settled in his profession at Washington, D. C., where he died March 31, 1850, in his 76th year; was one of the founders of the Columbian Institute and of the National Institute. (*Stryker's Am. Reg.*, iv, 456.)

MACY, JOHN B., representative from Wisconsin in congress from 1853 to 1855, and a citizen of Fond du Lac, Wis.; perished by the burning of the Niagara on Lake Michigan, Sept. 24, 1856.

MACY, REV. WILLIAM ALLEN, b. in city of N. Y., Jan 29, 1825; grad. at Yale in 1849, and became a teacher and missionary in China; an excellent scholar, and a devoted missionary; d. at Shanghai, China, April 9, 1859, a. 35.

MADDEN, REV. MICHAL, pastor of St. Vincent's church, Madison, N. J., May 17, 1868.

MADISON, MRS. DOLLY PAYNE, the accomplished widow of Pres. Madison, was born May 20, 1767, in Va.; she married Mr. Madison in 1794 as her second husband, and sustained her station in the executive mansion with grace and dignity; her influence upon the social world at Wash. was elevating and refining; d. at Washington July, 1849. (*Stryker's Am. Reg.*, iii, 235; *Hunt's Biog. Panorama*, p. 172.)

MAGEE, EUGENE, a native of Ireland, and member of the Miss. senate; d. at Vicksburg, July 20, 1835.

MAGEE, ENSIGN WILLIAM, Pa., killed in the rev. Sept. 20, 1777.

MAGOUN, THATCHER, d. in Medford, Mass., April 16, 1856, a. 81; a successful ship builder, laid the first keel of a ship at Medford, in 1802, and since then had built a fleet.

MAGRUDER, PATRICK, b. in Montgomery co., Md., in 1768; educated at Princeton, and became a lawyer; was in congress from Maryland from 1805 to 1807, and clerk of the house from 1807 to 1815; d. at Petersburg, Va., in 1819, or 1820.

MAGRUDER, RICHARD B., d. at Baltimore, Md., Feb., 11, 1844, a. 57; associate judge of the 6th judicial dist. of Maryland,

MAHON, ALEXANDER, d. in Harrisburg, Pa., Dec. 9, 1855, a. 75; served in both houses of the legislature and had been pres. of the senate and state treasurer.

MAHON, JOHN, of Irish birth, settled and married in Herkimer co., N. Y.; was sheriff in 1808–9, in 1811–13, and in 1815–16; from 1817–21 he was engaged in private pursuits, and upon the restoration of the republicans to power became county clerk, from 1821 to 1823, a county judge from 1823 to 1833; d. at Herkimer Oct. 1851, a. 78. (*Benton's Herkimer Co. N. Y.*, p. 342.)

MAHONI, JOHN, Dutch gov. of Surinam, from Jan. 22, 1716, till his death in 1717.

MAINE, DR. ZADOK P., b. in Plainfield, Conn.; practiced many years as a physician in Cooperstown, N. Y., and afterwards lived some time in Utica; d. at an advanced age, in Poughkeepsie, January 21, 1850.

MAITLAND, WILLIAM, a native of Montrose in Scotland; came to Montreal in 1775, and was at first successful, but about 1826, met with losses and was imprisoned; so strong was public sympathy in his favor that the legislature of Lower Canada passed a law for his benefit, that no debtor over 70 years of age should be imprisoned; d. at Montreal, Feb. 20, 1851, a. 96.

MALBONE, FRANCIS, was in congress from Rhode Island, from 1793, to 1795, and again from that state in 1809; d. June 4, 1809, a. 50.

MALLARY, FRANCIS, d. at Norfolk, Va., March 26, 1860, formerly member of congress.

MALLORY, SARAH, colored, d. in Virginia, Feb. 22, a. 120 years.

MALTRIE, REV. EBENEZER DAVENPORT, b. in Stamford, Ct., Jan. 20, 1799; spent his youth in N. Y. city; grad at Hamilton College in 1824; and entered the Andover Seminary; from 1826 to 1831 was tutor at Hamilton, was licensed, and served as college chaplain; m. a daughter of President Davis; preached at Hamilton four years; taught at the Hudson river seminary, Lansingburgh and elsewhere, and in 1849 settled at Syracuse where he d. July 10, 1858, in his 60th year. (*N. Y. Observer.*)

MALTBY, HENRY, teacher, from Richland, N. Y., was teacher of academy at Lowville, N. Y., in 1834–5 and many years at Flemingsburg, Ky.; d. at St. Paul, Min., July 1860. (*Lowville Acad. Semi-cent. Celeb.*, p. 82.)

MALTBY, REV. JOHN, b. in Northfield, Ct.; grad. at Yale in 1822; studied theology at Andover, Mass.; settled at Dutton, Mass., from 1826 to 1834, and over the Hammond street church in Bangor, Me., from 1834 till his death, May 15, 1860; d. in Worcester, Mass., a. 65.

MALTBY, T. A., late brig. gen. of U. S. vols., d. at Vicksburg, Miss., Dec. 12, 1867; was mayor of Vicksburg.

MANAHAN, REV. AMBROSE, D.D., b. in New York in 1814; he pursued ecclesiastical studies in Rome, Italy; in 1841 he was president of St. John's (catholic) College at Fordham, N. Y., and afterwards pastor of St. John's church New York city; subsequently lived at Boston, and also at Utica; d. Dec. 7, 1867.

MANDEVILLE, REV. HENRY, D.D., b. in New York state, grad. at Union College in 1826; professor of moral phil. and rhetoric at Hamilton, from 1841 to 1849; went to Mobile in 1852, and became pastor of a church; d. of yellow fever Oct. 1, 1856; was several years pastor of the 4th Pres. church Albany. (*Hist. Mag.*, ii, 348.)

MANDEVILLE, JOSHUA, d. at Waterville, N. Y., May 3, 1860, a. 78; member of assembly in 1829, and formerly a member of the county court.

MANLEY, JAMES R., M.D., prof. in Coll. of Phys. and Surg., N. Y.; b. in Phila., April 5, 1782, son of Capt. Robert M.; grad. at Columbia Coll. in 1799, and in 1803 was graduated as a physician and practiced many years in N. Y. city; was several years pres. of the St. Med. Soc., and 12 years resident physician by appointment of the gov.; in 1839 he became lecturer on obstetrics and diseases of women and children in N. Y., and filled many stations of honor in his profession; d. Nov. 21, 1851, a. 70. (*Tr. N. Y. St. Med. Soc.*, 1852, p. 51.)

MANLEY, THOMAS, b. in Dorset, Vt., Aug., 1763, came to Norway, N. Y., in 1789; in assembly in 1800, 1810, and 1821; d. Jan. 21, 1852, a. 89 years, at his home in Norway. (*Benton's Herkimer Co. N. Y.*, p. 344.)

MANN, Abijah, b. at Fairfield, Herkimer co., N. Y., Sept. 24, 1793, received an academical education; a teacher, merchant, postmaster and justice of the peace; during the years 1828-30, a member of the legislature, and actively opposed the Chenango canal; from 1833 to 1837 he represented his district in congress, and being placed on a committee to investigate the affairs of the U. S. Bank; when he was denied admission thereto, he forced its officers to admit him by employing men to excavate beneath the walls of the Bank; in 1838 was again a member of the state legislature; removed to Brooklyn, and in 1854 represented Queens co. in the democratic convention; the following year was nominated by the republicans for attorney gen., and in 1857 for the state senate; his death occurred Sept. 6, 1868.

MANN, Alexander, b. in Scottsville, Monroe co., N. Y.; grad. at the University of Vt., in 1838; studied law, and practiced at Rochester, and in 1843, took charge of the *American*, a daily whig paper, established by the Jerome bros.; in 1857 this paper was united with the *Democrat;* he went to N. Y., was an editor of the *Times;* went to St. Augustine for his health, and d. Dec. 6, 1860. (*N. Y. Times*, Dec. 10, 1860.)

MANN, Charles Addison, b. at Fairfield, Jan. 16, 1803, and was educated at Fairfield Academy; studied law at Utica, which was his place of residence, and admitted to the bar in 1825; in 1840 he was a member of assembly, and in 1850 of the state senate, but resigned in 1851 to prevent the passage of the canal bill; was a director of the Oneida Bank, for some time its vice president, and a short time its president; was director and two terms president of the N. Y., Albany & Buffalo Telegraph Co.; director in several manufacturing companies, and president of Utica steam cotton mills; was manager of the N. Y. State Lunatic Asylum, school commissioner, trustee of Utica Academy, of Utica Female Academy, &c.; d. Jan. 19, 1860.

MANN, James, member of congress from the 2d dist. of Louisiana; d. at New Orleans, Aug. 26, 1868, a. 46; b. in Maine, and resided at Gorhame, Me., many years; was capt. in a reg. of Maine vols., and became pay master, and was assigned to duty at New Orleans; after the war was made treasury agent by Lincoln and Johnson; in 1867 became active in reorganizing the democratic party south.

MANN, Joel K., from 1831 to 1835 representative in congress from Pa.; d. in Montgomery co., Pa. Sept. 5, 1837, a. 77.

MANN, Dr. John Milton, b. in Attlebury, Mass.; grad. at Brown University, and settled at Hudson, N. Y., in 1800; was drowned in crossing the Hudson to Athens, Aug. 24, 1809, a. 43. (*Barber & Howe's Hist. Coll. N. Y.*, p. 118).

MANNING, Alonzo W., a native of Missouri, d. May, 1847, a. 37; a judge of the criminal court of St. Louis, Mo., which office he had held for about five years.

MANNING, Dr. John, d. Nov. 6, 1841, in Rockport, Mass., a. 80; well known for successful practice in the medical profession, was surgeon in the army, and afterwards became distinguished as physician, merchant and agriculturist.

MANOUVRIER, George P., U. S. consul at Pernambuco; d. there Jan. 17, 1847.

MANWEE, EUNICE, last full blooded Indian of the Pishgachligoh tribe; d. March 15, 1860, a. 103, in Kent, N. Y. (*Hist. Mag.*, iv, 125.)

MARBLE, HENRY, d. at Westborough, Mass., Oct., 1841, a. 86; a lieut. in the 5th Mass. regiment in the revolution.

MARCHAND, ALBERT G., d. at Greensburg, Pa., Feb. 5, 1848; was in congress from 1839, to 1843.

MARDIS, SAMUEL W., b. in Alabama in 1801; and a representative from that state in congress from 1831 to 1835; d. at Talladega, Ala., Nov. 14, 1835, a. 34.

MAREUIL, PIERRE DE, Jesuit missionary arrived in Canada June 1706; at Onondaga in June 1709, was surrendered to the English and taken to Albany; d. Aug. 25, 1747.

MARKELL, JACOB, b. in Schenectady co., N. Y., May 8, 1770; settled at Manheim, and spent his life in farming: was 27 y. a supervisor, many years a co. judge; in 1813-5 in congress; 1820 in state assembly; d. at the home of his son John, in Manheim, Nov. 26, 1852, a. 82; his wife survived 5 mo. having lived with him 62 y. (*Benton's Herkimer Co. N. Y.*, p. 336.)

MARKS, MRS. LUCY, mother of Merriwether Lewis, who with William Clarke explored the country to the Pacific; d. in Albemarle co., Va., Sept. 8, 1837, a. 85.

MARLING, JOHN L., U. S. minister to Guatemala, d. at Oakland, near Nashville, Tenn., Oct. 16, 1856, a. 29; was bred a printer but became a lawyer, and edited the *Nashville Gazette* and afterwards the *Nashville Union*, in both of which he took strong union ground; was appointed minister in 1854, and was home on leave of absence at the time of his death.

MARRIOT, GEN. WILLIAM H., collector of the port of Baltimore under Polk; d. at Baltimore, May 13, 1851.

MARRON, JOHN, third assistant postmaster gen.; d. in Washington, D. C., March 3, 1859, a. 60.

MARRYATT, WILLIAM W., assistant astronomer of Lieut. Wheeler's exploring expedition; d. Oct., 1873, at Bozeman, Montana, of mountain fever; was buried there.

MARSDEN, CAPT. FRANCIS, of Col. Harvey's reg. of militia, May, 1780; was one of those who escaped alive, but badly wounded, from the action of Bunker hill, being then captain in 5th regt. of foot.

MARSH, REV. FREDERICK, for more than half a century, pastor of the Congregational church of Winchester Centre, near Hartford, Ct.; d. at that place, Feb. 7, 1873, a. over 90.

MARSH, DR. MARTIN MANVILLE, b. at Pompey, N. Y., in 1812; grad. at Hamilton Coll. in 1836, and became principal at Manlius Acad.; studied medicine and grad. at Albany in 1841; was employed as an agent of the Sanitary Commission and in Feb., 1863, went to Beaufort, S. C., where he remained till peace; in 1865, went to superintend the Lincoln Home for disabled soldiers in N. Y. city; in the spring of 1867, became prof. of applied chemistry and hygiene in the Rutgers Female Coll. but did not enter upon its duties, and d. at Carson, O., June 9, 1868. (*Regent's Report*, 1869, p. 812.)

MARSH, DR. METCALF, d. in Smithfield, R. I., April 10, 1854, a. 53; b. in Charlestown, Mass., but soon after receiving his medical degree removed to Rhode Island; was a prominent actor in the Dow rebellion, so called, and was obliged to absent himself for a time from the state.

MARSH, SAMUEL, for 20 years vice pres. of the N. Y. and Erie rail road, d. in N. Y. city, Nov. 30, 1872, a. 87.

MARSHALL, CAPT. CHARLES ALONZO, a well known commander of the Black Ball sailing packets; d. at sea, July 24, 1872, a. 42.

MARSHALL, HUMPHREY, ex-congressman, and minister to China; d. at Louisville, Ky., March 28, 1872, a. 60. (*Drake's Am. Biog.*)

MARSHALL, JOHN H., a lieut. in the U. S. navy, and native of La.; was at his death June 8, 1850, nearly at the head of the list of lieutenants; was in the navy nearly 30 years.

MARSHALL, JOHN M., d. March, 1848, in his 85th year; son of Col. Thomas M., commander of the 3d Virginia regiment in the revolution; became a lawyer; married a daughter of Robert Morris, of Phila.; was judge of the U. S. circuit court for the district of Columbia under John Adams; retired to his estate in Fauquier co., Va., and devoted himself to agriculture; was the oldest surviving brother of Chief Justice Marshall.

MARSHALL, THOMAS, eldest son of Chief Justice Marshall; killed by accident, June 28, 1835, at Baltimore, Md., a. about 50; grad. at Princeton in 1803, and was a distinguished scholar and lawyer.

MARSHALL, REV. THOMAS, d. at Sherburne Falls, Mass., June 7, 1842, a. 58.

MARSHALL, THOMAS, d. April 15, 1871, a. 77; was formerly member of congress, and judge of the court of appeals of Kentucky.

MARSHALL, DR. ——, of Baltimore; a volunteer in the yellow fever epidemic at Portsmouth, Va., in the autumn of 1855, and fell a victim to the disease.

MARSTON, J. W., d. in Newburyport, Mass., Aug. 28, 1873; was for 33 years justice of the police court at that place.

MARTIN, DANIEL, gov. of Md.; d. in Talbot co., Md., July 10, 1831.

MARTIN, DAVID, M.D., of Albany; b. in Argyle, N. Y., May 4, 1800; grad. at Fairfield Med. Coll. in 1828; settled in Albany in 1836, and d. in 1853, a. 53. (*Tr. N. Y. St. Med. Soc.* 1854, p. 64.)

MARTIN, F. AUGUSTINE DU BOIS, d. at Baltimore, Md., July 6, 1833, a. 91.

MARTIN, COL. GEORGE W., d. in Tallahatchie co., Miss., June 30, 1854, a. 65; was in the war of 1812; with Gen. Jackson in the Creek war, in 1813, 14, and 15, and in the last of these campaigns was aid of Gen. Coffee.

MARTIN, J. L., chargé d' affaires of the U. S. to the Pontifical states; d. at Rome, Italy, Aug. 26, 1848.

MARTIN, LIEUT. PETER, Penn., killed at Brandywine, Sept. 11, 1777.

MARTIN, VIVALDI R., a lawyer; d. at Lowville, N. Y., Aug. 8, 1850, a. 31.

MARTIN, WALTER, brig. gen. of N. Y. militia; b. in Sturbridge, Mass., Dec. 15, 1764; settled in Salem, N. Y., in 1787; bought and settled in the town of Martinsburgh, N. Y., in 1801, and died there, Dec. 10, 1834; was many years P.M., and served a short time on the frontier in the war, and in the state senate in 1809, 12. (*Hough's Hist. Lewis Co. N. Y.*, p. 172.)

MARTIN, WILLIAM B., judge of the court of appeals of Maryland; d. at Cambridge, Md., April, 1835, a. 65.

MARTIN, CAPT., of Hessian engineers dept., qr. mr. gen. to the Hessian troops in America; d. in N. Y. city, May 27, 1780; his funeral was attended by a large number of officers of the garrison, British and German.

MARTINDALE, HENRY C., long a prominent member of the bar, and in congress ten years (from 1823 to 1831, and in 1834 and 1835; d. at his residence in Sandy Hill, N. Y., April 22, 1860, having retired from business several years before.

MARTINDALE, REV. STEPHEN, d. May 23, 1860, at Tarrytown, N. Y., in his 73d year; was next to the oldest member of the N. Y. conference of the Methodist Episcopal church. (*Vincent's Semi-Annual Register*, p. 437.)

MARTINEZ, FRANCISCO PIZARRO, late envoy and minister from Mexico to the U. S.; d. at Georgetown, D. C., Feb. 9, 1840.

MARTUSCELLI, CHEVALIER ROCCO, envoy extraordinary from the court of Naples; d. in New York, Nov. 8, 1853, a. 52; served as chargé 14 years.

MARVIN, DUDLEY, d. in Ripley, N. Y., June 25, 1852; b. in Lyme, Conn.; removed to Canandaigua, N. Y., in 1807; began law practice about 1811, and acquired distinction; was in congress from 1823 to 1829; removed to Ripley, Chautauqua co.; and there was again chosen to congress.

MASON, ENSIGN CALEB, Md., killed at Brandywine, Sept. 11, 1777.

MASON, CHARLES W., d. in Concord, Mass., Dec. 12, 1873; a. 75; was a prominent member of the Masonic order.

MASON, DANIEL GREGORY, d. June 24, 1869, a. 49; son of Lowell M., musical composer, and senior member of the firm of music publishers, Mason & Bros., New York city.

MASON, GEORGE, member of parliament, sided with Charles I, and fought on his side till after the overthrow at Worcester, when he came to Va., in 1651, and was soon followed by his family; in 1676, he led a force against the Indians, and the same year represented the co. of Stafford in assembly; the co. of Stafford, Va., was named in compliment to him from his native co. of Staffordshire; he settled at Acohick Creek on the Potomac; his son George (2) married Mary, dau. of Gerard Fowke of Gunston Hall, Eng.; their son George (3) lived at Acohick and was buried there; George (4) married a dau. of Stevens Thomson of the Middle Temple, atty. gen. of Va., in the days of Queen Ann; lived at Doeg Neck on the Potomac, now in Fairfax co., and was in 1719, lieut. and chief commander of Stafford; he was drowned in the Potomac; he left two sons George (5), author of the Const. of Va., and Thomson, a member of the house of burgesses and an eminent lawyer.

MASON, GEN. JOHN, was a son of Col. Geo. Mason of Gunston Hall, Va.; held many public trusts and was widely known and esteemed; d. at Clermont, Va., March 19, 1849, a. 83 y. (*Striker's Am. Reg.* ii, 497.)

MASON, JOHN T., secretary of state of Maryland; d. in Elkhorn, Md., March 28, 1873.

MASON, JONATHAN, d. at Farnsworth, N. H., March 20, 1839, in his 94th year; was a rev. pensioner.

MASON, LOWELL, an eminent musical teacher and composer, b. Jan. 8, 1792: d. at Orange N. J., Aug. 10, 1872.

MASON, THOMAS, Unitarian minister at Northfield, Mass.; b at Princeton, that state, 1769; grad. Harvard Univrsity, 1796, where he is said to have been the greatest wrestler that was ever in college; ordained at N. Nov. 6, 1799; dismissed March 28, 1830; rep. in state legislature 8 years; d. Jan. 3, 1851, a. 82.

MASON, THOMAS F., d. at Alexandria, D. C., Dec. 31, 1838; judge of the criminal court of the District of Columbia.

MASSEY, HART, b. at Salem, N. H., Dec. 5, 1771; removed to Windsor, Vt., in 1792, to Saltash, now Lyme, in 1795 and in 1800 to Watertown, N. Y., where he bought a part of site of the present village; was collector of customs of Sacketts Harbor dist., during the embargo and war periods and was active in enforcing non intercourse; in 1820 he became county judge: d. in March 1853. (*Hough's Hist Jeff Co., N. Y.*, p. 447.)

MASSEY, SOLON, antiquarian, and known in northern New York by his numerous biographical articles printed in Watertown papers, over the signature of *Links in the Chain;* d. at Brownville, N. Y., Aug. 12, 1871, a. 73, son of Hart Massey, and formerly a police magistrate of Watertown; for the last few years of life lived in Osborne, Ohio.

MASTERS, JOSIAH, b. in Woodbury, Conn., Oct. 22, 1763; grad. at Yale in 1784; settled at Schaghticoke, Rensselaer co., N. Y., and was in assembly in 1793, 1800 and 1801; was then made associate judge of Rensselaer co.; and from 1805 to 1809, a representative in congress; in 1808 became first judge of Rensselaer co.; d. June 30, 1822.

MASTIN, JOHN WILLIAM, d. at Huntsville, Ala., Nov. 14, 1845, a. 37; b. in Frederick co., Va., in 1808; grad. at Yale in 1829; was a merchant at Huntsville, and a much respected citizen.

MATHER, DR. THADDEUS, b. in Windsor, Conn., March, 1778; son of Elihu M., and settled in Binghamton, N. Y., where he d. Oct. 8, 1855. (*Binghamton Democrat*, Oct., 1855.)

MATHEUS, CHARLES, an eminent English comedian, visited the U. S., twice; in 1823 and in 1834; d. at Davenport, Eng., on his 59th birth day June 28, 1835. (*Am. Almanac*, 1836, p. 296.)

MATHEUS, VINCENT, b. in Orange co., N. Y., June 29, 1766, was admitted to the bar in 1790, and settled at Elmira, now Chemung co., N. Y.; was in assembly in 1794, 5; in the senate from 1791 to 1803; in 1798, was appointed a com'r to settle bounty claims; from 1809 to 1811, in congress; in 1812, dist. atty. for several counties; in 1816 removed to Bath, and thence to Rochester; d. at Rochester, N. Y., Aug. 26, 1846.

MATHEWSON, ELISHA, several years a member of the Rhode Island legislature, and once a speaker of the house; was senator in congress from that state, from 1807 to 1811, and d. Oct. 14, 1853, at Scituate, R. I.

MATLACK, JAMES, d. at Woodbury, N. J., Jan. 15, 1840; member of congress from New Jersey, in 1821–25.

MATTESON, JOEL A., ex-governor of Illinois, d. at Chicago, Ill., Jan. 31, 1873.

MATTHEWS, REV. DR. JOHN, professor in the theological seminary of Indiana, d. May 18, 1848.

MATTHEWS, GEN. JOHN, d. near Port Tobacco, Md., May 4, 1854, a. 70; was in the war of 1812, and fifteen years in the state legislature of Maryland, where he served in both houses.

MATTHEWS, THOMAS, a firm supporter of the rev., and speaker of the house of delegates of Va.; d. at Norfolk Va., April 20, 1812. (*Rogers's Am. Biog.*)

MATTHEWS, REV. WILLIAM, d. in Washington, D. C., April 30, 1854; was for fifty years pastor of St. Patrick church in that city.

MATTOCKS, CAPT. JOHN, killed at Kings mountain Oct. 7, 1780.

MATTOCKS, JOHN, d. Aug. 14, 1847, at Peacham, Vt., a. 71; was many years a successful lawyer, and held many responsible offices; was three terms in congress, two years a judge of the supreme court, and one year a governor of the state and afterwards declined reëlection to the last mentioned office.

MAURY, ABRAHAM P., member of congress from Tennessee, from 1835, to 1839; d. at his home in Williamson co., Tenn., July 22, 1848.

MAURY, JOHN W., late mayor of Washington, D. C.; d. in that city Feb. 2, 1855; was an alderman from the time he became of age (except 1840 when he declined nomination), till 1852 when he became mayor; at the time of his death he was president of the Bank of the Metropolis.

MAURY, MATTHEW FONTAINE, LL.D., a distinguished astronomer and scientist; d. at Lexington, Va., Jan. 25, 1873. (*Drake's Am. Biog.*)

MAXWELL, HUGH, d. in New York city, March 31, 1873; b. in Scotland; came in childhood to the United States; grad. at Columbia Coll.; settled in N. Y. city and built up a lucrative practice. His first public position was that of assistant judge-advocate general in the United States army, he being appointed in the year 1814; in 1819 he was elected district attorney for this county, was again chosen under the new constitution, in 1822, and was successively reëlected until the year 1829; in 1823 occurred the famous "conspiracy trials," when Jacob Barker, the well-known banker, Henry Eckford, the shipbuilder, and others were charged with conspiring to defraud certain insurance companies; there was a strong array of counsel opposed to District Attorney Maxwell, yet he was successful, and a majority of the accused were convicted; during these trials he greatly distinguished himself, and added to his reputation as a clear and forcible speaker. For the twenty years succeeding his withdrawal from the office of district attorney, Mr. Maxwell was engaged in the practice of his profession, and was looked upon as one of the leaders of the bar in this city and state; he was for many years a prominent whig politician; in 1849 President Taylor appointed him collector of the port, and he held this position through the administrations of Presidents Taylor and Fillmore; on leaving this post he returned to the practice of his profession for a short time, and then withdrew from active life; for many years past he has lived during the summer on his farm near Nyack, and in winter in the old family mansion in St. Mark's place.

MAXWELL, John P. P., b. in N. J., in 1805; grad at Princeton in 1823, and admitted to the bar in 1827; was in congress from N. J., from 1837 to 1839 and from 1841 to 1843; d. at Belvidere, N. J., Nov. 14, 1845.

MAXWELL, Samuel, b. in Heath, Mass.; grad. at Yale in 1797; studied law and practiced in Charlemont, Mass., of which town for about 30 years he was actively engaged in municipal affairs; was frequently elected to the legislature, and served in both houses; d. Dec. 21, 1859, a. 82.

MAY, George W., late lieut in the U. S. army, and distinguished at the battles of Palo Alto, Resaca de la Palma, Cerro Gordo, at Monterey, and Vera Cruz; d. at New York, Jan. 8, 1860.

MAY, Col. Joseph, d. at Boston, Mass., Jan. 27, 1841, a. 41: was over forty years secretary of an insurance company.

MAY, Samuel, merchant, d. at Boston, Mass., Feb. 23, 1870, a. 94: b. in that city in 1776, a member and officer of various benevolent institutions, and in his younger days a citizen of enterprise.

MAYER, Charles F., d. in Baltimore, Md., Jan. 3, 1864, a. 68; a member of the bar, and much given to literary pursuits.

MAYER, Christopher, d. in Baltimore, Md., Sept. 14, 1842, a. 79; pres. of the Neptune Insurance Co., and consul general of Wurtemberg; came to America at the close of the revolution, and resided nearly 50 years at Baltimore.

MAYER, Henry C., a native of Maryland, and a member of the Baltimore bar; d. in Rochester, N. Y., March 1, 1846, a. 24.

MAYER, Rev. Lewis, professor in the Theological Seminary of the German Reformed church; d. at York, Pa., Aug. 19, 1849.

MAYER, Rev. Philip F., d.d., d. in Philadelphia, April 16, 1858, a. 77; pastor of the Evangelical Lutheran church of St. John; b. in Albany, N. Y., and resided in Albany before locating in Philadelphia; he was many years pres. of the Penn. Inst. for the Deaf and Dumb; pres. of the Phila. Dispensary, and a trustee of the University of Pennsylvania.

MAYHEW, William E., d. April 10, 1860, at Baltimore, a. 75; was president of the Farmers and Planters' Bank many years.

MAYNADIER, Col. Henry, d. at Annapolis, Md., Nov. 11, 1849, a. 93; was a surgeon in the revolution.

MAYNADIER, Henry E., maj. gen. U. S. A., d. at Charleston, S. C., Dec. 3, 1868, a. 38; a native of Va., grad. at West Point, in 1851; was in the Utah expedition of 1857–8, and the upper Missouri yellowstone expedition in 1859–61; was in the late war in several engagements, and was breveted for services.

MAYNARD, John, was a member of the New York assembly in 1822 and senate from 1838 to 40, and in the 20th and 27th congresses, from Seneca co.; was county clerk of Seneca co. from 1821 to 1825, district attorney in 1836, and elected a justice of the supreme court for the 7th district in June 1847, for a term of four years, in which office he d. at Auburn, N. Y., March 24, 1850. (*Stryker's Am. Reg.*, iv, 453.)

MAYNARD, Jonathan, d. at Framingham, Mass., July, 1835, a. 83.

MAYNARD, Needham, d. in Waterloo, N. Y., Oct. 20, 1844; served in the revolution, and settled after the war, as a farmer in Ipswich; in

1788, removed to Whitestown, N. Y., and resided there more than 40 years; removed to Seneca co., and d. a. 88.

MAYNARD, William H., was a native of Conway, Mass., graduated at William's Coll., in 1810, studied law with Gen. Joseph Kirkland of New Hartford, N. Y., and was several years editor of the *Utica Patriot;* he became a partner with Samuel A. Talcott, and in 1828 was elected to the state senate, and while attending a session of that body sitting in New York city as a court of errors, he died of cholera, Aug. 28, 1832, a. 45. By his will be gave $20,000 for the endowment of a law school at Hamilton College. (*Am. An. Reg.*, 1832–3, p. 417.)

MAYO, Joseph, d. in Richmond, Va., Aug. 9, 1872, a. 77; was commonwealth atty. of Richmond for 29 years, and member of the legislature, and served as mayor of Richmond for 15 years, until he was removed by the federal authorities. He was author of a legal work known as *The Mayor's Guide.*

MAYSON, Charles C., d. at Jackson, Miss., Aug. 27, 1837; was a native of S. C.

MAZUREAN, Stephen, a native of France and once an officer in the French navy; came to New Orleans in 1804, and long held a prominent position as a lawyer; was at different times member of the state legislature, secretary of state and attorney general; d. May 25, 1849, a. 77. (*Stryker's Am. Reg.*, ii, 496.)

MEACHAM, Joseph, Shaker leader; b. at Enfield, Ct.; became head of the Shaker community at New Lebanon, and d. Aug. 16, 1786. (*Evans's Shakers' Compendium*, p. 183.)

MEADE, George Gordon, major gen. U. S. A., d. in Philadelphia, Nov. 6, 1872; b. in Cadiz, Spain, where his parents were temporarily living, Dec. 31, 1815; grad. at West Point in 1835, and served in the Mexican war; was afterwards employéd on river and harbor improvements, and when the late war began, was on the lake surveys; he was ordered to report to Washington, and on the 31st of August, 1861, he received the appointment of brigadier-general of volunteers, with command of the second brigade of the Pennsylvania Reserve Corps; he took part in McClellan's advance on Richmond, and during the seven days' fight was struck by a ball, which caused a severe and painful wound; he soon recovered, and September, 1862, took command of a division in Reynolds's First Army Corps, which he conducted with great skill and bravery during the Maryland campaign; at Antietam his Reserves were in the hottest and thickest of the fight, and when Gen. Hooker was wounded, Gen. McClellan placed the general in command of the corps which had just been deprived of its gallant leader; during the action he received a slight contusion, and had two horses killed under him; he received the appointment of major-general of volunteers on the 29th of November, and took part in the battle of Fredericksburg (December, 1862), and displayed courage and coolness during the engagement; during the same month he was placed in command of the Fifth Corps, which, after being engaged throughout the battle of Chancellorsville, covered the retreat of the beaten army, and guarded the crossings until the whole army was safely over the river. In June, 1863, when Lee was advancing up the Shenandoah valley to invade Maryland and Pennsylvania, Gen. Meade was suddenly and unexpectedly called to succeed Gen. Hooker in the command of the army of the Potomac, numbering 100,000 men; he advanced through Maryland on parallel lines with Lee's army, which finally, marching eastward, struck (July 1) the head of Meade's column under Gen. Reynolds, near Gettysburg; the fight for position which occurred, and which resulted in the defeat and death of Reynolds, and the retirement of his column through Gettysburg to a strong position south of the town, is generally spoken of as the first day's fight of the great battle which ensued at Gettysburg; the whole army advanced to this position during the night, and the next day Sickles's corps went into action and was driven back, the day closing with the advantage on the side of the Confederates; the third day opened with an advance of the Union right under Slocum, who retook ground he had lost and rested upon it; soon after the Confederate artillery opened and plowed the Union lines for two hours, when the great Confederate column of assault emerging from behind the batteries pressed swiftly toward the Union lines, and was repulsed with great slaughter. This reverse decided the day, and when the Confederates regained their lines the battle had been won by the Union forces; Gen. Meade, who displayed masterly ability throughout the engagement, reported his loss in these three bloody days at 2,834 killed, 13,709 wounded and 6,643 missing. He took 13,621 prisoners and 24,978 small arms. Lee promptly retreated, and escaped before the detachments sent by Meade in pursuit could arrest his progress; Gen. Meade was promoted to be a brigadier-general of the regular army by a commission dated July 3, 1863. About the 18th of July he moved his army across the Potomac into Virginia, where he had several skirmishes with the enemy in October and November, 1863. He was second in command of the army of the Potomac in its operations against Richmond in 1864. "I tried as far as possible," observed Gen. Grant, "to leave Gen. Meade in independent command of the army of the Potomac; my instructions for that army were all through him, and were general in their nature, leaving all the details and the execution to him; the campaigns that followed proved him to be the right man in the right place;" the army of which he had immediate command fought great battles at the Wilderness, Spottsylvania Court-house, and Cold Harbor, and was employed many months in the siege of Petersburg; in August, 1864, he was appointed a major-general of the regular army; he was placed in command of the third military district, comprising Georgia, Florida, and Alabama, in 1867, and was subsequently appointed commander of the Atlantic Military Division having its headquarters at Philadelphia; was tall, and soldier-like in bearing. (*N. Y. Tribune.*)

MEADE, Richard Kidder, father of Bp. M., was an aid de camp to Washington in 1777, and held the rank of col.; was in the battle of Monmouth, and very narrowly escaped death. His brother Everard, was aid to Gen. Lincoln; the brothers were educated at Harrow, England, under Dr. Thackeray, at the same time with Sir Wm. Jones, Sir Joseph Banks and Dr. Parr. (*Campbell's Va.*)

MEADE, Richard W., commodore U. S. N., d. at Brooklyn, N. Y., April 16, 1870, a. 63; b. in Madrid, Spain; his father R. W. Meade being then minister to Spain; entered the Naval Academy in 1823, and at the beginning of the late war was a commander; commanded the U. S. receiving ship North Carolina, at New York, until 1864; and was then placed in command of the steamer San Jacinto, which was lost on the Florida reefs; was a brother of Maj. Gen. Geo. G. Meade of the army.

MEANDER, JOHN, minister and member of the society of Friends, d. in Providence R. I., June, 1860, a. 64 ; b. in Sandwich, N. H.; resided formerly in Maine, but for many years past at the place of his death. (*Vincent's Semi-An. Register*, p. 619.)

MEANS, REV. ROBERT, a Presbyterian minister of Fairfield dist., S. C., d. Jan. 20, 1836 ; he published several sermons, and an essay on the Pentateuch.

MEASE, JOHN, b. in Strabane, Ireland, came to America in 1754, and was an eminent shipping merchant of Philadelphia ; was an active partisan of the American cause in the revolution, and for the last thirty years of life one of the admiralty surveyors of the port of Philadelphia ; d. in 1826, a. 86. (*Simpson's Eminent Philadelphians.*)

MEASE, MATTHEW, b. in Strabane, county Tyrone, Ireland, and settled in early life in Philadelphia as a merchant ; he entered the navy, and became purser of the Bonhomme Richard ; in the conflict with the Serapis, he obtained command of the quarter deck guns, and was dangerously wounded ; d. at Philadelphia in 1787.

MEBANE, ALEXANDER, b. in Hawfields, Orange co., N. C., Nov. 26, 1767 ; was a member of the convention in 1776, that formed the first state constitution ; in congress in 1793–4 ; d. July 5, 1795.

MEBANE, JAMES, a prominent citizen of North Carolina, d. in Caswell co., N. C., Dec. 12, 1857, a. 84.

MEECH, EZRA, b. in New London, Conn., July 26, 1773 ; became an agent of the N. W. fur trade with J. J. Astor, and in 1809, an agent for supplying spars for the British navy ; in 1822–3 was elected chief justice of Chittenden co., Vt. ; was in the conventions of 1822 and 1826, and in the state legislature in 1805, 7; in congress from 1819 to 1821, and from 1825 to 1827 ; devoted his later years to farming, having 3000 acres, 3,000 sheep, and 800 head of cattle ; d. at Shelburne, Vt., Sept. 23, 1856.

MEIGS, JOSIAH, first pres. of the University of Ga., at Athens. (*White's Hist. Ga.*, p. 397.)

MELLEN, JAMES, d. at Hudson, N. Y., Oct. 3, 1839 ; a prominent citizen.

MELVILLE, GANSEVOORT, secretary to the U. S. legation to Great Britain ; d. in London, May 12, 1846.

MENARD, CLAUDE, Jesuit missionary, arrived in Canada, July 8, 1640 ; was with Lemercier at Onondaga, from 1656 to 1658, and afterwards with the Cayugas : said to have been killed Sept. 8, 1661. (*Liste Chron. des Evêques et des Prêtres du Canada ; Doc. Hist. N. Y.*, iv, 292.)

MENDENHALL, DR. GEORGE, d. at Cincinnati, O., June 4, 1874 ; b. in Sharon, Pa., in 1814, and settled in Cincinnati in 1843, where he acquired an extensive practice, and was especially successful in obstetrics, of which he was professor in the Miami and Ohio Medical Colleges.

MENEFEE, RICHARD H., d. at Frankfort, Ky., Feb. 21, 1841 ; a member of congress from Kentucky from 1837 to 1839.

MERCEIN, COL. THOMAS R., d. in New York city, Oct. 24, 1843, a. 51 ; was in the New York assembly in 1811 and 1812, and a distinguished and useful citizen.

MERCER, COL. HUGH, d. in Fredericksburg, Va., Dec. 1, 1853, a. 77.

MERCER, SINGLETON, conspicuously before the country some eighteen years before his death; from having avenged his sister's dishonor by shooting her seducer on a ferry boat near the Jersey shore, at Philadelphia; he was tried and acquitted on the ground of insanity; he went to Norfolk, Va., as a nurse in the yellow fever epidemic in the fall of 1855, and fell a victim to the disease.

MERCER, WILLIAM, d. at Fredericksburg, Va., Aug. 20, 1839, at an advanced age; born deaf and dumb, and was the eldest son of Gen. Hugh M., who fell at Princeton, in 1777.

MERCHANT, GEORGE, b. in Princeton, N. J., Oct. 21, 1757; graduated at Princeton in 1789, and the classic elegance of a salutatory address won him the appointment of principal in an academy in Princeton; in 1786, he became principal of an academy at Albany, N. Y., where he held the offices of alderman, police justice, county clerk, lottery manager, com. of bankruptcy and paymaster in the war of 1812; d. at Albany, Sept. 14, 1830, a. 73.

MEREDITH, REESE, father of Samuel Meredith, was a merchant of Philadelphia, and a prominent citizen of Phila.

MEREDITH, WILLIAM, b. in Philadelphia, Pa., June 2, 1772, and d. Sept. 1844; was an eminent lawyer, and continued to practice his profession till 1814, when he was elected president of the Schuylkill Bank; was many years one of the common council, and for a time city solicitor; was a prominent Episcopalian, and for many years in its diocesan and general conventions; was a trustee of the University of Pennsylvania; a member of the American Philosophical Society and a director of the Academy of Fine Arts. (*Simpson's Eminent Philadelphians*, with portrait.)

MEREDITH, WILLIAM M., an eminent lawyer of Pennsylvania; d. at Philadelphia, Aug. 17, 1873, a. 77.

MERIWETHER, JAMES, b. in Va.; served in the revolution; settled in Ga. in 1782, and d. in Jefferson co., Ga., Oct. 25, 1817.

MERRIAM, EBENEZER, printer; was apprenticed to Isaiah Thomas at Worcester in 1790; went to Boston in 1796, and in 1797 was established at Brookfield, where he published the *Mass. Repository* and *Farmer's Journal*; he became a book and job printer in 1800 and continued 51 years; d. at W. Brookfield, Mass., Oct. 1, 1858, a. 81. (*Hist. Mag.*, ii, 348.)

MERRIAM, GEN. ELA, d. in Leyden, N. Y., Nov. 11, 1873; b. in Meriden, Conn.; removed in childhood with his father's family to Lewis co., N. Y.; and was through most of his life a stage proprietor, and extensively known in northern New York; was much interested in agriculture, and internal improvements, and one of the founders of Port Leyden, N. Y.; was the father of Hon. Clinton L. Merriam, M. C., from New York 1871–5.

MERRIAM, NATHANIEL, judge; b. in Wallingford, Ct., June 3, 1769; settled in Leydon in 1800; removed to Indiana in 1838; returned in 1846, and d. Aug. 19, 1847; he was in assembly in 1811–19, and was made county judge in 1815; father of Gen. Ela M., of Leyden. (*Hough's Hist. Lewis Co.*, p. 122.)

MERRICK, RICHARD VAUGHAN, d. at Phila., Penn., Aug. 18, 1870; was senior member of the firm Merrick & Sons, manufacturers of marine engines and other machinery; one of the largest establishments in the

U. S.; first pres. of the Penn. Central rail road co., and one of its projectors; for a long time an officer of the Franklin Institute.

MERRICK, WILLIAM D., d. in Washington, D. C., Feb. 5, 1857; was of Charles co., Md., and was senator from Md. from 1838 to 1845; had filled several important stations in his own state, before his entrance upon the duties of senator.

MERRILL, FERRAND F., b. in 1811, and from 1835 mostly in public life; elected clerk of the Vt. house of representatives in 1835, and annually for the next 11 years; in 1849 became sec. of state and held five years; afterwards state atty. for the co., and a member of the state legisature; d. in Montpelier, May 2, 1859, a. 47.

MERRILL, TIMOTHY, secretary of state of Vt.; d. at Montpelier, Vt., July 27, 1836.

MERRITT, THOMAS, a loyalist in the revolution; d. May 12, 1842, at St. Catharines, Canada; held a commission in the British army; was sheriff of the district of Niagara, and for many years surveyor of woods and forests in Upper Canada.

MERVINE, CATHARINAR B., son of Admiral M.; b. at Litchfield, Herkimer co., N. Y., Jan. 12, 1805; in Apr., 1861, he enlisted as a private in the 12th reg. N. Y. state vols., and was made adjutant; he next served on the staff of Genl. McQuade, and after the seven days' battle before Richmond, was appointed assist. adj. gen. to Gen. Griffin; d. at City Point, Va., Aug. 17, 1864.

MERVINE, WILLIAM, rear admiral U. S. N., b. near Philadelphia March 14, 1791, and entered the navy in Jan., 1809; from this time until 1832, he made numerous cruises, was severely wounded in the battle of Black Rock, and as lieut., was in the guard ship that convoyed the first colony to Liberia; in 1832, he took his first command and was stationed in the harbor of Charleston; before war opened with Mexico, he captured a Mexican brig which had two American vessels under its guns; in Sept., 1841, he was appointed captain; in 1845 or 46, he went in the Cyane to California, and on the show of hostilities he attacked and took the fort at Monterey, remaining in charge until 1847; two years later, in the steam frigate Powhattan, he had command of the Mediterranean squadron, but was recalled by urgent duty at home; in 1854–7, in the flag ship Independence, he cruised in the Pacific; in 1861, while in command of the gulf blockading squadron, he planned the attack which was carried out by Lieut. Russell, but in consequence of illness was recalled; was appointed commodore in July, 1862, and rear admiral in 1866; was sixty years in the naval service, being 25 years at sea, and 4 years on duty ashore; d. at Utica Sept., 15, 1868.

MERWIN, JESSE, d. in Kinderhook, N. Y., Nov. 8, 1852, a. 70; in early life taught school, and was a companion of Washington Irving; was the original of Ichabod Crane, in the Legend of Sleepy Hollow.

MERWIN, DR. SAMUEL C., d. at Natchez, Miss., Nov. 4, 1839; formerly of Philadelphia.

MESSANT, PAUL, a well known French journalist and citizen of the U. S., d. on Long Island, N. Y., Jan., 26, 1873, a. 29.

MESSELIN, CHARLES FRANCOIS BAILLY DE, b. at Varennes, Canada, Nov. 4, 1740; became priest May 4, 1767, and was chosen coadjutor of M.

Hubert, R. C. bp. of Quebec, June 30, 1788, with the intention of succeeding him, but died before him, May 20, 1794. (*Liste Chron. des Evêques et des Prêtres du Canada.*)

MESZÁROS, LAZARUS, a Hungarian general; spent several years in America, became a citizen, returned to Europe in 1858, and died in Eywood, Herefordshire, England, Nov. 16, 1858, a. 62.

METCALF, DR. GEORGE W., b. in Owego, N. Y., July, 22, 1837; d. Oct. 28, 1874, served as a surgeon in the war of 1861–5.

METCALF, MICHAEL, one of the first settlers at Dedham, Mass., and emigrant and ancestor of this family in Am.; b. in Tatterford, Norfolk co., Eng., in 1586; admitted as a townsman at Dedham, July 14, 1637, a selectman in 1641; d. Dec. 27, 1664, a. 78. (*Goodwin's Notes*, p. 157.)

METCALF, SILAS, d. at Deposit, Delaware co., N. Y., Dec. 9, 1867; b. in Berkshire, Mass., and was well known as the superintendent of young ladies' institutes at Kinderhook, Parsipanny, and East Brooklyn.

MILAM, BENJAMIN R., a Texan patriot, b. near Frankfort, Ky.; was led by his fondness for adventure to engage in the Mexican revolution, but resigned his commission upon the crowning of Yterbide; was imprisoned, but at length returned, and became a pioneer in Texas; was killed at the storming of San Antonio in 1835. (*Texas Almanac*, 1857, p. 135.)

MILES, GEORGE H., poet and dramatist; d. at Thornton, Md., July 24, 1871, a. 47; prof. of belles lettres at St. Mary's Coll., Md.

MILES, CAPT. JOHN E., d. at Watertown, N. Y., Feb. 1, 1860, a. 78. (*N. Y. Reformer*, Feb. 16, 1860.)

MILET, PIERRE, Jesuit missionary; sent with de Carheil to Cayuga; left in 1684; was at Niagara in 1688; taken prisoner at Cataracouy in 1689, and held till Oct. 1694; was living several years after 1705.

MILLARD, REV. HENRY NORTON, b. Summer Hill, N. Y., Aug. 5, 1830; grad. at Hamilton Coll. in 1850; pastor of Presbyterian church at Eaton, Truxton, Williamstown and Holland Patent; d. at Auburn, Sept. 13, 1873.

MILLARD, WILLIAM, ex-member of congress from Delaware; d. at Kirkwood, Del., Nov. 26, 1871.

MILLEN, COL. JOHN, d. near Savannah, Ga., Oct. 15, 1843, a. 39; member elect in congress; was a young lawyer of great promise; was in the legislature in 1828. (*Am. Almanac* 1845, p. 307.)

MILLER, ANDREW J., d. in Augusta, Ga., Feb. 3, 1856: several years president of the state senate.

MILLER, AMOS, an early settler of Leyden, N. Y.; in assembly in 1826; d. Oct. 2, 1840, a. 64.

MILLER, BERNARD J., d. in Washington, D. C., Sept. 17, 1837; was several years surgeon major in the Columbian navy.

MILLER, DAVID, a pioneer of Leyden, N. Y.; d. in that town, March 19, 1833, a. 82.

MILLER, DAVID BRAINERD, pioneer settler in Leyden, N. Y.; d. March 19, 1833, a. 82.

MILLER, REV. GEORGE BENJAMIN, b. of Moravian ancestors at Enmaus, Lehigh co, Pa., June 10, 1795; was in early life in mercantile business, but in 1812, became associated with Rev. Dr. Hazelius in an acad. at Hartwick, N. Y.; was licensed to preach in 1818, and was 9 years at Canajoharie; again became a teacher at Hartwick Seminary, and in 1830, prin. and prof. of theology; accepted a call to the theological seminary at Gettysburg; d. at Hartwick, April 5, 1869. (*Regents' Report*, 1870, p. 593; *Hartwick Seminary Memorial*, with portrait.)

MILLER, DR. HENRY, one of the founders of the Louisville Medical College, and many years a member of its faculty; b. in Glasgow, Ky., Nov. 1, 1800; d. at Louisville, Ky., Feb. 8, 1874.

MILLER, REV. JAMES, a Baptist minister and pioneer in Turin, N. Y.; d. in West Turin, N. Y., March 1, 1843, a. 87.

MILLER, JAMES, a revolutionary soldier, d. at East Greenwich, R. I., May 19, 1849, a. 95 years.

MILLER, JAMES F., commodore U. S. N., d. at Charlestown, Mass., July 11, 1868; b. in N. H., and entered the service in 1826.

MILLER, JESSE, d. in Harrisburg, Pa., Aug. 20, 1850; was secretary of state in the term of Gov. Shank, and in congress from Pennsylvania, from 1836 to 1837.

MILLER, CAPT. JOHN, Penn., killed at Fort Washington, Nov. 16, 1776.

MILLER, DR. JOHN, d. at Truxton, N. Y., March 30, 1862, a. 87. (*Transac. N. Y. State Med. Soc.*, 1863, p. 449.)

MILLER, JOHN BLEECKER, son of Judge Miller, was b. Nov. 7, 1820; he studied law and practiced for a brief period; was for some time associate editor of the *Utica Observer;* in ——, he was appointed U. S. consul at Hamburg; April 6, 1861, at Marseilles in France.

MILLER, JOHN G., d. in Saline co., Mo., May 11, 1856, a. 44; b. in Kentucky, emigrated to Missouri in 1835, was elected to the state legislature in 1840, and from 1853, till the time of his death a representative in congress from Missouri.

MILLER, John J., judge of the Columbia county court, d. at Claverack, N. Y., Dec. 2, 1839.

MILLER, COL. JONATHAN P., d. in Montpelier, Vt., Feb. 17, 1847, a. 50; he entered warmly into the cause of the Greeks, when struggling for liberty, and in 1827, sailed from New York with a cargo of supplies which had been raised in this country, and of which he superintended the distribution; he was an ardent opponent of slavery.

MILLER, DR. LEWIS, b. in Glastonbury, Conn., Dec. 25, 1799; grad. at Hamilton Coll., 1833; settled at Moreland, N. Y.; d. at Jackson, Mich., Sept. 29, 1873.

MILLER, MORRIS SMITH, son of Dr. Matthias Burnet Miller, surgeon of the revolutionary army, was b. on Long Island in 1780; graduated at Union College in 1798, and studied law; was secretary of Gov. Jay, and afterwards agent at Lowville, of Nicholas Lowe; removed in 1806 to Utica and entered on the practice of his profession; March 5, 1810, he was appointed first judge of the county, and held the office until his death; in 1813–15 he represented his district in congress; in July, 1819, he acted as commissioner in a treaty with the Seneca Indians; at first an adherent of Governor Clinton, he became a bucktail, and was one of the so called, "high-minded gentleman;" d. Nov. 19, 1824.

MILLER, MORRIS S., lieut. col. and brevet brig. gen. U. S. A., son of the preceding, b. in Utica, April 2d, 1814; graduated at West Point in 1834; he participated in the Florida and Mexican wars, and in the war for the union; throughout the latter he was in the quarter master's department at Washington, and while there about $20,000,000 passed through his hands, yet upon examination of his accounts less than $20 was to be disallowed; d. March 11, 1870.

MILLER, SAMUEL, lieut. col. of U. S. marine corps; d. at Philadelphia, Dec. 9, 1856, a. 81, after a life spent in honorable service. (*Simpson's Eminent Philadelphians.*)

MILLER, DR. SYLVESTER, d. at Lowville, N. Y., from an accident, July 30, 1838, a. 54.

MILLER, THOMAS, presiding judge in Powhatan co. court, Va.; was a county magistrate 44 years, and repeatedly in the general assembly; he d. in Powhatan co., Va., Nov. 2, 1845, a. 65.

MILLER, THOMAS A., d. at Torringford, Conn., Oct. 16, 1861, a. 55; his wife Mary C. d. Oct. 13, and both were buried in one grave.

MILLER, WILLIAM H., d. at Harrisburg, Pa., Sept. 12, 1870; was clerk of the supreme court of Pa. middle dist., 1854–63, and member of the 38th congress.

MILLER, WILLIAM STARR, d. in New York city, Nov. 9, 1854; was in congress from New York from 1845 to 1847.

MILLS, ISAAC, d. at New Haven, Conn., Jan. 29, 1843, a. about 75; was a native of Huntington, Conn., and grad. at Yale in 1786; was many years a judge of the court for the county of New Haven, and judge of probate.

MILLS, JOHN, b. in Chatham, N. Y.; settled in Columbia, Herkimer co., N. Y., in 1790; was in assembly in 1800, filled town offices most of his life and d. in 1836, a. 76. (*Benton's Herkimer Co. N. Y.*, p. 348.)

MILLS, MARTHA, d. in Stanton, Del., Jan., 1842, in her 100th year.

MILLS, REV. SAMUEL J., b. in Derby, Conn.; grad. at Yale, and emigrated to the Genesee country in 1785; d. soon after 1800; was an early minister of Livingston co., N. Y. (*Turner's Phelps and Gorham Purchase*, p. 351.)

MILLS, WILLIAM A., son of Rev. Samuel J. Mills, a pioneer business man at Mount Morris, Livingston co.; was a commissioned officer in the war of 1812, and became a brigadier gen.; d. in 1844, a. 67. (*Turner's Phelps and Gorham Purchase*, p. 351.)

MINER, ASHER, d. at Wilkesbarre, Pa., March 13, 1841, a. 63.

MINER, PHINEHAS, an eminent lawyer, and member of congress from Connecticut in 1834–5, d. at Litchfield, Conn., Sept. 16, 1839, in his 60th year.

MING, ALEXANDER, one of the oldest printers in N. Y. city; d. at that city, Feb. 2, 1849, a. 76. (*Stryker's Am. Reg.*, ii, 254.)

MINOR, ISAAC, president of the board of canal commissioners of O.; d. at Columbus, Dec. 27, 1831.

MINOR, COL. THOMAS, d. at Fredericksburg, Va., July, 1834, a. 83

MINOR, WILLIAM G., a native of Va.; emigrated to Mo. in 1840; was one of the commissioners for running the northern boundary of that state, and was many years editor of the *Jefferson Inquirer;* was an effective speaker, and served as secretary of state senate and adjt. gen.; d. at Jefferson city, Mo., Feb. 20, 1851, a. 45.

MITCHELL, GEORGE E., member of congress from 1823 to 1827, and from 1829 to 1832; d. at Washington, D. C., June 28, 1832; he resided at Elkton, Md.

MITCHELL, HENRY, M.D., b. in Woodbury, Ct., in 1784; was licensed to practice in 1806, and settled in Coventry and soon after in Norwich, Chenango co., N. Y., where he d. Jan. 12, 1856, a. 72. (*Tr. N. Y. State Med. Soc.*, 1857, p. 85.)

MITCHELL, REV. JESSE, of St. Louis conference; d. Aug. 12, 1854. (*Deems's Annals of Southern Methodism*, p. 346.)

MITCHELL, GEN. JOHN, was twice a sheriff of Centre co., Pa., and elected to the 19th and 20th congresses; he was first engineer on the Erie canal extension and superintended the construction of the French creek feeder; was several years in the state legislature and once canal com'r. in Pa.; d. in Beaver co., Pa., August, 1849.

MITCHELL, THOMAS R., grad. at Harvard in 1802; in congress from South Carolina from 1821 to 1823; from 1825 to 1829, and from 1831 to 1833; d. in 1837.

MIX, EBENEZER, b. in New Haven, Conn.; settled as a mason at Batavia, N. Y.; in 1809, became a teacher, studied law and became a clerk in the Holland Land Company's office, where he afterwards became agent; was for 20 years surrogate of Genesee county; d. at Batavia.

MOALE, SAMUEL, d. in Baltimore, Feb. 21, 1857, a. 84, being at the time the oldest member of the Baltimore bar, cotemporary with Pinckney and Harper, and highly esteemed for his integrity of character.

MOFFAT, DR. THOMAS C., d. at New York, Dec. 17, 1870; had been for many years physician in chief of the Seaman's Retreat, on Staten Island.

MOLLESON, GEORGE P., d. at New Brunswick, N. J., May 17, 1844, a. 37; attorney general of the state; grad. at Princeton, 1827; admitted to the bar and gained a high standing; was several times a member of the state legislature.

MOMPESSON, ROGER, first chief justice of New Jersey; arrived in Phila. in 1703; was sworn into office as chief justice of Pa., April, 1706, but is not known to have acted; upon the arrival of Lord Cornbury he was made chief justice of New York and New Jersey, which he held during Cornbury's term, acting as his adviser in all points of law; he resigned upon Cornbury's removal, justly dreading a speedy end of his official relation with the colony; he disgraced his judicial office by the basest partiality. (*Coll. N. J. Hist. Soc.*, iii, 56.)

MONCRIEF, JAMES, ex-judge of the superior court; d. at New York, Feb. 1, 1870, a. 48; b. in Ohio, Sept. 16, 1822; studied law in New York and practiced there till 1858, when he was elected judge, and held that office 7 years.

MONCRIEFFE, THOMAS, was a lieut. at Oswego, and taken prisoner in 1756; joined the 1st Royals in 1757; was appointed aid to Brig. Monckton, lieut. gov. of Nova Scotia in 1758, and accompanied Gen. Prideaux to Niagara in 1759; he attended Amherst's expedition to Montreal as captain in 1760; returned to Ireland in 1764; came back to America in 1768, and in 1774, was made brigade major by Gen. Gage at Boston; he returned to N. Y., was taken prisoner at Brooklyn, but was soon released; he resided at Flatbush, was again taken prisoner, and exchanged; d. at N. Y., Dec. 9, 1791. (*Com. Wilson's Orderly Book*, 119.)

MONELL, ROBERT, judge; a native of Columbia co.; removed to Binghamton, N. Y., in 1808, and to Greene, N. Y., in 1811, where he succeeded Elisha Smith as agent of the Hornby estate; he resigned in 1819; was in the legislature in 1815–25–6–8, and in the 14th and 16th congresses; in 1831 he became circuit judge of the 6th circuit, and held 14 years; from 1845 to 1847 he was clerk of the supreme court at Geneva; he returned to Greene and lived to an advanced age. (*Chenango American*, Jan. 1858.)

MONEYPENNY, ALEXANDER, became capt. Aug. 29, 1756, and in 1757 joined the 55th foot from Cork for America; in 1758 he served in the unfortunate attack of Ticonderoga, and May 5, 1759 was a brig. gen. in the army against Crown Point; in 1760 he attended Amherst by way of Oswego to Montreal, and in 1761 marched against the southern Indians; he returned to Ireland, was made lieut. col. Sept. 1, 1762; was at Gibraltar in 1769, and remained until 1776; d. or resigned Sept., 1776.

MONGES, DR. JOHN ARMENTAIRE, b. in Thorembasse, France; came to America in 1781, as surgeon of a ship sent to aid the American revolution; remained for a time, went by the interior route to New Orleans and St. Domingo, in 1785, and to Philadelphia in 1793; was very successful with the yellow fever; d. in 1798. (*Simpson's Eminent Philadelphians.*)

MONI, REV. ABBÉ, d. at Mobile, Ala., Aug. 3, 1842; a professor of the Catholic worship, and much respected by all denominations.

MONROE, CAPT. EDMUND, Mass., killed at Monmouth, June 28, 1778.

MONROE, COL. JAMES, 3d son of Benjamin M., d. April 20, 1860, at Frankfort, Ky.; he was captain in the Mexican war, and afterwards represented Franklin co., in the Kentucky legislature.

MONROE, COL. JAMES, d. at Orange, N. J., Sept. 7, 1870, a. 71; b in Albemarle, Va., in 1799; grad. at West Point in 1815; and removed to New York; was in congress in 1839–41, and in the state legislature in 1850 and 1852, was a nephew of President Monroe; he served in the war with Algiers, and was wounded, served in the army till 1832; was alderman, and pres. of that board in 1833–4.

MONSON, LEVINUS, b. in Hampden, Conn., May 5, 1792; grad. at Yale in 1811; studied law and settled in Hobart, N. Y.; many years a judge of com. pleas of Delaware co., and in 1850, appointed to fill a vacancy on the bench of the supreme court of New York; d. at Hobart, N. Y., Sept. 23, 1859, a. 68.

MONTAIGUT, DAVID, speaker of assembly, in Ga., judge of the court of conscience, naval officer, vice consul of France and sec. to several societies in Savannah; d. in 1796, a. 80.

MONTGOMERIE, ARCHIBALD, 3d son of Alex., 9th earl of Eglinton; raised in 1757 the 62d afterwards 77th regiment of which he became lt.

col.; in 1758 he made the campaign against Fort Duquesne, and in 1759, accompanied Gen. Amherst; in 1760, he was sent against the Cherokees, and in 1762, became col.; he was equerry to the queen in 1763, and gov. of Dumbarton castle in 1764; in 1767 he became col. of the 51st reg., and became an earl; in May, 1772, he became maj. gen., and in 1777 lieut. gen.; d. a general in the army Oct. 30, 1796. (*Com. Wilson's Orderly Book*, 17.)

MONTGOMERY, Rev. Henry E., d.d., pastor of the Prot. Episc. church of the Incarnation, N. Y. city; d. Oct. 16, 1874, in his 50th year.

MONTGOMERY, John B., rear admiral in the U. S. navy; d. at Carlisle, Pa., March 25, 1873; he entered the navy in 1812, and was on the retired list; he served 21 years and 9 months at sea, and 17 years on shore duty; he was a midshipman on board of the flag-ship Niagara in the victory of Lake Erie; September, 1814, and commanded the Washington Navy-Yard from 1864 to 1865; was interred at Washington.

MONTGOMERY, John G., member of congress from the 12th dist. of Pa.; d. in Danville, Pa., April 24, 1857; said to be a victim of the National Hotel disease, which caused such alarm and loss of life soon before this date.

MONTGOMERY, William, d. at Washington, Pa., April 28, 1870, a. 51; b. at Canton, Bradford co., 1819; educated at Washington Coll.; studied law, was admitted to the law in 1832, and was a member of congress in 1856-60; was the author of the Crittenden-Montgomery Amendment, which was intended as a sedative measure on the slavery question.

MONTGOMERY, William, R., lieut. col. U. S. A., d. at Bristol, Pa., May 31, 1871; was brig. gen. of U. S. vols., in the late war, also served in the Mexican war.

MONTRESOR, James, became director of engineers and lt .col. in the British army, Jan. 4, 1758, and served against Ticonderoga under Abercrombie; he drew the plan of Fort Stanwix and grounds adjacent, the summer of the same year; superintended the construction of Fort George on Lake George in 1759, and in 1771 received a grant for 10,000 acres of land on Otter creek now in Panton, Vt.; in May, 1772, he became a col. in the army; d. Dec. 1775.

MOODY, Capt. Lemuel, d. at Portland, Me., Aug. 11, 1846, a. 79; was a successful shipmaster and a carefully observing man; kept a meteorological record many years, and published in 1825, a valuable chart of Casco bay, and the inlets from the mouth of the Saco to the Kennebec.

MOOERS, Dr. Benjamin, of Plattsburg, N. Y., d. May 20, 1869, a. 82; b. in Haverhill, Mass., Sept. 11, 1787. (*Transac. N. Y. State Med. Soc.*, 1870, p. 309.)

MOOR, John, said to have belonged to Londonderry, N. H.; two officers of this name served at Louisburg in 1745, one a capt. the other a lieut. (*Farmer and Moore's N. H. Coll.*, iii, 326.)

MOOR, Wyman B. S., d. at Lynchburg, Va., March 9, 1869; a citizen of the state of Maine, a senator from that state in congress, by governor's appointment, to fill an unexpired term in 1848–9, and afterwards U. S. consul general in Canada.

MOORE, A. B., ex-gov. of Ala.; d. at Marion, Ala., April 5, 1873, a. 68.

MOORE, AUGUSTUS, formerly a judge of the superior court of N. C., and a distinguished lawyer; d. at Edenton, N. C., March 24, 1851, of apoplexy.

MOORE, ELI, d. Jan. 16, 1860; a prominent democratic politician; member of congress from N. Y. from 1835 to 1839; marshal of the southern dist. of N. Y., then editor of the *Women's Journal*, at Belvidere, N. J., and Indian agent in Kansas; registrar of the land office in Kansas Territory at the time of his death.

MOORE, EPHRAIM, b. at Hollis, N. H., April 26, 1794; settled in Farmington, Ontario co., N. Y., in 1816, and in March, 1817, came to Rochester; was a cooper, and extended his business to 35,000 bls. a year; held several town and co. offices, and d. April, 1857.

MOORE, HEMAN A., d. at Columbus, O., April 3, 1844, a. 34; member of congress; b. in Vt.; studied law in Rochester, and began law practice at Columbus, O., where he soon obtained distinction.

MOORE, JAMES, d. at Metuchen, N. J., April 15, 1859, in his 100th year.

MOORE, REV. J. B., d. at Southampton, Eng., July, 1872; acting pastor of the church of the Unity at Springfield, Mass; in Concord, Mass.; and for six years pastor of the Unitarian church in Lowell.

MOORE, REV. JOHN, d. in Concord, N. H., Feb. 5, 1855; he fell suddenly dead in the street from heart disease; was nominated for gov. by the American party, a short time before, but his name withdrawn, because ineligible.

MOORE, JOHN M., a prominent citizen of Mississippi, d. at Vicksburg, Feb. 15, 1859.

MOORE, JOSIAH, U. S. consul for the Philippine Islands; d. at Manilla, March 18, 1848, a 37.

MOORE, LAVREY H., d. at Springfield, La., Oct. 3, 1836; was for several years a distinguished member of the senate of Louisiana.

MOORE, MAJ. WILLARD, Mass; killed at Bunker hill, June 17, 1775.

MOORE, WILLIAM, served in the British army in the French war as ensign, became captain, his name was dropped from the lists in 1776.

MOOREHEAD, CHARLES S., d. in Greenville, Miss., Dec. 23, 1868; b. in Nelson co., Ky., in 1802; was in the legislature of Kentucky in 1828; attorney general in 1832; speaker of the house from 1840 to 1844; member of congress from 1847 to 1851; was elected gov. of Kentucky in 1855, and was a delegate from that state to the peace convention of 1861.

MOOREHOUSE, EBEN B., was a justice of the supreme court of N. Y., in the 6th district, for a term of 8 years in June, 1847; died at Cooperstown, N. Y., Dec. 9, 1849.

MORALES, GEN., president of Bolivia, shot by his nephew La Faye, Nov. 27, 1873.

MORDECAI, DR. SOLOMON, d. at Mobile, Ala., May 7, 1869, having practiced there for nearly half a century.

MOREL, EDMUND, engineer in chief of the Japanese Imperial railway; d. at Yokohama, Nov. 5, 1871.

MORELAND, HARRY GEORGE, a successful actor; d. in New York, June 13, 1832.

MORGAN, CHARLES C., d. in New York city, Aug. 1867.

MORGAN, GEN. DANIEL, from 1831, to 1843 (with exception of one year), in the Ky. legislature; d. in Fleming co., Ky., May 19, 1851, a. 68.

MORGAN, EDWIN WRIGHT, d. at Bethlehem, Pa., April 16, 1869; grad. at West Point in 1837; was lieut. col. in the U. S. army in the Mexican war, superintendent of the Kentucky Institute until the beginning of the late war, and at the time his death, prof. of mathematics and mechanics in the Lehigh University.

MORGAN, JOHN J., the father-in-law of John A. Dix, was a leading democratic politician; was several years alderman of N. Y., and a member of the 17th, 18th and 23d congresses; d. at Port Chester, N. Y., July 29, 1849, in his 81st year. (*Stryker's Am. Reg.*, iii, 238.)

MORGAN, THOMAS J., secretary of the American legation at the court of Brazil; d. at Rio Janeiro, April 5, 1850.

MORGAN, WILLIAM A., d. in Lebanon, Conn., March 22, 1842 a. 77; a soldier of the revolution and at the battle of Bunker hill.

MORNAY, LOUIS FRANCOIS DUPLESSIS DE, third R. C. bp of Quebec; b. at Vannes in Brittany; selected as successor of St. Vallier in 1718; was consecrated at Paris coadj. of Quebec, April 22, 1714, and resided at Cambray; he became bp. of Quebec May 31, 1728, but sent M. Dorquet as coadjutor, and d. Nov. 28, 1741, a. 78, without ever having seen Canada. (*Liste Chron. des Evêques et des Prêtres du Canada.*)

MORRILL EZEKIEL, a member of the New Hampshire state council, in 1836; d. at Canterbury, N. H., July 28, 1837, a. 58.

MORRIS ANTHONY, son of Anthony, a prominent Quaker of Philadelphia; member of assembly one year and in 1739 mayor; d. in 1762.

MORRIS, ENSIGN BENJAMIN, Penn., killed at Brandywine, Sept. 11, 1777.

MORRIS, CHARLES F., lieut. 8th U. S. infantry, d. at U. S. hospital in Mexico, Sept. 17, 1847, a. 28, of wounds received in the storming of El Molino del Rey.

MORRIS, CHARLES W., d. Nov. 1, 1846, on board the U. S. frigate Cumberland, from wounds received in the attack on Tabasco, Oct. 26; was a son of Commodore Morris.

MORRIS, FREDERICK VAN BRAAM, U. S. consul; d. at Batavia, May 25, 1849.

MORRIS, HENRY, d. in Philadelphia, Pa., Dec. 1, 1842, a. 65; sheriff of Philadelphia; son of Robert Morris, the celebrated financier of the revolution.

MORRIS, JOHN COX, d. at Butternuts, N. Y., Feb. 2, 1849, a 67; was a prominent citizen of Otsego co., and second son of Gen. Jacob M., one of the earliest settlers of that region.

MORRIS, JOHN M., executive clerk of the U. S. senate; d. at Washington, Nov. 2, 1873, a. 37; native of Conn., and once editor of the *Charleston* (S. C.) *Republican*; and afterwards of the *Washington Chronicle.*

MORRIS, MAJOR JOSEPH, N. J., killed at Princeton, Jan. 3, 1777.

MORRIS, JOSEPH, b. in Green co., Pa., Oct. 16, 1795; was chosen sheriff in 1824, and in 1829 removed to Ohio, and became a merchant; was in the state legislature in 1833–4; co. treas. for Monroe co. one year; elected to congress in 1843, and 1845; d. at Woodfield, Ohio, Oct. 23, 1854.

MORRIS, LEWIS N., capt. in 3d infantry, killed at the battle of Monterey, Mex., Sept. 21, 1846; b. in N. Y.; grad. at West Point in 1820, and served in the Black Hawk and Florida wars. (*Am. Almanac*, 1848, p. 349.)

MORRIS, MATTHIAS, d. in Doylestown, Pa., Nov. 9, 1839, a. 54; was in congress from Pennsylvania in 1835–9.

MORRIS, RICHARD V., commodore in the navy, youngest son of Lewis M., of Morrisania, one of the signers of decl. of indepen. His widow d. at N. Y., April 18, 1858, a. 85. (*Hist. Mag.*, ii, 188.)

MORRIS, CAPT. SAMUEL, b. in Philadelphia, June 24, 1734; son of Anthony; d. July 7, 1812; was much given to sporting, an active partisan of the revolution, and although disowned by the Friends for the share he took in the war, he continued to use their dress and language, and to attend their meetings.

MORRIS, SAMUEL W., d. in Wellsborough, Tioga co., Pa., May 25, 1847, a. 59; served many years as a judge of the court in that district, and was twice elected to congress.

MORRIS, THOMAS, formerly U. S. marshal of the S. dist., N. Y., and a son of Robert Morris, the financier of the revolution; d. at N. Y., March 12, 1849.

MORRIS, REV. THOMAS A., D.D., senior bishop of the M. E. church; d. at Springfield, O., Sept., 1874; b. in Va., in 1794; joined the Ohio conference in 1817, as a traveling preacher and preached in Ohio, Tenn., Ky., until 1833, when he became editor of the *Western Christian Advocate*, and filled the duties of this office 3 y.; in 1836 became bishop.

MORRISON, DANIEL, of the *Toronto Telegraph;* d. at Toronto, Canada, April, 1870.

MORROW, COL. ROBERT, paymaster of one of the div. depts. of the army; committed suicide at San Francisco, Nov. 27, 1873.

MORSE, CYRUS, well known for many years as the driver of the omnibus between Harvard Coll. and Boston; d. Sept. 20, 1846, a. 51; the undergraduates made a characteristic pun to his memory: *Mors Communis est omnibus.*

MORSE, OLIVER ANDREW, son of Judge James O. Morse of Cherry Valley, N. Y., where he was b. March 26, 1815; grad. at Hamilton Coll. with valedictorian honors in 1833; studied law and practiced a few ys., but was more occupied with literary pursuits and with public affairs; in 1857–9 he was a representative in the U. S. congress; d. April 20, 1870.

MORSE, RICHARD C., one of the founders of the *N. Y. Observer*, which he assisted in editing till 1858; d. at Kissingen, Germany, Sept. 22, 1868, a. 74.

MORTON, ALVIN C., civil engineer, d. in N. Y. city, Feb. 25, 1871, a. 61; was engineer of many rail roads, among which was the N. Y. and Erie, Sacramento Valley, Grand Trunk, Great Western, Lower Canada and Nova Scotia rail roads.

MORTON, DANIEL O., was b. in Vermont; grad. at Middlebury Coll.; studied law and settled in Toledo, O., where he became U. S. dist atty. for Ohio; d. at Toledo, Dec. 6, 1859.

MORTON, EDMUND L., commodore of New Jersey Yacht Club; d. Oct. 15, 1873.

MORTON, GEN. JACOB, d. at N. Y. city, Dec. 3, 1836; he was for twenty years before his death clerk of the com. council and performed duty as an officer of the N. Y. Artillery every year since 1789; was assistant marshal under Morgan Lewis, at the grand reception of Gen. Washington, as first president, and held many civil offices with intelligence and acceptance.

MORTON, JAMES, d. in Charles co., Md., July 20, 1842, a. 56.

MORTON, MAJ. JAMES, d. at High Hill, Cumberland co., Va., Jan. 21, 1847, a. 90; was through the revolutionary war, and an officer of great bravery; was a trustee of Hampton Sidney College, and was a ruling elder of the Presb. church 60 years.

MORTON, SAMUEL L., d. in Adams, N. Y., Nov., 1856, a druggist and one of the proprietors of the *Jefferson County News.*

MORTON, CAPT. SILAS, d. at Pembroke, Mass., March 25, 1840, a. 85; served through the revolution.

MOSELY, EDWARD S., ex-state treas. of Conn.; d. at Hampton, Conn., June 22, 1873, a. 60.

MOSELEY, ELIZUR, M.D., a native of Westfield, Mass.; he grad. at Yale Coll. in 1786, and settled in Whitesboro, N. Y., as early as 1794, in which year he was made a justice of the peace; was asst. judge in 1798, and sheriff in 1799–1800; for many years he was post master of Whitesboro; d. in 1833.

MOSELEY, JONATHAN OGDEN, formerly of East Haddam, Conn., d. at Saginaw, Mich., Sept. 9, 1839, a. 77; grad. at Yale in 1780, and was in congress from Conn., from 1805 to 1821.

MOSELEY, WILLIAM ABBOTT, son of Dr. Elizur M., grad. at Yale in 1816, and made his home in Buffalo; was a member of N. Y. assembly in 1835, the state senate from 1838 to 1841, and a representative in congress from 1843 to 1847; d. in N. Y., Nov. 19, 1873.

MOSHER, JAMES, d. in Baltimore, Md., March 27, 1845, in his 85th year; was a soldier in the revolution; formerly president of the Mechanics' Bank; for many years surveyor of the port of Baltimore.

MOTT, JOSEPH O., a lawyer, and in 1830 in assembly; d. at Turin, N. Y., Dec. 26, 1843, a. 50.

MOTT, DR. VALENTINE, a distinguished physician and surgeon of N. Y. city, and a writer and lecturer on subjects within his profession; d. at N. Y., April 26, 1865, a. 79. (*Trans. N. Y. State Med. Soc.* 1866, p. 304.)

MOTTE, MAJOR CHARLES, S. C., killed in the assault on Savannah, Oct. 9, 1779.

MOWER, JOSEPH A., brevet brig. gen. U. S. A., commanding department of Louisiana; d. at New Orleans, La., Jan. 7, 1870; entered the army as a private of a company of engineers in the Mexican war, and was commissioned 2d lieut. in 1855, and 1st lieut. in 1857; commanded a company in the beginning of the rebellion; became col. of the 1st Mo. vols. in 1862; was wounded at Corinth; served at Vicksburg, Red river, Mo. and with Sherman, and at the end of the war commanded the 20th corps.

MOURY, Sylvester, an ex-officer of the U. S. army; d. in London, Oct. 17, 1811.

MOXLEY, Nehemiah, d. at Elkridge, Md., March, 1836, a. 99; he assisted in throwing tea overboard at Annapolis, at the beginning of the revolution.

MUDGE, Capt. Samuel, d. in Lynn, Mass., Feb. 16, 1849; was captain of drafted militia in 1812, and frequently a member of the state legislature.

MUHLENBERG, Henry A., b. in Reading, Pa, representative in congress from the 8th dist. of Pa., from 1853 to 1854; d. at Washington, D. C., Jan. 9, 1854.

MUIR, Robert, merchant and manufacturer of Auburn, N. Y., b. in Kilwinning, Scotland, March 25, 1790; d. in Auburn, Feb. 17, 1868. (*Hall's Auburn*, p. 555.)

MUIRHEAD, Col. John, d. April 11, 1860, at Lebanon, Tenn.; was many years a member of the state senate.

MULLANPHY, Bryan, was liberally educated; was judge of the circuit court and director of the Bank of Mo., and mayor of St. Louis; d. at St. Louis, June 15, 1851, a. 44. (*Stryker's Am. Reg.*, vi, 234; *Am. Almanac*, 1852, p. 341.)

MULLETT, James, one of the justices of the supreme court, for the 8th judicial dist. of N. Y.; d. in Fredonia, N. Y., Sept. 10, 1858.

MULLIKEN, George S., formerly judge of the municipal court in Augusta, Me.; d. in San Antonio, Texas, April 20, 1860.

MUMFORD, Major Augustus, killed in the revolution at Plowed hill, Aug. 27, 1775.

MUMFORD, George, b. in Rowan co., N. C.; was in the state legislature in 1810 and 1811; in congress from 1817 to 1819; d. Dec. 31, 1818.

MUNCY, Silas, d. near Babylon, N. Y., 1860, a. 85; his wife Sarah d. at the same time and place, a. 82; they had lived together 63 years.

MUNGOUR, Orren, d. in Northampton, Mass., Aug. 9, 1842; a member of the legislature at the time of his death.

MUNGER, Nelson H., b. in Colchester, Ct., in 1811; removed when young to S. C.; grad. at Chapel Hill, N. C.; studied law in S. C. and began practice in Mississippi; in 1840 he removed to Texas, where he practiced successfully till 1854, when he was elected judge of the first judicial dist. in which office he d. at San Felipe, Texas, Jan. 3, 1856.

MUNRO, Rev. Harry, b. in 1729, son of Dr. Robt. M., of Dingwall, Scot.; grad. at the University of St. Andrews; studied divinity at Edinburgh, and in 1757, was appointed chaplain to the 77th regt. foot; came to America in 1759 and served through the French war; resided at Princeton, N. J. some time; became Episcopal in 1764; was first pastor at Yonkers, N. Y., two years; and in 1767 was appointed minister of St. Peter's ch., Albany, where he settled Mar. 26, 1768; in 1775 he removed to Hebron, N. Y., where he owned land, obtained a pass to Canada in 1777, became rector of a ch. in Edinburgh and d. in 1801, a. 71. (*Doc. Hist. N. Y.*, iv, 410.)

MUNRO, PETER JAY, son of Rev. Henry M.; was a lawyer, and a member of the constitutional con. of 1821, from West Chester co., N. Y.; d. Sept. 22, 1833, a. 66.

MUNROE, COL. ISAAC, b. in Boston; was bred a printer and started the *Boston Patriot;* settled at Baltimore, Md., in 1812, and in Jan., 1813, founded the *Baltimore Patriot*, which he conducted many years; he was at the bombardment of Fort McHenry in 1814, and was aid to Gov. Veazey; d. in Baltimore, Md., Dec. 22, 1859, a. about 75.

MUNROE, JOHN ALEXANDER, of Bradford, a member of the junior class at Harvard University, d. in Cambridge, Jan. 2, 1846, a. 24.

MUNROE, THOMAS, d. in Washington, D. C., April 14, 1852, a. 80; one of the earliest commissioners of that city during the administration of President Washington; and after the removal of the seat of government in 1800, was appointed post master, and held till 1829.

MUNSON, ALFRED, b. at Barhamstead, Litchfield co., Conn., May 21, 1793; a miller and mill-wright by trade; he commenced the manufacture of burr mill stone, at Utica, N. Y., in 1823; fifteen years later he was occupied with the management of manufacturing corporations; was interested in packet-boat lines on the Erie canal, in steam-boat lines on Lake Ontario, in coal mines in Pennsylvania, and in other enterprises, and acquired a large fortune; was first president of the Oneida Bank, and one of the first board of managers of the N. Y. State Lunatic Asylum; d. May 6, 1854.

MUNSON, ELISHA, d. at New Haven, Conn., Aug. 27, 1842, a. 86 y. 5 mo; grad. at Yale in 1784, and in early life was engaged in mercantile pursuits; succeeded S. Bishop as clerk Dec. 15, 1801, and resigned in the summer of 1832.

MURDOCK, REV. JAMES, b. in Saybrook, Ct.; grad. at Yale, in 1774; removed to Lewis co., N. Y., in 1805, and was long a Presbyterian minister in Martinsburg, and in Gouverneur; d. Jan. 14, 1841, at Crown Point, N. Y., a. 86.

MURFREE, WILLIAM H., b. in Hertford co., N. C.; grad. at Chapel Hill in 1801; became a successful lawyer, and served in the state legislature in 1805, and in congress from 1813 to 1817; removed to Tennessee in 1825, and d. soon after at Nashville.

MURPHY, JAMES MCLEOD, an eminent English engineer, in the service of the U. S.; d. in New York city, June 1, 1844.

MURPHY, JAMES MCLEOD, d. in N. Y. city, June 1, 1871, a. 44; served in the U. S. navy as midshipman; was N. Y. state senator in 1860–1; and col. of the 15th N. Y. vols. (engineers) early in the late war; he entered the navy, and commanded the iron clad Carondelet, in 1863–4.

MURPHY, THOMAS, native of Ireland, and hardy pioneer of Schoharie co., N. Y., where he was noted for his bravery in the revolution; d. at Middlebury, N. Y., June 27, 1818. (*Hough's Northern Invasion of* 1780, p. 52.)

MURRAY, DAVID, d. in Elkridge, Md., April 19, 1842, a. 64.

MURRAY, HUGH C., settled in California in 1850, and was for a time a member of the city government of San Francisco; then presiding judge of the supreme court of that city, and then elected justice of the supreme court of California; of which for some time he was chief justice; d. at San Francisco, Sept. 18, 1857.

MURRAY, JAMES, d. in Alexandria, La., July 4, 1854; was mayor of the town; was killed in trying to suppress a disturbance at a barbecue.

MURRAY, NOAH, son of a lieut. of the revolution; b. Jan. 24, 1783; became a magistrate at Athens, Pa.; went west in 1831, and d. in Kosciusko co., Ind., Sept. 4, 1859. (*Hist. Mag.*, iii, 353.)

MURRAY, ROBERT J., son of John M.; a philanthropist, and nephew of Lindley M., the grammarian; was a manager in several benevolent institutions of N. Y. city, and d. there Jan. 28, 1858, a. 92.

MURRAY, THOMAS W., b. in Lincoln co., Ga.; was many years in the legislature, and once a speaker of the house.

MUSE, WILLIAM H., d. in Jackson, Miss., Jan. 9, 1855, a. 40; secy. of state of Miss.

MUSGROVE, MARY, alias CONSOPONAKEESO, an Indian woman; b. at Coweta, on the Ocmulgee; brought up by the English; m. Jno. Musgrove jr., son of Col. M., and in 1723 returned to S. C.; in 1732 he established a trading house on the site of Savannah, where Oglethorpe found her in 1733; he purchased her influence and her husband having died she married Capt. Jacob Mattheus, and after his death in 1742, Rev. Thos. Bosomworth; protracted difficulties arose from claims which these persons set up, founded upon Indian grants. (*White's Hist. Ga.*, p. 21.)

MUSGROVE, THOMAS, an Englishman over 70; killed on the Morris and Essex rail road at Rossville, N. J., April 19, 1873; was the father of the bankers composing the firm of Musgrave & Co., in Broad st., N. Y., and was one of the prominent men of Northampton, Mass.

MUSSEY, JOHN FITZ HENRY, a grad. of Harvard in 1835; d. at Portland, Me., April 14, 1846, a. 30.

MUTTER, THOMAS DENT, M.D., b. in Richmond, Va., March 9, 1811, and d. in Philadelphia, Mar. 16, 1859; was professor in the Jefferson Medical College, and for sixteen years with Dr. Pancost, conducted the most successful clinical course of instruction that had been known in the U. S.; he was especially successful in treating club feet, crooked limbs, tumors, strabismus, rhinoplastic operations, etc.; his collections were very extensive and valuable and belong to the coll. of physicians of Philadelphia. (*Simpson's Eminent Philadelphians.*)

MYERS, MICHAEL, b. at Auville, N. J., Feb. 1, 1753; served in the revolution and was wounded in the battle of Johnstown in 1781; upon the formation of Herkimer co., he was appointed a judge and justice, and held till 1805; was in assembly in 1790–1–2–3, and in the state senate from 1794 to 1801; he was many years an active politician and concerned in extensive purchases of land from the state; d. at Herkimer, Feb. 17, 1814, a. 61. His son Peter was some years a co. clerk. (*Benton's Herkimer Co., N. Y.*, p. 349.)

MYERS, SAMUEL, d. at Richmond, Va., Aug. 22, 1836, a. 82.

MYRICK, SAMUEL, d. at Woodstock, Vt., Dec., 1839, a. 82; was a lieutenant in the revolution.

NAGLE, WILLIAM T., d. in N. Y., Aug. 16, 1869; b. in that city in 1836, reared a merchant; raised a co. for the 88th N. Y. vols., was in several battles and after the war became deeply interested in the Fenian cause; went to England, as was thought for the purpose of exciting a revolution, and was arrested and held several months.

NANCREDE, DR. JOSEPH G., b. in Boston, June 1793; and d. in Philadelphia in the summer of 1856. (*Simpson's Eminent Phil.*)

NAPEHSHNEEDOOTA, first male Dakota convert to Christianity; d. July 1870, near Lac-qui-Parle, Minn. (*Memoir by Rev. T. S. Williamson; Coll. Minn. Hist. Soc.* iii, 188.)

NAPIER, wife of HON. CAPT. CHARLES, of 80th grenadiers; d. Jan. 1780, at Flushing, a. 23. (*Rivington's Gazette*, Jan. 15.)

NASH, JOHN W., several years in the Virginia legislature, for the last ten years of his life one of the circuit judges of the state; d. in Powhatan, Va., July 17, 1859.

NATHAN, BENJAMIN, stock broker, murdered in his house in N. Y. city, July 29, 1870, a. 54.

NAUDIN, ARNOLD, ex-senator of Del.; d. at Wilmington, Del., Jan. 4, 1872, a. 72.

NECKERE, REV. LEO DE, the 4th Roman Catholic bishop of N. O.; d. at N. O., September 4, 1833.

NEIL, CAPT. DANIEL, N. J., killed at Princeton, Jan. 3, 1777.

NEILSON, JOHN, a native of Ireland; many years a citizen of N. Y., and prominent in the Presb. ch.; he commanded a merchant ship in the European trade, which was blown up on the coast of France in 1762; he left a legacy to his favorite church. (*Miller's Life of J. Rogers*, p. 121.)

NELLIS, GEORGE, d. at Fort Plain, N. Y., May, 1855, a. 89; was in the revolutionary war, and war of 1812, serving as colonel of militia in the latter; was in assembly in 1811–12, and several years a county judge. (*Albany Argus.*)

NELSON, JOHN W., son of Judge N., of the federal supreme court; d. in N. Y. city, Oct. 3, 1857, a. 37.

NELSON, THOMAS A. R., d. at Knoxville, Tenn., Aug., 1873; a lawyer; in 1848 presidential elector, and in 1851 appointed a commissioner to China; was in the 36th congress, and elected to the 37th, but did not take his seat on account of the rebel government; in 1866 was in the Philadelphia national convention, and in 1868 one of President Johnson's counsel on the impeachment trial.

NELSON, MAJ. THOMAS M., d. near Columbus, Ga., Nov. 10, 1853, a. 71; grandson of Sec. N., of Va., and son of Maj. John N., of the revolution; entered the army in 1812, and was retained on the peace establishment; resigned in 1815, and served in congress from 1816 to 1819, from the Mecklenburg dist. in Va., when he declined re-election, and retired to private life.

NEPVEN, JAN, gov. of Surinam from Oct. 27, 1769, till his death Feb. 27, 1774.

NERINCKX, Rev. Charles, western R. C. missionary; b. Oct. 2, 1761 at Herffelinger, in Haynault; educated at the University of Lourain, and studied theology at the Seminary of Malines, where in 1785 he became pastor and 8 years after was sent to Evenberg, Meerbeke, Brussels; the revolution drove him into the hospital of Terremond; he escaped to the U. S. in 1804, and the next year was sent missionary to Ky.; was once offered the diocese of New Orleans, but preferred to continue his missionary labors; d. at St. Genevieve, Mo., Aug. 12, 1824. (*Metropolitan Cath. Almanac*, 1854, p. 43.)

NES, Henry, member of congress from Pa. from 1843 to 1845, and from 1846 to 1850; d. at York, Pa., Sept. 10, 1850; was born in Pa. in 1799; bred a physician, and held various town offices.

NESBITT, John Maxwell, an eminent Phil. merchant, emigrated from Ireland before the revolution; in 1777 he joined the first troop of Phil. cavalry; was patriotic and liberal in support of the war, and aided by raising money and necessaries for the army; was one of the founders of the Hibernian Society of Philadelphia.

NEUMAN, Rt. Rev. John, R. C. bishop of Philadelphia, ; d. in that city, June 6, 1860; b. in Bohemia, March 28, 1811; came to America in 1834. (*Vincent's Semi-An. Register*, pp. 19, 25, 26.)

NEVILL, Yelvaten, a revolutionary soldier; b. in Rutherford co., N. C., Dec. 25, 1763; d. in Jackson co., Tenn., April, 1860. (*Vincent's Semi-An. Register*, p. 351.)

NEVIUS, Rev. William, d.d., d. at Balt., Md., Sept. 14, 1836, a. 38.

NEWBOLD, George, president of the Bank of America, in New York; d. at Philadelphia, Pa., Sept. 8, 1858, a. 76.

NEWBURY, Walter L., of Chicago; d. at sea, Nov. 6, 1868; settled in Chicago in 1833, and was the first president of the Chicago Union rail road co.

NEWCOMB, Chr., bishop of the German Meth. soc.; d. at Hagerstown, Md., March 10, 1830, a. 58.

NEWCOMB, Kinner, d. at Plattsburg, N. Y., Feb. 6, 1840, in his 84th y.; many years judge of the county court; he entered the rev. army at the age of 17, and served through the war.

NEWELL, Francis, d. at Wilton, Conn., March 3, 1841, in his 101st y.; b. in France, July 11, 1840.

NEWKIRK, Matthew, d. at Philadelphia, May 31, 1868; b. in Pittsgrove, Salem co., N. J., in 1810; entered the mercantile profession in 1810; was first president of the Philadelphia, Wilmington and Baltimore R. R. Co., and a prominent citizen.

NEWMAN, Alexander, member elect from the 15th dist. of Va., to 31st congress; d. at Pittsburg, Pa., of cholera, Sept. 8, 1849.

NEWMAN, Daniel, served as a soldier in the early Indian wars of Georgia, and held various honorable offices in that state; was in congress from 1831 to 1833, and d. in Walker co., Ga.

NEWMAN, George H., d. March 20, 1847, near Baltimore, Md., 1851; was consul for Brazil, and a merchant of Baltimore.

NEWTON, Isaac, steam boat proprietor, b. at Schodack, N. Y., Jan. 10, 1794; witnessed Fulton's first steam trip on the Hudson, and his attention thus directed determined his course. Over ninety vessels, ocean and river steamers, barges, sloops, &c., were built under his direction; about 1815, he established the first line of tow boats on the Hudson; about 1825, he built the steamer Balloon, soon after the North America and South America, and in 1836, the People's Line from N. Y. to Albany was established, of which in 1840 he became supt.; the Hendrick Hudson, New World and Isaac Newton of this line, are widely known to the traveling public; he d. Nov. 22, 1858, at N. Y., having been some thirty years an active member of the Oliver st. Baptist church and most of the time a Sunday school teacher. (*Hist. Mag.*, iii, 27.)

NEWTON, John, b. at Colchester, Ct., April 8, 1758; went to Wyoming, Pa., just previous to the massacre, which he witnessed and narrowly escaped, and settled in Middlefield, Ct., where he afterwards resided. (*Hunt's Biog. Panorama*, p. 279.)

NEWTON, Thomas, b. in 1769; was in congress from Virginia from 1801 to 1829, and from 1831 to 1833; d. at Norfolk, Va., Aug. 5, 1847.

NICHOL, Josiah, president of the Branch Bank of the U. S.; d. at Nashville, Tenn., of cholera, May 31, 1833, a. 62.

NICHOLAS, Philip N., d. at Richmond, Va., Aug., 1849; formerly attorney general of Virginia, and at his death judge of the superior court of the city of Richmond.

NICHOLAS, Samuel Smith, of Louisville, Ky.; d. Nov. 27, 1869; b. in Lexington, Ky., April, 1797, and son of Col. Geo. N., of the revolution; was admitted to the bar in 1824, and was appointed judge of the court of appeals for Kentucky, and afterwards chancellor of the equity court for Louisville district; was commissioner for revising the case of Kentucky.

NICHOLLS, Thomas C., d. in Donaldsonville, La., July 12, 1847, a. 57; native of Maryland, and long a judge of the 4th district court of Louisiana, and lately one of the judges of the court of appeals.

NICHOLS, John Augustus, ll.d., b. in Monmouth co., N. J., Sept. 14, 1822; was employed in a stereotype foundery; was taken into the family of Prof. Charles Davies, and pursued mathematics with success; became for a time teacher, and in 1851, tutor in the free academy in N. Y. city; in 1852, was appointed prof. in a new college at Cleveland, but soon returned, and became prof. of nat. phil. in free acad.; he remained in this institution, with some change of duties, till his death, Nov. 25, 1868. (*Regents' Report*, 1870, p. 582.)

NICHOLSON, Jacob C., d. in Baltimore, Dec. 21, 1868, in his 64th year.

NICHOLSON, John, comptroller of Penn. from 1772 to 1794; was an owner of vast landed estates, and at one time owned about 3,700,000 acres in Penn. besides vast possessions, real and personal; his affairs became embarrassed, he was imprisoned, d. in confinement, and insane, in 1800. (*Simpson's Eminent Philadelphians.*)

NICHOLSON, Samuel, inventor of the Nicholson Pavement, of wooden blocks, and an improved apparatus for steering vessels, etc.; d. in Boston, Jan. 16, 1868, a. 76; was a native of Plymouth, Mass.

NICOLL, Charles, N. Y., d. Dec. 12, 1780, a. 89; merchant, loyalist.

NICOLL, WILLIAM, d. March 1, 1780, at Islip, L. I., a. 65; formerly mem. of the general assembly, of N. Y.

NIEMCEWIEZ, URSIN, a celebrated Pole, formerly aid-de-camp of Kosciusko, those imprisonment at St. Petersburg he shared; he emigrated to N. J., and settled at Elizabethtown, where he married, settled, and resided some years as a cultivator; he returned to Europe in 1807, and d. at Paris, France, May, 1840, a. 84.

NIMS, CAPT. ELIAKIM, a revolutionary pensioner; d. in Sullivan, N. H., March, 1846, a. 94 y., 6 mos.

NISBIT, EUGENIUS A., son of Dr. James N., who emigrated from N. C. to Ga., in 1791, and settled in Greene co.; b. Dec. 7, 1803, grad. at Franklin Coll. in 1821; studied law at Litchfield, Ct., and settled in Madison, Morgan co.; he was seven ys. in the legislature, took an interest in various public charities and literary subjects; from 1839 to 1842, he was in congress; in 1845, he was elected a judge of the supreme court of Ga., and in 1847, was reëlected; d. at Macon, March 19, 1871. (*White's Hist. Ga.*, p. 273, with portrait.)

NIXON, COL. JOHN, first prest. of the old Bank of North America; son of Richard N., native of Wexford, Ireland; he was born in Westchester, Pa.; became a merchant in Phila., was one of the founders of the soc. of the Friendly Sons of St. Patrick, in 1771, and was an ardent patriot; he was one of the committee of safety in Pa., often presided as chairman, and served on the committee of accounts; as lt. col. he commanded the city guard of Phila, from July 19, 1776, and was one of the navy board at Phila.; he commanded the 3d Pa. battalion in the defense of the Del., in 1776–7, and while at Valley Forge, his house was burned by the enemy; he was one of the directors of the old Bank of Pa., July 17, 1780, and was pres. of the Bank of N. A., at the time of his death about Jan. 1, 1809. (*Hist. Mag.*, iv, 371; v, 25.)

NOBILI, REV. JOHN, S. J., b. in Rome; entered the Soc. Jes. in 1828; taught in Italy, Oregon and New Caledonia, and labored as a priest in California; in 1851 he took charge of Santa Clara mission, and founded a college; d. there March 1, 1856. (*Metropolitan Cath. Almanac*, 1857, p. 298.)

NOBLE, JAMES, senator in congress from Ind. from 1816 to 1831; d. Feb. 26, 1831, a. 48; b. in Clark co., Va.; removed in his youth to Ky., and thence to Ind.

NOEL, JOHN Y., an eminent lawyer; d. in Savannah, Ga.

NONEZ, H. B., capt. of U. S. revenue cutter service; d. at Wilmington, Aug. 25, 1868, in his 65th year; entered the merchant service at the age of 18, and in 1830 joined the revenue service; in the rebellion was on blockade duty in Chesapeake bay, and other places.

NORCROSS, NICHOLAS G., a native of Orono, Me., and largely concerned in lumbering business in that state, and afterwards on the Merrimack, in Mass.; aided to develop the resources of the Canadian forests, and was the inventor of a planing machine; d. at Lowell, Mass., July 14, 1860, a. 54.

NORFLEET, COL. R. J., member of the Miss. legislature; d. at Holly Springs, Miss., April, 1859.

NORRIS, JOSEPH PARKER, b. in Phil., May 5, 1763; d. Jan. 1766; was a prominent citizen of Phil., and he formed a fine library, which became the property of Dickenson Coll. at Carlisle. (*Simpson's Eminent Philadelphians.*)

NORRIS, MOSES, b. in Pittsfield, N. H., in 1799; grad. at Dartmouth, in 1828; became a lawyer, and in 1839 was elected to the house, and in 1840 became speaker; in 1841 was elected one of the council, and in 1844 and 1846 was elected to congress; in 1847 again speaker in the house, and elected to the U. S. senate, where he remained from 1849 to 1855; d. at Washington, D. C. Jan. 11, 1855.

NORRIS, ROBERT, d. in Phil. June 3, 1874; was over twenty years engaged as a locomotive manufacturer; although he sustained heavy reverses, he left a very large estate.

NORRIS, N. H., ex-member of congress from Alabama; d. at Montgomery, Ala., Jan. 27, 1873.

NORRIS, REV. THOMAS W., d. in Somerville, Mass., Dec. 21, 1853; for many years editor of the *Olive Branch.*

NORTH, DR. ERASMUS DARWIN, d. in Westfield, Mass., June 17, 1858, a. 51; he was b. in Goshen, Ct., grad. at the University of North Carolina in 1826; studied medicine and practiced a few years; was instructor of elocution in Yale Coll. from 1830 to 1854, and the author of *The Practical Speaker;* at the close of his life he was engaged in preparing a biographical sketch of his friend James G. Percival, and an edition of his poems.

NORTH, THEODORE, d. at Elmira, N. Y., April 21, 1842, a. 62; grad. at Williams Coll.; began the practice of law, and was several years in the Connecticut legislature.

NORTHROP, LIEUT. ISAAC, d. at Woodbridge, Conn., Jan. 19, 1841, a. 81; was a revolutionary pensioner, and one of the last nine surviving officers of the Connecticut line.

NORTON, A. H., lieut. in 4th infantry; lost on the steamer Atlantic, Nov. 4, 1846; grad. at West Point in 1842, and was several years stationed at West Point, as an assistant instructor of tactics.

NORTON, ALMON N., prominent merchant in Denmark, N. Y., for many years; d. at Lockport, Ill., Nov. 23, 1859, a. 73.

NORTON, DANIEL S., U. S. senator from Minnesota; d. at Washington, D. C., July 15, 1870, a. 41; b. in Mount Vernon, O., April 12, 1829; educated at Kenyon College; served as a volunteer in the Mexican war, and visited California and Nicaraugua; returned to Ohio, where he studied and practiced law; went to Minnesota; was in the state senate in 1857-8-60-1-2-3-4; was elected to the senate of the United States in 1865.

NORTON, REV. JACOB, was b. in Abington, Mass., Feb. 12, 1764; grad. at Harvard in 1786, and d. in Billerica, Mass., Jan. 17, 1858, being at the time the oldest graduate living; he was a Congregational preacher, and much esteemed. (*Am. Almanac*, 1859, p. 356.)

NORTON, JOHN PITKIN, b. July 19, 1822, in Farmington, Ct.; 1842 began chemical studies in New Haven, and two years after went to Scotland, where he studied agricultural chemistry under Prof. Jas. F. W. Johnston, at Edinburgh; his analysis of the oat here won the prize of 50 guineas from the Highland Society; in the fall of 1847 he joined Prof. B. Silliman in the analytical laboratory of Yale Coll., and in 1848 began his first course of lectures; in 1851-2 he entered zealously into the plan of a university at Albany, and while traveling from New Haven to Albany twice each week giving lectures at both places, he contracted a disease of which he died Sept. 5, 1852, at his father's residence, at the age of 30 years; he fell a sacrifice to an honorable ambition to promote an interest in a science in which he had evinced a brilliant capacity for original research. (*Am. Jour. Sci. & Arts*, 2d ser., xiv, 448; *Memorial* 1853.)

NORTON, MERRET M., formerly a merchant of Lowville, N. Y.; d. at Brattleboro, Vt., Oct. 17, 1846.

NORTON, MILFORD PHILLIPS, judge of the fourteenth dist. court of Texas; formerly a lawyer in Bangor, Me., and a member of the Maine senate, and land agent; lived twenty years in Texas, and d. at Corpus Christi, Texas, June, 1860.

NORTON, DR. WILLIAM S., of Fort Edward, N. Y.; d. Feb. 20, 1863, a. 67. (*Transac. N. Y. State Med. Soc.*, 1863, p. 392.)

NORVELL, JOHN, a printer and editor in early life; was post master at Detroit; in congress from Mich. from 1835 to 1841; was several years atty. for the state of Mich., and in 1837 was appointed regent of the university; d. of apoplexy in April, 1850.

NOXON, B. DAVIS, a distinguished lawyer of Syracuse, N. Y.; killed by being run over by the R. R. cars, May 13, 1869; was engaged nearly half a century in his profession. (*In Memoriam, B. D. N.* Syracuse, 1869.)

NOYES, GEORGE F., d. in N. Y., Jan. 9, 1868; b. in Maine; grad. at Bowdoin; practiced law in Boston and San Francisco; was on Gen. Wadsworth's staff in the late war, and at the time of his death was practicing in the city of N. Y.

NOYES, JOHN, grad. at Dartmouth in 1795, and afterwards tutor; in congress from Vermont, from 1815 to 1817; d. in 1841, a. 78.

NUCELLA, REV. JOHANNES PETRUS, early Dutch minister at Albany, began in 1699, and continued three or four years; he left or d. in 1702. (*Rogers's Hist. Discourse*, p. 18.)

NUNAN, JOHN, of the Bowery Theatre, N. Y.; d. Feb. 24, 1870, a. 38.

NURSE, BENJAMIN, d. at Keene, N. H., April 26, 1841, a. 97; on the 28th his wife, a. 91; having lived together 69 years.

OAKES, WILLIAM, was b. at Danvers, Mass., July 1, 1799; grad. at Harvard in 1820; studied law with the Hon. L. Saltonstall at Salem, and settled at Ipswich where he afterwards resided; while a student, he acquired a strong fondness for botanical studies, to which in a few years he entirely devoted himself, especially in the region of the White mountains; he was preparing an illustrated volume for the press, when he was drowned on a ferry boat at Boston, July 31, 1848. (*Am. Jour. Sci. and Arts*, 2d ser., vii, 138.)

O'BANNEN, DR. J. D., d. at Prattsville, Ala., May 31, 1860; was in the Mexican war. (*Vincent's Semi-An. Register*, p. 465.)

O'BRIEN, JOHN, secretary of the Catholic Total Abstinence Society of America; d. at St. John, N. B., Aug. 27, 1873.

ODEN, BENJAMIN, d. at Bellefield, Prince George co., Md., Sept. 7, 1836, a. 74.

O'DONNEL, DANIEL KANE, poet, author and journalist, d. at Phil., Sept. 8, 1871, a. 30.

O'DONELL, JACQUES LOUIS, first vicar apostolic of Newfoundland, consecrated Sept. 21, 1796 at Quebec; transferred to the bishoprick of Derry in Ireland about 1818. (*Hist. Chron. des Evêques et des Prêtres du Canada.*)

O'DONOHOE, PATRICK, d. in Brooklyn, N. Y., Jan. 22, 1854; one of the Irish exiles who had recently escaped to America from Van Dieman's Land.

O'FLANAGAN, REV. PETER B., S. J., from Ireland; became priest at Georgetown, D. C., where he was some time employed; he d. at Loyola Coll., Balt., Feb. 19, 1856, a. 49. (*Metropolitan Cath. Almanac*, 1857, p. 297.)

OGDEN, ABRAHAM, U. S. dist. atty. for N. J.; of Morristown, N. J., where his house was used by Washington as winter quarters, while the army lay there; he held the post of U. S. dist. atty., from Jan. 4, 1791, till his death in 1798.

OGDEN, DR. BENJ., d. at College Point, L. I., June 18, 1867, a. 70.

OGDEN, DAVID A., land proprietor, judge, &c.; son of Abraham O.; bought lands in St. Lawrence co., N. Y.; having practiced law some years in N. Y., removed in 1812 to an island in the St. Lawrence in Madrid; he engaged in extensive improvements, served in the 15th congress, was 8 years first judge of St. Lawrence co., and d. at Montreal, June 9, 1829. (*Hough's Hist. St. Law. and Fr. Cos. N. Y.*, p. 599.)

OGDEN, JAMES DE PEYSTER, merchant, at New York; d. April 7, 1870, a. 87.

OGDEN, OLIVER W., d. at New Germantown, N. J., Nov. 14, 1839, a. 61; formerly U. S. marshal for the dist. of N. J.

OGDEN, THOMAS L., d. in N. Y. city, Dec. 17, 1844, a. 71; was a highly esteemed member of the bar, and in early life a partner of Alexander Hamilton.

OGDEN, UZAL, d. at Newark, N. J., July 25, 1780, a. 68. (*Rivington's Gazette.*)

OGILBY, REV. JOHN, rector of St. Mark's ch., N. Y., and nine years prof. of ecclesiastical hist. in the P. E. Sem. of N. Y.; d. at Paris, Feb. 2, 1851.

OGLE, ANDREW J., d. in Somerset, Pa., Oct. 14, 1852; representative in congress.

OGLE, CHARLES, member of congress from Pa. from 1837 to 1841; d. at Somerset, May 10, 1841; author of a speech famous for misrepresentation of the extravagance of the government, which was used for electioneering purposes.

OLDS, JOSEPH, d. in Circleville, Pickaway co., Ohio, April 27, 1847, a. 52; was many years a member of the Ohio legislature, and as early as 1825 began to urge a system of internal improvements.

OLIPHANT, George Talbot, d. April 24, 1873, in New York city; b. in that city June 29, 1819; resided some ten years in Mount Morris, N. Y., and in 1849 sailed for China; in 1850, became engaged at New York in an extensive China trade; he was prominently connected with the Del. & Hud. Canal Co.; was one of the governors of the New York Hospital, and a director in the Erie railway.

OLIVER, Dr. A. F., of Penn Yan, N. Y., d. 1857, a. 65.

OLIVER, Francis Johonnot, son of Ebenezer O., b. Oct. 10, 1777; grad. at Harvard in 1795; began as a merchant in Boston in 1805; in 1818 was elected 1st pres. of the Am. Insurance Co., and held till 1835, when he resigned and was elected pres. of the City Bank; in 1840 he removed to Middletown, Ct., and d. Aug. 21, 1858; he was in the Mass. legislature in 1822–6; a member of the Boston com. council in 1823, 4, 5, 8, and its pres. in 1824–5. (*Hist. Mag.*, ii, 314.)

OLIVER, John M., ex-major gen. U. S. A.; d. March 30, 1872.

OLMSTED, David, a pioneer settler of Minnesota, b. in Fairfax, Vt., May 5, 1822; went west at the age of 20, and in 1839 settled at Prairie-du-Chien; was concerned in various public affairs, and d. Feb. 2, 1861. (*Collec. Minn. Hist. Soc.*, iii, p. 231.)

OLMSTED, David, d. in Albany, N. Y., May 31, 1842, a. 72; b. in Ridgefield, Conn.; many years city superintendent at Albany.

OLMSTEAD, Denison Jr., a son of Prof. D. Olmstead of Yale Coll.; evinced an early profficiency in mineralogy and chemistry; in 1845, was appointed chemist on the geological survey of Vermont; he was a few months after appointed to the same office in Canada, but died soon after of consumption at New Haven, August 15, 1846, a. 22 years. (*2d Am. Rep. Geol. Vt.*, 252; *Vt. Chronicle, Sept.* 2, 1846; *Am. Jour. Sci. & Arts*, 2d ser., ii, 297.)

OLNEY, Jesse, geographer, and author of school books; d. at Stratford, Conn., July 30, 1872, a. 74; was late comptroller of Connecticut.

OLNEY, John, judge, d. at Catskill, N. Y., Dec. 30, 1869.

O'LOUGHLIN, Rev. James, R. C. priest of Boston diocese, d. Jan. 1856, after two years labor at Quincey and E. Boston. (*Metropolitan Cath. Alm.*, 1857, p. 294.)

ONDAYAKA, an aged Onondaga Indian chief, d. near Oneida Castle, N. Y., Sept. 20, 1839, a. 96.

ONDERDONK, Dr. John, d. in New York city, 1832.

OPECHANCANOUGH, brother of Powhatan; became chief of a powerful tribe of Indians in Va., and was many years the scourge of the early colonists, and the fierce and implacable enemy of the whites. He was at length captured in April 1644, taken to Jamestown, kindly treated by the governor; but in a few days shot in the back by one of his guards for some private revenge and d. of the wound; he was nearly a hundred years old, and very infirm. His successor was Necotowance.

ORD Thomas, became a capt. in the British service, March 1, 1746, and commanded the artillery in Braddock's expedition; in 1759 he was major, and in Nov. became lt. col.; he was with Amherst in 1759, and 1760, and in 1762, attended the expedition to Martinico; he became col. comd't of 4th battalion of royal artillery in 1771 and d. in 1777. (*Com. Wilson's Orderly Book*, p. 41.)

O'REILLY, DON ALEXANDER, first Spanish governor of Louisiana; was b. in Ireland about 1735; entered the Spanish navy at an early age, and served with distinction in Italy where was maimed for life; in 1755 he was permitted to enter the Austrian service, and made two campaigns against the Prussians; in 1751 he volunteered in the French army, where his services secured him the recommendation of the Duke de Broghlie to the king of Spain, by whom he was promoted to lieut. col., brig. gen., and in 1862, to major general, in which capacity he was sent to Havana to rebuild the fortifications that the English had destroyed; on the 24th of July, 1769, he arrived with a strong fleet at the mouth of the Mississippi to take possession of the colony, which was done Aug. 18; his despotic treatment of the leaders in the late revolts, rendered him odious to the French inhabitants, and the regulations he adopted were considered severe and oppressive; he was superseded a year after by Don Antonio Bucarelly; in 1774 he commanded an unsuccessful expedition against Algiers, and afterwards served as governor of Cadiz; he fell into disfavor on the death of Charles III, but afterwards was appointed to the command of the army of the Pyrennes, on his way to join which, he d. at an advanced age. (*B. F. French's Hist. Memoirs of La.*, p. 193.)

O'REILLY, RT. REV. BERNARD, D.D., 2d bp. of Hartford, R. I.; b. in Longford co., Ireland, 1803; came to America in 1825, entered the eccl. sem., Montreal, was made priest in 1831; served in N. Y. city in the cholera season of 1832; labored in Rochester and Buffalo, and in 1850 became bp. of Hartford; he sailed for Europe in Jan., 1856, and perished in the Arctic on his return Jan. 23, 1856. (*Metropolitan Cath. Almanac*, 1857, p. 294.)

O'RIELLY, REV. WILLIAM, pastor of St. Mary's ch., in Newport, and vicar gen. of the R. C. diocese of Hartford; d. at Hartford, Conn., Dec. 20, 1868.

ORMSBEE, CHARLES WILBUR, b. in Paris, N. Y., Aug. 24, 1831; studied law and removed to St. Joseph, Mich., in 1861; d. at Salt Lake city Nov. 12, 1872.

ORR, ALEXANDER D., in congress from Ky., from 1792 to 1797; d. at Paris, Ky., June 21, 1835, a. 70.

ORR, REV. JOHN, d. in Melrose, Mass., Jan. 25, 1869, a. 55; was a son of Hon. Benjamin Orr, of Brunswick, Me., and for more than 20 years pastor of the congregational church at Alfred, Me.

ORR, ROBERT, formerly judge in the court of common pleas; d. at Kittaning, Pa., Sept. 4, 1833, a. 89.

ORRICK, COL. GEORGE, d. at Winchester, Va., Jan. 31, 1840; was long cashier of the Farmers' Bank at that place.

ORSEN, JOHN, ex-sheriff of N. Y.; d. May 15, 1870, a. 62.

ORTIZ, V. REV. JOHN F., vicar apostolic of Santa Fe; b. at Santa Fe, N. Mex. 1798; was ordained in 1822; appointed pastor at Cabelleros in 1823, and Santa Fe in 1825; in 1832 he was appointed administrator of N. Mexico, and Nov. 24, 1850 vicar apostolic; d. of apoplexy, Jan 20, 1858, a. 61. (*Metropolitan Cath. Almanac*, 1859, p. 248.)

ORVIS, DR. CHARLES, in the N. Y. assembly in 1830 from Jefferson co.; afterwards co. clerk of Lewis co; d. at Warren, Ill., May 31, 1858.

OSBORNE, REV. CHARLES F., F. W. Bap. preacher; b. at Lee, N. H., March 12, 1808; ordained Sept. 4, 1840; preached at Scarboro and West Limington, and d. at Gorham, Me., Jan. 23, 1856. (*F. W. Bap. Reg.* 1857, p. 88.)

OSGOOD, DR. ERASTUS, d. at Norwich, Conn., Dec. 22, 1867, in his 88th year; b. in Pomfret, Conn., and in practice from his 24th year.

OSGOOD, ISAAC, d. at North Andover, Mass., Sept. 30, 1847, a. 92.

OS-SA-HIN-TA, Captain Frost, an Onondaga chief; was head man in his nation from 1830 to 1846; d. Jan. 24, 1846, a. 86. (*Clark's Onondaga*, i, 109, with portrait.)

OSTRANDER, REV. DAVID, d. at Plattekill, N. Y., Dec. 8, 1843; had been 50 years in the Methodist Episcopal ministry.

OTERO, MIGUEL A., d. in New Mexico, Nov. 30, 1870, a. 90; was a member of the legislature, and attorney gen. of New Mexico; a delegate in congress in 1855.

OTIS, JAMES, SEN., of Barnstable, Mass.; farmer and glazier; became well informed in history; had a commission for the peace and as judge of the co. court; he was was often a representative and an earnest friend of the colonies; was in the legislature most of the time from 1763 to 1775; his son was an eminent orator. (*Bradford's N. E. Biog.*)

OTIS, JOHN, b. in Maine in 1801; grad. at Bowdoin Coll. in 1823; was in congress from Maine in 1849–51; d. in 1856.

OTIS, MARY, widow of Samuel Allyne O., formerly sec. of U. S. senate; d. at Boston, April 18, 1845, a. 85.

OTIS, WILLIAM FOSTER, d. in Versailles, France, May 29, 1858, a. 56; he was the third son of Harrison Gray Otis; grad. at Harvard in 1821; studied law, and practiced at the Suffolk bar; he was in the state legislature from 1830 to 1833, and for several years president of the Young Men's Temperance Society.

OTIS, WILLIAM S., of Philadelphia, Pa., d. at Westfield, Mass., Nov. 13, 1839; principal contractor on the Western rail road.

OTTO, JACOB S., an agent of the Holland Land Company of western New York; was formerly a merchant in Philadelphia; became agent in 1821; d. May 2, 1826, at Batavia, N. Y. (*Turner's Holland Land Company*, p. 441.)

OUDIN, LUCIEN d. May 18, 1868, a. 40; was instructor of French at the college of the city of New York.

OVIDEO, SENOR, of diamond wedding notoriety; d. in Cuba, Feb. 6, 1870.

OWEN, REV. JOHN J., D.D., LL.D., pres. of the college of the city of New York; d. in that city, April 19, 1869, a. 66; b. in Vermont and grad. at Middlebury, was a superior Greek scholar and author of several text books in Greek and Latin.

OWENS, GEORGE W., d. at Savannah, Ga., 1856, was a prominent member of the Georgia bar, and a representative in congress from that state from 1835 to 1839.

OWENS, WILLIAM, d. in Va., Aug. 25, 1859, a. 100.

OXLEY, JOHN A., tragedian; d. at N. Y., Dec. 27, 1869.

PADDOCK, REV. BENJAMIN GREEN, b. in Bennington, Vt., Jan. 24, 1789; d. at Metuchin, N. J., Oct. 7, 1871. (*Northern Christian Advocate*, Nov. 16, 1871.)

PADDOCK, REV. BENJAMIN S., d. at Metuchin, N. J., Oct. 7, 1871, a. 83; was 63 years a preacher of the M. E. church.

PADDOCK, EPHRAIM, formerly judge of supreme court of Vt.; son of James P.; b. Jan. 4, 1780 in Brimfield (now Holland), Mass.; was admitted to the bar in Jan., 1809, and settled at St. Johnsbury, Vt.; was a representative in 1821, 23, 24, 25, 26; was in the constitutional convention in 1828, and the same year was elected a judge of the supreme court; in 1841 was one of the council of censors; retired from practice in 1847, and d. July 27, 1859, in his 80th year. (*Hist. Mag.*, iii, p. 286.)

PAEZ, GEN. JOSÉ ANTONIO, ex-pres. of Venezuela; d. at N. Y. city, May 6, 1873, a. 82.

PAGE, HUGH NELSON, capt. in U. S. navy; d. at Broad Creek, Va., June 3, 1871, a. 73; was in the battle of Lake Erie under Com. Perry in 1813.

PAGE, JAMES W., formerly an extensive commission merchant; d. in Boston, May 19, 1868.

PAGE, JOHN, capt. 4th reg. infantry U. S. army; b. in Freyburg, Me., in 1797; was appointed 2d lieut. 8th infantry, Feb. 13, 1818; 1st lieut. Jan. 1819, and capt. April 30, 1831; was emigrating and disbursing agent for the removal of Choctaws; was wounded at the head of his division at the battle of Palo Alto, in which he lost his whole lower jaw; d. July 13, 1846, on a steamer on the Mississippi. (*Thorpe's Army of the Rio Grande*, p. 193.)

PAGE, HENRY, lawyer; d. in Turin, July 15, 1843.

PAGE, DR. MATTHEW, d. in Edenton dist., S. C., Oct. 18, 1853.

PAIGE, JOHN KEYES, grad. at Williamstown Coll. in the class of 1807; served as a capt. in the war of 1812, and in 1823 was appointed clerk of the supreme court; in 1829 was appointed a regent of the University of N. Y., which office he held till his death; in 1844 was a presidential elector, and in 1845 was the mayor of Albany; removed to Gilboa, N. Y., in 1849 and to Schenectady (his early residence) in 1856; d. at Schenectady, Dec. 10, 1857, a. 69; was a brother of the Hon. Alonzo C. Paige formerly reporter in the court of chancery. (*Alb. Eve. Jour.*, Dec. 15, 1857.)

PAINE, BYRON, associate justice of supreme court of Wisconsin; d. at Madison, Wis., Jan. 20, 1871.

PAINE, MRS. JANE T., widow of Lemuel P.; d. at Winslow, Me., Apr. 19, 1860; was a dau. of Hon. Ebenezer Warren, brother of Gen. Joseph Warren. (*Vincent's Semi-An. Register*, p. 312.)

PALFREY, EDWARD, projector of the *Salem Advertiser* ,Mass., and many years its editor; d. at Worcester hospital, April 14, 1846, a. 41.

PALFREY, JOHN, d. near St. Martinsville, La., Oct. 19, 1843, in his 77th year; b. in Boston, and a member of one of the first Am. mercantile houses established in New Orleans; was a planter of Attakapas from 1811; a member of the legislature in 1819–1820; was youngests on of Col. William P., who was pay master in the revolution.

PALMER, JOHN, b. in Hoosick, N. Y., in 1785; settled at Plattsburg, N. Y., as a lawyer in 1810, and was a partner with the late Chancellor Walworth till 1820; in congress from 1817 to 1819, and from 1837 to 1839; dist. attorney of Clinton co., 1818–32; first county judge, 1832 to 1837; d. at St. Bartholomew in the West Indies, Dec. 8, 1840.

PALMER, DR. JOSEPH, journalist, d. in Boston, March 3, 1871.

PALMER, LEWIS, an architect of talent, d. at Lewisburg, Pa., June, 1860; he built the court house and college edifices at Lewisburg.

PALMER, MRS. SUSANNAH, mother of Gov. P., of Vermont; d. at Franklin, N. Y., March, 1835, a. 94.

PANET, BERNARD CLAUDE, R. C. bp. of Quebec; b. at Quebec, Jan. 9, 1753; became priest Oct. 25, 1788; was chosen coadjutor of Bp. Plessis in Jan., 1806, and succeeded him Dec. 12, 1825; he retired in 1832, and d. at Quebec, Feb. 14, 1833, a. 80. (*Liste Chron. des Evêques et des Prêtres du Canada.*)

PAPEN, JULES RENÉ, b. in Paris, Fr.; educated at the Polytechnic School; was government civil engineer, and d. in Le Ray, N. Y., July 27, 1862, a. 62.

PARDO, RAIMUNDO, one of the victims of the Virginius expedition; shot at Santiago de Cuba, Nov. 7, 1873, a. 25; b. in Colon, and belonged to a prominent family.

PARADOL, LUCIEN ANATOLE PREVOST, French minister to the U. S.; committed suicide at Washington, D. C., July 20, 1870; b. in Paris, Aug. 8, 1829, had been a professor, and editor, and published several historical, political and educational works.

PARISH, DAVID, financier and wealthy land proprietor in northern New York; son of John Parish, Am. consul at Hamburgh; was educated as a banker, and about 1808 came to America as agent for a house in Amsterdam, to conduct a great financial operation under a contract with the elder Napoleon; he purchased the site of Ogdensburg and extensive tracts of land, built furnaces, ware houses, vessels &c., and was largely engaged in improvements when the war occurred; with Stephen Girard he loaned to the U. S. $7,000,000; in 1816 he returned to Europe, became entangled in a partnership with Fries & Co., of Vienna, who became insolvent; believing himself ruined, he committed suicide by drowning in the Danube. (*Hough's Hist. St. Law. & Fr. Cos., N. Y.*, p. 600, with portrait.)

PARISH, GEORGE, land proprietor of northern N. Y.; br. of David and son of John P., settled at Ogdensburg in 1816; had been a collector in the East Indies and engaged in finances; he engaged in mining, and improvements on his extensive estates; spent several years in traveling in Europe; d. in Paris, April 22, 1839, a. 58. (*Hough's Hist. St. Law. & Fr. Cos., N. Y.*, p. 604.)

PARISH, RUSSELL, lawyer, b. at Branford, Ct., Oct. 27, 1789; grad. at Yale in 1813; settled in Lowville, N. Y., taught acad. a year, and engaged in the law business; he was in the state convention of 1846; d. Feb. 21, 1855. (*Lowville Acad. Semi-cent. Celeb.*, p. 80.)

PARKER, AMASA, d. in Delhi, N. Y., March 1, 1855; was b. in Litchfield co., Conn.; grad. at Yale, and removed to Delhi, N. Y., in 1812, where he practiced law till his death; was surrogate of Delaware co., from 1832 to 1840, and many years master in chancery.

PARKER, REV. BENJAMIN CLARK CUTLER, b. in Boston, in 1796; grad. at Harvard in 1822; and for the last 15 years of his life, pastor of the Floating Chapel for Seamen, in the city of New York, where he d. Jan. 28, 1859, a 62.

PARKER, GEN. DANIEL, chief clerk in the war department; d. in Washington, April 5, 1846; was from Mass., and came to Washington before the beginning of the war of 1812, to fill the part of chief clerk in the war department; was transferred in Madison's term to the office of adj. and inspector gen. of the army, and held till 1821 when he was returned to his former place.

PARKER, DANIEL P., d. in Boston, Aug. 31, 1850, a. 60; a successful merchant and extensive ship owner.

PARKER, EDMUND, d. in Claremont, N. H., Sept. 8, 1856, a. 73; was b.in Jaffrey, Feb. 7, 1783; grad. at Dartmouth in 1803; was admitted to the bar in 1807, and settled in Amherst, N. H.; was 11 years in the legislature, and in 1824 speaker of the house; was judge of probate of Hillsborough co., from 1826 to 1835; removed to Nashua in 1836, and became agent of the Jackson company, and afterwards was pres. of the Nashua and Lowell rail road; represented Nashua in the legislature 5 years, and was a member of the constitutional convention of 1850.

PARKER HENRY, col. gov. of Ga.; was in 1714 bailiff at Savannah, Ga.; settled on the Isle of Hope at an early day, and in 1741 was made an assistant; in 1750 he succeeded Mr. Stephens as pres. of the colony of Ga.; in Jan. 1751 he called an assembly; he discharged the executive office till the surrender of the charter in 1754; he then retired to the Isle of Hope, and d. at an advanced age. (*White's Hist. Ga.*, p. 181.)

PARKER, JAMES, one of the provincial council of N. J., and leading member of the board of proprietors of that colony; resided at Perth Amboy, and d. in 1797.

PARKER, JAMES, native of Boston, and a physician; was in congress from Mass. from 1813 to 1815, and from 1819 to 1821; was for 50 years a resident of Gardiner, Me., and d. there Nov. 9, 1837, a. 69.

PARKER, LIEUT. JAMES L., aid of Com. Perry; d. on board the U. S. steamer Miss., July 12, 1847.

PARKER, JOHN, one of the oldest and wealthiest of the merchants of Boston; d. in that city May 29, 1840, a. 83.

PARKER, JOHN AVERY, d. in New Bedford, Mass., Dec. 30, 1853; was a distinguished merchant, and a millionaire.

PARKER, JOHN M., d. at Oswego, N. Y., Dec. 16, 1873; was a lawyer, and in 1859 elected a justice of the supreme court of N. Y., in the 6th district.

PARKER, JOHN W., d. near Zutphen, Holland, Aug. 14, 1842, a. 61; he was from Boston, Mass., and for many years U. S. consul at Amsterdam.

PARKER, JOSEPH, d. at Philadelphia, Pa., June 22, 1841; late president of the Bank of Philadelphia.

PARKER, JOSEPH, a veteran actor and scenic artist; d. Dec. 30, 1871

PARKER, LIEUT. COL. MOSES, Mass., killed at Bunker Hill, June 17, 1775.

PARKER, PETER, merchant, d. at Boston, Sept. 7, 1870, a. 71.

PARKER, Dr. Richard H., from North Carolina, had resided some years at Portsmouth, Va., and fell a victim to the yellow fever August 10, 1855, at an advanced age.

PARKER, Samuel Franklin, printer, d. Dec. 6, 1779, at Woodbridge, N. J., a. 34; son of the late James Parker formerly secretary and comptroller of his majesty's post office for the northern department.

PARKER, Samuel J., formerly a state senator in Pennsylvania; d. at Williamsport, Pa., Oct., 1834.

PARKER, Gen. Severn E., d. in Northampton co., Va., Oct. 21, 1836; he was a lawyer, and had formerly been a member of the state legislature, and from 1819 to 1821, a member of congress from Virginia.

PARKER, Thomas, d. in Farmington, Me., Feb. 4, 1860, in his 77th year.

PARKS, Rev. Isaac, d.d., d. at Whitehall, N. Y., April 15, 1869, in his 66th year; was 35 years a Methodist minister, and from 1857 till his death, a regent of the university. (*Regents' Report*, 1869, p. 587.)

PARMELEE, William, d. in Albany, N. Y., March 15, 1856; was mayor of that city; b. in Lansingburgh; grad. at Yale in 1826, and admitted to the bar in 1830 at Albany; in 1839 was appointed a judge of the county court, and in 1840 recorder, which office he held till 1841, when he was elected mayor; in 1847 was chosen judge of the county court, and held till 1852; in 1855, again elected mayor, and in this office at the time of death; he was a son-in-law of Dr. T. Romeyn Beck.

PARMELIE, Capt. Josiah, Conn., killed March 24, 1778.

PARMENTIER, Nicholas S., native of France, and prof. of French in the University of Nashville; d. July 15, 1835, a. 59.

PARRIS, Samuel, revolutionary patriot; b. Aug. 31, 1855, at Pembroke, Mass., and during the revolution was an officer; at the peace settled in Hebron, Me., was a judge of court of com. pleas for Oxford co., several years, and repeatedly a representative to the general court; in 1812 he was presidential elector; he d. at Washington, Sept. 10, 1797, a. 92; his son Albion K., was governor of Maine. (*Hist. Mag.*, i, 130.)

PARRIS, Virgil D., member of congress from Maine, in 1838–41; d. at Paris, Me., June 14, 1870.

PARRISH, Henry, d. in New York city, March 2, 1856, a. 68; a well known and wealthy merchant.

PARRISH, Dr. Isaac, b. March 19, 1811; grad. at the University of Penn. in 1832; was elected one of the surgeons of Will's Hospital, Philadelphia, and was interested in its affairs for the rest of life; he d. July 31, 1852. (*Simpson's Eminent Philadelphians.*)

PARRISH, Jasper, emigrated from Connecticut to Luzerne co., Pa.; was captured at the age of 11, by the Delawares, and remained seven years a prisoner with the Six nations where he acquired their language; he was released at Fort Stanwix in 1784; speaking five different Indian languages, he was appointed an interpreter and sale agent, for thirty years, and assisted at many Indian treaties; he d. at Canandaigua, N. Y., July, 1836, a. 69 years. (*Turner's Phelps and Gorham's Purchase*, p. 311.)

PARROTT, John F., in congress from New Hampshire; from 1817 to 1819; and senator in congress from 1819 to 1825; and in 1826 appointed post master at Portsmouth, N. H.; d. at Greenland, N. H., July 9, 1836, a. 68.

PARRY, RT. REV. THOMAS, D.D., bishop of Barbadoes; d. in England March 16, 1870, a. 75.

PARROLE, CHARLES T., SEN., pantomimist; d. at New York, Sept. 22, 1870, a. 66.

PARSONS, ICHABOD, formerly a judge of the courts of Lewis co., N. Y.; b. in Middletown, Conn., 1777; was a pioneer of the Black river valley; and d. at Denmark, Lewis co., Sept. 9, 1867.

PARSONS, LORENZO, b. at Utica, N. Y., in 1806; grad. at Hamilton Coll. in 1833; was prin. of the Springville Acad. N. Y.; from 1837 to 1841 at Westfield, N. Y., and from 1841 to 1845 supt. of schools in Chautauqua co.; was afterwards in business at Westfield; d. Feb. 4, 1866.

PARSONS, SAMUEL, b. in Va.; entered the revolution a. 15; was engaged in the battle of Guilford C. H., at the siege of Little York and that of Yorktown; he d. in Fayette co., Ga., in 1832, a. 70.

PARSONS, REV. STEPHEN, pioneer Baptist preacher in northern N. Y.; Sept. 5, 1748; ordained in 1788; removed from Middletown, Ct., to Whitestown, N. Y. and in 1802 to Lewis co.; he d. in Denmark, N. Y., from a fall, Jan. 7, 1820, having but a few hours before preached from the text, II Sam., xix, 34, "How long have I to live?" (*Hough's Hist. Lewis Co., N. Y.*, p. 93.)

PARTON, MRS. SARAH WILLIS, "Fanny Fern"; d. in New York city, Oct. 10, 1872, a. 61.

PARVIN, REV. ROBERT, lost in the collision and burning of the steamboats North America and United States, on the Ohio river, Dec. 4, 1868; was sec. of the Prot. Episc. Evangelical Education Soc.; had been rector of several churches in Pa., and N. Y., and was last in charge of St. Paul's church, Cheltenham.

PASTORIUS, FRANCIS DANIEL, arrived in Philadelphia, in 1683, and was the founder of Germantown; was a chief magistrate there. (*Simpsons Eminent Philadelphians.*)

PATERSON, WILLIAM, supposed to be a native of Ireland; removed to Westminster, Vt., in 1723; he was prominent in the Westminster massacre, was imprisoned, sent to Northampton, and detained till November following; he was sheriff of Cumberland co., from Oct. 1, 1773, till 1775. (*Hall's Eastern Vermont*, p. 678.)

PATIN, VICTOR, president of the Citizens' Bank; d. at New Orleans, La., Sept. 15, 1839.

PATTERSON, ANGUS, d. in Barnewell, S. C., May 26, 1854; was for a long time president of the state senate of South Carolina.

PATTERSON, HENRY STUART, M.D., b. in Phil., Aug. 15, 1815; d. April 27, 1854; grad. at the Med. Dep. of University of Pennsylvania; became in 1839, resident physician of the Phila. Alms House, and in 1843, prof. of materia medica in the Pa. Coll.; in 1846, was appointed physician in chief of the Phil. Alms House. (*Simpson's Eminent Philadelphians*, with portrait.)

PATTERSON, MATTHEW C., district attorney for the U. S. district court, for the southern dist. of N. Y.; d. at New York city, Jan. 26, 1846.

PATTERSON, SAMUEL D., formerly a well known democratic politician, d. at Evensburg, Montgomery co., Pa.; was formerly navy agent at Phil. and at various times connected with the press; he contributed poems and other articles of moderate merit to several literary and religious jour.

PATTERSON, WILLIAM, d. at Warsaw, N. Y., Aug. 14, 1838; member of congress from New York.

PATTERSON, CAPT. WILLIAM, d. at Savannah, Ga., Aug. 14, 1842, a. 54.

PATTERSON, WILLIAM, member of congress from the 29th dist. of N. Y.; d. at Warsaw, N. Y., Aug. 14, 1838.

PATTERSON, WILLIAM, merchant at Balt.; d. Feb. 7, 1835, a. 85.

PATTERSON, WILLIAM D., U. S. consul-gen. for Belgium; d. at Antwerp, July 4, 1836, a. 68.

PATTON, JOHN M., b. in Va.; was a lawyer, and in congress from 1830 to 1838; d. Oct., 1858, a. 62.

PATTON, REV. SAMUEL, of the Holston conference; b. in Lancaster dist., S. C., Jan. 27, 1797; d. in Aug., 1854, at Knoxville, Tenn., where he was for a time editor of the *Holston Christian Advocate.* (*Deems's Annals of Southern Methodism*, p. 347.)

PATTON, LIEUT. WILLIAM, Pa.; killed at Germantown, Pa., Oct. 4, 1777.

PAUL, J. J., Venezuelan minister to the U. S.; d. at Washington, March 7, 1870, a. 45.

PAUL, WILLIAM, acting lieut. in British navy; killed in battle of Plattsburg, Sept. 11, 1814.

PAULDING, WILLIAM, b. in Tarrytown, Westchester co., N. Y., in 1769; engaged in law practice in N. Y. city; was in the convention of 1821, and in congress from 1811 to 1813, but absent on militia service after war was declared; mayor of N. Y. in 1824, and 1827; d. at Tarrytown, Feb. 11, 1854.

PAWLING, COL. ALBERT, son of Levi P., of Dutchess co.; an officer of the revolution; joined the army in 1775 as 2d lieut. in Col. Jas. Clinton's reg. and marched to Canada; served under Montgomery; was appointed brig. major under Gen. Geo. Clinton in 1776, and in 1777 became major in Col. Malcom's reg.; resigned in 1779; became col. of a reg. for the defense of the frontier, and served till the peace; became a merchant at Troy; was first sheriff of Rens. co., and first mayor of that city from 1816 to 1820; d. Nov. 10, 1837, a. 88. (*Woodworth's Troy*, 53.)

PAXON, STACY A., treasurer of N. J.; d. May 26, 1847, at Trenton.

PAYNE, WORDEN, settled in Houndsfield, N. Y., in 1803 from Mass.; was capt. of an infantry company in the war of 1812-15; d. March 3, 1849, a. 55. (*Hunt's Biog. Panorama*, p. 475.)

PAYNTER, SAMUEL, formerly governor of Delaware; d. near Milton, Del., Oct. 1, 1845.

PAYSON, ARTHUR L., d. Jan. 10, 1855, a. 31, at Boston, Mass.; was although young favorably known as a merchant; was versed in several modern languages, having resided in the south of Europe several years where his father was consul.

PAYSON, HENRY, merchant in Baltimore; d. Dec. 26, 1845; was a native of Roxbury, Mass., and settled in Baltimore during the revolution; was one of the founders of its commercial prosperity, and saw many reverses in fortune, but with integrity unimpaired.

PEABODY, REV. JAMES A., financial secretary of the board of education of the Presb. church; d. at Lynn, Mass., Oct. 12, 1839, a. 35.

PEABODY, JOSEPH, shipowner and merchant; b. at Middleton, Mass., Dec, 9, 1757; a volunteer to Lexington, but too late for service, and engaged as a privateer; was successful in two cruises; devoted some time to study and again went to sea; was taken prisoner, was exchanged, and on board the Ranger of seven guns, was very successful; continued in the merchant service till 1791 when he retired from the ocean; m., engaged in commerce, and gradually increased the number of his ships until they floated on every sea; built and owned 83 ships, which in every instance he freighted himself, and for their navigation, shipped at different times over 7000 seamen; after 1811 he had advanced 35 to masters, who had entered his employ as boys; had performed 38 voyages to Calcutta, 17 to Canton, 32 to Sumatra, 47 to St. Petersburg, 10 to other ports of northern Europe and 20 to the Mediterranean, besides unnumbered voyages to the West Indies and South America, the north-west coast &c. His aggregate taxes were $200,000 and the business brought to Salem above calculation; d. Jan. 5, 1844, a. 86. (*Hunt's Lives of Am. Merchants*, i, 367.)

PEABODY, JOSEPH AUGUSTUS, eldest son of Joseph P.; an eminent ship owner of Salem, Mass., grad. at Harvard in 1816; after extensive foreign travel engaged with his father in business; and d. in 1828.

PEABODY, STEPHEN, formerly judge of the court of common pleas, of Hancock, co., Me.; d. at Bucksfort, Me., April 13, 1851, a. 77.

PEALE, FRANKLIN, d. at Phil.; May 5, 1870, a. 75; son of Charles Wilson Peale, in 1833; was appointed assistant assayer of the U. S. mint, and afterwards held the office of melter, refiner and chief coiner; left the mint in 1854.

PEARSE, O. P., a merchant of Phila.; was drowned at Cape May, June 29, 1848.

PEASE, SETH, mathematician and astronomer, b. Suffield, Conn., about 1770; d. Washington city, 1818; surveyor of Mass., wild lands in Maine 1794-5; for the Connecticut Land Co.; in Ohio 1796-7; for the Holland Land Co., N. Y., 1798-9; ran southern boundary of the western reserve in Ohio, 1796 and 1806; surveyor general in Mississippi, 1806; a special genius and devotee in astronomy and mathematics, often in the employ of the U. S.; a good sketcher and penman, leaving numerous diaries and journals of his expeditions.

PEARSON, JOSEPH, member of congress from North Carolina; d. at Salisbury, N. C., Oct. 27, 1834, a. 54.

PEASE, DIODATE, land agent, surveyor, and formerly member of the New York assembly; d. in Martinsburg, March 25, 1862, a. 47.

PEASE, REV. LORENZO W., d. in the Island of Cypress, Aug. 28, 1839; was late of Auburn; a missionary.

PECKHAM, RUFUS W., one of the judges of the court of appeals of the state of New York, and a citizen of Albany; lost with his wife in the wreck of the French steamer, Ville du Havre, Nov. 22, 1873, a. 66; was a member of congress from 1853 to 1855; a distinguished lawyer of Albany.

PEDRO I, ANTONIO JOSE D'ALCANTARA, emperor of Brazil; b. Oct. 12, 1798; crowned Oct. 12, 1822; abdicated in favor of his son in 1831, and returned to Portugal, where he d. Sept. 24, 1834; he m. Amelia, 3d dau. of the Duke of Leuchtenberg, son of Viscount Beauharnois and Josephine, afterwards empress of France; she d. Jan. 26, 1873, at Lisbon.

PEET, HARVEY PRINDLE, LL.D., principal of the New York Institution for the Deaf and Dumb; d. in New York city, Jan. 1, 1873, a. 79.

PEETS, GEORGE W., one of the most prominent of the citizens in north western Louisiana; d. in the parish of Claiborne, La., Dec. 12, 1852.

PEGRAM, GEN. JAMES W., d. Oct. 23, 1844, by accident on board the steamboat Lucy Walker; was president of the Bank of Virginia.

PEIRCE, CHARLES, b. in Kittery, Maine, July 29, 1770; became a printer, and after living in Portsmouth and Boston, several years, settled in Philadelphia in 1814, and in 1816 in Germantown; in 1825, returned to Philadelphia, and in 1848 removed to Bristol, Pa.; he d. there Sept. 23, 1851. (*Simpson's Eminent Philadelphians.*)

PEIRCE, JAMES R., d. in Dorchester, Mass., July 25, 1842, a. 24; grad. at Harvard in 1838, and was a student in the Divinity School at time of death.

PEIRCE, LIEUT. TIMOTHY, Pa., killed in the revolution, July 3, 1778.

PEIRE, COL. H. D., d. at New Orleans, La., Dec. 2, 1848, a. 68; was in the war of 1812, and conspicuous as major comd't of the 44th infantry, at the capture of Pensacola, in 1814; he enjoyed various civil appointments, and discharged their duties with credit.

PELBY, WILLIAM, d. in Boston, May 28, 1850; for many years proprietor and manager of the National Theatre at Boston.

PENA, Y PENA, president of Mexico at the close of the war with the United States; d. in Mexico, Jan. 26, 1850. (*Stryker's Am. Reg.*, iv, 447.)

PENDLETON, JOHN S., b. in Va. in 1841, was chargé d'affaires to the republic of Chili, and in 1845–9, a member of congress; d. at Culpepper co., Va., Nov. 19, 1868.

PENDLETON, MICAJAH, d. in Nelson co., Va., Feb. 9, 1844, a. 86; a soldier of the revolution; a prominent Methodist and temperance reformer; before the year 1800, he circulated a temperance pledge; his theory of reform extended to the exclusion of wine and cider, differing from whiskey only in strength.

PENDLETON, WILLIAM F., b. in Va.; entered the army as ensign of 20th infantry, June, 1812; rose to the rank of 1st lieut., May, 1814; was retained in 1815; resigned Dec., 1816, and held the office of member of executive council of Va. 14 y.; d. Sept. 11, 1860, at Washington, a. 76.

PENDLETON, WILLIAM M., d. near Coffeeville, Clarke co., Ala., Sept. 21, 1842 in his 45th year; b. in Spottsylvania co., Va.; was founder of the Pendleton Academy, and a teacher of high classical attainments. (*Am. Almanac*, 1844, p. 314.)

PENET, PETER, confidence man of the revolution; came from Nantes, France, in Dec. 1775, and succeeded in imposing upon several public functionaries and procuring advances for arms that he was to supply in the greatest abundance; afterwards went among the Oneida Indians; gained the confidence of many and got from them, as the fulfilment of a pretended dream, a gift of 10 miles square of land, since known as Penet's Square, in Jeff. co., N. Y.; was a trader for a time at Schenectady; went to St. Domingo and there again continued his impostures by selling lands on Oneida lake, which he had never owned. (*Hough's Notice of Peter Penet*, Lowville, N. Y., 1866.)

PENNEL, DR. RICHARD, of N. Y. city; d. April 11, 1861, a. 62.

PENNICOCK, THOMAS, d. in Eng., March 27, 1849, a. 102; fought and was wounded at Bunker hill.

PENNINGTON, SAMUEL, d. at Newark, N. J., March 3, 1835, a. about 70.

PENNINGTON, WILLIAM S., sec. of legation at Paris, under Pres. Lincoln; d. at Newark, N. J., Sept. 4, 1868; was a son of a former gov. of N. J.

PENNOCK, BARCLAY, known as a traveler and linguist; d. young at Kennett, Chester co., Pa., March 15, 1858. (*Hist. Mag.*, ii, p. 156.)

PENNYBACKER, ISAAC S., d. in Wash., D. C., Jan. 12, 1847, a. 41; U. S. senator from Va.; b. in Shenandoah valley in 1806; educated to the law, and practiced with high reputation until called to represent his dist. in congress; at the end of his first term was transferred to the dist. court of Western Va., and thence to the senate of the U. S.

PENROSE, CHARLES BIDDLE, b. in 1791, and d. April 6, 1857; was state senator from the Cumberland dist. 8 years (1833–41); was made solicitor of the treasury under Pres. Harrison in 1841, and held till the end of Tyler's term; in 1849 was appointed assistant sec. of the treasury, but soon resigned, and returned to law practice in Phil.; was prominently interested in internal improvements, and the projector of the Cumberland Valley rail road. (*Simpson's Eminent Philadelphians.*)

PENTLAND, JOSEPH, a popular American clown; d. in the city of N. Y., Jan. 1, 1873, a. 79.

PERKINS, ELIAS, grad. at Yale in 1786; member of congress from Conn. from 1801 to 1803; d. in 1845.

PERKINS, ELIPHALET, d. at Kennebunk Port, Me., Aug. 22, 1842, a. 77; a ship owner and merchant; was several years in the legislature of Mass., and a member of the Maine constitutional convention of 1820.

PERKINS, GEORGE, d. in China, May 5, 1854; b. in Boston, and a retired partner of the house of Russel & Co., of Canton and Shanghai; was murdered by the Chinese crew of a boat which he had engaged to take him ashore at Macao, from the Hamburg barque Concordia, in which he had just arrived from San Francisco.

PERKINS, MAJ. HARDIN, d. in Tuscaloosa, Ala., Dec. 31, 1850, a. 59; b. in Tenn.; removed to Ala. in early life, and was in the convention that formed a state constitution; was often a member of the legislature; for some time state treasurer, and for several years president of the State Bank.

PERKINS, JACOB, of Cleveland, O.; d. in Havana, Cuba, Jan. 12, 1859, a. 38; was a native of O.; grad. at Yale, and was a member of the state convention for revising the constitution.

PERKINS, SAMUEL, a worthy and highly esteemed citizen; d. in Roxbury, Mass., Aug. 1, 1846, a. 75; had been president of the Mass. Charitable Mechanic Association.

PERKINS, THOMAS C., a lawyer; d. at Hartford, Conn., Oct. 11, 1870.

PERLE, RICHARD, philanthropist; d. at Phil., May 6, 1870, a. 74.

PEROT, ELLISTON, b. in the Bermuda islands, March 16, 1747; sent to New York city when 7 years old to be educated by his uncle Elliston, then comptroller of customs; having finished his education returned to Bermuda; in 1772, became a partner with his brother John in the Island of Dominica; in 1778 at St. Christophers; then at St. Eustatius; settled in Phil. as merchants in 1784; d. Nov. 28, 1834. (*Simpson's Eminent Philadelphians.*)

PEROT, JOHN, merchant of Phil.; b. at Bermuda, May 3, 1749; spent his youth in Va., and in 1772 came to Phil. where he finally settled as a merchant in 1781; d. Jan. 8, 1841.

PERRINE, DR. HENRY, physician and consul; b. in N. J.; educated to the medical profession, which he practiced in Ill.; in 1826 was appointed consul at Campeachy, where during several years he studied tropical agriculture with the view of transfer to the southern states; his services during the cholera gained him the thanks of the Mexican government, and many warm friends; brought to Florida, among other tropical plants, the sisal hemp, the cochineal, cactus and banana, and procured aid from congress towards their introduction; perished at the hands of the Seminole Indians at Indian Key. (*Griswold's Biog. An.*, 1841, p. 288.)

PERRY, CHARLES B., an early settler and well known citizen of Auburn, N. Y.; d. at that city, Dec. 30, 1859.

PERRY, DR. DAVID, d. in Rutland, N. Y., Aug. 31, 1862, a. 87; he spent the greater part of his life in medical practice at Lowville, N. Y. (*Hough's Hist. of Lewis Co.*, p. 154.)

PERRY, CAPT. ELNATHAN, a soldier of the revolution; present at Bennington, Saratoga, Monmouth, Eutaw, Yorktown and other battle fields; d. at Rush, Monroe co., N. Y., June, 1849, a. 90.

PERRY, DR. MARSHALL SEARS, b. in Barre, Mass., June 16, 1805; grad. with degree of M.D. at Harvard in 1830; settled in Boston in 1832, where for 27 years he practiced with great success, devoting himself strictly to his prof. and holding no public office; d. Nov. 19, 1859, a. 54.

PERRY, THOMAS, native of Md.; in congress from 1844 to 1847, and circuit judge in 1851–61, and 1864–67; d. at Cumberland, Md., June 23, 1871, a. 63.

PETER, WILLIAM, d. in Phil., Pa., Feb. 6, 1853; British consul for that place for 13 years; formerly a member of parliament, and an active politician of the liberal party; was an accomplished scholar, and a talented poet; his last work was a translation of the Prometheus of Æschylus.

PETERS, CHARLES, comedian belonging to Booth's theatre; d. in N. Y., Nov. 3, 1870, a. 35; had performed in all the principal theatres of the United States.

PETERS, GEORGE P., army officer; son of Gen. Absalom P., cadet 1807; served in war as 1st. lieut., and was wounded in battle of Tippecanoe, Nov. 7, 1811; became asst. adj. gen. in 1813; capt. of infantry in

1814; was retained in 1815 as capt. of artillery; d. in East Florida, Nov. 28, 1819, a. 31.

PETERS, JOHN R., oldest son of Gen. Absalom P., of Hebron, Ct.; b. at Wentworth, N. H., 1783; began business at Groton, Mass.; went to Troy, N. Y., and in 1814 to N. Y., where he was a leading merchant, and had extensive connections in the cotton trade; in 1816 he began the first trade of note with Mobile; was a member of the council, and com'r of the almshouse; was instrumental in forming the establishment known as Long Isl. Farms; he devoted much attention to charitable institutions; d. Apr. 26, 1858. (*N. Y. Herald.*)

PETERS, JOHN S., d. in Hebron, Conn., April 11, 1858, a. 80; was several years in the state legislature, and lieut. gov. from 1827 to 1831, when he was elected gov., and held this office two years.

PETERS, NATHAN, major in the revolution; joined the Ct. troops at the beginning of the war; rose from lieut. to maj., and was engaged at Long Island, York Island, Princeton, Trenton and Newport; was the first to enter Groton fort after the enemy left, and extinguished a train leading to the magazine; returned to the law after the war and practiced many years at the New London bar; d. at Norwich, Ct., in 1823. (*Rogers's Am. Biog.*)

PETERS, SAMUEL J., d. in New Orleans, La., Aug. 11, 1855, a. 54; was a native of Canada, but for many years had resided in New Orleans, which city owes much to him for its prosperity in that day; was for a long time pres. of two banking institutions; pres. of the chamber of commerce, and during the terms of Presidents Taylor and Filmore, collector of the port.

PETERSON, REV. JOHN DIEDRICH, d. Jan. 18, 1848, a. 91; late pastor of the German Lutheran congregations of Markham, and Vaughan in Upper Canada; b. in Bremen, Germany, Nov. 23, 1756; came to Am. in 1795, and first had charge of a church in Harrisburg, Pa.; removed in 1803 to Canada. (*Am. Almanac*, 1849, p. 336.)

PETERSON, MRS. LOUIS, d. in Colerain, Mass., July 2, 1842, a. 93, leaving numerous descendants of three generations.

PETRY, DR. WILLIAM, revolutionary surgeon; b. near Oppenheim, Germany, Dec. 7, 1733; came to Am. in 1763, having been a surgeon in the Prussian army; was a merchant at Herkimer, N. Y., before and after the revolution; served on committees of safety several years, and was surgeon at Ft. Dayton in 1776–79; in 1782 was appointed surgeon to the levies under Col. Willett, having previously served professionally in various expeditions, and throughout the Mohawk valley as occasion demanded; d. at Herkimer, Aug. 6, 1806, a. 73. (*Benton's Herkimer Co., N. Y.*, p. 352.)

PETTICOLAS, DR. ARTHUR E., supt. of the Eastern Lunatic Asylum of Va.; committed suicide, Nov. 28, 1868, at Williamsburg, Va., being himself at the time insane.

PETTIS, SPENCER, member in congress from Mo. in 1829–31; killed in a duel near St. Louis by Tho. Biddle, pay master in the army, who was also killed, Aug. 26, 1831.

PETTIT, ANDREW, a merchant of Phil., Pa.; d. in that city March 5, 1837, a. 77.

PETTIT, THOMAS M., director of the U. S. mint at Phil.; d. in that city, May 31, 1853.

PETTUS, CAPT. THOMAS, joined the revolutionary army in 1781; was a representative in the Va. legislature in 1800–1; d. in Charlotte co., Va., May 2, 1850, a. 91.

PEYTON, DR. JOSEPH H., member of congress from Tenn. in 1843–45, and elected for the 29th cong.; d. at Gallatin, Texas, Nov. 12, 1845; had served his state in the senate and in other public stations with acceptance.

PEYTON, LIEUT. ROBERT, Va.; killed at Brandywine Sept. 11, 1777.

PFEIFFER, MADAM IDA, eminent traveler and author; b. in Vienna in 1797; m. Dr. P. in 1820; traveled over 130,000 miles by sea, and 18,000 by land, and wrote many books; d. in Vienna, Oct. 27, 1858; her Am. travels were in South America in 1846; in 1853, 54, in California, Oregon, and the Atlantic states; left N. Y. for Europe Nov. 1854.

PHAROUX, PIERRE, a distinguished French architect and engineer; was employed on the surveys of the Castorland tract on the Black river in Lewis and Jefferson counties, N. Y., and was drowned in the cascade of Black river, in the present city of Watertown, N. Y., Sept., 1795. (*Hough's Hist. Lewis Co., N. Y.*, p. 52.)

PHELAN, MICHAEL, a noted billiard player; d. in N. Y. city, Oct. 7, 1871.

PHELPS, ANSEL, Jr., d. at Springfield, Mass., June 2, 1860, a. 44; b. in Greenfield, Mass.; was a lawyer, and for some 16 years had resided in Springfield; was closely identified with the Western rail road; was mayor of that city several years; after the breaking up of the old whig party he joined the democrats.

PHELPS, CHARLES, son of Nathaniel P.; b. in Northampton, Mass., Aug. 15, 1715; removed to Hadley, and in 1764 to Marlborough, Vt., of which he was a patentee; was a lawyer, very excentric in some respects; his zealous and indiscreet attachment to the N. Y. interests subjected him to inconvenience; he importuned the governor of N. Y., and the congress at Phil., with a garrulity which had little effect; was at length imprisoned in 1784 at Westminster, and soon removed to Bennington; was pardoned by the legislature in Oct. 1784; d. April, 1789 in his 73d year. (*Hall's Eastern Vermont*, p. 679.)

PHELPS, CHARLES JR., second son of C. P.; b. in 1744; was educated to the law; removed to Hadley, Mass., from Vt., and continued to sympathize with and aid his father and brother who remained; d. in Hadley, Dec. 4, 1814, a. 70. (*Hall's Eastern Vermont*, p. 692.)

PHELPS, CHARLES B., judge of co. court of Litchfield co., Ct.; member of both houses of legislature, and speaker in the house of representatives; judge of probates &c.; was politically a democrat; stout in person, and weighed 380 pounds; d. suddenly, Dec. 21, 1858, at Roxbury, Mass., where he was attending to the erection of a monument to Seth Warner. (*Hist. Mag.*, iii, p. 60; *N. Haven Jour.; Hartford Times.*)

PHELPS, CHARLES PORTER, b. in Hadley, Aug. 8, 1772; grad. at Harvard in 1791; became a lawyer, and in 1816 a representative from Boston in the state leg.; in 1817 he returned to his native town, and spent the remainder of his life, being often honored with tokens of public confidence; served in both houses of the leg.; d. at Hadley, Mass., Dec. 21, 1857, a. 85. (*Am. Almanac*, 1859, p. 349.)

PHELPS, ELISHA, b. in Simsbury, Conn., Nov., 1779; grad. at Yale in 1800; studied law at Litchfield; was elected several times to the leg., where he was speaker of the house, and senator; was in congress from 1819 to 1821, and from 1825 to 1829; comptroller of the state from 1830 to 1834; in 1835 appointed to revise the statutes of Conn.; d. at Simsbury in April, 1847.

PHELAS, DR. JAMES L., of N. Y. city; d. Oct. 17, 1869, a. 84.

PHELPS, NATHANIEL, son of William P.; b. in England; was an early settler of Northampton, Mass.; d. May 27, 1802. (*Hall's Eastern Vermont*, p. 689.)

PHELPS, OLIVER LEICESTER, son of Oliver Phelps the great land proprietor of western N. Y.; was educated at Yale Coll.; m. a granddau. of Roger Sherman, and resided for a time in Paris, France; returned after the death of his father; became a resident of Canandaigua, N. Y.; was major gen. of militia; d. ——, 1813.

PHELPS, SOLOMON, 1st son of Charles; b. in 1742; grad. at Harvard Coll. in 1762; studied law and was admitted in 1768 to the courts of Cumberland co., Vt.; was a member of the committee of safety of that co. in the early part of the revolution; preached at Marlborough in 1776; became insane and committed suicide in 1790. (*Hall's Eastern Vermont*, p. 691.)

PHELPS, TIMOTHY, 3d son of Charles of Marlborough, Vt.; b. Jan. 25, 1747; was ardent in his attachment to N. Y.; was thrown into prison, and never after could yield hearty assent to this authority although he continued to reside there; d. at Marlborough, July 3, 1817; was the last sheriff of Cumberland co., under the authority of Vermont. (*Hall's Eastern Vermont*, p. 693.)

PHELPS, WILLIAM, one of the first settlers at Dorchester, Mass., in 1630; removed to Windsor, Ct., in 1635, where he was a judge; d. July 14, 1672. (*Hall's Eastern Vermont*, p. 689.)

PHIFER, JOHN, grad. at the University of N. C., in 1790; and was many years a distinguished member of the legislature of North Carolina, and a ruling elder of the Presbyterian church; he d. in Cabarrus co., N. C., Oct. 18, 1845, a. 67.

PHILBRICK, SAMUEL, a native of Seabrook, N. H.; settled in Boston as a merchant, and amassed a fortune; d. in Brookline, Mass., Sept. 19, 1859, a. 70.

PHILIPS, HORATIO GATES, b. in N. J., in 1773; son of Capt. Jonathan P., of the army; he settled at Dayton, O., in 1805; was a merchant and d. Nov. 10, 1859. (*Hist. Mag.*, iv, 26.)

PHILLIPS, REV. EBENEZER, fifth pastor of Presb. church at East Hampton, L. I.; d. March 16, 1830, at Carmel, N. Y. (*Prime's Hist. L. I.*, p. 181.)

PHILLIPS, EDWARD B., d. at Brattleboro, Vt., June 24, 1848; leaving $100,000 to Harvard University; with a fortune which could have commanded worldly comforts without stint, he at the early age of 23, weary with the limited enjoyment in which he indulged, was driven by ennui to insanity and became a self murderer; he left an estate of $900,000. (*Stryker's Am. Reg.*, i, 501.)

PHILLIPS, Eleazer, first printer in South Carolina; b. in Boston, removed to Charleston, S. C., in 1730; d. in 1731.

PHILLIPS, Hannah, d. in New Jersey, Feb. 22, 1859, a. 118 years.

PHILLIPS, Capt. Henry T., d. at Fredericksburg, Va., May 1, 1842, a. 75.

PHILLIPS, James, d. at Jackson, Miss., Aug., 1838, a. about 50; treasurer of the state of Mississippi.

PHILLIPS, John, d. at Sturbridge, Mass., Feb. 25, 1875, a. 104 y. 7 m. 26 d.; he was of the sixth generation from Rev. George Phillips, who came from England, 1630, in the Arabella, with Gov. Winthrop, and Sir Richard Saltonstall; he occupied offices of trust and responsibility in his native town, and in 1816 was in the state legislature.

PHILLIPS, Jonathan, b. April 24, 1778, was many years in the dry goods and hardware business at Boston, and in the legislature; he was nearly sixty years prominently identified with Boston, by his public spirit, his generous benefactions, and his private munificence; he was the largest contributor to the exploring expedition under Mr. Hays, gave $10,000 to the Boston library, the same to the Music hall, and a chime of bells to the church which he attended; he d. at Boston, July 29, 1860. (*Boston Transcript*, July 30, 1860; *Hist. Mag.*, iv, 284.)

PHILLIPS, Ensign Noah, Conn., killed in the rev. March 16, 1778.

PHILLIPS, Thomas Walley, was b. in Boston, Jan. 16, 1797, and was a son of Hon. John Phillips, first mayor of Boston; he grad. at Harvard, in 1810, was admitted to the bar in 1817; practiced law in Boston, until appointed clerk of the municipal court in 1830, and filled this office till his death Sept. 8, 1859; he was a member of the com. council in 1827, and of the state legislature in 1834 and 1837.

PHŒNIX, J. Phillips, b. in Morristown, N. J.; was long a merchant in N. Y. city; in 1843 to 45, and from 1849 to 51, he was in congress, and in 1848 in assembly; he d. May 4, 1559.

PICKENS, Francis W., d. at Edgefield, S. C., Jan. 25, 1869; b. in Toagadoo, S. C., April 7, 1807; educated at Columbia Coll.; was in the legislature, and in congress from 1834 to 1845; in the state senate for a short time and U. S. minister to Russia in 1857; was gov. of S. C., in 1860; was in early life a nullifier, and in the late war a secessionist.

PICKMAN, Benjamin T., pres. of the Mass. senate; d. at Boston, Mass., March 21, 1835, a. 44.

PICKMAN, Charles Gayton, d. at Boston, May 11, 1860; he bequeathed his large and valuable library to Harvard College; was b. in Salem, Nov. 22, 1791, and grad. at Harvard in 1811.

PICQUET, François, French missionary in Canada (Sulpician); b. at Bourg in Bresse, Dec. 6, 1708; studied theology at Paris, and in 1733, came out as a Catholic missionary, founded the station at Two Mountains in 1740, and at the mouth of the Oswegatchie (now Ogdensburg, N. Y.), in 1748; where Fort Presentation was built and a large Indian settlement formed; this place was the head quarters of scalping parties during the French war; and, Picquet himself led many expeditions against the English; he retired to La. on the approach of Amherst in 1760, and was several years in the ministry near Paria, and elsewhere in France; in 1777 he visited Rome; he d. at Verjon, July 15, 1781.

(*Lettres Edifiantes et Curieuses*, Lyons, 1819, iv, 262; *Hough's Hist. St. Law & Franklin Cos.; Doc. Hist., N. Y.*, i, 428.)

PIERREPONT, Hezekiah Beers, landed proprietor in northern New York, and eminent shipping merchant; b. in New Haven, Ct., Nov. 3, 1768, descendant of Rev. James P., first minister in that colony; in 1790 he went to N. Y., and became concerned in trade, and in 1793, with Wm. Leffinwell engaged in European trade; he visited France, India and China, and in returning his ship was taken by French privateers; he witnessed some of the excesses of the French revolution; returning after seven years absence he m. a daughter of Wm. Constable; was an executor of his immense landed estates in northern N. Y., of which he became a large proprietor, in Lewis, Oswego, Jefferson, St. Lawrence and Franklin cos.; in 1802 he settled in Brooklyn, occasionally visiting his northern agencies, and d. Aug. 11, 1838; the care of his lands in Lewis, St. Lawrence and Franklin cos., devolved upon his son Henry E., of Brooklyn, and those in Jefferson and Oswego upon his elder son Wm. C., of Pierrepont Manor, N. Y. (*Hough's Histories of St. Law & Fr. Cos.*, p. 713; *Jeff. Co.*, p. 448, and *Lewis Co.*, p. 243, with portrait.)

PIERRON, Jean, Jesuit missionary; arrived in Canada, June 27, 1667; sent to the Mohawks the next month; returned to Quebec, and again arrived among the Mohawks, Oct. 7, 1668; left in 1670, and was sent to the Senecas after 1672–3; where he was still in 1679.

PIERSON, Job, a lawyer of Troy, N. Y., member of congress from 1812 to 1823; d. at Troy, April 9, 1860, a. 69.

PIKE, Samuel N., a millionaire; d. in New York city, Dec. 7, 1872, a. 50.

PILCHER, William S., a native of Virginia, and mayor of Louisville, Ky.; d. in that city, Aug. 14, 1858.

PILLSBURY, Timothy, b. in Newbury, Mass., April, 12, 1789; became a sailor and coasting trader; settled in Maine, and was a member of the executive council, and of the legislature; removed to Ohio, thence to Louisiana, and to Texas; where he was several years in the house and senate of the Texan republic; was a member of congress from that state, from 1846 to 1849; and d. near Danville, Texas, Nov. 23, 1858.

PILSBURY, Moses C., b. in Newbury, Mass., worked in a smith's shop and on a farm till of age; began without resources other than a strong native genius, and acquired distinction as a firm and successful keeper of prisons; he d. at Derry, N. H., June 1848, a. 70; he was the father of Amos P., the celebrated prison keeper. (*Newgate of Ct.*, p. 125.)

PINCIN, Simeon, d. in Scituate, Mass., May 2, 1850, a. 97; his wife who survived him was 102; they had been m. 75 years.

PINCKNEY, Charles, junior editor of *The Sun;* d. at Washington, D. C., March 26, 1835, a. 38.

PINCKNEY, Henry, commander in the U. S. navy, drowned by the swamping of a boat on the bar of Tuspan.

PINCKNEY, Richard Shubrick, d. in Charleston, S. C., July 9, 1854, a. 57; was of the navy; a native of South Carolina; entered the navy in 1814, and was made commander in 1841; was engaged against the Algerine pirates of the Mediterranean, when he received several severe wounds, commanded the Decatur, during the Mexican war.

PINEDA, GEN., d. at Rivas, Sept. 21, 1853; late president of Nicaragua.

PINHORNE, WILLIAM, a distinguished merchant of N. Y.; councilor in Sloughter's administration and till 1692; removed to New Jersey near the Hackensack; he was appointed by Cornbury a judge of the supreme court of N. J., and took his seat Nov., 1704; he shared the odium that attached to Chief Justice Mompesson who became his son-in-law; he d. in retirement about 1719. (*Coll. N. J. Hist. Soc.*, iii, 73.)

PINKHAM, REV. DANIEL, F. W. Bap. preacher; b. at Madbury, N. H.; resided in Jackson, Lancaster, &c., N. H.; preached 41 years; d. of cancer at Lancaster, June 25, 1855, a. 76. (*F. W. Bap. Reg.*, 1857, p. 89.)

PINNEY, BENJAMIN, a prominent citizen of Tolland co., Conn.; d. June 9, 1860, in his 80th year; he had formerly served in the state legislature and senate; was judge of county court, and in 1841, democratic candidate for lieut. governor. (*Vincent's Semi-An. Register*, p. 514.)

PINTO, MANUEL, of California, d. April 1, 1860, at Benito, Cal., having just passed his 120th birthday.

PIPHEO, MRS. SUSANNAH, d. at Baltimore, Md.; in her 108th year, native of Germany.

PITCAIRN, JOSEPH, b. in Fifeshire, Scot., came to the U. S., in early life, and afterwards resided in the East Indies; was at one time U. S. consul at Paris; resided mostly at Hamburg as a merchant; in 1817 he acquired an interest in lands in northern New York and the town of Pitcairn, St. Lawrence co., is named from him; d. in New York, June, 1844.

PITCHER, NATHANIEL, was in the New York assembly in 1806, 1815, and 1817; in the constitutional convention of 1821, and in 1826, was elected lieutenant governor; he succeeded to governor on the death of De Witt Clinton, Feb. 11, 1828, and held the office for the unexpired term; he was in congress from 1819 to 1823, and from 1831 to 1833; d. at Sandy Hill, Washington co., N. Y., May 25, 1836, a. 59.

PITCHER, DR. ZINA, of Detroit, many years an army surgeon; d. in Detroit, April 5, 1872, a. 75.

PITCHLYNN, JOHN, d. in Mississippi, July, 1835, a. 71; he had lived a long time with the Choctaws, and was an interpreter.

PITKIN, REV. JOHN B., native of Massachusetts and pastor of the First Independent ch. at Richmond; d. at St. Augustine, Fla., Feb. 9, 1835.

PIXLEY, COL. DAVID, was an officer of the revolution, and served at Quebec; was the first settler of Owego, N. Y., in 1790, and d. there Aug. 25, 1807 in his 65th year.

PLANT, DAVID, b. in Stratford, Conn.; grad. at Yale in 1804; was speaker of the house in Conn., in 1819 and 1820; a state senator in 1851, and twice reëlected; lieut. gov. from 1823 to 1827, and in congress from 1827 to 1829; d. at Stratford, Conn., Oct. 18, 1851.

PLATT, ANANIAS, an innkeeper at Lansingburg, N. Y., in 1790 procured from the legislature an exclusive privilege of certain stage routes and did a large passenger business for his day. (*Woodworth's Troy*, 19.)

PLATT, CHARLES, an early settler of Plattsburg, N. Y., first county judge of Clinton co., 1797–1804, and clerk from 1808 to 1823; was in assembly in 1797, was a native of Long Island and a brother of Zephaniah Platt.

PLATT, REV. CHARLES H., D.D., rector of Christ church (Episc.), and chaplain of the grand lodge of New York, A. Y. M.; d. at Binghamton, N. Y., Feb. 25, 1869.

PLATT, ISAAC, journalist, d. in Poughkeepsie, N. Y., June, 1872; he had been an editor about 44 years; in 1827 he established the *Dutchess Intelligencer*, opposed to the Jackson party, and was through the subsequent years a prominent whig and republican partizan.

PLATT, JAMES, d. at Oswego, N. Y., May 8, 1870, a. 83; was state senator in 1852–3; first mayor of the city of Oswego, and at the time of his death, president of the Lake Ontario National Bank.

PLATT, JONAS, a son of Zephaniah Platt, was b. at Poughkeepsie, N. Y., June 30, 1769; studied law with Col. Varick, was admitted to the bar in 1790 and in 1791 settled at Whitesboro, N. Y.; here he was appointed first county clerk of Herkimer and in 1798 of Oneida co.; in 1796 he was chosen to assembly; from 1796 to 1801 was in congress, and from 1810 to 1813 in the state senate; in 1810 ran for governor but was defeated by Tompkins; in 1813 was a member of the council of appointment and Feb. 25, 1814, was appointed justice of the supreme court of New York; in 1821 he was chosen to the state convention from Oneida co.; after the expiration of his term upon the bench of the supreme court, Jan. 29, 1823, he engaged in practice at Utica and afterwards at New York; he d. at Peru, Clinton co., N. Y., Feb. 22, 1834, in his 65th year. (*Street's Council of Revision*, p. 195.)

PLATT, ZEPHANIAH, patentee and early proprietor of Plattsburg, N. Y., was in provincial congress from Dutchess co., and from 1777 to 1783, in the state senate from that county; removed from Poughkeepsie to Plattsburg in 1801, and d. there Sept. 12, 1807. (*Albany Gazette*, Oct. 28, 1807.)

PLEASANTS, HUGH ROGER, the Richmond whig; d. at Richmond, Va., April 27, 1870, a. 58.

PLUMMER, FRANKLIN E., d. in Jackson, Miss., Sept. 24, 1852; representative in congress from 1831 to 1833, and from 1834 to 1835; had been a circuit judge; d. in great destitution.

POHLMAN, REV. WILLIAM J., b. in Albany, Feb. 17, 1812; went as missionary to Borneo, and perished at sea, while passing from Hong Kong to Amoy, in January, 1849. (*Rogers's Hist. Discourse, R. P. D. Church Albany*, 114.)

POLK, CHARLES, native of Delaware and repeatedly chosen to places of trust, being twice governor of the state; he d. in Kent co., Del., Oct. 28, 1857, a. 70. (*Am. Almanac*, 1859, p. 349.)

POLK, EDWARD, president of the senate of Tennessee; d. April 4, 1854.

POLK, COL. WILLIAM, served at the battles of Camden, Eutaw Springs, Brandywine and Germantown; held the office of lieut. col. at the end of the revolution; he was the last surviving field officer of the N. C. line and one of the Mecklenburg signers May 20, 1775; he d. at Raleigh, N. C., Jan. 14, 1834, in his 76th year.

POLLARD, EDWARD A., journalist, and author of southern histories of the late war; d. at Lynchburg, Va., Dec. 17, 1872, a. 45.

POLLARD, HENRY RIVES, editor of the *Southern Opinion;* was assassinated at Richmond, Va., Nov. 24, 1868, in his 35th year; b. in Nelson co., Va., and formerly editor of the *Richmond Examiner and Times.*

POLLARD, RICHARD, formerly chargé to the republic of Chili, and a resident of Albemarle co., Va.; d. at Washington, D. C., Feb. 19, 1851.

POMET, JOSEPH, d. at Natchez, Miss., Aug. 30, 1839, in his 95th year; a native of France.

POMFRET, DR. JAMES E., b. in Preston, Eng., March 26, 1826; became pastor at Haverhill, N. H., in 1853; grad. at Albany Med. Coll. in 1859; settled in that city; was appointed prof. of chemistry in the Albany Female Academy; was a surgeon in the 113th N. Y. vols., surgeon gen. of N. Y., in 1865, and in 1867, prof. of physiology in the Albany Med. college; d. at Albany, Feb. 22, 1869. (*Regents' Report*, 1870, p. 598.)

PONCET, JOSEPH ANTHONY, Jesuit missionary; arrived in Canada, Aug. 1, 1639; prisoner among the Iroquois from Aug. 20, to Oct. 3, 1652; started for Onondaga, Aug. 28, 1657, but recalled at Montreal; left Canada, Sept. 18, 1657; d. at Martinique, June 18, 1675.

POND, SAMUEL M., d. at Bucksport, Me., Jan. 23, 1849; judge of probate for the county of Hancock, and a prominent member of the bar; was long known for his efforts in behalf of the temperance reform, and common school education.

POOLE, FITCH, d. at Peabody, Mass., Aug. 19, 1873, a. 70; he was for many years connected with the press, and his writings were characterized by the same genial spirit of humor and good sense that made him everywhere a welcome guest; he belonged to the Whig party, and was the author of several satirical and pointed ballads, that were much quoted and much enjoyed at the time; among these was *Giles Corey's Dream;* he was thoroughly conversant with the habits and manners of those who lived at the time of the Salem witchcraft, and was the editor of a certain manuscript that turned up at the tearing down of the old First Church, and from its exact similarity to those of a more ancient date was treasured for some time as a rare discovery; Mr. Poole at different times represented the town of Peabody in the legislature; was a member of the school committee and board of selectmen; was editor of *The Danvers Wizzard* when that paper was established in 1859 and retained the position until 1868; he was formerly member of the Jordan Lodge of Free and Accepted Masons; perhaps the matter of greatest interest in his life was his connection with the Peabody Institute; he was the founder of the Mechanics' Institute Library, an institution which Mr. Peabody afterward endowed with his name and $20,000, and for the last seventeen years of his life has been the librarian of that institution, always obliging and attentive, and holding the esteem which he merited. Though not a rich, he was always a liberal man, was a friend and associate of Mr. Peabody when the latter was at home, and was well able to recite to him many of the minor incidents that took place during his absence.

POPE, ANNA, d. in Massachusetts, July 14, 1859, a. 105.

POPE, REV. AUGUSTUS RUSSELL, d. in Somerville, Mass., May 24, 1858, a. 39; he was b. in Boston, Jan. 25, 1819; grad. at Harvard in 1839; studied theology, and was settled in Kingston, Mass., where he resided until 1849, when he was installed at Somerville; he was state agent and lecturer of the Mass. Board of Education for the last two years of his life; he edited the first educational year book, and published several discourses and sermons.

POPE, PATRICK H., in congress from Kentucky from 1833 to 1835; d. at Louisville, Ky., May, 1841.

POPE, WORDEN, one of the oldest citizens of Louisville, Ky.; d. at that place, April, 1838.

PORTER, BRIG. GEN. ANDREW, d. in Paris, France, Jan. 4, 1872; formerly of the U. S. army.

PORTER, AUGUSTUS, b. in Salisbury, Ct., Jan. 18, 1769; was the son of Dr. Joshua P.; in 1806 located at Niagara Falls, where he afterwards resided; he acted a prominent part in the early settlement of the western country; was the first judge of Niagara co.; was a heavy loser from the British invasion of 1813; was a brother of Gen. Peter B. Porter; d. at Niagara Falls, June, 1849. (*Stryker's Am. Reg.*, ii, 504; *Turner's Holland Purchase*, 358, with portrait.)

PORTER, GEORGE, formerly editor of the *N. Y. Spirit of the Times*, and afterwards of the *Picayune;* d. at New Orleans, May 24, 1849.

PORTER, GEORGE W., known for his many inventions, and especially the Porter rifle; d. near Memphis, Tenn., Nov. 7, 1856, a. about 50.

PORTER, JAMES, the Ky. giant; d. in Louisville, Ky., April 23, 1859; was seven feet nine inches high, and weighed 300 pounds.

PORTER, MOSES, of Hadley, Mass.; b. Sept. 19, 1768; was a grandson of the elder Pres. Edwards, and lived a long life in the house in which he was born; he often represented Hadley in the legislature; was a member of the state const. conven. of 1820; held various civil and military offices of trust; d. Feb. 14, 1843, a. 71. (*Goodwin's Notes*, p. 173.)

PORTIER, RT. REV. MICHAEL, D.D.; 1st R. C. bp. of Mobile; b. in Montbrison, France, in 1795; was consecrated bp. of Mobile at St. Louis, Nov. 5, 1826; d. May 14, 1859, a. 64. (*Metropolitan Cath. Almanac*, 1860, p. 260; *Dunigan's Am. Cath. Almanac*, 1860, p. 37.)

POST, REV. REUBEN, native of Vt.; grad. in 1814; studied theology at Princeton, and was ordained pastor of the First Presbyterian ch. in Washington, D. C., where he remained till 1836; was then called to Charleston, and settled as pastor of the Circular ch. in that city, where he remained till his death, Sept. 22, 1858, a. 66.

POTT, BENJAMIN, d. at Pottsville, Pa., Nov. 12, 1868, in his 76th year; was one of the oldest residents of Schuylkill co., and one of the soldiers of the war of 1812.

POTTER, CHANDLER EASTMAN, distinguished as a scholar and jurist in N. H.; d. Aug. 3, 1868, at Flint, Mich.; b. March 7, 1807; grad. at Dartmouth in 1831, and soon commenced the study of the law with Ichabod Bartlett of Portsmouth; from 1844 to 1848 was editor and proprietor of *The Manchester Democrat;* was subsequently connected with *The Farmers' Monthly Visitor*, and *The Granite Farmer and Visitor*, publishing in these journals many biographies of eminent men, and sketches of N. H. hist.; for the preparation of the latter articles, his antiquarian researches gave him facilities which few possessed; as a gentleman, a jurist, a scholar, and a journalist, he was highly respected throughout the state.

POTTER, HENRY, b. in Mecklenburg, Va., in 1765; was appointed judge of the U. S., dist. court of N. C., by Mr. Jefferson, in 1801, and held this office till his death, which occurred in Fayetteville, N. C., Dec. 20, 1857, a. 92.

POTTER, JOHN, d. at Princeton, N. J., Oct. — 1849, a. 84; native of Ireland, but from early life a resident of Charleston, S. C., where he was long a successful merchant; he had lived many years in Princeton, and was of late years principally employed in promoting the Delaware and Raritan canal, and other improvements.

POTTER, PARACLETE, journalist, elder brother of Bishops P. of N. Y., and Pa.; conducted the *Poughkeepsie Journal* nearly thirty years, and was a book-seller; he d. at Worcester, Mass., Feb. 3, 1858, a. 78. (*Hist. Mag.*, ii, 155.)

POTTER, SAMUEL J., senator in cong. from Rhode Island, in 1803–4; d. Oct. 1 1804, a. 54.

POTTER, DR. URIAH, of Fort Plain, N. Y.; d. Dec. 16, 1869, a. 60. (*Transac. N. Y. State Med. Soc.*, 1870, p. 312.)

POTTER, William W., member of congress from the 14th dist. of Pa.; d. at Bellefort, Pa., Oct. 28, 1839.

POUCHOT, ——, French officer in Canada, b. at Grenoble in 1712; was distinguished in the wars of Italy, Flanders and Germany; came to America in the French war; was at Oswego and Ticonderoga, and made a gallant defense at Fort Niagara; in 1760, he was in command at Fort Lewis on Isle Royal, known as Oraconenton by the Indians, and now as Chimney island, 3 miles below Ogdensburg in the St. Lawrence; he made a gallant resistance but was obliged to surrender; this was the last resistance of the French against the English in Canada; he returned to France, wrote a memoir of the war in America, in 3 vols.; narrowly escaped the Bastile, and fell in Corsica, May 8, 1769, while still only captain. (*Hist. Mag.*, vi. 259.)

POWELL, CUTHBERT, d. at Langollen, Loudon, co., Va., May 8, 1849; formerly mayor of Alexandria; represented Loudon co. in the Virginia legislature, and in the 27th congress; was many years a magistrate.

POWELL, HORATIO, M.D., physician, b. in Hartford, Vt.; settled at Malone, N. Y., in 1811; d. Nov. 12, 1849. (*Hough's Hist. St. Law. & Fr. Cos. N. Y.*, p. 605.)

POWELL, JEREMIAH, revolutionary patriot, of North Yarmouth, Me.; was chosen by the provincial cong. in 1774, a member of the council, and in July 1775 an executive counselor, and held several years by annual choice; d. in 1784. (*Bradford's N. E. Biog.*)

POWELL, JOSEPH, Moravian missionary, b. near Whitechurch, Shropshire, Eng., 1710; came to America in 1742; d. at Sichem in the oblong, Dutchess co., N. Y., Sept. 23, 1774; was several years at Wechquadnach, a missionary station in Litchfield co., Ct. (*Moravians in N. Y. and Ct.*)

POWELL, THOMAS, d. at Newburg, N. Y., May 12, 1856, a. 87; b. at Hemstead, Long Island, in 1799; while in business in N. Y., was driven out by the yellow fever, and settled at Newburg, where he engaged in freighting and was the owner of steamers on the Hudson; he took an active interest in the growth and prosperity of Newburg.

POWER, Rev. John, was educated at Maynooth, Ireland, in the class with Father Matthew, the celebrated temperance reformer; he served 32 years as pastor of St. Peter's church, N. Y., and d. April 14, 1849, a. 57.

POWER, Rt. Rev. ———, Roman Catholic bishop of Toronto, C. W., d. Oct. 1, 1847, a. about 42; b. in Halifax, N. S.

POWERS, Charles, of Davenport, Iowa, while returning home from Chicago, d. at Ottawa, Ill., Feb. 3, 1860; b. in Dutchess co., N. Y.; grad. at Middletown, Conn., and settled as a lawyer at Poughkeepsie; in 1855, removed to Davenport, and became an active partner of the banking house of Tallman, Powers & McLean.

POWERS, Hiram, an eminent American sculptor; d. at Florence, Italy, June 27, 1873.

POWERS, James M., formerly canal commissioner in Pa.; d. at Pittsburg, Pa., May 13, 1850.

POZER, d. at Quebec, June 12, 1848, a. 95; he was a native of Welstade in Baden; went to England in 1773, from thence to Phila. and Schoharie, N. Y.; he was a staunch tory and removed to Quebec in 1785, with a large stock of goods and commenced business; he was the largest landholder in that city and was regarded as the Astor of Quebec. (*Stryker's Am. Reg.*, i, 501.)

PRATT, Henry, an eminent shipping merchant of Philadelphia; b. May 14, 1761; son of Matthew, a portrait painter; he amassed a large fortune; was fortunate in the purchase of real estate; d. Feb. 6, 1838. (*Simpson's Eminent Philadelphians*, with portrait.)

PRATT, Capt. Joseph, was commander of several privateers in the revolution, and was remarkably successful; he took the Providence, Capt. Hancock, a brig of 16 six pounders and several rich prizes in one cruise; he made three cruises in a vessel named the Grand Turk, and after the peace, built and launched a large ship at Salem, which he named after his favorite vessel; this ship, under Capt. Benj. Hodge, opened a commerce with the East Indies; Capt. Pratt d. at Oxford, N. H., in 1832. (*Am. An. Reg.*, 1832–3, p. 427.)

PRAY, Dr. Orestes M., d. in New York city, June, 1869.

PREBLE, Mrs. Margaret, d. in Pendleton co., Ky., May 3, 1860, a few days less than 100 years old, leaving numerous descendants.

PRENTISS, George D., d. in Louisville, Ky., Jan. 22, 1870; b. in Preston, Conn., Dec. 18, 1802; grad. at Brown University; studied law but did not practice, and edited the *New England Review* at Hartford, from 1828 to 1831; then went to Kentucky and established the *Louisville Journal*, which he continued to edit till his death; he was a forcible, witty and sarcastic writer.

PRENTISS, Capt. James H., of the 1st U. S. artillery; d. at Point Isabel, of yellow fever, Sept. 22, 1848.

PRESCOTT, Rev. Edward G., rector of the Prot. Epis. church in Salem, N. J.; d. April 11, 1838, a. 38.

PRESCOTT, James, revolutionary statesman, of Groton, Mass.; many years representative in gen. court before the war; he was chosen a counsellor in 1774, but rejected by Gov. Gage, and in 1775 was an executive counsellor; he was in county convention, and prov. congresses, and several years after a representative and counsellor; in 1780 he became a justice of the court of com. pleas for Middlesex co. (*Bradford's N. E. Biog.*)

PRESTON, DR. JONAS, son of Jonas, who emigrated from Wales before the revolution; he settled in the medical practice in Phil., and acquired a fortune of about $400,000; d. in 1836, a. 72; endowed the Preston Retreat with $200,000, as a lying-in hospital. (*Simpson's Eminent Philadelphians.*)

PRICE, STEPHEN, a distinguished tragedian and manager of theatres; d. in N. Y. city, Jan. 20, 1840.

PRICE, GEN. THOMAS, L., d. at Jefferson city, Mo., July 16, 1870; was member of congress in 1861–3, and democratic gov. of Missouri in 1864.

PRINGLE, JAMES, d. July 11, 1840, at Charleston, S. C.; was collector of the port for upwards of 20 years; formerly president of the senate of S. C., and intendant of Charleston.

PRINGLE, JOHN JULIUS, d. at Charleston, S. C., March 7, 1843, a. 90; was speaker of the state house of representatives from 1787 to 1789, and atty. gen. from 1792 to 1801; was a member of state constitutional convention.

PROCTOR, JABEZ, late judge of the probate court, and a councillor of the state; d. at Cavendish, Vt., Nov. 23, 1839.

PROFIT, GEORGE H., d. at Louisville, Ky., Sept. 5, 1847; recently minister to Brazil, and representative in congress from Indiana from 1839 to 1843.

PROILEAU, SAMUEL, revolutionary patriot; b. in Charleston, S. C.; served in the revolution; was captured and sent to St. Augustine, while his family was banished and transported to Phil.; d. in Charleston, March 23, 1813, in his 71st year. (*Rogers's Am. Biog.*)

PROILEAU, S., d. at Pendleton, S. C., May 8, 1839; was formerly judge of the Charleston city court.

PROBASCO, JOHN, b. in N. J., but from boyhood resided in Lebanon, O., where he d. Sept. 18, 1857, a. 43; was a lawyer; in 1840 and twice afterwards, was chosen to the legislature; in 1849 was chosen a judge of the court of com. pleas, which office he held till a change in the consitution; was for a time a distinguished member of the Cincinnati bar.

PROUDFIT, REV. ALEXANDER, d. at Salem, N. Y., Sept. 7, 1831, a. 87.

PROUDFIT, REV. JAMES, pastor of the Asso. Ref. congregation at Salem, N. Y.; d. Oct. 22, 1802; was in the ministry over 50 years.

PROUDFIT, REV. ROBERT, d. at Schenectady, N. Y., Feb. 11, 1860; emeritus prof. of Greek and Latin in Union College for many years.

PRUYN, DR. JOHN M., of Kinderhook; d. Feb., 1866, a. 60. (*Trans. N. Y. State Med. Soc.*, 1867, p. 464.)

PUFFER, REV. ISAAC, b. in Westminster, Mass., June 20, 1784; removed to Otsego co., N. Y., in 1789, and to Watson, N. Y., in 1800; became a M. E. minister in 1809, and labored over a large and newly settled region many years, chiefly in Black River conference; d. in Ogle co., Ill., May 25, 1854; was remarkable for the facility and correctness with which he quoted scripture, always giving the chapter and verse; his citations sometimes exceeded a hundred in a discourse. (*Hough's Hist. Lewis Co. N. Y.*, p. 227.)

PUGH, Ensign Willis, Va.; killed in the revolution, May 1, 1777.

PURCHASE, John, capt. in British army; killed in battle of Plattsburg, Sept. 11, 1814.

PURDY, Elijah, politician; d. in the city of N. Y., Oct. 7, 1871.

PURDY, Dr. Jotham, b. in Spencer, N. Y., May 4, 1799; began practice in 1820; removed from Spencer to Elmira, N. Y., in 1824, and d. there, Aug. 11, 1858. (*Tr. N. Y. State Med. Soc.*, 1860, p. 172.)

PURNELL, Lemuel, d. Nov. 15, 1846, in Queen Anne's co., Md., Nov. 15, 1846, a. 72; late associate judge of the 2d judicial district of Maryland.

PUTNAM, George Peabody, publisher in N. Y. city; d. Dec. 20, 1872; b. at Brunswick, Me., Feb. 21, 1814; went at 14 to Boston, and thence to New York, as a clerk in a bookstore; he afterward entered the employ of John Wiley, whose partner he became about 1840; in 1841 he went to London as representative of the firm, and remained there seven years in charge of the English branch of the house; he was one of the first to build up the business of importing English books, a business which has since been largely developed, and he was probably the first to introduce the sale of American publications into England; during his sojourn in London he wrote and published a book called *American Facts* which, by giving a great deal of information concerning the condition of affairs in the United States, contributed greatly to produce a better understanding and appreciation of this country in English minds; this work was a source of considerable pride to Mr. Putnam from the beneficial influence he felt it had exerted abroad; his most important literary work was the *World's Progress; or, Dictionary of Dates*, which he began at the age of 14 and completed when 22; revising it, however, from time to time, to keep the record even with the time. The last revision, just finished, brings it down to date, and constitutes his last literary work. Mr. Putnam returned to New York from London in 1848, and soon afterward dissolved the partnership with Mr. Wiley and engaged in business by himself; he soon began the publication of Washington Irving's works — his most important enterprise, if the character and number of the volumes, their extensive sale and wide influence are considered, and this proved a very successful venture; among other various standard works which he has published are the writings of J. Fenimore Cooper, Bayard Taylor, Charles Lamb, Thomas Hood, John P. Kennedy, Edgar A. Poe, and others; one of his early publishing enterprises was a library of choice reading, in 25 cent volumes, selected from the best authors, whereby he hoped to bring them within the reach of all classes. This undertaking was only partially successful in a business point of view, but he was partial to the idea till his death. Mr. Putnam early interested himself in the production of fine illustrated books, publishing, among others, the Artists' Edition of *Irving's Sketch Book*, and the *Book of American Scenery;* in 1852, with the assistance of George William Curtis and James Briggs, and others, he established *Putnam's Magazine*, the aim of which was to be, what no other monthly in this country then was, a strictly American magazine; it met with immediate success, and in 1856, while still prospering greatly, was sold to other publishers, who failed in the financial crisis of 1857, when the publication of the magazine was suspended. In 1863, Mr. Putnam retired from active business to become collector of internal revenue, a position which he held till 1866, when, in conjunction with his sons, he formed the publishing house of G. P. Putnam & Sons; the magazine was reëstablished in 1867 and continued till 1870, when it was sold to Scribner & Co., and merged in *Scribner's Monthly*. Mr. Putnam was one of the first members of the Century club, and was for several years chairman of the art committee of the Union League club; he has also been very active in the organization of the Metropolitan Museum of Art, of which he has been honorary superintendent during the past year, beside being busily engaged on the committee for the preparation of a representation of American art at the Vienna exposition. (*N. Y. Tribune.*)

PUTNAM, HARVEY, d. at Attica, N. Y., Sept. 21, 1855, a. 62; was for more than a quarter of a century a leading member of the bar of Genesee co., and a representative in congress from New York from 1847 to 1851; served in the senate in 1843–4–5–6.

PUTNAM, REV. JONATHAN W., b. in Leyden, N. Y., July 31, 1815, and d. in Middlesex, Yates co., N. Y., Sept. 9, 1871. (*Northern Christian Advocate*, Nov. 23, 1871.)

PUTNAM, MOSES, of Danvers, Mass., was 58 years a shoe manufacturer, and d. Sept. 10, 1860, a. 85; he retired from business in 1854.

PYKE, ———, was b. in Nova Scotia in 1774; settled as a lawyer at Quebec; was appointed a prothonotary, received the honor of queen's counsel, and in 1820 was elevated to the bench of the dist. of Montreal as puisne judge; in April, 1839, upon the death of Chief Justice O'Sullivan, he became president of the court, but in 1842 he resigned; he d. at Mount Victory, Vaudreuil, C. E., Feb. 3, 1851, a. 76.

QUARLES, CAPT. AUGUSTUS, killed in battle at Cherrubusco, Mexico, Aug. 20, 1847; was of Southport, Wis., and an officer of merit; his remains were brought home and buried at the expense of the state.

QUASH, FRANCIS DALLAS, native of Charleston, S. C., grad. at Harvard in 1814; studied law, became a planter, and was 18 years in the state legislature; d. in Charleston, S. C., Feb. 17, 1857, a. 63.

QUICK, THOMAS, Indian slayer of the Minisink and Delaware country, b. 1734; became a celebrated hunter and a mortal enemy of the Indians who had murdered his father; d. in 1795 or 6. (*Tom Quick and the Pioneers of Minisink and Wawarsink, Monticello, N. Y.*, 1851, 18mo, pp. 264.)

QUIGGLEY, DANIEL, a citizen of Mobile, Ala., d. March 8, 1860, a. 85; native of New Jersey.

QUIGLEY, EDWARD V., journalist, d. in Williamsburg, N. Y., Nov. 17, 1873, a. 42.

RADCLIFF, THOMAS, a distinguished officer under Wellington in the peninsular war, and commander of the Canadian militia on the western frontier in the patriot war; d. at Kingston, Canada, June 6, 1840, a. 47.

RADIÈRE, MONS. DE LA, one of the four engineers employed in France, Feb. 13, 1777, under authority of congress; was made lieut. col. July 8, and col. Nov. 17, 1777; was retained Jan. 1, 1779, and d. in service that year; the defenses by booms, etc., in the Hudson were against his advice, and he was succeeded by Kosciuszko; his representatives were entitled to the benefit of certain resolutions of congress, Aug. 3, 1785. (*Munsell's Hist. Series*, v, 137.)

RADWAY, JOHN D., patent medicine man, d. at N. Y., March 14, 1870, a. 45; b. in England in 1824; came to America in his 6th year, and at 21, engaged in business as a chemist and druggist; was proprietor of several well known patent medicines.

RAFEIX, PIERRE, Jesuit missionary, arrived in Canada, Sept. 22, 1663; chaplain in Courcelle's expedition in 1665; sent to Cayuga in 1671, thence on Carheil's return to Seneca, where he was in 1679; he was at Quebec in 1702–3.

RAGAN, COL. E. S., d. at Williamsburg, Miss., Aug. 9, 1841; formerly a representative in the state legislature.

RAGUENEAU, PAUL, Jesuit missionary; arrived in Canada, June 28, 1636; superior from 1650 to 1653; sent to Onondaga, July 26, 1657; left March, 1658, and d. at Paris, Sept. 3, 1680.

RAINE, JOHN B., d. at Paris, Ky., April 10, 1860, a. 72; for twenty-four years (with short intervals excepted), president of the Northern Bank of Kentucky.

RAMSEY, JOHN, surgeon, Penn.; d. Sept. 4, 1776, in the rev. service.

RAMSEY, WILLIAM, b. at Sterrett's Gap, Cumberland co., Pa., Sept. 7, 1779; in 1803 was appointed surveyor of that county, and was prothonotary, register, recorder, and clerk of the orphan's court; practiced law with success; in 1826 was elected to congress, and again in 1828 and 1830; d. at Carlisle, Sept. 29, 1831.

RAMSEY, WILLIAM S., b. in Carlisle, Pa., June 10, 1810; educated at Dickinson Coll., but did not graduate; was attaché at London, and after his return, was admitted to the bar in 1832; elected to congress in 1838 and 1840, but d. at Baltimore, Oct. 17, 1840, a few weeks after his last election.

RANDALL, ALEXANDER W., ex-post master general; d. at Elmira, N. Y., July 25, 1872, a. 53.

RANDALL, BENJAMIN, b. in Mass. in 1789; grad. at Boudoin in 1809; studied law, and was admitted to the bar in 1814; practiced law at Bath 45 years, except as withdrawn by public duties; was in the state senate in 1833; in congress from 1839 to 1843, and collector at Bath, under Taylor's appointment; d. at Bath, Oct. 14, 1857.

RANDALL, CHARLES, b. in Sharon, Mass., in 1816; pub. the *Northern Star* many years in R. I., and was state senator in that state; he d. at Warren, R. I., Dec. 11, 1859. (*Hist. Mag.*, iv, 60.)

RANDALL, NICHOLAS P., b. in Stonington, Conn., July 25, 1779; grad. at Yale in 1803; was admitted to the bar and in 1807 located at New Hartford, Oneida co., N. Y.; in 1811 settled in Manlius where he practiced as a lawyer till his death, March 7, 1836. (*Clarke's Onondaga*, ii, 201, with a portrait.)

RANDOLPH, EDWARD, b. in 1754, at Perth Amboy, N. J.; became a printer at New York, and served as an officer in the revolution; settled at Philadelphia after the war, as a merchant, and from small beginnings grew to be one of the most extensive East India merchants of the city; he d. in 1837.

RANDOLPH, SIR JOHN, son of Wm. R., of Warwickshire, Eng., a poor carpenter who came to Va., and by industry acquired a good estate; he was a burgess for Henrico co.; John R. was educated at William and

Mary's Coll.; studied law at Gray's Inn and the Temple; settled in Va., and by his talents gained great eminence; he was speaker of the house of burgesses, treasurer of the colony and representative for Wm. and Mary's Coll.; he d. March, 1737. (*Campbell's Va.*)

RANDOLPH, Richard K., d. in Rhode Island, March 21, 1849, a. 67; was a lawyer and politician, and a native of Virginia.

RANDOLPH, St. George, last of the Randolphs, eldest son of Richard R. and nephew of John R., of Roanoke; was a deaf mute, and from the death of his brother Theodoric Tudor R., in 1814, a hopeless maniac; he d. at Charlotte C. H., Va., Dec. 5, 1857. (*Hist. Mag.*, ii, 36.)

RANDOLPH, Thomas Jefferson, contractor on the Chesapeake and Ohio R. R., killed Aug. 8, 1872, near Hawk's Nest, Fayette co., Va., by a premature blast; he was great grandson of Thomas Jefferson.

RANKIN, Christopher, b. in Washington co., Pa.; was in congress from Mississippi from 1819 to 1826, and d. March 14, 1826.

RANSOM, Epaphroditus, receiver of public moneys at Port Scott., Kan.; d. there Nov. 11, 1859; in 1848 and 1849, he was governor of Michigan.

RASBACH, Frederick Helmer, b. in Herk., July 22, 1847; grad. at Ham. Coll., in 1873; d. at Canastota, N. Y., Oct. 9, 1873.

RATHBUN, Acors, d. at Verona Mills, Oneida co., N. Y., Sept. 15, 1855, in his 84th year; was a pioneer of Verona, and a native of Rhode Island. (*Rome Sentinel.*)

RAVIDEN, James, b. in Kentucky, and an early settler of the White River Valley, was self educated, and became a lawyer; was in congress from Indiana from 1837 to 1841; d. at Cambridge city, Ind.

RAWLINGS, James, d. at Richmond, Va., Feb. 19, 1838; president of the Farmers' Bank of Virginia.

RAY, Dr. Charles H., of the *Chicago Post;* d. Sept. 24, 1870.

RAY, Gilbert, revolutionary soldier; b. at Wrentham, Mass.; lived 20 years in Tinmouth, Vt.; settled in North Russell, N. Y., March 17, 1849, in his 85th year.

RAY, Jean, gov. of Surinam, from July 6, 1735, till his death in 1737.

RAY, Martin M., prominent lawyer at Indianapolis, Ind.; d. there Aug. 5, 1872.

RAYMOND, Benjamin, pioneer agent and surveyor of Potsdam, N. Y.; b. at Richmond, Mass., Oct. 19, 1774; was first settler at Potsdam in 1803, founded the St. Lawrence Acad. in 1816; was an early surveyor, and explored a canal route from Lake Champlain to the St. Lawrence; he d. at St. George's, Del., while surveying the Del. & Chesapeake canal, Sept. 26, 1824. (*Hough's Hist. St. Law. & Fr. Cos., N. Y.*, p. 605, with portrait.)

RAYMOND, Jarvis, father of Henry J. R., of the *N. Y. Times;* d. at Detroit, Sept., 1868; formerly resided in Lima, N. Y., and in Ypsilanti, Mich.

RAYNORD, Capt. James, an officer of the revolution; d. in Westchester, N. Y., Aug. 9, 1842, a. 88.

READ, Almon H., d. in Montrose, Susq. co., Pa., June 3, 1843; a member in congress, a. 33; native of Vermont, and a grad. of Williams

Coll.; in 1814, removed to Montrose, Pa., and became a lawyer; in 1827, was elected to the legislature, and five years afterwards became a member of the senate; in 1840 was appointed state treasurer, and afterwards elected to fill a vacancy in congress.

READ, AMASA, d. at Baton Rouge, La., June 10, 1849, a. 34; b. in Ohio; grad. at Ohio Univ., and in 1837, removed to La., where he was soon chosen a professor in the college at Baton Rouge; he soon after engaged in law practice; was made state attorney for the parish; a member of the state convention for revising the constitution and a member of the legislature; he took great interest in the cause of education, drafted the bill which became a law, and at the time of his death held a commission to select and report a site for the state seminary required by the new constitution.

READ, HENRY E., b. in Larue co., Ky., in 1824; served in the Mexican war; studied law, and was in the confederate congress at Richmond from Kentucky; committed suicide at Louisville, Ky., Nov. 9, 1868.

READ, REV. THOMAS, d. in Montgomery co., Md., Jan. 5, 1838, a. 90; was 40 years rector of Prince George's parish.

READ, THOMAS BUCHANAN, d. in N. Y. city, May 11, 1872; b. in Chester co., Pa., March 12, 1822; his instincts for art were awakened at an early period, and when only 17 years old, he entered the studio of a sculptor in Cincinatti, intending to make that his profession for life; was diverted from this purpose, however, by the superior attractions of painting, although in after life, he occasionally indulged in the practice of sculpture as an amateur, among the fruits of which was an admirable portrait bust of Gen. Sheridan, which Am. visitors in Rome will remember as a striking ornament of his studio; in 1841 removed to N. Y., where he commenced his career as a painter, and subsequently, after a brief residence in Boston, settled in Phil. in 1846; his first visit to Europe was made in 1850, since which time, with the exceptions of intervals mostly spent in Cin., his home was in Florence and Rome, where he was the centre of a large social circle, dispensing an elegant hospitality on the most generous scale, and unwearied in his attentions to Americans who made a temporary sojourn in those capitals; his studio in Rome especially, during the last few years, was the resort of numerous American and English visitors, together with many distinguished personages from various European countries, who learned to prize his portraits and other productions of his pencil for the delicate refinement of their execution and the soft ideal charm which he threw around his favorite subjects; his chief pleasure was in the delineation of scenes of aërial lightness and grace, though diversified at times by such pieces as his vigorous portrait of Sheridan and his horse, which has attained almost equal celebrity with his singularly popular poem on *Sheridan's Ride;* his most successful paintings are, perhaps, Undine, The Lost Pleiad, The Star of Bethlehem, and others of a similar character, which exhibit a peculiar unity of conception amid every variety of detail; was also known by his poetry, which for the most part presents the same traits as his paintings, and which has given him an honorable rank among the minor poets of this country; his first collection of poems was published in Boston in 1847, which was followed by a volume of *Lays and Ballads* in 1848, and an illustrated edition of his poems in 1853; two years later he brought out his most elaborate poem, *The New Pastoral;*

43

The Home by the Sea was issued in 1856, and a new collective ed. of his poems in 1860; of his miscellaneous productions, the patriotic lyric of *Sheridan's Ride*, written in 1864, has attracted the most attention, both by the interest of its subject and the fervor of its composition. (*N. Y. Tribune.*)

READE, SAMUEL J., d. at Mount Holly, N. J., Oct. 2, 1836, a. 65.

REAMER, DAVID D., iron manufacturer in Lewis co., N. Y.; d. in Watertown, N. Y., Aug. 12, 1858. (*Hough's Hist. Lewis Co. N. Y.*, p. 98.)

REDDING, ANDERSON, revolutionary soldier of Monroe co., Ga.; d. Feb. 9, 1843, a. 80. (*White's Hist. Ga.*, p. 563.)

REECE, REV. RICHARD, one of the oldest preachers of the Wesleyan ch., and a representative from that body to the Meth. Ep. ch. in the U. S.; d. in England, April 26, 1850.

REDPITH, LIEUT. JOHN, N. C., killed Oct. 13, 1777.

REED, REV. FITCH, b. March 28, 1795; d. at Ithaca, N. Y., Oct. 10, 1871. (*Northern Christian Advocate* Nov. 9, 1861.)

REED, COL. ISAAC G., b. in Littleton, Mass., Nov. 16, 1783; grad. at Harvard in 1803, and settled at Waldoboro, Me., as a lawyer in 1808, where he acquired a large practice; was chief justice of the court of sessions, county treasurer, inspector of state prison, post master 12 years, and delegate to the convention of 1820; was many years in the state legislature, and author of the state seal of Maine; d. Feb. 26, 1847.

REED, JOHN, was for 20 years president judge of the Cumberland dist., La., and filled several other offices of trust; he represented Westmoreland co., in the senate, and about the close of his term was appointed pres. judge of the courts of Adams, Cumberland and Perry, which office he held about twenty years; after leaving the bench he resumed the practice of the law, and he was a professor in the law school attached to Dickinson College; he d. at Carlisle, Pa., Jan. 19, 1850, a. 64.

REED, TIMOTHY, d. in Barnstable, Mass., Jan. 12, 1855, a. 61; b. in Warwick, Mass.; settled as a lawyer in Winchester, N. H., but removed to Yarmouth, Mass., in 1829, and became a law partner with Gov. Reed; was afterwards cashier of the Barnstable Bank, register of probate, and at the time of his death was clerk of the courts for the county.

REED, WILLIAM, an eminent merchant and native of Mass.; in congress from 1811 to 1815; president of the Sabbath School Union, of Mass. and of the Am. Tract Soc.; vice president of Am. Education Soc.; member of several boards of charitable and educational objects; gave $17,000 to Dartmouth Coll.; $10,000 to Amherst Coll.; $——— to A. B. C. F. M.; $9,000 to the 1st church and soc. of Marblehead; $7,000 to 2d ch. do; and $5,000 to library of Theol. Sem., Andover; d. at Marblehead, Feb. 18, 1837.

REEDER, ABNER, d. at Trenton, N. J., Oct. 25, 1841, a. 75.

REES, JAMES, a pioneer of western N. Y.; settled at Geneva, about 50 years before his death, which occurred March 24, 1851, a. 86.; he was deputy quarter master gen., under Washington in the whisky rebellion of western Pa.

REESE, REV. DANIEL E., one of the oldest Meth. Epis. ministers in Baltimore; d. Aug. 17, 1849.

REESE, REV. WM. J., d. of cholera at Buffalo, N. Y., Sept. 6, 1834.

REGNIER, PIERRE, lieut col. of N. Y. troops in the revolution; removed to New Orleans after the war; was employed as a police officer; d. there in the summer of 1810. (*Bleeker's Order Book*, p. 26.)

REID, REV. HORACE H., formerly rector of St. Stephen's ch. at Millburn, N. J.; d. March 17, 1860, at Geneva, Switzerland, a. 37. (*Vincent's Semi-An. Register*, p. 190.)

REID, SIR WILLIAM, K.C.B., maj. gen. in the British army, and for a time employed in Barbadoes; was gov. of Bermuda, Barbadoes, and Malta; author of a work on the Law of Storms; d. in England, Oct. 21, 1858.

REIGART, EMANUEL C., d. at Lancaster, Pa., Dec. 17, 1870, a 74; b. in that place in 1795; admitted to the bar in 1822; member of the convention of 1837, and candidate for gov. on the native American ticket in 1847.

REILLEY, DR. B. S., acting asst. surgeon, U. S. A.; d. of yellow fever at Rio Grande city, Texas, Sept. 20, 1867.

REINICK, CHRISTOPHER, surgeon, Penn.; d. in the revolutionary service, Sept. 21, 1777.

RENSHAW, REV. CHARLES, d. in Richmond, Mass., Jan. 8, 1860; served in the navy in his youth; became religious, studied theology, and went on a mission to Jamaica; preached at Phil., and came north on account of the climate, and had resided at Richmond some six years.

REYNOLDS, BENJAMIN, b. in Caroline co., Va.; served towards the close of the revolution; settled in S. C., and afterwards in Jones co., Ga., where he d. a. 73.

REYNOLDS, EDWARD, d. at Lafayette, Ind., Aug. 13, 1868, a. 92; was father of Maj. Gen. J. J. Reynolds, and of W. F. Reynolds, formerly pres. of the Lafayette and Indianapolis rail road.

REYNOLDS, DR. HENRY, a native of Columbia co., N. Y., and son of Joel J. Reynolds; studied medicine with Dr. Daniel Hicks of Northumberland, and grad. at Fairfield in 1810; was elected pres. of the Saratoga Co. Med. Soc. in 1853; d. at Wilton, Dec. 20, 1857, a. 69. (*Tr. N. Y. State Med. Soc.*, 1858, p. 47.)

REYNOLDS, JOHN, d. at Whitehall, N. Y., Sept 16, 1840, a. 100; was pensioned as a lieut. of the army.

REYNOLDS, DR. JOHN HENRY, of Saratoga co., N. Y.; b. in Wilton, Sar. co., N. Y. Aug. 17, 1828, and d. in that town, April 3, 1870. (*Transac. N. Y. State Med. Soc.*, 1872, p. 349.)

RHINELANDER, DR. JOHN R., of N. Y. city, d. May 8, 1857, a. 65.

RHOADS, SAMUEL, an original member of the Am. Phil. Soc.; d. April? 29, 1784.

RIBAS, FLORENCIO, Venezuelan consul at N. Y.; April 9, 1873, in N. Y. city; was instrumental in introducing into Caraccas in a great measure, the police and school systems of the United States.

RICE, J. W., d. in Mobile, Ala., Feb. 25, 1857, a. 35; a member of the state senate, and an accomplished gentleman and scholar.

RICE, VICTOR MOREAU, b. in Mayville, N. Y., April 5, 1818; grad. at Alleghany Coll., Meadville, in 1841; studied law, but became a teacher; was supt. of schools for Buffalo, and in 1854 chosen first superintendent of public instruction of the state of New York, and held 3 years; was in assembly in 1861; again chosen supt. of public instruction, in Feb., 1862, and April, 1865; at the end of this six years' service, he went to New York city, and became pres. of the Guardian Savings Institution; d. at Oneida, N. Y., Oct. 17, 1869.

RICH, JOSIAH, d. in Denmark, N. Y., June 24, 1831, a. 92.

RICHARDS, ALEXANDER, agent and collector of customs; b. at New London, Ct.; went to N. J., and in 1803 to Madrid, N. Y., where in 1811 he became dep. collector; he d. at Waddington, N. Y., Oct. 16, 1834, a. 69. (*Hough's Hist. St. Law. & Fr. Cos. N. Y.*, p. 609.)

RICHARDS, BENJAMIN W., son of William; b. at Batsto iron works, Burlington co., N. J., in Nov., 1797; grad. at Princeton at the age of 19; became a merchant in Philadelphia; served in both houses of the legislature, and in 1830 and 1831 was elected mayor; was prominently concerned in various financial affairs, and was actively engaged in promoting the public schools. (*Simpson's Eminent Philadelphians.*)

RICHARDS, GAY, one of the oldest merchants in the city of New York; d. March 28, 1873, a. 85.

RICHARDS, DEA. JAMES, d. in Plainfield, Mass., March 1, 1842, a. 85.

RICHARDSON, CAPT. ADDISON, of the Union line of Havre packets; d. in New York city, Nov. 27, 1871.

RICHARDSON, DANIEL, d. in Tyngsboro, Mass., Feb. 12, 1842, a. 59; counselor at law, and one of the oldest members of the Middlesex bar; he was a member of the general court several years, and served both in the house and senate.

RICHARDSON, GEORGE R., attorney general of Maryland; d. at Baltimore, Md., Feb. 10, 1851.

RICHARDSON, JAMES, d. in Dedham, Mass., June 7, 1858, a. 86; b. in Medfield, Mass., Oct. 6, 1771; grad. at Harvard in 1797; studied law with Fisher Ames, and was for a time his partner; a state senator in 1813, in the convention of 1820, in the Executive Council in 1834–5, and often honored by his fellow citizens by being chosen to places of trust; was a man of scholarly tastes and well acquainted with classical literature and the early English poets.

RICHARDSON, J. B., d. on St. Mary's river near Fort Wayne, Ind., Aug. 13, 1841, a. about 80; was principal chief of the Miami nation and left a large estate and $200,000 in specie.

RICHARDSON, COL. JOHN, b. in Taneytown, Md., Dec. 19, 1780, and d. in Auburn, N. Y., April 20, 1849; was a furniture manufacturer; in the war of 1812, raised a rifle company, and served on the Niagara frontier. (*Hall's Auburn*, 570.)

RICHARDSON, JOHN F., prof. of literature in the University of Rochester, N. Y.; d. Feb. 10, 1868, a. 60; b. in Oneida co., N. Y.; author of valuable works on Latin pronunciation.

RICHARDSON, JOHN P., b. in Vernon, N. Y.; Feb. 7, 1808; pursued classical and theological studies, at Hamilton, where he became tutor, and then prof. of Latin; in 1850 became prof. at Rochester University; d. Feb. 10, 1868. (*Regents' Report*, 1869, p. 810.)

RICHARDSON, JOHN S., president of the S. C. law court of appeals, and a prominent member of the bar; d. at Charleston, S. C., May 11, 1850, a. 73; he had been a member and speaker of the house of representatives of S. C.; attorney general of the state; was elected to congress from the Sumter dist. in 1820, but from an unforeseen exigency in his private affairs he declined to qualify and retained his seat on the bench.

RICHARDSON, JOSEPH L., b. in Frederick co., Md., in 1776; came to Cayuga, co., N. Y., in 1802; settled in Auburn as a lawyer in 1805; in the war of 1812, was paymaster; in 1827, was appointed first judge of Cayuga co., and held till 1846; d. in Auburn, April, 1853. (*Hall's Auburn*, p. 564.)

RICHARDSON, TILLEY, a soldier of the revolution; removed from New Hampshire to Watertown, N. Y.; d. there, Jan. 14, 1852, a. 93.

RICHMOND, JONATHAN, d. in Aurora, N. Y., July 29, 1853, a. 79; one of the pioneers of western N. Y.; in 1813, was United States collector; in 1818, a member of congress.

RIDDLE, COL. THOMAS, member elect of the state senate; d. at Springfield, Ala. Aug., 1840.

RIDGELY, RANDOLPH, brevet capt.; killed at Monterey, Oct. 27, 1846, by a fall from a horse.

RIDGLEY, HENRY MOORE, d. at Dover, Del., Aug. 7, 1847, a. 69; was an eminent lawyer, and for many years in public life; was twice elected to congress, and on the death of Mr. Van Dyke, in 1827, he succeeded him in the senate of the United States.

RIDGEWAY, ROBERT, member of congress from Virginia; d. Oct. 17, 1870.

RIGGS, SAMUEL, d. in New York, Dec. 26, 1852, a. 52; was a prominent merchant and banker.

RIKER, LIEUT. ABRAHAM, N. Y., killed, May 7, 1778.

RIKER, RICHARD, formerly recorder of the city of New York; d. Sept. 26, 1842, a. 69; he had held this important office nearly 30 years.

RILEY, CAPT. JOHN, d. in Dover, N. H., May 21, 1842, a. 61; he had held several town offices, and served in the legislature.

RILEY, PERRY, shot by Geo. W. Swope, a state senator of Kentucky, Aug. 3, 1874, in a quarrel growing out of an election.

RIPLEY, HEZEKIAH, late judge of probate for Windham co., Conn.; d. at Windham, Nov. 11, 1836.

RISING, REV. FRANKLIN S., sec. of the Am. Church Missionary Soc.; lost in the collision and burning of the steamers North America and United States, on the Ohio river, Dec. 4, 1868.

RITCHIE, WILLIAM F., many years editor of the *Richmond Examiner*; d. at Washington, D. C., Oct. 2, 1868.

RITTENHOUSE, CLAUS or NICHOLAS, first paper maker in British America; came from Holland in 1687 or 1688, and built a paper mill at Germantown, Pa.

RITTER, JACOB, JR., b. Jan. 2, 1784; was a merchant, and made several voyages to the East and West Indies, and to South America; met with a serious accident in 1832, which disabled him from active life; d. June 27, 1840. (*Simpson's Eminent Philadelphians.*)

RITTER, John, d. Nov. 24, 1831, in Reading, Pa.; representative in congress from Pennsylvania, from 1843 to 1847.

RITZIUS, M., d. in Tennessee, June, 1860; is said to have written down his sensations while dying. (*Vincent's Semi-An. Register*, p. 619.)

RIVERS, Dr. Henry W., d. at Providence, R. I., Dec. 3, 1869, a. 50; was educated at Harvard, and the Penn. U.; practiced at Providence; was an army surgeon in the late war, in N. C., at Harpers Ferry, and at the head quarters of the army of the Potomac.

RIVES, Dr. Landon C., d. at Cincinnati, O.; June 3, 1870, a. 79.

RIVES, Robert, d. at Oak Ridge, Nelson co., Va., March 9, 1845, a. 81; was the father of Hon. William C. Rives.

RIZO, Leopold, one of the victims of the Virginius expedition; shot at Santiago de Cuba, Nov. 7, 1873, a. 27; son of a wealthy planter and lawyer.

ROACH, Isaac, b. in Phil. county, Feb. 24, 1786; entered the army in 1812, and served with honor in the war; in 1813 became captain in the 33d Infantry; in 1815 was transferred to the artillery; in 1823 was made brevet major; in 1824 resigned; in 1838 was elected mayor of Phil., and some time afterwards was appointed treasurer of the mint; d. Dec. 29, 1848.

ROBARDS, Col. William, d. in Granville, N. C., June 17, 1842; he was formerly public treasurer, and held various state offices.

ROBARDS, William A., attorney general of Missouri; d. of cholera, at St. Louis, Aug., 1852, a. 32.

ROBB, Rev. Henry, d. at Washington, D. C., Feb. 25, 1869, a. 78; was chief clerk in the treasury department under Gen. Jackson, having served on his staff at New Orleans.

ROBBINS, Amos, ex-senator from New Jersey; d. at New Brunswick, N. J., June 27, 1871; was formerly collector of customs at Perth Amboy.

ROBBINS, Archibald, was b. in Wethersfield, Ct.; was a mariner; captured in the war of 1812, and detained 18 months at Halifax, as a prisoner of war; in May, 1815, he sailed with Capt. James Riley in the brig Commerce and was wrecked on the coast of Africa, where he was captured by the Arabs and held 19 months as a slave, and until redeemed by the English consul at Mogadore; his sufferings are familiar to the readers of *Riley's Narrative;* after some years service at sea, he settled in his native village, where he was post master; in 1836, he removed to Solon, O., became the first p. m. there, and d. Dec. 27, 1859, a. 67.

ROBERTS, Charles, a native of Oxfordshire, Eng., but who had resided nearly 80 years in America; d. in Berkeley county, Va., in 1796, a. 116; during his long life he had not known sickness, and rode to church alone two years before his death; he d. while eating his supper, without any previous indisposition. (*Kirby's Museum*, ii, 273.)

ROBERTS, Elijah J., a native of western New York; while young edited the *Western Courier* at Homer, N. Y., and after, other papers; he removed to Michigan where he held the office of adjutant general and member of the house of rep., and at the time of his death he was a state senator; he d. at Detroit, April 30, 1851, a. about 55 years. (*Stryker's Am. Reg.*, vi, 229; *Am. Almanac*, 1852, p. 342.)

ROBERTS, DR. GEORGE C. M., LL.D., minister of the Meth. Epis. church, and physician; d. in Baltimore, Jan. 15, 1870, a. 64.

ROBERTS, MAJ. JOHN, d. in Rappahannock co., Va., Nov. 30, 1843, a. 85; served in the revolution, in which he attained the rank of major; and negotiated for the exchange of prisoners after the battle of Saratoga, was member of the legislature 13 years.

ROBERTS, JONATHAN, d. in Phil., Pa., July, 1854, a. 83; b. in 1771, and in the early part of this century in the state legislature, where he served with distinction in both houses; was in congress from 1811 to 1814; in 1814, elected to the U. S. senate, and served till 1841, when he was appointed collector of the port of Phil. by Pres. Harrison, but was removed by Pres. Tyler.

ROBERTS, JOSEPH, d. in Phil., Pa., April 23, 1856, a. 81; one of the trustees under the will of Stephen Girard, and cashier of Stephen Girard's Bank; trustee of the first bank of the United States the affairs of which he assisted in closing up.

ROBERTS, CAPT. MOSES, Mass., killed Feb. 11, 1780.

ROBERTS, COL. OWEN, S. C., d. in the rev. service, June 20, 1779

ROBERTSON, ALEXANDER, early printer in N. Y., Albany and Norwich, Ct.; loyalist, and settled in Nova Scotia after the revolution; d. 1784.

ROBERTSON, GILBERT, British consul at Phil.; d. at that place, Oct. 1836, a. 78.

ROBIE, COL. OLIVER P., formerly of the U. S. army; d. by suicide in San Francisco, Cal., March 16, 1874.

ROBIE, SAMUEL BRADSTREET, d. at Halifax, N. S., Jan. 3, 1858, a. 87; was the oldest member of the Halifax bar, and had been master of the rolls of the court of chancery of Nova Scotia.

ROBINSON, DR. BENJAMIN, d. near Fayetteville, N. C., March 8, 1857, a. 81; was a medical practitioner 52 years, was formerly mayor of Fayetteville, and once U. S. marshal for Florida; in 1825 he was appointed by Pres. Adams to treat with the Southern Indians; b. in Benington, Vt., Feb., 1776.

ROBINSON, HEZEKIAH D., d. at Bedford, N. Y., Sept. 19, 1870, a. 42.

ROBINSON, MAJ. JAMES, d. in Tuscaloosa co., Ala., Aug. 28, 1838, in his 79th year; better known as Horse Shoe Robinson, the hero of Mr. Kennedy's novel of that name.

ROBINSON, JOHN, the oldest merchant in Charleston, S. C.; d. at that place May 19, 1849, in his 74th year; he was 53 years in trade. (*Stryker's Am. Reg.*, ii, 503.)

ROBINSON, JOHN M., d. at Ottawa, Ill., April 26, 1843, a. 50; was one of the judges of the supreme court of Illinois, and twelve years (1830 to 1842) a senator in congress; he had been elected one of the judges of the supreme court not long before his death.

ROBINSON, ROBERT, was appointed searcher of the customs in Newport, R. I., about 1706; d. at Narraganset, R. I., Jan. 8, 1761, a. 84.

ROBINSON, THOMAS, member of congress from Delaware from 1839 to 1841; d. in Sussex co., Delaware, Oct. 28, 1843.

ROBINSON, REV. WILLIAM, got involved while in youth and came to America; taught in N. J., and was ordained by the presbytery of New Brunswick, as a preacher on the frontiers of Va.; d. at St. George's, Del., April, 1746. (*Miller's Life of J. Rodgers*, p. 36.)

ROBINSON, WILLIAM JR., d. at Pittsburg, Pa., Feb. 25, 1868, in his 83d year; son of a pioneer settler; grad. at Princeton; a lawyer and an early friend of rail road improvements, and several years pres. of the Pittsburg, Fort Wayne and Chicago rail road co.

ROBY, DR. JOSEPH, b. in Boston; grad. at Brown University, in 1828; studied medicine, and settled in Boston; was prof. of anatomy at the same time, at the Dartmouth and Bowdoin Med. Schools, and also lectured upon theory and practice; was appointed prof. of anatomy and physiology in the University of Md., and spent the last years of his life there; d. in Baltimore, June 3, 1860, a. 51.

ROCHESTER, NATHANIEL, b. in Westmoreland, Va., Feb. 21, 1752; settled in N. C., and served in the rev.; was a member of the provincial conven. of N. C.; became a maj. of militia, in active service; was in the conven. at Halifax that prepared a state constitution in S. C.; became col.; was after the war clerk of the court, but soon engaged in mercantile business at Phil., and then at Hagerstown, Md.; became largely concerned in buying wheat, and established rope factories; in May 1785, visited Ky. to look after lands held by himself and partners; went again in 1800, and the same year with others visited western N. Y.; in 1802 bought a hundred acre lot now in the city of Rochester, and afterwards other lands in Livingston co.; in 1810 settled in Dansville, N. Y., and built a large paper mill, and other extensive improvements, and made extensive purchases of land; in 1818 took up his residence in Rochester, N. Y., then a village; took an active interest in the construction of the Erie canal; was first county clerk of Monroe co., in 1821, and in assembly in 1822; in 1824 was elected first pres. of the Bank of Rochester, but retired from active business soon after, on account of declining health and the growing infirmities of age; d. May 17, 1831. (*O'Reilly's Rochester*, with portrait.)

ROCKWELL, PHILO, an early merchant of Martinsburg, N. Y., and afterwards of Utica; d. at Utica of cholera, Aug. 13, 1832.

ROCKWELL, THOMAS, cashier of the Branch Bank at Utica, N. Y.; d. Aug. 19, 1849, in his 74th year.

ROCKWELL, WILLIAM, d. New Utrecht, N. Y., July 26, 1856, a. about 56; b. in Sharon, Conn.; grad. at Yale in 1822; studied law and settled in Brooklyn; in Nov., 1853 was chosen judge of the supreme court of N. Y., and held this trust at the time of his death.

ROCKWELL, DR. WILLIAM, of N. Y. city; d. Dec. 30, 1868, a. 68. (*Transac. N. Y. State Med. Soc.*, 1869, p. 256.)

ROCKWELL, WILLIAM J., d. in Harford co., Md., Jan. 23, 1870; was U. S. dist. judge for Georgia; before the rebellion; was a prominent free mason.

RODDAN, REV. JOHN T., ordained R. C. priest at Rome; in 1848, took charge of the ch. at Quincy, and in 1865 of St. Vincent's ch., Boston; d. Dec. 3, 1858, a. 42. (*Metropolitan Cath. Almanac*, 1860, p. 261.)

RODMAN, THOMAS I., brev. brig. gen. U. S. A., and inventor of the Rodman gun; d. at Rock Island Arsenal, June 7, 1871, a. 75.

RODMAN, WILLIAM, b. in Bensalem, Bucks co., Pa., Oct. 7, 1756; was of the Society of Friends, but served in the war, and raised a company to put down the whisky rebellion of 1798; was in congress from 1811 to 1813, and d. at the place of his birth, July 27, 1824.

RODMAN, W. M., d. in Providence, R. I., Dec. 11, 1868; was mayor of Providence in 1857–8.

ROGERS, REV. AMMI, b. in Branford, Ct., May 26, 1770; grad. at Yale in 1790, and was ordained a deacon in Trinity ch., N. Y., June 24, 1792, and a priest, Oct. 19, 1794, and preached in N. Y. city, Ballston and Schenectady, N. Y., Branford, etc., Ct.; was imprisoned at Norwich, Ct., two years. (*Memoirs written by himself.*)

ROGERS, CHARLES O., proprietor of the *Boston Journal;* d. at Boston, April 15, 1869.

ROGERS, DAVID, Col. in the Va. line, while ascending the Ohio, in Oct., 1779, was killed by a party of Indians, near the mouth of the Licking. (*Hist. Mag.*, iii, 267.)

ROGERS, EDWARD, b. in Conn.; studied law and settled in Madison, Madison co., N. Y.; was in congress from 1843 to 1845, was many years a county judge, and d. in Galway, N. Y., May 23, 1857, a. 70.

ROGERS, JONATHAN P., of Boston, d. in Roxbury, Mass., Nov. 26 1846, a. 45; b. in Wakefield, N. H., was a lawyer, and began practice in Bangor, Me.; was a member of the Maine senate, and for several years was attorney general; removed to Boston about four years before his death. (*Am. Almanac*, 1848, p. 350.)

ROGERS, JOSEPH, a judge of the county court; d. at Waterford, Gloucester co., N. J., Oct. 12, 1840.

ROGERS, REV. JOSHUA M., first rector of St. Paul's church, West Turin, N. Y.; b. in Hudson, N. Y., May 15, 1782; was for a time in Utica, and in 1851, went to Easton, Pa., where he d. March 1, 1858. (*Hough's Hist. Lewis Co.*, p. 248.)

ROGERS, JOHN, commodore in the navy, and senior commander in the American navy; d. at Philadelphia, Aug. 1, 1838; was for fifteen months a resident of the Naval Asylum, and the greater part of the time in close confinement as a maniac.

ROGERS, CAPT. JOHNSON, d. April 16, 1841; his wife Jemima D., d. Dec. 3, 1832; he served in the revolution, and in 1797 was one of the pioneers in beginning a settlement in the place where he died.

ROGERS, THOMAS, d. in New York city, April 19, 1856, a. 64; b. in Conn., and a well known manufacturer of cotton machinery; turned his attention to the construction of iron work and machinery for rail roads; in 1835, begun the manufacture of locomotives, in the construction of which he excelled.

ROGERS, REV. THORNTON, d. in Albemarle co., Va., Aug. 6, 1835, a. about 37.

ROLFE, JOHN, a Canadian statesman; d. Oct. 20, 1870, a. 84.

ROLFE, THOMAS, son of Pocahontas, the Indian maiden who saved the life of Capt. Smith of Va., in 1607; he became a prominent and wealthy citizen of Va., and left a daughter; he was buried at Farmingdale, Prince George co., Va.

ROMAINE, Ralph, d. at Big Pond, Franklin township, Bergen co., Pa., April 17, 1860, a. 89; was a soldier in 1812.

ROMAYNE, Dr. Nicholas, d. in New York city, July 20, 1817, a. 61.

ROOSEVELT, James, d. in New York city, Feb., 1847, a. 88; was formerly a prominent citizen of New York.

ROOT, Prof. Edward Walstein, b. at Clinton, N. Y., July 4, 1841, and son of Prof. Oren Root, of Hamilton Coll.; grad. at Hamilton in 1862; went to Germany to continue his studies, and on his return in 1865 was appointed assist. prof. of analytical chemistry at the school of mines in N. Y. city; in 1868, became prof. of agricultural chemistry at Hamilton Coll.; d. at Clinton, N. Y., Nov. 15, 1870. (*Regents' Report*, 1873, p. 639.)

ROPER, William P., judge of the 1st judicial dist. of Ky.; d. Aug. 11, 1833.

ROSA, John H., of Fishkill, N. Y.; one of the projectors of the Bank of Fishkill, and for years its vice pres.; d. Sept. 18, 1860, a. 57.

ROSE, Robert S., a representative from N. Y., in cong. from 1823 to 1827, and from 1829 to 1831; d. at Waterloo, N. Y., Nov. 24, 1835, a. 63 years.

ROSE, William J., on the editorial staff of the *N. Y. Herald*; d. in Brooklyn, April 6, 1871.

ROSECRANTS, Rev. Abraham, b. and educated in Germany; settled in German Flats, N. Y., about 1754; and labored among the Germans of the Mohawk valley extensively; married a sister of Gen. Herkimer; d. on Fall Hill in the town of Little Falls about the close of the last century, and was buried near his brother, the first German minister of the upper Mohawk; their graves were within the church. (*Benton's Herkimer Co.*, p. 404.)

ROSECRANTS, George, son of Rev. Abraham R., b. Nov. 15, 1764, on Fall hill near Little Falls, N. Y.; his mother was a sister of Gen. Herkimer; in 1801, he served in the state convention; in 1805, he became co. judge, and held till 1821; in 1812, he was a presidential elector; in 1817–18, he was in assembly; in 1819–20–21–22, in the state senate; d. at the place of his birth, Dec. 21, 1838, a. 74; he had three brothers, Abraham, Joseph and Nicholas. (*Benton's Herkimer Co.*, p. 356.)

ROSECRANTS, Mortimer, brevet capt. 5th infantry, d. at Ypsilanti, Mich., Oct. 7, 1848, a. 29; grad. at West Point in 1741; was distinguished in the Mexican war, especially in the battle of Cherrubusco.

ROSS, Henry H——, b. May 9, 1790; was son of Daniel Ross, and grandson of William Gilliland, the pioneer of the Champlain valley; was highly educated in Montreal and grad. in 1808 from Columbia Coll.; studied law with David B. Ogden; andse ttled on the frontier in his native village Essex, in Essex co., N. Y.; he occupied a commanding position in all the affairs of the region; was a member of the 19th congress; was elected co. judge in 1847; was president of the electoral coll. of N. Y., in 1848; was in the campaign of Plattsburg in 1814, acting on the staff of Gen. Macomb; was subsequently a brigadier and major general in the state militia; d. at Essex, Sept. 13, 1862. Judge Ross, on the death of Samuel Jones, was tendered and declined the office of chancellor.

ROSSEAU, Lovell H., brig. gen. U. S. A.; brevet maj. gen., d. at New Orleans, Jan. 8, 1869; b. in Lincoln co., Ky., in 1818; studied law, was in the legislature of Ky., and Ind. and in congress; was capt. in an Indiana regt. in the Mexican war, and raised the first Union troops in Kentucky in the late war; was appointed maj. gen. of vols., and was in various battles.

ROSSELL, William, d. at Mount Holly, N. J., June 20, 1840, a. 79; judge of the U. S. court for the dist. of New Jersey; and for many years judge of the supreme court of that state.

ROSSELL, Gen. Zachariah, d. in Trenton, N. J., July 21, 1842, a. 55; was in the war of 1812, and rose to the rank of major; in 1817, was appointed clerk of the supreme court of New Jersey, and held by 4 successive appointments till his death; was many years adjutant general of militia.

ROSSITER, Gen. David, of Richmond, Mass., was captain of a company of minute men at Cambridge, in 1775; d. March 8, 1811, a. 75.

ROTHACKER, William, a native of Baden; graduated at Heidelberg and was involved in a revolution in 1848, which obliged him to leave Germany; he edited a newspaper in Pittsburg, Baltimore and Cincinnati, and d. at the latter place, Nov. 23, 1859, a. 31.

ROWAN, John, chargé de affaires to Naples during Polk's administration; d. in Kentucky, Aug., 1855.

ROWELL, Dr. Isaac, professor in the Pacific Med. Coll., at San Francisco, Cal.; d. Jan. 4, 1871, a. 53.

ROWLAND, Maj. Thomas, d. at Detroit, Mich., Aug. 1848; was formerly secretary of state, and post master at Detroit under Gen. Harrison.

ROWLEY, John, lawyer, d. at Claverack, N. Y.; May 9, 1868, a. 64; grad. at Union Coll., and settled as a lawyer at Redhook; in 1846, was appointed a judge of the court of common pleas of Dutchess county; afterward elected county judge, which position he occupied for four years, but since then physical debility compelled him to retire in some measure from the practice of his profession.

ROWSON, William, d. in Boston, Mass., July 21, 1842, a. 77; native of England, and for over 40 years a clerk in the Boston custom house.

RUFFER, Col. David, d. in Kanawha Salines, Va., Feb. 1, 1843, a. 76; was frequently in the state leg., and held various public offices.

RUFFIN, Thomas Sen., ex-chief justice of N. C.; d. Jan. 24, 1870, a. 83.

RUGGLES, Almon, d. at Vermillion, O., July 17, 1840, in his 70th year; was an early settler in northern O., and when the co. of Huron was founded in 1810, was appointed first recorder; held various public offices, among which were those of state senator, and associate judge.

RUGGLES, Nathaniel, b. in Mass.; grad. at Harvard in 1781; was in congress from Mass. from 1813 to to 1819; d. ——, 1819.

RULAND, John, b. in 1789 on the banks of the river Raisin, in Mich., and lived many years at Detroit; entered the N. W. army at the age of 19, and served reputably several years; d. at St. Charles, Mo., Jan. 1, 1849.

RUNK, G. W., lieut. 6th U. S. infantry; killed in battle of Plattsburg, Sept. 8, 1814.

RUNYARD, THOMAS, of Runyard, in Staffordshire; was the first representative of Gov. Barclay of N. J.; his conduct in the laying out and granting of lands was not approved by the proprietaries in England, who removed him from office and annulled his grants; he retained the office of sec. and register till 1685, when he left the province for Jamaica; d. in 1692; his daughter Anne, married John West, and Margaret, Samuel Winder. (*Coll. N. J. Hist. Soc.*, i, 123.)

RUSH, WILLIAM, b. in Phil., July 4, 1756; his father was a ship carpenter, and at a proper age was apprenticed to a carver, and far excelled his master; his figureheads were the admiration of foreign ports, and sketches and casts were made as objects of art; besides being a skillful sculptor in wood, he was often selected as a member of the city councils; d. Jan. 27, 1833. (*Simpson's Eminent Philadelphians.*)

RUSH, PHŒBE ANN, dau. of Jacob Ridgeway; d. in 1857, a. about 60; was a lady of extensive information, fine talents, and well versed in literature. (*Simpson's Eminent Philadelphians.*)

RUSSELL, ABRAHAM D., ex-judge; d. at N. Y., April 25, 1870, a 68.

RUSSELL, CHRISTOPHER, a captain in the British army in the French war. (*Com. Wilson's Orderly Book*, 109.)

RUSSELL, GEORGE W., d. in Baltimore, Md., March 16, 1869; was many years captain of the steamers on the bay line, from Baltimore to Norfolk, and port warden of Baltimore.

RUSSELL, MRS. HEPSIBETH, d. at Nantucket, Mass., April 25, 1836, a. 100.

RUSSELL, JOHN, d. at Urbana, Ohio, Dec. 17, 1870; had been secretary of state of Ohio, and at the time of his death was a member elect of the state senate.

RUSSELL, PROF. WILLIAM, d. Aug. 16, 1873, a. 75; native of Scotland, and came to this country in his twentieth year; he was editor of the first series of *The American Journal of Education*, published from 1826 to 1829, and was afterward for more than 40 years actively engaged in educational pursuits, giving special attention to elocution; he was so well liked that his friends and former pupils purchased for him the house in which he lived and gave him a liberal annuity.

RUST, ALBERT, native of Virginia; member of congress from Arkansas from 1855 to 1857; d. April 3, 1870.

RUTHERFORD, JOHN, d. at Ederston, N. J., Feb. 23, 1840, in his 80th year; native of New York city, and nephew of Wm. Alexander, Earl of Stirling; grad. at Princeton in 1776; educated to the bar; was elector of president in 1788; U. S. senator from N. J., from 1791 to 1798; was the last survivor of the senators in congress during the administration of Washington; he early retired from public life, and being one of the largest landholders in New Jersey, was actively engaged in the promotion of public improvements.

RUTLEDGE, MAJ. HENRY M., d. at Nashville, Tenn., Jan. 20, 1844, a. 68; only son of Edward R., signer of the declaration of independence; b. in 1775; was sec. to Gen. C. C. Pinckney; embassador to France in 1797; commissioned major in the U. S. army in 1799; was several times in the legislature of his native state, and in 1816 removed to Tennessee where he held many responsible offices.

RYCKMAN, LEWIS W., socialist; was concerned in the war of 1812–15; he was interested in a socialist experiment in Pike co., Pa., which failed, and became an advocate of a certain land-reform movement; he was once a candidate for congress; d. April 25, 1857, in N. Y.

RYERSS, JOSEPH WALTER, d. at Philadelphia, Pa., Jan. 20, 1868, a. 62; of the firm Lincoln & Ryerss; pres. of the Tioga rail road co., in 1852, and pres. of the Philadelphia Exchange at the time of his death.

RYERSON, MARTIN F., d. at Pompton, N. J., Aug. 20, 1837, a. 85; many years owner of extensive iron works.

RYERSON, THOMAS C., d. in N. J.; Aug., 1838; judge of the supreme court of N. J.

SABIN, NOAH, b. at Rehoboth, Mass., Nov. 10, 1714; in 1764 removed to Putney, Vt.; became town clerk, and in 1772 was appointed judge of the inferior court; he was imprisoned soon after the affray at Westminster, sent to N. Y., and about a year after returned home; he suffered much from suspicions of his attachment to the British; d. March 10, 1811, a. 96, having outlived much of the prejudice which had existed toward him. (*Hall's Eastern Vermont*, p. 694.)

SABIN, NOAH JR., was b. at Rehoboth, Mass., April 20, 1750; removed with his father to Putney, Vt.; register of probate for Windham co., from 1761 till 1891, when he became judge of probates till 1808; he was nearly 50 years justice of the peace; represented Putney in general assembly in 1782, 3, 4, 5, 7; d. Dec. 5, 1827. (*Hall's Eastern Vermont*, p. 697; *Brattleboro Messenger*, Dec. 21, 1827.)

SACKET, AUGUSTUS, founder of Sackets Harbor, N. Y.; b. in N. Y. city, Nov. 10, 1769; became a lawyer; purchased a tract in Houndsfield, N. Y., and settled on Lake Ontario in 1801; was first collector of the dist. of S. H., but was removed for cause; was first judge of Jeff. co. from 1805 to 1810, and in 1812 removed to Jamaica, N. Y., and thence to Meadville, Pa.; in 1820 went to Rutherford co., N. C.; returned to the St. Lawrence where he claimed some islands, and in 1827 removed to Newburg, N. Y.; d. at Albany, April 29, 1827. (*Hough's Hist. Jeff. Co., N. Y.*, p. 451.)

SACKETT, ADNAH, d. at Providence, R. I., Feb. ——, 1860; native of Westfield, Mass.; came to Providence in boyhood, and was successful in business; was pres. of the Bank of America, from the date of its organization.

SACKET, DR. GIDEON S., d. at Cape Vincent, N. Y., Sept. 24, 1860, in his 68th year.

SACKETT, SAMUEL, capt. 4th N. Y. reg.; d. April 15, 1780.

SAFFORD, REUBEN, d. in Dallas co., Ala., Feb. 15, 1848, a. 60; b. in Wilkes co., Ga., Sept. 4, 1788; practiced law for a time in Ga.; in 1813 removed to Jackson, Clark co., Ala., then Miss. Terr., and was engaged in the Indian war; was in the territorial leg. conv., and first state legislature; in 1819 became a circuit judge, and in 1832 one of the three judges of the supreme court; resigned in 1843. (*Am. Almanac*, 1849, p. 337.)

SAGE, ELIAS, d. in Denmark, N. Y., Feb. 29, 1852, a. 94.

SAILLY, PETER, native of Loraine, France; came to the U. S. in 1784, and a year or two after brought on his family and settled at Plattsburg,

N. Y., where he was elected to congress in 1804, and held from 1805 to 1807; afterwards appointed collector of the port, and held over 18 years; d. in 1826; was first county judge from 1804 to 1806.

ST. CLAIR, REV. JOHN T., b. in Goochland co., Va.; d. in Franklin co., Va., July 3, 1854; was of the M. E. church, south.

ST. JOHN, SAMUEL, d. in New Haven, Conn., Nov. 4, 1844, a. 78; a wealthy merchant.

SALISBURY, NICHOLAS, pioneer of Adams, N. Y., from Westm., Oneida co., N. Y.; d. Dec. 11, 1834, a. 71.

SALMON, REV. MARTIN, b. in Pauling, N. Y.; settled when a child in Turin, N. Y., became a Baptist minister of the sect known as old school; d. Sept. 13, 1847, a. 53.

SALTER, MRS. MARY, d. May, 1838, a. about 100, at Farmington, Me.

SALTER, WILLIAM, commodore in U. S. N. d. at Elizabeth, N. J., Jan. 3, 1869, in his 74th year; was appointed midshipman in 1809, and was in the engagement between the Constitution and the Guerriere, Aug. 19, 1812.

SALTONSTALL, MRS. ANNA, widow of the late Dr. S., and sixth in descent from William White, who began settlement at Haverhill in 1640; d. at that place, Oct. 21, 1841, a. 89.

SALTONSTALL, DR. GURDON, d. at Tuscaloosa, Ala., Sept. 11, 1834, a. 37.

SAMUELS, GREENE B., d. in Richmond, Va., Jan 5, 1859, a. 65; was for eleven years judge of the supreme court of appeals of the state of Virginia.

SANBORN, MRS. ANN, d. in Charleston, Me., March 29, 1860, a. 87; her surviving husband Theophilus was then 90; had been married 63 years.

SANBORN, TRISTAM, d. in Cumberland, Me., Jan. 14, 1842; member of the house of representatives of Maine.

SANDYS, SIR EDWIN, treasurer of the colony of Va.; b. in 1577; spent some time in the University at Oxford; traveled in Europe &c., in 1610; in 1615 published a book of travels; was the first poet of Va., and translated parts of Ovid and Virgil; d. in 1643, in Bexley Kent, Va.,

SANFORD, GEORGE H., senator in the N. Y. senate; d. at Oneida, N. Y., Nov. 25, 1871, a. 34.

SANFORD, JOHN, b. in Ct., settled early in Montgomery co., N. Y., as a teacher; afterwards merchant and contractor; was in congress in 1841–3; d. at his home in Amsterdam, N. Y., Oct. 4, 1857, a. 55.

SANFORD, JONAH, b. in Vermont; member of assembly from St. Lawrence, co., N. Y., in 1829–30; in cong. in 1830–31; raised the 92d regt. N. Y. vols., and was its first col.; d. at his home in Hopkinton, N. Y., Jan. 1868.

SANFORD, REUBEN, of Wilmington, Essex co., N. Y., d. May 19, 1855, in Columbus, O.; b. in Connecticut; settled in Wilmington in 1803; was in assembly in 1814–15; in constitutional convention in 1821; in the state senate from 1828 to 1831; on the British invasion of 1814, was major of a battalion of vols., and served with honor. (*Clinton County Whig*, June 2, 1855.)

SANFORD, WILLIAM T., d. in St. Charles co., Mo., July 29, 1842 a. 45; late of Hampshire co., Va.

SANTA ROSA AUGUSTINE, one of the victims of the Virginius expedition; shot at Santiago de Cuba, Nov. 7, 1873; b. in Havana and previously engaged in efforts for securing Cuban independence. (*N. Y. Tribune* Semi Weekly, Nov. 14, 1874.)

SAPP, HENRY, revolutionary soldier of Ga.; d. in Twiggs co., Ga., Oct. 29, 1829, a. 83; his wife d. the same day, a. 93.

SARGEANT, REV. JOHN, missionary to the Indians; missionary among the Stockbridge Indians in Mass., d. July 27, 1749; his daughter Sarah, was the first child born in Stockbridge, 1740; Erastus S., a son, b. 1742, was a distinguished physician at that place, and d. Nov. 14, 1814, a. 72; John S., another son, b. 1747, became a preacher to the Indians of Stockbridge, Oneida co., N. Y., where he d. Sept. 8, 1824, greatly esteemed. (*Goodwin's Notes*, p. 131.)

SARGENT, DANIEL, d. in Boston, April 2, 1842; having held at various times, office in the legislature, and the treasury of the state.

SARGENT, WINTHROP, author, d. at Paris, France, May 15, 1870.

SAUL, JOSEPH, a citizen of Louisiana since 1803; formerly cashier of the Branch Bank of the U. S., and pres. of the first insurance co. incorporated by the state of La.; d. at New Orleans, Dec. 6, 1856.

SAUNDERS, AUGUSTUS B., d. at Jackson, Miss., Feb. 25, 1842, a. about 55; was at the time of his death auditor of public accounts.

SAUNDERS, REV. DANIEL CLARK, b. in Sturbridge, Mass., in 1768; grad. at Harvard in 1788; ordained at Vergennes, Vt., in 1794; elected pres. of the University of Vt. in 1801; resigned in 1813, the college being occupied by Gen. Wade Hampton's army; was installed in Medfield in 1818, and dismissed in 1829; in 1812 published a Hist. of the Indians; in 1820 was in the Massachusetts convention; d. in Medfield, Mass., Oct. 18, 1850, a. 82.

SAUNDERS, JOHN, prof. in the Phil. High School; d. April 5, 1844, a. 57; author of *Biography of the Signers of the Declaration of Independence*, and several volumes of a book entitled *The American in Paris.*

SAUNDERS, MRS. SARAH, d. at Bristol, Me., Jan., 1835, a. 101.

SAUVAN, JEAN BAPTISTE AMEDÉE, d. at Richmond, Va., 1870; was consul for the French government, and had served in consular offices in Philadelphia, Baltimore, and Civita Vecchia.

SAVAGE, DR. JOHN H., d. at Rodney, Miss., Oct., 1843, of yellow fever; was a distinguished physician, and held the office of prof. of chemistry at Oakland College.

SAWTELL, JOSEPH, a revolutionary pensioner; d. in Groton, Mass., March 21, 1842, a. 78; was a sexton, and had buried between 1100 and 1200 persons.

SAWYER, FRANKLIN, d. at Cambridgeport, Mass., Nov. 18, 1851, a. 41; grad at Harvard in 1830; was editor at New Orleans, and Detroit; while in Mich. was supt. of public instruction; for the last two years was an editor of the *Watchman and Reflector* at Boston, and in the leg. the session before his death.

SAWYER, REV. JOHN, d. in Bangor, Me., Oct. 14, 1858, a. 103 y. and 5 days.

SAWYER, REV. JOHN, b. at Hebron, Ct., Oct. 9, 1755; entered the army a. 22; grad. at Dartmouth in 1785, and in 1787 settled in Oxford,

N. H., where he resided till 1795; was more than 50 years a resident of Maine, chiefly at Bangor, where he was one of the founders of the Theological Seminary; d. Oct. 14, 1858, over 103 years of age. (*Hist. Mag.*, ii, 366.)

SAWYER, NATHANIEL L., of Gardiner, Me.; d. in Greene, Me., Oct. 13, 1845, a. about 36; he grad. at Bowdoin Coll. and at the law school in Harvard, and was a young man of excellent talents.

SAWYER, MRS. SYBILL, widow of Dr. Micajah S.; d. at Newburyport, Mass., July 8, 1842, a. 95.

SAWYER, DR. WILLIAM, grad. at Harvard in 1788; and after the death of Dr. Abbot (Jan. 31, 1859), was the oldest graduate of that college; he studied medicine, practiced a few years, and then entered the mercantile business in which he acquired a fortune; he withdrew from active business a quarter of a century before his death; and d. in Boston, April 18, 1859, a. 88.

SAWYER, WILLIAM, b. in Westminster, Mass.; grad. at Harvard in 1800; studied law at Dover, N. H., and settled at Wakefield in 1804; he was several years in the New Hampshire legislature, and on the division of Strafford co., was chosen president of the Carroll county bar; he d. at Wakefield, N. H., July 5, 1860, a. 84.

SAYER, BENJAMIN, d. Oct. 26, 1874, in Warwick, N. Y.

SCANTLAND, MAJ. JAMES M., a volunteer in the Mexican war, fought at Monterey and Cerro Gordo; he d. at Red Sulphur Springs, Tenn., July 22, 1849.

SCARRITT, JEREMIAH MASON, U. S. engineer, from Ill.; grad. at West Point in 1838; in 1839 became 1st. lieut. of engineers; was assistant prof. of engineering at W. P., Sept., 1839 to Aug., 1841; served honorably in Mexico and was made captain by brevet in 1847, for bravery in the battles of Monterey, Palo Alto and Resaca de la Palma; received a sword from Ill.; retired from the army; in 1853 he took charge of the works on Ft. Taylor, Key West; d. June 22, 1855. (*N. O. Picayune*, July 3, 1855.)

SCHAATS, REV. GIDEON, second Dutch minister at Albany; b. 1607; was a schoolmaster in Holland; was ordained and sent over in 1652, and labored at Albany over thirty years; his eldest son was killed in the massacre at Schenectady in 1690; in 1675, Mr. Niewenhuysen was a colleague, and in 1683 the Rev. G. Dellius. (*Rogers's Hist. Discourse*, p. 13.)

SCHACHIPAKA, or DECARI THE WHITE HEAD, a Winnebago chief; d. in Wisconsin Territory, April 20, 1836, in his 90th year.

SCHANCK, ZELPHY, d. in New Jersey, Feb. 18, 1859, a. 119 years.

SCHENCK, FERDINAND S., M.D., a highly respected citizen of Somerset co., N. J.; d. at Camden, N. J., May 18, 1860, a. 72; he was a member of the house of representatives from 1833 to 1837; a member of the constitutional convention in 1844, and was several times in the state legislature; he was also a judge of the court of errors and appeals.

SCHERMERHORN, ABRAHAM M., d. in Rochester, N. Y., Aug. 22, 1855; was in the N. Y. assembly in 1848, and a member of congress from New York, from 1849 to 1853.

SCHIMMELPENNICK, RUTGER JAN, one of the Holland land company of western New York; d. at Amsterdam, Holland, Jan. 15, 1825.

SCHLEY, GEORGE, a native of Md., and 25 years post master at Savannah, Ga.; d. at that place April 17, 1851, a. 59.

SCHLEY, JOHN, d. in Georgia, May 26, 1847, a. 62; he was many years judge of the supreme court of the middle district of Georgia.

SCHLOSSER, JOHN W., d. at York, Pa., Feb., 1860.

SCHMUCK, CAPT. JACOB, an officer in the war of 1812, and native of Penn.; d. at St. Augustine, Fla., April 10, 1835, in his 43d year.

SCHOOLCRAFT, JOHN L., a citizen of Albany, and from 1849 to 1853, mem. of cong.; d. at St. Catharines, Canada West, June 7, 1860.

SCHOPPE, MADAME AMALIA, eminent German novelist and poet; daughter of Dr. Weise; b. on the island of Fehman in the Baltic, Oct. 19, 1791; was long a resident of Hamburg, where she published a weekly journal many years; the titles of her books number nearly two hundred, chiefly historical romances; in 1848 she accompanied her only son Alphonse S., an engineer, to America; resided at Utica, Albany, and Schenectady, and d. there Oct. 10, 1858; she was a lady of much refinement, and gifted with great intellectual powers. (*Hist. Mag.*, ii, 349.)

SCHOULER, GEN. WILLIAM, journalist; b. in Scotland in 1814; d. at Jamaica Plains, Mass., Oct. 24, 1872.

SCHRŒTER, GEORGE, b. at Lilienthal near Bremen in Hanover; grad. at Göttingen and became private secretary of Prince Adalbert of Prussia, son of the late Prince William; in 1848 he sided with the liberals, and was obliged to take refuge in the U. S., the next year; he was employed in connection with the Am. Geog. & Statist. Soc., and in 1856 completed a map of the U. S., 30 by 17 feet, of great minuteness in detail, which was sent to the stock exchange in London; he also executed models in wax, of considerable regions of the U. S.; d. at Paterson, N. J., Oct. 25, 1860, a. 43. (*N. Y. Times*, Oct. 27, 1860.)

SCHRUGAM, WILLIAM H., one of the justices of the supreme court of New York, residing in Yonkers; d. August 9, 1867.

SCHUYLER, PHILIP, many years a merchant in Boonville, N. Y.; d. there, Feb. 10, 1854.

SCHUYLER, PHILIP J., member of congress in 1817–19; d. at New York city, Feb. 21, 1835, a. 67.

SCHUYLER, PHILIP PIETERSEN, first of the family in America, came in 1650 from Amsterdam and held an important position in New Netherland; he d. at Albany March 9, 1684; he was father of Peter S., first mayor of Albany and grandfather of Gen. Philip S., of the revolution. (*Munsell's Ann. Alb.*, ii, 177.)

SCHWARTZ, JOHN, d. in Washington, D. C., June 20, 1860; member of congress from Berk's co., Pa.

SCORERBY, REV. WILLIAM, celebrated as an Arctic explorer and eminent philosopher; d. at Torquay, Eng., March 31, 1857.

SCOTT, CHARLES, d. at Charleston, Kanawha co., Va., March 21, 1860; was a relative of Gen. Winfield Scott, and a native of Powhatan co., Va.

SCOTT, JOHN, d. near Potosi, Mo., July 26, 1839, in his 109th year.

SCOTT, COL. JOHN, d. at Powerville, N. J., Nov. 29, 1839, a. 57; pres. of the Dover Bank, and a distinguished officer of the war of 1812; he was a most efficient officer in the prosecution and completion of the Morris canal.

SCOTT, CAPT. MARTIN, b. in Burlington, Vt., Jan. 17, 1788; served as lieut. in the war of 1812; was disbanded in 1815, but again entered the army in 1818, and served in the north west and became well known in Minnesota; was killed at the head of a reg. at the battle of El Molino del Rey, Mexico, Sept. 8, 1847. (*Collections of Minnesota Hist. Soc.*, iii, part 2d, p. 180.)

SCOTT, REV. ORANGE, b. in Vermont in 1800; became a traveling M. E. preacher in 1822; withdrew from the church in 1842, and assisted in organizing the Wesleyan Methodist connection of America, by a conv. of which he was president; d. July 31, 1847.

SCOTT, THOMAS, d. at Chillicothe, O., Feb. 15, 1856, a. 84; b. in Md. in 1772; became an itinerant Meth. minister in 1789, when but 17 ys. old; in 1798 began thes tudy of law, and settled at Chillicothe; was sec. of the constitutional convention of Ohio in 1802; was for a time clerk of the courts; sec. of the senate till 1809, when he was elected a judge of the supreme court of O.; in 1810 became chief justice, and held till 1815, when he resumed the practice of law.

SCOVEL, REV. SYLVESTER, b. March 3, 1796; grad. at Williams Coll. in 1822; studied theology at Princeton, and preached a few years in N. J. and Pa.; in 1830 went west as a missionary of the board of missions, and in 1846 became president of Hanover Coll.; d. July, 1849. (*Stryker's Am. Reg.*, iii, 233.)

SCOVILLE, SAMUEL, an early settler of West Turin, N. Y.; d. in that town March 26, 1863, a. 96.

SCRANTON, JOSEPH H., d. June 9, 1872, at Baden Baden, Germany; was founder of the city which bears his name, and one of the most able and eminent citizens of Pa.; went abroad with part of his family in Jan., 1872, in the hope that residence and travel in Europe would restore his health, which had been for a year or more somewhat impaired; he spent the winter amid the bland airs of the Mediterranean coast, visiting successively Nice, Genoa, Rome, Naples, and Florence; but without deriving permanent advantage; was 58 years old at the time of his death; the last 30 years was spent in building up the town which bears his name; he found it not even a hamlet; one or two farm houses and a country tavern stood by the border of the stream, and surrounding them were bleak and sterile mountains; it is now the third city in Pa., its prosperity being based on coal-mining and iron manufactures, in which Mr. Scranton bore the most active and influential share; he early perceived the wealth that lay latent beneath the surrounding hills, and after unremitting effort and many delays and failures, succeeded in enlisting the coöperation of some capitalists in this city, who were induced to risk a moderate sum in his enterprise; it was barely $30,000 — a small sum in these days, but Mr. Scranton often spoke to his friends of the delight and exultation with which he received this first modest installment of the vast sums which have since been expended under his influence and direction; he had the faculty of distinguishing the practicable from the visionary or plausible; his energy was direct and instant, and his executive capacity of the highest order; there will be sadness and mourning in the city which he helped to build, to which it was hoped he would return with his health and vigor restored, and where his memory will long be held in affection and honor. (*N. Y. Tribune.*)

SCRIBA, GEORGE, a native of Germany, and formerly an eminent merchant of N. Y.; d. at Constantia, Oswego co., N. Y., Aug. 14, 1836, a. 84; had resided in Oswego co. for 30 years, and was patentee of a large tract of land east of the Oswego river and bordering on Lake Ontario, known as Scriba's Patent; the town of Scriba, near Oswego, is named from him.

SCRIBNER, CHARLES, publisher, N. Y. city; d. at Luzerne, Switzerland, Aug. 25, 1871, a. 50.

SCUDDER, DR. JOHN A., a native of New Jersey; d. in Davis co., Ind., Nov. 6, 1836, a. 79.

SCUDDER, ZENO, d. in Barnstable, Mass., June 26, 1857; had filled many places of trust; was pres. of the state senate, and from 1851 to 1854 in congress, where his declining health obliged him to resign; was a good lawyer, and much esteemed.

SEAMAN, NOAH, a native of Swanzey, Mass., d. in Jackson co., Mich., Aug. 18, 1831, a. 100 years 1½ month.

SEATON, GALES, son of Wm. W. S., was b. in Washington, D. C., July 27, 1817; grad. at Harvard, in 1837; studied law, but did not practice; became proprietor and editor of the *Raleigh (N. C.) Register;* he spent several years in Europe; d. in Washington, D. C., Feb. 9, 1857, a. 39.

SEAVER, BENJAMIN, d. in Roxbury, Mass., Feb. 14, 1856, a. 60; b. in Roxbury, in 1795; engaged in merchandise in Boston in early life; was a state representative from 1846 to 1848; state senator in 1850 and 1851; was a member of the common council of Boston, from 1845 to 1849, and its president from 1847 to 1849, and mayor in 1852 and 1853.

SEAVER, EBENEZER, d. in Roxbury, Mass., March 1, 1844, a. 81; b. 1763; grad. at Harvard in 1784; in congress from Mass., from 1803 to 1813.

SEDGWICK, CHARLES, d. in Lenox, Mass., Aug. 3, 1851, a. 64; b. in that town, and bred to the bar, was early in his professional life, appointed clerk of the courts for Berkshire co., and removed to Lenox, where he resided till his death.

SEDGWICK, ROBERT, d. at Sachem's Head, Conn., Sept. 2, 1841; long a member of the N. Y. bar, and a son of Theodore S. of Stockbridge Mass.

SEEBER, HENRY, d. at German Flats, N. Y., May 15, 1845, a. 104, 2 mo; b. at Indian Castle, Tryon co., N. Y., March 15, 1741; served in the French and rev. wars, and was in the battle of Oriskany.

SEELEY, EBENEZER, d. in Weston, Ct., May 21, 1842, a. 82; was a rev., soldier and many years a deacon in the Congregational church.

SEELY, ELIAS P., d. at Bridgeton, N. J., Aug. 23, 1846, a. 55; was several years a member of the council and assembly, and in 1833, governor of New Jersey.

SEGER, FRANCIS, b. in Guilderland, N. Y., March 12, 1797; from 1828 to 1833, clerk of assembly, when he was elected state senator and served till 1837; was a lawyer; settled in Lewis co., N. Y., where he held the office of county judge; often supervisor of the town of Greig; d. at Albany, April 30, 1872.

SELDON, DUDLEY, was in assembly from Rensselaer co., in 1831; removed to N. Y., where he was elected to the 23d cong. by the democrats, but resigned in 1834, and became thenceforth a whig; was a prominent member of the N. Y. bar; and upon the death of Mr. Packard, his father in-law, who was a wealthy Cuban planter, he received a large estate; he removed to the city of Paris, and d. there, Nov. 8, 1855.

SELDEN, DR. WILSON C., a surgeon of the rev. war, d. March 14, 1835, a. 73.

SELMER, TILDEN R., merchant, d. at Quincy, Ill., April 21, 1870, a. 66.

SEMPLE, DR. ROBERT, killed by an accidental fall from his horse, near Colusa, Cal., Oct. 25, 1854; one of the pioneers of California; and president of the constitutional convention of 1849.

SENTER, MAJ. ASA, an officer of the rev.; d at Windham, N. H., Jan.—, 1835, a. 79.

SENTER, WILLIAM T., d. in Grainger co., Tenn., Aug. 28, 1849, a. 47; from 1843 to 1845, he was a representative in congress.

SERGEANT, JOHN THOMAS, late a judge of the supreme court of Pa.; d. at Philadelphia, May 5, 1860, a. 78.

SETTLE, THOMAS, d. in Rockingham co., N. C., April 5, 1857, a. 65; was in the state leg. in 1815, 1826–27–28; in 1828, was speaker of house of commons; was in congress in 1817 to 1821; in 1832, was chosen judge of the superior court of law and equity, and held the office for twenty years, when he resigned.

SEVER, WILLIAM, of Kingston, Mass., son of Nicholas S., former fellow in Harvard; grad. in 1745 at Harvard; was in the council in Hutchinson's day; in 1775 was in prov. cong.; was several years afterwards in the council, and took a deep interest in pub. affairs; d. in 1809. (*Bradford's N. E. Biog.*)

SEWALL, DANIEL, d. at Kennebunk, Me., Oct. 14, 1842; many years clerk of the courts of register and probate in York co.; b. at York March 28, 1755; was appointed register of probate in 1783, and held till 1820; in 1822, was appointed p. m., at York, and remained so for 15 years; was made clerk of com. pleas in 1791, having been assistant clerk 11 ys. afterwards recording clerk of S. J. court. (*Am. Almanac*, 1844, p. 315.)

SEWALL, HENRY, one of the judges of the supreme court of North Carolina; d. near Raleigh, N. C., Oct. 12, 1835.

SEWALL, REV. JOTHAM, d. in Chesterville, Me., Oct. 3, 1850, a. 90; b. in York, Me., Jan. 1, 1760, was in mercantile life when young; studied divinity and was licensed to preach; was employed as a home missionary by the Massachusetts and afterwards by the Maine Missionary Society.

SEWARD, SAMUEL S., father of Hon. Wm. H. Seward, ex-governor of N. Y.; d. at Orange co., N. Y., Aug. 24, 1849; he was the founder of the S. S. Seward Institute, to which he bequeathed $20,000 besides their house and lot.

SEWARD, William Henry, d. in Auburn, N. Y., Oct. 10, 1872, a. 71; a most distinguished statesman. (*Drake's Am. Biog.*)

SEXTON, Charles, d. in Sparta, Mich., Oct. 23, 1858; b. in Lebanon, Vt., June 25, 1777; settled in Lowville, N. Y., but lived most of his life in Jefferson co., N. Y.

SEYE, Hendrick, one of the Holland Land Company of western New York; d. near Utrecht near the village of De Bilt, Holland, Aug. 14, 1823.

SEYMOUR, Frederick, gov. of British Columbia; d. June 10, 1869, on board the Sparrow Hawk, on the north-western coast of British Columbia; was sec. of Tasmania in 1843; stipendiary of Antigua in 1848; pres. of the island of Nevis, the same year; gov. of British Honduras, 1857–63, and gov. of British Columbia, from 1863 till his death.

SEYMOUR, Henry, canal com'r and state senator; was a merchant in Pompey, N. Y., was appointed canal com'r March 24, 1819, while the principal canals of N. Y. were under construction, and held till 1833; in 1820 he was in assembly, and from 1816 to 1819, and in 1822 was state senator; in 1819 he removed to Utica, and d. there, Aug. 26, 1837; his widow survived till Sept. 16, 1859; his son Horatio S., has twice been governor of New York. (*Hist. Mag.*, iii, 353.)

SEYMOUR, Hezekiah C., civil engineer, and formerly state engineer and surveyor of N. Y.; d. July 24, 1853, a. 42; was constructing engineer of the Maysville and Lexington, the Ohio and Mississippi and the New York and Boston rail roads; was engineer on the Ontario, Huron and Lake Simcoe rail road in Canada.

SEYMOUR, Horatio, b. in Litchfield, Ct.; grad. at Yale in 1797; was a lawyer of Middlebury, Vt., and from 1821 to 1833, a member of the U. S. senate from Vermont; d. at Middlebury, Vt., Nov. 21, 1857, a. 79.

SEYMOUR, John, b. at New Canaan, Ct., Nov. 20, 1786; removed in 1812 to Northville, N. Y.; then to N. Y., and in 1831, to Genoa, N. Y., where he was post master; he took a prominent part in the Freemason excitement of 1828–32; d. at Auburn, N. Y., Sept. 11, 1860. (*N. Y. Times*, Sept. 17, 1860.)

SHACKLEFORD, John, sergeant at arms of the United States senate; d. at St. Louis, Mo., Aug. 16, 1837.

SHACKLEFORD, William H., d. in Exeter, N. H., March 5, 1842, a. 28; grad. at Harvard, and prof. of math. in Phillips Exeter Academy.

SHACKFORD, Capt. John, a soldier of the revolution; d. at Eastport, Me., Dec., 1840, a. 86.

SHAFF, Frederick, a soldier of the revolution; d. in May, 1860, in Berkshire, Tioga co., N. Y., about 100 years old.

SHAFFER, John Wilson, gov. of Utah; d. at Salt Lake city, Oct. 31, 1870; b. in Lewisburg, Pa., July 5, 1827.

SHALER, Joseph, was a lieut. in Col. Meigs's corps, and afterwards raised a company in Meriden, Ct., and as captain joined St. Clair's expedition against the Miami Indians; his son was killed and scalped; Capt. Shaler settled in Ohio after the war and died there. (*G. W. Perkins's Hist. of Meriden, Ct.*, p. 85.)

SHALER, Nathaniel, merchant of Middletown, Ct.; became agent and part owner of four townships in Turin, N. Y., in 1796, and settled the larger part; he spent much time on the tract, but did not remove; he owned extensively on the Western reserve, O., where the town of Shalersville bears his name; he d. in Middletown, Ct., May, 1816. (*Hough's Hist. Lewis Co., N. Y.*, p. 228.)

SHALLUS, JACOB, b. in Philadelphia, and d. there, April 18, 1796; served as a vol. quartermaster to the 1st Penn. reg't, in the expedition to Canada, and afterwards in the revolution; was for many years assistant clerk of the assembly, and of the convention of 1790; he was the father of Francis Shallus, who in 1817, published in 2 vols., *Chronological Tables for Every Day in the Year.* (*Simpson's Eminent Philadelphians.*)

SHANNON, GEORGE, formerly a circuit judge in Kentucky and U. S. dist. atty., for Missouri; d. at Palmyra, Mo., Aug. 30, 1836, a. 49; he was a native of Pennsylvania, and accompanied Lewis and Clark at the age of 16, on their expedition to the Pacific ocean in 1803; he afterwards studied law, settled in Kentucky, and in 1828 removed to St. Louis.

SHANNON, JOHN R., d. at Beaver, Pa., Feb. 18, 1860; for over fifty years a prominent lawyer in that county; came from Washington co., Pa., in 1806, and represented Beaver co., several times in the legislature.

SHARKEY, WILLIAM L., ex-governor of Mississippi; d. in Washington, D. C., April 29, 1873, a. 83.

SHARP, JOSEPH, was a member of the legislature of New Jersey 15 successive years, and d. at Vernon, Sussex co., N. J., Sept. 14, 1845, a. 88.

SHARPE, SOLOMON P., b. in Va.; removed to Kentucky when a child; was admitted to the bar, and was several times elected to the state legislature; attorney general of the state, and from 1813 to 1817, in congress; was assassinated Nov., 1835, while a member of the legislature, a. 35.

SHARSWOOD, JAMES, b. in Philadelphia, March 24, 1747, 8 (O. S.), and d. Sept. 14, 1836; held various public offices and trusts, and wrote much for the press. (*Simpson's Eminent Philadelphians.*)

SHATTUCK, LEMUEL, M.D., statistician and historian; b. at Ashby, Mass., Oct. 15, 1793; resided in Detroit; was many years a resident of Boston, where in 1837–8–40–1, he was in com. council, and several times in the legislature; in 1845 he directed the census of Boston, and in 1850, with others made an able sanitary report to the legislature; he published *Memorials of the Descen. of Wm. Shattuck*, a *Hist. of Concord, Mass., and of the Towns of Bedford, Acton, Lincoln and Carlisle*, a system of family registration &c., and was particularly active in promoting a system of registration of births, marriages, and deaths, and in organizing the N. E. Historic-Genealogical Soc.; he d. at Boston, Jan. 23, 1859, in his 65th year. (*Hist. Mag.*, iii, 95.)

SHAUGNESSEY, MARY, d. in Mass., March 14, 1859, a. 112.

SHAW, HENRY, studied law in Albany; at an early age removed to Lanesboro, Mass., and was chosen to congress in 1816 and 1818; he was 18 years in the Massachusetts legislature where he served in both branches; was prominently interested in manufacturing enterprises in western Massachusetts; in 1848 he removed to New York city, where he became a member of the board of education, and of the common council and assembly; in 1854 he removed to Newburg; he d. at Peekskill, N. Y., Oct. 17, 1857, a. 68.

SHAW, Rev. Joseph Coolidge, a native of Boston; grad. at Cambridge in 1840; traveled in Europe; became a Catholic and studied theology at Rome; he returned to Boston, was ordained a priest by Bp. Fitzpatrick, and officiated till his death; he d. at the novitiate, Frederick, Md., March 10, 1851, a. 30. (*Stryker's Am. Reg.*, vi, 216.)

SHAW, Joshua, landscape painter; b. in Bellingbroke, Lincolnshire, Eng.; was early left an orphan, and was farmer boy, post boy, and apprentice to a sign painter; he found the latter to afford opportunities for indulging a native taste, and he became known as a landscape painter; he came to America in 1817; he was an inventor; received grants from congress for an improved gun lock, and from Russia for improvements in naval warfare; he lost an arm in his experiments in gunnery; for seven years was affected with paralysis, and for the last two years was confined to bed; he d. at Burlington, N. J., Sept. 8, 1860, a. 83. (*N. Y. Times*, Sept. 17, 1860.)

SHAW, Capt. Sylvanus, R. I.; killed in the rev., Oct. 22, 1777.

SHAW, Tristram, d. at Exeter, N. H., March 14, 1843, a. 57; lately a representative in congress from New Hampshire.

SHEARMAN, Sylvester G., associate justice of R. I.; d. at Providence, Jan. 3, 1868, a. 66.

SHEFFEY, Daniel, b. in Frederick, Md., in 1770; settled at Augusta, Va., and studied law; was often elected to the legislature, and in 1809–17 was in congress; was opposed to the war of 1812; d. at his home Dec. 3, 1830.

SHELDON, Frederick, d. in Westchester co., N. Y., April 28, 1859, a. 76; he had been for forty years prominently engaged in commercial, educational and religious movements, and was one of the founders of the U. S. Life Insurance Co., and of the U. S. Trust Co., and for many years was a director in the Bank of America.

SHELDON, Capt. Pardon, d. at Providence, R. I., Feb. 3, 1838, in his 99th year.

SHELLMAN, Col. John, d. at Savannah, Ga., May, 1838; a revolutionary officer; long a citizen of Savannah; was a captain in the Maryland line in the early part of the war, and was at the battle of White Plains.

SHEPARD, Charles B., d. in Newbern, N. C., Oct. 31, 1843; b. in Newbern, Dec. 5, 1807; grad. at Chapel Hill in 1827; was elected to congress in 1837 and served till 1841.

SHEPARD, Maj. Gideon, a militia officer of the war of 1812; d. in Turin, N. Y., Dec. 11, 1850. (*Hough's Hist. Lewis Co., N. Y.*, p. 211.)

SHEPARD, Lorenzo B., corporation council of New York city; son of David B. S., a lawyer of N. Y.; he was b. in Cairo, Greene co., N. Y., in 1820; read law in N. Y. with Ulysses D. French, and early engaged in politics as a democrat; he was licensed in 1841; became a partner of his preceptor, was a delegate to the state convention in 1846, and was the youngest of that body; in 1848 he became U. S. dist. att'y for the south dist. of N. Y., until removed by Taylor; in 1855 he was elected council to the corporation of N. Y.; d. Sept. 19, 1856; he was the author of two or three law books.

SHEPARD, Samuel, came to Massachusetts, a. 22, and settled at Cambridge; in 1639 he was one of the supt's for erecting the first college building; he returned to Eng. after 1645, and in 1658 was a major and living in Ireland. (*Young's Chron. Mass.*, p. 541.)

SHEPARD, WILLIAM BIBBLE, d. in Elizabeth city, N. C., June 20, 1852, a. 51; b. in Newbern, N. C., in 1799; was in congress from 1827 to 1837.

SHEPARD, CAPT. WINTHROP, an officer of the war of 1812, and an early settler of Turin, N. Y.; d. in that town, Sept. 24, 1854, a. 82.

SHEPHERD, JAMES L., president of the Union Bank; d. in New Orleans, La., July 27, 1837 of apoplexy.

SHERBURNE, ANDREW, b. at Portsmouth, N. H., Sept. 30, 1765; shipped on board the Ranger, a continental vessel, at 14, and afterwards on privateers; was captured and imprisoned during the war; became a Baptist minister, and a chaplain in the war of 1812–15, with the Maine militia; afterwards traveled and preached in the west, and drew a navy pension from government. (*Memoirs of A. S., Written by Himself, Utica,* 1828, 12mo., pp. 272.)

SHERMAN, CONGER, printer; d. at Phil., Nov. 25, 1867, in his 74th year; b. near Albany; went to Phil. in 1811; worked as a journeyman till 1830, when he set up business for himself and was quite successful.

SHERMAN, ROGER, son of the signer of the declaration of independence of this name; d. in New Haven, Conn., March 5, 1856, a. 88.

SHERWOOD, CHARLES, U. S. consul at Messina, Sicily; d. at that place Jan. 2, 1848.

SHERWOOD, ISAAC, lieut. 2d N. Y. reg.; d. Oct. 10, 1777.

SHERWOOD, ISAAC, b. in Williamstown, Mass., Oct. 13, 1762; settled in Norway, N. Y., and in 1798 in Aurelius; was a merchant, hotel-keeper and stage proprietor; d. in 1840. (*Hall's Auburn*, p. 549.)

SHIELDS, WILLIAM C., b. in Richmond, Va., Sept. 2, 1855, a. 64; was a native of Phil., and served in the navy in the war of 1812; founded the *Richmond Compiler*, and was afterwards for many years joint proprietor and editor of the *Norfolk Beacon;* in 1844 begun the *Norfolk Courier;* d. of the yellow fever epidemic.

SHILE, LIEUT. PETER, Penn. killed Nov. 5, 1777.

SHINE, JOHN, b. in N. C., in 1759; served in the revolution, under Gen. Caswell; was at the battle of Camden in 1780; d. in Twiggs co., Ga., in 1832. (*White's Hist. Ga.*, p. 656.)

SHINGLEDECKER, MRS. ABIGAL, d. near Sharon, Ohio, Aug. 8, 1838, in her 104th year.

SHIPMAN, DR. AZARIAH B., of Syracuse, N. Y.; d. Sept. 15, 1868, a. 65. (*Transac. N. Y. State Med. Soc.,* 1869, p. 247.)

SHIVERS, JONAS, a revolutionary soldier, d. Nov. 12, 1826, a. 77; at Warren co., Ga.

SHOCK, THOMAS A., chief engineer, U. S. N.; d. at Charlestown, Mass., Jan. 21, 1873, a. 41.

SHOEMAKER, DR. NATHAN, d. in Phil., Pa., June 18, 1868, a. 80.

SHORTER, JOHN GILL, ex-gov. of Alabama; d. in Eufaula, Ala., May 29, 1872.

SHORTRIDGE, CAPT. BENJAMIN, N. H., killed in the revolution, July 8, 1776.

SHRIVER, DAVID, d. in Cumberland, Md., April 28, 1852, a. 84; b. in Frederick, now Carroll co.; became an engineer, located and superintended construction of the National road from Cumberland to Wheeling; was one of the commissioners of public works of the general government; planned and constructed other public and private works.

SHOBER, EMANUEL, d. at Salem, N. C., June 13, 1846; was a lawyer, and had represented Stokes co., for many years in the house of commons; was also a member of the constitutional convention of 1835.

SHOVER, WILLIAM H., brevet major, and capt. in 3d artillery, and instructor of artillery and cavalry at West Point; d. there Sept. 7, 1850, of a disease contracted in the Mexican war, in which he served as a subaltern in Ringold's (afterwards Bragg's) battery, under Gen. Taylor, and after promotion in the valley of Mexico.

SHREVE, HENRY W., of St Louis, started flat boats in 1808, and in 1814 took charge of a steam boat, performing the voyage from Pittsburg to New Orleans in 14 days; he was the first to ascend the Mississippi by steam; served under Jackson in 1814, 15, and manned one of the field pieces that destroyed the advancing column of Gen. Kean, Jan. 8, 1815; he also served with his steamer in conveying troops and supplies for the relief of Ft. St. Phillip; under J. Q. Adams and Van Buren he was U. S. supt. of western improvements, and was 40 years connected with commerce; d. at St Louis, Mo., March 6, 1851.

SHUBRICK, JOHN TEMPLE, son of Col. Thomas S., was b. on Bull's Island, S. C., Sept. 12, 1788; studied law at Charleston, with Col. Drayton; Aug. 19, 1806, entered with his younger brother William as a midshipman in the navy, and was on board the Chesapeake, when fired upon by the Leopard; he served with intrepidity in various engagements during the war, and in 1815, was sent from Algiers to the U. S., as the bearer of a treaty with that power; he sailed in the Epervier, and passed the straits of Gibraltar about July 10, 1815, but never was heard from after; it is supposed his vessel foundered at sea in a heavy gale that it encountered. (*J. F. Cooper's Lives of Distin. Am. Naval Officers*, i, 147.)

SHUBRICK, CAPT. RICHARD, S. C., killed in revolution, Nov. 8, 1777.

SHUBRICK, WILLIAM B., rear admiral in the U. S. navy; d. at Washington, May 27, 1874, in his 84th year; the general order issued by the navy department on the occasion says: "Born in South Carolina in 1790, Admiral Shubrick entered the navy in 1806, and has served his country faithfully and well for 68 years; four times he has commanded squadrons, twice navy-yards, has twice served as chief of naval bureaus, and for many years presided over the Light-house board; he won his early renown in battle as a lieutenant of the frigate Constitution in the war of 1812, and his last service afloat was as commander of the Paraguayan expedition; in every trust committed to him during life he has deserved well of the republic, and dying, he leaves to the service the conspicuous example of a life of wisdom, courtesy, courage, and spotless honor."

SHURLDS, HENRY, d. in St. Louis, Mo., Aug. 1, 1852; was from Gloucester co., Va., and held the offices of auditor of public accounts, secretary of state, judge of the circuit court, and cashier of the State Bank.

SHURTLIFF, JAMES, a pioneer settler of Theresa, N. Y.; d. at Plessis, N. Y., Aug. 1, 1846, a. 79.

SIBLEY, JONAS, member of congress from Mass., in 1812, 13, 15; d. at Sutton, Worcester co., Feb. 10, 1834, a. 72.

SIBLEY, MARK H., b. in great Barrington, Mass., in 1796; removed to Canandaigua, N. Y. in 1814, and became a distinguished lawyer; was in the N. Y. assembly in 1835 and 1836; in congress in 1837–9; state senator in 1840–1, and elected county judge and surrogate of Ontario county, in 1847; d. at Canandaigua, N. Y., Sept. 8, 1852.

SICKLES, NICHOLAS, d. in Kingston, N. Y., May 13, 1845; was a native of Kinderhook, N. Y., and a member of congress in 1835–37.

SIGOURNEY, CHARLES, merchant; d. in Hartford, Conn., Dec. 30, 1854; was husband of the poetess and writer, Mrs. Lydia H. S.

SIGUR, L. J., noted fillibuster; was a devoted friend of Narciso Lopez, who perished in Cuba; d. at New Orleans, Sept. 18, 1858, a. 42. (*Hist. Mag.*, ii, 347.)

SILL, REV. FREDERICK, pastor of the Protestant Episcopal church of St. Ambrose, N. Y. city; d. Dec. 13, 1874, in his 62d year.

SILL, JOSEPH, b. in Carlisle, Eng., May 14, 1801; came to Phil. in 1819; became a merchant; d. Nov. 2, 1854. (*Simpson's Eminent Philadelphians.*)

SILL, SETH E., a justice of the supreme court of N. Y. for the 8th judicial district; d. at Buffalo, N. Y., Sept. 15, 1851.

SILLIMAN, GEORGE W., d. on a voyage home from Eng., Oct. 28, 1842, a. 34; was of Coshocton, Ohio; counselor at law.

SILVESTER, FRANCIS, d. at Kinderhook, N. Y., Jan. 30, 1845, a. 76; was a lawyer; a man of retired habits, and but once called into public life, being elected a delegate to the convention of 1821. (*Am. Almanac*, 1846, p. 332.)

SILVESTER, PETER, of Columbia co., N. Y.; was one of the Albany committee of safety, and in provincial congress; judge of com. pleas; in assembly from Columbia co. in 1788, 1803, 1805, and 1806; in the state senate from 1797 to 1800, and in congress in 1789–91; d. at Kinderhook, N. Y., Jan. 30, 1845.

SIMMONS, DAVID, rail road engineer on an express train wrecked at New Hamburg, N. Y., Feb. 5, 1871; d. adhering to his post of duty, and saved many lives; the accident cost 22 lives as it was.

SIMMONS, DAVID ALLEN, b. in Boston, Nov. 7, 1787; removed when a child with his parents to Keene, N. H., but afterwards settled in Boston as a lawyer; was frequently a representative from Roxbury; was a senator from the Norfolk dist. in 1848–49; one of the exec. council, in 1839–40; in 1824, he received the honorary degree of A.M. from Dartmouth; d. in Roxbury, Nov. 20, 1859, a. 72.

SIMMONS, GEORGE A., b. in Lyme, N. H., Sept. 8, 1791; d. at Keeseville, N. Y., Oct. 28, 1857; unaided he prepared himself for coll.; was an alumnus and LL.D. of Dartmouth; conducted an academy for some years at Lansingburg; while studying law, began the practice at Keeseville in 1825; established the highest reputation for ability and learning; was elected three successive terms to the legislature, and two congresses; in each of which bodies he was chairman of the judiciary com. was also a member of the state constitutional convention of 1846.

SIMMONS, George A., was in assem. from Essex co., in 1840–41–42; in congress from 1855 to 1857; was also in the const. conven. of 1846; was a lawyer, and enjoyed a fair reputation for professional skill; d. at Keeseville, N. Y., Oct. 27, 1857.

SIMMONS, William, d. in Boston, Mass., June 17, 1843, a. 61; senior justice of the police court; held various responsible offices.

SIMMONS, William H., d. at Boston, Mass., Aug. 10, 1841, a. 29; grad. at Harvard in 1831.

SIMMS, John Douglas, d. in Washington, D. C., March 2, 1843; for some years chief clerk in the navy department; b. in Virginia, educated at Princeton; practiced law with success several years.

SIMON, Michael, d. at Boardman, Ohio, May 20, 1839, in his 99th year; leaving upwards of 400 descendants living, 81 having died.

SIMONDS, Col. Nathaniel, emigrated to the western shore of the Mississippi in 1800; shared in the perils of Indian warfare; held several offices of trust in Missouri; d. at Troy, Mo., April 7, 1850.

SIMONDS, William, an editor of the *N. E. Farmer;* son of Joseph S., of Charlestown, Mass.; where he was b. in 1822; was editor and prop. of the *Saturday Rambler;* author of the Aimwell stories, and of several Sunday school books; d. at Winchester, Mass., July 7, 1859. (*Hist. Mag.*, iii, 256.)

SIMONS, Abraham, a soldier of the revolution, d. in Wilkes co., Ga., a. 79; was a captain.

SIMONS, Keeting, served in the revolution as an aid to Gen. Marion; d. at Charleston, S. C., Sept. 18, 1834, in his 82d year.

SIMONS, Samuel, in congress from Conn. from 1843 to 1845; d. at Bridgeport, Conn., Jan. 13, 1847, a. 55.

SIMONSON, Capt. James, d. in Cuba, Aug. 7, 1839, a. 45; formerly of the U. S. army.

SIMONTON, Capt. Isaac P., U. S. dragoon; d. at Fort Wayne, Cherokee Nation, Feb. 21, 1842, a. 46; grad. at West Point and entered the army in 1827, from which time he was constantly in service till his death.

SIMONTON, William, d. in South Hanover, Pa., May 18, 1846; was a representative in congress from Pa. from 1839 to 1843.

SIMPSON, Benjamin, a member of the celebrated Boston tea party of the revolution; d. at Saco, Me., March 27, 1849, a. 94.

SIMPSON, George, b. in Phil., Dec. 12, 1759; d. Nov. 30, 1812; was many years cashier of Mr. Girard's Bank, and honorably connected with various public enterprises of his day. (*Simpson's Eminent Philadelphians.*)

SIMPSON, Dr. Josiah, a surgeon of the army; d. at Baltimore, Ind., March 3, 1874; had been in the medical service nearly 37 years, having been appointed asst. surgeon from Pa. in 1837; was with the troops in the Florida and Mexican wars, and during the rebellion was successively med. director of two departments; in 1867 was transferred to Baltimore, being appointed attending surgeon and med. officer at Fort Henry; was promoted in 1865 to the rank of brevet col. for meritorious service.

SIMPSON, MAJ. THOMAS, an officer of the revolution; d. at New Hampton, N. H., Nov. 27, 1835, a. 81.

SIMPSON, THOMAS, arctic explorer; native of Dingwall, Scotland, and companion of Mr. Dease in the discovery of a north west passage; shot himself in a fit of temporary insanity at Turtle river, British America, after shooting two of the company, Messrs. Bird and Legros, June 29, 1840, a. 32.

SIMS, A. D., a member of congress from South Carolina, and a native of Brunswick co., Va.; d. at Kingstree, S. C., Nov. 16, 1848, a. 45.

SIMS, WILLIAM, d. in New York, Sept. 24, 1859, a. 102.

SINGLETON, THOMAS D., of S. C.; on his way to Washington as member of congress, d. at Raleigh, N. C., Dec., 1833.

SINNETT, GEORGE, sole survivor of the army of Gen. Wolfe, and a native of Germany; d. at Brighton, N. S., Jan. 6, 1849, a. 120.

SISCO, JAMES, d. at Olmstead, O., April 15, 1836, a. 108 y. 5 m.

SIXBURY, ROBERT, d. in Le Ray, Jeff. co., N. Y., Oct., 1873, a. 110 y. 7 m.; Mr. S. had acquired great reputation as a hunter on John Brown's tract, in northern New York, where he had slain more than 2,200 deer; the funeral was attended by several of his children of the ages of from 80 to 90 years; the deceased had enjoyed comparatively good health up to the day of his death.

SKILLINGS, CAPT. JOHN, Mass; killed in the rev., April 2, 1777.

SKINNER, AARON NICHOLS, was b. in Woodstock, Ct., 1800; grad. at Yale in 1823; was tutor there from 1825 to 1829; studied law, but did not practice and continued to teach; he established a school for classical instruction of a high order in New Haven, and continued in this employment to the close of life, being occasionally called into the public service; he d. at New Haven, Oct. 26, 1858.

SKINNER, CHARLES M., commodore in the U. S. navy, and nearly 50 years in the service; he entered in 1809, as midshipman, and in 1855 was placed on the retired list; about 36 years of his life was passed on shore unemployed, and 14 on the sea; his principal command was in relieving the African squadron under Perry; he d. at Richmond, Va., Nov. 15, 1860. (*Hist. Mag.*, iv, 373.)

SKINNER, MRS. HANNAH, widow of Benjamin Skinner, a lawyer and former county clerk of Jefferson co., N. Y., and sister of Major Gen. Jacob Brown, of Brownville; d. in Pamelia, N. Y., Oct. 25, 1862, a. 78; she was a pioneer of Jefferson co, and in old age retained a remarkably clear recollection of early events in that section of the state.

SKINNER, JOHN H., b. in Prince George co., Md.; was for some years purser in the navy, and during the war visited the British fleet with a flag of truce with Francis S. Key, and was with him during the bombardment that inspired the "Star Spangled Banner;" he resigned soon after, devoted himself to agriculture, established in 1817 at Baltimore the *American Farmer* and conducted it many years; he was p. m. in Balt. 20 ys., and assistant p. m. gen. under Harrison and Tyler; he returned to N. Y., established the *Journal of Agriculture* and two years after at Phila. began the *Plow the Loom and the Anvil* to which he devoted the rest of his life; he d. at Baltimore, Md., March 21, 1851, a. 63 years. (*Stryker's Am. Reg.*, vi, 212.)

SKINNER, JOSEPH B., d. at Edenton, N. C., Dec. 22, 1851, a. 70; was a lawyer in early life, but devoted himself to agriculture, and was at various times in the state legislature; was in the constitutional convention of 1835.

SLACK, DR. J. H., d. in N. J., Oct., 1874, a. 39; grad. at the Pennsylvania University, and was a prof. in a Phila. med. coll.; was a man of extensive and varied information, and a naturalist; also gave especial attention to the quadrumania. (*N. Y. Tribune*, semi-weekly, Oct. 9, 1874.)

SLADE, CHARLES, elected member of congress from Illinois in 1832; sickened and d. in Knox co., Md., July, 1834, on his way home.

SLICER, REV. HENRY, D.D., d. at Baltimore, April 23, 1874; was at one time an active and distinguished divine of the Methodist church; he was b. at Annapolis, Md., in 1801, and entered the Baltimore Methodist conference in 1822; in early life he was elected chaplain of the United States senate, and was retained in that position during eight sessions; in 1835 he published an *Appeal on Christian Baptism*, and the next year *A Further Appeal*, which went through five or six editions; he made in 1838 a notable discourse against dueling, occasioned by the duel fought near Washington between Mr. Graves of Kentucky and Mr. Cilley of Maine, in which the latter was killed; Dr. Slicer's argument was read extensively, and aided in causing congress to pass Senator Prentiss's bill declaring duels illegal.

SLOAN, LIEUT. THOMAS T., entered the U. S. marine corps in 1834; served through the Florida campaign, and during the last three years was on the African station; he d. at the naval hospital, Brooklyn, Feb. 11, 1850. (*Stryker's Am. Reg.*, iv, 449.)

SLOANE, COL. JOHN, d. in Wooster, O., May 5, 1856, a. 77; b. in Pennsylvania, and removed to Ohio while it was under a territorial government; was a member of the state legislature in 1804, and in 1805–6, was speaker; was receiver of public moneys at Canton, from 1808 to 1816, and afterwards at Wooster till 1819; was in congress from 1819 to 1829; clerk of com. pleas of Wayne co., from 1831 to 1838; sec. of state three years from 1841, and treasurer of the United States under Filmore.

SLOCUMB, JESSE, member of congress from North Carolina from 1817 till his death Dec. 20, 1820, a. 40.

SMALL, JACOB, revolutionary partizan, native of Germany; he was a capt. of Tryon co. militia in the upper Mohawk country, and for some time stationed at Fort Dayton; he resided at Herkimer. (*Benton's Herkimer Co.*, p. 414.)

SMEALLIE, REV. JAMES M., b. in Princetown, N. Y., June 12, 1820; grad. at Union Coll. in 1847; was licensed to preach in 1850, and went as a home missionary to Michigan; settled at Oakland, Mich., and in 1861, was installed pastor at North Kortright, Delaware co., N. Y., and in 1867, succeeded his brother Peter, at the Andes Collegiate Institute; d. Sept. 7, 1868. (*Regents' Report*, 1870, p. 594.)

SMEALLIE, REV. PETER, b. in Princetown, N. Y.; grad. at Union Coll. in 1853, went to Mississippi, but returned and was prin. of the

Acad. at Johnstown, N. Y., for 10 years; in 1864 became prin. of the Andes Collegiate Inst.; d. there, Feb. 4, 1867. (*Regents' Report*, 1868, p. 707.)

SMITH, ARTHUR, b. in the county of Isle of Wight, Va., Nov. 15, 1785; educated at the Coll. of Willtam and Mary; served in the war of 1812, at the head of a militia force at Norfolk; was a member of the privy council of Virginia, and of the legislature; in 1831–25, was in congress; was a lawyer but never practiced; d. in Va., March 30, 1853.

SMITH, A. M. C., d. at Greenpoint, L. I., Nov. 23, 1870; was one of the directors and managers of the American Express Company.

SMITH, BENJAMIN, d. in North Kingston, R. I., Nov. 18, 1849, a. 85; had held many public offices; was 14 years in the house, and 7 in the senate, of the state; was one of the judges of the court of com. pleas, for Washington co., R. I.; was 21 years member of the town council of North Kingston, and most of the time president of that body.

SMITH, BUCKINGHAM, d. in N. Y. city, Jan. 6, 1871; was a member of the state senate of Florida; formerly a judge in that state; was a man of literary and antiquarian tastes; and well versed in Spanish American history.

SMITH, REV. BUEL A., principal of the Union Acad. at Belleville; d. 1867.

SMITH, CHARLES, d. in Talbot co., Md., Oct. 1, 1839, a. 77; was in the revolutionary service.

SMITH, REV. DANIEL, d. in Stamford, Conn., June 11, 1846, a. 78; was b. in New Canaan, Conn., Aug. 9, 1767; grad. at Yale, in 1791; was ordained and installed pastor of the Congregational church in Stamford, in June 1793; where he labored the rest of his life; was elected a member of the corporation of Yale Coll. in 1818.

SMITH, DANIEL, d. in Harrisonburg, Va., Nov. 8, 1850, a. 72; one of the senior judges of the general court of Virginia; as such a member of the special court of appeals, in that commonwealth. (*Am. Almanac*, 1852, p. 329.)

SMITH, DAVID, pioneer settler at Adams, N. Y., originally called Smith's Hills, from him; d. March 18, 1844, a. 73.

SMITH, REV. ELI, d. at South Frankfort, Ky., Oct. 23, 1839; grad. at Dartmouth Coll., in 1809, and a Presbyterian minister.

SMITH, ERASTUS, Texan pioneer; known as Deaf Smith; b. in N. Y., April 19, 1787; moved a. 11 to Mississippi ter., and settled near Natchez; in 1817 he went to Texas, and finally settled there in 1821; d. at Fort Bend, Nov. 30, 1837. (*Texas Almanac*, 1857, p. 136.)

SMITH, FREDERICK, one of the judges of the supreme court of Pa; d. at Reading, Pa., Oct. 6, 1830.

SMITH, GERRIT, b. in Utica, N. Y., March 6, 1797; son of Peter S., an extensive dealer in lands in central New York and elsewhere; grad. at Hamilton Coll., 1818; was educated as a lawyer, but devoted himself largely to benevolent objects, and conspicuously to the anti-slavery movement, of which he became one of the earliest and ablest advocates; he was an effective public speaker, a fluent and powerful writer, and a man of great influence in political affairs, but not for personal advancement, as he avoided office for the most part; he was elected to the 33d congress, but resigned at the close of the 1st session; d. Dec. 28, 1874, at New York city.

SMITH, HENRY, pres. of board of police, N. Y. city; d. Feb. 23, 1874; the *Tribune* of the next day has the following notice: H. S. was b. Oct. 20, 1820, in the village of Amsterdam, Montgomery co., N. Y.; the son of a farmer, he began life as a driver on the Erie canal; when quite young he opened a shop in the village of Fultonville, where he sold groceries and canal stores; he was subsequently employed as an agent of the Albany Merchants' line of canal boats; he did so well that he was induced, about 1843 or 1844, to come to New York as the agent for the Fultonville line of canal boats; he filled this position for several years and purchased an interest in the line; by his efforts he built up an extensive forwarding and commission business; he was subsequently connected with Abram Van Santvoord in running a line of tow-boats, and afterward with Albert Van Santvoord in the same business; Van Santvoord and he, built the handsome steamboats Chauncey Vibbard and Drew, and organized a day line to Albany; Mr. Smith has been for 25 years one of the most active politicians in the whig and republican parties, and for several years past has been one of the most influential republican politicians in the state; he was for many years extremely popular with the working classes in the lower part of the city, and was on several occasions elected over his democratic opponent in a strong democratic district; in 1853 he was chosen councilman from the 1st district, and was reëlected two years later; serving in the board of councilmen during the years 1854, 1855, 1856, and 1857; he was defeated for alderman in the latter year, but was elected two years later, and served in the board of aldermen until 1863, having been reëlected on the expiration of his first term; in 1863 he was chosen one of the board of supervisors, and six years later was again elected; his seat was contested by John Foley, but while the case was before the courts the charter of 1870 was passed, abolishing the board of supervisors on July 4 of that year; in the winter of 1868 Mr. Smith was chosen by the legislature to fill the vacancy occasioned by the resignation of Police Commissioner Thos. C. Acton; when the police board was reorganized in 1870, under the provisions of the charter passed by the legislature of that year, Mr. Smith was reappointed by Mayor Hall, and drew the long term; under the provisions of the present charter he retained his office with several other heads of departments; he served two years as treasurer of the board of police; in 1870, on the reorganization of the board of police, he was chosen president; Mr. Smith has also been a member of the board of health ever since he entered the police board under the new charter, by virtue of his position as president of the board of police.

SMITH, HENRY L., capt. of corps of top. engineers U. S. A.; d. at Madisonville, La., Sept. 13, 1853, a. 44; had been in command of Forts Pike, Wood, Jackson and St. Philip.

SMITH, REV. ISAAC, served in many battles of the revolution; became a Methodist preacher, and d. in Monroe co., Ga., in 1834, a. 76.

SMITH, JAMES S., d. in Orange co., N. C., Dec. 7, 1852, a. 65; was in congress from the 8th dist. of N. C. 2 terms.

SMITH, DR. J. AUGUSTINE, of Va.; d. Feb. 9, 1865, a. 83.

SMITH, DR. J. CLARKSON, of Columbia, Pa.; a volunteer in the yellow fever epidemic at Portsmouth, Va., in the autumn of 1855; fell a victim to the disease.

SMITH, DR. JESSE, d. at Cincinnati, Ohio, July, 1833.

SMITH, CAPT. JESSE, d. in Salem, June 11, 1844; was in the battle of Bunker hill, and served in the battles of Brandywine, Trenton, Germantown and Monmouth.

SMITH. JONATHAN, d. at Bath, N. H., Aug. 10, 1840, a. 43; a prominent member of the Grafton co. bar.

SMITH, J. HOWARD, passed asst. surgeon U. S. N.; d. at naval hosp., Island of Salmadina, of yellow fever, Sept. 5, 1847; was one of the med. officers in charge of sick, and fell in the discharge of his duty.

SMITH, JOHN, of Burlington, N. J.; an original member of the Am. Phil. Soc.; d. March 26, 1771, a. 49.

SMITH, JOHN, of Brookhaven, Suffolk co., N. Y.; in congress from N. Y. from 1799 to 1803, and senator in congress from 1804 to 1813; marshal for N. Y. under Madison; d. in 1816.

SMITH, JOHN, b. in 1835; senator in congress from Ohio from 1803 to 1808; d. July, 1816.

SMITH, GEN. JOHN, formerly a member of congress; d. at Rockville, Md., March 3, 1836, a. 86.

SMITH, GEN. JOHN, d. at Ulysses, N. Y., Jan. 2, 1839, a. 72.

SMITH, JOHN, b. in Barre, Mass., in Aug., 1789; removed in early life to St. Albans, and was admitted to practice law in 1810; was 9 years in the state legislature; was elected state's atty. of Franklin co. in 1826, and served 6 years; was in 1831, 32, 33, speaker in general assembly; was in congress in 1839–41, and after his term expired returned to practice; in 1846 became engaged in important rail road enterprises; d. at St. Albans, Nov. 20, 1858.

SMITH, GEN. JOHN K., d. in Portland, Me., Aug. 7, 1842; he was an officer of the revolution, and for a time aid-de-camp to Lafayette.

SMITH, JONATHAN, d. in Peterborough, N. H., Aug. 29, 1842, a. 79.

SMITH, JOSEPH BROWN, b. in Dover, N. H., and when an infant a week old became blind; when 9 years old he was placed at the Inst. for the Blind, in South Boston, under Dr. Samuel G. Howe; at the age of 17, entered Harvard Coll., where he grad. in 1844; he evinced a talent for music, and became a teacher at Louisville, Ky, in an institution for the blind, where he d. May 6, 1859, a. 36.

SMITH, JOSEPH W., M.D., pioneer physician in St. Law. co., N. Y.; b. at Cheshire, Mass., Feb. 22, 1781; removed to Vt., and thence to Lisbon, N. Y.; was eminent as a surgeon; d. at Ogdensburg, July 4, 1835. (*Hough's Hist. St. Law. & Fr Cos. N. Y.*, p. 610.)

SMITH, JOSHUA HETT, alleged confederate in Arnold's treason; brother of Wm. Smith, early historian of N. Y.; resided in the revolution below the Highlands on the west side of the Hudson; was a lawyer, and man of consequence; he brought André ashore from the Vulture, afforded a place for interview with Arnold, at his house; exchanged clothing with André and conducted him towards N. Y., as far as he thought neccessary, under passes from Arnold; was arrested Sept. 25, 1780, at Fishkill and tried in Oct. 1780 by a court martial which continued several weeks; was acquitted, but detained many months by civil authority, when he escaped in woman's clothing to N. Y., and went to England; was treated with suspicion by both governments, and wrote a vindictive account of André's trial and execution. (*Chandler's Am. Crim. Trials,* ii, 183); d. in N. Y., 1818. (*Drake's Biog. Dict.*)

SMITH, JOTHAM, editor of the *Yonkers Statesman;* d. at Yonkers, N. Y., Feb. 9, 1869; was a lawyer by profession and had been one of the editors of the *N. Y. Courier and Enquirer.*

SMITH, LEONARD, d. in Newburyport, Mass., Aug. 1842, a. 95; many years a merchant at that place.

SMITH, NATHAN, removed from Mass., to Herkimer co., N. Y., in 1790, and opened a store a few miles from Fairfield and afterwards in the village; was in assembly in 1798, 1801, 2; was several years a county judge; was in the senate from 1807 to 1814, and in 1808 was one of the council of appointment; from 1814 to 1821 was first judge of Herkimer co.; d. at Fairfield, N. Y., Oct. 7, 1836, a. 67. (*Benton's Herkimer Co. N. Y.*, p. 357.)

SMITH, DR. NATHANIEL, prof. of theory and practice of medcine in Yale Coll.; was b. at Rehoboth, Mass., Sept. 30, 1762; at 24 accidentally witnessed a surgical operation which created an ardent desire to study anatomy; studied medicine, grad. at Harvard Medical School; practiced with success and founded the med. school at Dartmouth Coll.; subsequently visited Edinburgh and London to perfect his medical education, and in 1813, became a prof. in the newly founded medical school at Yale Coll; d. at New Haven, Jan. 26, 1829, in his 67th year. (*Am. Jour. Sci. and Arts*, 1st ser., xvi, 211.)

SMITH, PERRY, U. S. senator from Connecticut; d. June 3, 1852.

SMITH, PETER, d. Schenectady, N. Y., Aug. 13, 1837, of apoplexy; was formerly first judge of the Madison co. court; an enterprising and wealthy citizen; in the early settlement of Central New York, was largely concerned in land speculations, and dealt largely in lands sold at tax sales.

SMITH, PHEBE, d. at Providence, R. I., Aug. 1836 in the 100th year of her age.

SMITH, PLINY, b. Dec. 19, 1761; settled in Orwell, Vt., in 1784; was town clerk and land register 30 years; member of the legislature 20 years in succession; county judge 18 years; chief judge of Rutland co., for 8 years; d. July 5, 1840. (*Family Reg. of Descendants of Nathaniel Smith, Jr.*, p. 28.)

SMITH, REBECCA, d. at Selingsgrove, Pa., March 15, 1855, a. 105 ys.; she was b. a slave at Havre de Grace, in 1730; went to Pa., in 1800.

SMITH, LIEUT. RICHARD H., of Tennessee; swept from the deck of the San Francisco, Dec. 25, 1853; was appointed to one of the additional infantry regiments, authorized in 1847, the 14th; was transferred to the artillery in June 1848.

SMITH, SAMUEL, d. in Peterborough, N. H., May, 1842, a. 75; was largely concerned in manufactures in that town, of which he was the father; was in congress from N. H., from 1813 to 1815; d. in 1842; held various public offices.

SMITH, SHELDON, a lawyer of Buffalo, N. Y.; d. there, June 1, 1835, a. 96.

SMITH, THOMAS, d. at Hartland, Me., Aug., 1872, a. 80; he had been librarian of the Bangor Mercantile Library, 23 years.

SMITH, THOMAS P., first auditor of the treasury; d. at Washington, D. C., Dec. 4, 1871.

SMITH, LIEUT. WILLIAM, Va., killed at Germantown, Oct. 4, 1777.

SMITH, WILLIAM, d. at Huntsville, Ala., July, 1840, a. 78; was member of congress from South Carolina in 1797–9; U. S. senator in 1816–23, and in 1826–31; afterwards removed to Alabama; he was a distinguished supporter of the doctrine of state rights.

SMITH, WILLIAM H., (Sedley) actor and manager; d. at San Francisco, Cal., Jan. 19, 1872.

SMITH, WILLIAM HENRY, agent of the Western Associated Press at Nashville, Tenn., and an old journalist of that city; d. April 9, 1873; he had been at different times editor of *The Huntsville Advocate*, *The Nashville Gazette*, *The Nashville Banner*, *The Nashville Patriot*, and during the war *The Nashville Union.*

SMITH, WILLIAM PRESCOTT, president of the Baltimore and Ohio rail road co.; d. at Baltimore, Oct. 1, 1872.

SMITH, REV. W. P., D.D., d. near Fayetteville, Tex., March 18, 1870; had been in the M. E. church, a resident of Texas for 40 years; was surgeon gen. of the army of the republic of Texas, and served through the whole of that war.

SMITH, CAPT. ZEBINA, d. in Winsted, Conn., Feb. 4, 1842, a. 82; a revolutionary pensioner.

SNODGRASS, JOHN TRYALL, d. in Parkersburg, Va., June 5, 1854, a. 50; member of congress from the 11th dist. of Va.; b. in Berkeley co., Va., March 2, 1804; settled at Parkersburg, as a lawyer, and lived there through life; was a member of the convention in 1850.

SNOW, EPHRAIM, removed from Killingworth, Ct., to Herkimer co., N. Y., before 1800, and was sheriff in 1806; he lived and d. in Herkimer village. (*Benton's Herkimer Co. N. Y.*, p. 361.)

SNOW, MRS. JANE, d. at Gorham, Me., March, 1837, a. 102.

SNOW, CAPT. PETER W., d. in Providence, R. I., May 7, 1843, a. 58; late U. S. consul at Canton, China.

SNOW, DR. SIMEON, of Root, Montgomery co., N. Y.; d. Sept. 20, 1865, a. 62. (*Transac. N. Y. State Med. Soc.*, 1866, p. 347.)

SNYDER, ADAM WINDER, d. in Bellevue, Ill., May 14, 1842, a. 41; had served frequently in the state leg., and was from 1837 to 1839 in congress; was a candidate for the office of governor at the time of his death.

SNYDER, ANDREW, d. at Intercourse, Lancaster co., Pa., Nov. 1, 1845, a. 112; was a soldier of the revolution.

SOMMERVILLE, DR. JAMES, d. at Tuscaloosa, Ala., Feb. 3, 1842; an eminent physician.

SOUTHARD, HENRY, d. in Baskenridge, N. J., June 2, 1842, a. 95; served in the revolution; was 9 years in the leg., and from 1801 to 1811, and from 1815 to 1821 in congress from N. J.

SPAFFORD, HORATIO GATES, b. in Tinmouth, Vt., Feb. 18, 1778; is celebrated as the author of the first *Gazetteer* of N. Y., of which editions were published in 1813, and 1824; d. of cholera at Lansingburg, N. Y., Aug. 7, 1832.

SPAFFORD, JOHN, revolutionary patriot; an early settler of Tinmouth, Vt., and with Allen and Arnold in the capture of Ticonderoga, and Crown Point, and received at the latter the sword of the officer in charge; d. at Lowville, N. Y., where he was a pioneer settler, March 24, 1823, a. 71; was father of Horatio Gates S., author of the first *N. Y. State Gazetteer*. (*Hough's Hist. Lewis Co. N. Y.*, p. 142.)

SPALDING, CATHARINE, 1st. superior of sisters of charity of Nazareth; b. Dec. 23, 1793, in Charles co., Md., and in 1814 was chosen superior of a house of the sisters of charity in Ky.; in 1831 she was sent to Louisville in charge of a school, and an orphan asylum grew out of her labors; she d. Mar. 20, 1858. (*Dungan's Am. Cath. Almanac*, 1859, p. 42.)

SPALDING, JAMES R., journalist, d. at Dover, N. H., Oct. 11, 1872.

SPALDING, MOST REV. MARTIN JOHN, archbishop of Baltimore; d. at Baltimore, Md., Feb. 7, 1872, a. 62.

SPALDING, THOMAS, b. at Frederica on the island of St. Simond's, Ga., March 26, 1774; studied law with Tho. Gibbons of Savannah, but possessing an ample fortune he did not practice; he was elected to the legislature, lived two years in London, and on his return was in congress from 1805 to 1807; he was many years in the state senate, and was several times state commissioner with important duties; he was a ready writer, and prepared a memoir of Oglethorpe; d. at his son's residence near Darien, Ga., Jan. 4, 1851, in his 77th year; being then the oldest survivor of the convention that revised the constitution of Ga. in 1798; Spalding co., Ga., was named from him. (*White's Hist. Ga.*, p. 634.)

SPANGLER, DAVID, in congress from Ohio from 1833 to 1837, and in 1844 offered the nomination of governor by the whig party, but declined; he d. at Coshocton, O., Oct. 18, 1856.

SPANGLER, JACOB, d. at York, Pa., June 17, 1843, a. 75; formerly a representative in congress, and surveyor general of Pennsylvania under Governors Findley and Wolf.

SPARHAWK, EDWARD V., d. at Richmond, Va., a. about 36, Jan. 6, 1838; editor of the *Petersburg Intelligencer*.

SPARHAWK, SAMUEL, formerly secretary of state of New Hampshire; d. at Conway, N. H., Nov. 22, 1834.

SPAULDING, CORNELIUS, d. in New Orleans, La., March 10, 1851, a. 79; said to be the wealthiest man in that city.

SPAULDING, MISS L. L. K., missionary to Africa; d. at Cape Palmas, early in 1860. (*Vincent's Semi-An. Register*, p. 619.)

SPAULDING, RT. REV. MARTIN JOHN, D.D., archbishop of Baltimore and primate of the Roman Catholic church in the United States; d. at Baltimore, Feb. 7, 1872; b. in Marion co., Ky., May 23, 1810; became bishop in 1848, and archbishop May 6, 1864. (*Hist. Record*, i, 190.)

SPEARS, NOAH, a prominent merchant of Paris, Ky.; d. May, 1868.

SPEIGHT, JESSE, senator in congress from Mississippi, and formerly a representative in congress from North Carolina, his native state; d. in Lowndes, Miss., May 1, 1847.

SPENCER, DR. GORDON P., a surgeon in the war of 1812, and for many years a practicing physician in Champion, N. Y.; d. at Watertown, N. Y., March 26, 1859; he was b. in Salisbury, Litchfield co., Conn.;

was the father of senator George E. Spencer of Alabama. (*New York Reformer*, April 12, 1859.)

SPENCER, ISAAC, an officer of the revolution, and from 1818 to 1835, treasurer of Connecticut; d. at Hartford, Conn., Oct. 16, 1840, a. 81.

SPENCER, JAMES B., judge; settled at Ft. Covington, N. Y., from Vt., in 1810; was captain in 29th regt. U. S. infantry, from April 30, 1813 till 1815; held many county offices, was in assembly in 1831-2; in congress in 1837–9; d. March, 1848, a. 64. (*Hough's Hist. St. Law. & Fr. Cos., N. Y.*, p. 611.)

SPENCER, JOHN C., JR., d. at sea, off the coast of Africa, on board the U. S. ship Marion, of which he was purser, Dec. 29, 1845, a. 23.

SPENCER, JOSHUA AUSTIN, LL.D., son of Eliphalet S.; b. at Gt. Barrington, Mass., May 13, 1790; learned the clothier's and wagon makers' trades, in Madison co., N. Y.; served as captain in the war of 1812–15; studied law, and near his thirtieth year was admitted to the bar; he became distinguished as a lawyer at Utica; was U. S. dist. att'y under Harrison and Tyler; was in the state senate in 1846–7; d. April 28, 1857, a. 67. (*N. Y. Jour.*, April 29, 1857.)

SPENCER, PHILIP, son of John C. Spencer, sec. of war; sailed in the U. S. brig Somers, with Alex. Slidell McKenzie, Aug., 1842, for the coast of Africa as midshipman; was arrested on the return voyage, Nov. 26, for an alleged intention to seize the vessel and turn pirate; was tried by court martial, and hung at the yard arm., Dec. 1, 1842, with Samuel Cromwell and Elisha Small. (*Cruise of the Somers, illustrative of the Despotism of the Quarter Deck*. . . N. Y., 1844, 12mo, pp. 102.)

SPENCER, THOMAS, M.D., prof. in Geneva Med. Coll.; b. in Gt. Barrington, Mass., Oct. 22, 1793; was a son of Eliphalet S.; at the a. of 11 he removed to Lenox, N. Y., and at 18 entered the office of Dr. Dix of Delhi; was licensed at Fairfield, in 1815, and settled in Lenox, where he soon acquired an extensive practice; in 1821 received the degree of M.D., and in 1824 was elected to assembly; in 1832, 33, was elected pres. of the State Med. Soc., and in 1834 was appointed prof. of the theory and practice of medicine in Geneva Coll., in which a med. dept. had been just established; remained in this station 15 years, discharging its duties with great ability; was appointed in 1847 surgeon of the 10th N. Y. reg. N. Y. and N. J. volunteers in the Mexican war, under Col. Temple of Albany, and served nearly a year and a half on the northern line of the army; soon afterwards settled in Syracuse, but soon removed to Milwaukee, having been appointed prof. of the theory and practice of medicine in the Rush Med. Coll. of Chicago; after delivering one course of lectures he resigned from ill health, and returned to Syracuse, and engaged in practice chiefly as a consulting physician; about 1852 was elected to a professorship in the Phil. Coll. of Med., to which city he removed, and there d. May 30, 1857; in 1832 published a small treatise on cholera, and in 1844, 45 delivered several lectures on Animal Heat, which were published and highly commended; was a brother of the Rev. Eliphalet Spencer, Ichabod S. Spencer of Canistota, and Joshua A. Spencer of Utica. (*Tr. N. Y. State Med. Soc.* for 1858, p. 35.)

SPENCER, THOMAS, formerly an extensive dealer in hardware; d. at Athens, N. Y., Jan. 19, 1840, a. 88.

SPENCER, DR. T. RUSH, U. S. surveyor general for the territory of New Mexico; d. at Santa Fé, N. M., June 19, 1872, a. 54.

SPENCER, WILLIAM W., publisher; d. at Boston, Mass., May 27, 1870.

SPINK, CYRUS, b. in Berkshire co., Mass., in 1793; removed to O. in 1815; was successively county surveyor, county auditor, state representative, land register, presidential elector, member of the state board of equalization, and director of the Ohio penitentiary; d. at Wooster, O., being then a member elect to the 36th congress from the 14 dist. of Ohio.

SPINK, CAPT. OLIVER, d. in Wickford, R. I., Nov. 11, 1846, a. 92; was an officer of the revolution.

SPINNER, REV. JOHN D., b. at Warback in the electorate of Mentz, Jan. 18, 1768; received a clerical education, and in 1789 was admitted to holy orders in the R. C. church; about 1800 he became a protestant, and soon after m. and removed to America; began clerical duties at Herkimer and German Flats, Sept. 1801, and labored among the Germans of the Mohawk country about 40 years; for a time he taught a high school at Utica; was accustomed to preach both in German and English; d. at Herkimer, N. Y., May 27, 1848 in his 81st year. (*Benton's Herkimer Co.*, p. 407.)

SPITFATHAM, JOHN, d. June 13, 1839, at Lovingston, Nelson co., Ky., a. 89; was an ensign in the revolution.

SPOFFORD, PAUL, member of the firm of Spofford & Tileston, merchants and importers, N. Y. city; d. in Westchester co., N. Y., Oct. 28, 1869, a. 78; b. in New England; went to N. Y. in 1817, and was very successful in the shipping trade.

SPOONER, JUDAH PADDOCK, first printer in Vt. in company with Timothy Green; they published *The Vermont Gazette*, or *Green Mountain Post Boy*, beginning Feb. 1781, at Westminster.

SPOONER, PAUL, was a member of the Vt. council from 1778 to 1782, when he was chosen lieut. gov. till 1786; was a judge in the supreme court in 1779–80; and from 1782 to 1788; in 1781, 82 he was judge, and register of probates in Windsor; removed to Hardwick where he served as town clerk, and in 1797, 98, 99, was in assembly. (*Hall's Eastern Vermont*, p. 698.)

SPOONER, SAMUEL A., d. in Albany, N. Y., Nov. 1, 1868, a. nearly 69.

SPOONER, WALTER, revolutionary patriot of Dartmouth, now Fairhaven, Mass., and one of the Friends; was in prov. cong. and executive council in 1775; in 1775, he with others were sent to divert an expedition against Ticonderoga and Crown Point; was active and useful through the war. (*Bradford's N. E. Biog.*)

SPORCKE, BARON DE, provisional gov. of Surinam, from March 1751, till his death, Sept. 7, 1752.

SPOTSWOOD, JOHN, son of Gen. Alex. S., gov. of Va.; married Mary, dau. of Wm. Dandridge, of the British navy, in 1745; left two sons, Gen. Alexander S. and Capt. John S. of the revolution.

SPOTSWOOD, ROBERT, younger son of Gov. Alex. S. of Va.; was an officer under Washington, in the French and Indian war; was detached with a scouting party from Ft. Cumberland, in 1756; was supposed to have been killed by the Indians; his remains were found near Ft. Du-Quesne. (*Campbell's Va.*)

SPRAGUE, DR. ALDEN S., of Buffalo, N. Y.; d. Jan. 8, 1863, a. 62. (*Transac. N. Y. State Med. Soc.*, 1868, p. 311.)

SPRAGUE, HORATIO, U. S. council at Gibraltar; d. at that place, March 30, 1848.

SPRAGUE, JOHN, b. at Rochester, Mass.; grad. at Harvard in 1765; settled as a lawyer in Worcester co.; came very slowly into the measures of the revolution; was in the gen. court, and a sheriff of Worcester co., and a chief justice of com. pleas; d. in 1800, a. 60. (*Bradford's N. E. Biog.*)

SPRAGUE, RALPH, came to America, a. 25; was prominent in the early settlement of Charlestown, Mass., where he was several years a selectman; in 1630, first constable, in 1639 lieut. and in 1637 and 8 years after, a representative; d. in 1650. (*Young's Chron. Mass.*, p. 373.)

SPRAGUE, RICHARD, merchant, and one of the founders of Charlestown, Mass., where he was several years a selectman; from 1659 to 1666, was a representative; d. Nov. 25, 1668. (*Young's Chron. Mass.*, p. 373.)

SPRAGUE, SETH, b. in Duxbury, Mass., Nov. 21, 1787; was a representative from that town in the legislature in 1827 and 1833; senator from Plymouth, dist. in 1828–30 and 1840–42; was interested in agricultural improvements; for several years was pres. of the Plymouth co. Agricultural Society; d. in Boston, Dec. 12, 1856, a. 69.

SPRIGG, MICHAEL C., representative in congress from Maryland, from 1827 to 1831; d. at Cumberland, Me., Dec., 1845; he had been repeatedly in the Maryland legislature, and was at one time pres. of the Chesapeake and Ohio canal.

SPRING, REV. GARDINER, D.D., long pastor of the old brick church in the city of New York, and afterward of the church on Murray Hill; d. in New York city, Aug. 18, 1873, a. 89.

SPROAT, JAMES, for thirty years clerk of the courts of Bristol co., Mass.; d. at Taunton, Sept. 8, 1857.

SPROUSE, MRS. MARY, d. in Albemarle co., Va., May 7, 1838, a. 90.

STAATS, BARENT, lieut. col. of militia in Albany co., in the revolution; d. April, 1796, in Bethlehem, N. Y.

STAATS, DR. BARENT P., a prominent physician of Albany; d. July 9, 1871, a. 74.

STACY, CAPT. JOHN, d. at Harvard, Mass., Aug. 31, 1840, a. 83; was a soldier through the revolution.

STAFFORD, JAMES B., d. at Trenton, N. J., Aug. 19, 1838 in his 103d year; formerly a merchant in New York; b. in 1736; was in the French war, and served in the navy through the revolution; in the latter part of it a midshipman on board the Alliance frigate.

STALLARD, CAPT. RANDOLPH, a soldier of the revolution; d. in Culpepper co., Va., March 26, 1843, a. 86.

STAMPS, COL. SAMUEL, sec. of state of Mississippi; d. at Jackson, Miss., March 22, 1850; had been twice elected to that office.

STANDIFER, COL. JAMES, a member of congress from Tennessee from 1823 to 1825, and again from 1829 till his death, which occurred near Kingston, Tenn., Aug. 20, 1837.

STANFORD, Rev. John, d. at N. Y., Jan. 14, 1834, a. 81.

STANFORD, Richard, in congress from North Carolina, from 1797 to 1816; d. April 19, 1816, a. 48.

STANLEY, Edward, d. in San Francisco, Cal., July 12, 1872; he was b. in North Carolina, received a portion of his education in Connecticut, and afterward devoted himself to legal pursuits; served three years in the house of representatives of North Carolina, and represented a district of that state in congress during six terms; 1852 he removed to California, where he attained great success in his profession, and was one of the founders of the republican party in that state; was its nominee for gov. in 1857, but was defeated; during the war President Lincoln evinced his esteem for him by appointing him military governor of North Carolina. Mr. Stanley gave up lucrative pursuits to accept this office, and discharged its duties with eminent success for about a year, when he resigned; he then returned to California and resumed the practice of his profession. (*N. Y. Tribune.*)

STANLEY, Horatio N., a prominent merchant of Batavia, N. Y. d. Dec. 1850, a. 48.

STANLEY, John, member of the 7th and 11th congresses from N. C.; and a distinguished member of legislature; was an eloquent and able debater; while delivering a speech in the N. C. legislature, in the session of 1826–7, he was suddenly stricken with paralysis of one side from which he never found relief; d. at Newbern, N. C., Aug. 3, 1833.

STANSBURY, E. A., of Passaic co., N. J.; d. at his residence in Holidon, a suburb of Paterson, N. J., Nov. 4, 1873; was born in Vermont in 1811, and after being grad. at an eastern coll. edited a newspaper for several years; subsequently he practiced law in N. Y., and in 1856 removed to Holidon, or as it was then called Oldham; here he became an active worker in the republican party and a zealous advocate of abolition; in 1866 he was elected to the assembly.

STANSBURY, John, a lieut. in U. S. navy; killed in naval battle before Plattsburg, Sept. 1, 1814.

STANTON, Col. David, auditor gen. of Penn.; d. Nov. 5, 1871, a. 42.

STANTON, Henry, brigadier gen. U. S. army; b. in Vt.; entered the army as 3d lieut. June 29, 1813, and served through the war, a part of the time as sec. to Gen. Izard; retained in 1815, served as adj. gen. to M. J. Jessup, in the Florida war; was made brevet brig. gen. Jan. 1, 1847; d. at Ft. Hamilton near N. Y., Aug. 1, 1856.

STANTON, John (Corry O'Lanus), one of the editors of *Brooklyn Eagle;* d. Nov. 2, 1870, a. 40; was a humorous writer for *Vanity Fair* and *Punchinello.*

STAPLETON, George, b. in Va.; served in the revolution, was in several battles; d. in Jeffeson co., Ga., May 30, 1832.

STARBUCK, Calvin W., of the *Cincinnati Times*, d. Nov. 15, 1879, a. 48.

STARK, John, d. in Manchester, N. H., Nov. 24, 1843, a. 82; third son of Gen. John S., d. in the house where he was b.; was a magistrate of Hillsborough co., N. H., for more than half a century.

STARLING, LYNE, one of the original proprietors of Columbus, O.; patron of the Medical Coll. of that city, which bears his name; d. at Columbus, Nov. 21, 1848, a. 70 years. (*Stryker's Am. Reg.*, ii, 148.)

STARR, DR. HENRY, lately of Newton, Mass.; at Tremont, Ill., Jan. 21, 1838, a. 31.

STARR, HENRY, d. in Burlington, Iowa, Aug. 31, 1851, a. 69; b. in Warren, Conn.; son of Rev. Peter Starr; grad. at Williams College; studied law at Litchfield law school, and at Troy, N. Y., where he was admitted to the bar; removed to Cin. some 25 years before his death.

STARR, JONATHAN, d. at New London, Conn., Feb. 9, 1838, a. 95; was a merchant.

STARS, VERY REV. DR.——, vicar general of the Catholic diocese, of N. Y.; d. Feb. 6, 1873, a. 72.

STAUGHTON, DR. JAMES M., d. at Cincinnati, O., Aug. 8, 1833.

STAUNTON, COL. PHINEAS, vice chancellor of Ingham University; d. at Quito, Ecuador, Sept. 5, 1867, a. 50; b. in Wyoming, N. Y.; son of Gen. Phineas S.; evinced a talent for painting, and without instruction, while still a minor, had gained considerable success as a portrait painter; in June, 1867, became a member of an expedition sent out by Williams Coll. and the Smithsonian Inst. to explore parts of the Andes, and the Amazon, and collect specimens of natural history; but lived only to reach the capital of Ecuador, where he d. (*Regents' Report*, 1868, p. 809.)

STEARNS, EDWIN, d. at Middletown, Conn., Sept. 4, 1867, a. 63; was a prominent merchant, manufacturer and politician; served in both houses of the state legislature; in 1852–3, was elected state treasurer, and held various other public offices.

STEARNS, JONATHAN, a lawyer in eastern Vermont; was concerned in the Westminster massacre; escaped to Boston and went to New York; he removed to Nova Scotia, and was afterwards attorney secretary of that province. (*Hall's Eastern Vermont*, p. 699.)

STEBBINS, JOHN, a revolutionary soldier; d. in Martinsburg, N. Y., May 25, 1838, a. 80.

STEDMAN, WILLIAM, grad. at Harvard in 1784; was in congress from Massachusetts in 1803–10; d. in 1831.

STEELE, LIEUT. AARON, Mass.; k. in the revolution, Nov. 24, 1777.

STEELE, DR. EBENEZER, of Delhi, N. Y.; d. 1856.

STEELE, OSMAN N., deputy sheriff of Delaware co., N. Y.; killed by anti-rent ruffians, disguised as Indians, while he was in the discharge of his duty, at a sale of property taken for debt, Aug. 7, 1845; the armed party in disguise were led by Big Thunder (Daniel W. Squires). (*Hough's N. Y. State Gazetteer*, 1872, p. 250.)

STEELE, WILLIAM, entered the revolutionary army in 1778; in 1794 he commanded a troop of horse from N. J., in an expedition into western Pa.; he d. at Big Flats, Steuben co., N. Y., April 4, 1851, a. 89; a native of N. Y. city. (*Am. Almanac*, 1852, p. 343.)

STEPHEN, JOHN, d. at Annapolis, Md., June 26, 1844; was for twenty years one of the judges of the court of common pleas of Maryland; formerly of the executive council, and often in the state legislature, before his appointment as judge in 1824.

STEPHENS, MAJOR CHARLES, an officer of the war of 1812, and a volunteer in the Florida war; was appointed to various civil offices, and was appraiser of customs at the time of his death, which occurred at Savannah, Ga., Jan. 23, 1849.

STEPHENS, MRS. DOLLY, d. at Roxbury, N. J., Oct. 1, 1839, a. 97; leaving alive 244 descendants, some of the 5th generation.

STEPHENS, EHUD, a pioneer of Lowville, N. Y.; d. in Copenhagen, Lewis co., Aug. 21, 1852; he was a native of Westfield, Mass. (*Hough's Hist. of Lewis Co. N. Y.*, p. 139.)

STEPHENS, JAMES, b. in Fairfield, Conn.; served in congress from Connecticut from 1819 to 1821; in 1822, was appointed post master at Stamford, where he d. April, 1855, a. 67.

STEPHENS, LINTON, brother of Alexander H. Stephens, d. at Spartan, Ga., July 14, 1872; b. in Taliaferro co., Ga., in 1823; studied law, and became a judge; was opposed to the ordinance of secession, but subsequently withdrew his opposition, and during the war served in the state legislature; he continued to take much interest in politics after the war.

STEPHENS, PHILANDER, member of congress from Pennsylvania from 1829 to 1833; d. in Springfield, Pa., July 8, 1842, a. 54.

STEPHENS, MRS. HARRIET MARION, d. in East Hampden, Me., Aug. 27, 1858, a. 35; she was author of many tales, sketches and poems, a collection of which has been published under the title of *Home Scenes and Home Sounds.*

STEPHENS, WILLIAM, dist. judge of Georgia, son of Wm. S., pres. of the colony of Ga.; d. a. 67, at Savannah.

STEPHENSON, BENJAMIN, removed to Illinois from Kentucky in 1809; was sheriff of Randolph co. many years; colonel in the war of 1812; and delegate in congress from Illinois ter., in 1815–16; was appointed receiver of public moneys at Edwardsville, and d. at that place.

STEPHENSON, JAMES, b. in Gettysburg, Pa., March 20, 1764; removed at an early day to Virginia; was many years in the Virginia legislature, and in congress from 1803 to 1805, and from 1809 to 1811, and from 1822 to 1825; d. Aug., 1833.

STEPHENSON, JAMES S., in congress from Pennsylvania, from 1825 to 1829; d. at Pittsburg, Oct. 17, 1831.

STEPHENSON, DR. T. G., of Boston, d. at White Sulphur Springs, Va., June, 1835, a. 36.

STEPHENSON, ROBERT, a distinguished English engineer; was concerned in the construction of Victoria bridge over the St. Lawrence; d. in London, Oct. 12, 1859, a. 56.

STEPHENSON, ROWLAND, d. in Bristol, Pa., July 2, 1856, a. 83; b. in England; had resided 30 years in this country; was formerly a member of the British parliament, and for many years a banker in London.

STERIGERE, DAVID, d. near Washington, Franklin co., Mo., Sept. 24, 1843; b. in Pa.; was several years in the general assembly of Mo., and a judge of the 9th judicial dist. of that state.

STERLING, MICAH, congressman and senator; b. in Lyme, Ct., Nov. 5, 1784; grad. at Yale in 1804; studied law at Litchfield; settled at

Adams, and the year after at Watertown, N. Y., where he resided from about 1809 till his death, April 11, 1844; was in congress in 1821–23, and in the state senate in 1836–9. (*Hough's Hist. Jeff. Co. N. Y.*, p. 452.)

STERRETT, SAMUEL, member of congress in 1791–93 from Baltimore, Md.; d. in that city July 12, 1833, a. 77.

STEVENS, ROSWELL, formerly judge of probate for the county of Merrimack; d. at Pembroke, N. H., Jan. 13, 1836, a. 53.

STEVENS, EDWIN A., d. at Paris, France, Aug. 7, 1868; was one of the projectors of the Camden and Amboy, rail road, and pres. of that co. from 1830 to 1867; builder of the iron clad battery for harbor defense at Hoboken.

STEVENS, JAMES, b. in Fairfield, Conn.; served in congress from that state from 1819 to 1821, and in 1822; became post master at Stanford; d. at that place, April, 1835, a. 67.

STEVENS, JAMES W., b. in N. J.; grad. at Princeton; was long employed as a clerk in the Holland company's land office, at Batavia, N. Y.; was a judge of the county court; d. in 1841.

STEVENS, JOHN H., millionaire; d. at Newark, N. J., Jan. 22, 1870, a. 82.

STEVENS, DR. GUSTIN E., d. in Boston, Mass., Dec. 17, 1852, a. 30; late surgeon of the 9th or New England regiment in the Mexican war.

STEVENS, PARAN, hotel proprietor, N. Y. city; d. April 25, 1872.

STEVENS, SAMUEL, d. in New York city, Nov. 24, 1844, a. 60; a distinguished member of the bar and son of Gen. Ebenezer S.; had been president of the board of aldermen in New York, and one of the commissioners for construction of Croton waterworks.

STEVENS, SAMUEL, d. in Rochester, N. Y., Sept. 12, 1854, a. 56; was a well known lawyer and politician of New York.

STEVENS, MRS., d. in Clearfield co., Pa., May, 1841, a. 108; leaving posterity to the 6th generation.

STEVENSON, CARTER L., d. at Fredericksburg, Va., June 3, 1840; pres. of the branch of the Farmers' Bank, and for several years a member of the house of delegates.

STEVENSON, JAMES, one of the oldest of the Seneca chiefs; d. on the Cataraugus reservation; d. Dec. 23, 1846, a. about 81; he was a son of an English officer, who vainly endeavored to persuade his Indian wife to return with him to England.

STEVENSON, JAMES S., member of the 19th and 20th congresses; d. at Pittsburg, Pa., Oct. 17, 1831.

STEWART, ALVAH, formerly of Utica; in 1844 the liberty party candidate for vice-president; d. at N. Y., May 1, 1849.

STEWART, DAVID, a prominent member of the Baltimore bar; in 1849–50 senator in congress by executive appointment; d. in Balt., Jan. 6, 1858.

STEWART, GILBERT, portrait painter, b. at Newport, R. I.; evinced an early talent for painting and in 1784 (a. 26) went to England, and became a pupil of West; he returned in 1790, and passed some time in N. Y., Phila., Newport and Boston, where he spent the last 15 years of life; he excelled in portraits, and d. in 1828, a. 70. (*Bradford's N. E. Biog.*)

STEWART, Harriet Bradford, wife of Chas. S. Stewart, missionary to Sandwich islands, maiden name Tiffany; b. near Stamford, Ct., June 24, 1798; m. at Albany, June 3, 1822, arrived at the S. island, April, 1823; sailed for London in 1826, returned to the U. S., and d. Jan., 1830, at Cooperstown, N. Y. (*Hunt's Biog. Panorama*, p. 273.)

STEWARD, Rev. Ira R., b. in New London, Conn., in 1805; was minister at the mariner's temple, N. Y., from 1843 to 1865; and d. at New York city, Dec. 26, 1868.

STEWART, Dr. James, b. in N. Y. city April 7, 1799; d. Sept. 12, 1864, in that city. (*Transac. N. Y. State Med. Soc.*, 1865, p. 304.)

STEWART, Patrick Somerville, b. in Edinburgh, Scotland, Aug., 1791; came to America when a young man; was a clerk in Mr. LeRay's land office and afterwards for many years his general agent at LeRaysville and afterwards at Carthage, Jeff. co., N. Y.; was in the N. Y. assembly in 1859; d. at Carthage, N. Y., Oct. 31, 1874.

STEWART, Robert, a pioneer of the west, and in early life concerned with Astor in the fur trade; he resided many years at Detroit but more recently was connected with the management of the Illinois and Michigan canals; d. at Chicago, Oct. 28, 1848. (*Stryker's Am. Reg.*, ii, 246.)

STEWART, Col. William, d. at Baltimore, Md., Feb. 12, 1839, in his 59th year.

STEWART, Col. William Montgomery, d. in Washington, D. C., Nov. 9, 1872, a. 74; grad. at Harvard, studied law at Washington, D. C., and settled at Rockville, Md., as a lawyer; was twice in the Maryland legislature; was a pioneer in California, and assisted in forming the constitution of that state; was appointed judge; and was nominated for gov.; returned to Washington, and resided there till death; commanded the cavalry escort that conducted Pres. Buchanan to the depot; received Pres. Lincoln, but disbanded this troop rather than serve against the south.

STILLÉ, Benjamin, b. Oct., 1779; d. Aug., 1854; his family was of Swedish ancestry, and settled on the Delaware in 1638; Mr. S. was a merchant of Philadelphia for more than fifty years; retired about twenty years before his death with a competency; took an interest in various philanthropic enterprises of his day. (*Simpson's Em. Philadelphians.*)

STILWELL, Gen. Garret, d. in N. Y. city May 6, 1843, a. 86; formerly of Monmouth, N. J.; served with reputation in the rev., and a prisoner in N. Y. city; after the war was for many years in the militia, in which he acquired the rank of general.

STIMPSON, Joseph, of Elliot, Me.; d. May, 1860, a. 89 y. 10 m.; b. in Charlestown, Mass.

STIMSON, John J., of Providence, R. I., an eminent merchant; d. Jan. 19, 1860, in his 62d year.

STOCKMAN, John R., d. in Natchez, Miss., Nov. 11, 1850; mayor of the city; was b. in Pennsylvania, but for the last sixteen years resident of Natchez; was elected mayor in 1843, and retained this office till the time of his death.

STOCKTON, Dr. Ebenezer, an eminent physician; d. at Princeton, N. J., Dec. 8, 1837, a. 77.

STOCKTON, Miss Fannie, vocalist and actress; d. at New York, Dec. 25, 1870.

STOCKTON, L. D., judge of the supreme bench of Iowa; d. at Burlington, Iowa, June 9, 1860; was appointed to this office in 1856, by Gov. Grimes, and afterwards elected.

STOCKTON, LUCIUS H., lawyer; d. at Trenton, N. J., May 26, 1835.

STOCKTON, SAMUEL, a lieutenant in the U. S. navy; d. at Princeton, N. J., Nov. 29, 1836, a. 35.

STOCKTON, WILLIAM S., founder and editor of the *Wesleyan Repository*, in 1821; d. near Burlington, N. J., Nov. 20, 1860.

STODDARD, CHARLES, of the firm of Stoddard & Loring, Boston; d. April 20, 1873; he was for many years senior deacon of the old South Church, and prominently identified with Congregationalism and the American Board of Foreign Missions.

STODDARD, REV. DAVID TAPPAN, d. at Oroomiah, Persia, Jan. 22, 1857, a. 38; b. in Northampton, Mass.; grad. at Yale in 1838; after completing his theological studies went as a missionary to the Nestorians, where he labored through life, with great zeal and success.

STODDARD, CAPT. JOSIAH, Conn.; killed Aug. 24, 1779.

STODDARD, CAPT. NATHAN, Conn.; killed in the rev., May 27, 1777.

STODDART, EBENEZER, b. at West Woodstock, Conn., May 6, 1786; grad. at Brown, U. in 1806; was a lawyer of extensive practice; was several years in the state legislature; was lieut. gov. one year; in congress from 1821 to 1825; d. at Woodstock, Aug., 1848.

STODDART, JOHN T., member of congress, from Maryland, from 1833 to 1835; d. in Charles co., Md., July 19, 1870, a. 80; b. in that co., in 1790; grad. at Princeton, in 1810; was admitted to the bar; served as a militia officer in the war of 1812; was several years in the Maryland leg.

STOHLMANN, REV. CHARLES F. E., D.D., pastor of St. Matthews German Evangelical Lutheran ch.; d. in N. Y. city, May 3, 1868, in his 59th year.

STONE, BALTIS, a revolutionary pensioner; d. at Phila., Oct. 22, 1846, a. 103 ys. 16 days.

STONE, REV. P., B. D.D., treasurer of the N. H. Bible and Missonary Soc.; d. at Concord, N. H., Nov. 28, 1871, a. 70; formerly editor of the *Congregational Journal, and Christian Reporter.*

STONE, REV. COLLINS, d. at Hartford, Conn., Dec. 23, 1870, a. 58.

STONE, DR. DANIEL, d. in Sharon, Mass., Aug. 27, 1842, a. 69; grad. at Harvard, in 1797; and much esteemed as a physician and citizen.

STONE, DANIEL, professor of language and literature in the University of Pennsylvania; d. in Chicago, Ill., August 7, 1846.

STONE, COL. HENRY D., d. in Calhoun co., Fla., Jan. 24, 1841, a. 77; was a soldier of the revolution, and for a time president of the legislative council of Florida.

STONE, JAMES W., d. in Kentucky, Oct. 13, 1854, a. 41; was in congress from the 5th district of Kentucky, from 1843 to 1845, and from 1851 to 1853.

STONE, REV. WILLIAM, Presbyterian clergyman, b. Guilford, Ct.; was a soldier of the revolution; spent 1 y. at Dartmouth Coll. and three at Yale, where he grad. in 1786; he studied theology, was licensed by the Ct. asso., and labored thirty-five years in the ministry; he spent several years in the southern states, and preached on Long Island, at New Paltz (where he was ordained), Jericho (now Bainbridge, N. Y.) and at Cooperstown, and other towns in Otsego co.; in 1817 he removed to Junius, and in 1819 to Sodus, N. Y., where he d. March 20, 1840, a. 83; he was father of Wm. L. Stone the author and editor. (*Griswold's Biog. Annual*, 1841, 200.)

STONER, NICHOLAS, famous hunter in northern N. Y.; b. about 1762, settled at Fonda's Bush, 10 m. north of Johnstown, N. Y.; served in the revolution, and spent his life in the north woods of New York. (*J. R. Simms's Trappers of N. Y.*, pp. 15–174, with portrait.)

STORER, CLEMENT, U. S. senator from N. H., from June 17, 1817 to March 3, 1819; d. at Portsmouth, N. H., Nov. 22, 1830, a. 70 years.

STORER, WOODBURY, a prominent lawyer, d. at Portland, Me., June 24, 1860, a. 76.

STORMS, ABRAHAM, d. May, 1842, a. 87; served in the revolution and for more than six months a prisoner of war; for the last twenty-five years he resided at Lebanon, O., where he d.

STORMS, GEN. HENRY, d. at Tarrytown, N. Y., April 11, 1874, a. 79; was formerly prominent in New York city politics, being an active supporter of the democratic party; he was an alderman as far back as 1825, and was for a number of years a member of the Tammany Society; in his youth he joined a cavalry regiment of the state militia, and while acting as first commandant received Gen. Lafayette at Castle garden, his company acting as escort to Putnam hill; he finally rose to brigadier general of the first division of the national guard of this state, and held that rank for twenty years; Gen. Storms was commissary general of the state in 1842, and some years later was elected inspector of state prisons; upon retiring from public life he moved to Tarrytown, where for several years past he was senior warden of St. Mark's Protestant Episcopal church.

STORMS, REV. WILLIAM, b. Feb. 2, 1772, and d. in Plessis, N. Y., Dec. 30, 1859. (*New York Reformer*, Feb. 10, 1859.)

STORRS, LEMUEL, son of Lemuel S.; b. April 26, 1753; resided in Colchester, Ct.; m. a dau. of Col. Henry Champion, Oct. 5, 1783; was concerned in the titles and settlement of lands in northern N. Y., and in Ohio; d. Nov. 29, 1816. (*Goodwin's Notes*, p. 220.)

STORY, BENJAMIN, d. Dec. 25, 1847; a distinguished financier of New Orleans, La.; pres. of the Bank of La., and a millionaire.

STOUGHTON, EDWARD H., d. at Boston, Mass., Dec. 28, 1868; grad. at West Point in 1859; was col. of the 4th Vt. vols. in the late war, and promoted to brig. gen.; was captured at Fairfax C. H., by Moseby, and imprisoned at Richmond some time; after his release he resigned, and entered upon the practice of law.

STOUGHTON, REV. WILLIAM, formerly president of Columbia Coll.; d. on a journey to Ky., Dec. 12, 1829.

STOW, ALEXANDER W., chief justice of Wisconsin; b. in Lowville, N. Y.; son of Silas S.; lived many years at Rochester, N. Y.; went to Wisconsin in 1841; on the organization of the judiciary of that state; he was chosen circuit judge, and subsequently was elected by his associates, chief justice; d. Sept. 14, 1854, at Milwaukee. (*Milwaukee Sentinel*, Sept. 15, 1854.)

STOW, HORATIO J., N. Y. senator; son of Silas S., of Lowville, N. Y.; settled at Buffalo as a lawyer; was elected recorder, and member of the const. conv. of 1848; removed to Lewiston, N. Y.; was elected to the senate of 1858–9; d. at Clifton Springs, Feb. 19, 1859. (*Murphy's Biog. of Legis.*, 1858, p. 102.)

STOW, JOSHUA, d. at Middletown, Conn., Oct. 9, 1842, in his 81st year; was many years post master in Middletown; was chief judge of Middlesex co., a state senator, and had filled many other public offices.

STOW, SILAS, judge and land agent; b. in Middlefield, Ct., Dec. 21, 1773; studied law; became an agent in Leyden in 1795, and in 1797 in Lowville, where he bought a valuable tract known as Stow's Square; was first judge of Lewis co. from 1815 to 1823, and in congress in 1811, 13; d. at Lowville, July 19, 1827, a. 54; his sons were Alex. W., chief justice of Wis., Horatio J., eminent lawyer and senator of Lewiston, and Marcellus J., a merchant of Wis. (*Hough's Hist. Lewis Co., N. Y.*, p. 139.)

STOWE, REV. PHINEAS, pastor of the Bethel church in Boston; d. Nov. 14, 1868.

STRADER, CAPT. JACOB, b. in N. J. in 1795, and settled in Cincinnati, O., 1817; he first engaged in banking, and afterwards in mills; was one of the pioneers in steamboating on the Ohio, and from 1830 to 1846 held a mail contract between Cincinnati and Louisville; was one of the promoters of rail roads in Ohio, and in 1844 aided in establishing a large cotton manufactory; was for a time at the head of a banking house at Cincinnati, which bore his name; d. there Aug. 28, 1860, a. 65.

STRAIGHT, HENRY, d. in Springfield, O., Jan. 10, 1858, a. 97; he was a native of R. I.; had served in the war of the revolution, and in 1812 was a lieutenant; he had voted at every presidential election.

STRAIT, REV. JOHN, a revolutionary soldier. d. at Gallipolis, O., Jan. 7, 1860, a. 101 y. 9 mo. 7 d. (*Vincent's Semi-An. Register*, p. 20.)

STRANG, JAMES J., Mormon leader, of the settlement on Beaver I., Lake Huron; was assas., June 15, 1856. (*Detroit Adv.*, June 20, 1856.)

STRANG, JESSE L., Mormon leader of the settlement on Beaver Island; assassinated June 16, 1856. (*Detroit Advertiser*, June 20; *N. Y. Tribune*, June 25.)

STREET, GEN. JOSEPH M., U. S. agent for the Sac and Fox Indians; d. May 5, 1840, on Des Moines river.

STREET, RANDALL S., settled early in life in the state of N. Y. from Ct.; studied law at Poughkeepsie, where he married and resided 30 y.; he was dist. att'y of several river counties, Feb. 9, 1810, and held one year, having served in the 16th congress (1807–9); in 1824 he removed to Monticello, Sullivan co., N. Y., where he d. in 1839; he was the father of Alfred B. Street of Albany.

STREETER, SAMUEL, a revolutionary pensioner; d. in Plainfield, Sept. 7, 1844, a. 90 y. 3 m. 15 d.; had lived in town 68 years.

STRICKLAND, FREDERICK, a wealthy English gentleman, about 30 years of age; in visiting the White mountains, got separated from his companions, wandered and perished Oct. 25, 1849; his lifeless body was found on the mountains two days after.

STRONG, GEORGE W., d. in New York city, June 28, 1855, a. 74; b. in East Hampton, N. Y.; grad. at Yale in 1802; resided in city of New York, and became eminent as a lawyer.

STRONG, JAMES, of the city of New York; d. in Chester, N. J., Aug. 8, 1847, a. 64; was in congress from Columbia co., N. Y., from 1819 to 1821, and from 1823 to 1831, being then a resident of Hudson.

STRONG, JULIUS L. member of congress from the Hartford district, Conn.; d. in Hartford Sept. 5, 1872, a. 47.

STRONG, NATHAN, a prominent settler of Rodman, N. Y.; d. in that town, Jan. 21, 1841. (*New York Reformer*, May 19, 1859.)

STRONG, NATHANIEL T., an educated Seneca chief; d. Jan. 4, 1872 on the Cattaraugus Reservation in Chautauqua co., N. Y. (*Hist. Record*, i, 143.)

STRONG, OLIVER, of Rochester, N. Y., d. at Detroit, July 9, 1832

STRONG, OLIVER R., one of the pioneers of Onondaga co., N. Y., d Oct. 3, 1872, a. 91 y. 2 mo; b. in Conn.; went to Syracuse in 1802; was formerly county sheriff and during 22 years county treasurer; was pres. of the 1st National Bank of Syracuse; was judge of com. pleas, and in 1834 was in assembly.

STRONG, OLIVER S., who was identified with various educational and 'benevolent movements of the day; d. in N. Y. city, April 30, 1874, in his 68th year.

STUART, ALONZO C., a lawyer, b. in Clermont, N. H.; grad. at Dartmouth; removed from Reading, Pa., to Belleville, Ill., in 1816; was killed by accident in 1817.

STUART, REV. JULIUS WALKER, d. at Beaufort, S. C., Oct. 30, 1856, a. 28; grad. at Harvard, in 1849; was ordained associate rector of Grace church in Charleston.

STUART, GEN. PHILIP, an officer of the revolution; d. at Washington, D. C., Aug. 14, 1830.

STUART, SIDNEY H., d. in N. Y. city, Sept. 18, 1871, a. 60; had been a police magistrate several years; was afterwards distinguished as a criminal lawyer.

STURDEVANT, JAMES MONROE, M.D., b. in Tinmouth, Vt., March 11, 1800; removed with his father's family to Ellisburg, N. Y., in 1813; attended med. lectures at Fairfield; settled in practice at Copenhagen, in 1825; in 1832, removed to Martinsburg, N. Y.; in 1848 to Rome, where he d. suddenly, Aug. 10, 1873. (*Memorial of J. M. S., N. Y.*, 8vo, pp. 44, with portrait.)

STURGES, JONATHAN, identified with various benevolent organizations in the city of New York; a prominent citizen; d. Nov. 28, 1874, in his 73d year.

STURGES, LEWIS BURR, d. at Norwalk, O., March 30, 1844, a. 82; b. in Fairfield, Conn.; grad. at Yale in 1782; from 1805 to 1817, a representative from Conn. in congress.

STURGIS, CAPT. JOSIAH, d. in Boston, July 28, 1850, a. 56; commander of the revenue cutter Hamilton.

STURGIS, RUSSELL, a prominent shipping merchant of N. Y. city; d. in that city, May 7, 1872, a. 68; was a native of Barnstable, Mass., where his early life was spent; came to this city when a young man; was engaged for years in the East India trade, as captain of a merchant ship, gaining a high reputation as a skillful navigator, and a man of unflinching honesty and uprightness; subsequently he established a shipping house in this city, of which he remained the head until his death; has always been at the head of the pilot commissioners; was for some time chairman of the harbor-masters; and took the most lively interest in everything pertaining to the welfare of the merchant marine of New York; during the war he rendered efficient service to the government in procuring and fitting out vessels; his youngest son was killed in Virginia while with the army of the Potomac; since the war Mr. Sturgis had been the chief proprietor of one of the lines of steamers to Savannah. (*N. Y. Tribune.*)

STUYVESANT, Gerard, a descendant of the last Dutch gov. of Netherland; a man of ample fortune, and liberal in its use; d. at N. Y., Feb., 1859. (*Hist. Mag.*, iii, 96.)

STUYVESANT, Nicholas W., d. New York, at his seat in the Bowery, Sept. 28, 1780, a. 58; many years a magistrate; great grandson of the Dutch governor.

SUDAM, John, of Kingston, N. Y.; member of the New York senate; d. at Albany, April 13, 1835.

SULLIVAN, John Turner Sergeant, a son of Wm. Sullivan of Boston; a member of the Phila. bar; known as a successful author; d. at Boston, Dec. 30 1848, a. 35 years. (*Stryker's Am. Reg.*, ii, 250.)

SULLY, Thomas, d. in Phila., Nov. 5, 1872; was a portrait painter; came to America when 9 years old in 1792., with his parents, who were English players; he began the study of painting at a very early age, and in 1803 established himself as an artist in Richmond, Va., whence he soon removed to New York; he did not remain long here, however, but soon betook himself to Philadelphia, where he spent the rest of his long life; his greatest successes were attained many years ago, although he has never entirely laid down the pencil; among his best known works are portraits of Thomas Jefferson, Lafayette, Commodore Decatur and Dr. Benjamin Rush; in 1838 was commissioned to paint a portrait of the queen of England; his principal historical picture is Washington crossing the Delaware, now in the Museum at Boston; his son, Gen. Sully of the United States army, is a gallant and accomplished officer, who has distinguished himself in our Indian wars on the frontier. (*N. Y. Tribune.*)

SUMMERS, Levi, d. at Sulphur Springs, Va., Aug. 27, 1843, a. 65; was a member of constitutional convention in 1829; in that body and on the bench, his services were highly important.

SUMNER, Charles, an illustrious statesman of Massachusetts; d. while a senator in congress, March 11, 1874.

SUMNER, Charles P., late sheriff of Suffolk co.; d. at Boston, April 2, 1839, a. 63.

SUMNER, Hezekiah, son of Wm. S. of Middletown, Ct., b. about 1732; was a lieut. of rangers at first, and afterwards of the 1st Ct. regt.; he settled in Berkshire co., Mass., about 1802, and d. May 13, 1822, a. 90.

SUMNER, Rev. William, Meth. Episc., d. in Housatonic, Mass., Nov. 12, 1869, a. 64. (*Christian Advocate*, Jan. 13, 1870.)

SUMTER, Col. Thomas, only son of Gen. Sumter of the revolution; d. June, 1840, near Statesburg, S. C.

SURGET, Capt. Francis, d. near Natchez, 1857, a. 72; he was largely engaged in business, and at the time of his death was the wealthiest man in Mississippi, being reputed worth $7,000,000.

SUTHERLAND, John, d. at Mirigonishe, N. S., in his 116th year; b. in Clyne, Sutherlandshire, North Britain; lived under six sovereigns and in 1746, emigrated to Nova Scotia, where he lived till his death.

SUTTLES, William, a revolutionary soldier; d. in 1839, a. 108, in De Kalb co., Ga.; it was estimated that his descendants at his death numbered 300; his wife Margaret, d. June, 1839, a. 104; she had been seventy years a member of the Baptist church.

SUYDAM, Abraham, was murdered, Dec. 3, 1840, just as he was about to go to church on thanksgiving day; was president of the Farmers and Mechanics' Bank.

SWACKHAMER, Conrád, b. in 1814; conspicuous as a leader of German democrats in the city of New York; was navy agent under Pierce, and d. in New York city, Nov. 7, 1867.

SWAIM, William M., b. in Onondaga co., N. Y.; came to Philadelphia in 1836, and was one of the originators of the *Public Ledger;* d. at Philadelphia, Pa., Feb. 16, 1868, in his 59th year.

SWAN, Benjamin, d. at Woodstock, Vt., April 11, 1839, a. 76.

SWAN, Gustavus, settled in Columbus, O., in 1812; was a representative in the state legislature; judge of the court of com. pleas; one of the state fund commissioners, and the first president of the state bank of Ohio; he d. at Columbus, Feb. 6, 1860, a. 71.

SWAN, Thomas, d. at Morven, near Leesburg, Va., Jan. 19, 1840, in his 75th year; an eminent lawyer, and formerly attorney of the U. S., for the Dist. of Columbia. (*National Intelligencer.*)

SWAN, Dr. Samuel, d. at Boundbrook, N. J., Aug. 24, 1844, a. 73; was several years a representative in congress from New Jersey.

SWANTON, John B., collector at Bath, Me., under the administration of J. Q. Adams; d. at Dresden, Me., June 1, 1851, a. 69; was a representative in the general court of Mass. from Bath, in 1816.

SWARTWOUT, Gen. Robert, quarter master general of the U. S., in the war of 1812; succeeded Gen. Covington after the death of Gen. Covington after the battle of Crysler's field; he d. in New York, July 19, 1848. (*Stryker's Am. Reg.*, i, 502.)

SWARTWOUT, Samuel, once collector of the port of New York, and noted for his defalcations in office; d. in that city, Nov. 21, 1856, a. 73.

SWAYNE, Rev. David L., ll.d., president of the University of N. C., and well versed in the history of that state; d. Aug., 1868, from injuries received by being thrown from a carriage.

SWEENY, Thomas, d. in Pa., Feb. 27, 1859, a. 122.

SWEET, Gen. Benjamin J., deputy com'r of internal revenue; d. at Washington, Jan. 1, 1874, a. 41; formerly col. of the 21st Wis. vols.

SWEET, Rev. William Gray, d. in Charlestown, Mass., Feb. 15, 1843; pastor of the Unitarian church at Lynn, Mass.

SWEETSER, Philip, d. at Indianapolis, Ind., April 29, 1843, in his 46th year; distinguished at the bar of Indiana; grad. at Harvard.

SWEETSER, SETH, d. in Guayaquil, S. C., Sept. 7, 1848, a. 54; was U. S. consul for the republic of Equador.

SWEETZER, HENRY E., of *The N. Y. World;* d. at N. Y., Feb. 17, 1870, a. 33; b. in Mass.; grad. at Yale, and was one of the founders and publishers of the *Round Table.*

SWEEZY, REV. MOSES, Presb. pastor at Riverhead, N. Y.; ordained in 1808; d. Jan. 28, 1826, a. 55.

SWIFT, CAPT. ALEXANDER J., of the engineer corps; d. in New Orleans, La., April 24, 1847; entered at West Point in 1826, and grad. in 1830, and in 1838 he became capt.; in 1840 was selected by the war department to visit France, and acquire practical information as to the organization and exercises of engineer soldiers; returned in 1841, and in 1846 organized a company of these soldiers; was present at the seige of Vera Cruz, but his health failing returned to New Orleans and died.

SWIFT, BENJAMIN, b. in Amenia, Dutchess co., N. Y., April 5, 1781; began law practice in Bennington, Vt., in 1806, and was settled for a time at Manchester, and then at St. Albans, where he became eminent in his prof.; was in general assembly of Vt. from 1827 to 1831; was U. S. senator in 1833–39; d. suddenly in an open field on his farm, Nov. 11, 1847.

SYKES, FRANCIS, a soldier of the revolution; d. at Springfield, N. Y., Sept. 5, 1837, a. 75.

SYLVESTER, FRANCIS, a lawyer of Columbia co., N. Y.; b. July 22, 1767; d. Jan. 31, 1845.

SYME, REV. ANDREW, D.D., d. in Petersburg, Va., Oct. 26, 1845, a. 91; oldest citizen in that town, and said to be oldest clergyman in the state; was b. in Lanarkshire, Scotland, Sept., 1754; came to Petersburg, before 1800, and lived there till his death; was of the Protestant Episcopal church.

SYMMES, REV. WILLIAM, D.D., grad. at Harvard in 1750; was tutor several years, and settled over a church at Andover Mass., where he d. in 1807. (*Bradford's N. E. Biog.*)

SYMOCKS, HENRY, was a lieut. in the English army in the French war in America.

TACON, Y. ROSISQUE DON FRANCISCO, minister from Spain to the U. S., d. at Phila., June 22, 1835. (*Am. Almanac*, 1836, p. 311.)

TAGERT, JOSEPH N., for 40 years president of the Farmers and Mechanics' Bank of Phila.; d. at Germantown, Pa., Aug. 1, 1849, at the age of 92 years.

TAGGART, DR. CHARLES, d. in Jersey city, N. J., Sept., 1867.

TALBOT, ISHAM, b. in Bedford co., Va. in 1773; in the Kentucky senate from 1812 to 1815, and from 1815 to 1837, a member of the U. S. senate; d. near Frankfort, Sept. 27, 1837.

TALBOT, MATTHEW, state senator and acting gov. in Georgia; b. in Va.; settled in Wilkes co., Ga. in 1785, and afterward removed to Oglethorpe; was often in the legislature, and was a framer of the state constitution; in 1808 was elected to the state senate; was pres. from 1818 to 1823 and acted a short time as gov. in 1819; d. in Wilkes, Sept. 17, 1827, a. 60. (*White's Hist. Ga.*, p. 229.)

TALBOT, MICAH J., d. in East Machias, Me., Jan. 17, 1869, a. 80; served in both branches of the legislature, and on the governor's council.

TALCOTT, George H., brevet maj.; capt. in ordnance corps, U. S. A.; d. at Indian Springs, Ga., June 8, 1854, a. 43; b. in Maryland; entered the service from Delaware, and grad. at West Point in 1831.

TALCOTT, Hezekiah, pioneer of Talcottville, Leyden, Lewis co., N. Y.; d. Mar. 16, 1813, a. 74.

TALCOTT, Samuel Austin, attorney gen. of N. Y.; b. in Hartford, Ct., 1790; grad. at Williams in 1809; studied law and settled at Lowville, N. Y.; removed in a few years to Utica was appointed atty. gen. of N. Y., Feb. 12, 1821; held till 1829; d. in N. Y., March 19, 1836, the admiration and sorrow of friends; his talents were of the most brilliant kind and his oratory seldom excelled. (*Hough's Hist. Lewis Co. N. Y.*, p. 152.)

TALLMADGE, Daniel Bryant, b. April 6, 1793, in Chatham, N. Y.; was a lawyer at Hudson, and in N. Y. city; was appointed a judge of the superior court of N. Y.; was a legal writer of eminence; d. at Richmond, Va., on a journey for his health, Oct., 1847. (*Raymond's Distinguished Men of Columbia Co.*, p. 87.)

TANEY, Joseph, d. near Emmetsburg, Md., Nov. 24, 1844, a. 89; was for some years a member of the state legislature.

TAPPAN, John, for 40 years president and treasurer of the American Tract Society at Boston; d. March 25, 1871, a. 90.

TAPPEN, Lewis, a pioneer in the free church movement; and the great abolition agitator; d. in Brooklyn, N. Y., June 21, 1873, a. 85.

TARASCON, Louis Anastasius, a French merchant at Philadelphia where he established himself in 1794; was a large importer of silks, and all kinds of French and German goods; in 1801 established an extensive mercantile house at Pittsburg and built ships for foreign trade, in 1801–4. (*Simpson's Eminent Philadelphians.*)

TARPLEY, Colin S., an eminent lawyer; d. in Jackson, Miss., April, 1860, a. about 60.

TAYLER, John, lieut. gov. of N. Y.; b. in N. Y. city, July 4, 1742; the only child of respectable parents of limited means; at the age of 17 he removed to Albany and with some adventitious funds was able to procure some goods and removed to Lake George to supply the British garrison in which business he was successful and won the esteem of many of the officers; the next year he followed the army to Oswego on the same business and there acquired the Indian language which proved very serviceable in after life; 1771 he married Miss Margaret VanValkenburgh of Albany; some time after removed to Stillwater; but in 1773, he returned to Albany and became a merchant; early in the revolution he was sent by Gen. Schuyler to Canada on an important mission; he served through the war as a member of provincial congress and member of assembly; in 1802 and from 1804 to 1814, he was in the state senate when he was elected lieut. gov. and served 9 years, during which period he served a short time as governor upon the election of Tompkins to the vice-presidency; in 1802 he was elected a regent; in 1814 a chancellor; d. 1829.

TAYLOR, Allen, judge of the general court of Virgina, 17th circuit; d. June 3, 1836, in his 53d year.

TAYLOR, DR. AUGUSTUS R., d. at New Brunswick, N. J., Aug. 19, 1840, a. 59; was a member of the legislative council, and a prominent physician.

TAYLOR, CREED, late chancellor of the Richmond and Lynchburg district; d. at Needham, Va., Jan. 7, 1836, in his 70th year.

TAYLOR, MAJ. GEORGE, swept from the deck of the San Francisco, Dec. 25, 1853; b. in Georgia, grad. at West Point in 1833; served in the Florida war, and was asst. prof. of mathematics at West Point in 1842; served in Mexican war, and was distinguished in the battle of Allixco; Mrs. T. was lost with him in the wreck of the San Francisco.

TAYLOR, CAPT. G. W., d. in Washington, D. C., April 28, 1850, a. 42; proprietor of the famous diving bell, and the inventor of the India rubber camels.

TAYLOR, JAMES B., politician d. at New York, Aug. 23, 1870, a. 64.

TAYLOR, REV. JOHN, missionary of Westfield, Mass., grad. at Yale in 1784; settled at Deerfield, Mass., and in 1802 went on a missionary tour through the Mohawk and Black river valleys; in 1806 he engaged in farming at Enfield, Ct., in 1817, settled in Mendon, N. Y., and in 1832 in Michigan; he d. at Bruce, Macomb co., Mich., in 1840, a. 78. (*Doc. Hist. N. Y.*, iii, 1106.)

TAYLOR, MAJ. JOHN, d. in Chesterfield, Mass., Dec. 26, 1843, a. 81; formerly of Northampton; grad. at Harvard in 1786, and for several years a member of the legislature.

TAYLOR, JOHN E., American consul at Sierra Leone, Africa, native of Phila., a. 53.

TAYLOR, DR. LEWIS, surgeon in U. S. army; d. at Fort Wadsworth, Dakota Ter., Jan. 5, 1868.

TAYLOR, NAJAH, a merchant of New York city; d. March 23, 1860; b. in Ridgefield, Conn., Oct. 31, 1769.

TAYLOR, NATHAN, d. at Sanbornton, N. H., April, 1840, a. 84; was an officer of the revolution.

TAYLOR, RICHARD, revolutionary officer; father of Pres. Z. Taylor; b. in Va., March 22, 1744; held a col's commission in the Va. line, and served through the war; settled near Louisville, where he gained a large estate; was a collector at that place; a framer of the constitution of Ky.; member of both houses of legislature, and of several electoral colleges; d. near Louisville.

TAYLOR, COL. THOMAS, b. in Amelia co., Va., in 1743; d. at Columbia, S. C., Nov. 17, 1833, a. 90; has been styled the patriarch of the state rights party of S. C.

TAYLOR, DR. WILLIAM, of Manlius, N. Y.; d. Sept. 16, 1865, a. 74. (*Transac. N. Y. State Med. Soc.*, 1861, p. 267.)

TAYLOR, WILLIAM, a representative in congress from Va.; d. in Washington, D. C., Jan. 17, 1846; was a native of Alexandria, D. C.

TAYLOR, WILLIAM, d. at Estill Springs, Ky., Sept. 1, 1850; late of Point Coupee, La.; b. in Va., but soon removed with his family to Ky., where his father, Edmund T., was a pioneer settler; was left an orphan at an early age; went to Louisiana and became marshal, after the formation of a territorial government; was afterwards consul at St. Domingo, and Vera Cruz; was a relative of Gen. Z. Taylor.

TAYLOR, WILLIAM B., post master of N. Y. in 1860–62, and for many years before and after asst. post master; d. March. 12, 1871, a. 71.

TEACH, JOHN, a pirate known as Blackbeard; established himself in 1718 at the mouth of the Pamlico, in N. C.; surrendered himself to Gov. Eden, who was suspected of being in collusion with him; wasted his ill gotten treasure in debauchery; again entered in piracy, and was captured Nov. 21, 1718, in Pamlico bay by Lieut. Maynard; the vessel returned to the James river with his head hanging from the bowsprit; 13 of his men were hung; Benj. Franklin, then an apprentice in Boston, wrote a ballad on his death which he peddled through the streets.

TEMMINCK, HENRI, gov. of Surinam, from Oct. 1, 1721, till his death in 1721.

TEMPLE, JOHN, d. at Bowdoin, Me., Jan. 13, 1846, a. 86; b. in Concord, Mass., Oct. 6, 1756 and served in the revolutionary war, at the close of which he was capatin.

TEMPLE, ROBERT EMMET, adjutant general of New York; b. in Vt.; cadet in 1824; 2d. lieut. 3d artil., July 1, 1828; acting assist. prof. math. at West Point, Oct., 1828 to Sept., 1829, when he became acting assist. prof. of nat. and eper. philosophy, till Feb., 1830; he was aid to Gen. Scott from 1832 to 1836; he served in the Florida war; was adj. gen. of N. Y., from Feb. 4, 1846, to Jan. 1, 1847; was col. of 10th infantry in the Mexican war, from March 3, 1847, to Aug. 26, 1848; he was again appointed adj. gen. of N. Y., Jan. 4, 1853, and d. in office at Albany, July 20, 1854.

TEMPLE, STEPHEN, d. in South Adams, Mass., 1854, a. 91; served in the revolution, and had voted at every presidential election.

TEMPLEMAN, CAPT. ANDREW, Ga.; killed at the siege of Charleston, May 12, 1780.

TEN BROECK, GEN. ABRAHAM, an officer of the revolution and a descendant from one of the most ancient of the Dutch families of Albany; many years mayor, state senator in 1780–82, and a prominent merchant; b. May 13, 1734; d. at Albany, Jan. 19, 1810. (*Hough's Northern Invasion*, 1780, p. 113.)

TEN BROECK, CORNELIUS P., deputy clerk of the court of appeals; d. Oct. 7, 1874, at Albany, N. Y., a. 63; had filled many places of trust; was formerly deputy state treasurer.

TEN BROECK, LEONARD W., was in assembly from Columbia co., N. Y. in 1832, and sheriff from 1834 to 1837; he d. at Livingston, N. Y., Jan., 1852.

TEN EYCK, ANDREW J., d. April 26, 1842, a. 84, at Readington, N. J.; a revolutionary soldier.

TEN EYCK, EGBERT, judge; b. April 18, 1779 at Schodack, N. Y.; grad. at Williams Coll., in 1799, and settled in law at first in Champion, and soon after in Watertown, N. Y.; in 1813 he served in assembly; in 1822 in state convention, and in 1823–5 in congress; he was five years first judge of Jefferson co., and many years sec. of the county Ag. Soc.; he d. April 11, 1844. (*Hough's Hist. Jeff. Co.*, p. 452.)

TERRELL, JAMES, captain in the revolution; was an early patriot in Ga., and served till disabled by a wound; he d. in Franklin co., Ga., a. 77.

TERRETT, John Chapman, lieut. in 1st infantry; killed in battle of Monterey, Sept. 21, 1846; native of Fairfax co., Va.; entered the army in 1839, and served in the Florida war.

TESCHEMACHER, James Englebert, b. in Nottingham, Eng., in 1790; entered a commercial career which he continued through life, but found time to devote to science; settled in Boston about 1832; rendered valuable contributions to the sciences of mineralogy, botany and geology; d. near Bost., Nov. 9, 1853. (*Am. Jour. Sci. and Arts.* 2d ser., xvii, 150, 292.)

TEST, John, member of congress from Indiana, from 1823 to 1827, and from 1829 to 1831; d. near Cambridge city, Ind., Oct. 9, 1849; was a presiding judge of the circuit courts; resided some years in Mobile, Ala., as a lawyer.

THACHER, Anthony, a tailor from Salisbury in Wiltshire, where his bro. Peter was rector of the church of St. Edmond, as early as 1622; came to Boston, Mass., in 1635; in Aug., 1635, he embarked with 22 others for Marblehead, in a pinnace; was wrecked, and most of the par y perished, including all of his children; resided at Marshfield until Jan., 1639, when he removed to Yarmouth, on Cape Cod, where he d. in 1668, a. 80. (*Young's Chron. Mass.*, pp. 483–494.)

THACHER, Benjamin B., lecturer, editor and author; b. in Maine; grad. at Bowdoin Coll. in 1826; began the study of law, but turned his attention to literature; after admission to the bar, devoted much of his time to writing for the periodicals, editing a daily paper, and in lecturing; had much at heart African colonization, temperance and the claims of the Indians; wrote an *Indian Biography* in two vols. — and *Indian Traits;* application to study, having impaired his health, he visited Europe in 1838, and spent two years, but soon after his return home, d. of lingering sickness, July 14, 1840, a. 31. (*Griswold's Biog. Annual*, 1841–5.)

THACKER, Henry, son in law of Daniel Boon of Kentucky; d. in California, Dec. 1871, a. 123.

THAXTER, Samuel, d. in Boston, Mass., April 18, 1842, a. 72.

THAYER, Edwin N., d. at Philadelphia, Pa., April 4, 1870, a. 73.

THAYER, Rev. John, after laboring as a protestant, was ordained a catholic priest at Paris; returned to America in 1790; remained at Boston for some time, where he engaged in a controversy with the Rev. Mr. Leslie; was in Albany in 1798; spent two years in Kentucky; left there in 1803 for Europe to procure funds for a convent at Boston; d. at Limerick, Ireland, Feb. 17, 1815, a. 56. (*Hist. Mag.*, i, 159.)

THAYER, John Eliot, banker and financier; b. at Lancaster, Mass.; went to Boston, penniless, a. 17; on attaining his 21st year, announced himself worth more than the whole of his native town; his financial operations were on an immense scale; was largely concerned with railroads; left a bequest of $50,000 to aid poor students at Harvard; d. at Boston, Oct. 1857, a. 54. (*N. Y. Eve. Post.*)

THAYER, Jonathan, d. in Camden, Me., Sept. 20, 1853, a. 74; b. in Milford, Mass.; grad. at Brown, in 1803; filled various public offices in Maine; the last of which was that of judge of probates of Waldo co.

THAYER, Nathaniel E., d. in Braintree, Mass., April 18, 1842, a. 64.

THAYER, SYLVANUS, brig. gen. U. S. A.; d. at Braintree, Mass., his native place, Sept. 7, 1872.

THOMAS, A. G., d. at Havre de Grace, Md., Aug. 31, 1841.

THOMAS, REV. DR. ELEAZER, U. S. commissioner to the Modocs; killed at the Lava beds, Oregon, with Gen. Canby, April 11, 1873.

THOMAS, GEORGE, b. in St. Marys co., Md., resided forty years at Washington, and was cashier of the Bank of the Metropolis for a long time; he d. at Washington, Sept. 29, 1858, a. 67.

THOMAS, ISAAC B., d. in Chicago, Ill., Feb., 1850; of the supreme court of Illinois.

THOMAS, J. ADDISON, assist. sec. state, under Marcy, b. in Tenn., grad. at West Point, in 1834, commandant of cadets, at the academy with the rank of captain; studied law, and was appointed by W. L. Marcy, while sec. state, council in disputed claims between Eng. and the U. S.; was afterwards assist. sec. state.; d. at Paris, March 20, 1858. (*Hist Mag.*, ii, 187; *N. Y. Evening Post*, April 13, 1858.)

THOMAS, JESSE B., served on the supreme bench of Illinois; held other offices; d. at Chicago, Feb. 27, 1850; one of the senators of Illinois, from 1818 to 1829.

THOMAS, COL. JOHN, father of ex. Gov. Francis Thomas; d. at Frederick, Md., a. 85.

THOMAS, LIEUT. COL. JOSEPH, N. H., killed at Bemis Heights, Sept. 19, 1777.

THOMAS, JOSEPH, d. at Plymouth, Mass., Aug. 19, 1838, a. 84; was a capt. of artillery in the revolutionary war.

THOMAS, JUDGE JOSHUA, of Plymouth, Mass.; grad. at Harvard in 1772; was aid to Gen. Thomas in May, 1775, and attended him to Canada; returned to Plymouth, where he settled as a lawyer; was chosen to the gen. court in 1781, and to the senate in 1784; became judge of probate for Plymouth co., and held till his death Jan., 1821, a. 70; was in the Hartford convention of 1814. (*Bradford's N. E. Biog.*)

THOMAS, RICHARD, many years a member of both houses of the Md. legislature, and six years president of the senate; d. in St. Mary's co., Md., Oct. 30, 1849.

THOMAS, SAMUEL, member of the Va. leg. from Warren co.; found dead in his bed at Richmond, Va., Sept. 25, 1873.

THOMAS, STEPHEN, d. at Charleston, S. C., June 17, 1839, in his 89th year; b. in the village of Eymet, in France, in 1750; fled with an elder maiden sister in 1764 to Charleston, S. C., to seek an asylum from persecution; served in the revolution, and was in the battle of Ft. Moultrie, and afterwards with Gen. Marion.

THOMPSON, ALEXANDER, a member of the 18th and 19th congresses; d. at Chambersburg, Pa., July 2, 1848, a. about 63.

THOMPSON, DR. ALEXANDER, of Aurora, N. Y.; d. Sept. 21, 1869, a. 60; b. in Cambridge, N. Y., May 2, 1809. (*Transac. N. Y. State Med. Soc.*, 1871, p. 362.)

THOMPSON, ALEXANDER, member of congress from Penn. from 1824 to 1826; d. at his home in Chambersburg, Pa., Aug. 2, 1848, a. 63.

THOMPSON, Benjamin, d. in Charlestown, Mass., Sept. 24, 1852, a. 54; held many offices of trust in that town, and was several times in the state legislature; served in congress from 1845 to 1847, and from 1851 till his death; his services in the legislature on the committee on military affairs during the Mexican war were especially valuable.

THOMPSON, Benjamin F., favorably known as the historian of L. I.; was a lawyer, resident at Hampstead, and in 1812–13 and 1816 was in assembly; from 1826 to 1836 was dist. atty. for Queens co.; d. March 21, 1849. (*Stryker's Am. Reg.*, ii, 298; *Griffin's Journal*, p. 247.)

THOMPSON, Charles, d. in Hanover co., Va., March 21, 1836, in his 93d year.

THOMPSON, David, a pensioner of 80 years standing; d. at Easton, Mass., Oct., 1836; he enlisted in the French war at the age of 16; and was at the massacre of Fort William Henry in 1757, where he lost an arm, for which a pension was granted; he was the last pensioner of that war and his age was not known accurately, but was between 98 and 102 years.

THOMPSON, Rev. Edward, d.d., bishop of the Methodist Episc. church; d. at Wheeling, W. Va., March 22, 1870, a. 50.

THOMPSON, Hedge, member of congress from New Jersey in 1827–8; d. July 23, 1828.

THOMPSON, Dr. Horatio, of Belchertown, Mass.; d. Oct. 4, 1860, a. 57. (*N. Y. Times*, Oct. 16, 1860.)

THOMPSON, James, d. in Milton, Saratoga co., N. Y., Dec. 26, 1845, a. 70; he was fourteen years first judge of the county, and a native of Stillwater and son of Hon. John T., of that town.

THOMPSON, James, d. in Washington, D. C., Oct. 16, 1856, a. 87; he was b. in Georgetown in 1769; was appointed a lieut. in the Marine corps in 1798–9, and served most of the time as pay master till 1811; he was appointed chief clerk in the third auditor's office in 1817, and served till July, 1853.

THOMPSON, Col. John, d. in Philadelphia, Pa., July, 1840, a. 66; candidate for presidential elector.

THOMPSON, John, b. in 1777; was in congress from Ohio, from 1825 to 1827, and from 1829 to 1837; d. at New Lisbon, Ohio, Dec. 2, 1852.

THOMPSON, John Edgar, pres. of the Pennsylvania R. R.; d. at Philadelphia, Pa., May 27, 1874, a. 68; b. in Chester co., Pa., and devoted himself to civil engineering, and when young went to Georgia where he built the principal part of the Georgia Central R. R.; returned to Penn. some 30 years before his death; became chief engineer, and for the last 2 years pres. (*N. Y. Tribune*, semi-weekly, May 29, 1874.)

THOMPSON, John R., d. at New York city, April 30, 1873; b. at Richmond, Va., on the 23d of October, 1823; he was graduated at the University of Virginia in 1845, and after devoting some time to the study of the law, his bent for literature led him to assume, in 1847, the chair of editor of *The Southern Literary Messenger*, which he conducted with such taste and skill as to give it at once the place it always occupied as the leading literary magazine of the south; more recently he was connected with *The New York Evening Post.*

THOMPSON, PHILIP R., d.. in Kanawha co., Va., July 22, 1837, a. 71; member of congress from Virginia, in 1801–7.

THOMPSON, SAMUEL H., d. at Washington, D. C., Aug. 25, 1839; an aid-de-camp of Gen. Jackson at the battle of New Orleans.

THOMPSON, MISS SARAH, d. in Concord, N. H., Dec. 2, 1852, a. 70; Countess of Rumford and dau. of Benjamin Thompson, Count Rumford.

THOMPSON, THOMAS, lieut. of N. Y. artillery; killed in action in 1781.

THOMPSON, THOMAS W., grad. at Harvard in 1786; was in cong. from N. H., in 1805–7, and in the U. S. senate from 1814 to 1817.

THOMPSON, WILLIAM, a native of St. Mary's co., Md.; d. at Hickory Hill, Md., July 22, 1833, in his 112th year; he left 11 or 12 surviving children, the oldest 91 and the youngest 25 years of age.

THOMPSON, WILLIAM, a pioneer of eastern Maine; d. at Eddington, Me., March 23, 1851, a. 83.

THOMPSON, DR. WILLIAM, d. in Lowville, N. Y., Sept. 9, 1845, a. 45.

THORN, CAPT. HERMAN, of the U. S. army; was drowned near Gila in crossing the Colorado in California, Oct. 16, 1849.

THORNDIKE, ROBERT, native of Beverly; d. at Camden, Me., Dec., 1834, in his 104th year.

THORNTON, THOMAS GILBERT, d. at Madison, Wis., Nov. 4, 1868, a. 45; grad. at Bowdoin in 1844; practiced law at Biddeford, Me., till 1854; then went to Kansas, taking an active part as a free state man; was pres. of the senate of the first free state legislature.

THORNTON, REV. T. C., D.D., president of Madison Coll., Mississippi; an eminent Methodist divine; d. at Sharon, Miss., March 22, 1860, a. about 73.

THROOP, ENOS THOMPSON, b. in Johnstown, N. Y., Aug. 21, 1784; was admitted to the bar in 1806; settled in Cayuga co., N. Y.; was county clerk in 1811–13; was in congress in 1815–16, and circuit judge from 1823 to 1828; was then elected lieut. gov. on the ticket with Martin Van Buren, and a few months after succeeded as governor on the resignation of the latter; in 1830, was elected governor; at the end of his second term was appointed naval officer at New York; in 1838 was appointed by Mr. Van Buren chargé d' affaires to the kingdom of the two Sicilles, where he remained till Harrison's administration; he then returned, and spent the rest of life at Willow Brook on the banks of Owasco lake near Auburn, N. Y., where he d. Nov. 1, 1874. (*Jenkins's Lives of the Governors of New York*, with portrait.)

THROOP, COL. THOMAS, d. in Flemingsburg, Ky., Aug., 1847; was democratic candidate for the 9th congressional dist. of Ky.

THURMAN, JOHN R., d. July 24, 1854; was from 1849 to 1851, a member of congress from the 15th dist. of New York; resided in Chestertown, Warren co.

THURSTON, BUCKNER, b. in Va., about 1763; removed when young to Ky., was appointed a federal judge in the Territory of Orleans in 1805; was elected to the U. S. senate, but resigned in 1809 on being appointed

U. S. judge for the dist. of Columbia, which office he held till his death, Aug. 30, 1845.

THURSTON, SAMUEL R., delegate to congress from Oregon; d. on the steamer California on her passage from Panama to San Francisco, April 9, 1851.

THURSTON, THOMAS B., b. in Maine; grad. at Bowdoin Coll., in 1843; was a delegate in congress from Oregon from 1849 to 1851; d. on board a California steamer on her passage from Panama to San Francisco, April 9, 1851.

TIACKS, DR. JOHN LEWIS, F.R.S., British astronomer to the American boundary line; d. at Jever in Oldenburg, his native place, May 1, 1836, in his 48th year.

TIBBITS, GEORGE, son of John T., who settled at Lansingburg, N. Y., from Warwick, R. I., soon after the revolution; he was b. Jan. 14, 1763; began trade at Troy, N. Y., in 1797; was in congress in 1803–5; in the state senate from 1815 to 18, and in assembly in 1800 and 1820; he was mayor of Troy from 1830 to 1836; was a director of the Farmers' Bank more than 40 years, and an officer in St. Paul's church, Troy, 44 years; he d. July 19, 1849, a. 86; his brother Benjamin, b. 1765, was several years his partner in trade, and d. Sept. 11, 1802. (*Woodworth's Troy*, 36.)

TIERNAN, LUKE, d. at Baltimore, Nov. 10, 1839, in his 81st year; native of Ireland, and one of the most opulent and benevolent men in that city.

TIFFANY, OSMOND C., d. in Baltimore, Md., June 11, 1851, a. 57; b. in Attleborough, Mass.; was bred a merchant, and settled in Baltimore in 1815; in connection with the late William C. Shaw, he established himself in domestic trade and an extensive business.

TILGHMAN, ELIZABETH, widow of late Chief Justice T.; d. in Philadelphia, Pa., April 4, 1842, a. 91; she was dau. of Chief Justice Chew, and related to many distinguished persons in Pennsylvania.

TILLINGHAST, HENRY, son of Benjamin T.; b. in east Greenwich, R. I., May 22, 1772; went to Vt., became a tanner, and settled in Norway, N. Y., in 1792; was an active republican politician, and served in assembly in 1823 and 1825, and was nearly 30 years in succession a supervisor; he was also many years a magistrate; he d. July 29, 1841. (*Benton's Herkimer Co., N. Y.*, p. 362.)

TILTON, DR. JOSEPH, d. at Exeter, N. H., Dec. 5, 1837, a. 94; had been a surgeon in the revolutionary war.

TILTON, JOSEPH, d. in Exeter, N. H., March 27, 1856, a. 81; native of East Kingston, N. H.; grad. at Harvard in 1797; admitted to the bar in 1801, and settled first in Wakefield, then in Rochester and then at Exeter, N. H.; resided at Exeter from 1809 till his death; was from 1815 to 1823, a representative from Exeter in the legislature.

TIPPEN, ANDREW H., d. in Phila., Feb. 6, 1870; served as lieut. in the 1st reg., in the Mexican war; went into service as major of the 20th Pa. militia at the beginning of the late war; was elected colonel of the 68th Penn. vols., and served during the war.

TIPTON, JOHN, United States senator from Louisiana in 1832–9; d. April 6, 1839, at Logansport, Ind., a. about 35.

TOBEY, HENRY L., of the *Utica Morning Herald;* d. April 18, 1860.

TOBEY, THOMAS, a native of Phil.; d. at New Orleans, July 14, 1849; was one of the oldest and most respectable merchants in the city.

TOBIN, CAPT. GEORGE, of Irish birth; was educated at Trinity Coll., Dublin, and served under Gen. Persifer Smith, in Florida; was also under Gen. Taylor on the Rio Grande; d. at Stockton, California, Jan. 3, 1849. (*Stryker's Am. Reg.*, iv, 441.)

TOD, JOHN, one of the judges of the supreme court of Pa.; d. at Bedford, Pa., March 27, 1830, a. 51.

TODD, MRS. LUCY P., mother of Wm. Temple Washington, and only surviving sister of Mrs. Madison; d. in Jefferson co., Va., Jan. 30, 1846; she had been the wife of George S. Washington, nephew of Gen. W., and afterwards of Hon. Thomas Todd, of Ky., one of the judges of the supreme court of the U. S., whom she survived many years.

TODD, DR. STEPHEN, b. in Wallingford, Ct., Dec. 23, 1773; removed to Salisbury, N. Y., in 1792; studied and practiced medicine, and as a farmer was prominent as an early grazier; in 1814 as capt. of militia he was called to the frontiers, and in 1822 served in assembly; d. at Salisbury, N. Y., in 1827, a. 54. (*Benton's Herkimer Co., N. Y.*, p. 367.)

TODD, WILLIAM W., d. in New York city, Jan. 10, 1872, a. 90.

TOLAND, ROBERT, an eminent merchant of Phil; d. Dec. 20, 1848.

TOLER, EDWARD H., d. at Richmond, Va., May 15, 1848, a. 49; was 23 years editor of the *Lynchburg Virginian*, and in the house of delegates from the county of Campbell from 1838 until his removal to Richmond in 1846.

TOLME, KENNETH, a lieut. and afterwards a captain in the English army in the French war.

TOMBLING, DR. ABIJAH, settled in Norway, N. Y., about 1800 as a physician; removed to Herkimer; became a collector of direct tax for U. S., and in 1816 was appointed surrogate; held till April, 1821; d. at Herkimer. (*Benton's Herkimer Co., N. Y.*, p. 368.)

TOOLEY, JAMES JR., a miniature painter of much promise; d. at Natchez, Miss., Aug. 10, 1844, a. 28.

TOOMER, JOHN D., d. in Chatham co., N. C., Sept. 27, 1856, a. 72; he was often elected to the state legislature; was in the convention of 1835, and twice elected judge of the superior courts of law, and courts of equity; for a short time he was a judge of the supreme court of his state.

TORRENCE, JOHN, revolutionary soldier of Warren co., Ga.; d. July 4, 1827, a. 78. (*White's Hist. Ga.*, p. 675.)

TORRY, SYLVIA, d. at Kingston, R. I., Nov. 1, 1849, a. 112; her youngest child living with her was 87.

TOTTEN, JAMES, brevet brig. gen. U. S. A.; d. at Sedalia, Mo., Oct. 2, 1871.

TOULMIN, J. B., d. at Bowden, England; a merchant of Mobile, Ala., a. 72.

TOWERS, JOHN T., d. at Washington, D. C., Aug. 11, 1857, a. 46; he was a native of Alexandria, but for thirty years had lived in Washington, where he had been a member of the common council, and one term a mayor.

TOWNLEY, Daniel O. C., business manager of Grand Opera House, N. Y. city; d. Dec. 28, 1872; came to America in 1860; was an assistant editor for a time on the *New York Times*, and editor of the *Evening Mail.*

TOWNSEND, Charles D., m.d., of Albany, b. in Goshen, N. Y., April 15, 1778; studied medicine in Albany with Drs. Mancius and Woodruff; attended lectures at Columbia Coll. in 1802; settled in Rhinebeck, N. Y., but soon removed to Albany; he was first sec. of the state med. soc. and d. at Albany, Dec. 19, 1847. (*Tr. N. Y. St. Med. Soc.*, 1857, p. 30; *Munsell's Ann. Alb.*, ix, 94.)

TOWNSEND, Dr. Howard, of Albany, formerly a professor in the Albany Medical College; d. in Albany, Jan. 15, 1867, a. 43. (*Transac. N. Y. State Med. Soc.*, 1867, p. 466.)

TOWNSEND, Isaac, a wealthy merchant of N. Y., and from the beginning one of the ten governors of the N. Y., alms house establishment; d. April, 1860; he was president of the bank of the state of New York and a director in the New York Central rail road; he was a native of Orange co., and at his death in his 55th year.

TOWNSEND, John, b. at Stirling Iron Works, Orange co., N. Y., June 14, 1783; came to Albany in 1802, and in 1804 with his brother Isaiah, began the hardware and iron foundry business and continued many years; in 1814, he m. a daughter of Ambrose Spencer; in 1829, 30, 2, he was mayor of Albany; with Joshua Foreman and others he established the first solar salt works at Syracuse and at his death he was pres. of the Syracuse Coarse Salt Co., and of the Commercial Bank of Albany, the Albany Exchange Bank, the Board of Water Comr's of Albany, the Albany Savings Bank, the Albany Pier Co., the Watervliet Turnpike Co., and acting pres. of the Albany Insurance Co.; he d. at Albany, Aug. 26, 1854. (*Munsell's Ann. Alb.*, vi, 338.)

TOWNSEND, Josiah, d. in Savannah, Wayne co., N. Y., March 19, 1860, a. 90; was formerly of Champion.

TOWNSEND, Micah, was b. at Cedar Swamp, Oyster Bay, L. I., May 13, 1749; grad. at Princeton in 1766, and in 1770 was admitted to the bar; he settled at White Plains, N. Y., was clerk of the Westchester com. of safety and in June, 1776, was appointed captain of a militia company in the service; he removed to Brattleboro, Vt., supported the N. Y. interest, but became a citizen of the state of Vt., and in 1785, was secretary of convention; in 1781, he became sec. state, aud served till 1788, when he resigned; he removed in 1802 to Farnham, L. C., and in 1816, to Clarenceville to the residence of his son where he d. June 27, 1831, a. 71 years. (*Hall's Eastern Vermont*, p. 700.)

TOWNSEND, Moses, d. in Salem, Mass., Feb. 14, 1842, a. 82; president of the Union Marine Insurance Co., for the last 38 years; he was a soldier of the revolutionary war.

TOWNSEND, Richard, pioneer agent and settler of Gouverneur, N. Y.; removed from Hebron, N. Y., to Delhi, and thence in 1810 to G., as agent of Gouverneur Morris; he d. in 1826, near Phila., N. Y. (*Hough's Hist. St. Law & Fr. Cos.*, *N. Y.*, p. 611.)

TOWNSHEND, Roger, 4th son of Charles Viscount Townshend, became lieut. col. Feb. 1, 1758; served as adj. gen. against Louisburg, and dep. adj. gen. in 1759; he was killed by a cannon shot in the trenches before Ticonderoga, July 25, 1759; and removed to Albany for burial. (*Com. Wilson's Orderly Book*, 77.)

TOURTELOT, Dr. Freeman, of Middle Grove, Saratoga co., N. Y.; d. Dec. 14, 1868, a. 62. (*Transac N. Y. State Med. Soc.*, 1869, p. 260.

TYLER, Gould, Capt. in Col. Samuel Blakesle's regt.; killed in the invasion of Niagara frontier, Dec. 30, 1813.

TRACY, Albert H., b. at Norwich, Ct., June 17, 1793; settled in western N. Y., in 1811, and in 1815 was admitted to the bar; from 1819 to 1825, he was in congress; in 1826 he was appointed circuit judge of the 8th dist. but declined; in 1829 he was elected to the senate by the anti-masons, and held till 1837; he adhered to the whig party, but was not a partizan; he d. at his home in Buffalo, N. Y., Sept. 17, 1859. (*Hist. Mag.*, iii, 321; *Am. Almanac*, 1861, p. 391.)

TRACY, Henry E., a Boston journalist; d. in that city Nov. 5, 1873; was formerly connected with the New-York and Washington press, and more recently with *The Boston Herald*; was in his fiftieth year, and had attained prominence in his profession.

TRACY, William H., judge of the marine court of N. Y.; d. in N. Y. city Jan. 25, 1873, in his 37th year; he was born in Grand st., and in boyhood lived alternately in this city and NewJersey, where his mother still resides; in 1856 he entered the office of Luke F. Cozzens, then a practicing lawyer at No. 41 Ann st.; in 1858 he was admitted to the bar, and was soon elected school trustee in the thirteenth ward, an office which he held for several years; was elected a member of the assembly, representing the thirteenth, and parts of the tenth and seventeenth wards; the object of his ambition was a seat on the bench, and at the last election for civil justices he was a prominent candidate for the nomination for justice of the fifth district court, but failed to obtain the nomination; when the act relative to the marine court was passed, making three new seats, Judge Tracy received the nomination and was elected with Judges Shea and Joachimsen; this was his last year of office; his decisions have been reversed less frequently than those of any judge of the marine court and by his death the bench has lost one of its most energetic and serviceable members.

TRASK, Dr. Nahum, d. at Windsor, Vt., March 5, 1837, a. 76.

TREADWELL, Thomas, b. in Smithtown, L. I., in 1742; grad. at Princeton, in 1764; a member of the provincial congress of N. Y.; was surrogate of Suffolk co., N. Y., from 1787 to 1791 and 4 years state senator from 1786 to 1789; removed to Plattsburg N. Y.; was again senator in 1804–6; surrogate of Clinton co. from 1807 to 1831; d. Jan. 30, 1832.

TREANOR, Rev. Thomas, d. at N. Y., Nov. 29, 1870.

TRÉMIN, Jacques, Jesuit missionary; arrived in Canada, in 1655; at Onondaga, from 1656 to 1658; sent to the Mohawks, in July 1667; left there for Seneca, Oct. 10, 1668 and remained a few years; he d. at Quebec, April 20, 1691.

TRENOR, Thomas, d. Sept. 6, 1848, a. 86; b. in Monaghan, in Ireland, March 17, 1761; became a merchant, and involved in the Irish rebellion; was treasuer of the United Irish Soc.; arrested, confined in Dublin castle, escaped, and after hiding for some time, escaped in one of his own ships to Norway; went to England, was arrested again, kept 4 ys.

in prison, and in 1806 went to Portugal, and in 1807 to the U. S.; resided some years in in Lansingburg; established the iron manufacture in Vermont; during the last fifteen years, he held a place in the N. Y. custom house.

TRENTLEN, JOHN ADAM, a revolutionary gov. of Georgia; was in gen. assembly of Georgia under Gov. Wright, and in the revolution was foremost on the side of freedom; was in the first prov. cong. of Ga., in 1775, from the parish of St. Andrews; May 8, 1777, was elected gov. of Ga. by a large majority over B. Gwinnett; in 1780 the royal government of Ga. placed him on the list of persons disqualified from holding office; during his administration a proposition was made by letter through Wm. Henry Drayton, for the union of Ga. with S. C. which led to a spirited proclamation offering £100 for his arrest. (*White's Hist. Ga.*, p. 202.)

TREZVANT, JAMES, b. in Sussex co., Va.; a lawyer and attorney for the state; member of the legislature and constitutional convention of 1830; in congress from Va., in 1825–31, and d. in 1838.

TRIMBLE, DAVID, d. at Trimble's Furnace, Ky., Oct. 26, 1842, a. about 60; b. in Va., educated at William and Mary College; studied law, and when he came of age removed to Kentucky; was in the war of 1812; in congress from 1817 to 1827, and then devoted himself to agriculture and the iron manufacture; in the latter did much to develop the resources of the state.

TRIMBLE, JAMES, late deputy secretary of Pa.; was appointed a clerk in the executive department of the proprietary government in 1769, and continued a clerk among the records until within a few weeks before his death, which occurred at Harrisburg in Feb., 1836, a. 89.

TRIPLER, DR. CHARLES A., surgeon in the army; d. Oct. 20, 1866.

TRIPNER, MAJ. GEORGE, a soldier of the revolution and war of 1812; b. in Baltimore April, 1762; d. at Phil. June 7, 1848, a, 87; served at Bunker hill, White plains, Monmouth, Germantown, Brandywine and Stony Point. (*Stryker's Am. Reg.*, i, 500.)

TROOP, GEORGE M., d. in Lawrence co., Ga., May 3, 1856, a. 75; was in congress from 1807 to 1815, and senator from 1816 to 1818, and from 1829 to 1834; from 1823 to 1827 was gov. of Ga.

TROTT, JOHN, chief justice of the court of common pleas; d. at Warren, R. I., Sept. 3, 1836, a. 61.

TROTTER, MATTHEW, an officer of the revolution; was with Gansevoort and Willett at the siege of Ft. Stanwix, and afterward aid to Lord Stirling; engaged in trade at Albany after the war, and for some years was capt. of a sloop on the Hudson; held several city offices in Albany, and in 1824 was chosen with Gen. John H. Wendell to proceed to N. Y. and invite Lafayette to the hospitalities of the city; d. Dec. 9, 1830, at his home corner of Market and Patroon streets, Albany.

TROUSDALE, WILLIAM, ex-gov. of Tenn.; d. in Gallatin, Tenn., March 27, 1872, a. 82.

TROWBRIDGE, DR. AMASA, b. in Pomfret, Conn., May 17, 1779; was a surgeon in the war of 1812, and a prominent surgeon and medical practitioner at Watertown, N. Y., many years; was for a time professor of surgery at the Willoughby Med. Coll., O.; d. at Watertown, N. Y. (*New York Reformer*, 1859.)

TROWBRIDGE, DR. JOHN F., of Syracuse, N. Y.; d. 1872.

TROY, ALEXANDER, d. in Anson co., N. C., April, 1841; was a lawyer, and many years solicitor of the 5th judicial circuit of N. C.

TRUESDELL, SAMUEL, d. at North Salem, N. Y., Oct. 2, 1839, a. 80; was a soldier of the revolution, and wounded at Yorktown.

TRUGIEN, DR. JOHN W. H., d. of yellow fever at Portsmouth, Va., Aug. 29, 1855; b. in that place in Feb., 1827. (*Report of Portsmouth Relief Asso.*, 1855, p. 167–71.)

TRUMBULL, GEORGE A., d. in Worcester, Mass., Aug., 1868, a. 77; was at one time one of the proprietors and publishers of the *Massachusetts Spy;* afterwards cashier of the Central Bank, and still later, of the Citizens' Bank of Worcester.

TRUYNS, REV. CHARLES, D.D., a Jesuit, d. at St. Louis, Mo., Dec. 14, 1868, in his 65th year; b. in Belgium in 1813; came to America in 1837; was an officer of St. Louis University, and of St. Charles Coll., La.; a missionary to the Indians, and later in life pastor of St. Joseph's church, Bardstown, Ky.

TUCKER, EBENEZER, b. in New York in 1758; settled in New Jersey, and served in the revolution; was collector, postmaster, and from 1825 to 1829 member of congress; was judge of common pleas, justice of the court of quarter sessions, and judge of the orphans court; d. at Tuckertown, N. J., Sept. 5, 1845.

TUCKER, GEORGE STERLING, member of congress from 1817 to 1831, from S. C.; d. Feb. 4, 1834, in Laurens district, S. C.

TUCKER, ICHABOD, d. in Salem, Mass., Oct. 22, 1846, a. 81; was late clerk of the courts of Essex co.; grad. at Harvard, in the class of 1791.

TUCKER, LUTHER, editor and proprietor of the *Country Gentleman;* d. at Albany, Jan. 26, 1873.

TUCKER, CAPT. W. A., an experienced sea captain and 17 years pres. of the Baltimore Fire Insurance Co; d. at Baltimore, March 21, 1849.

TUCKERMAN, HENRY THEODORE, d. Dec. 17, 1871; celebrated literary scholar; b. in Boston, April 20, 1813; spent much of his life abroad; removed from Boston to New York in 1845, and resided there till death, excepting that his summers were spent in Newport. (*Hist. Record*, i, 93.)

TUNIS, CAPT. BENJAMIN, d. in Stockton, Cal., Jan. 22, 1860, a. 65. (*Vincent's Semi-An. Register*, p. 53.)

TUOMEY, PROF. MICHAEL, state geologist of Alabama; d. at Tuscaloosa, March 30, 1857, a. 46; was a native of Virginia; had been supt. of the Petersburg, R. R.; was appointed state geologist of South Carolina, in 1844; four years after published his final report in one quarto volume; was subsequently appointed prof. of geology in the University of Ala.; held this office at his death. (*Am. Jour. Sci. and Arts*, 2d ser., xxiii, 448.)

TUPPER, JAMES, a prominent citizen; d. at Summerville, S. C., Aug. 28, 1868; youngest son of Tristram T., a merchant of Charleston, S. C.; was b. in that city in 1819; at twenty-one he was admitted to practice law in the courts of the state, and gained a reputation in his profession; in 1848, was elected to the state legislature, remaining there two years; in 1851, was appointed one of the masters of equity in the Charleston district; in 1862, was elected state auditor, while holding this office effected a tohrough reconstruction of the state finances; Mr. Tupper, while so busily and actively engaged in the affairs of this life, ever remembered as his principal duty, obedience to God; joined the First Baptist church in 1835, was chosen deacon, and contributed more than $5,000 toward its support.

TURLEY, WILLIAM B., judge of the Memphis court of common law and chancery; was transferred 18 months before at his own request from the supreme court, of which he had long been a member; was a profound lawyer and commanded much esteem; his death occurred at Raleigh, Shelby co., Tenn., May 27, 1851.

TURNBULL, COL. WILLIAM, of the corps of topographical engineers, U. S. A.; d. in Washington, D. C., Dec. 9, 1857.

TURNER, CAPT. JACOB, N. C., killed at Germantown, Oct. 4, 1777.

TURNER, DR. L. S., of Fallsburg, Sullivan co., N. Y.; d. 1860, a. 49.

TURNER, NAT., leader of a slave insurection in Southampton co., Va.; taken, Oct. 30, executed Nov. 11, 1831.

TURNER, PETER, commodore in U. S. navy; d. Phila., Feb. 19, 1871; b. in R. I.; appointed midshipman in 1823; lieut. in 1832; commander in 1861; commodore in 1862; commander of the U. S. Naval Asylum, in 1863–68.

TURNER, ROBERT, an early Irish colonist in Phila.; became a member of the society of Friends; was one of the 24 purchasers of East Jersey, from the owners of the Carteret estate; was one of the 5 commissioners for governing the colony of Pa., in Penn's absence. (*Simpson's Eminent Philadelphians.*)

TURNER, DR. WILLIAM, d. at Newport, R. I., Sept. 27, 1837, a. 62; a surgeon in the U. S. army.

TURNER, DR. WILLIAM, practitioner, and advocate of the chrono-thermal system, on which he wrote a book; he was a son of John T., associate of John Lang in the *N. Y. Gazette;* d. in N. Y., Mar. 8, 1858, a. 56. (*Hist. Mag.*, ii, 155.)

TURNEY, HOPKINS L., b. in Smith co., Tenn., Oct. 3, 1797; acquired his education after coming to manhood; studied law, was about 10 years in the Tennessee legislature (1828 to 1838); in congress from Tenn., from 1837 to 1843, and in the U. S. senate from 1845 to 1851; d. at Winchester, Tenn., Aug. 1, 1857.

TURPIN, WHITE, d. near Natchez, Miss., April 4, 1842, a. 65; native of Delaware, and emigrated to Mississippi with Gov. Holmes in 1809, by whom he was appointed sheriff of Adams co.; in 1817, he was again elected to that office, and continued till chosen to the legislature; he was afterwards president of the Agricultural Bank of Mississippi until obliged to resign from ill health.

TURRELL, JOEL, d. at Oswego, N. Y., Dec. 26, 1859, a. 64; he was a member of congress from 1833 to 1837, and afterwards minister to the Sandwich islands.

TUTE, AMOS, one of the pioneers of Vernon, Vt., and a man of wealth and influence; in 1755 Mrs. Jemima Howe, the fair captive, was taken prisoner, who on her return married Mr. Tute; in 1768 he was appointed by Lieut. Gov. Colden of N. Y., coroner of Cumberland co.; d. April 17, 1790 in his 60th year. (*Hall's Eastern Vermont*, p. 706.)

TUTTLE, NORMAN, printer; in 1828 was proprietor of the *Troy Sentinel*, edited by O. L. Holley, and in 1839 was an owner of the *Troy Daily Mail;* he d. at Troy, N. Y., Feb. 20, 1858. (*Hist. Mag.*, ii, 155.)

TUITSHELL, GERSHOM, of Milford, Mass., a miser, who, owning one of the finest farms in town, persisted in living in squalid poverty. (*Vincent's Semi-An. Register*, p. 614.)

TWO GUNS, (See Hajaongueh.)

TYLER, COMFORT, was b. at Ashford, Ct., Feb. 22, 1764; entered the army at 14 and served a short time; in 1783 he went to Caughnawaga where he began as a surveyor and teacher, and becoming acquainted with the projectors of the leasee project in 1788; settled in Onondaga where he made the first piece of turnpike west of Ft. Stanwix; he was engaged in land surveys; was sheriff of Onondaga co., in 1798, and co. clerk in 1799; in 1797–8 he was in assembly where he became acquainted with Aaron Burr, with whose schemes he became involved and by which he lost much property; in 1811 he removed to Montezuma for the manufacture of salt and in the war he served as assistant commissary gen., with the rank of colonel; he d. at Montezuma, N. Y., Aug. 5, 1827. (*Clark's Hist. Onondaga Co.*, i, 365, with portrait.)

TYLER, RUFUS, d. at New Orleans, La., Sept. 7, 1839; chief coiner at the branch mint at that place.

ULTINGER, JOHN, d. in Tennessee, Oct. 12, 1859, a. 104.

UNDERWOOD, GEORGE, b. in Cooperstown, N. Y., Jan. 4, 1816; came in childhood to Auburn; grad. at Hamilton Coll. in 1838; became a lawyer at Auburn, and many years attorney for the Auburn and Syracuse rail road; was in assembly in 1850–1; mayor of Auburn in 1854; d. May 25, 1849. (*Hall's Auburn*, p. 542.)

UNDERWOOD, JOHN C., federal judge in Virginia; d. at Washington, D. C., Dec. 7, 1873; b. in 1808, at Litchfield, Herk. co., N. Y., and long before the war settled in Clarke co., Va., where he was a farmer; became concerned in dealings in southern lands; in 1861, President Lincoln nominated him as consul at Callao, Peru, but he accepted instead the office of fifth auditor in the treasury department, and while such was appointed judge of the district court of Virginia; in that position he zealously favored the union interests by a just interpretation of the law, and braved the hostility of the confederates by decisions which enlarged the war powers of the government; he affirmed early in the war the right of the government to confiscate rebel property, and also maintained the civic rights of colored citizens; his decisions were given in terse and forcible language, and showed an enlightened sense of the rights of the colored people and the absurdity of discrimination based on color or race; it was in this district that Jefferson Davis was indicted, and it was he who refused, in June, 1866, to admit the prisoner to bail on the ground that he was in custody of the military authorities; he still presided in May, 1867, when the confederate leader was released; Judge Underwood was very bitterly assailed because of his zeal in enforcing the federal laws, and was latterly forced into litigation because of a decree sanctioning confiscation;

he was, however, greatly misunderstood by his opponents; for he entertained kindly feelings toward them, and sought as well as he could to promote harmony in the south, and to advance her material interests. (*N. Y. Tribune.*)

UNDERWOOD, John Curtis, b. in Litchfield, N. Y., March 14, 1809; grad. at Ham. Coll., 1832; appointed 5th auditor, treasury dep., in 1861; U. S. dist. judge of Va., in 1863–73; pres. of con. convention, Va., 1867; d. at Washington, D. C., Dec. 7, 1873.

UPDIKE, Daniel, a son of Gilbert Updike; visited Barbadoes in his youth; studied law, and began practice at Newport, R. I.; in 1722 he was elected attorney general of R. I., and re-elected annually till May, 1732, when he became a candidate for governor, but was defeated; he was employed in the controversy with Mass., and in 1741, was appointed attorney gen. for Kings co., R. I., and in 1743 for the colony; he was one of the founders of the Redwood library in 1730; he d. May 15, 1757. (*W. Updike's Memoirs of the R. I. Bar*, p. 34.)

UPFOLD, Rt. Rev., bishop of the Prot. Epis. church in Indiana; d. in Indianapolis, Ind., Aug. 26, 1872.

UPHAM, George B., grad. at Harvard in 1789; was in congress from New Hampshire from 1801 to 1803; d. in 1848.

UPHAM, Jabez, b. in Mass.; grad. at Harvard in 1785; was in congress from Massachusetts from 1807 to 1810; d. in 1811.

UPHAM, Col. Timothy, d. in Charlestown, Mass., Nov. 2, 1855, a. 71; b. in Deerfield, N. H., in 1783; began mercantile life at Portsmouth, N. H., in 1807; in March, 1812, was appointed major in the army, and soon after was placed in command of the forts and harbor of Portsmouth, and superintended the recruiting service; in July, 1812, was commissioned in the eleventh infantry, and in Sept., joined the army at Plattsburg; was made lieut. col. in the 21st regt., and was in the sortie at Fort Erie; after the war was collector of customs at Portsmouth, and from 1816 to 1829; in 1841 was navy agent, and held till 1845, when he removed to Charlestown. (*Am. Almanac*, 1857, p. 349.)

UPHAM, William, d. at Washington, D. C., Jan. 14, 1853, a. 56; was a state senator from Vt. from 1843 till his death.

UPSON, Stephen, an eminent lawyer of Oglethorpe co., Ga.; d. in 1824.

UPTON, Miss Hannah, dau. of Rev. Timothy Upton; b. in Deerfield, N. H., July, 1789; became a teacher, and in 1830 became principal of the Ontario Female Seminary at Canandaigua; conducted this institution 18 years, and in 1848 resigned her charge; d. at Canandaigua, Aug. 20, 1868. (*Regent's Report*, 1870, p. 595.)

UPTON, John, d. at Lynnfield, Mass., May, 1838, a. 92; an officer of the revolution.

VAIL, David W., d. in New Brunswick, N. J., Jan. 18, 1842; at various times in the state leg., and mayor of New Brunswick.

VAIL, George H., of Troy, N. Y.; a young man of intelligence and talent; d. at San Francisco, Cal., Dec. 25, 1849, at the a. of 30.

VALENTINE, William, formerly a member of the Rhode Island senate; d. at Fall River, Mass., June 21, 1839, a. 80.

VALERNAIS, M. DE, d. July 22, 1780, at Newport, of wounds received in an engagement with the British frigate Isis; 1st lieut. of the Hermione frigate.

VAN ALLEN, ISAAC, d. at Rockingham, Iowa, Oct. 16, 1839, in his 24th year; native of Kinderhook, N. Y., and U. S. dist. atty. for Iowa.

VAN ALLEN, LUCIUS J., d. at Kinderhook, N. Y., Sept. 28, 1858, a. 81; was a highly respectable citizen of Columbia co.

VAN BRUNNE, LIEUT. JOHN DE LA, Md.; killed in the revolution Sept. 12, 1781.

VAN BUREN, DEWITT, of the *New York Leader;* d. Oct. 5, 1870, a. 30.

VAN CORTLAND, STEPHEN, d. at Newark, N. J., Sept. 30, 1839, a. 90.

VAN CORTLANDT, GEN. PHILIP, an officer of the revolution; he was commissioned colonel at the beginning of the war; raised a large regiment in N. Y. and N. J.; was at the battles of Saratoga and in other active service; in 1793 he entered congress and remained 16 years; he d. Nov. 5, 1831, a. 82.

VAN CORTLANDT, GEN. PIERRE, a son of the first lieut. gov. of N. Y.; was b. Aug. 29, 1762; was a member of assembly in 1792, 4, 5; presidential elector in 1800, and 1840; in 1811–12, a member of congress; he was first president of the Westchester Co. Bank in 1833 and held this office till his death, which occurred at Croton, the seat of his ancestors and descendants, June 13, 1848. (*Stryker's Am. Reg.*, i, 501.)

VAN CURLER, ARENT, early Dutch settler at Schenectady, where he acquired the confidence of the Indians and was long held in affectionate remembrance; he was drowned in Lake Champlain in 1667 on his way to Canada. (*Munsell's Ann. Albany*, i, 205.)

VANDENBERGH, PETER, of Jersey city; d. at St. Augustine, Fla., March 24, 1873; was b. in Somerset county; grad. at Rutgers College in 1826, and was admitted to the bar in 1829; he began practice at Freehold, Monmouth county, and was at one time a member of the leg. council, under the old constitution; in 1854 he was appointed justice of the supreme court by Gov. Price, and reappointed in 1862 by Gov. Olden, the former a democrat and the latter a republican; he was a lawyer of eminent ability, and some of his opinions now on record are among the most carefully prepared ever read from the bench of New Jersey.

VANDERGRIFT, CAPT. JOHN, d. in Delaware city, Del., June, 1860, a. about 60.

VAN DER HEYDEN, DIRCK, inn keeper of Albany early in the last century; became engaged in land speculations and leased lands at Schaghticoke of the city of Albany; he is said to have d. in Oct. 1738; his descendants became proprietors of the present site of Troy; Derick V. H., his grandson, owned the northern and middle allotments.

VAN DER HEYDEN, JACOB D., patroon of Troy; b. Oct. 20, 1758, owned a large part of the present city of Troy, then a farm; and d. Sept. 4, 1809. (*Woodworth's Troy*, 71.)

VAN DER MEER, PIETER ALBERT, gov. of Surinam, from March 6, 1754, till his death, Aug., 1756.

VANDERPOOL, AARON, d. in New York city, July 19, 1870; b. Feb. 5, 1799, admitted to the bar in 1820; in assembly in 1825 to 1828, and in congress from 1833 to 1841; judge of the superior court of New York city from 1841 to 1848.

VANDERPOEL, JAMES, b. at Kinderhook, N. Y., Jan. 10, 1787; studied law and practiced in Columbia co.; he was several times in assembly; in 1812–14 was surrogate; he d. Oct. 3, 1843, at Albany, where he then resided. (*Raymond's Dist. Men of Colum. Co.*, p. 90.)

VAN DER SCHEPPER, GERARD, gov. of Surinam, from Sept. 11, 1737 till his death, Nov. 1, 1741.

VANDEVENTER, MAJ. EUGENE, d. in New York, July 3, 1854; served in the Mexican war with distinction, and was promoted from captain to major.

VANDERVEER, Dr. HENRY, d. at Vanderstedt, N. J., May 22, 1868, in his 92d year.

VAN DRIESSEN, REV. PETRUS, became Dutch minister at Albany in 1712, and remained till his death, Feb. 1, 1738; he organized the church at Kinderhook in 1712, and the one at Claverack in 1716; during his ministry the old stone Dutch church formerly at the foot of State street Albany was erected. (*Rogers's Hist. Discourse*, p. 20.)

VAN DYCK, ABRAHAM, a lawyer of Coxsackie, N. Y.; d. at that place, Feb. 5, 1835, a. 56.

VAN DYCK, DR. ANDREW, b. in Kinderhook, N. Y., Jan. 27, 1801; d. at Oswego, N. Y., Aug., 1871; first settled in practice on the bay of Quinte in Canada; removed to Belleville, and sympathizing with the rebellion of 1837, but without taking any part, became unpopular and returned to his native place; in 1843, settled at Oswego, where he became a prominent physician. (*Tr. N. Y. State Med. Soc.*, i, 1872, p. 336.)

VAN ESGHEN, PIETER, one of the Holland Land Company of western New York; d. at Amsterdam, Holland, Jan. 13, 1815.

VANHOOK, ROBERT, long a member of the senate of North Carolina; d. at Preston, N. C., Oct. 21, 1834, a. 64.

VAN HORNE, RICHARD, b. in Sussex co., N. J., Nov. 15, 1770; son of Abraham V.; in 1791 he removed to the head of the Otsquaga creek, now known as Van Hornesville, and engaged in trade with his brother Daniel, which became a business of great amount; he was in assembly in 1809, 10, 3, 6; in 1821, he was in the state convention, and voted against the constitution therein adopted; he d. in Van Hornelsville, Stark, Herk. co., N. Y., March 12, 1823, in his 73d year. (*Benton's Herkimer Co., N. Y.*, p. 370.)

VAN HOVENBURGH, DR. HENRY, of Kingston, N. Y.; d. July 27, 1868, a. 77.

VAN NESS, JOHN P., b. in Ghent, N. Y., formerly Claverack; d. in Washington, March 7, 1846, a. 76; grad. at Columbia Coll.; began the study of law; in 1801, was elected to congress; in 1802 married a daughter of David Burns, an heiress to a large amount of real estate in Washington, where he spent the rest of life. (*Raymond's Distinguished Men of Columbia Co.*, p. 32; *Am. Almanac*, 1847, p. 344.)

VAN NESS, WILLIAM P., b. in what is now Ghent, N. Y., about 1778; grad. at Columbia Coll.; settled in law at N. Y., about 1800; was appointed U. S. judge of southern dist. of N. Y., by Madison; d. in N. Y., of apoplexy, Sept. 6, 1826. (*Raymond's Distinguished Men of Columbia Co.*, p. 33.)

VAN OLINDA, DR. HENRY, b. in Charleston, N. Y., April 9, 1805; began practice in Montgomery co., in 1826; removed to Albany; d. Sept. 30, 1846, a. 46. (*Munsell's Ann. Alb.*, ix, 107.)

VAN OLINDA, DR. PETER, of Albany; d. Aug., 1872.

VAN RENSSELAER, CHARLES M., first officer on the steamer Central America; son of Gen. John S. V. R. of Albany.

VAN RENSSELAER, JACOB RUTSEN, son of Gen. Robert V. R.; b. at Claverack, N. Y., in 1767; d. Sept. 22, 1835; was several times in the assembly, and in 1812, was speaker; in 1814, was appointed secretary of state, and while in this trust made a thorough rearrangement of the records; in 1821, was in the constitutional convention.

VAN RENSSELAER, KILIAN K., son of Kilian V. R. of Greenbush; was educated as a lawyer, and practiced several years in Albany; was in congress from 1801 to 1811; was several years in the city councils; d. June 18, 1845, a. 82. (*Rogers' Hist. Discourse*, p. 109.)s

VAN RENSSELAER, PHILIP SCHUYLER, wealthy citizen of N. Y.; d. June 1, 1871.

VAN RENSSELAER, RENSSELAER, a son of Solomon V. R. of Albany; commander of the patriots on Navy Island, in 1838; d. a suicide at Syracuse, Jan. 1, 1850.

VAN RENSSELAER, GEN. ROBERT, was a militia general in the revolution, and commanded an unsuccessful expedition in charge of Sir John Johnson in the fall of 1780, up the Mohawk valley; he died at his home in Claverack, N. Y., Sept. 11, 1802, a. 61. (*Hough's Northern Invasion* of 1780, p. 104.)

VAN RENSSELAER, SOLOMON, col. in the war of 1812–15; b. in Greenbush, Aug. 6, 1774; son of Gen. Henry K. V. R., of the revolution; at 18 he became cornet of dragoons and before 20 commanded a troop of horse; he was wounded at the Miami while serving under Wayne, Aug., 1794; he became adj. gen. of N. Y., in 1801, and served till 1809, and in 1810, and 1813 to 1821; he was aid to Maj. Gen. Stephen V. R., in 1812, and served as col., in the battle of Queenstown, in which he was wounded six times; he was in congress from 1819 to 1822, was p. m. at Albany under J. Q. Adams and Jackson, and in 1840 was a presidential elector; he was again appointed p. m. at Albany and was removed by Tyler; he resided at Cherry Hill near Albany, till his death, April 24, 1852. (*Alb. Atlas*, April 25, 1852; *Rogers's Hist. Discourse*, p. 110.)

VAN RENSSELAER, GEN. STEPHEN, d. in Albany, May 25, 1868, in his 80th year, was the 6th in descent from Killian V. R., the first patroon of Rensselaerwyck, and served in the war of 1812.

VAN SANTVOORD, ANTHONY, in early life was captain of a Hudson river sloop, and was the last of the skippers who run a passenger sail vessel on the river before the introduction of steamboats; he died March 17, 1852 at Albany, a. 91. (*Alb. Daily St. Reg.*, April 5, 1852; *Munsell's Ann. Alb.*, v, 222.)

VAN SCHAACK, HENRY, brother of Peter V. S., of Kinderhook, N. Y.; was lieut. in the French war, and present in several engagements; he was several years in the western fur trade; d. in 1823, a. 90. (*Life of Peter Van Schaack*, p. 2.)

VAN SCHAICK, JOHN BLEECKER, literary writer and editor, b. at Albany, and a grand son of Col. Gosen V. S., of the revolution; he studied law with Harmanus Bleecker, and in 1826 visited Europe; preferring literature, he became editor of the *Albany D. Advertiser;* he was distinguished by a fervid eloquence and a high poetic talent; d. at Albany, Jan. 3, 1839, a. 36. (*Griswold's Biog. Annual*, 1841–55).

VAN SCHIE, REV. CORNELIUS, colleague and successor of the Rev. Mr. Van Driesen in the R. P. Dutch church at Albany, having previously labored at Fishkill and Poughkeepsie; called at Albany in 1733; d. Aug. 15, 1744, a. 41. (*Rogers's Hist. Discourse, R. P. D. Church Albany*).

VAN STAPHORST, JAN GABRIEL, one of the Holland Land Company of western New York; d. at Amsterdam, Holland, Aug. 23, 1804.

VAN STAPHORST, NICHOLAS, one of the Holland Land Company of western New York; d. at Amsterdam, Holland, June 19, 1801.

VAN STAPHORST, ROELOF, the younger, one of the Holland Land Company, of western New York; d. at the village of Leyderdorp, in Holland, June 1, 1802.

VANUXEM, LARDNER, son of James Vanuxem, an eminent merchant of Phila. was educated at the School of Mines in Paris, where he acquired a strong taste for the study of mineralogy and the allied sciences; he was soon after connected with Columbia College, S. C., and in 1826, he resigned the chair of chemistry, to take charge of a gold mine near the city of Mexico; he soon returned and settled on a farm at Bristol, Pa., devoting a large part of his time to his favorite studies; in July, 1836, he was appointed geologist to the 4th dist., on the N. Y. geological survey, from which he was transferred in 1837 to the 3d dist.; upon the completion of this labor, he returned to Bristol where he died Jan. 25, 1848; his wife was the daughter of John Newbold, of Bristol. (*Am. Jour. Sci. and Arts*, 2d ser., v, 445.)

VAN VECHTEN, ABRAHAM, statesman and lawyer; b. at Catskill, N. Y., Dec. 5, 1762; studied law under Chancellor Lansing; settled in Montgomery co., but soon after in Albany and gained great distinction at the bar; was in the state senate from 1798 to 1805, and from 1816 to 1819, and in assembly in 1806, 8, 9, 10, 11, 12, 13; was atty. gen. of N. Y., in 1810, 11, 13, 14, 15; recorder of Albany from 1797 to 1808, and a member of the convention of 1821; d. at Albany, Jan. 6, 1837. (*Munsell's Ann. Alb.*, x, 382, with portrait; *Roger's Hist. Discourse*, p. 104.)

VAN VEGHTEN, TOBIAS, lieut. 1st N. Y. regiment; killed in action in 1778.

VAN VLEILAND, LIEUT. CORNELIUS, killed at the storming of Savannah, Oct. 9, 1779.

VAN VOORHEES, ELIAS W., d. in N. Y. city, Aug. 17, 1869; b. in Fishkill, N Y., in 1790; went to the city of N. Y., in 1814, and was largely engaged in the Savannah trade in dry goods and oil.

VAN WINKLE, PETER G., ex-senator from West Virginia; d. in Parkersburg, Va., April 15, 1872.

VAN ZANT, COL. ISAAC, formerly minister from the Texan republic to the U. S.; d. at Houston, Texas, Oct. 11, 1847.

VARNEY, DR. ALFRED E., of Middleville, Herkimer co., N. Y.; b. Dec. 29, 1807; d. 1871. (*Transac. N. Y. State Med. Soc.*, 1872, p. 357.)

VARNEY, EDMUND, b. in Amenia, N. Y., June 6, 1778; son of John V.; settled in Herkimer co. in 1809; was a justice of the peace 25 years; was 5 years a county judge, and many years supervisor, town clerk, &c.; in 1826 was in assembly, and in 1842, 43, 44, 45, in the state senate; d. at Russia, N. Y., Dec. 2, 1847. (*Benton's Herkimer Co. N. Y.*, p. 369.)

VARNEY, SAMUEL J., journalist; started the *Vox Populi*, at Lowell, Mass., in 1841; sold and bought the *Journal and Courier* in 1850, and in 1855 returned to the former; d. Nov. 11, 1859, a. 45. (*Hist Mag.*, iv, 26.)

VARNAM, JOHN, b. in Mass.; grad. at Harvard; was a representative in congress from Mass. from 1825 to 1831, and practiced law at Haverhill, which he repeatedly represented in the legislature; removed to Niles, Mich.; d. there July 23, 1836, a. 63.

VAUGHAN, JOHN DANIEL, d. in Nassau co., Fla., May, 1860, in his 98th year; was a revolutionary soldier. (*Vincent's Semi-An. Register*, p. 469.)

VAUGHAN, JOHN, secretary of the American Philosophical Society; d. at Philadelphia, Dec. 30, 1841, a. 85; was a native of England; had resided in America about 65 years; was extensively acquainted with the prominent characters of his day. (*Am. Almanac*, 1843, p. 306.)

VAUGHAN, LIEUT. WILLIAM, Del., killed in the revolution March 22, 1777.

VAUX, GEORGE, was a lawyer of Philadelphia, and a member of the society of Friends; served in the municipal councils; d. in 1836. (*Simpson's Eminent Philadelphians.*)

VEEDER, LT. COL. VOLKERT, of the N. Y. militia, in the revolution; was in assembly from Tryon, and after its change of name from Montgomery co., N. Y. in 1784, 5, 6, 8, 9 and 1790; afterwards became brigadier general of militia; d. Feb. 22, 1813.

VELAZQUEZ, MARIANE, DE LA CADENA, b. in Mexico, June 28, 1778; sent a. 7 to Madrid and educated at the Royal Seminary of the nobles; 1799, he received the degree of Bachelor of Philosophy and crown cases; in 1800 was admitted royal notary of the chambers and Indies; afterwards a proprietary office analagous to accountant general or curator of the estates of minors and deceased persons; returned to Mexico, but in 2 years came to N. Y. where he established himself as prof. of Spanish; wrote several elementary works in that language; d. in N. Y. in 1860. (*Hist. Mag.*, iv., 156.)

VENABLE, WILLIAM E., minister resident of the U. S. in Guatemala; d. in that country, of cholera, Aug. 22, 1857.

VERPLANCK, ISAAC A., chief judge of the superior court of Buffalo, N. Y.; d. in that city April 16, 1873; born in Coeymans, Albany co., Oct. 16, 1812; grad. at Union Coll.; became a lawyer, and practiced in Batavia from 1831 to 1847, when he removed to Buffalo, where he resided until his death; 1854 he was elected one of the judges of the superior court of Buffalo, and was made chief thereof by his associates; he discharged his judicial duties with ability and unimpeachable integrity, and was twice reëlected; was one of the ablest members of the constitutional convention of 1867–8.

VERREN, REV. ANTOINE, D. D., many years rector of the French Protestant Episc. church N. Y. city; d. March 17, 1874, in his 73d year.

VICK, MAJ. B., d. at Vicksburg, Miss., April 23, 1844; a native of Virginia, removed to Miss. in 1807.

VIGO, COL. FRANCIS, d. in Knox co., Ind., March 22, 1836, a. over 90 years; was a native of Sardinia; came early to America, amassed a large fortune, and expended it in charitable and hospitable objects; before his death, congress granted money to pay claims for services he had rendered to Virginia troops in the early wars of the west. (*Am. Almanac*, 1837, p. 309.)

VINING, WILLIAM HENRY, son of Senator V. of Delaware; removed to Waddington, N. Y.; studied law, and in 1821 was elected to assembly but sailed to the W. I., and d. at St. Croix, in 1822; evinced exalted talent and had a brief but brilliant career. (*Hough's Hist. St. Law. and Fr. Cos. N. Y.*, p. 611.)

VINTON, DAVID H., major gen. U. S. army; d. at Stamford, Conn., Feb. 21, 1873, a. 55.

VINTON, REV. FRANCIS, D.D., d. Sept. 29, 1872, a. 63, at Brooklyn, N. Y.

VINTON, JOHN ROGERS, brevet maj. 3d artil. U. S. A.; killed at the bombardment of Vera Cruz, March 22, 1847, a. 46; b. in Providence, R. I., June 16, 1801; grad. with honors at West Point and served in Florida.

VOLLENHOVEN, HENDRICK, one of the Holland Land Company of western N. Y.; d. at the village of Marsen, Holland, June 4, 1826.

VON DER LAUNITZ, ROBERT EBERHARD SCHMIDT, d. in N. Y., Dec. 13, 1870; b. in Riga, Russia, Nov., 1806; studied sculpture under Thorwaldsen; came to America when young; executed the Pulaski monument, battle monument at Frankfort, Ky., and various other works of art.

VON GILSA, COL. LEOPOLD, late of the U. S. army; d. at N. Y., March 1, 1870.

VON, SCHOULTZ, NEILS SCOLTERCKI, a Polish exile; came to N. Y. in 1836; lived at Syracuse; was engaged in the patriot war of Canada; commanded at the wind mill when attacked by Canadian troops; captured, tried and hung at Port Henry, Kingston, Dec. 18, 1838.

VOORHEES, CAPT. PETER, N. J., killed in the rev. Oct. 26, 1779.

VOORHEES, RALPH, commander in the U. S. navy; d. at Smyrna, Turkey, July 27, 1842.

VOSE, HENRY, a native of Mass.; was educated at West Point, but left without graduating in 1822; was connected at various times with the press of Mississippi, to which he contributed much in geography, statistics and history; was a man of sanguine temperament, ardent in the pursuit of knowledge, but wanting in qualities that insure success; d. near Woodville, Miss., April 17, 1837, of small pox.

VOSE, ROBERT R., secretary of the convention that formed the constitution of Maine, in 1821; clerk of the court of the county of Kennebec; d. at Augusta, Me., June 28, 1836, a. 53.

VOSE, ROGER, grad. at Harvard in 1790; in cong. from N. H., from 1813 to 1817; d. in 1841.

VOSE, GEN. RUFUS CHANDLER, d. in Augusta, Me., Aug. 14, 1842, a. 44.

VREDENBURG, PETER, ex-judge of the sup. court of New Jersey; d. at St. Augustine, Fla., March 27, 1873, a. 82; b. in Somerset co., N. J.; grad. at Rutgers Coll. in 1826.

VROOM, PETER D., ex-governor of N. J.; d. in Trenton, N. J., Nov. 18, 1873, a. 82.

VROOMAN, DR. CORNELIUS, b. at Schenectady; became the agent of Mrs. Campbell; d. Dec., 1811, a. 30. (*Munsell's Ann. Alb.*, ix, 93.)

VROOMAN, CAPT. WALTER, of Col. J. Harper's levies N. Y. militia; was prisoner with the enemy; d. in Guilderland, N. Y., Feb. 17, 1817, a. 70.

WADE, GEN. MELANCTHON S., d. at Avondale, Mo., Aug. 11, 1868; son of David W., one of the first settlers of Cincinnati; at the beginning of the late war, was appointed a brigadier general, and was in command at camp Dennison for some time.

WADSWORTH, JOHN, tutor in Harvard Coll.; native of Duxbury, Mass.; grad. at Harvard in 1762; taught several years; was tutor from 1770 to 1777, when he d. (*Bradford's N. E. Biog.*)

WAINWRIGHT, LIEUT. GEORGE, distinguished at the battle of Molino Del Rey; d. at Brooklyn, N. Y., from wounds received on that occasion, Aug. 4, 1848.

WAIT, JOSEPH, lieut. col. in the revolution; d. Sept. 28, 1776.

WAKEFIELD, CYRUS, d. in Boston, Oct. 26, 1873, a. 62.; he was b. in Roxbury, N. H., in 1811; he began life poor, but in time became one of the most extensive importers in Boston; he owned a manufactory at Wakefield which gives steady employment to 1,300 workpeople, and was largely interested in the Boston and Maine Iron Foundry, the American Rattan Company of Fitchburg, and other large industrial establishments; he owned real estate in Boston and Wakefield estimated to be worth $2,000,000 above all liabilities.

WALCOT, CHARLES M., SR., d. at Phil., May 13, 1868; was an actor of ability, and many years employed at Wallack's theatre, N. Y.

WALDO, DR. ALBIGENCE, surgeon in the continental army; b. in Pomfret, Ct., Feb. 27, 1750; studied the classics and medicine, and served as a surgeon through the revolution; enjoyed an extensive practice in Ct., Mass. and R. I.; d. in Feb. 1794, leaving an interesting collection of MSS. upon professional subjects. (*Hist. Mag.*, v, 104.)

WALES, DR. HENRY WARE, d. in Paris, France, June 8, 1856, a. 37; b. in Boston in 1818; grad. at Harvard in 1833; went to Paris to study medicine, but devoted himself to the languages; made himself master of French, Italian, German, modern Greek, Sanscrit and various oriental languages; was absent 8 years, and returned home; went a second time and extended his travels to the east; returned and went a third time, but his health soon failed; collected a large and valuable library which he bequeathed to Harvard College.

WALKER, BENJAMIN, a presidential elector in 1836; d. at Lowell, Mass., Sept. 7, 1840, a. 39.

WALKER, DAVID, in congress from Ky. from 1817 to 1820; d. March 1, 1820.

WALKER, DIONYSSIUS, of Yazoo, Miss.; d. Feb., 1859, while on his way as consul to Genoa; was formerly editor of the *Vicksburg Sentinel*, and subsequently practiced law.

WALKER, FELIX, b. in Hampshire co., Va., July 19, 1753; in congress from N. C. from 1817 to 1823; explored Ky. with Boone; settled in Tryon co., N. C., and was many years in the state legislature; removed to Miss., and d. there in 1830.

WALKER, FREEMAN, senator in congress from Ga., in 1819–21, took an active part in the Mo. compromise measures; he lived in Augusta, Ga., and d. there Sept. 23, 1827.

WALKER, REV. JAMES, D.D., formerly pres. of Harvard University; d. at Cambridge, Mass., Dec. 23, 1874, a. 80.

WALKER, JAMES P., ex-senator from Wisconsin; d. in Wisconsin, March 29, 1872.

WALKER, JOSEPH, d. in New Orleans, La., Jan. 24, 1856; from 1850 to 1854, governor of Louisiana.

WALKER, JOSEPH BREWSTER, d. in Cincinnati, O., Dec. 31, 1846, a. 37; was a member of the St. Louis bar; grad. at Harvard in the class of 1832.

WALKER, SAMUEL, late speaker of the house of representatives in Ala.; d. in Madison co., Ala., Jan. 23, 1841.

WALL, JAMES W., d. in Elizabeth, N. J., June 9, 18—; b. in Trenton in 1820; his father, Garret P. Wall, was a U. S. senator from N. J.; grad. at Princeton in 1839; studied law, practiced in Trenton, and was appointed commissioner in bankruptcy; in 1847 removed to Burlington, gave some attention to literary pursuits, and in 1854 visited Europe, and published an interesting account of the famous places he visited; came into collision with the administration during the war, and was imprisoned for a few weeks in Ft. Lafayette; in 1863 was elected to the U. S. senate by the democrats for a short term of six weeks; was a member of the Cincinnati Society of New Jersey, and late pres. of the Citizens' Gas Light Company of Elizabeth.

WALL, WILLIAM, ex-member of congress from N. Y. city; d. April 20, 1872, a. 71.

WALLACE, CAPT. ANDREW, Va.; killed in battle of Guilford, March 15, 1781.

WALLACE, REV. CRANMORE, of Charleston, S. C.; an eminent Episcopal clergyman formerly of New England; d. Feb. 3, 1860.

WALLACE, J. B., b. in Edgefield dist., S. C., and settled in Alabama where he was judge, and held many important offices; d. at Tuscaloosa, Ala., Aug. 4, 1853.

WALLACK, HENRY, veteran actor; d. at N. Y., Sept. 2, 1870, a. 70.

WALLACK, JAMES WILLIAM, a well known actor; d. in N. Y. city, May 24, 1873, a. 56.

WALLACK, RICHARD, a distinguished lawyer of Washington, D. C.; d. in that city, Dec. 3, 1835.

WALLBRIDGE, ARTHUR D., of the Rochester bar; d. in Rochester, Dec. 14, 1872; was a son of S. D. Wallbridge; b. in Gaines, Orleans co., in 1843; grad. at Princeton in 1867; after devoting some time to journalism, he studied law and was admitted to the bar; he evinced poetic abilities of great promise, and was author, among others, of the well-known melodies, *Now I Lay Me Down to Sleep*, *Sleeping where the Daisies Grow*, *Baby Meets Me on the Stairs*, *Gone;* the first of these was once very popular.

WALLER, JOHN, d. Oct. 22, 1780, at Jamaica, N. Y., of fever; maj. of brigade to Gen. DeLancey.

WALLEY, THOMAS, d. in Boston, Mass., Aug. 2, 1848, in his 80th year; son of Thomas W., and fourth in descent from the Rev. Thomas W. of Barnstable, one of the non conformist exiles of the time of Charles II.

WALN, JACOB S., b. in Monmouth co., N. J. in 1776; became extensively concerned in mercantile affairs in Phil.; held many public trusts, and was a member of the legislature; d. at Phil., April 4, 1850. (*Simpson's Eminent Philadelphians.*)

WALN, S. MORRIS, merchant at Phil.; d. Dec. 22, 1870, a. 63.

WALSH, ALEXANDER, many years an active merchant, and an early and devoted friend to agriculture; d. at Lansingburg, N. Y., Aug., 1849, in his 61st year.

WALSH, WILLIAM, d. at Newburg, N. Y., Nov. 2, 1839, a. 67; president of the Bank of Newburg.

WALSH, MOST REV. WILLIAM, D.D., R. C. archbishop of Halifax; b. in Waterford, Nov. 1804; educated at St. Johns Coll. at that place; ordained priest March 25, 1828; in 1838 was offered the place of bp. of Calcutta, which he declined; 1842 he became coadjutor vicar apostolic of Nova Scotia; afterwards bp. of Halifax, and in 1852 first arch bp. of that diocese; d. Aug. 10, 1858, a. 54. (*Dungan's Am. Cath Almanac*, 1859, p. 41.)

WALTER, LYNDE, d. in Boston, Mass., July 25, 1842, a. 43; editor of the *Boston Transcript;* grad. at Harvard in 1817.

WARD, ABRAHAM, an old and much respected citizen of Newark, N. J.; d. at that place Dec. 26, 1833, a. about 87.

WARD, CLEMENT L., d. at Towanda, Pa., May 14, 1870; was an early settler of Tioga co.; printer by trade, and had been president of the Towanda Bank; 1864 he was chairman of the democratic central committee.

WARD, REV. ELIJAH, of Ohio, d. in Willoughby, O., Jan. 16, 1860, a. 94; joined the N. Y. conference in 1801, and was more than half a century a Methodist preacher of no common order of talent.

WARD, JOSHUA H., d. at Salem, Mass., May 29, 1848, a. 39; judge of the Mass. court of com. pleas; a grad. of Harvard in 1829.

WARD, JOSHUA JOHN, d. on his plantation in South Carolina, Feb. 27 1853, a. 53; was lieut. governor of that state,

WARD, NAHUM, of Marietta, O.; d. April 6, 1860, a. 75; came from Shrewsbury, Conn., in 1811.

WARD, SAMUEL, banker, b. at Newport, R. I., May 1, 1786; in 1790 removed to N.Y.; at 14 he became a clerk in the banking house of which he was afterwards the head; 1808 he was taken into partnership with Nathaniel Prime, and the firm of Prime, Ward & King became widely known as enterprising bankers; in 1828 he lent an active hand in behalf of the N. Y. Hist Soc.; in 1830 to the founding of the N. Y. University, and at a later day entered warmly into various temperence, mission, tract and other beneficent movements; in the commercial crisis of 1836, 7, he was particularly active in supporting the commercial credit of the city, in 1838 he aided in founding the Bank of Commerce, of which he was afterward president; d. Nov. 27, 1839. (*Griswold's Biog. Annual* 1841, 266; *Hunt's Lives of Am. Merchants*, i, 295.)

WARD, SAMUEL, d. in Salem, Mass., April 27, 1842, a. 54; for several years a member of the general court.

WARD, THOMAS, d. at Newark, N. J., Feb. 4, 1842, a. 83; member of congress from N. J. from 1813 to 1817.

WARD, THOMAS, in congress from N. J. from 1813 to 1817; d. at Newark, N. J., Feb. 4, 1842, a. 83.

WARDSWORTH, DANIEL, brother-in-law of Prof. Silliman; d. at Hartford, Conn., Aug. 4, 1848, in his 77th year.

WARE, NICHOLAS, began his professional career at Augusta, Ga.; was in the U. S. senate from 1821 to 1824; d. in the city of N. Y., Sept., 1824.

WARFIELD, HENRY R., d. at Frederick, Md., March 18, 1839; member of congress in 1819–25.

WARNER, ANDREW E., d. in Baltimore, Jan. 16, 1870, a. 84; was a soldier in the war of 1812; a prominent odd fellow; and had held high offices in that order.

WARNER, HIRAM, b. in Mass. Oct. 29, 1802; settled in Ga., a. 17; was assistant teacher in the Sparta Acad.; studied law and settled at Knoxville, Crawford co., Ga.; in 1828 he was elected to the legislature and held till 1831; was opposed to nullification; in 1833, he was elected judge of the Coweta circuit and held till 1840; in 1848 the supreme court of Ga. was organized and he was elected and again elected in 1849. (*White's Hist. Ga.*, p. 557, with portrait.)

WARNER, JAMES COOPER, *N. Y. Tribune* correspondent; d. at Panama, April 15, 1868, a. 23.

WARNER, CAPT. WILLIAM H., of the topographical engineers; was shot by nine arrows by the Indians at the east fork of the Sacramento, while leading a command, Sept. 20, 1849.

WARREN, CORNELIUS, member of congress from the 8th dist. of N. Y. in 1847–49; d. at Cold Spring, Putnam co., N. Y., July 28, 1849.

WARREN, REV. IRA D., b. in Oswegatchie, N. Y., April 4, 1802; d. in Cortland, N. Y., Nov. 18, 1869. (*Northern Christian Advocate*, Jan. 13, 1870.)

WARREN, DR. J. MASON, d. in Boston, Mass., Aug. 19, 1867, in his 56th year.

WARREN, REV. PETER, F. W. bap. preacher; b. in Limerick, Me.; grad. at Readfield Sem., Me.; went to Wis. in 1845; taught at Sheboygan Falls; was ordained in 1850; preached at Utica, N. Y., and Greenbush, Wis., where he d. March 10, 1856, a. 38. (*F. W. Bap. Reg.*, 1857, p. 86.)

WARREN, Col. Samuel, d. in Pendleton, S. C., Nov. 29, 1841, a. 80; was an officer in the revolutionary war; had served in the legislature, and was at one time pres. of the senate.

WARRINER, Maj. Gad, d. in West Springfield, Mass., May 19, 1842, a. 84; a revolutionary soldier.

WASHBURN, Rev. Cephas, d. at Little Rock, Ark., March 17, 1860; came to Arkansas some 30 years before as missionary to the Cherokees, and lived among them till 1840, when he removed to Benton co., and about 1847 to Ft. Smith, and was pastor of the Presb. church there; in 1856 went to Norristown, which was his home till death.

WASHBURN, Ichabod, originator and manager of the Washburn & Moen Manufacturing Co. at Worcester, Mass.; d. at Worcester, Dec. 10, 1869.

WASHINGTON, Dr. Bailey, d. in Washington, D. C., Aug. 4, 1854, a. 67; b. in Westmoreland co., Va., in 1787; senior surgeon in the navy, having entered the navy in 1810; was surgeon on the Enterprise when captured by the Boxer; afterwards served with efficiency on Lake Ontario under Chauncey; was fleet surgeon under Com. Rogers, Elliott and Patterson, in the Mediterranean, and was last in sea service in the Mexican war; was consulting and visiting surgeon of the navy yard and marine barracks at Washington at the time of his death.

WASHINGTON, George C., d. in Georgetown, D. C., July 17, 1854; b. in Va.; served in congress from Md. in 1827–33, and in 1835–37; pres. of the Ohio and Chesapeake Canal Co., and commissioner for the settlement of Indian claims.

WASHINGTON, Henry A., of Williamsburg, Va.; prof. of hist. in William and Mary's Coll., and editor of an edition of Jefferson's works; d. at Washington, D. C., Feb. 28, 1858, a. 36. (*Hist. Mag.*, ii, 123.)

WASHINGTON, John Macrae, brevet lieut. col.; major 3d artil. U. S. A.; lost on board the San Francisco, Dec. 25, 1853, a. about 60; b. in Va.; grad. at West Point in 1813, and rose to the rank of major in 1847; served with honor in the Mexican war; was a thorough tactician in the artillery service, and as early as 1824, was made instructor in the artillery school at Ft. Monroe; from Oct. 1848 till Oct. 1849, acted as military governor of New Mexico. (*Am. Almanac*, 1855, p. 328.)

WASHINGTON, Lund Jr., was for many years connected with the press, and afterwards a clerk in the state department; d. at Washington, D. C., Aug. 20, 1849, a. 56.

WASHINGTON, Samuel, brother of Gen. Geo. W.; b. Nov. 16, 1734; was 5 times m.; d. in 1781, at Harewood, Berkley co., Va.; in 1778 was appointed by congress com'r to proceed westward on public business, but declined from ill health, and a successor was appointed. (*Sparks's Life and Writings of Washington*, p. 550.)

WASHINGTON, Thomas Bushrod, d. in Albany, N. Y., Aug. 4, 1854, a. about 40; a grand nephew of Gen. Geo. Washington.

WASHINGTON, W. D., prof. of fine arts in the Va. Inst. at Lynchburg, Va.; d. Nov. 30, 1871.

WATERBURY, Charles, over 12 years supt. of the Naugatuck rail road; d. in Bridgeport, Conn., Sept. 3, 1868.

WATERBURY, HENRY, b. at Stamford, Ct.; served on the lakes as lieut. of rangers in 1755, and through the French war in one of the Ct. regiments; in 1775 commanded a Ct. reg. under Montgomery in Canada; in 1776 was appointed brig. gen. by the state of Ct., and was next to Arnold in command on Lake Champlain, where he was taken prisoner in a naval engagement, Oct. 13, 1776; was released on parole and exchanged.

WATERHOUSE, HENRY S., M.D., prof. in Vt. University; b. at Salisbury, Vt.; settled at Malone, N. Y., about 1812, and became well known as a surgeon; in 1826 became prof. in the med. dept. of Vt. University, and held 2 years; removed to Key West and drowned a few years after at Indian Key. (*Hough's Hist. St. Law. and Fr. Cos., N. Y.*, p. 612.)

WATERMAN, JOHN, d. at Warwick, R. I., Aug. 21, 1837, a. 78; was a soldier in the revolution, and afterwards chief justice of the court of common pleas of R. I.

WATERMAN, CAPT. ROBERT, one of the oldest ship-masters of the country, d. at New Orleans, La., April 29, 1860. (*Vincent's Semi-Annual Register*, p. 342.)

WATERS, MRS. ABIGAIL, d. in Boston, Nov. 22, 1816, in her 96th yr. (*Memoir of Mrs. A. W. by Joshua Huntington.*)

WATERS, DR. CHARLES, a volunteer physician from Baltimore in the yellow fever at Portsmouth, Va., in the autumn of 1855; fell a victim to the disease.

WATERS, DR. WILSON, a surgeon in the navy during the revolutionary war; d. in Ann Arundel co., Md., Feb. 5, 1836, aged 78.

WATSON, MALBONE, justice of the supreme court of N. Y.; was a prominent lawyer at Catskill, N. Y.; several years dist. atty. of Greene co.; in 1847 he was elected a justice of the supreme court for the 3d dist. drew the term of 6 years; was reëlected in 1853; d. at New Orleans, April 1857.

WATSON, DR. GEORGE, d. in Richmond, Va., Oct. 12, 1853, a. 70; an eminent physician.

WATSON, JAMES, b. in Woodbury, Conn., April 6, 1750; fitted for college with Rev. A. R. Robbins; grad. at Yale in 1776, settled in New York city as a merchant; was in assembly in 1794–5–6, and the first of these years speaker; was in the state senate in 1797–8; and U. S. senator from 1798 to 1800; d. May 15, 1806, and buried in Litchfield; he purchased a large tract of very poor land in Lewis and Herkimer counties, which is still partly a wilderness; his son, James Talcott Watson, undertook expensive improvements with barren results.

WATSON, JAMES, county auditor; d. at New York city, Jan. 30, 1871.

WATSON, JAMES TALCOTT, son of James, and proprietor of the town of Watson, N. Y.; committed suicide in N. Y. city, Jan. 29, 1839, a. 50.

WATSON, JOSEPH, d. in Philadelphia, Pa., April 9, 1841, a. 57; president of the Lehigh Company, and formerly mayor of Philadelphia.

WATSON, SAMUEL EDMISTON, d. at Vera Cruz, Mex., Nov. 16, 1847; was lieut. col. of marine corps.

WATTS, ALARIC A., an English artist, poet, critic and journalist; d. at Kensington Park, London, April 5, 1864; he was the originator in England of the system of literary annuals, once so popular, beginning with *The Literary Souvenir for* 1824; in 1853, the queen bestowed upon him a pension of £100 for his services through thirty years in literature and the fine arts.

WATTS, CHARLES, a native of N. Y.; removed to La., and held the office of judge of the commercial court, at the time of the adoption of the new constitution; he d. at Biloxi, La., January 14, 1851, a. 62. (*Stryker's Am. Reg.*, vi, 207.)

WATTS, JACOB, a pioneer of the Miami valley, and native of New Jersey; d. at Gallatin, Ky., July, 1849, in the 93d year of his age; he settled at the village of Columbia at the mouth of the Little Miami in the fall of 1788. (*Stryker's Am. Reg.*, iii, 232.)

WATTS, JOHN, b. in New York city; was a member of assembly from New York city and speaker in 1791–2–3; was in congress from 1793 to 1795; d. in New York city, Sept. 3, 1836.

WATTS, DR. JOHN, JR., of New York city; d. Feb. 4, 1831, a. 45.

WATTS, ROBERT (see Leake, John G).

WATTS, WILLIAM, became lieut. in the 17th foot of British army, Feb. 2, 1757; d. in 1759.

WAUGH, REV. BEVERLY, senior bishop of the Methodist Episcopal church; d. at Baltimore, Md., Feb. 9, 1858, a. 69; he had served as bishop since 1836.

WAY, REV. RUSSELL, Free Will Baptist preacher; d. near Collinsville, Lewis co., N. Y., July 23, 1848; his father, Moses W., d. in West Turin, April 7, 1813, a. 67.

WEBB, COL. B. R., secretary of state of Mississippi, and for some years before in the state senate from Pontotoc co.; d. at Jackson, Miss., Jan. 16, 1860, a. about 48.

WEBBER, EDWARD A., d. in Rumney, N. H., April, 1842, a. 50; late a judge of probate for Grafton co.

WEBBER, RICHARD W., d. at the Bay of St. Louis, Miss., Sept. 29, 1843, a. about 45; a lawyer, formerly a member of the legislature.

WEBER, THOMAS, d. at Baltimore, Md., April, 1860; the largest man in Baltimore, weight 460 lbs. (*Vincent's Semi-An. Register*, p. 354.)

WEBSTER, ALEXANDER, a prominent Scotch settler of Charlotte, now Washington co., N. Y.; commanded a militia regiment in the revolution; served in provincial congress; was two years in assembly, 1788–89, and from 1777 to 1785; from 1790 to 1793 in the state senate; was 5 years one of the council of appointment; in 1786–88, was first judge of Washington co.; d. at Hebron, N. Y., Sept. 17, 1810, a. 75.

WEBSTER, LIEUT. AMOS, d. in the revolution, Oct. 7, 1777.

WEBSTER, CHARLES R., eminent Albany printer; b. Sept. 38, 1762, at Hartford, Ct.; was apprenticed to the printing trade; served a short time in the revolution; went to Albany in 1781 or 1782; became a partner of Solomon Balentine, and began a paper, but in 1783 dissolved; in 1784 began the *Albany Gazette;* continued in the trade through a long period, being for a time a partner of George W., a twin brother, and his nephews, Elisha W., Hezekiah and Daniel Skinner; d. July 18, 1834. (*Munsell's Ann. Alb.*, v, 230.)

WEBSTER, Ebenezer, father of Daniel W.; b. in Kingston, N. H., in 1739; served in the French war; settled in Stevenstown afterwards Salisbury, as early as 1761; held various town offices; was a representative in 1778–80–90–91; senator in 1785–86–88; in 1778 a del. to const. convention; was a presidential elector in 1789; 1791 became judge of com. pleas for Hillsborough co., and held till his death in April, 1806; in the revolution was a captain, and afterwards held military offices many years. (*Hist. Mag.*, ii, 324.)

WEBSTER, Maj. Edward, d. at St. Angel, 8 miles from Mexico, Jan. 25, 1848, a. 27; of the Mass. regiment of volunteers.

WEBSTER, Ephraim, was b. at Hempstead, N. H., in 1752; removed in 1773, to N. Y. near the North river; served three years in the revolution; soon after the peace engaged in trade with the Iroquois, at first at Oriskany, and in 1786 at Onondaga; resided here many years, a lonely pioneer, acquired the language and confidence of the natives, with whom he intermarred, and engaged extensively in the purchase of furs and ginseng; was many years Indian agent, and interpreter; received a mile square of land in Onondaga Hollow; held several town offices; was generally esteemed; d. at Tuscarora, in 1825, and was buried at Onondaga. (*Clark's Hist. Onondaga Co.*, i, 337.)

WEBSTER, Horace, ll.d., b. in Vt., Sept. 21, 1784; d. at Geneva, N. Y., July 12, 1871; grad. at West Point in 1818; was assist. prof. of mathematics at West Point, from 1818 to 1823; in Sept., 1823, became prof. of mathematics at Geneva Coll.; in 1848, was appointed principal of the Free Academy at New York, which under his supervision became thoroughly organized. (*Regents' Report*, 1872, p. 692.)

WEBSTER, James, m.d., prof. of anatomy, and journalist; b. at Warring, Eng., Dec. 24, 1803; came with his father's family to Phila., when an infant; grad. at Phila. in 1824; succeeded Dr. Godman, as lecturer on anatomy; became concerned in medical journals, and in surgery; settled in N. Y., where he made diseases of the ear a specialty, and lectured; succeeded Prof. Parker, at the Geneva Med. Coll., and held till 1853; in 1839, removed to Rochester; in 1845, was appointed prof. in the med. dep. of the University of Buffalo, where he remained till 1850; d. at Lousville, Ky., July 18, 1854. (*Tr. N. Y. St. Med. Soc.*, 1855, p. 165.)

WEBSTER, Lucien B., brevet lieut. col., maj. 4th U. S. Artil.; d. at Fort Brown, Tex., Nov. 4, 1853; b. in Vermont; grad. at West Point in 1823; served on the eastern frontier in the Aroostook troubles; in command of the fort at the mouth of Fish river; served with distinction in the Mexican war.

WEBSTER, Samuel C., high sheriff of Grafton co., N. H.; d. at Haverhill, N. H., July 21, 1835, a. 47.

WEED, Hiram, secretary of state of Connecticut; d. at Danbury, June 7, 1850.

WEED, Jared, grad. at Harvard in 1807; settled as a lawyer in Petersham, 1813; reached a respectable standing in the profession; was for some years chairman of the board of county commissions; d. at Petersham, Mass., Aug. 6, 1857, a. 74.

WEED, Monroe, b. near Sacketts harbor, N. Y., Jan. 18, 1817; grad. at Madison U., in 1846; in 1852, took charge of Middlebury Acad. and taught 15 years; in 1866, went to Fisherville, N. H.; but soon sickened and died. (*Regents' Report*, 1868, p. 710.)

WEED, DR. SAMUEL, b. in Amesbury, Mass.; grad. at Harvard in 1800; settled at Portland, Me., in the practice of medicine, which he continued till he was disabled by an injury, in 1852; d. Nov. 24, 1857, a. 83.

WEEDEN, MRS. JOHN, d. in Lorain co., O., March 30, 1860, a. 93; she escaped from the Wyoming massacre, and remembered that occurence. (*Hist. Mag.*, iv, 157.)

WEEDEN, MRS. P., last survivor of the Wyoming massacre; d. March 30, 1860. (*Vincent's Semi-An. Register*, p. 226.)

WEEKS, REV. HOLLAND, from Abingdon, Miss.; formerly a Congregationalist, and afterwards Swedenborgian preacher; came to Henderson, N. Y., in 1821; d. July 24, 1843, a. 75.

WEEKS, JOHN, d. at New London, Conn., in 1798, a. 114; m. his tenth wife at the age of 106; shed his gray hairs, which were replaced by dark hair, and several new teeth made their appearance. (*Kirby's Museum*, ii, 279.)

WEIR, EDWARD, doorkeeper in the U. S. senate; fell suddenly dead, Feb. 21, 1839.

WEISSENFELS, FREDERICK H. BARON DE, native of Prussia; settled in Dutchess co., before the revolution; was naturalized Dec. 20, 1763; served as lieut. col. with credit till the peace; subsequently removed to New Orleans, accepted an humble office in the police, and d. Aug., 1806. (*Hough's Northern Invasion*, 1780, p. 147.)

WEISSINGER, GEORGE W., associate proprietor and editor of the *Louisville Journal*; d. at Louisville, Ky., Feb. 25, 1850.

WELCH, H. R., a lawyer; d. at Hartford, Conn., Nov. 28, 1870.

WELCH, REV. WHITMAN, of Williamstown, Mass.; chaplain in the American army; d. near Quebec, March, 1776.

WELCKER, CAPT. GEORGE L., d. at Savannah, Ga., May 24, 1848; of the U. S. corps of civil engineers.

WELLES, DR. BENJAMIN, removed from Kinderhook to Steuben co., N. Y., in 1798; had been a surgeon in the revolution; d. in Wayne, Steuben co., N. Y., in 1812.

WELLES, SAMUEL, of Glastonbury, Ct.; d. Nov. 12, 1834, a. 80.

WELLES, WILLIAM H., senator in congress from Delaware, from 1799 to 1804; from 1813 to 1817; d. March 11, 1829.

WELLMAN, JAMES, d. in Salem, Mass., March 3, 1869, a. 86; b. in Lyndeboro, N. H., Feb. 25, 1783; lived 59 ys. in Farmington, Me; and for the last 5 years in Salem; in 1867, he published a genealogy of the Wellman family.

WELLS, ALEXANDER, d. in San José, Cal., Oct. 30, 1854, a. 40; judge of the supreme court of California, formerly a lawyer of New York city; in 1846, in assembly; had resided in California 5 years.

WELLS, DANIEL JR., b. in Maine; was a lawyer, and settled in Wisconsin; was in congress from 1853 to 1855; afterwards held the offices of judge of probate, and county judge; d. in 1858.

WELLS, MAJ. MELANCTHON W., d. in Lowville, N. Y., Feb. 27, 1857, a. 56; settled at that place in 1809; was from Lanesboro, Mass.

WELLS, SAMUEL, son of Jonathan Wells, was b. at Deerfield, Mass., Sept. 9, 1730; settled in Brattleboro on a farm of 600 acres in July, 1762; was appointed judge of the inferior court of Cumberland co. in 1766; in 1773 was chosen to the gen. assembly of N. Y. and sided with the loyalists, although he did not openly avow his principles; he promoted the negotiation with the British in 1782 having as an ostensible object the annexation of Vermont to Canada; he suffered many vexations and losses in consequence of his loyalty but held out to the last; d. at Brattleboro, insolvent, Aug. 6, 1786, in his 56th year. (*Hall's Eastern Vermont*, p. 718.)

WELLS, REV. TIMOTHY, first pastor of the Presb. church at Riverhead, N. Y.; d. at Catchogue, Jan. 15, 1783, a. 62; was ordained Oct. 25, 1759.

WELLS, WILLIAM, b. in England; came to this country in 1793; grad. at Harvard, in 1796; taught, and was a bookseller in Boston; removed to Cambridge in 1830, and kept successfully a classical school there for many years; d. at Cambridge, Mass., April 21, 1860, a. 86.

WENDELL, CORNELIUS, formerly government printer at Washington, D. C.; d. at Northampton, Mass., Oct. 8, 1870.

WENDELL, OLIVER, grad. at Harvard, in 1753, and was many years a merchant in Boston; belonged to the 2d and 3d prov. congresses, and was several years after in the legislature, serving in both houses; he was a judge of probate for Suffolk; d. in 1818. (*Bradford's N. E. Biog.*)

WENDELL, DR. PETER, chancellor of the regents of the university, and oldest resident physician at Albany; d. Oct. 31, 1849, in the 64th year of his age; b. in Albany, June 3, 1786; studied with Dr. William McClelland, and attended lectures in Phil., and practiced medicine at Albany through life. (*Tr. N. Y. State Med. Soc.*, 1850, p. 230; do. 1857, p. 39; *Munsell's Ann. Alb.*, ix, 98.)

WENDELL, ROBERT U., d. at his residence on College hill, Schenectady, N. Y., July 7, 1848, a. 88.

WENTWORTH, FRANCES, widow of late Hon. Asahel Stearns; d. in Cambridge, Mass., Sept. 28, 1842, a. 70.

WEREAT, JOHN, an acting executive of Ga. in the revolution; took an early stand in the revolution on the side of the colonies; was in the Ga. prov. congress in 1775; speaker in 1776, and active through the war; when Savannah fell into the hands of the enemy he, as president of the executive council, continued the functions of government and ordered an election of members of assembly; was a man of much financial talent; was pres. of the conv. in Ga. that ratified the fed. const. at Augusta, Jan. 2, 1788; d. in Bryan co., in 1798. (*White's Hist. Ga.*, p. 210.)

WESNER, FREDERICK E., d. in Greene co., Ala., July 11, 1842, a. 19; was a native of S. C. and a teacher.

WESSELHOEFT, DR. WILLIAM, homœopathic physician, and formerly pres. of the Mass. soc. of this school of medicine; b. in Chemintz Saxony; lived 34 years in U. S; d. in Boston, Sept. 1, 1858, a. 65.

WEST, Dr. Eli, b. in Hampton, N. Y., July 26, 1792; settled as a physician at Carthage, N. Y., in May, 1816, and resided there till his death, June 23, 1866.

WEST, George Augustus, youngest son of the 1st earl of Delaware; b. in 1733; became capt. Nov., 1755; came to Am. in 1757, and served against Ticonderoga in 1758; succeeded Maj. Proby; ranked as lieut. col. Nov. 6, 1759, and became col. in the army, and aid-de-camp to the king June 25, 1766; col. of the 58th foot, Oct. 18, 1775; d. childless, Feb., 1776. (*Com. Wilson's Orderly Book*, 93.)

WEST, Rev. George W., d. in Groton, Mass., March 17, 1843, a. 38; pastor of the First Congregational church of that town; grad. at Harvard in 1823.

WEST, Nathaniel, d. at Salem, Mass., Sept. 7, 1843, a. 55; was of Indianapolis, Ind., but native of Salem; grad. at Harvard in 1807; was a commissioner for settling claims under the treaty with Naples; in 1835 removed to Ind., where he was engaged in agriculture and manufactures, and held several offices of trust.

WEST, Robert Athow, an editor of *N. Y. Commercial Advertiser* for many years; in June 1863 became editor of the *Chronicle* at Washington, and afterwards held an office in the bureau of military justice; d. Feb. 1, 1865.

WEST, Silas, m.d.; b. in Watervliet, N. Y., March 11, 1793; removed at 13 to Paris, Oneida co.; studied with Dr. Elnathan Judd; settled at Vernon Centre, in 1819, and in Binghamton in 1823; d. there suddenly Aug. 27, 1859, a. 67. (*Tr. N. Y. State Med. Soc.*, 1860, p. 168.)

WEST, Thomas Barnard, d. in Salem, Mass., Oct., 1842, a. 26; grad. at Harvard in 1836, and principal of Beverley Academy.

WESTCOTT, James D., d. at Trenton, N. J., March 2, 1841, a. 66; was for the last 10 years sec. of state, and had filled other public offices.

WESTCOTT, Col. David M., d. at Goshen, N. Y., April 21, 1841, a. 72.

WESTERLO, Rev. Eilardus, b. in Groningen, in Oct. 1738; was installed in Holland in March 1760, as pastor of the R. P. Dutch church of Albany, and arrived in the autumn of that year; in 1775, he married the widow of Stephen Van Rensselaer, then patroon of Rensselaerwyck and resided at the Manor house till 1784; d. Dec. 26, 1790, a. 53. (*Rogers's Hist. Discourse, R. P. D. Church Alb.*)

WESTERN, Helen, d. in Washington, D. C., Dec. 11, 1868; b. in N. Y., and made her first appearance on the stage in *Uncle Tom's Cabin;* had played in nearly every city in the Union.

WESTON, Ezras, d. in Duxbury, Mass., Aug. 15, 1842, a. 70; a prominent merchant.

WESTON, Capt. Jonathan, d. at Reading, Mass., April 24, 1839, a. 82; was a soldier of the revolution.

WETHERBEE, David, d. in Lunenburg, Mass., Jan. 18, 1842, a. 85; a revolutionary pensioner.

WETHERBEE, E. B., state senator of Michigan and a native of Marlborough, Mass.; d. at Detroit, Feb. 20, 1847, a. 42.

WETHERILL, John Price, b. in Phil. Oct. 17, 1794; was engaged in the lead and chemical business, and much devoted to science; was vice pres. of the Academy of Nat. Sci.; a member of the Am. Phil. Soc. (*Simpson's Eminent Philadelphians.*)

WETMORE, Thomas, b. in Boston Aug. 31, 1795, grad. at Harvard in 1814; studied law, but left the bar; devoted much time to the interests of his native city, being 3 ys. a member of the com. council, and for 11 ys. an alderman; was some years one of the board of water commissioners; d. in Boston, March 30, 1860, a. 64.

WETMORE, William Chauncey, commander in the U. S. navy; d. at Bergen Hill, N. J., Aug. 8, 1846, a. 49; had served in the navy since he was thirteen years old, and with Com. Chauncey's flag ship on Lake Ontario.

WEYMAN, William, early printer in N. Y.; son of an Episc. clergyman at Oxford, Pa.; served with Wm. Bradford; in Jan. 1753, became a partner of John Parker of N. Y., till Jan. 1759; published the *N. Y. Gazette*, till Dec. 1767; in 1760, became public printer; d. in N. Y., July 18, 1768. (*Doc. Hist. N. Y.*, iv, 327.)

WHACOAT, Rev. Richard, Methodist bishop; b. in Glocestershire, Eng.; began a traveling preacher in 1769, in Eng. and Ireland; in 1784, came to the U. S. and assisted in the ordination of Mr. Asbury; labored till 1800, when he was ordained bishop; d. at Dover, Del., July 5, 1806. (*Lee's Hist. Meth.*, p. 341.)

WHARRY, Evans, b. near Wallkill, N. Y., in 1749; left an orphan at an early age; made several voyages to the West Indies, and became a surveyor; the revolution found him in the prime of life; commanded a company in Montgomery's army in Canada, and served through the war; about 1785–86, settled in Herkimer co., N. Y., surveyed lands many years; was a county judge, and justice a long time; a member of the state convention of 1801; in assembly in 1804–5; d. in Little Falls, April, 1831, a. 82 years. (*Benton's Herkimer Co., N. Y.*, p. 373.)

WHARTON, Rev. Charles Henry, d. at Burlington, N. J., July, 1833, a. 86 years.

WHARTON, Geo. Mifflin, d. at Philadelphia, Pa., Feb. 5, 1870, a. 63; a distinguished member of the Phila. bar, and U. S. dist. atty. under Buchanan.

WHARTON, Jesse, in congress from Tennessee, from 1807 to 1809; U. S. senator in 1814 and 1815; d. at Nashville, Tenn., July 22, 1833.

WHARTON, Robert, b. in the dist. of Southwark, Phila., Jan. 20, 1757; d. in 1834; held the office of alderman; was fifteen times elected mayor; was a colonel, and afterwards general of militia. (*Simpson's Eminent Philadelphians.*)

WHEELER, Charles, d. in Phila. June 16, 1858, in his 71st year; was a prominent lawyer, and churchman; many years a member of the original board of managers of the Domestic and Foreign Missionary Soc., of the P. E. ch. and of the soc. for the advancement of Christianity in Penn. (*Simpson's Eminent Philadelphians.*)

WHEELER, Grattan H., son of Silas; was a prominent politician of Steuben co., N. Y.; served in assembly in 1822–24–26 : in the state senate in 1828–31; in congress in 1831–33; d. 1852.

WHEELER, DR. HORACE K., asst. physician of Bloomingdale Asylum for the Insane, N. Y. city; d. May 7, 1868.

WHEELER, SAMUEL, b. in Weccacoe, Phil. co., Pa., in 1742; d. in Phil. May 10, 1820; was a most eminent iron smith, and made cannon from iron bars by welding; made the chain across the Hudson in the Highlands. (*Simpson's Eminent Philadelphians.*)

WHEELER, CAPT. SILAS, pioneer and namesake of the town of Wheeler, Steuben co., N. Y.; b. in R. I., and emigrated from Albany in 1800 or before; bought several thousand acres of land; d. in 1828 a. 78.

WHEELWRIGHT, WILLIAM, founder of the Pacific Mail Steamship Co.; d. in London, Sept. 25, 1873, a. 76.

WHIPPLE, CHARLES W., d. in Detroit, Mich., Oct. 25, 1857; was an accomplished jurist and one of the judges of the supreme court of Mich.

WHIPPLE, DANIEL, was appointed sheriff of Cumberland co., April 17, 1770; conflicting accounts have been preserved of his capacity and integrity; he probably d. about 1775. (*Hall's Eastern Vermont*, p. 725.)

WHIPPLE, THOMAS, d. June 7, 1859, a. 71, at Coventry, R. I.; had frequently held the office of representative in the state legislature; was a judge of the court of common pleas from 1820 to 1822, and in 1849 lieut. governor.

WHITAKER, WILLIAM, d. in Boston, Mass., Jan. 22, 1844, a. 56; member of the Mass. senate from the Franklin dist.

WHITCOMB, ASA, revolutionary col.; citizen of Lancaster, Mass., which he represented in 1766–7; was in county conv. in Aug., 1777, and in the prov. congresses of Oct., 1774 and Feb., 1775; was made col. in May, 1775, and commanded a company at Carson Point and Ticonderoga; d. in poverty at an advanced age. (*Bradford's N. E. Biog.*)

WHITCOMB, JOHN, a revolutionary pensioner; d. at Swansea, N. H., March 31, 1835, a. 104.

WHITE, CAPT. AARON, killed in invasion of Niagara frontier, Dec. 30, 1813.

WHITE, ANDREW, financier; b. at West Middleton, Pa., in 1803, of Irish parents; was apprenticed to the book binders' trade in Albany; and in 1830 was concerned in the establishment of the *Albany Eve. Jour.* and conducted its financial affairs; in 14 years retired with an ample fortune; was receiver to the Albany Canal Bank, cashier of the Commercial Bank, and was connected with this bank till his death, Nov. 17, 1857. (*Alb. Eve. Jour.* Nov. 18, 1857.)

WHITE, DR. BARTON, of Fishkill, N. Y.; d. Dec. 11, 1862, a. 87. (*Transac. N. Y. State Med. Soc.*, 1863, p. 393.)

WHITE, DANIEL APPLETON, b. at Methuen, Mass., Jan. 7, 1776; grad. at Harvard in 1797; began to practice law at Salem; for many years was judge of probate for Essex co.; member of the Mass. Hist. Soc. and Am. Acad. Sci.; he d. March 30, 1861. (*Hist. Mag.*, v., 192.)

WHITE, DAVID, one of the judges of the circuit court of Kentucky; from 1823 to 1825 a member of congress from that state; d. in Franklin co., Ky., Feb. 17, 1835, a. 50.

WHITE, GEORGE, land agent; b. at Hatfield, Mass., Oct. 10, 1775; removed to Trenton, N. Y.; in 1800 to Rutland, N. Y., where he d. Mar. 9, 1833; in 1823–5, he was in assembly and several years agent for settling his town. (*Hough's Hist. Jeff. Co.*, p. 452.)

WHITE, GREENLEAF, d. in Portland, Me., July 17, 1852; adjutant-gen. of the state of Maine.

WHITE, JOSEPH, a wealthy merchant in Salem, Mass., a. 81 years; was assassinated in bed April 6, 1830.

WHITE, DR. JOSEPH, a distinguished surgeon; d. at Cherry Valley, N. Y., June 2, 1832, a. 70.

WHITE, COL. JOSEPH M., d. Oct. 18, 1839; for several years a delegate in congress from Florida; a prominent lawyer; d. at St. Louis, Mo., Oct. 18, 1839.

WHITE, LEONARD, d. in Haverhill, Mass., Oct. 10, 1849, a. 82; grad. at Harvard in 1787; many years town clerk and treasurer; was a representative in the legislature and from 1811 to 1813 in congress; was first cashier of the Merrimack Bank; held this office for a quarter of a century.

WHITE, DR. MENZO, a brother of Dr. Delos White; was a surgeon of much celebrity and long practice of Cherry Valley, N. Y., where he d. Jan. 16, 1848.

WHITE, NATHANIEL, grad. at Harvard; d. at Middleton, Conn., Aug. 27, 1711, a. 82.

WHITE, PHILIP, a revolutionary soldier; d. at Longacoming, N. J., May 2, 1850, at the a. of 104.

WHITE, DR. SAMUEL, principal of Hudson Lunatic Asylum; b. at Coventry, Ct., Feb. 23, 1777; studied with Dr. Philip Turner of Norwich, Ct., and began practice at Hudson, N. Y., in 1797; acquired eminence as a surgeon, and in 1828 was elected prof. of obstetrics and prac. surg. at Pittsfield Med. Coll.; resigned, in 2 years, and gave his chief attention to the treatment of insanity, and in 1830 established a private asylum at Hudson, which was continued by his son; d. Feb. 10, 1845, a. 68. (*Am. Jour. Insanity*, i, 384.)

WHITE, STEPHEN, d. at N. Y. city, Aug. 10, 1841, a. 54; formerly a prominent merchant of Salem.

WHITE, DR. S. POMEROY, d. June 6, 1867, in N. Y. city, in his 66th y.

WHITE, THOMAS, b. Nov. 12, 1779; an active member of the Ep. ch. and last surviving son of Bp. White; d. Oct. 15, 1859, at Phila. (*Hist. Mag*, iii, 355.)

WHITE, THOMAS L., law bookseller of New Orleans; d. Sept. 23, 1867, a. 54; formerly of N. Y. city.

WHITE, MRS ———, widow of Hon. Henry White, and daughter of Lieut. Governor Van Courtland; d. in N. Y. city, Aug. 19, 1836, in her 100th year.

WHITEHEAD, ASA, a native of New Jersey; studied law; was repeatedly elected to the legislature; d. at Newark, N. J., May, 1860, a. 66.

WHITEHEAD, SIMPSON, d. at Norfolk, Va., Oct. 13, 1839; president of the Exchange Bank of Virginia.

WHITEHEAD, WILLIAM, formerly of New York, and afterwards cashier of the Newark Banking and Insurance Co. and the Commercial Bank at Perth Amboy; d. at Pittsburg, Pa., Jan. 10, 1837, a. 64.

WHITEHOUSE, RT. REV. HENRY JOHN, bishop of Illinois; d. Aug., 1874, at Chicago; the *New York Tribune* says: this distinguished prelate of the Protestant Episcopal church was born in Park-place, in this city, in 1802, and was educated at Columbia Coll.; after graduation, in 1821, he studied three years at the General Theological Seminary, becoming a deacon in 1824; in 1827 he received full orders, and ministered to a parish at Reading, Penn., for three or four years; he then, at the earnest request of Bishop Hobart, accepted the rectorship of St. Luke's church, Rochester, and retained charge of the parish fifteen years; in 1844 he accepted the rectorship of St. Thomas's parish in this city and held that position until 1851, when he was elected assistant bishop of the diocese of Illinois; on the death of Bishop Chase, in 1852, he succeeded to the bishopric. Bishop Whitehouse visited England in 1867 and preached the opening sermon before the Pan-Anglican council held at Lambeth palace; during his visit he was treated with marked atttention, and received degrees from both the Oxford and Cambridge Universities; he was an accomplished scholar, an eloquent preacher, and earnest defender of his church; he discharged efficiently his episcopal duties, claiming no exemption because of his advanced years; his views were accorded great weight in the council of bishops and generally favored conservatism; in late years, however, he encouraged high church principles, and by doing so was to some extent instrumental in causing the dissensions which led to the withdrawal of the Rev. Mr. Cheney and others from the regular Episcopal church.

WHITELY, L. A., d. in Washington, D. C., July 20, 1869; b. in Kentucky, in 1825, edited a newspaper in that state, and afterwards the *Little Rock Journal;* was correspondent of the *N. Y. Herald;* and an editor of the *National Intelligencer;* and *Washington Sunday Herald.*

WHITESIDE, JOHN D., b. at Whiteside's Station, Monroe co., Ill., in 1794; d. there in 1850; was at various times in the state legislature, and for many years state treasurer, and fund commissioner.

WHITESIDE, WILLIAM B., b. in N. C., was capt. in the war of 1812; went with his father, Col. William Whiteside, to the Illinois country, in 1793; was sheriff of Madison co. many years; d. in that co.

WHITING, BOWEN, d. in Geneva, N. Y., Dec. 28, 1850, a. 63; resided in Ontario co., N. Y., more than thirty years; was in assembly in 1824, 1825; district attorney in Ontario co. from 1823 to 1832; first judge of that county from 1838 to 1844; circuit judge of 7th circuit from 1844 till the office was abolished by the constitution in 1846.

WHITING, CHARLES, capt. in the revolution; killed July 10, 1779.

WHITING, HANNAH CONANT, widow of Col. Wm. W., fifth in descent from Roger Conant first gov. of the Cape Ann Colony; she was b. Oct. 20, 1788, on the same day and hour as her husband; d. Nov. 19, 1859, a. 71. (*Hist. Mag.*, iv., 28.)

WHITING, JAMES R., lawyer; d. at Spuyten Duyvil, N. Y., March 16, 1872, a. 69.

WHITING, GEN. JOHN, d. at Great Barrington, Mass., Jan. 13, 1846, a. 75; was a native of that town, lived there through life; was a lawyer

52 years, and was for many years the oldest attorney in the county; was for some time county attorney, and for a long time president of the bar of the county.

WHITING, TIMOTHY, founder of the town of Whiting, Me., son of Nathan W. of Medway, Mass.; b. Aug. 5, 1767, removed in 1815 to Washington co., Me., where he owned a tract of land. (*Goodwin's Notes*, p. 46.)

WHITLEY, ESTHER, widow of Col. W.; accompained her husband to Kentucky, among the early settlers, and was his companion and assistant in many bloody conflicts with the Indians; she d. in Ky., Nov. 20, 1833, in her 85th year.

WHITMAN, BENJAMIN, d. at. Boston, Mass., Aug. 31, 1840; the first justice of the Boston police court when it was established; for many years a lawyer of extensive practice.

WHITMAN, REV. JASON, d. at Portland, Me., Jan. 25, 1848, a. 49; grad. at Harvard in 1825; some years Unitarian preacher at Saco; removed to Boston and became sec. of the Am. Unitarian Assocation till 1835 when he accepted a call from Portland and remained ten years; was installed at Lexington, in 1845, and continued in this connection till death.

WHITMAN, LEMUEL, d. at Farmington, Conn., Nov. 18, 1841, a. about 60 years; grad. at Yale, in 1800, and was a representative in congress from Connecticut from 1823 to 1824.

WHITNEY, ALEXANDER, d. in East Cambridge, Mass., May 13, 1842, a. 32; grad. at Harvard in 1831.

WHITNEY, ASA, a well known car manufacturer; d. at Philadelphia, Pa, June 4, 1874.

WHITNEY, ELIAS, of Poughkepsie, N. Y.; d. June, 1860, a. 91. (*Vincent's Semi-An. Register*, p. 619.)

WHITNEY, JAMES P., d. Jan. 24, 1847, a. 44; native of Shirley, Mass.; lately a member of the state senate.

WHITNEY, STEPHEN, merchant in N. Y.; amassed a colossal fortune; was remarkable for the tenacity with which he held on to his down-town residence; was many years the last person who retained a mansion fronting the bowling green, once the aristocratic quarter of the town; d. Feb. 16, 1860, a. 84. (*Vincent's Semi-An. Register*, p. 112.)

WHITON, EDWARD V., chief justice of supreme court of Wisconsin; d. at Janesville, Wis., April, 1859, a. 54; was a native of Mass.; emigrated to Wisconsin in 1825; had been a county judge.

WHITTAKER, JAMES, early leader among the Shakers; b. at Oldham near Manchester, Eng., Feb. 28, 1751; came with Mother Ann to America; d. Enfield, Ct., July 20, 1787. (*Evans's Shakers' Compendium*, p. 160.)

WHITTLESEY, ASAPHA, native of Conn.; settled in Tallmadge, O., in 1813; was the next year appointed post-master, and held through life; d. March 17, 1842, a. 61.

WHITTLESEY, ELISHA, b. New Tuston, Ct., Oct. 19, 1783; m. Polly Mygott, Danbury, Ct., Jan. 5, 1806; education, common school, Salisbury, Ct., and academy at Danbury; attorney at law Canfield, O., 1806; brigade inspector, rank of major, under General Simon Perkins, 6 months levies 1812 on north western frontier; Ohio legislature 1821–22; member of congress 1822–41; first comptroller and auditor, Washington city, under Harrison, Pierce, Buchanan and Lincoln; scrupulously correct and uncorrupted by forty years of public survice; d. suddenly at Washington, D. C., Jan. 7, 1863.

WICKES, WILLIAM H., formerly captain in the 169th regt. N. Y. vols.; post master at Sand Lake, N. Y.; d. at that place, Jan., 1871.

WICKLIFF, ROBERT, d. at Lexington, Ky., Sept. 1, 1859, a. 85.

WICKLIFF, ROBERT JR., d. in Ky., Aug. 29, 1850; late chargé de affaires to Sardinia.

WIDRIG, GEORGE, of Herkimer co., N. Y.; was in assembly from 1801 to 1807, inclusive; in the war of 1812 was major gen. militia, but was not in active service; lived and d. in Frankfort, N. Y. (*Benton's Herkimer Co., N. Y.*, p. 377.)

WILBER, REV. P. W., d. in Ohio, June 11, 1859, a. 52; having, since 1842, been principal of the Wesleyan Female College.

WILCOX, MAJ. DE LAFAYETTE, of the U. S. army; d. at Palatka, Fla., Jan. 3, 1842; was from Connecticut, and entered the army in 1812; was distinguished at the battle of Bridgewater, where he was severely wounded, and in other engagements on the Niagara frontier; served in the army till his death. (*Am. Almanac*, 1843, p. 325.)

WILCOX, JEDUTHAN, member of congress from New Hampshire in 1813–17; d. at Oxford, N. H., July, 1838, a. 69.

WILCOX, LEONARD, b. in N. H.; grad. at Dartmouth, in 1817; was a member of the state legislature; a judge of the superior court, and a senator in congress from New Hampshire in 1842–3; d. in 1850, a. 50.

WILCOX, SAMUEL DARWIN, b. at Napoli, N. Y., May 10, 1846; grad. at Ham. Coll., 1866; tutor at Robert Coll., Constantinople, in 1867–8; prof. in Ham. Coll., in 1870–2; editor of the *Florida Agriculturist* in 1872–3; d. at Napoli, N. Y., March 31.

WILCOX, THOMAS H., ex-confederate major gen.; killed at Richmond, Va., April 27, 1870, by the falling of the floor of the court of appeals.

WILDER, JOHN N., a retired merchant, resided at Ballston Spa and devoted much time to philanthropic and literary pursuits; he was pres. of trustees of Rochester Univ., and a trustee of the Dudley Observatory; he died suddenly at Albany, July 15, 1858. (*Hist. Mag.*, ii, 252.)

WILKESON, SAMUEL, of Buffalo, N. Y.; died at Kingston, on the Tennessee river, July 7, 1848, in his 68th year; he was one of the oldest and most enterprising citizens of Buffalo and an active promoter of the colonization cause.

WILDMAN, TALMON, of Danbury, Conn., and member of congress from Connecticut; d. in Washington, D. C., Dec. 10, 1835.

WILDMERDING, HENRY A., merchant; d. at New York, Feb. 3, 1868, a. 68.

WILKINS, MRS. ANN, d. at Fostertown, N. J., Feb. 1840, in her 100th year.

WILKIN, GEN. JAMES W., b. in 1762; was in assembly from Orange co., N. Y., in 1796, 1808 1809; and in the latter year speaker; in the state senate from 1801 to 1804, and from 1811 to 1814; in congress from 1815 to 1819; d. at Goshen, N. Y., Feb. 23, 1845.

WILKINS, MARTIN S., long a member of the New York bar; d. at West Farm, Westchester co., N. Y., Oct. 27, 1836, a. 73.

WILKINSON, ROBERT., d. at Poughkeepsie, N. Y., Aug. 20, 1849, a. 62.

WILKINSON, SIMON, of Boston; a distinguished citizen; d. Feb. 19, 1860, a. 83; he had a seat in the board of aldermen, and had been in the state legislature.

WILLARD, ASHBEL, gov. of Indiana; native of Oneida co., N. Y.; son of Erastus W., sheriff of Oneida in 1832–5; grad. at Hamilton Coll. in 1842; was governor of Indiana; d. at St. Paul, Oct., 1860.

WILLARD, DR. AUGUSTUS, of Greene, Chenango co., N. Y.; d. March 12, 1868, a. 68, at Ellicottville, N. Y.; b. in Stafford, Conn., in 1800. (*Transac. N. Y. State Med. Soc.*, 1869, p. 264.)

WILLARD, DR. DAVID, d. at Wilton, Conn., Feb. 9, 1860, a. 71.

WILLARD, DR. ELIAS, revolutionary surgeon; b. at Harvard, Mass., Jan. 7, 1756; he served as assist. hospital surgeon, and in 1777, became surgeon of a Maine reg't and served through the war; d. in Albany, March 20, 1827, a. 71, and the 51st of his professional life. (*Tr. N. Y. St. Med. Soc.*, 1857, p. 31; *Munsell's Ann. Alb.*, ix, 95.)

WILLARD, GEN. JOSEPH A., b. in Hubbardton, Vt., April 26, 1803; d. at Lowville, N. Y., where he spent the most of his life, Aug. 18, 1868; was state senator in 1858–9, and many years brigadier general of militia; was a clothier, and manufacturer of woolen yarn.

WILLARD, JOSIAH, son of Henry Willard, was b. at Lancaster, Pa., about 1693; was one of the first settlers of Lunenburg, Mass.; he d. Dec. 8, 1750, having been honored with both civil and military offices. (*Hall's Eastern Vermont*, p. 726.)

WILLARD, JOSIAH, JR., was b. in 1716; was several years in charge of a garrison at Ashuelot, now Keene, N. H., and in 1749 removed to Winchester, N. H.; upon his father's death he was promoted to his office as commander of Ft. Dummer; he was in assembly; d. at Winchester Nov. 19, 1786. (*Hall's Eastern Vermont*, p. 727.)

WILLARD, DR. MOSES, d. at Albany, N. Y., Dec. 6, 1826, a. 66.

WILLARD, PAUL, d. in Charlestown, Mass., March 18, 1856, a. 60; b. in Lancaster, Mass.; grad. in Cambridge in 1817; was a lawyer, and in 1822 was appointed post master in Charlestown, which place he held seven years; in 1823, was elected clerk of the senate and held seven years; he was entrusted by his fellow citizens with various municipal offices.

WILLARD, DR. SYLVESTER D., surgeon general of New York; d. at Albany, N. Y., April 2, 1865, a. 39; b. June 19, 1825, in Wilton, Conn.; son of Dr. David Willard; settled in Albany, and was several years sec. of the State Medical Society; he was a ready writer, fond of biographical researches, and a contributor to medical periodicals; in 1865, he reported the results of inquiries made under his direction, by order of the State Medical Soc. as to the condition of the insane in poor houses, and which resulted in the establishment of the Willard asylum at Ovid, N. Y. (*Transac. N. Y. State Med. Soc.*, 1866, p. 329.)

WILLERS, CALVIN, son of Rev. Diederich Willers, of Varick, N. Y., and formerly county clerk of Seneca co.; d. at Albany, April 9, 1875, being at the time chief clerk in the office of secretary of state.

WILLETS, JACOB, author of various educational works popular in their day, and a member of the Soc. of Friends; he d. at Mechanic, Dutchess co., N. Y., Sept. 12, 1860, a. 76.

WILLEY, CALVIN, b. in East Haddam, Ct., in 1776; studied law, was admitted to the Tolland co. bar in 1793, and was frequently a member of the legislature, where he served in both branches; he was many years post master in Tolland, and seven years judge of probate for Stafford district; presidential elector in 1824, and member of the U. S. senate from 1825 to 1831; he d. at Stafford, Ct., Aug. 23, 1858, a. 81.

WILLIAMS, MRS. ABIGAL E., dau. of late Chief Justice Oliver Ellsworth, of Conn.; d. at Hartford, March 5, 1860. (*Vincent's Semi-An. Register*, p. 164.)

WILLIAMS, REV. ARTHUR, a venerable Baptist minister of South Carolina; d. May 13, 1860.

WILLIAMS, DR. B. BROWN, well known in Pennsylvania as a lecturer on psychology; a Fillmore stump-speaker in 1856; d. at Little Rock, Ark., May, 1860.

WILLIAMS, REV. BENJAMIN, d. in Vicksburg, Miss., Sept. 27, 1855, a. about 37; grad. at Princeton, and soon after removed to Mississippi, and preached at Pine Ridge church, Adams co., till 1854 when he was called to the Presbyterian church in Vicksburg.

WILLIAMS, DAVID, one of the captors of André; was b. at Tarrytown, Oct. 21, 1754; entered the army in 1775; was with Montgomery at the taking of Ft. St. John's and served six months; he again served by different enlistments until 1779; his patriotism, as shown on the 23d of September, 1780, secured him the lasting gratitude of his country, a medal and pension, from congress, and a farm valued at $1250; in 1830 the corporation of New York invited Mr. Williams to be present at celebration of the French revolution and while there received great attentions from individuals and societies; in 1805 he removed to Broome, Schoharie co., N. Y., where he d. Aug. 2, 1831, a. 77. (*Simms's Hist. Schoharie Co.*, p. 646.)

WILLIAMS, DAVID, d. at Elizabethtown, N. J., Aug. 1, 1841, a. 84; was in the whole of the revolutionary war and present at the battles of Long Island and Monmouth.

WILLIAMS, DURRELL, d. in Albany, N. Y., Aug. 13, 1854, a. 90; b. in Pennsylvania, and served in the revolutionary war.

WILLIAMS, EDWARD P., commander of U. S. corvette Oneida; drowned near Yokohama, Japan, Jan. 24, 1870, a. 40.

WILLIAMS, ELIJAH D., d. in Chelsea, Mass., June 24, 1842, a. 24.

WILLIAMS, ELIPHALET, d. in Boston, Mass., June 12, 1855, a. 77; was chairman of the last board of selectmen, before Boston became a city; a member of the common council for 15 years, and in 1829, president of that board.

WILLIAMS, ELISHA, was b. in New York city, Aug. 29, 1773; studied law, and settled at Spencertown, N. Y.; he became eminent at the Columbia county bar; in 1799 removed to Hudson; was an influential federalist;

a member of the state convention for revising the constitution in 1821, and was 9 years in the assembly; he was a man of great eloquence and of great power in debate; d. June 29, 1833, at New York city. (*Raymond's Distinguished Men of Columbia Co.*, p. 1.)

WILLIAMS, HEZEKIAH, b. in Vermont; grad. at Dartmouth in 1820; was in congress from Maine, from 1845 to 1849, and d. in 1856, a. 58.

WILLIAMS, JAMES G., d. at Jackson, Miss., Feb. 25, 1840; treasurer of Mississippi; the fourth incumbent of this office that had d. within 2 years.

WILLIAMS, JAMES W., d. Dec. 2, 1842, a. about 55, on his way to Washington; was a representative from Maryland; had been many years a prominent member of the legislature and for a time speaker of the house of delegates; in May, 1841, was elected to congress.

WILLIAMS, JESSE, d. in Woodstock, Vt., Jan. 27, 1842, a. 80; he was for many years an active citizen; for seven years a judge of the county court, and twelve years a judge of probate.

WILLIAMS, JOEL, a revolutionary soldier; d. at Orange, N. J., March, 1849, a. 85 years.

WILLIAMS, DR. JOHN, late of Cambridge; d. in Walpole, N. H., May 8, 1846, in his 98th year; he was b. June 20, 1748, (O. S.); during the revolution was a practicing physician of Hanover, N. H.; he afterwards practiced at Barre, and at Provdence, R. I., and about 1810, removed to Cambridge, where he became an apothecary.

WILLIAMS, JOHN, d. at Boston, Mass., Sept. 9, 1845, a. 72; counselor at law; grad. at Harvard in 1792.

WILLIAMS, COL. JOHN, d. in Currituck co., N. H., Nov. 7, 1835, a. 85.

WILLIAMS, JOHN, U. S. senator from Tennessee, from 1815 to 1823; d. at Knoxville, Aug. 7, 1837.

WILLIAMS, JOHN MASON, formerly chief justice of the court of com. pleas, Mass.; d. at New Bedford, Mass., Dec. 28, 1868, in his 89th year.

WILLIAMS, JOHN STODDARD, d. at Salem, Mass., Sept. 11, 1848, a. 42; b. in Wethersfield, Conn.; grad. at Yale in 1827, and settled as a lawyer in Salem; was elected to the state senate, and held other important offices.

WILLIAMS, JOHN W., a member of the Philadelphia bar; d. in that city, Aug. 29, 1837; he was a native of Connecticut; grad. at Yale in 1822, and was a man of superior talents; he distinguished himself as a writer, in the *North American Review*, of which he was for some time the editor. (*Am. Almanac*, 1838, p. 321.)

WILLIAMS, JOSEPH, of Norwich, Ct., took an active part with the patriots of the revolution, and spent much time in organizing the militia of his county; his son Edwin W., became known as a literary man, and published a *New York State Register* several years. (*Cymri, of* 76, p. 26.)

WILLIAMS, LEWIS, b. in Surrey co., N. C.; grad. at the University of N. C. in 1808; served in the house of commons in 1813 and 1814; was in congress from N. C. from 1815 to 1842; d. in Washington, D. C., Feb. 23, 1842, a. nearly 60. (*Am. Almanac*, 1843, p. 325.)

WILLIAMS, MARMADUKE, b. April 6, 1772, in Caswell co., N. C.; was a lawyer, and in congress from N. C. from 1803 to 1809; in 1810 removed to Madison co., Ala., and thence in 1818 to Tuscaloosa; was repeatedly in the leg., and a delegate in the convention that formed the state constitution; was a candidate for gov. but not elected; in 1826 was appointed a com'r to adjust the unsettled accounts between Ala. and Miss. growing out of their territorial connection; in 1832 elected judge of the county court, and held till April, 1842, when he resigned, having reached the age of 70; d. at Tuscaloosa, Ala., Oct. 29, 1850.

WILLIAMS, LIEUT. NATHAN, Md.; killed at Camden, Aug. 16, 1777.

WILLIAMS, NATHAN, formerly one of the circuit judges of N. Y. state, and a lawyer of Utica, N. Y.; d. at Geneva, N. Y., Sept. 24, 1835.

WILLIAMS, PUTNAM T., a member of the Miss. conv. of 1832; d. at Jackson, Miss., July 10, 1834.

WILLIAMS, DR. ROBERT, d. in Pitt co., N. C., Nov. 12, 1840, in his 83d year; was a surgeon in the revolution, and a delegate in the convention that adopted the constitution of the U. S.; was also in the state conv. of 1835, and was repeatedly a member of the state legislature.

WILLIAMS, REV. SOLOMON, d. at Northampton, Mass., Nov. 9, 1834, a. 82.

WILLIAMS, THOMAS, alias TEHORAGWANEGEN, Caughnawaga chief, and descendant of Rev. John Williams of Deerfield, Mass.; served with the French in the war of 1755–60, and in the British army in the revolution; acted in several treaties with the state of N. Y.; d. at Caughnawaga, Aug. 16, 1849; was the reputed father of the Rev. Eleazer W., of St. Regis; by some reputed the Bourbon Prince Louis XVII of France. (*Life of Tehoragwanegen, by Eleazer Williams*, Albany, 1859, 8vo, pp. 92; *Hough's Hist. St. Law. and Franklin Cos. N. Y.*, p. 200.)

WILLIAMS, COL. THOMAS, of Stockbridge, Mass.; d. at Skeenesborough, N. Y., July 10, 1836, a. 30.

WILLIAMS, THOMAS L., a lawyer and judge; d. near Nashville, Tenn., Dec. 11, 1856, a. 70.

WILLIAMS, WILLIAM, removed from Northboro, Mass., to Marlborough in Vt. about 1769, where he built the first framed building; had served as a captain of rangers in the French war; was elected to the first provincial congress of N. Y.; was a citizen of Wilmington, Vt., in 1777; frequently changed his residence in the years that followed, at last settling in Lower Canada, where he d. in 1823. (*Hall's Eastern Vermont*, p. 728.)

WILLIAMS, REV. WILLIAM, d. in Virginia, Feb., 1848; he had preached more than fifty years.

WILLIAMS, COL. WILLIAM, became a resident of Utica, in 1800 and published for some years the *Utica Patriot;* in the war of 1812, he was aid to Gen. Oliver Collins; in 1832 became a devoted attendant upon the sick of cholera; he was actively concerned in religious movements; was well known as a publisher and bookseller; he d. June 12, 1850, in his 63d year. (*Striker's Am Reg.*, iv, 468.)

WILLIAMSON, CHARLES, b. in Balgray, county of Dumfries, Scotland; was a captain in the British service in the revolution; captured on the passage and kept a prisoner in Boston; became an agent of the Pultney estate; and a distinguished pioneer in the settlement of western N. Y.; begun settlement at Bath, Steuben co., and at many other places; opened roads, built mills and other improvements and made the Genesee country famous by his accounts; he regarded the Susquehannah as the natural outlet for the produce of the country, and Baltimore and Philadelphia as the future markets of western N. Y.; among his enterprises was a large hotel at Geneva, a settlement at Sodus, on Lake Ontario, and elsewhere; was in assembly in 1797, 8, 9, 1800; his past enterprises proved too expensive for his patrons, and his agency was withdrawn in 1802; he returned to England, was employed by the British government in some service in the West Indies; d. in 1808, on a return passage from Havana to England. (*Turner's Phelps and Gorham Purchase, and Holland Purchase; McMaster's Steuben Co.*)

WILLIAMSON, JAMES C., captain in the U. S. navy; d. at Jersey city, N. J., July 24, 1871.

WILLIAMSON, CAPT. JOHN, of the ordnance department, U. S. A.; d. at Cannonsburg, S. C., Dec. 23, 1849, a. 44; was employed in superintending erection of government works on the Chattahoochee in Florida, and the arsenal near Charleston, where he resided at the time of his death.

WILLIAMSON, JOHN G. A., d. Aug. 7, 1840, at Puerto Cabello; chargé d'affaires of the U. S., to Venezuela.

WILLING, RICHARD, b. Dec. 25, 1775, d. in Philadelphia, Pa., June 18, 1858, was a man of great wealth, and never engaged in active business; he declined public office, and in early life had made several voyages to Europe and the East Indies.

WILLINGTON, JAMES, brevet. lieut. col.; capt. of 3d Buffs, in British army; killed in battle of Plattsburg, Sept. 6, 1814.

WILLINK, JAN, one of the Holland Land Company of western New York; d. at Amsterdam, Holland, in 1826.

WILLINK, JAN (the younger), of the above company; d. at Amsterdam, Holland, Oct. 3, 1827.

WILLINK, WILLIAM, one of the Holland Land Company, of western New York; d. at Amsterdam, Holland, Feb. 13, 1840, a. 91.

WILLIS, FRANCIS, b. in Frederick co., Va., Jan. 5, 1825; was in congress from Georgia in 1791–3 (having removed to that state in 1784) and in 1811, removed to Tenn., where he d. in Maury co., Jan. 25, 1829.

WILLIS, HENRY, d. at Newark, N. J., April 29, 1842, a. 85; revolutionary soldier, and present at the battles of Long Island, White Plains, Trenton, Princeton and Monmouth.

WILLIS, JOHN R., d. in New York city, Dec. 7, 1844, a. 65, by an accident; was pres. of the board of com's of the almshouse.

WILLIS, NATHANIEL, d. in Boston, May 26, 1870, a. 90; was one of the founders of the *Boston Recorder*, a religious paper, in 1816, and of the *Portland Argus*; was father of the poet, N. P. Willis, and of Mrs. Parton (Fanny Fern).

WILLOUGHBY, DR. WESTEL, b. in Ct.; resided for a time in Mass., and settled in Norway, N. Y., at an early period; after practicing here for a time, he removed to Newport village; he was about 20 years prof. of midwifery and the diseases of women and children, at the Medical Coll. in Fairfield, N. Y.; was in assembly in 1808–9, and in congress in 1815–17; from 1805 to 1821 he was a county judge; in the war of 1812–15, he was in the medical staff of the army at Sackett's Harbor, and elsewhere; d. at Newport, N. Y., in 1844, a. 75. (*Benton's Herkimer Co.*, p. 378.)

WILLS, JAMES, JR., d. Jan. 22, 1825, a bachelor, at Philadelphia, Pa., leaving $1000 to each of his tenants, and other legacies, of which $5000 were for the Friends' Asylum for the Insane; $2,500 for four monthly meetings of Friends; $1000 to the Phila. Soc. for support of charity schools; $5000 to the Magdalen Soc.; to the Orphan Society, the house in which he lived; to the city dispensary, and dispensaries of Southwick, and Northern Liberties two other houses, and the remainder (amounting to $122,000), to found the Wills Hospital for the relief of the indigent blind and lame; his heirs at law undertook to defeat these intentions, but in 1831, the supreme court of Pennsylvania, confirmed the will, and the Wills Hospital has been since established in accordance with its founder's plans. (*Simpson's Eminent Philadelphians.*)

WILLYAMOZ, CHARLES, served as lieut in the campaign on Lake Champlain in 1759; went on half pay in 1763, and continued on the army rolls till 1799.

WILMOTT, WILLIAM, capt Md. Line; killed by a British foraging party in a skirmish on John's Island, S. C., Nov. 14, 1782; said to have been the last killed in battle in the revolution.

WILSON, DR. ALLEN, d. at Plainfield, N. J., May 26, 1842, a. 36; a man of superior talents.

WILSON, CLARA, d. near Alton, Ill., Dec. 13, 1859; said to be 125 years old; had been a slave in S. C., and was carried west some 70 years before her death.

WILSON, CLARENDON J. L., lieut. of 1st reg. dragoons; d. in Albuquerque, Mex., Feb. 21, 1853; was brevetted for bravery in the conflicts at El Embado and Taos, N. M.

WILSON, DAVID, author of *Solomon Northrop*, and formerly clerk of assembly; d. at Albany, N. Y., June 9, 1870, a. 52.

WILSON, EDGAR C., of northern Va.; a lawyer and formerly in congress from the Wheeling district; d. at his home in Morgantown, April 24, 1860.

WILSON, ISAAC, d. at Batavia, Ill., Oct. 25, 1848; during the war of 1812 commanded a company of cavalry, and was actively engaged in the north west; served in both houses of the N. Y. legislature; in 1823 was elected to congress, and at the end of his term was appointed first judge of Genesee co., N. Y., and held until his removal to Ill.

WILSON, JAMES, b. in Adams co., Pa., April 28, 1779; d. at Gettysburg, Pa., July, 1868; had been a justice of the peace from 1811 till 1859, and a member of congress in 1823–29.

WILSON, JAMES J., U. S. senator from N. J., in 1815–21, and post master at Trenton, N. J.; d. July 28, 1824.

WILSON, LIEUT. JOHN, Va.; killed at Eutaw Springs, Sept. 8, 1781.

WILSON, JOHN, d. at Plainfield, N. J., March 11, 1840, a. about 65; late judge of the county court.

WILSON, JOHN, b. in 1777; grad. at Harvard in 1799; attained to eminence as a lawyer, and was in congress from Mass. from 1813 to 1815, and from 1817 to 1819; d. at Belfast, Me., July 9, 1848.

WILSON, JOHN, a vocalist; d. at Quebec, July 8, 1849; was well known in the United States as a musical composer.

WILSON, JOHN, d. in Maine, Nov. 1, 1859, a. 103 years.

WILSON, JOHN A., d. Sept. 14, 1841, at Washington, D. C.; formerly U. S. marshal for the Dist. of Columbia.

WILSON, JONATHAN, capt. Mass. troops; killed at Concord, Mass., April 19, 1775.

WILSON, CAPT. J. D., of the steamer Sierra Nevada; d. at Panama, March 1, 1853.

WILSON, LOUIS D., col. 12th infantry; d. at Vera Cruz, Mex., Aug. 13, 1847; was for twenty years a member of the legislature of North Carolina; was in 1842–43, speaker of the senate.

WILSON, MRS. NATHANIEL, d. a. 103 ys. 8mo. 3 d. at Wilson's mills, Oxford co., Me., Nov. 1, 1859. (*Hist. Mag.*, iv, 26.)

WILSON, CAPT. ROBERT, d. in Charleston, S. C., Oct. 31, 1846, a. 82; pres. of the Marine Soc.; for the last 25 years boarding officer for the custom house; b. in Pa., and in his youth on board a privateer; was captured, and settled in Charleston, after his release.

WILSON, GEN. ROBERT, d. at St. Louis, Mo., May 9, 1870, a. 68.

WINANS, REV. WILLIAM, D.D., d. in Amite co., Miss., Aug. 31, 1857, a. 68; b. in Penn., Nov. 3, 1783; nearly half a century of his life he devoted to the Methodist ministry; in 1812, went to Mississippi as a missionary, and labored in that state the rest of life.

WINCHESTER, GEORGE, a distinguished lawyer and a judge in one of the higher courts of Mississippi; d. at Natchez, where he had lived 32 years, March 29, 1851, a. 54 years; b. in Salem, Mass., and grad. at Yale in 1816.

WINCHESTER, JACOB B., formerly of Salem, Mass.; d. at Plainfield, N. J., August, 1842, a. 80; a revolutionary soldier, and several years in the legislature of Massachusetts.

WINCHESTER, LEMUEL, d. at Danvers, Mass., Jan. 19, 1841, in his 101st year; a revolutionary pensioner.

WINDHAM, SIR CHARLES A., lieut. gen., commander in chief of the British army in Canada; d. Feb. 18, 1870, a. 60.

WINEPRESS, WILLIAM, was an adjutant of a regiment in the French war; became capt. June 9, 1762; in 1775, was again ordered to America.

WING, AUSTIN E., b. in New York, a delegate from Michigan territory in the 19th, 20th and 22d congresses; afterwards the incumbent of several offices in that state; d. at Cleveland, O., Aug. 25, 1849, a. 58 years; he had until near his death been U. S. marshal.

WING, JOEL A., M.D., of Albany; b. in Dalton (now Hinsdale), Mass., Aug. 13, 1788; studied with Dr. John Delamater, and began practice in 1811 in Columbia co., and in 1814 in Albany where he remained through life; he was pres. of N. Y. Med. Coll., in 1843, and a manager of the Utica Asylum from 1847; in 1848 he was in assembly; his health failed in 1851, and he d. at the Retreat in Hartford, Ct., Sept. 6, 1852. (*Tr. N. Y. St. Med. Soc.*, 1853, p. 345; Do., 1857, p. 47, with portrait; *Munsell's Ann. Alb.*, ix, 101.)

WING, MATTHEW GREGORY, d. in Santa Fé, New Mexico, July 5, 1860, a. 34; son of Dr. Joel A. W., of Albany. (*Alb. Eve. Jour.*, July 31, 1860.)

WINGATE, MOSES, d. at Haverhill, Mass., June 6, 1870, a. 106; was at one time a member of the Massachusetts legislature, and in the constitutional convention of 1820.

WINN, JAMES C., captain in the Texan army from Gwinnett co., Ga.; was shot by order of the Mexican commander, March 27, 1830, among those taken at Goliad; a monument is erected to him and others at Lawrenceville, Ga.

WINN, COL. JOHN THOMAS, shot near Washington, Miss., July 8, 1840, by an unknown person, while sitting at tea.

WINN, RICHARD, entered the revolution in 1775, and fought at Hanging Rock where he was wounded; he served through the war and at its close was appointed brigadier, and then major general of militia; he d. in Tennessee in 1812 or 1813.

WINSHIP, CAPT. JONATHAN, d. in Roxbury, Mass., Aug. 6, 1847; was a skilful horticulturist.

WINSHIP, MAJ. OSCAR F., U. S. A.; d. in Troy, N. Y., Dec. 13, 1855, a. 40.

WINSLOW, JOHN A., rear admiral U. S. N.; d. at Boston Highlands, Mass., Sept. 29, 1873; was b. in North Carolina, Nov. 9, 1811, and at an early age entered the United States Naval Academy, receiving his commission through the influence of Daniel Webster; he was commissioned in 1827, and first served as midshipman on board the sloop-of-war Falmouth in the West India squadron; his promotion to the rank of passed midshipman was dated June 10, 1833, and the next six years of his service were about equally divided between the South Atlantic fleet and the Charlestown navy yard; in 1839, with the rank of lieutenant, he sailed on the steamer frigate Missouri, which was burned at sea. During our war with Mexico he served in the United States fleet operating against Vera Cruz, and, at the close of hostilities, was assigned to the sailing frigate Saratoga, of which he was executive officer; after a long leave of absence, he was ordered to the frigate St. Lawrence in 1852, and, with that vessel, which was the flag-ship of Commodore Dulany, joined the Pacific squadron immediately; the navy was reorganized in 1855, and Winslow then received the rank of commander, and was again ordered to the Boston station, where he remained until 1859; he had a brief term of service in the lighthouse department; and at the breaking out of the rebellion was thus employed; his first important active duty after that time was with the flotilla on the Mississippi river, but his service on inland waters was brief, and, early in 1862, he was ordered to the command of the Kearsarge, then a new third-rate screw sloop-of-war, built at Portsmouth, N. H., and a twin ship with the Wachusett, which has also won great fame; at this time he was promoted to be captain, his commission being dated July 16, 1862; the Kearsarge was built for speed, carried eight guns, was 1,550 tons displacement, and was at once ordered on special service in pursuit of the confederate cruiser Alabama; after many vexatious elusions by the enemy, the audacious sea-rover was found in the harbor of Cherbourg, France, in June, 1864; cruising off that port, Capt. Winslow received a note from Semmes, commanding the Alabama, begging him not to leave until the two vessels could have an opportunity to measure their strength; this challenge, of course, was promptly accepted and the Kearsarge laid off and on waiting for her expected adversary; the Alabama was principally manned by English seamen, and her artillerists were trained men from the British practice-ship Excellent; Capt. Winslow protected the machinery of his vessel by the use of chain cables, and made every possible preparation for this novel sea-duel; the Alabama steamed out of the harbor at 10:20, Sunday, June 19, accompanied by the French iron-clad Couronne and the English yacht Deerhound; the last-named vessel was, as it afterward appeared, a tender to the Alabama, its owner, Mr. Lancaster, being on board; the fight took place about seven miles from shore, the Alabama opening the fire when one mile from her adversary; the details of this engagement are familiar to our readers; the firing of the Kearsarge was reserved, steady, and well-directed; that of the Alabama was wild and hurried; after performing many desperate manœuvers, the fight was ended by the complete disabling of the confederate cruiser, which was abandoned by Semmes, who fled to the Deerhound, after casting his sword into the sea; this duel was observed by thousands of persons from the French coast, and the particulars of the remarkable affair created a profound impression in Europe; the Alabama sunk, carrying down a portion of her crew; some of the men were picked up by the Deerhound and other vessels near the scene of the action, and 69 were taken on board the Kearsarge; some of the minor details of the engagement have been subjects of controversy; but its conduct by Capt. Winslow gave him at once a wide and well-merited reputation; in the United States the news was received with a delirium of joy; and the public pulse, which had been beating high with recent successes on land, throbbed even more wildly when it was known that the scourge of the seas was at last destroyed by the guns of an American man-of-war; on his return to this country, Capt. Winslow was received with every mark of national esteem and affection; various honors were heaped upon him by states and municipal corporations; congress voted him the thanks of the nation; the president and senate gave him the rank of commodore, dating from the memorable June 19, 1864, and he was subsequently made rear-admiral; soon after the close of the war he took command of the North Pacific squadron, with a rendezvous at San Francisco, at which city he was received with enthusiastic demonstrations of respect. Admiral Winslow early formed ties which bound him to Massachusetts, and made his home in that state while he was on duty at the Charlestown navy yard; his residence was on what was formerly known as Roxbury Highlands, now part of the city of Boston; he was fifth of the active list of rear-admirals until his retirement, which took place quite recently; the evening of his days was passed tranquilly, though his health had been undermined by repeated nervous attacks; like Farragut and all other true heroes, Winslow was modest and reserved in speech; he considered that the honors given him were justly due his officers and men; he disclaimed the possession of any shining merit, and was glad to claim for the naval service of his country all the praise which was sounded for him; his exploit was a notable event of those stormy times; it was invested with the heroic and poetic interest which always surrounds a famous sea fight, and it will forever endear his name to the hearts of his grateful countrymen. (*N. Y. Tribune.*)

WINSLOW, RICHARD, b. near Saybrook, Ct., July 24, 1771; settled at Troy, and about 1800 at Albany; was for 20 years master of a packet on the Hudson, and later a merchant; d. at Albany, Jan. 9, 1847. (*Hunt's Biog. Panorama*, p. 472.)

WINSTON, FOUNTAIN, formerly lieut. gov. of Mississippi; d. at Natchez, Dec. 1, 1834.

WINSTON, HORATIO G., an eminent lawyer of Virginia and lately a leading member of the state legislature; d. at Louisville, Ky., Oct. 24, 1836.

WINSTON, COL. JOHN, a near relative of Patrick Henry; served with distinction under Jackson in the Creek war; was well known in Alabama in which state he d. April 8, 1850, a. 65.

WINSTON, GEN. JOSEPH, d. in Missouri, March 24, 1840, a. 53; supposed to have been drowned in the Missouri, near the mouth of the Platte, where he was preparing for his future residence; had lately removed from Stokes co., N. C., where he had filled several offices, both civil and military.

WINTER, ELISHA J., formerly president of the Lexington & Ohio R. R.; d. at Lexington, Ky., June, 1849. (*Stryker's Am. Reg.*, iii, 232.)

WINTHROP, MRS. ELIZA C., wife of Hon. Robert C. Winthrop; d. in Boston, June 14, 1842, a. 33; she was a dau. of the late Francis Blanchard, and adopted dau. of Samuel P. Gardner.

WINTON, DR. NELSON, of Havana, N. Y.; b. in Fairfield co., Conn., in 1800, and d. at Havana, Aug. 27, 1864. (*Transac. N. Y. State Med. Soc.*, 1865, p. 299.)

WIRT, DR. HENRY GRATTAN, a son of William Wirt; d. near Monticello, Fl., June 26, 1850.

WISE, MAJOR SAMUEL, S. C., killed at Savannah, Ga., Oct. 9, 1779.

WISE, TULLY R., first auditor in the treasury department; d. at Washington, D. C., July 22, 1844, a. 47.

WISNER, HENRY G., d. in Goshen, N. Y., Feb. 27, 1842, a. 64; a lawyer.

WISNER, JOHN W., settled early in Elmira, N. Y., was many years a supervisor and justice; was elected judge of Chemung co., in 1847, twice democratic candidate for congress; d. at Elmira, April 24, 1852, a. 51. (*Elmira Gazette.*)

WISTAR, RICHARD, b. in Philadelphia, July 20, 1756; was many years an iron monger and hardware merchant; engaged in real estate purchases; d. in Philadelphia, June 6, 1821. (*Simpson's Eminent Philadelphians*, with a portrait.)

WISWALL, JOSEPH, an aged citizen of Mobile, Ala.; d. April 20, 1860.

WITHALL, JOHN N., a prominent citizen of Waterbury, Conn., and manager of the Great Brook Woolen co., d. in that town, Feb. 7, 1869.

WITHERSPOON, JAMES, brigade major, killed at Germantown, Oct. 4, 1777.

WOENKLER, JOHN, a native of Wirtemberg, Germany; died at Beaver, O., Jan. 1, 1850, aged 100 years; he came to this country in 1776.

WOLCOTT, FREDERICK, brother of Gov. Oliver, son of Oliver W., who d. in 1797, and grandson of Gov. Roger W.; d. at Litchfield, Conn., May 28, 1837; he grad. at Yale in 1786, and was many years a member of the council and senate of Connecticut; he held important public offices for 45 years, and died in his 70th year.

WOLCOTT, OLIVER, son of the signer, and gov. of Ct., b. Jan. 11, 1760, grad. at Yale in 1778, was admitted to the bar in 1781; was one of the committee of pay tables at Hartford, Jan., 1782; joint com'r to settle acc'ts with the U. S., May, 1784; sole com'r, May, 1787; comptroller of public accts., of Ct., May, 1788; auditor of the treasury of the U. S., Sept. 12, 1789; comptroller of the same June 17, 1791, and sec., of U. S. treas., Feb. 2, 1795; he resigned in 1800; he was appointed judge of the 2d circuit of the U. S., Feb. 20, 1801; gov. of Ct., from 1817 to 1827, and died June 1, 1833. (*Am. An. Reg.*, 1832–3, p. 447; *Goodwin's Notes*, p. 25.)

WOLCOTT, SAMUEL BAKER, d. in Boston, Dec. 4, 1854, a. 59; born in Bolton, Mass.; grad. at Harvard, in 1819; was tutor there in 1821–2; lived some time in Boston, but for a greater part of his life in Hopkinton; more recently he had lived in Salem; was frequently in the legislature, and had been a state senator, one of the executive council, and delegate to the constitutional convention of 1853.

WOOD, ABIEL, of Wiscasset, Me.; merchant and formerly member of congress; d. at Belfast, Me., Nov. 2, 1834, a. 62.

WOOD, AMOS E., b. in Ellisburg, Jeff. co., N. Y., in 1800; removed with his father's family to Portage co., O., in 1812, and settled permanently in Woodville, Sandusky co.; was twice in the state legislature and two years in the state senate; entered congress in 1850, and d. at Fort Wayne, Ind., Nov. 19, 1850.

WOOD, GEORGE, of the New York bar; d. in New York city, March 17, 1860, a. 71; native of Burlington, N. J., and studied law with Richard Stockton; began practice in New Jersey, where he became eminent as a chancery lawyer.

WOOD, MRS. GEORGE (Eliza Logan), actress, d. at New York, Jan. 15, 1872.

WOOD, JAMES, iron manufacturer; b. in Bedford co., Pa., in 1790; became a builder of steamboats on the western waters; was one of the wealthiest men of western Pa.; d. at Pittsburg, Pa., Dec., 1867.

WOOD, JAMES, a confectioner; d. in Philadelphia, Pa., April 3, 1860; became painfully prominent in Oct., 1839, for the murder of his daughter. (*Vincent's Semi-An. Register*, p. 256.)

WOOD, JOSEPH, ex-mayor of Trenton, N. J.; d. May 8, 1860; was uncle of Fernando Wood, formerly mayor of N. Y.

WOOD, ROBERT, lieut. in 2d N. Y. reg.; d. Oct. 10, 1777.

WOOD, STEPHEN, a revolutionary pensioner; d. at Salem, Mass., Nov. 19, 1841, a. 94; entered the service early in the revolution, and was present in the battles of Bunker hill, Saratoga, Princeton and White Plains.

WOOD, LIEUT. SYLVANUS, d. at Woburn, Mass., Aug. 12, 1840, a. 93; a soldier of the revolution.

WOOD, THADDEUS M., b. in Lenox, Mass., March 9, 1772; grad. at Dartmouth in 1790; settled as a lawyer at Onondaga Hollow in 1794, and was the first lawyer in Onondaga co.; was an officer in the war of

1812, and became maj. gen. of militia in 1820; d. Jan. 10, 1836, a. 64. (*Clark's Onondaga*, ii, 118, with portrait.)

WOOD, WILLIAM, a brother of Mrs. Nathaniel Gorham of Canandaigua, N. Y.; b. in Charlestown, Mass., and had been in early life an importing merchant at Boston, and a cotton dealer in New Orleans; was known by his deeds of philanthropy and benevolence, and was instrumental in organizing mercantile library associations, and other agencies of public utility; his residence at Canandaigua is recollected with pleasure, and a library has been named in his honor.

WOOD, WILLIAM, managing editor of the *Brooklyn Eagle;* d. Feb. 21, 1872, a. 37.

WOODBURY, LUKE, d. in Antrim, N. H., Aug. 27, 1851; was a well known merchant; son of Mark W., of Antrim; grad. at Dartmouth; studied law, and frequently represented his town in the leg.; in 1836 was appointed judge of probate for Hillsborough co., which office he held till his death. (*Am. Almanac*, 1852, p. 344.)

WOODBURY, PETER, father of Levi W., secretary of treasury, and formerly a senator in the state legislature; d. at Francestown, N. H., Sept. 13, 1834, a. 65.

WOODHOUSE, GEORGE, (colored,) d. in Va., Dec. 17, 1859, a. 120.

WOODIS, HUNTER, mayor of Norfolk, Va., d. of yellow fever while remaining in the discharge of his duties, Aug. 26, 1855.

WOODRUFF CHAUNCEY, resided in Herkimer, N. Y., was sheriff of Herk. co., from 1798 to 1802; d. May 10, 1810, a. 41.

WOODRUFF, Dr. HUNLOKE, revolutionary surgeon; b. in Elizabethtown, N J.; educated at Princeton and studied with Dr. Malaci Treat; served as surgeon in the N. Y. line through the war; was at Fort. St. John, Fort Stanwix, and with Sullivan's expedition; settled at Albany and d. July 4, 1811, a. 59., (*Tr. N. Y. St. Med. Soc.* 1857, p. 28; *Munsell's Ann. Alb.*, ix, 91.)

WOODRUFF, JOHN, d. at New Haven, Conn., May 25, 1868, a. 43; b. in Hartford, Conn., Feb. 12, 1826; in early life he was a hard-working, industrious mechanic, and for a long time was an active member of the Hartford fire department; subsequently he filled various positions in the government of that city; in 1854 was elected to the lower house of the Connecticut legislature; in 1855 was sent to the federal house of representatives by the American party, but failed to receive his reëlection in 1857; was, however, again chosen congressman in 1859, and served a second term; for several years before his death, Mr. W. held the office of collector of internal revenue for the 2d. congress. district, and in that capacity gave the public much satisfaction; also took a prominent part in the Brooks-Sumner difficulty, having acted throughout that affair as the friend of the latter gentleman; was a man of high culture, though self-educated, and in private life was remarkable for his kindness and benevolence.

WOODRUFF, JOHN O., a prominent merchant of New Orleans; d. April, 1860. (*Vincent's Semi-An. Register*, p. 350.)

WOODRUFF, GEN. MORRIS, d. in Litchfield, Conn., May 17, 1840, a. 63.

WOODS JOHN, b. in Dauphin co., Pa., in 1794; removed to Ohio, in infancy with his parents; was admitted to the bar in 1819; settled in Hamilton, O.; in 1824 elected to cong. and served two terms; in 1829, became publisher of the *Hamilton Intelligencer*, and continued till 1832, when he returned to his profession, and practiced till 1845; was then elected state auditor, and held 2 years; d. at Hamilton, Ohio, July 30, 1855.

WOODS, JOHN S., 2d lieut. of 2d infantry; killed in the battle of Monterey, Sept. 21, 1846; grad. at West Point in 1844.

WOODWARD, ABNER, d. at Ashford, Conn., Jan. 28, 1840, a. 78; a patriot of the revolution.

WOODWARD, ELIJAH, d. at Watertown, N. Y., Oct. 2, 1840, a. 93; was the last of a family of 7 brothers and 2 sisters, whose average ages were 85 years.

WOODWARD, THEODORE, prof. of surgery, in the Vermont Academy of Medicine; d. at Castleton, Vt., Oct., 1840.

WOODWORTH, SOLOMON, became lieut. in Col. Harper's regiment of N. Y. levies, May 11, 1780, and March 8, 1781, was appointed 1st lieut. in Col. Fisher's regiment of Tryon co. militia, in place of Wm. Lard, deserted; with 40 rangers he was stationed at Ft. Dayton (now Herkimer village) and engaged in scouring the wilderness, north of German Flats; he was once taken prisoner and escaped, and at another time defended a block house near Johnstown; leaving Ft. Dayton to reconnoitre on the royal grant he fell into an ambuscade, and was killed 3 miles north of Herkimer village, east of Canada creek, in a deep ravine; a mound of earth marks the spot; this occurred in 1781. (*Benton's Herkimer Co., N. Y.*, p. 92.)

WOOLLEY, AARON K., for many years state senator from the Fayette district; formerly judge of the circuit court, and at the time of his death, law professor in Trannsylvania University, and one of the candidates for the convention in his district; d. at Lexington, Ky., of cholera, Aug. 3, 1849, a. 50.

WOOLEY, JOSEPH, Delaware Indian; entered Mr. Wheelock's school at Lebanon, April 9, 1757; spent the winter of 1764 at Onoboghquage, leaving the Iroquois, and was licensed to teach in 1765; he d. the same year. (*Doc. Hist. N. Y.*, iv, 342.)

WOOLWORTH, ORRIN, many years a merchant in Turin, N. Y.; b. in that town, July 20, 1803; d. July 22, 1872.

WOOLWORTH, REUBEN, a pioneer settler of Turin, N. Y.; d. there June 28, 1872, a. 83; native of Westfield, Mass.

WOOSTER, SHERMAN, b. in Danbury, Ct., Feb. 17, 1779; removed to Ballston Spa in 1787, and was apprenticed to a hatter; in 1801 he went to Utica, and in 1804 to Newport, N. Y., where he afterward resided; he was many years a supervisor, justice and judge; in 1821 he was in the state convention; in 1823–4–5–6, in the state senate, and in the passage of the electoral law was one of the 17 senators who voted for its postponement, and incurred a temporary persecution; in 1833 he was in assembly; d. at Newport, N. Y., May 21, 1833, in his 55th year. (*Benton's Herkimer Co.*, p. 380.)

WORCESTER, Rev. Evarts, d. at Peacham, Vt., Oct. 21, 1836, a. 29; he was ordained pastor of the Congregational church at Littleton, N. H., March 17, 1836, and had been a tutor in Dartmouth College.

WORCESTER, Benjamin, d. at Littleton, Mass., Nov. 24, 1836, a. 99.

WORCESTER, Rev. Leonard, d. at St. Johnsbury, Vt., May 28, 1847; was pastor of the Congregational church in Peacham, Vt., for nearly half a century; was a brother of Dr. Samuel W. of Salem, and Noah W. of Brighton.

WORDEN, Alvah, d. in Canandaigua, N. Y., Feb, 16, 1856; was a prominent lawyer, and a delegate to the constitutional convention of 1846.

WORMLEY, Ralph, rear admiral of the British navy; for some time resident of Boston, having retired from active service on the half pay list.

WORTENDYKE, J. R., d. at Jersey city, N. J., Nov. 7, 1868; b. in Bergen co., N. J., in 1818; grad. at Rutgers; studied law, and was member of congress from 1858 to 1860.

WORTH, Gorham A., d. in N. Y. city, April 3, 1856, a. 72; was a skilful and successful financier and had been cashier of various banks; at the time of his death was president of the N. Y. City Bank; was author of *Random Recollections of Albany and of Hudson.*

WORTHINGTON, Brice T. B., a distinguished member of the Maryland bar; d. at Annapolis, Md. Nov. 29, 1856.

WORTHINGTON, William C., d. in Charleston, Jeff. co., Va., Sept. 22, 1854; was a prominent lawyer, and formerly member of the legislature of Va.

WRIGHT, Gen. Ambrose R., member elect to congress from the 8th dist. of Ga.; d. at Augusta, Ga., Dec. 21, 1872, a. 47.

WRIGHT Dr. Amos C., of Tallmadge, O.; d. May, 1845, a. 63. (*Tallmadge Semi-Centennial*, p. 70.)

WRIGHT, Azariah, bore a prominent part connected with the Westminster massacre, and was noted for the boldness of his nature and the eccentricity of his conduct; had served as a ranger in the French war, and was a fast friend of liberty in the revolution, bold, rough, uncouth and outspoken. (*Hall's Eastern Vermont*, p. 730.)

WRIGHT, Benjamin, land surveyor and 1st engineer on Erie canal, and other public works; b. at Weathersfield, Ct., Oct. 10, 1770; settled in Rome, and was several years engaged in sub-dividing the large tracts owned by Wm. Constable, H. B. Pierrepont and others in northern N. Y.; he with James Geddes surveyed the Erie, and other early canals of N. Y., and afterwards directed or aided in the Farmington, Blackstone, Del. & Chesapeake, James river, Chesapeake & Ohio, Kanawha, Delaware & Hudson, Welland, Chicago and Ill., and other canals, and the Harlem, and the N. Y. & Erie rail road; was an early surveyor of the Croton water works, N. Y., and in 1835 visited Cuba to decide upon a rail road question; d. in N. Y. city, Aug. 24, 1842, a. 72. (*Hough's Hist. Jeff. Co. N. Y.*, p. 453.)

WRIGHT, Maj. Ben, d. in Purdy, Tenn., Jan. 31, 1860; b. in Chatham co., Ga., in 1787; an officer in the war of 1812, and in the Texan struggle for independence, joined his fortunes with that republic; served in the Mexican war. (*Vincent's Semi-An. Register*, p. 73.)

WRIGHT, E. V. R., d. at Jersey city, N. Y., Jan. 19, 1874; b. at Hoboken; a prominent democrat politician; state senator in 1844–48, and candidate for gov. in 1859; member of congress.

WRIGHT, JOHN, a soldier under Braddock in 1755, and in the revolution; d. in Wilkes co., Ga., March 28, 1831, a. 102.

WRIGHT, JABEZ, accidentally drowned at Huron, O., Dec. 16, 1840; was an early settler; formerly in the state senate, and an associate judge of the county.

WRIGHT, JOHN FERNANT, d. at Throgs Neck, N. Y., Nov. 1, 1868; b. in Leeds, England, Feb. 15, 1800; was a sea capt., and had commanded many ships between N. Y. and the south, Cuba and the West Indies.

WRIGHT, JOSEPH H., d. at Philadelphia, Pa., April 11, 1874; was a son of John Wright, one of the oldest merchants in Philadelphia, a prominent member of the commercial exchange, and was a young man of great promise.

WRIGHT, LUCY, prominent Shaker; b. in Pittsfield, Mass., Feb. 5, 1760; became head of the Shakers and founded several societies in Ohio and Ky.; she d. Feb. 7, 1821.

WRIGHT, NATHANIEL, b. in Sterling, Mass.; grad. at Harvard, in 1808; studied law, and was admitted to the bar in 1811; when Lowell was organized as a town, he was made chairman of the selectmen, and held this office 5 years; was the first representative from that town in the state legislature; was senator from Middlesex co. and mayor of Lowell, in 1841–2; for more than thirty years he was president of the Lowell Bank; d. Nov. 5, 1858, a. 73.

WRIGHT, SAMUEL, removed from Vermont to Russia, N. Y., about 1793; engaged in farming and trade, was in assembly in 1803, 4, 5, 6, 7; his course with regard to the passage of the charter of the Merchant's Bank of N. Y., procured by bribery, closed his political career. (*Benton's Herkimer Co.*, p. 385.)

WRIGHT, SAMUEL G., b. in 1787; at the time of his death member of congress elect from N. J.; d. near Allentown, N. J., July 30, 1845.

WRIGHT, WILLIAM B., justice of the court of appeals of New York; d. at Albany, Jan. 11, 1868; was in the constitutional convention of 1846 and in the legislature in 1847; elected a justice of the supreme court the same year.

WYETH, JOHN, b. in Cambridge, Middlesex co., Mass., March 31, 1770, and d. in Philadelphia, Jan. 23, 1858; was a newspaper publisher at Harrisburg many years and post master under Washington and Adams.

XUAREZ, RT. REV. JOHN, bp. elect of Rio de las Palmas in 1527; of the order of St. Francis; came to Vera Cruz in 1515, and labored among the natives. (*Dunigan's Am. Cath. Almanac*, 1860, p. 39.)

YALE, BARNABAS, b. in Salem, N. Y.; spent most of his life in Martinsburg, N. Y., as a lawyer and magistrate; d. at Norfolk, N. Y., Oct. 11, 1854. (*Hough's Hist. Lewis Co.*, p. 180.)

YANCY, BARTLETT, b. in N. C.; grad. at the University of N. C., in which he was for a time tutor; was in congress from 1813 to 1817, and many years in the state legislature, in which he was repeatedly chosen speaker; d. in 1828.

YARDLEY, Dr. Thomas H., d. at Philadelphia, Pa , Jan. 4, 1860, in his 60th year.

YARROW, John, d. in Savannah, Ga., Dec. 20, 1855; had been a merchant in Philadelphia, and at the time of his death, held several important offices of honor and trust.

YATES, Abraham, Jr., was a colonial sheriff of Albany co., and early known as opposed to British measures; his letters signed *Rough Hewer* had a great influence in preparing the way for the revolution and was in all the prov. congresses and conventions of N. Y.; in 1777, and from 1779 to 90, he was in the state senate; in 1788 he was in congress, and from 1790 to 1796 mayor of Albany; he died while in this office June 30, 1796, a. 73. (*Rogers's Hist. Discourse*, p. 100.)

YATES, Col. Christopher, d. at Schenectady, Sept. 1, 1785, leaving a widow and 9 children.

YATES, Christopher P., col. of militia in Tryon co., N. Y., in the revolution, and chairman of the county committee of correspondence; first county clerk, and in assembly in 1784–5–9, 1801–2; d. on his farm 3 miles west of Canajoharie, N. Y., Jan. 21, 1814, a. 65.

YATES, Rev. John Austin, grad. at Union Coll. in 1821; was tutor in 1823–27, and professor of oriental literature till his death, which occurred at Schenectady, Aug. 25, 1849, from cholera.

YATES, Richard, d. at St. Louis, Mo., Nov. 27, 1873, on his return from Fulton, Ark., as U. S. com'r for examining the lower end of the Cairo and Fulton rail road; was b. in Kentucky, Jan. 18, 1818; removed to Illinois, and grad. at the Ill. College; afterward studied law; served in the legislature of his state several terms, and a representative in congress from Illinois in 1851 to 1855; was elected governor of Ill. in 1861 for a term of four years, and took an active part in raising troops for the Union army during the rebellion; was elected United States senator from Ill., for the term beginning in 1865 and ending in 1871; served on the committees on the district of Columbia, the Pacific rail road, territories, pensions, manufactures, and mines and mining; also served as chairman of the comittees on revolutionary claims and territories; was a delegate to the loyalists' convention, held in Phila., in 1866. (*N. Y. Tribune.*)

YATES, Rev. William, third president of William and Mary's Coll., Va., from 1761 till his death in 1764; followed by Rev. James Horrocks.

YEATMAN, Thomas, a banker at Nashville, Tenn.; d. on board the steam boat Mount Vernon of cholera, June 13, 1833, in his 45th year.

YEOMANS, Rev. Edward D., d.d., pastor of the Central Presbyterian church at Orange, N. J.; d. at that place, Aug. 26, 1868, a. 39.

YERGER, George S., an eminent lawyer of Mississippi; d at Yazoo city, April, 1860, a. 60.

YORK, Joseph, sheriff of St. Law. co., N. Y.; b. in Clarendon, Mass., Jan. 8, 1781; went to Randolph, Vt.; in 1805 to Ogdensburg, N. Y.; was sheriff from 1814 to 1818, and in assembly in 1819–20–21; d. May 6, 1827, a. 46; the town of York, Livingston co., N. Y., was named from him. (*Hough's Hist. St. Law. and Fr. Cos. N. Y.*, p. 612.)

YOUNG, Augustus, d. at St. Albans, Vt., June 17, 1857, a. 72; b. at Arlington, Vt., March 20, 1785; admitted to the bar in St. Albans in

1812, and held various state offices; in 1841–43, was a member of congress, from the St. Albans district; afterwards was appointed state geologist.

YOUNG, EBENEZER, b in Killingly, Conn., in 1784; grad. at Yale in 1806; was elected to the state senate in 1823, and twice re-elected; was two years speaker of the house; in congress from 1829 to 1835; d. at West Killingly, Aug. 18, 1851.

YOUNG, IRA, prof. in Dartmouth Coll.; many years prof. of astronomy, and nat. phil.; d. at Hanover, N. H., Sept. 14, 1858; a few hours after undergoing the operation of lithotomy. (*Hist. Mag.*, ii, 346.)

YOUNG, REV. JACOB, early Methodist preacher; b. in Alleghany co., Pa., Mar. 19, 1776; Sept., 1801, was licensed to preach; he began in Shelby co., Ky., as an itinerant, was placed on the Wayne circuit in 1802, the Marietta circuit in 1806; was sent to Tenn., and thence to Miss., Va. and Md.; in 1812 he came to Ohio, and was presiding elder in most of the districts; he preached till 1856; d. at Harrisburg, Pa., Sept. 15, 1859, a. 83. (*Hist. Mag.*, iii, 353.)

YOUNG, DR. JOHN S., b. in Va.; resided in Tennessee a quarter of a century; in 1839 he was elected sec. of state, and again in 1843; he was one of the commissioners to erect the new state Capitol, and new Lunatic Asylum; d. at Nashville, July 7, 1857.

YOUNG, CAPT. PETER, d. at Harmony, N. J., March 14, 1842, a. 86; served in the revolution, and present at the battles of Trenton, Princeton and Monmouth.

YOUNG, SAMUEL, was in the N. Y. assembly in 1814–15 and 1826, in which he was in 1815–26 speaker; was in the state convention in 1821; was appointed a canal com'r in 1816, and held until 1840; in the state senate from 1818 to 1820, and from 1835 to 40, and in 46–7; was secretary of state from 1842 to 1846; he sustained these various trusts with ability and probity; d. at Ballston Spa, N. Y., Nov. 3, 1850, a. 72. (*Stryker's Am. Reg.*, v, 188; *Am. Almanac*, 1852, p. 331.)

YOUNG, DR. SAMUEL, d. at Hagerstown, Md., July 23, 1838, in his hundredth year.

YOUNG, WILLIAM H., d. in Cobleskill, N. Y., Aug. 23, 1874, a. 45; he was a native of that town; was a prominent lawyer, and dist. att'y for Schoharie co., for 6 years.

YOUNGLOVE, DR. MOSES, a native of N. J.; removed to Washington co., N. Y.; in 1776, leaving his medical studies, he joined the army at Albany, as surgeon's mate in Col. Elmore's reg't; in 1777 was appointed surgeon, and in 1777 was taken prisoner in Herkimer's retreat; the following winter returned from Canada, on parole, and soon exchanged; settled at Stone Arabia, his house was burned and farm desolated by the enemy; in 1780, he removed to New Lebanon, Columbia co., N. Y., where he resided till his death in 1828, at his 77th year; in 1778–9 he was in assembly from Tryon co., and in 1802 from Columbia co.

YOUNGS, REV. DANIEL, second pastor of Presb. church, Riverhead, N. Y., called, March, 1782; d. in 1814, a. 70.

ZABRISKIE, ABRAM O., ex-chancellor of New Jersey; d. in California, June 28, 1837, a. 67.

ZENDER, REV. J. D. L., D.D., editor of the *French Almanac;* d. in Brooklyn, N. Y., Jan. 16, 1873.

www.ingramcontent.com/pod-product-compliance
Lightning Source LLC
LaVergne TN
LVHW021133110826
845150LV00005B/1012

* 9 7 8 1 4 2 5 5 4 9 2 7 5 *